One of *Kirkus Reviews/Rolling Stone*'s Top Music Books of 2020

One of NPR's Best Books of 2020

One of the Best Music Books of 2020, *Variety*

One of *No Depression*'s Best Music Books of 2020

Praise for Peter Guralnick's

Looking to Get Lost

Adventures in Music and Writing

"Peter Guralnick's *Looking to Get Lost* — a literary masterpiece — takes the reader on a fantastic journey through the very best of America's musical landscape. His jewel-like personal stories about Skip James, Bill Monroe, Doc Pomus, Solomon Burke, Joe Tex and others are priceless. *Looking to Get Lost* proves that *nobody* knows more about rhythm and blues, bluegrass, rockabilly, and soul music than Guralnick. This pulsing jukebox of a memoir and cultural history certifies that mighty claim."
— Douglas Brinkley, author of *The Great Deluge: Hurricane Katrina, New Orleans, and the Mississippi Gulf Coast*

"In his new book, Guralnick has tracked down unlikely subjects…building human connections and bringing their worlds to life in novelistic detail. *Looking to Get Lost* is full of new insights on musical legends [as he] traces the personal experiences that led him to become a writer, and the creative revelations he discovered along the way." — *Rolling Stone*

"A series of deeply knowledgeable and heartfelt profiles, portraits, and perspectives on some of the greatest musicians of the past seventy-five years. It unfolds like a series of *New Yorker* articles — with Guralnick at the wheel, all you need to do is sit back and enjoy the ride."
— Jem Aswad, *Variety*

T0028364

"In *Looking to Get Lost,* Guralnick explores everything from the edifying enigma of blues icon Robert Johnson to the Appalachian absurdity of writer Lee Smith as he taps the veins of their, and other artists', combustible originality — all while fashioning his own inimitable aesthetic and sublime style as a formidable master of American letters."

— Michael Eric Dyson, author of *Long Time Coming:*
Reckoning with Race in America

"Be warned: the chapters on Solomon Burke, Doc Pomus, and Dick Curless just might squeeze tears out of you...Willie Dixon, Merle Haggard, Johnny Cash, I imagine their spirits all around Guralnick, seeking what the author feels is the 'one common denominator for all great music, its capacity to bring a smile to your lips.'...If this is what it means to get lost, it's a wonder anyone would ever care to be found."

— Brett Marie, *Pop Matters*

"Enlightening and engrossing."   — *People*

"Guralnick has always been particularly passionate about music that transcends categorization...He seems to prize most of all the intuitive individuality that distinguishes artistry — what makes a Jerry Lee Lewis, a Ray Charles, or a Merle Haggard more than the sum of their influences. 'Simply put,' the author writes at the beginning, 'this is a book about creativity,' and the sort of creativity that he appreciates in others can be seen throughout his work as well...[This is] a collection that clearly expresses the passion of musical discovery and lasting legacy."

— *Kirkus Reviews* (starred review)

"The chapter on Maine's Dick Curless stands out not only for its scope but for the emotional impact left upon the reader at its conclusion."

— Mike Dow, *Maine Edge*

"Peter Guralnick's new book is a slow read — slow because it's impossible not to keep stopping and listening to music. Many of the blues and country artists he covers in this collection are huge figures, but because Guralnick is such a fine-grained storyteller and so driven by a deep passion for the music, even familiar characters emerge in a revealing new light."

— Hugo Lindgren, *GQ*

"Peter Guralnick is important for, and to, musicians—essential, in fact. There are music critics without the depth of feeling he has, and there are critics with true feeling who lack his razor-sharp analysis. He is a dedicated explorer, and like all explorers with true mastery of their quest, he is singular and tenacious. He goes deep into the difficult emotional undercurrents, and the contradictions of success, in the lives of artists, and by subtle extension, into his own life. He is a writer of great sensitivity and intuition, who lyrically untangles the network that exists between artist and art, persona and humanity, rhythm and melody, the mortal desires that underscore it all, and, crucially and seamlessly, his own relationship to everything and everyone he contemplates." —Rosanne Cash

"Not a summation so much as a culmination of his remarkable work...It covers old ground from new perspectives, offering deeply felt, masterful, and strikingly personal portraits of creative artists, both musicians and writers, at the height of their powers. *Looking to Get Lost* is such a treat, however, because it's not only about music; the book gives us a glimpse at Guralnick the writer and Guralnick the reader and comes as close as we're likely to get to something like an autobiography. What connects these pieces is Guralnick's creativity, his love of getting lost in a story or a song, and his desire to write." —Henry Carrigan, *No Depression*

"A captivating anthology of music figure portraits, from household names such as Ray Charles, Johnny Cash, and Eric Clapton to more obscure blues, country, and soul legends like Lonnie Mack, Dick Curless, and Solomon Burke...Curless receives the lengthiest treatment with seventy-one pages that read like a gripping novella that will, I should warn, break your heart."

—Wade Tatangelo, *Sarasota Herald-Tribune*

"Guralnick is America's preeminent musical chronicler because he possesses—as he notes of Johnny Cash—the 'gift of empathetic transference.' His first two collections, *Lost Highway* and *Sweet Soul Music* stand as literary touchstones in the study of American roots music. His latest book uses his own journey as a musical seeker for its narrative thread, [beginning] with a prologue that imagines a party populated by his many musical heroes and end[ing] with deeply personal reminiscences of his forefathers." —Bob Mehr, *Memphis Commercial Appeal*

"In the introduction to this collection of profiles, American roots music chronicler Peter Guralnick plays that old game of imagining his favorite dinner party, composed of the subjects of his book. And what a gathering! Guralnick writes with deep empathy and respect about legends like Johnny Cash and Willie Dixon, lesser-known key figures like bluesman Lonnie Mack and music-adjacent kindred spirits like the novelist Lee Smith. This book will make you feel nostalgic for up-close conversations as Guralnick gently reaches the heart and soul of his subjects."

—Ann Powers, *NPR Music*

"Peter Guralnick views his job as telling the Great American Story through the accomplishments of those who [have] the ability to make the nation feel as one through their music. What I love most about this anthology is Peter's Zip-Stripping of the synthetic veneer that cakes up on notable artists over time, masking the natural grain of their triumphs. He rebuilds the true legacy of these artists and personalities by slowly revealing the factors that made them tick and the creative impulses that drove them. [He] reminds us that exceptional rock writing is essentially sublime storytelling."

—Marc Myers, *Jazzwax*

"Charlie Rich once wrote a beautiful song called 'Feel Like Going Home.' It's an extraordinary, yearning ballad. What is more remarkable, it was composed in response to a portrait of the singer written by Peter Guralnick, from an anthology with the same name. It is more common for music to inspire prose of various shades of purple...I can think of no finer compliment to a writer on the subject of music and humanity than to inspire a song in this way."

—Elvis Costello

Looking to Get Lost

Looking
to Get Lost

Adventures in Music and Writing

Peter Guralnick

Back Bay Books

Little, Brown and Company | NEW YORK | BOSTON | LONDON

Back Bay Books / Little, Brown and Company
Hachette Book Group
1290 Avenue of the Americas, New York, NY 10104
littlebrown.com

Originally published by Little, Brown and Company, October 2020
First Back Bay trade paperback edition, October 2021

Back Bay Books is an imprint of Little, Brown and Company, a division of Hachette Book Group, Inc. The Back Bay Books name and logo are trademarks of Hachette Book Group, Inc.

The Hachette Speakers Bureau provides a wide range of authors for speaking events. To find out more, go to hachettespeakersbureau.com or call (866) 376-6591.

Copyright acknowledgments appear on page 531.

All photographs are copyrighted by the photographer and/or owner cited, all rights reserved.

PAGE I: Solomon Burke, gesturing to the skies. *Courtesy of Bill Millar*
PAGE VIII: Chuck Berry, late 1930s. *Photograph by Harry Davis © Bill Greensmith Collection*
PAGE 1: Dick Curless, with his younger brother, Phil (*on left*), Gilbertville, Massachusetts, ca. 1942. *Courtesy of Terry Curless Chinnock*
PAGE 496: Dick Curless at 17: "He's the best-dressed cowboy in town." *Courtesy of Terry Curless Chinnock / Richard Weize — ... and more bears*

Designed by Susan Marsh

ISBN 978-0-316-41262-9 (hc); 978-0-316-41260-5 (pb)
LCCN 2020937314

Printing 1, 2021

LSC-C

Printed in the United States of America

For Susan and Tommy, Betty and Wally,

Phil and Rose, Ruby and Nina

Contents

Having a Party

S IMPLY PUT, THIS IS A BOOK about creativity. Like so many other things in my life, this is a realization I have come to only after the fact. When I first started writing profiles (see "Falling into Place" and "Whose Skip James Is This?"), it was with the idea of putting what gifts I had at the service of a greater cause. But gradually over the years I have come to recognize that what has always fascinated me, apart from the very idiosyncratic nature of each and every person that I've ever written about, was the imaginative impulse that drove them all, not the material dreams (even in the case of a fabulist like Colonel Tom Parker, I would argue that this was by no means his primary motivation) but what it was in their makeup that led them to express themselves in so particular and individuated a manner.

And so in a way this is what all my profiles from first (Skip) to last (Dick Curless) have been about, however different the particulars of the lives may be. In some cases, as with the unique collaboration between Elvis Costello and Allen Toussaint, the artist may be exceedingly self-aware—but then, so, too, in his own way, was Howlin' Wolf, who saw his music as an expression not just of personal freedom but of personal *difference*. It is that almost inextinguishable drive to self-expression that, to paraphrase John Lee Hooker, was, simply, in them and had to come out. I'm reminded sometimes of what Stoney Edwards, a singular black country singer who could neither read nor write, said to me on the subject of other people's attempts to educate him. "I'm glad I can't read," he said. "It scares the shit out of me sometimes how close I came to being an educated man. What I'm saying is, when I think about how many things that's written about that's copied—well, I *can't* copy anybody else. What I write about comes from a natural feeling inside myself. What I write has to be true."

Well, maybe so. Though that is not, of course, the only way. And yet it is one way to discover that state of abandon which all artists, whether knowingly or not, are searching for, that momentary sense of "lostness" that leads an author like Henry Green to forgo grammatical niceties, and sometimes even linear sense, for the same kind of lyrical rapture (in Green's case it might best be described as verbal drunkenness) that permits a musician like Jerry Lee Lewis or Ray Charles to discover places he might never otherwise have sought to go.

I toyed with the idea of calling this book *Creativity: An Autobiography*, because in one sense that is what it is. But then I figured no one would really get the joke (is it a joke—and if it is, how certain am I that *I* get it?)—and besides, it might take away from the seriousness of my point. Which is that there is no one in this book, or any other that I have written, who was not lifted up in some way on the wings of imagination.

You won't find anyone more dedicated to their writing, or more ambitious about the precision of its expression, than Merle Haggard or Chuck Berry. To Lee Smith, "I guess my favorite thing is before you even start writing, when you're sitting down every day just thinking about [it], and it's all completely fluid in your head and there're all these people running around, and there's infinite possibilities of what they might or might not do. . . . Everything is all intensely alive, and it's just total possibility." Doc Pomus, who experienced a late-in-life renaissance that freed him from the more self-conscious restrictions of genre and craft, describes writing one of his early songs in an almost trance-like state ("I definitely remember writing the song in a car. I was still living on and off with my family, and I was riding somewhere. It has a kind of quasi-heartbeat, it's almost like subliminal writing"), but in the end he had no interest in explaining the song, because "it's like with Edward Hopper, when they asked him, 'Who are those paintings about, all those late-night diners?,' he said, 'They're all me.'" Henry Green was so inflamed by his fears for the demise not just of himself but of everything that he knew and loved as the Battle of Britain began (he was driven, he said, "to put down what comes to mind before one is killed, and surely it would be asking much to pretend one had a chance to live") that he wrote what could arguably be considered his three greatest masterpieces in the course of little more than two years. Bill Monroe, widely hailed as the "Father of Bluegrass," saw a long lifetime as an opportunity to refine the ever-developing arc of the revolutionary new music that he had pioneered in his mid-thirties. And if you listen to the dialogue between Elvis Costello and Allen Toussaint, you will overhear a conversation that returns again and again to the work ethic of the artist (simply put, this might be summarized by writers and musicians from Ernest Hemingway to Robert Johnson as, You'd better be there just in case inspiration arrives, because if you're not, it may never choose to show its face again) — a conversation leavened and uplifted, in a manner that Lee Smith and Bill Monroe would certainly approve, by visionary arrivals like the Archangel Gabriel in the midst of an otherwise wholly secular (and, up to that point, almost frivolous) song.

Many of the subjects of this book are people that I've known for years — in a number of cases, I've simply written new profiles of artists that I have written about before. Jerry Lee Lewis, for example, I met originally in 1970, when he was living on Coro Lake, outside of Memphis, still married to his first cousin once removed, Myra Gale, whom he had married some fourteen years earlier when she was thirteen. (The revelation of their marriage in 1958 had virtually ended his career for the next decade.) Over the years I continued to talk to, and write about, Jerry Lee, and I like to think I gained additional insight not only into what he was saying to me at the present moment but into what he had told me long ago. The same with Howlin' Wolf — I interviewed him just months before Jerry Lee, as I was putting together my first book, *Feel Like Going Home*, but though he died in 1976, I never ceased to be fascinated by both the man and his music. And Solomon Burke — well, as I say, someday I'm going to write an *epic* about Solomon Burke (not really, but I wish I could), and I have tried once again here to suggest some of the illimitable dimensions of his world.

All of these portraits, old and new, tell stories that are just as exciting to me today as when I first encountered them, and they connect with one another now in ways that I might not always have suspected. The most recent piece, the chapter on Dick Curless, which I have been working on for the last two or three years, turned into something altogether different from what I had imagined — and told a story that, while it began and ended in the same place that it had originally started, took a number of unexpectedly tortuous twists and turns. In similar fashion, I found myself exploring another side of Ray Charles, whom I've written about extensively over the years, by focusing on the moment in his life when everything changed. Or, in another newly written piece, which, like the Ray Charles chapter, started out as a talk and then evolved, I sought to place

Elvis' manager, Colonel Tom Parker, in a different, deeper, and I hope more entertaining perspective by utilizing my own interaction (and correspondence) with him over an almost ten-year period.

With all of the profiles, old and new, I wanted to maintain a "present-ness" in the writing, even while doing everything that I could to avoid unintentional anachronisms or inaccuracies. It's funny, the challenges that sometimes arise. You may note, for example, in the profiles of both Leiber and Stoller and Tammy Wynette how I've tried to address looming issues that never came up at the time (I simply didn't have the information to ask the questions)—but I hope never at the expense of that first wide-eyed moment of meeting. Sometimes, in rereading and rewriting, I've found myself embarrassed most of all by—well, by *myself.* (I must confess, this could happen just as easily with something I'm writing today as something written twenty or thirty years ago.) But I never want to deny that first, fresh impression—however much I might be tempted, I would never want to touch up the truth, or the tone, of an instant that I can so vividly recall but could never fully re-create in the same terms that presented themselves so startlingly to me at the time.

And then there was the matter of how exactly to present the portraits, how best to order them and introduce old friends and new not only to the reader but to each other. At first I thought, well, why not just try to put them into some kind of thematic sequence—but then I realized that far too many of the themes intertwined and overlapped to even consider that kind of arrangement. The centrality of home, for example, as the starting point for every creative endeavor, yoked to the implicit understanding that there was no way of ever getting back there again. (See previous paragraph.) Dick Curless, I think, put it most poignantly when he spoke of quitting school and leaving home at eighteen to go out on his first musical tour, just weeks before high school graduation. There's little doubt in my mind that, given the opportunity, he would have done it again. And yet, "If I could go back and find that boy," he said almost fifty years later, "knowing all the things that would happen to him, I'd tell him, 'Boy, stay and sing with your family. They're not going to be there very long. Yeah, you stay home and sing. Be happy in your little town.'" I'm not sure anyone else would have expressed themselves in such stark emotional terms (well, maybe Lonnie Mack), but Lee Smith spoke movingly of some of that same sense of regret (she described it as a kind of "intense ambivalence"). So did Allen Toussaint and Tammy Wynette, among others. Or, as Ernest

Tubb once said, speaking of the origins of his own deliberately spare country style, "I want my music to be simple enough so that the boy out there on the farm can learn it and practice it and try to play it." But as he himself would have been the first to acknowledge, it was a long time since he had visited that farm, and for all he knew neither the boy nor the farm was still there.

The one thing that united every one of them was the breadth and conviction of their democratic views—and I'm not talking politics here, even if like Chuck Berry you are inclined to argue that *everything* is politics. I mean, let me be clear: I am not prepared to vouch for anyone's political views—in many cases I have no idea, and in the case of someone like Merle Haggard (whose views ran the full gamut, from left to right and back again), I couldn't possibly begin to interpret them. But I *can* say confidently that none of the people I have written about—whatever their articulated political or social views might be—have ever voiced their aesthetic views, their views about art or music or self-expression, in anything but purely democratic terms. Howlin' Wolf, Jerry Lee Lewis, Ray Charles, Johnny Cash, Chuck Berry, Allen Toussaint, Merle Haggard, Bill Monroe— every one of them listened with his ears wide open, all of them expressed their admiration, often in the most expansive terms, for their acknowledged peers and predecessors, irrespective of genre, irrespective of class or color. And all in some sense would tend to subscribe to the view most explicitly voiced by Sam Phillips and Solomon Burke—that music, or in the case of Henry Green and Lee Smith the meticulous reimagining of all that they saw or heard around them, has the power to save (or at least *preserve*) the world.

Oh, yes, and sequencing the book? Well, I knew I wanted to start with some kind of statement of purpose, so I revisited two of the first subjects I ever wrote about, Robert Johnson and Skip James, to present them in a somewhat different, but no less fiercely partisan, light. They were among the very first to wake me up to the music, and in many ways they could each be said to have started me off on my own adventures. As far as the rest of it goes, the order of the book from Ray Charles on, well, I mean, what other choice did I have but to fall back on the tried-and-true method that so many of these artists called upon in their own work? In the end I did it simply by feel.

I spoke at a college not too long ago, and at the reception afterwards I was asked by my host who I would like to have at my ideal dinner party.

Solomon Burke and Rufus Thomas at *Sweet Soul Music* book release party, Memphis, Tennessee, 1986. *Photograph by Pat Rainer*

Oh, Solomon Burke, I said, limiting the invitations to people I have actually known. And, of course, Sam Phillips, even if they didn't seem to get along when I introduced them in real life. Don't forget Johnny Shines. And Sleepy LaBeef — Sleepy would get along with everybody. All eyes turn when Carla Thomas, Stax's own Queen of Memphis Soul (she sang with Otis Redding while studying for her master's degree in English at Howard University), arrives. Sam wants to know right away where her father, Rufus, is. Which raises the question, Where *is* Rufus? After all, not only was he the originator of Sun Records' very first hit, he is never anything less than the life of the party. I guess we'd better send out a call to him, too. Charlie Rich and his songwriter wife, Margaret Ann, come in together, a study in contrasts. Margaret Ann, the author of some of Charlie's deepest, most personal songs, is an inveterate reader (as it happens, she's a big fan of Lee Smith, whom she's thrilled to see across the room) and a natural mixer who fits right in. Charlie, on the other hand, one of the most introverted people I've ever met, might have to be coaxed out of his corner, but I'm sure if anyone could do it, Lee Smith could. Lee might in fact have to do double duty with Merle Haggard. (This was evidently going to be quite a party.) Not to mention Howlin' Wolf, even if he might appear to be sulking at first (or maybe "brooding" might be the better term) — Sam would just be so happy to see him. My mind was really working overtime now. I think Doc Pomus and Colonel Parker, with their mutual (while very different) dedication to the proposition that you can't hip a square, would get a big kick out of each other. Though on second thought Doc and Sam Cooke's friend and business partner J. W. Alexander, who never met but should have, had so much in common that maybe they should be seated together. And what about Jack Clement, who could play Falstaff (or at least ukulele) to his onetime mentor Sam Phillips' Lear, while Dick Curless could entertain everyone with his cowboy songs and courtly manner. Well, this had gotten a little out of hand (particularly with all the embellishments that my mind, if not my mouth, was adding), and I could see everyone's eyes beginning to glaze over — but it was only when I got to Jerry Lee Lewis that my host held up his hand with a look that suggested, Surely you can't be serious. But I was — and I am. All of these people are to be celebrated for their wit and wisdom, their humanity, and, yes, their genius. And I would like to present them all to you, without ascribing any more to it than I do in the pages of my books, in some cases as friends, in all cases as people I admire, people from whom I have learned, people whose work has deeply moved and influenced me.

Art is meant to be shared and treasured, borrowed and altered, too. Bobby "Blue" Bland took equally from the fiery sermons of Aretha Franklin's father, the Reverend C. L. Franklin, and Perry Como's easygoing pop balladry. Ray Charles could cite both Hank Williams and the apocalyptic Five Blind Boys lead singer Archie Brownlee as models. Bill Monroe, often seen as the keeper of a very isolated, Appalachian tradition, always pointed to a black blues player named Arnold Shultz as one of the formative influences of his life. Even more surprisingly, Howlin' Wolf, one of the most distinctive exemplars of the pure African American blues tradition, never failed to credit the profound influence of Jimmie Rodgers, the Father of Country Music. Listen to Solomon Burke talk about Gene Autry (and Brother Joe May) and Jerry Lee Lewis about B.B. King (and Gene Autry) — and then simply immerse yourself in the incalculable diversity of their music, which derived from a melting-pot culture that came to its fullest flowering in the twentieth century. Because, of course, with the invention of the radio and the phonograph and ever-broader agents for the mass dissemination of information and music, all effective barriers to the integration not just of culture but of the imagination were down — no matter how isolated the community (and just think of Skip James growing up in

Bentonia, Mississippi, Dick Curless in Caribou, Maine, Lee Smith in Grundy, Virginia, and Johnny Cash in Dyess, Arkansas) there was bound to be a crossover, not to the obliteration of one tradition or another, but to their *extension,* in much the same way that Sun Records founder Sam Phillips (Elvis, Howlin' Wolf, Ike Turner's "Rocket 88") confidently predicted the arrival of rock 'n' roll well before the music had been named.

This is a book about individual difference — it is about a world in which, for so many of the people I am writing about, the possibilities seemed limitless, a world that through the gift of imagination continued to expand for them, in some cases right up until the moment of their death. And I'd like to think, whatever the challenges of the world that we see around us today, in which, like it or not, we have all been incorporated into the global marketplace, that somehow or another (and not by going back to where we were but by listening to the inner voice that we all possess), those same possibilities for individuation and freedom still exist. As Joe Tex, one of the most extroverted philosophers I have ever met, cheerfully declared, "I've enjoyed this life. I was glad that I was able to come up out of creation and look all around and see a little bit, grass and trees and cars, fish and steaks, potatoes. Everywhere I've gone, I can always go back, and I can always find a friend. I don't go trying to make nobody like me, I just be me, you know, and it has worked out." Or, in the somewhat more measured words of Allen Toussaint, after losing nearly all of his material possessions to Hurricane Katrina, "The things I had served me well when I had them. . . . I'll have to write some more."

Looking to Get Lost

ONE

Falling into Place

I COULD ACT as if I don't really know how it happened, but it wouldn't be true. I know exactly how I got to this place, whether for good or for ill, and I can't pretend otherwise.

I wanted to be a writer. Not a rock writer — there was no such thing. I wanted to write novels and stories. And so I did — and occasionally still do. When I was fifteen, I first read the *Paris Review* interview with Ernest Hemingway in which he spoke of his working methods, and I took note of the fact that he set himself a quota of something like 500 words a day. With as much self-doubt as temerity, I did the same, committing myself to the idea that should inspiration ever deign to visit I was not going to be absent from my post. And so I began a daily vigil that has persisted more or less to this day.

When I was around fifteen, too, I fell in love with the blues: Lightnin' Hopkins and Big Bill Broonzy, Leadbelly and Muddy Waters, Howlin' Wolf and Blind Willie McTell. I lived it, breathed it, absorbed it by osmosis, fantasized it — don't ask me why. It was like the writing of Italo Svevo or Henry Green: it just turned me around in a way that I am no more inclined to quantify or explain today than I was then. But I never dreamt of writing about it. There was nowhere to write about it *in*. And besides, I'm not sure I could have imagined a way in which to truly evoke just what I was feeling at the time. *Experience, don't analyze,* my inner voice told me. Though that didn't stop my friend Bob Smith and me from scrutinizing liner notes, poring over the one book we knew to exist on the subject (Sam Charters' *The Country Blues*), and talking about the blues — *all the time*. It was almost as if by the time we saw our first bluesman, Lightnin' Hopkins, live and in person in the fall of 1960, we had created a virtual world that ignored the complexities of the real one. All of a sudden we were forced to adjust to the idea that there were actual people who made the music, subject to neither our preconceptions nor our fantasies and, of course, far more interesting than either.

I won't bore you with all the mundane details of my awakening to that music and that world. Everyone has a similar story. Suffice it to say that I almost literally held my breath every time I went to see Muddy Waters, Big Joe Williams, Sleepy John Estes, Chuck Berry, Bo Diddley, and Mississippi John Hurt in those days, for fear that all of this beauty, all of this wit, all of this gloriously undifferentiated reality might somehow disappear as suddenly as it had first manifested itself in my life.

I was perfectly happy as a mere acolyte, expanding my world to the soul and gospel shows that came through town, when a series of related events conspired to rob me of my innocence. First I stumbled upon the English blues magazines *Blues Unlimited* and *Blues World* in 1964 and 1965. I started writing to the editors of both and, inspired by the recognition that there were others out there like me, began to file reports on the shows I went to. It was this sense of a larger community, as hungry as I for insights and information, that led me to approach the great Mississippi bluesman Skip James in the summer of 1965. There could have been no more unlikely interviewer than I, and certainly no one burdened with a greater degree of self-consciousness, but I had witnessed Skip's astonishing performance at the Newport Folk Festival the previous summer, just after his rediscovery in a Tunica, Mississippi, hospital, and his even more astonishing reclamation onstage of the weird, almost unearthly sound that characterized his remote 1931 recordings. So I presented myself as best I could, asked questions at whose obviousness I winced even as they were being greeted with a kind of courtly gravity by the person to whom they were addressed, and persisted in this exercise in self-abasement because, I told myself, greatness such as this would not pass my way again.

That was my entire motivation. I wanted to tell the world something of the inimitable nature of Skip James' music, I wanted to proclaim Muddy Waters' and Bo Diddley's genius, I wanted to find some way to describe the transcendent drama of the rhythm and blues revues that I had witnessed, featuring astonishing performances by such virtuosic entertainers as Solomon Burke, Otis Redding, Joe Tex, Jackie Wilson, and Little Richard, sometimes even on the same bill. When in 1966 an underground music press began to emerge — first with the appearance of *Crawdaddy! The Magazine of Rock 'n' Roll*, Paul Williams' utopian embrace of the revolution, then, in the same year, with the arrival of *Boston After Dark*,

"Boston's Only Complete Entertainment Weekly," and finally, in late 1967, with *Rolling Stone* — my course was set. In each case someone at the publication knew of my love for the blues (and who within the sound of my voice could *fail* to be aware of it?) and asked if I would like to write about the music. I never saw it as a life decision (I had no intention of abandoning my novels and short stories), but I never hesitated either. How could I refuse the opportunity to tell people about this music that I thought was so great? How could I turn down the chance simply to put some of those names down on paper?

Muddy Waters, Howlin' Wolf, James Brown, Solomon Burke, Robert Pete Williams, Jerry Lee Lewis, Bo Diddley, Elvis Presley, Chuck Berry, and Buddy Guy — these were among the first stories I wrote, some of them no longer than 150 or 200 words. They were intended to *sell,* not a product but an unarticulated belief, a belief in the intrinsic worth of American vernacular culture. Writing down these names even today evokes some of the same secret thrill, but it could never fully suggest the tenor of a time when merely to name was to validate, when so much of this music was not simply ignored but reviled in the mainstream press. To be able to write in my perfectly serious, if not altogether unself-conscious, way of James Brown's "brilliant sense of theatrics," his "genius for showmanship," and the "passionate conviction" with which he transformed his show into something like a religious ritual, to proclaim Solomon Burke an artist "whose every song seems to [possess] the underlying belief that somehow or other by his investment of emotion he might alter the world's course," to describe Muddy Waters as the creator of a seminal style whose songs were our contemporary classics, to speak of the "existential acts" with which Elvis "helped to liberate a generation" — these were my own intentional acts of subversion, by which I was clearly attempting to undermine ingrained cultural prejudices and, no doubt, declare my own.

The more I wrote, of course, the more I found the need to seek out a vocabulary that could suggest something of the experience that I found so compelling. Writing about music is, as more than one dismissive wag has pointed out, a little like dancing about architecture, and for someone almost entirely lacking in musical training or knowledge, it is even more so. What I was trying to capture, though, I realized from the start, was the *feeling,* not the technique. I was not trying to provide deconstructive analysis of the breathtaking swoops and glissandos of Aretha Franklin's singing style any more than I would have attempted to break down

My First Trip to Memphis: at the Memphis Country Blues Festival, Overton Park, 1969. *Courtesy of Augusta Palmer*

the sentence structure of Henry Green's *Pack My Bag*. What I was interested in was exhortatory writing, writing that would bring the reader to the same appreciation of Ray Charles, Skip James, and Charlie Rich that I felt, that would in a sense mimic the same emotions not just that I experienced but that I believed the musician had put into the music in the first place. Just how ambivalent I was about this whole enterprise can be gleaned from the epilogue to my first book, *Feel Like Going Home*. "I consider this chapter a swan song," I wrote in 1971, "not only to the book but to my whole brief critical career. Next time you see me I hope I will be my younger, less self-conscious and critical self. It would be nice to just sit back and listen to the music again without a notebook always poised or the next interviewing question always in the back of your mind."

Well, perhaps it's unnecessary to admit but, save for a brief interlude, that never really happened. After writing another novel, two years later I was back, lured by the siren song of Bobby "Blue" Bland and Waylon Jennings. My moment of abject self-recognition in fact came while I was writing the Bobby "Blue" Bland story, spending my time shuttling back and forth between teaching Classics at Boston University and hanging out at the somewhat seedy soul club downtown where Bobby was playing a weeklong engagement. My teaching job was running out, and I thought I'd better look for a new one, so I arranged for an interview at a nearby prep school, where I met with the head of the English department and talked about some of my favorite books, like *Tristram Shandy* and Thomas Pynchon's *V*. That night Bobby's bandleader, Mel Jackson, called a horn rehearsal for after the show, and I sat around for an hour or two as the

Bobby "Blue" Bland,
1976. *Photograph by*
Steve Tomashefsky

lights were turned up, the club emptied out, and all of its tawdry glitter was unmasked. Finally it became obvious that the rehearsal was never going to happen. Bobby had gone back to the hotel, the horn players had drifted off to various unspecified assignations, and in the end Mel Jackson just shrugged and walked up the stairs to the deserted street.

I was exhausted and, I suppose, frustrated, too. But I realized in that moment that I would rather sit around in this club watching all the transactions that were taking place and waiting for an event that was not going to occur than spend a lifetime teaching English in a muted, well-bred academic setting. And so my fate was sealed. It involved an admission I had never wanted to make: that I was drawn not just to the music but to the life. I had discovered what Murray Kempton called the lure of "going around." That was forty-five years ago, and since then I have never really tried to escape.

I don't mean to suggest in any way that my experience has been without pitfalls or regrets — but it has been enormous fun. To meet and write about my heroes, diverse and unreconstructed figures all, has been as exciting an adventure as anything I could ever have imagined as a kid, except maybe playing big-league baseball. As far as the pitfalls go, they are, I suppose, just the pitfalls of life: as soon as you start out doing *something*, you can no longer do everything. As soon as you set words down on screen or paper (the moment in fact you embark upon any kind of real-life adventure), you have to let go of the dream of perfection, you are forced inevitably to make do with reality.

The reality that anyone who writes about music (or film, or literature) has to come to terms with is this: How do you sustain enthusiasm, how do you avoid repetition, how do you keep from tangling up in the web of your own words and ideas? Maybe that's the dilemma of writing in general — or just of life. I know that early on I stumbled upon a strategy that seemed to accommodate both my strengths and weaknesses. I started writing about people primarily, presenting the music within the context of their backgrounds, their aspirations, their cultural traditions. That helped solve a number of problems. It allowed me to seek a colloquial language suited to each subject and better suited, I thought, to the subject as a whole than generational enthusiasm (the "groovy" / "far out" / "awesome" syndrome) or academic pretension. It allowed me, in other words, to *reflect* the music without trying to dissect it, something I was neither prepared nor willing to do. It also gave me a fresh path to pursue every time I started a new project, since each artist stakes out their own territory, every artist has his or her own story to tell, no matter how it may connect with a common tradition or fuse in certain elemental ways with that of others. But the pursuit of endless byways can carry with it its own price, as any writer, as anyone who appreciates the digressive and the strange, inevitably finds. You listen to music for a living, and you no longer hear with the ears of the teenager who once discovered it. You pursue your curiosity, and it tends to carry you further and further afield, until the question arises: How do you get back to the place you once were? How do you rekindle that simple enthusiasm for the music, the ardor I sought to describe in that same 1971 epilogue to my first book as "an emotional experience which I could not deny. It expressed for me a sense of sharp release and a feeling of almost savage joy."

The short answer is that you can't — at least not without assuming a kind of disingenuousness as embarrassing as any other transparent attempt to deny age or experience. But in another sense, who knows what disingenuousness I was capable of even at fifteen, when I first discovered the music, or at twenty-seven, when I wrote those words? I'm not convinced we are ever wholly ingenuous. But whether we are or not, what other hope is there except in surrender, whatever indignities surrender may entail? So in the end that is my advice: surrender to the music. That is what I hope the underlying message of my writing to be. Surrender to Muddy Waters. Surrender to Solomon Burke. Surrender to Sam Cooke and Bob Dylan and Sleepy LaBeef and the Mighty Clouds of Joy. We are all just looking to get lost.

TWO

Robert Johnson and the Transformative Nature of Art

EVER SINCE his earliest discovery by a mass white audience in 1961, Robert Johnson has been a lightning rod for the blues. Not just his music but his myth. Not just the startling originality of his work but his iconic status in a world that accorded him no status while he was alive, with only sidelong acknowledgment of the tradition from which he sprang. Robert Johnson, in other words, was posthumously "rediscovered" and enshrined, his music reclaimed with a boxed set of his complete recordings that was certified gold in 1990, more than fifty years after his death. Not long after that, his image appeared on the face of a stamp, airbrushed of any trace of the cigarette that lay curled between his lips in the photograph on which that image was based, and the blues, for nearly a century a cultural stepchild, officially entered the mainstream.

We are, of course, constantly rediscovering things, not just in history but in our own individual memories and experience. It has to do, I suppose, not simply with what we have forgotten or overlooked but with alterations in our perspective as well: our own past looks different to us from different vantage points, certainly, but I think rediscovery of a past in which we did not share inevitably carries with it broader implications. For the person making the discovery, it is all too easy to imagine that the subject has never existed before. For the artist, for the individual being rediscovered, on the other hand, what does it mean? In some cases, little more than a weary shrug and the logical question, What took you so long? If, as in the case of Robert Johnson, the artist is long dead, rediscovery can still have an enormous effect on the currency of his or her work, even after hundreds of years (look at the case of seventeenth-century metaphysical poet John Donne, hailed as a contemporary voice in the 1920s, or Herman Melville, taken up, like Robert Johnson, after a mere half century of neglect). There are any number of variations on both the nature and the impact of this process. But in no case, I would argue, does redis-covery have anything to do with the intrinsic power of art. It neither adds to nor subtracts from the value of the work. It is art that has drawn us, not the other way around.

The point is that Robert Johnson never went away. We may congratu-late ourselves on our perspicacity in finding our way to the music—but in fact the music has always had the power to find its way to us. Virtually at the time of Robert Johnson's death—before it was even known outside his immediate circle of family and friends—record pioneer John Ham-mond advertised his upcoming appearance at the December 23, 1938, From Spirituals to Swing concert at Carnegie Hall, which was billed as "An Evening of American Negro Music" and dedicated to the memory of Bessie Smith. When he learned that Johnson, too, had died, Hammond incorporated his music into the program, reading a brief tribute and play-ing two of his recordings from the stage.

It was in pursuit of the Robert Johnson tradition in the Mississippi Delta that folklorist Alan Lomax found both Son House and Muddy Waters in 1941, the one perhaps Johnson's most direct progenitor, the other the most prominent heir to his style, and it was Lomax's recordings of them for the Library of Congress that in many ways helped pave the way for House's own rediscovery some two decades later and Muddy's entry into the commercial recording field. At a time when jazz critic Rudi Blesh was writing of the song that may well be Johnson's masterpiece, "Hellhound on My Trail," with all the romantic fervor that Johnson's work so often summons up ("the notes paint a dark wasteland, starless, ululant with bit-ter wind, swept by the chill rain," Blesh wrote in 1946, "[while] over a hilltop trudges a lonely, ragged, bedeviled figure . . ."), Muddy Waters was transforming Johnson's music, bringing it into the nascent world of ampli-fied Chicago blues, with no thought of nostalgia or rediscovery in mind. That music reached an audience of transplanted Mississippians, Mem-phians, Arkansans, Georgians who embraced it for its immediacy, its sug-gestiveness (like all great art, in every sense), its unblinking realism, its direct emotional impact. And Muddy Waters became a star.

Johnny Shines, Robert Jr. Lockwood, Sonny Boy Williamson, Howlin' Wolf, Honeyboy Edwards, Calvin Frazier, Sunnyland Slim, Baby Boy War-ren, Elmore James—the list could certainly go on—were not *memorial-izing* the music of Robert Johnson when, in the early '50s, they sang songs that echoed his style or even performed his signature compositions. They

Photograph by Marion Post Wolcott, Library of Congress, F.S.A.

were making music that moved them, they were singing songs that continued to live on in their own terms, whether or not their audience — or the singer himself, for that matter — knew of Robert Johnson or even recognized the name. And, of course, as the music grew in popularity, as it fanned out in ever-widening gyres, it reached people who would be newly moved by its power, and newly moved to create music of their own. So whether one is speaking of Boyd Gilmore in the Delta or Keith Richards in Dartford, England, the effect of the music is the same: it's moving, inspiring, *living* art.

I know how I felt when I first listened to Robert Johnson in 1961 at the age of seventeen. Well, I should backdate that a little. I had heard "Preachin' Blues" on Sam Charters' 1959 compilation, *The Country Blues,* as well as excerpts of "Cross Road Blues" and "From Four Until Late" on another Charters anthology, *The Rural Blues,* which offered brief, but tantalizingly incomplete, selections of various styles and approaches to the blues. But to pick up an album called *Robert Johnson: King of the Delta Blues Singers* (Columbia 1654 — I could never forget that number!) with, literally, no preparation for it — no coverage in *Rolling Stone, People, Entertainment Weekly, USA Today* — was one of those rare experiences that gives validation to the term "truly awesome." Listening to songs like "Cross-roads," "Me and the Devil," "Hellhound on My Trail" over and over, trying to absorb the locutions, getting some sense not just of the strangeness of the music but of the unmistakable familiarity of its emotional terrain, was an unrecapturable experience. But—and I think this is a point that cannot be emphasized too much—it was *my* good fortune, not Robert Johnson's, that I stumbled upon that album. It has been *all* of our good fortune to experience—I'm tempted to reach for a Rudi Blesh-like line—the exaltation of his music.

This is the thing I think we have to keep straight. Art is always there to be found. It's up to us to open up our eyes and ears. Even now there is some contemporary Robert Johnson, some painter, some poet, some unac-knowledged novelist, performance artist, musician, waiting to be discov-ered, and if we are fortunate enough to make that discovery, we are uplifted by it. But our presence in the room makes not the slightest dif-ference to the vitality of the work.

Art is a mystery. Where does it come from? It arrives unbidden, out of nowhere; it shows up when we least expect it. If it is too calculated a bid for greatness, most likely it will reveal its seams. It is not the product of a finishing school or a creative writing program; it springs full-blown from the head of Zeus.

This is the manner in which Robert Johnson's gifts emerged. Son House said: "We'd all play for the Saturday night balls and there'd be this little boy standing around . . . and when we'd get a break and want to rest some, we'd set the guitars up in a corner and go out in the cool. Robert would watch and see which way we'd gone and he would pick one of them up. And such another racket you never heard! It'd make the people mad, you know." Then, in House's account, Robert went away for a time, and when he came back he showed up at a little juke joint House was playing outside of Rob-insonville. "I said, 'Well, boy, you still got a guitar, huh? What do you do with that thing? You can't do nothing with it.' He said, 'Well, I'll tell you what. . . . Let me have your seat a minute.' So I said, 'All right, and you bet-ter do something with it, too.' . . . So he sat down there and finally got started. And man! He was so good! When he finished, all our mouths were standing open. I said, 'Well, ain't that fast! He's gone now!'"

To this day people say the same things about Robert Johnson that they have said about other unlettered geniuses from Shakespeare to Hank Wil-liams to Elvis Presley: What is there in this person's background that can explain his gifts? In Shakespeare's case, the argument has been repeatedly advanced since the middle of the nineteenth century that nothing could account for so vast and untrammeled an imagination other than that someone else — more sophisticated, better educated, higher born — had written his plays. With Robert Johnson it has been suggested with varying degrees of literal intent that he sold his soul to the devil — not really all that different from what some of his contemporaries said of a nineteen-year-old Elvis Presley who burst forth not just out of the same anonymity but out of what was widely perceived among his peers as the same kind of dedicated mediocrity that Son House and Willie Brown assigned to Robert Johnson. In the words of Jesse Lee Denson, who grew up in the same public housing project as Elvis but was seen as a kind of golden boy with a sure ticket to success both as a musician and as an athlete: "The difference between me and him was, I went for it. I drove for it. New York, Hollywood — I went everywhere for it. And he fell into the shithole and came up with the gold watch and chain."

There are people who *still* believe that — about both Elvis and Robert Johnson. The unspoken question always remains: What does he have that I don't have? A perfectly understandable question for anyone who trusts in yearbook prophecies. But what is perhaps more significant than contemporary reaction is the extent to which posterity embraces the same answers: the devil theory in the case of Robert Johnson, the idiot savant explanation in the case of Elvis (which posits that he would have been nothing had it not been for the genius of his discoverer, Sam Phillips — and that he was undone by the machinations of his manager, Colonel Tom Parker). In each of these cases, it should be understood, we are merely witnessing a natural, a very *human* need to explain the inexplicable. To say that Robert Johnson sold his soul to the devil is to pay him the highest compliment we can pay any artist — which is to say that his art defies explanation, it rises above its surroundings.

But with that said, what is it about Robert Johnson's music that makes it stand out so dramatically from the rest? While some in the blues community have argued that it is simply the result of the star treatment accorded his afterlife, surely it cannot be marketing strategies alone that have enabled Robert Johnson's blues to transcend such formidable barriers of class and culture, time and place.

Perhaps the first barrier to overcome is the idea that art is in any respect a competitive enterprise, that history is no more than a tear-off calendar, to be jettisoned when confronted with the latest style or trend. Robert Johnson, in other words, represents the extension of a tradition in which he had been thoroughly schooled, no less than Elvis Presley, Jimi Hendrix, Aretha Franklin, or Tupac Shakur spring from specific, readily ascertainable influences. Listening to Charley Patton's blues from an earlier generation, picking up various threads of the Delta blues tradition in the music of Son House, Tommy Johnson, Willie Brown, or Bukka White, recognizing the sources of some of Robert Johnson's greatest compositions in the strange harmonics of Skip James or the sophisticated piano-guitar duets of Leroy Carr and Scrapper Blackwell does not take anything away from either the synthesis or the source. Each stakes out its own territory, and each honors a shared tradition that ranges far beyond the blues itself—a tradition not just of music but of storytelling and preaching, a tradition that prizes resourcefulness of language and rhythm alike, a tradition that was born of the need to invent itself outside the cultural mainstream and in the process has come in many respects not just to influence but to *define* that mainstream. In that sense Robert Johnson's music unquestionably reflects the rich tapestry of African American culture as much as it reflects Robert Johnson alone. You cannot separate Robert Johnson's music from its roots any more than any of us can deny his or her own past, if only to trace how we got to where we are today.

But at the same time there is also something undeniably unique about Robert Johnson's blues, there is a kind of limpidity, a conscious fashioning of notes and images, words, sound, and emotional effect that sets his blues apart from any other music you will ever hear. If I were to point to one thing that stands out most about Robert Johnson's music—and I'm not talking here about his *hommages* to Lonnie Johnson or some of his more pedestrian exercises within the tradition—it would be this sense of focus, the way in which his best songs are conceived of as discrete pieces, cohesive compositions that exist in and of themselves, without sacrificing any of the fluency or emotional spontaneity of the blues. Take a song like "Crossroads," perhaps Johnson's most familiar recording and one that has been covered by everyone from Eric Clapton to the Cowboy Junkies. What strikes us most about the original, I think, what is most unduplicatable no matter how many covers attempt to mimic its delivery and form, is the manner in which all of its parts—voice, guitar, lyrics—tend toward a single point, create a single indivisible whole, but a whole not limited to any one background or culture, a whole that translates by its carefully considered craft and sensibility into other contexts, other lives. This is undoubtedly what all art aspires to in one form or another, to offer a window on experience, a window that is left open for anyone to enter by the very calculation of its making. With "Crossroads," for example ("Standing at the crossroads / I tried to flag a ride / Didn't nobody seem to know me / Everybody pass me by"), the singer may or may not be thinking of an actual crossroads, the song may or may not stem from some literal experience — but if it does, it transcends that experience by offering a metaphor and a sense of encroaching darkness (literal? figurative?) that any of us can understand.

I don't mean that you won't find examples of the same kind of pooled tradition in Robert Johnson's work that you find in any blues singer's, great or otherwise. Even Bob Dylan falls back on common rhymes, and certainly we can point to the same kind of "floating verses" in Robert Johnson's blues that we find in Son House's — it is the common property of a culture. But that same common property — words *and* music — is used in Robert Johnson's case to fashion a unique vision. In Son House's or Howlin' Wolf's work, in Muddy Waters', for that matter, as inspired as he may have been by Johnson's example — the point is not so much the integrity of the individual composition as it is to wring every last ounce of feeling from the song; it's not the lyrics specific to this or that setting or the marriage of each particular element so much as finding a way to enter a realm beyond meaning, beyond language, beyond translation. An emotional realm which Robert Johnson's music, too, inhabits on one level, while at the same time offering access to a multiplicity of other levels, of both meaning and feeling.

Charley Patton would offer another point of comparison. There is no greater, fiercer, or more versatile blues singer/"songster" than Patton, perhaps the best-known voice of the Mississippi blues generation prior to Johnson's as well as the most influential. Like Robert Johnson and Son House, he sang blues, spirituals, "folk" material like "Frankie and Albert," and he was in addition a chronicler of local characters and mores, not excluding his own. When he sings of his arrest for public drunkenness ("Tom Rushen Blues") and even gives details of the trial ("High Sheriff Blues"), it is not that you will ever forget the tale or the raucous, highly entertaining manner of its delivery; it is simply that it is rooted forever in a time and place that may seem comic, exotic, or racially regressive, that may gain in power by the very specificity of its detail, but that cannot be said to cross over into the illimitable, the *indefinable* realm of poetry. Just listen, in contrast, to even so commonplace a song of Robert Johnson's as "Come On in My Kitchen." There is no question that Johnson's song is based melodically on "Sittin' on Top of the World," probably as popular a number, and as familiar a tune, as the blues has ever known. Nor is the subject matter any more exalted than Patton's—it is a simple song of seduction. And yet somehow the combination of Johnson's voice, his guitar, his entire *approach* to the song creates an effect that in fellow bluesman and close friend Johnny Shines' description affected his audience "in a way that I could never understand. One time in St. Louis we were playing [it], he was playing very slow and passionately, and when we had quit, I noticed no one was saying anything. Then I realized they were crying— both women and men."

Take a much greater song like "Hellhound on My Trail." With its tortured imagery, its tormented delivery, it's hard to imagine him even singing it to a contemporary audience—a crowd gathered on a street corner, juke-joint celebrants drinking, dancing, gambling on a Saturday night. And yet he *continues* to sing it to a contemporary audience, to convey to us a tale of metaphysical terror in which the "hellhound" on his trail may well derive from a literal reading of Scripture but the feeling of unease, the sense that there is neither sanctuary nor resting place, is an abiding image with which we can all identify, an unforgettably chilling moment that stands forever fixed in its frame.

Robert Johnson's blues, like any art that moves us, should be taken as a beginning, not an end, an inspiration, not a public monument. As Johnny Shines never tired of pointing out, you have to build your house on a solid foundation, "if you forget your beginnings you can't do much with the future." At the same time, as Johnny was equally quick to remind his listeners, you can't honor the past without embracing the present. It's exciting, Johnny said, recalling his travels with Robert, to live a life without conventional boundaries. "It's really, I mean, if a person live in an exploratory world, then this is the best thing that ever happened to him." That's what art does for us. It removes boundaries, it *puts* us in that exploratory world. That's what is most exciting about Robert Johnson's music: where it takes us. Where it can take us still.

Whose Skip James Is This?

I FIRST MET Skip James at Dick Waterman's apartment in Cambridge in the summer of 1965. I sought him out because, quite simply, his music had overwhelmed me: the blues that he had recorded for Paramount Records in 1931 on piano and guitar, four of whose sides had been reissued on collectors' labels in the early '60s, had struck me as unfathomably strange, beautiful, and profound. Then in June of 1964 the singer himself was rediscovered in a hospital in Tunica, Mississippi, and when he appeared at the Newport Folk Festival some five or six weeks later, his music was just as haunting, just as profound, his pure falsetto floated out over that festival field with all the ethereal power of the records but with a new and eerie reality. When, a year later, he was booked into Club 47 in Cambridge and I found out that he would be staying with Dick Waterman, who managed Mississippi John Hurt and Son House at the time and would very shortly take over Skip's booking and management, too, I felt an obligation to seek him out. I'm not sure what exactly emboldened me. I didn't know Dick, except as one of the blues elite who could hang out backstage at Newport or stride past the waiting lines at Club 47 and walk right in the door. I certainly didn't know Skip. And at twenty-one, I was temperamentally disinclined to approach *anyone* outside the realm of my immediate circle of acquaintance. But I felt, not without an ironic recognition of my own foolishness and insignificance — for no other reason but my overwhelming admiration for his work, the scope of his imagination, I simply felt *compelled* to do it.

I had never formally interviewed anyone before. The closest I had come was when I went to see the English novelist Henry Green two years earlier under similar circumstances, and for much the same reasons. He was a writer I admired so much that I wrote to him when I arrived in England and asked if I could come visit. When he wrote back and agreed

to my importunity, I was panic-stricken—but I remained committed to my belief in art. So I summoned up what little courage I possessed, overcame every existential scruple I had about actually declaring myself (I was a fully signed-up member of the mumbling school of self-effacement), and spent an excruciatingly self-conscious, gloriously transcendent afternoon listening to Henry Green expound upon his views of life and art.

That is more or less what I did with Skip. I called up Dick and told him that I wanted to interview Skip for an article in *Blues Unlimited,* an English fanzine which was the first—and, with Jim and Amy O'Neal's *Living Blues,* which didn't come along until 1970, probably the most adventurous—of all the blues periodicals. Now, I should explain that at the time I had not yet seen *Blues Unlimited,* which had begun its mimeographed publication two years earlier. I had in fact only recently learned of its existence, through a Nat Hentoff column in *The Reporter,* and I had been in touch with its two editors, Simon Napier and Mike Leadbitter, by mail for the past six months without ever having received the first issue of my subscription. It came as something of a surprise, then, when Dick expressed skepticism that *Blues Unlimited* should want to undertake another story on Skip so soon after completing a three-part series. I'm not sure just how I recovered from that, but in the end I found myself sitting in my car on Concord Avenue nervously contemplating my future. I was in fact trying to decide whether or not to take the bulky Norelco tape recorder that was sitting on the front seat beside me out of the car and down the street to Dick's apartment, and it was a spirited inner debate. My father, who had been the editor of his college newspaper, had urged me to leave the tape recorder at home, a *real* reporter relied solely on his notes, he said—but that was not my primary consideration. What really disturbed me was a much simpler issue: How could I walk in and introduce myself to someone carrying all this *baggage*? In the end I left the tape recorder in the car, squared my shoulders, and marched in to meet my fate, to present myself to Skip James, unencumbered if not unafraid.

The man that I met was gracious and reserved, quietly observant but somewhat amused, too, and patient with my foolishness. I knew at the time that the questions I had put together were tiresome both in their obviousness and in their abstraction, but I couldn't think of any others, and Skip dealt with every one of them in a dignified, almost ceremonious

Skip James at the Newport Folk Festival, 1964. *Photograph by Dick Waterman* way. He would counter the naive wonderment of a twenty-one-year-old with the concrete experience of a man forty years my senior. Why'd he quit? "I was so disappointed. Wouldn't you be disappointed, man? I cut twenty-six sides for Paramount in Grafton, Wisconsin. I didn't get paid but $40. That's not doing very good. Wouldn't you be disappointed?" At other times he would brandish a polysyllabic vocabulary at total odds with the stereotype of the "primitive" bluesman but very much in keeping with what I took to be the dark secrets of his music. When I left, it was with the same sense of conflicting excitement and relief that I've come to recognize from countless subsequent interviews over the years: the feeling that I had done it, I had escaped without revealing myself as a *total* fraud, but without having gotten to the heart of the matter either.

I saw Skip James several dozen times over the next few years. His comeback was truncated by illness (he died in 1969) and was not in any case a major marker of success. Generally there would be twenty or thirty people at his performances, sometimes less. Often one felt an obligation to attend, if only out of loyalty. As Dick Waterman observed: "He was a man of intense pride in his ability. He was a genius, and he knew it." He was also aware, Dick pointed out, that "his good friend Mississippi John Hurt's music was much more widely accepted, that John played to wider and larger audiences, that John was an artist in demand, that John made more money. That, however, did not under any circumstances alter his appraisal of John's music. Which was that it was play-party, ball-less, pleasant music, good music for dances and country reels but not to be taken seriously as great blues."

You could see the effect on his music: it appeared to be hampered not just by the cancer that was eating away at him but by disappointment, and the unquestionable seriousness with which he took himself. The first time I saw him play after Newport, in the fall of '64, he was booked for a week into a folk club, the Unicorn, in Boston with John Hurt, and they sang just about everything you could imagine, from Jimmie Rodgers yodels (on which they would duet) to Skip's knocked-out versions of "Lazybones," "Silent Night," and "Girl of My Dreams" at the piano. Later on he would grow visibly more constrained, seeming to view his bookings almost as concert recitals, patiently instructing his audience about a way of life and a musical tradition with which they could not possibly be familiar, in a manner that was both disconcertingly and almost touchingly formal. ("As I first said, it's a privilege and an honor and a courtesy at this time and at

Skip and Mississippi John Hurt, Newport Folk Festival, 1964. *Photograph by Dick Waterman*

this age to be able to confront you with something that may perhaps go down in your hearing and may be in history after I'm gone.") He never failed to sing his trademark number, "Devil Got My Woman," the inspiration for Robert Johnson's "Hellhound on My Trail" (it is a peculiar footnote to history that Skip James, whose Paramount releases were among the most obscure "country blues" sides, should have provided the impetus for two of Robert Johnson's blues, and that his greatest song should have been the inspiration for Johnson's greatest), which he played in the hauntingly dissonant "cross-note" tuning that made Skip's music sound so supernally and indisputably itself. It would be a rare evening that he did not play his chilling Depression-era blues, "Hard Time Killing Floor," or the mournful "Cypress Grove." Generally he would present "I'm So Glad," his "little, tiny" children's song that Cream covered in 1966, at least once during the evening, explaining that while he could no longer play it as fast as he once had, in "sixty-fourth" notes, he could still perform it in "thirty-seconds." He would then take the song at breakneck speed and smile at the applause that washed over him. When I wrote to the editors of *Blues Unlimited* about my recent blues experiences, I always mentioned Skip and cited him as one of my favorite "live" performers. It was always edifying in one way or another to see him—there was never any question that you took something away from the performance, even if it was only a melancholy sense of human limitations, as reflected both in Skip's music and in his increasingly dour mien.

In 1994 a biography of Skip James appeared. It was called *I'd Rather Be the Devil* after his most famous song, and it proposed to offer "new insights into the nature of the blues, the world in which it thrived, and its fate when that world vanished." To do that, the author, Stephen Calt, proposed to demolish the "myth" of Skip James and, by extension, the romantic myth which he suggested had grown up around the blues; he would tell the true story of a bluesman, and the blues milieu, unvarnished and unembellished.

This would certainly be a worthy enough project taken at its face; it is one which was undertaken admirably, for example, by Jeff Titon in his *Early Downhome Blues,* which explores the origins of the blues, both folk and commercial, and the inevitable intersection of the two in the vernacular culture of their time. Mike Bloomfield's *Me and Big Joe,* which tells the tale of the young white guitarist's adventures and misadventures with Big Joe Williams, would be yet another corrective to the romantic view, cast in a first-person, scatological account not suitable to every taste perhaps but utterly convincing in its mix of love and confusion.

This is not the course that Stephen Calt chose to follow. Instead, he produced a book written out of what appears to be little but fear and loathing. He sets out in fact to systematically attack not just Skip James, a figure with whose achievement the world is scarcely familiar enough to justify such heavy-duty demolition, but everyone whose life Skip James ever touched. Skip himself is, in Calt's view, "a figurative white man trapped in a black skin," "cold-blooded," "obsessive," and the possessor of a "delinquent lifestyle." He is misogynistic, "a shameless braggart," "emotionally stunted," a gangster and bootlegger who was the plantation equivalent of "a successful drug dealer in a modern-day housing project," a "rank" exaggerator, "jaundiced," "humorless," "predatory," hypocritical, mendacious, pretentious, and just plain *bad.*

Lest you think that Skip James was any exception to the general rule of knavery and tomfoolery that was abroad in the land, here are just some of the characterizations that Calt offers of some of the book's other characters. In the course of the few pages surrounding Skip's 1964 Newport appearance, we discover Robert Pete Williams "looking like a caricature of a pimp," a "buffoonish" Hammie Nixon, an "embittered" Jesse Fuller, a "bleating" Fred McDowell whose unnamed wife "had a pop-eyed deranged look," a "boorishly bragging" Reverend Robert Wilkins, and a "dim-witted" Son House, "a surly drunk [who was] the laughing stock of his neighbors." (Son House, as much as anyone the inspiration for Robert Johnson's and Muddy Waters' style, appears to be a particular bête noire of Calt's.) And believe me, this is only skimming the surface. On other pages Ishmon Bracey, a contemporary of Skip's who produced a handful of matchless pre-Depression sides, is a "shameless name-dropper" and a "pest," Skip's fellow Bentonia, Mississippi, native Jack Owens an "unwitting bearer of another set of false pretenses" and, perhaps worse, a "derivative amateur"; Skip's father was "a man of primitive anger," Bukka White lacks personal and musical integrity, Mississippi John Hurt is another hopeless amateur, without any real talent or pride. And that's not even getting into all the white people who discover and represent all these "criminals" and buffoons and are even more lacking in integrity and seriousness themselves. Everyone is dismissed, from John Hammond and Alan Lomax to blues record collectors in general (effete "wine sniffers" and "connivers") to folklorists (racists all) to the Beat Generation (if you want four ways to recognize a beatnik, turn to pages 257–259) to the whole folk movement (greedy, stupid, "pretentious," and "nonsensical") to the entire U.S. ("No country could be more inhospitable to the [already dismissed] values of folk music scholars than the commercially oriented society of America, in which what was obsolete was valueless.")

What are we to make of all this? Why even bother with it at all? you might ask. Well, I suppose for me it was the seriousness with which the book was taken in many quarters — and for that I have no explanation at all. About two-thirds of the way through, though, we begin to catch glimpses of what it is all about, as suddenly the author himself appears, an awkward, "gawking," eighteen-year-old blues enthusiast, on his way to Newport in 1964 to see his idol, Skip James. In retrospect, he declares, his "infatuation with blues was a solitary, thoughtless preoccupation." And while he is "intoxicated" when he first hears Skip sing, years later he recognizes "the sentimental, juvenile nature of my joyous excitement [at] the soap-opera triumph of an impaired performer." The final, chilling judgment? "Had I known how our lives would intersect over the next four years, I would not have initiated that first conversation."

Is this a "thorough, clear-headed, and insightful" view, as one review had it, "the best book on the subject of country blues for the layperson"? Is it, as even some negative reviews have tended to suggest, a book deserving of respect because it unflinchingly reveals a truth at odds with observation, decency, and common sense? I don't think so. Not because the book that Calt purportedly set out to write would not have been a fascinating one. And not because there are not occasional nuggets of information, glimmers of idiosyncratic truth as presented in Skip's own words and views throughout. But the entire book is so colored by the language of indiscriminate rage, the sense of imagined slights so infects its very marrow, that there is nothing left but bile, universal loathing, and utter, and abject, self-contempt. In the end this is a terribly sad book, not because of its subject but because of its author. It may perhaps be deserving of our pity but surely not of our attention or respect.

So don't look to this book for a picture of Skip James. Look to the music instead. And if Skip, whose work never ceased to proclaim the beauty of what Gerard Manley Hopkins called "all things counter, original, spare, [and] strange," found himself set apart both from the world of his peers and, in later years, from the moment of time into which he had somehow inexplicably slipped, well, so be it. That was his self-acknowledged lot in life: engrossed in his music, he seemed well aware that he was destined never to fit in.

As Skip himself once declared:

"Now you know sometimes it seem like to me that my music seem to be complicated to some of my listeners. But the one thing that seem to be complicated to me, and that is that they can't catch the ideas. Now I have had some students that are very, very apt—they can catch ideas very quick—and other children, you cannot instill it in them, I don't care, no matter how hard they tried. Well, there are some people, they just don't have a calling for it. Now I might have wanted to do some things I've seen other people do and are prosperous at it, and I would like to take it up myself. But it just wouldn't fit into my life, it wasn't for me. So the thing that a person should do, seemingly, while they're young, is to seek for your talent wherever it is at, and then when you find where it is most fit to put it in execution, do *that*. Well, for myself, I been out traveling ever since I quit school. I've had quite an experience at different ages and different times. And that's the best teacher I found. That's something they cannot take away from you. Personal experience."

FOUR

COSMIC RAY:

How Ray Charles' "I Got a Woman" Transformed the

Music of Ray Charles, Allowed Him to Keep His Band,

and Created a Musical and Social Revolution

Music is not just my life, it's my total existence.
I'm deadly serious, man. I'm not just trying to feed you words.

NERVOUS, INTENSE, compulsively polysyllabic, Atlantic Records' recently installed vice president and minority owner Jerry Wexler could sense the excitement in the voice at the other end of the line. It was not unusual for him and his new partner, thirty-one-year-old Atlantic Records founder Ahmet Ertegun, to receive calls from their recording artists from the road. Usually it was the result of some kind of foul-up, as often as not they were looking for money, but this call from Ray Charles in November of 1954 was different. He was going to be playing the Royal Peacock in Atlanta in a few days, Ray announced in that curious half-stammer in which words spilled over one another to convey energy, certitude, deference, and cool reserve. He still had that same little seven-piece outfit he had put together a few months earlier as a road band for Atlantic's premier star, Ruth Brown—but he had changed the personnel around a little, he told Wexler. The sound was better, tighter, and they had worked up some new original material. He wanted Jerry and Ahmet to come down to Atlanta. He was ready to record.

There was no hesitation on Wexler's or Ertegun's part. Ertegun, a sardonic practical joker who had first been exposed to the deep roots of African American culture as the son of the wartime Turkish ambassador

Ray Charles in Seattle,
ca. 1950. *Courtesy of
Dave "Daddy Cool"
Booth / Showtime
Archives*

to the U.S., had started Atlantic in 1947 on a shoestring with veteran
record man Herb Abramson out of their mutual passion for the music.
He had purchased Ray's contract from the Swing Time label in California
five years later without even meeting his new artist or seeing him in person. Twenty-five hundred dollars was not easy to come by in those days,
but such was his belief in the dimensions of Ray's talent, he was so
"knocked out by the style, vocal delivery, and piano playing" of this
twenty-one-year-old blind, black blues singer whose popularity so far had
derived primarily from nuanced interpretations of the sophisticated styl-
ings of Nat "King" Cole and Charles Brown, that he had no doubt he could
make hit records with him. "I was willing," he told Ray Charles biographer
David Ritz, "to bet on his future."

So far, though, that bet hadn't really paid off. Atlantic had released half
a dozen singles from four sessions to date, with just one of them, a novelty
tune called "It Should've Been Me," released earlier that year, making any
real dent in the charts. More tellingly, Ahmet's direct attempts to move
Ray away from the politely stylized approach with which he had up to this
point made his mark could not be said to have fully succeeded. They had

in fact met with only faint approval from Ray, who, as pleased as he was with his recent progress ("All I wanted was to play music. Good music"), was not particularly "ecstatic" about his present situation either. He had started out imitating Brown and Nat "King" Cole both because he was drawn to their music and because they were popular. "If you could take a popular song and sound like the cat doing it, then that would help you get work. Shit, I needed work, man!" But now he wanted to get work on the basis of his own sound, with the kind of music he heard in his head, every kind of music from Chopin to Hank Williams, from the Original Five Blind Boys of Mississippi to Artie Shaw and Benny Goodman, with "each music," he said, "[having] a different effect." He just wasn't sure where, or how, to find it.

Ahmet and his original partner, Herb Abramson, had tried to help him. Initially they recorded Ray in New York, using, Ahmet said, "the formula we had used so successfully with artists like Big Joe Turner": a house band made up of the best New York studio musicians, with a&r chores assigned to veteran black songwriter and arranger Jesse Stone, who had been involved in nearly every one of Atlantic's hits to date. But Stone and Ray had clashed ("I respected Jesse Stone," Ray told David Ritz, "but I also respected myself"), and no one was fully satisfied, not even when Ray was given more leeway at the second New York session in the spring of 1953, exuberantly driving the boogie-woogie pastiche that Ahmet had written for him, "Mess Around," and throwing himself into the part of a slick, jive-talking jitterbug on the slower, but just as emphatically rhythm-driven, "It Should've Been Me."

Then, a few months later, he found himself in New Orleans—"I never lived there," he told me in response to any attempt on my part to make something more of it. "I spent some *time* there. Let's not get the two confused. I got *stranded* there is the best way to put it. Meaning, I got there, and I didn't have any money, and the people there took me in."

It was a situation that he absolutely hated. He had lost his sight at the age of six, but his mother had taught him that there was nothing he could not do; she refused to allow him to consider himself "handicapped"; she insisted fiercely that he always assert his independence. He was educated at the Florida School for the Deaf and Blind in St. Augustine, but he had been on his own since his mother's death when he was fifteen and had made his way in the world as a professional musician ever since. He had had a hit record on Swing Time at eighteen, then gone on the road with blues singer Lowell Fulson for two years, where he soon became the leader of Fulson's nine-piece band. He prided himself justifiably on his resourcefulness and intelligence — but here he was stuck in New Orleans in the summer of 1953, just *scuffling*. He was twenty-two years old, a heroin addict almost from the time he entered the music business, a musician with a certain measure of success but clearly not strong enough to carry a band to play his music or support himself as a single. He was, in short, dependent on the kindness of strangers.

Sometimes you can do things, and it'll be too soon. The people ain't ready for it. It can be all kinds of things, but if it's good, that's the main thing. At least you won't have to be embarrassed.

WHATEVER THE CIRCUMSTANCES of his arrival, New Orleans proved a fortuitous landing place. He moved into Foster's Hotel on LaSalle ("The guy let me stay there sometimes [when] I couldn't pay, and he didn't throw me out on the street"), got bookings at local clubs while playing gigs occasionally out of town, in Slidell and Thibodaux, and every day, with neither a cane, a seeing-eye dog, nor the assistance of anyone else, negotiated the four-block journey from Foster's to local club owner Frank Painia's Dew Drop Inn for a lunch of red beans and rice. Asked how he could find his way in life so confidently and precisely, he told a fellow musician it was easy. "I do just like a bat. You notice I wear hard-heeled shoes? I listen to the echo from my heels, and that way I know where there's a wall. When I hear a space, that's the open door."

In August of 1953 Ahmet and his new partner (Jerry Wexler, a one-time journalist and fellow jazz and r&b enthusiast, had joined Atlantic after Herb Abramson was drafted just two months earlier) went down to New Orleans for a Tommy Ridgley session that represented the thirty-six-year-old Wexler's first foray into the field. As Wexler described it in his autobiography, this was the first of many such trips, in which they would hit town after a rocky flight and Ahmet, who had either slept through the turbulence or kept "his head buried in Kant's *Critique of Pure Reason* or the latest issue of *Cash Box,* [would] be ready to roll [and] I'd be ready to crash. . . . The next thing I knew it was morning and Ahmet was just get-

Ahmet Ertegun, Jerry Wexler, Big Joe Turner. *Courtesy of Jerry Wexler*

ting in, brimming over with tales of . . . existential happenings." Given Ray's current residence and his obvious need for work, Ahmet got in touch with him to play on the session, at whose conclusion Ray cut a couple of blues with the all-star New Orleans band that Ahmet had assembled for the occasion.

The first, "Feelin' Sad," was a song written and originally recorded by a twenty-seven-year-old New Orleans-based bluesman who went by the name of Guitar Slim and whom Ray had met through Dew Drop proprietor (and Slim's manager and landlord) Frank Painia. Slim, whose real name was Eddie Jones, frequently dressed in a fire-engine-red suit, used a two-to-three-hundred-foot-long guitar cord that permitted him to stroll out the door of the Dew Drop and entertain passersby on the street, and occasionally dyed his hair blue — but the eight-bar blues that Ray chose to record didn't really stand out from the traditional blues material with which Ray had always worked, except for the churchy, exhortatory feel that Slim had imparted to it.

Ray brought some of the same fiery passion to his performance, wailing the words with an almost tearful break in his voice, calling out to the musicians — and presumably his listeners — to "Pray with me, boys, pray with me," and concluding with a hummed chorus that burst into a rough-edged gospel shout, with a bed of horns standing in for the amen corner. Even the second song, "I Wonder Who," a much more conventional composite blues, carried with it some of those same hints — though they were only hints — of the gospel pyrotechnics that Ray so admired in singers like Archie Brownlee of the Five Blind Boys of Mississippi. It was a slow, almost doleful blues, enlivened only by the passion in Ray's voice, and while Jerry and Ahmet were both glad to see Ray abandoning some of his stylistic refinements, neither felt they had made any real progress toward establishing a new direction in Ray's music, a new voice of his own.

Ray certainly didn't take it as any great turning point — he would have been the first to admit that at this point he was still just feeling his way. At the same time he recognized that if he ever expected to get anywhere, he'd better *find* his way pretty damn quick. He wasn't all that sure how he felt about the new man either. He had always taken Ahmet's wry enthusiasm — for him *and* the music — at face value. With his dry nasal voice, his sharp wit and parrying intelligence, above all the unmistakable respect and belief he had shown in Ray from the start ("[He] never, ever said to me I couldn't record a piece of music. That kind of tells you"),

Ahmet could never be deflected from the ironic assurance of his outlook or the certitude of his goals. Wexler on the other hand seemed edgy, almost jittery in his need to show who was in charge. At one point when Ray was playing behind Tommy Ridgley, Wexler told him, "Don't play like Ray Charles, you're backup." Which might have been the first and last straw if Ray had been dealing with anyone else, but he could see that Jerry was the same with Ahmet and Cosimo Matassa, the recording studio owner and engineer, both of whom seemed to just laugh it off as part of the makeup of a man who clearly was passionate about what he was doing but just wasn't cool.

He remained in New Orleans for the next few months, taking gigs as far away as Baton Rouge but generally returning to the Foster Hotel on the same night, even if it meant getting home not long before the break of day. He played blackjack, using Braille-marked cards, with fellow musicians ("Best blackjack player I ever saw," said one), maintained his drug connection, but kept to himself a good deal of the time, sometimes listening to his spiritual records and gospel music on the radio all day long, "the best singers I ever heard in my life [with] voices that could shake down your house and smash all the furniture in it. Jesus, could they wail!"

Gradually he put together a group of like-minded musicians, fellow eclectics to play and jam with on a semi-regular basis. "Feelin' Sad," his fourth Atlantic release, came out in September and did nothing. Then in October of 1953 he was approached by Frank Painia to play on a Guitar Slim session, Slim's first for the West Coast label Specialty. Painia asked him, would he mind listening to some of the songs that Slim wanted to do, maybe he could write some arrangements. "See, everybody knew I could write," Ray said. And everybody knew Slim's utter lack of organization. That was how Ray Charles became leader, arranger, and taskmaster for a series of stark, Guitar Slim–composed compositions whose riveting centerpiece was a number called "The Things That I Used to Do."

"The Things That I Used to Do," Eddie Jones claimed, had been presented to him by the devil in a dream and was a fiery, gospel-laced number with little sense of form until Ray got hold of it. It was not, Ray insisted, an easy task. "I liked Guitar Slim, he was a nice man, but he was not among the musicians that I socialized with. Believe me, we worked our ass off for that session. We started in the morning and worked well into the night, and once we got through it, I said, 'Okay, I'm glad to be part of it.' But my music had absolutely nothing to do with what we did with Guitar Slim."

There was more to it, though, despite the emphatic disclaimer. The unrestrained way that Slim attacked the material, the loose, spontaneous feel that he brought to the session, above all the sheer, uninhibited preacher-like power of his voice must have struck some kind of common chord, for all of Ray's vehement denials. And — something he denied even more vehemently, to the end of his life — the way that Guitar Slim *attacked* his songs surely must have had some kind of liberating effect. There was, it seemed, something almost inevitable in the feelings that it would come to unleash in his own music, feelings that up till now he had experienced only in his passion for gospel music. And the gargantuan success of Slim's record in the early days of 1954 (it went to number one on the r&b charts in January, remaining there off and on for fourteen weeks and becoming one of the biggest-selling blues records of all time) must surely have left its mark, too.

Ray continued to rehearse and play with some of the musicians who had provided the nucleus for the Guitar Slim session, and when Ahmet and Jerry Wexler came back to town for a Big Joe Turner session on December 3, 1953, he was ready to record. They couldn't get the use of Cosimo's studio the next day, so they went to radio station WDSU, where Ray opened with an exuberant falsetto whoop in his takeoff on a traditional blues composition, "Don't You Know." This was no knee-jerk approach to the blues, though, interspersed as it was with his own preacherly gruffness and churchy squeals, while the band followed right along without prompting from Ahmet or Jerry. It was, clearly, a very different kind of session, with even the more somber traditional blues that followed expressing itself with that weeping, wailing sound that had first manifested itself on Slim's "Feelin' Sad" at the last New Orleans session. It was, as Jerry Wexler would come to realize afterward, "a landmark session . . . because it had: Ray Charles originals, Ray Charles arrangements, a Ray Charles band. . . . Ahmet and I had nothing to do with the preparation, and all we could do was see to it that the radio technician didn't erase the good takes during the playbacks."

Ray moved his home base to Texas and went back on the road as a single at $75 a week early in the new year. "It Should've Been Me," the novelty song from the second New York session, hit the charts at the beginning of April 1954, rising as high as number five, while Guitar Slim's "The Things That I Used to Do" remained at number one. Which was all very well, but the musical exigencies of life on the road as a single were

becoming more and more unendurable for Ray. He played a gig in Philadelphia, and "the band was so bad," he told *New Yorker* writer Whitney
Balliett, "I just went back to my hotel and cried."

I was going crazy, man. I was losing my fucking head. Because, you know,
you go into a town, and the guy says he got the musicians, and the
musicians weren't shit. And if you're a very fussy person like me — and,
I mean, I'm fussy even about good musicians — well, I just couldn't take it.

THAT WAS THE FINAL IMPETUS for putting his own band together.
"I pestered the Shaw [booking agency] to death," he told Balliett, "and
they loaned me the money to buy a station wagon, and I had enough
money to make a down payment on a car for myself. I went down to Dallas
and put a band together out of people I had heard one place or another."
But the booking agency, Ray told me, said he still wasn't strong enough to
be booked on his own. "Which they were right. They said, 'In order for
you to work, we gonna put your band with Ruth Brown.' I said okay, and
we worked four or five dates with her. In fact, we only did four, because
the second date we missed. That first date we drove all day doing a
hundred-and-some-odd miles an hour, from Dallas to El Paso, it's amazing
we didn't burn [the engines] up, because they both were new cars. The
next job was in Louisiana, all the way back from where we just came from
and then some. Drove our ass off, and we were late and we missed it. We
got there at eleven o'clock at night, and the people canceled the job on us.
Now you talk about sick — we was SICK." Then they worked a few dates
in Mississippi and Florida, "and that was it. Ruth Brown left and went in
[one] direction, and we went in another."

There was no question of the direction that he had set for himself.
With the band, he wrote in his autobiography, *Brother Ray*, he was able
at last to become himself. "I opened up the floodgates, let myself do things
I hadn't done before. . . . If I was inventing something new, I wasn't aware
of it. In my mind, I was just bringing out more of me." His immediate
problem, though, in the fall of 1954 was to figure out a way to sustain the
band. And for that, there was no question, he needed a hit.

He appointed trumpeter Renald Richard, whom he had originally met
in New Orleans, musical director for an extra five dollars a week, then
paid him an additional five dollars to write out the charts according to

Ray's dictation as they drove along in his brand-new '54 DeSoto. "Ray dictated fast," Richard told Charles biographer Michael Lydon. "And he didn't work out the chart in the concert key, the chords as he played them on the piano. No, he'd give me the parts transposed . . . do one instrument, on to the next, and I'm writing and writing!" They listened to the radio, too. "Ray loved blues singers like Big Joe Turner," Renald Richard told Lydon, "but most of all he loved gospel singers. He used to talk all the time about Archie Brownlee, the lead singer with the Five Blind Boys of Mississippi, how much he liked him. Then he started to sound like him, turning his notes, playing with them to work the audience into a frenzy."

They were out on tour in early October. They had just played South Bend and were on their way to Nashville, with the radio tuned to whatever gospel music they could pick up as the stations faded in and out in the middle of the night. All of a sudden a song called "It Must Be Jesus" by the Southern Tones came on the air. It was a simple midtempo variation on the old spiritual, "There's a Man Going Around Taking Names," with the kind of tremolo guitar accompaniment that had come into fashion lately in a music that had up till now been sung mostly a cappella. The tenor singer took the lead on a pair of verses which began at the high end of his range, with the first line ("There's a man going around taking names") repeated in a slightly higher register and the third ("You know, he took my mother's name") rising yet again to the point where the singer's voice broke intentionally, the same way that Ray broke his voice in a kind of "yodel" on "Feelin' Sad" or "Don't You Know."

Almost without thinking about it, Ray and Renald Richard started singing along, but where the Southern Tones started out their second verse ("There's a man giving sight to the blind"), Ray and Renald broke into a secular verse ("I got a woman / Way across town / Who's good to me") with Ray's voice echoing exactly the Southern Tones' lead singer's intense intro and resolution. Then, after the second verse, the gospel number broke into a kind of syncopated patter between the tenor and the bass singer, the kind of give-and-take that the Golden Gate Quartet used for novelty effect but which in the contemporary gospel mode could be drawn out in live performance, building in tension until at last it was resolved by returning to the verse. Ray and his band director broke themselves up on this part as they substituted secular and profane variations on the spiritual message ("He's my rock / He's my mighty power") along the lines of "She gives me money / When I'm in need. . . ." Ordinarily that would have been the end of it, just a bit of late-night foolishness, but there was something about the song, and their lighthearted extemporization, that got to Ray in a way he couldn't quite put his finger on, and, rather than explore it himself, he asked Renald if he thought he could formally write out a song that was structured around their improvisation. "I said, 'Hell, yes,' and the next morning, ten o'clock, I was in his room with [it]. I didn't really write it all that night. I stuck in the bridge from another song I had written years back."

Ray sketched out an arrangement and started singing the new song, "I Got a Woman," in the show almost immediately. Renald Richard left shortly thereafter, largely over the way drugs seemed to be taking over the band, but the song continued to get a stronger and stronger response. Ray worked up a couple of other originals, along with "Greenbacks," a novelty number that Renald had contributed to the band's book, until he felt like he was ready for a full-scale session. That was when he called up Atlantic Records and announced to Jerry Wexler that he was coming to Atlanta and was ready to record. It was the first time he had called a session on his own, and he may have seemed more confident than he was. After all, he was not about to reveal his insecurities to just anyone, least of all someone like Ahmet Ertegun, who had treated him with so much respect and consideration. But if he wanted to keep the band together—and that was just about like saying if he wanted to keep on breathing—he needed a fucking hit.

Ahmet and Jerry met him at his hotel, just a few doors down from the club, the Royal Peacock, on "Sweet Auburn" Avenue, the hub of black life in Atlanta. It was a street humming with life, there were dozens of independent black businesses of greater and lesser repute, clubs, bars, beauty shops, and shoeshine stands, all packed together up and down the street, with the Peacock, along with Martin Luther King Sr. 's Ebenezer Baptist Church less than half a mile away, one of the twin centers of that life. The club was owned and operated by sixty-four-year-old Carrie Cunningham, an imposing woman of considerable entrepreneurial imagination and ambition (she owned the hotel, also called the Royal, in which Ray was staying), who had originally come to town as a circus rider after leaving her home in Fitzgerald, Georgia, in her teens with the Silas Green from New Orleans traveling show. She had opened the club in 1949 as a means of keeping her errant musician son at home, and it had almost immediately become a way station for every musician of any repute who passed

The Ray Charles Orchestra, San Francisco, 1968. *Photograph by Jonas Bernholm*

through Atlanta, from Duke Ellington to Big Maybelle. True to its name, it was resplendent with hand-painted images of peacocks and flamboyant color combinations that seemed to come to Miss Cunningham in visions that she had her regally attired staff carry out.

Ahmet and Jerry didn't have time to notice the decor, Ray was in too much of a hurry. They could barely keep up with him as he practically ran down the street, and when they entered the club he already had his seven-piece band set up onstage, two trumpets, two saxes, bass, drums, with a local pickup on guitar, all just sitting there as if waiting for their cue. Ray took his place at the piano and counted off, and the sound of the new song filled the room, a sound for which Ahmet and Jerry were totally unprepared.

It opened with a long, drawn-out, unaccompanied "Wellllll . . ." from Ray, with the band falling in solidly behind him three words into the first line. Ray's voice was altogether commanding but controlled as he sang the words that he and Renald Richard had fooled around with, but he was bearing down in a way that, while it was a recognizable elaboration on everything he had done before, was also something new. And when he got to the part where his voice ascended, with the horns ascending behind him, his voice rose to a kind of controlled climax.

The second verse drove just a little bit harder until, when he reached

Zenas Sears at WAOK, July 1968. *Photograph by Jonas Bernholm*

his highest natural pitch, it rose to a falsetto that was not so much an imitation as a tribute to Archie Brownlee's all-out attack, ending in a kind of discreet groan that signaled a honking solo from Donald Wilkerson on tenor sax. Then Ray took it back, delivering the syncopated recitatif that substituted for a bridge, with his own discreet version of the preacher's trick of a sharp expelling of breath, a pronounced huffing and chuffing that served to mark a kind of ecstatic release. Whereupon it was back to the first verse, his voice commandingly roughened, until he took it out with a tag that announced, "Don't you know she's all right? She's all right, she's all right."

Ahmet and Jerry sat there for a moment, stunned — but they knew right away. Ray ran through his three other new songs, and there was no question about it. Everything was ready, the band was fully rehearsed — it was as if, Ahmet said, he was simply announcing, to himself as much as to them, "This is what I'm going to do." "It was such a departure," Wexler said. "The band was his voice." All that was left was to set up a session.

This turned out to be easier said than done. There was no recording studio in Atlanta readily at hand (the recent regional success of Elvis Presley's first Sun record had not yet set off the explosion of local recording facilities that would soon follow in the mid-South), so they turned to their old friend Zenas "Daddy" Sears, a white New Jerseyan who had moved to Atlanta just before the Second World War, then took to the airwaves upon his return from the service, where he had acquired a love for gospel music and rhythm and blues while operating a little fifty-watt radio station in the hills of India for the mostly black troops who were stationed there. Just eight months earlier he had moved to a brand-new station, WAOK, dedicated exclusively to black programming, which before long he would come to own. It would have been logical to use the new radio studio, but WAOK had a full programming schedule, and eventually Zenas set up the session at WGST at Georgia Tech, his old station, the only catch being that they would have to break every hour for the news. There was some talk of Zenas bringing in a female singer he had worked with, Zilla Mays, to underscore the gospel sound, but nothing came of it. Jerry meanwhile tried to prep the less-than-enthusiastic radio engineer on the uniqueness of what they were about to do, but he quickly gave up on the idea when he realized that however earnestly he cued him for a sax solo that was coming up, all he got for his efforts was a quizzical shrug after the solo was past.

Ray kicked off with "Blackjack," an impassioned minor-key blues he had been working on while out on tour with T-Bone Walker, the consummate guitar stylist of the age. (B.B. King was one of his many disciples, as was, evidently, Wesley Jackson, the local guitarist on the session.) "T and I were up all night at a boarding house in Hattiesburg, Mississippi, playing blackjack," Ray told the co-author of his autobiography, David Ritz. "I'm winning big, over $2,000. T is down to his last 80 bucks . . . and just as he hits 16 with a 5, the Christian lady who owns the house sees him taking my money and starts yelling, 'How dare you take advantage of this poor blind man?' She was so irate she wouldn't let T touch my bread. Afterwards T told me, 'That shit's so funny you oughta write a song about it.' Well, I did." A song that ended with the horns coming in only on the last two drawn-out notes for an ironically sober Amen.

Jerry and Ahmet were no less impressed than they had been the day before. The arrangement was perfectly calibrated to the new rough-edged sound of Ray's vocals. But "I Got a Woman" was what they were waiting for — that was the reason for the session — and from the deliberate, almost stately pace of the count-off, and the elegantly elongated "Wellllll" that would soon become the musical catchphrase of a generation, their expectations were not just confirmed but exceeded. The guitar had by now dropped out — if it was present at all for the rest of the session, it was strictly as another element in the percussive mix. "Ray had every note that was to be played by every musician in his mind," said Ahmet, who had recorded some of the signature sounds of the past decade. "It was a real lesson to me to see an artist of his stature at work. You could lead him a little bit, but you really had to let him take over. For the first time, we heard something that didn't have to be messed around with, it was all there."

Even Ray, as determined a non-determinist as I have ever met ("My thing, man, has always been to do what I do, that's all," was about as much as you were ever going to get from him in the way of causative explanation), recognized the significance of the occasion. This was the moment, he said, that "I started being me." From this point on, whatever vicissitudes life might have in store for a blind heroin addict living by his wits in an indifferent world (a tendentious formulation with which Ray, who before long would quite rightly come to be called "The Genius" by his record company, would contumaciously disagree), there was no turning back. "The minute I gave up trying to sound like [someone else] and said, 'Okay, be yourself,' that was all I knew. I couldn't be nothing else but that."

How the shit can you explain a feeling? Everything, as far as I'm concerned is notes. Every [song] ain't sad, every song ain't funny, every song is not a dramatic-type thing. I don't believe the world is like that.

THE RECORD CAME OUT at the end of December 1954, and it hit like an atom bomb. "It has a rocking, driving beat and a sensational vocal," *Billboard* enthused about its Spotlight Pick for the new year. This record, it proclaimed, was unquestionably "one of the most infectious blues sides to come out on any label since the summer." But even the unqualified ardor of its endorsement could scarcely have predicted the effect the song would have not just on gospel and r&b but on rock 'n' roll (which had yet to be officially recognized) and the whole course of popular music still to come. "Records like [these] almost gospel-styled blues disks . . . don't come along often," *Billboard* would declare five months later of the follow-up single, a fervently delivered double-sided hit (one side was a direct transliteration of the spiritual standard "This Little Light of Mine," with "girl" substituting for "light"), and went on to wonder at the almost hypnotic and "commanding quality" that the artist was able to put across on disk. But even that degree of recognition failed to fully grasp the almost unimaginable impact, both commercial and aesthetic, the irreversible signal that "I Got a Woman" provided to the entire pop marketplace.

Twenty-year-old Elvis Presley, with just two Sun singles to his credit, added a freewheeling version of "I Got a Woman" to his live repertoire virtually from the day it came out and made a number of attempts to record it for Sun in early 1955, although he wasn't able to get a version that he liked until a year later, when he recorded it as the first song on his first RCA session.

Little Walter, the incomparable blues harmonica player, had recorded a song called "My Babe" by Willie Dixon in mid-1954 in a format that Dixon called a "Howlin' Wolf type" of blues, but once Willie heard "I Got a Woman," he rewrote the song and took Walter back into the studio to cut it to the tune of Sister Rosetta Tharpe's classic spiritual, "This Train." In that form it rose to number one on the r&b charts, where it remained for seven weeks, challenged each week by the source of its inspiration, Ray's "I Got a Woman," which reached number one in Juke Box Plays (one of the three Best-Seller categories) on May 7.

Art Rupe, the head of Specialty Records, one of the country's two leading gospel labels, and home of the Soul Stirrers, whose young lead singer, Sam Cook, had gained a reputation as the "matinee idol" of quartet singing for both his looks and his voice, saw the future open up in front of his eyes.

"Try to write words in the blues field," he wrote to one of his star spiritual singers and composers, Sister Wynona Carr, "to songs in the Gospel field that have been hits in the past. For example, you know what Ray Charles did with 'I Got a Woman.' Also, Little Walter took 'This Train' and made it into 'My Babe,' and it was a big hit. That seems to be what the people are buying today, and even if you cannot sing these numbers in your style [yourself], we certainly need them desperately for our other artists."

Almost simultaneously Rupe contacted a twenty-two-year-old performer named Little Richard Penniman from Macon, Georgia, who had been pestering him incessantly about a demo he had sent to the Specialty office a few weeks earlier. Up until that time Rupe had been unable to see the commercial potential of an overtly secular performer performing in a style somewhere between gospel singers Marion Williams and Professor Alex Bradford. Now he did. He signed Little Richard right away, and before the year was out released "Tutti Frutti," an ear-shattering fusion of driving gospel and r&b that reached the Top 20 of the pop charts and stands as one of the cornerstones of rock 'n' roll.

Sam Cook was the last link in the chain. He was twenty-four years old, with a velvety voice that Ray Charles recognized as utterly unique ("Nobody sound[ed] like Sam Cooke. He hit every note where it was supposed to be, and not only hit the note but hit the note with *feeling*"), and it would have been impossible to imagine any young singer achieving a greater degree of popularity or status in the gospel world. From the day that "I Got a Woman" was released, however, he was under constant pressure — both internal and external — to cross over.

It started in earnest in the summer of 1955, when Bill Cook, an influential black DJ and talent manager from Newark, and Specialty's a&r head, Bumps Blackwell, started courting Sam separately, with each one telling him that with their guidance he would be able to go places in pop he could never go in gospel, break through to a level of popular acceptance inaccessible even to Ray Charles. Bill Cook, who in the past two years had discovered and guided Roy Hamilton, a big-voiced, gospel-rooted singer, to a preeminent position in the r&b world, brought Sam not just to the attention but to the offices of Atlantic Records, again and again — but nothing ever came of it due to Sam's own persistent feelings of ambivalence. It wasn't until the end of 1956 that he was able to make up his mind even to enter the studio for a pop session — and then only under the name of *Dale* Cook. The number that he recorded, "Lovable," was a direct translation of his current gospel hit, "Wonderful," and while sales were only moderately successful, less than a year later "You Send Me," his first pop single under his own name (with an *e* added to his surname to lend a touch of elegance), went to number one on the pop charts.

But let me just back up for a moment, not simply for the sake of chronological verisimilitude but also to suggest some of the foundations for a movement that had been building stealthily for some time. Certainly there had been gospel-inspired r&b songs before, and the rate and impact of their success had accelerated rapidly in the last year or two, with the chart success of such "inspirational" numbers (as they were called) as Sonny Til and the Orioles' "Crying in the Chapel" (number one r&b, number eleven pop in the summer of 1953), Faye Adams' "Shake a Hand" (number one r&b a month or so later), and Roy Hamilton's version of "You'll Never Walk Alone," the Rodgers and Hammerstein message of unwavering reassurance from the musical *Carousel* (number one r&b in early 1954, number twenty-one pop). In fact, as *Billboard* reported in early 1954, with something of a hint of incredulity, "'Shake a Hand,' a common greeting among followers of spiritual and gospel music, is being uttered more so today by other facets of the entertainment industry . . . largely because the religious field continues to gain recognition as a growing bonanza."

The phenomenon had been duly noted, then. But not until the arrival of "I Got a Woman" had any other song so explicitly embraced its gospel roots. Anyone with even a cursory knowledge of the music could tell where the inspiration for all these songs was coming from — but with "I Got a Woman," the lineage came right out and declared itself, not just the lineage but its proud and unabashed Afro-American roots. As a still-unpublished Albert Murray, soon to become known as a leading literary proponent of black cultural pride, wrote to his friend Ralph Ellison of two recent "dance dates" by Ray: "Man, that cat operates on these Los Angeles Negroes like Reverend Ravazee at revival time. . . . That goddamned Ray ass Charles absorbs everything and uses everything. Absorbs it and assimilates it with all that sanctified, stew meat smelling, mattress stirring, fucked up guilt, touchy violence, jailhouse dodging, second hand American dream shit, and sometimes it comes out like a sermon by one of them spellbinding stem winders in your work-in-progress, and other times he's extending [Count] Basie's stuff better than Basie himself. Who knows maybe some of that stuff will help to set a number of people up for old BLISS!" To which Ellison, author of what is universally acknowledged as one of the great American novels of the twentieth century, *Invisible Man,* simply replied, "Just reading your description makes me homesick."

At the same time, and for many of the same reasons, nobody else's work came in for the kind of vilification and castigation that Ray's "I Got a Woman" received from diverse elements of the black community, including blues singers and preachers alike. "He's mixing the blues with spirituals," declared Big Bill Broonzy, the most cosmopolitan of blues singers, and someone who from all appearances was not averse to doing the same. "I know that's wrong." And Josh White, who had been criticized for taking the blues to sophisticated supper clubs and parading himself as a kind of deracinated "sex symbol," agreed. In the words of Brother Joe May, known as "The Thunderbolt of the Middle West" and one of the most compelling of all gospel singers: "Failure to recognize r&b for what it is may cause a general undermining of all true gospel singing everywhere."

Even Martin Luther King felt compelled to weigh in, in an advice column in *Ebony* magazine in 1958, with the stern admonition that "the profound sacred and spiritual meaning of the great music of the church must never be mixed with the transitory quality of rock and roll music [which] often plunges men's minds into degrading and immoral depths."

For all of his respect for Dr. King, however, and for all of his pragmatic commitment to the civil rights movement (he pretty much took Albert Murray and Zora Neale Hurston's all-American point of view that he didn't have to go begging outside his own community to find a full measure of cultural, if not economic, satisfaction), from where Ray sat, the music spoke for itself. It was only with the commercial success of "I Got a Woman," Ray remarked drily, that his booking agency was finally willing to concede that "maybe we can do something with you." But it was the increasingly charismatic nature of his live performances, the "incredible spell," as *Billboard* remarked, "that Charles wields over his live audiences," that permitted him to perform his own music in his own way, a pure distillation of everything he had ever heard or felt, incorporating blues, jazz, pop, country, and gospel, exuberant celebration and "more despair," too, he wrote in his autobiography, "than anything you'd associate with rock 'n' roll." It was, in short, *Ray Charles music,* by his own or anyone else's definition.

If he chose to answer his critics at all, it was merely to point out, as he did in *Brother Ray,* that he had been "singing spirituals since I was three, and I'd been hearing the blues for just as long. So what could be more natural than to combine them? It didn't take any thinking, didn't take any calculating. All the sounds were there, right at the top of my head. . . . Imitating Nat Cole had required a certain calculation on my part. I had to gird myself; I had to fix my voice into position. I loved doing it, but it certainly wasn't effortless. This new combination of blues and gospel was. It required nothing of me but being true to my very first music." People could say whatever they liked, everyone, as his mother always pointed out to him, is entitled to their own opinion. But in the end, he concluded, after wrestling with the subject for two full pages, "I really didn't give a shit about [their] criticism."

He cared just as little, he insisted, about the effect that his music had on others. Jerry Wexler brought him a copy of Elvis Presley's version of his song, thinking he would be knocked out by it—but he couldn't have cared less, he was simply indifferent. "To be blunt with you, Peter," he told me some twenty-five years later on the subject of his recognition as a near-universal force in contemporary popular music, "I understand what you mean, but I've never given any thought as to who's been doing what, as far as what I'm into. I mean, it's nice to have people say, 'Hey, Ray, I love your music,' or, you know, 'Joe Cocker really sounds a lot like you, Billy Preston idolizes you' — those are nice words, those are very beautiful things, but, you know, it just never occurred to me in any form, I swear to God, to say, 'Now, let's see, Ray, there are some people beginning to emulate what you are doing.' Because — and I don't want you to think I'm selfish, but I'm telling you the truth — I'm just always thinking about what *I'm* doing."

And, to tell you the truth, I believed him. The proof was in the work, which came to represent over the years the entire spectrum of *Ray,* from the deep-seated, almost ineffable sadness of "Hard Times," "Lonely Avenue," and, perhaps most of all, "Drown in My Own Tears," in which time and tempo come to a complete stop, all the way up to and beyond the orgiastic ululations of "What'd I Say," the very definition of everything that Martin Luther King had warned against and, perhaps not coincidentally, in 1959 his first big pop hit. This would be succeeded the following year by a new sound with a new record company, a string-laden treatment of Hoagy Carmichael's moody 1930 composition, "Georgia on My Mind," which gave him his first number-one pop hit in the fall of 1960, just in advance of Elvis Presley's deeply felt revival of another thirty-year-old pop standard, "Are You Lonesome Tonight?"

He would go on to achieve the kind of iconic success he could never have imagined, or, if he is to be believed, even cared about, while at the same time suffering some of the slings and arrows of outrageous fortune to which he professed equal indifference. Of a bad drug bust in Boston in late 1964, which forced him to take a full year off from performing, he was willing to concede only that, after quitting cold turkey ("I can stand almost anything for three days"), the real challenge was to convince the court. "I was a junkie for seventeen years," he wrote in *Brother Ray* with more than a little bravado, "[but] looking back, I can't say that kicking was a nightmare or the low point in my life."

None of it in any case impeded his sense of musical growth or self-progress. "In my life," he declared to me at the end of a long day, "everything I did, I did what I thought was right at the time. I hope I don't sound the same now as I did when I was eighteen. If I do, there's something

Ray Charles at the New Orleans Jazz & Heritage Festival, 1995. *Photograph by David Gahr*

wrong. One thing about my music, it must knock me out. Because if I don't feel it, I can't expect you to feel it. With my music, as egotistical as it may sound, *I must enjoy me.*"

And the world enjoyed Ray, whether he was singing country and western (his *Modern Sounds in Country and Western Music* held the number-one spot on the pop album charts for fourteen weeks in 1962 and remained on the best-selling lists for almost two years) or gutbucket blues, whether he was playing jazz or transforming pop standards like "Come Rain or Come Shine" or even reinventing a patriotic evergreen like "America the Beautiful" as a carefully constructed expression of emotional spontaneity. As Ahmet Ertegun once suggested, referring back to the remarkable metamorphosis in Ray's fortunes after the aesthetic breakthrough of "I Got a Woman, "he only got better. He got more commercial without trying to make hits. He was doing what he wanted to do naturally, but the music and the songs became better and stronger."

He became a universally embraced, almost mythic figure in a way that no other popular African American entertainer, with the possible exception of Louis Armstrong, has ever approached. He was the Bishop, the High Priest of Soul, The Genius, and (his favorite) Brother Ray. But always there was that restless sense of self-exploration, and in the background there always hovered that moment when, with the discovery not just of his own but of a communal voice, he became himself, when, in civil rights pioneer Julian Bond's tribute, "The Bishop of Atlanta," "he seduce[d] the world with his voice. . . ."

Screaming to be ignored, crooning to be heard
Throbbing from the gutter
On Saturday night
Silver offering only
The Right Reverend's back in town
Don't it make you feel all right?

FIVE

Hag at the Crossroads: Portrait of the Artist in Midlife

MERLE HAGGARD seems to occupy a permanent niche in the eye of the storm. The last time I saw him, in the fall of 1978, he was just about to get married, to Leona Williams, but had somehow neglected to arrange the details of his divorce from Bonnie Owens some three days before the wedding. This time, in the spring of 1980, he is in the midst of a well-publicized and protracted misunderstanding with Leona which started virtually on the day of their marriage. "I wouldn't give the marriage till Wednesday," says one insider drily. "And this is Monday." With which Merle seems inclined to agree. He is also at a point in his career when everything seems up for grabs: management, musical direction, lifestyle (he has given up drinking recently, he says, but not "carousing"), movie and television options, art.

Perhaps this is Merle's own brand of midlife crisis. Perhaps it is simply that he enjoys having people fight over him. Certainly he does nothing to interfere when longtime intimates vie for his attention, when veteran members of his band, the Strangers, smolder with resentment over the favored treatment accorded to newer recruits, when rumors swirl that he will soon be leaving his record company, MCA, because Jimmy Bowen, the head of Elektra's Nashville office, is producing his new album. If anything, Merle seems to promote all this conflict, to enjoy the sound of battle raging all about, and unquestionably there exists a deep ambivalence within Merle himself, a clear sense of what he *doesn't* want to do but an uncertainty about what he does, which reflects itself even in an appearance that can alter radically (from scruffily bearded to dapperly mustached to conventionally clean-shaven, from glittering star to seedy barfly) almost from day to day. Perhaps, as Merle says, "The more that's going on, the more life I'm able to be involved with and learn about, the more it seems to replenish my well of ideas." Perhaps, as friends suggest, he enjoys orchestrating all this drama simply because he is bored. About a year ago, he says, he nearly gave up performing and then changed his mind, not out of any love for what he knew but, typically, out of fear of what he didn't. "I found myself wanting to get out of the business simply because I wanted to see if I could do anything else. But I got just far enough away from the business to realize I *couldn't* do anything else. So I decided to stay with it."

He announces this in concert at the Jimmie Rodgers Memorial Festival in Meridian, Mississippi; he says it in his songs; he reflects upon it in his most private moments. But you'll notice that what he's talking about is not music but "business," not songwriting but self-promotion, not playing the guitar, his first and most abiding ambition, but selling himself as a product. For Merle Haggard is perhaps the last true outlaw, the one hold-out against wrapping up and merchandising feelings, the last rebel against high-gloss packaging. The music industry today, it almost goes without saying, speaks less of music than it does of industry, but for Merle Haggard, clearly, the only truth lies in art. Even after twenty years in "the business," he still lives, breathes, sleeps — he is *consumed by* music.

You can hear it in his records. The diverse subject matter and lyrics of his songs declare it. You even see it in the sound check rehearsal for his Saturday night performance at the Jimmie Rodgers Memorial Festival. Arriving shortly after one, the ten-piece band (complete, like Willie Nelson's band, with two drummers and two lead guitars) sets up on the stage of the Temple Theater, whose flashing marquee proclaims the arrival of the stars in downtown Meridian. The theater, built in 1927 (though it never saw the presence of native son Jimmie Rodgers, universally hailed as "the Father of Country Music" — *he* played the old Opera House), boasts such features as a painted railroad backdrop, ornate friezes, hardback seats, the pervasive smell of popcorn, and something that looks like a marble birdbath set off in a lighted alcove. Meridian, a pleasant town of 50,000 with a park dedicated to the memory of its most famous citizen and a museum built as a replica of the Mobile and Ohio railroad depot in Stonewall, Mississippi, is obviously geared up for the annual weeklong event, and Merle is geared up to play it, since Jimmie Rodgers — along with Bob Wills, Bing Crosby, and Lefty Frizzell — is one of his few genuine,

Merle on *The Johnny Cash Show*, August 2, 1969. *Photograph by J. T. Phillips.*
Courtesy of Sony Music Archives

publicly acknowledged heroes. Nonetheless it seems a little incongruous for the star himself to show up early for a sound check, normally the most perfunctory of ceremonies in which a balance is struck for the various mikes and instruments and voice levels are checked.

The few Shriners and Festival organizers who happen to be about (the Hamasa Shrine Temple owns the theater, and throughout the performance security is provided by a fez-topped Hamasa Patrol) are understandably thrilled, and several shake hands and introduce their wives, but for Merle this is obviously more than a star turn. For the next three hours he puts his band through their paces, working out arrangements, calling for slight modifications, picking up clinkers, but mostly just savoring the opportunity to hear the band, to use this collection of remarkable soloists and ensemble players as an instrument to express his own voice. Duke Ellington was once asked what kept him on the road, why he would continue to put up with all the turmoil, emotional and financial, involved in maintaining the kind of big band that he kept. He replied that it was more a matter of self-indulgence than anything else—he simply wanted to hear his music played right—and one gets the feeling that with Merle Haggard it is little different. As the band warms up on Bob Wills numbers and Merle Haggard hits, as they ramble easily through a limitless catalogue of standards and original compositions, you realize that for Merle Haggard this is his reason for being. Merle sways motionlessly in place, knees bent, face for once relaxed and even smiling, directing the action with his fiddle bow, while the band takes off on an extended jam, white-bearded guitarist Grady Martin contributes an exquisite solo, and original Stranger Roy Nichols responds with an equally compact, even more sizzling break. Longtime associate and sometime bus driver Lewis Talley does a couple of Ernest Tubb numbers after much encouragement from Merle, and Merle himself tosses off vocals as casual as they are deeply felt. It's as close as you're going to get to the spirit of Jimmie Rodgers or Bob Wills in the streamlined '80s.

Toward the end of the afternoon, just as Merle is nearly done working out an arrangement of "Miss the Mississippi and You" with Roy Nichols and Norm Hamlet, the only members of the band who played on Merle's classic 1969 Jimmie Rodgers tribute album, a blind man named Van Williams, who lost his sight in the Second World War, is led in by his wife. The man is wearing a Jimmie Rodgers railroad cap and, it is explained to Merle, knows all of Jimmie Rodgers' songs. He is a fixture at the Festival and appeared briefly the night before. Merle is obviously intrigued, announces to the band that he wants everyone to meet Van Williams, and then coaxes Van to do a number. For the next forty-five minutes Jimmie Rodgers' arching blue yodels float out over the Temple Theater, while Merle expresses encouragement, astonishment, delight, and finally determines that he will feature Van on his show that evening. It is an odd sight to see this most undemonstrative of men waxing so enthusiastic, all kindliness and courtliness as he takes on the part of the dutiful son. The afternoon ends with Merle coaxing Van to do "Miss the Mississippi" and finally "Never No Mo' Blues" for Lewis, throwing in a guitar fill now and then, adjusting Van's mike, knocked out again and again by the older man's near-perfect mimicry, oblivious to the band's obvious boredom.

The audience at the Saturday night show gets to see almost none of this side of Merle. Merle seems to close off, as he so often does in live performance, become stiff and standoffish and almost formal in presenting the kind of show that he thinks is expected of him. When I first started seeing him in the mid-'60s, he used to feature imitations in his act, almost as if he couldn't believe that people had come to see him, and now he seems to run through his own hits equally mistrustfully, disturbed perhaps by the feuding in the band, possibly thrown off by the mismatched rhythms of the drummers, irritated when a woman in the audience calls out, "Smile, Merle," and he replies, "Why? I only smile when something's funny." There are no really personal songs, there is nothing from his recent autobiographical masterpiece, *Serving 190 Proof,* and in fact one sees little of the simple enthusiasm that was evident all through the afternoon until he introduces Van Williams toward the conclusion of the first show. The audience responds with suitable politeness (it is an audience made up of the faithful, after all, with one contingent of Australians who have planned their U.S. tour around the Jimmie Rodgers Festival and Nashville Fan Fair) but is less than thrilled to have their star do little more than orchestrate the cheering for a local musician. Merle for his part couldn't care less. He lets Van close out the show with "Miss the Mississippi and You," the song that he'd rehearsed with the band that afternoon, and spends the entire time between shows not with his wife, who is out in front of the theater signing autographs, nor with any of the celebrities who clamor for his attention, but picking Jimmie Rodgers songs and exchanging self-deprecating small talk with Van Williams on his bus. When he finally has to go in for the second show, he brings Van back with him and insists once again that Van end the evening with "Miss the Mississippi." Some in the audience might suspect that they are being shortchanged, the band, dressed in black Western suits and white cowboy hats, just looks uncomfortable, but really Merle is convinced that he is giving people a priceless opportunity to hear *the real thing*. You know that if some Hollywood producer were to come along right now and offer him a chance to score and star in the next Clint Eastwood movie, he'd pass it up just for the chance to pick some more with Van Williams.

I live the kind of life most men only dream of
I make my living writing songs, and singing them

"PEOPLE DON'T REALIZE," says Merle Haggard almost resentfully, "that entertainers go through the same hardships of life as everyone else. When a plumber has someone close to the family pass away, they don't go to work—but an entertainer. . . . At five minutes to nine, they called me one night and said Lefty Frizzell had passed away. I went on. That's hard to do. You can't project how an entertainer will feel for an engagement that was planned months ago and predict his mood. Entertainers have the same feelings as anyone else, but they have to be phony about them. You have to go out and smile when you don't feel like smiling; somebody points a camera at you, and you put on that old Instamatic grin. Which is part of the profession, I guess. But sometimes part of the profession makes you feel like a prostitute. That's what that song is about. I've had letters that say, 'I hope that isn't—I would be very disappointed to find that as many people as love your singing that you really feel that way. I hope it's just a passing mood, I'm sure that it is.' Well, *life* is a passing mood. You know, when I see an artist like Lefty who had everything, every ingredient it took to become a monster, a legend, a Presley, with the exception of management—that was the only thing he lacked, but the people he came by made him hate the business before he ever really got into it, they killed his desire and ambition. I guess maybe 'Footlights' started that night when I got the call."

Needless to say, it's one of the songs he's proudest of, perhaps because, like so many of his most intimate personal songs, it pulls no punches. "'I live the kind of life most men only dream of,'" he quotes ruminatively. "You know, he says, "it's not even particularly about what it says. 'I'm

With Lefty Frizzell and DJ T. Tommy Cutrer. *Courtesy of Richard Weize —...and more bears*

forty-one years old, and I ain't got no place to go when it's over.'" He shakes his head.

Back in Nashville a few days later he is working on the final mix of one of the new tunes from his new album with producer Jimmy Bowen, himself an exile from L.A. and rock 'n' roll. Bowen is calm and professorial, and Merle, whose restless creativity generally outstrips his patience to read or study, is genuinely intrigued by the technology, a more than willing student, and an apt one, too. Work begins around seven o'clock in the evening, and when it is over at 2 A.M. only the one number will have been wrapped up, but Merle never loses interest, his attention never flags, and he even manages to write a new song during a break. When he goes into the sound booth to overdub his vocal, there is none of the coldness that you might associate with a canned sound, and although the song itself seems a little slick and pedestrian, Merle invests it with a feeling and an ardor that show up in each minute variation, in each new vocal twist. It is a true marriage of craft and passion, art and instinct, and here, just as at the sound check, there is no question that Merle Haggard is fully engaged, able to forget for a moment the embarrassment of his duet with Clint Eastwood in *Bronco Billy,* or even the compromise that this meticulously produced album itself represents in its attempt to transform Merle Haggard from country music legend to genuine pop star. Obviously Merle is going to have to face a lot of tough decisions in the next few months: Will he really dedicate himself to crossover success? Will he look for more media exposure, streamline his organization, get rid of the hangers-on, tone down an autobiography that promises to tell the unvarnished truth so that it will be more acceptable to public and publisher? Merle strains against the mold, clings desperately to the irrational response, however outrageous. He makes brave statements that indicate he will *never* tailor his beliefs to fit the proper image, never rein himself in to do what he is supposed to do. He lashes out wildly at an enemy he cannot quite identify, an invisible enemy who has transformed the American dream from the great westward migration to the move to the suburbs, transformed the hero from rugged individualist to armchair cowboy.

"It seems like if you do well on TV," he says, doing his best to put his finger on just what it is that's disturbing him, "you lose a lot of your mystique, a lot of your drawing power. I've argued and argued this point with people who are a lot smarter than I am, that for you to do well enough to get the type of shows that you want, you must be on there so much that the people in New York know who you are. And when you get to where the people in New York know who you are, you've usually done too much of it. Really I don't see any way of doing a happy medium, but there's no way to prove my point. So we go ahead, we attack television like we're planning to do now, and when the bottom falls out of the whole thing, well, they're going to say it's this or it's that, but I think it's very simple: people get sick of seeing you every time they turn on the TV.

"Well, you take some performers," he says, then singles out one prominent country music entertainer in particular. "I feel sorry for him. He's been so overexposed at this point, people turn on their television and they see him—they're sick of him. He can't get a hit record. The disc jockeys themselves are tired of seeing him. So this man's only alternative is to work the fairs and such things where there's a built-in crowd to begin with. Oh, he makes big money, but he knows I'm sure as well as anybody else what he is and who he is—he's a piece of, he's a product of the industry. He's not really a creative artist at all."

The Talley Whackers at the Porthole Bar, Ridgecrest, California, ca. 1961: Lewis Talley at the mike, Merle (seated) on right. *Photograph by Kenny Statler. Courtesy of Tex Whitson*

And that's really what it all comes down to for Merle Haggard. That's probably the worst fate that he can imagine, to become "a product of the industry," to give up the freedom of the creative artist, perhaps the last frontier. His emotional reaction to the fear of selling out takes many forms and perhaps as much as anything else is the explanation for his instinctual politics. Whenever he feels cornered, whenever he has begun to feel boxed in, Merle Haggard has lashed out, and probably he would be the last to

deny that his behavior has been destructive, reckless, ill-considered at times. It has never caused him to abandon his music, though. The one constant in his life has been music.

> *I've been running from life*
> *I keep running from life*
> *Hey, I'm still running from life*
> *But I can't get away*

"A lot of these people around me," says Merle Haggard a little sorrowfully of the retinue that has surrounded him off and on for twenty years now, "are sometimes not nearly as responsible as they need to be. They let me down in a lot of ways that other people would not allow. But their heart was always in the right place. They were always there to pick me up when other people wouldn't give a shit. They're not trying—I don't think—to get in my pocketbook. Because of some of their irresponsibility—and the irresponsibility I shoulder as much as anybody—it's not just their fault, it's my fault. It's their fault for allowing me to be that way, and my fault for allowing them to be that way, that we have not reached the height in our career that might have been available. But I really don't care. I've enjoyed this career, I think, a lot more than I would have if I'd tried to capitalize on every damned thing that happened to me. There were times when I could have jumped on a television special. I could have had my own network show if I'd pursued it. There were many directions I could have gone in, many things I could have done, but I chose to attack it on a low-key basis and to enjoy it and fuck off and write songs and make records and run up and down the highway in buses and stay with the people I wanted to be with rather than take that other route—I'm sure you know what route that is. And there's lots of other reasons why I didn't go that way. There was so many people wanting me to go one way or another that I couldn't be sure of what direction to go in. I had no way of knowing who was ready to fuck me and who was wanting to do me right. So I just stayed where I was, and I just stayed with the people I was with."

As he speaks, you get a momentary vision—a vision of Merle and his ex-wife Bonnie (still on the road singing with him) and Lewis Talley, of Fuzzy Owen, who first recorded Merle for his own and his cousin Lewis'

Teen Merle. *Courtesy of Richard Weize—...and more bears*

Tally label, and Tex Whitson, Merle's new manager, who has more or less replaced Fuzzy. It was Lewis who brought Merle, fresh out of prison, to the Porthole Bar and Café, where Tex's uncle ran the poker room, in Ridgecrest, California. Lewis Talley was, according to Tex, "the biggest thing in Southern California, California's answer to Hank Williams, I believe he could go back today, he was that popular. Merle was trying to be a lead guitarist, that was all he cared about, and Lewis just kept raving about, 'This kid . . . this kid.' It turned out to be Merle." Fuzzy coached Merle endlessly—on diction, on mannerisms, on what makes up a hit song. Merle met Bonnie at the Blackboard in Bakersfield, where she was waitressing and sang on Tuesday nights, and Merle played the relief shift. At the Porthole, "we checked for knives and guns at the door," says Tex. "If they didn't have 'em, we issued 'em." It all seems so much simpler, so much more innocent in a way, bathed in the light of nostalgia, though Tex, a self-admitted felon, claims that it is far easier now. "If I'd known then how easy the music business was, I could have saved myself seven years in the pokey!" It is the longest-running hit on Broadway, in which the actors shuffle about, exchange roles, take a temporary leave of absence, but one doubts they will ever quit the show.

"As a kid I never even thought about growing up," says Merle. "I just enjoyed being a kid. I got away with as much as I could get away with, I guess I didn't think about growing up because I thought I was grown. I never dreamt about success. Really, all I ever intended to do was to make a living. I've had far more success than I ever could have imagined—I guess I didn't set my sights high enough! Sometimes," says Merle Haggard, with only a hint of wistfulness in his voice, "I wish maybe I hadn't had as much success as I have. You know, it kind of ruins your incentive." But then, with that hard-won Okie sense of self-mocking good humor, he recovers: "I guess you've just got to keep making up goals."

SIX

Bill Monroe: Hard Working Man Blues

S ITTING OUT on an undivided highway not far from the site of Opry-
land is a little Quonset hut with a sign that warns: No Solicitors. This
is the home of Monroe Enterprises, a two-man operation which
encompasses father and son, whose business vehicles are parked to either
side of their construction-trailer office. Bill Monroe, Father of Bluegrass,
it says on the tour bus; James Monroe and the Midnight Ramblers reads
the legend on the more modest camper. Not surprisingly, Bill Monroe is
right on time for the scheduled appointment. He alights from his Ford
pickup impeccably turned out in a blue pin-striped suit, handkerchief
peeking from his breast pocket, longish white hair curled up on his collar
and emerging from under the familiar white Western hat. (It's almost
impossible to find anyone in Nashville anymore who'll do a decent job
cleaning hats, he volunteers later in the interview.) With his stiff, formal
manner, his erect bearing, and his deep-seated reserve ("Yes, sir," and "No,
sir," are expansive answers in Bill Monroe's vocabulary, and for the most
part he speaks in a gentle, almost faint tone of voice), he is, at sixty-nine,
an imposing figure — formidable, really — and meeting him is quite unlike
meeting your ordinary run-of-the-mill country music legend, simply
because he is so self-contained. "This story that you're taking, what are
you going to do with it?" he asks once in the middle of the interview, and
at the end he expresses an interest in what the last lines of the story are
going to be, whether they will provide a fitting summary of our discussion.

Other than that, it is softly murmured assents and deflections ("Maybe
it would be better off leaving that alone"), warm memories elliptically
expressed and old quarrels icily disdained. There is no question that he
loosens up as the conversation proceeds, but there is equally little question
that he would rather be out on his farm working with his prize horses and
bulls. Practically his first words in fact relate to work and its value. "I can't

slow down. Don't you like to work? If I haven't got anything to do, I look for something else. I couldn't ever make so much money that I wanted to stop, you know, and just loaf around." Everything that he has ever done in his life attests to his discipline and drive. Those who have worked with him have their stories of eccentricities and paradoxes, and there is no question in his own mind or anyone else's that Bill Monroe can be a harsh taskmaster. From the time that he was a young boy Bill Monroe has followed his own lights, gone his own way, rejected emotional excess and lack of resolve, and yet given himself over wholeheartedly to a passionate, almost uncontrollable strain in his nature that took its form in bluegrass music. He is a strange combination of fire and ice, which continue to war in a sternly mellow visage fortified by a steadfastly steely gaze.

He was born William Smith Monroe on September 13, 1911, on a 655-acre farm in Rosine, Kentucky. His father was fifty-four, his mother forty-one, and he was the youngest of eight, with his two closest brothers, Charlie and Birch, eight and ten years older than he. The tale of his early years has been recounted often: his solitary nature; his poor eyesight and sensitivity to the taunts of his schoolmates; the death of his mother, Malissa Vandiver, who played fiddle and accordion, when he was only ten; how her brother, Pendleton Vandiver, a trader and noted old-time fiddler, moved in with the family a couple of years later after his wife and two children died. By this time Bill's brothers, Charlie and Birch, who played guitar and fiddle respectively (as much as anything, their choice of instruments would eventually dictate his taking up the mandolin), had moved to Whiting, Indiana, and gone to work in an oil refinery. Then, when he was sixteen, his father, Buck, died, and he and his Uncle Pen were, effectively, left alone.

> My father had a wonderful farm. As far as being rich or having a lot of money, he didn't have that. He had eight children to raise. That takes a lot of money, and back in them days, you know, you didn't see a five-dollar or ten-dollar bill anyplace hardly. He was a good father and a good man. When he died, I lived a little while with my Uncle Jack Monroe, and then I went to stay with Uncle Pen. In his last days he was a crippled man. He'd been throwed by a horse. He could still get around and do a little cooking, though, and we bached together and he'd cook for us, and I got him wood and water. He could fix us breakfast, fix beans and stuff like that. All we had sweet was sorghum and molasses. We just made out. That was hard days, man. Hard days.

Bill Monroe shows me his restored mandolin, October 15, 1980. *Photograph by Russ Barnard*

He played backwoods square dances with his uncle and a black blues player from McHenry named Arnold Shultz (whose style was also a strong influence on the Everly Brothers' father, Ike, and Merle Travis), seconding the two older men on guitar. Shultz worked at the local coal yard as a loader and lived by the railroad track, but Monroe must really have been drawn to the bluesman's style to gain his attention since, as he told Ralph Rinzler, "probably any guitar man in the country could've beaten me." Between his uncle and Shultz, Monroe got a solid musical education.

There's a lot of people that don't know how to play for square dancing. They might think they do, but they don't. You have to really know how to dance yourself to understand how it should be played, because you can get it too fast and the dancers can't keep up with you and you'll hurt the whole thing. You got to think about the other man all through life, though; you can't just think about yourself, you got to help the other man, too. So that in the square dances you have got to play to where the timing is right and he can dance to it, just set the time and

let it stay there. Arnold played with me some; me and him used to play the square dances. He could fiddle some, too, and I could play guitar just well enough to get by. I never heard him sing. He could really play the blues, man, best bluesman I ever heard in my life — with a guitar. A lot of people around, you know, probably didn't like the blues, they'd rather hear the other kind of singing or music, but it give me a great feeling, man — I love the blues. It's played a big part in my life.

When he was eighteen he left Kentucky to join his two older brothers, working at oil refineries in Whiting and then in East Chicago, Indiana.

I could've stayed in Kentucky and been a farmer. I'd have been satisfied with that. I could've probably planned a married life and raised a family. But my people went and talked me into leaving Kentucky and going up to where there was money. I was afraid to leave Kentucky, because I'd never been around no place like that, I didn't know whether I could find my way around or not. Just like I told you, I would have taken any kind of life, being a farmer, doing what I was raised up to do, what I thought I would do. It was a long time before I ever got a job at Sinclair, probably three months. But I was never afraid of hard work. I learned how to handle those barrels just like a man throwing a ball, throwing a curve. I got to where I could handle a drum — you'd be surprised at what I could do with it and how far I could throw it and make it set up. I believe I could clean thirty-six drums in fifteen minutes and have them all sitting in the dryer.

He and his brothers were concentrating on their music, too. With a friend, Larry Moore, they were discovered at a square dance in Hammond — not playing but *dancing* — and were signed on as exhibition square dancers for the Chicago-based WLS National Barn Dance road show. They were working as a trio on a Gary radio station as well ("We was trying to learn how to play on the side. We wasn't learning too fast"), and when the opportunity arose to play full-time, with the Texas Crystal company, a popular laxative manufacturer, as their sponsor, Birch dropped out, and the Monroe Brothers became a guitar-and-mandolin duo.

The Monroe Brothers, Charlie and Bill. *Courtesy of Richard Weize — . . . and more bears*

Bill Monroe and His Original Blue Grass Boys: Art Wooten, Bill Monroe, Cleo Davis, Amos Garren, late 1939–early 1940. *Courtesy of Bluegrass Unlimited*

One of the most remarkable things about the Bill Monroe story is that he was a star before he ever hit upon the formula (rhythm plus blues on top of the old-timey style inherited from his Uncle Pen) for which he is renowned today. He and Charlie moved from Shenandoah, Iowa, to Omaha, Nebraska, to Spartanburg, South Carolina, changing sponsors in South Carolina (Crazy Water Crystals picked up the show) and recording for the first time for RCA Victor in Charlotte in 1936. By his own account Bill was not all that impressed with how far they had come; in fact he and Charlie seem to have been reluctant to record initially, and he still makes a sharp distinction between making music and making records. "We didn't have to have records. There was so much work, and we had such a great following that I felt I could have made it without records. You see, back in my young days, you'd have heard people on record, you know, but you kind of shunned a lot of that stuff yourself. You didn't have a manager, you didn't have somebody shoving you along. I guess there's been a lot of people who played but never had the chance to record—or they might have had the chance but didn't even want to, they just didn't want to fool with it."

In any case Eli Oberstein prevailed upon Bill and Charlie for Victor, and their first release, "What Would You Give in Exchange?," was a hit.

In all they recorded sixty songs in a two-year period, and their clean, sharply etched performances of well-known hymns, Jimmie Rodgers and Carter Family material, and traditional folk songs and ballads ("Nine Pound Hammer," "Foggy Mountain Top," "Darling Corey") sound as fresh and vigorous today as they must have when they were first recorded. Personal and professional differences ended the partnership in 1938, and Bill Monroe was once again on his own, this time for good.

When we were working together, I didn't even study a new style, because we had a style of our own. Charlie had a good lead voice, and I learned to sing tenor, but I never thought about a new style till we broke up. I wanted to build it around myself and have a drive to my music. I wanted that touch of the blues in it. I wanted musicians that could play up and down the neck, where back in the early years just B and C and D was all they could play. I wanted the guitar player to get something out of his instrument, I wanted to hear it ring, I wanted to put some runs in it that would match my music. You see, to me bluegrass is a music that'll let you know you can do things in music, that you don't have to sit still and go along with the old-time mountain style or folk style. Bluegrass is a challenge. You got to get out and work hard, you got to go out and do your best, or it's gonna outdo you. I don't think country music is like that, really. Just like I told you, bluegrass is a music that'll learn you a lot. It's more like a school of music for a lot of people.

Indeed he developed a dazzlingly virtuosic but deeply felt style on mandolin that not only revolutionized the music but extended both the range and power of the instrument. ("You've got to whip it like a mule," he said of the thrust he sought to impart to his music, whether it was played fast or slow.) And he created his own school for any number of musicians who not only went on to make a name for themselves but to enlarge the province of bluegrass itself. Lester Flatt, Earl Scruggs, Vassar Clements, Jimmy Martin, Sonny Osborne, Carter Stanley, Mac Wiseman — the list could go on and on. Like Miles Davis in jazz, or Muddy Waters in blues, Bill Monroe provided a training ground for every musician who aspired to any sort of recognition in the field. Every little town the show passed through had its own Blue Grass Boys copy band; there must have been hundreds of pickers who learned the entire Bill Monroe repertoire note by painstaking note, doing their best to puzzle out the records and every so often realizing a lifelong ambition when they had the opportunity to fill in for a night for an ailing band member and even dream of leaving town with the band. It was more than money, it was love—for Monroe and for his apprentices. And all the while the music was evolving through the contributions of its newer members. As Monroe says, "If a man had something to teach me, I like to think I learned something from him. If it was no good, I wouldn't listen to it. I'd never use a man's music to where he could say Bill Monroe's copying it, but if they had something good in there, a way of making notes, the slur of the music, why all I had to do was hear it one time and then I'd keep that."

More than with almost any other kind of music that I can think of, you can see how Monroe consciously fashioned his, and how it grew by leaps and bounds in both popularity and ambition even as he did. In 1939 Monroe joined the Opry and was told by its founder, George Hay, the "Solemn Ol' Judge," "If you ever leave the Opry, it'll be because you've fired yourself." Needless to say, Monroe never left. The recordings he made for Columbia in 1946 and 1947 with Lester Flatt and Earl Scruggs, who at this point was in the midst of reinventing banjo playing in much the same way that Bill Monroe had reinvented the role of the mandolin, may represent a peak of form and popularity, but he never ceased to set himself new challenges, and his music would remain as full of feeling in his seventies as it was when he first began taking his show out in a giant tent that could hold 6,000, reaching a whole generation of country people in Arkansas, Mississippi, Alabama, and Tennessee who may have had no other exposure to "professional" entertainers.

Back in days like that, say you played here today, you might play five or ten miles down the road the next day—you see, back in those days there wasn't no TV, there wasn't hardly no radio, so you didn't have to go so far then. We would leave in the morning and pull into the next town around ten or eleven o'clock. We had, I believe, seven trucks and a long stretched-out bus we traveled in. The people would be watching for you, they knew you were coming because you'd been advertised for two or three weeks, and they'd be standing on the street corners and sidewalks, you know, watching the show come in. Around 10:30 or 11:00 we'd go on out to where the tent would be put up. First you'd stretch the tent out, then drive the stakes down to where you could put the ropes up, just like the old carnival days. When the people got through

The Blue Grass Boys on the road: Birch Monroe, Chubby Wise, Bill Monroe, Lester Flatt, Earl Scruggs, ca. 1947. *Courtesy of Bluegrass Unlimited*

with work, they would shave and clean up and come on out to the show. Back in those days everybody wore a white shirt, it seemed like. They were just good, down-to-earth, working people, you know. We started out charging twenty-five and seventy-five cents admission; after a while it went up to ninety cents tops, and for a long time we went on with that. We played in some places there hadn't been a tent show allowed in years.

The theme of the show was variety, just as the dominant thread of Bill Monroe's music was intricacy, variety, versatility. "If I had got up there," Monroe told author and musician Jim Rooney, "and sang everything [by myself] with a little fiddle music behind me or a guitar like Ernest Tubb does, it would have got awful old." Instead Monroe alternated lead vocals and traded off solos with fellow musicians who, while clearly under his direction, were never just relegated to the role of sidemen. In a similar way the tent show presented a variety of entertainment, with Robert Lunn the "Talking Blues Boy," "Harmonica Wizard" DeFord Bailey (the Opry's only Negro member, and proudly advertised over WSM as "our

The Blue Grass Ballclub: Howard Watts, Chubby Wise, Dave "Stringbean" Akeman, Clyde Moody, Bill Monroe. *Courtesy of Bluegrass Unlimited*

little mascot"), and Uncle Dave Macon among its most prominent stars, and for almost a decade a baseball game was included among the festivities. For a while Monroe carried thirteen or fourteen ballplayers on the road, including his banjo player, Stringbean, a first-class utility man, and he maintained a team in Nashville, the Blue Grass Ballclub, as well. Monroe himself, who had been excluded from baseball games as a child because of his crossed eyes, enjoyed playing first or third and even pitched on occasion. If someone was needed to help set up the tent, as often as not it was Monroe who pitched in. "Bill loved to work," guitarist Don Reno told Jim Rooney. "Nobody could work him down. . . . Bill was more interested in ball than he was music at this time. I reckon that this was a way of resting his mind from music. But he liked to kill me playing ball. We would work on a show one night and drive to the next town and usually get in at an early morning hour, and he'd have a ball game set up by ten o'clock with the local team!"

It was undoubtedly this same combination of imagination and hard work, competitive drive and creativity that gave him his staying power. When his best musicians left to go off on their own, he replaced them with men as good or better, who always brought something different to the music. When times got tough, with the advent of rock 'n' roll, although he was forced to cut back and the tent show turned into appearances at the local drive-in theater, he may have been discouraged, but he never gave up. When in the '60s he was discovered by a new college audience, he was more ready for them than they for him — not least because his repertoire had never stopped expanding, both forward and back. At the beginning of his career he wrote very little; his first big hit was his distinctive version of Jimmie Rodgers' "Mule Skinner Blues," and many of his most familiar songs were reworkings of traditional old-timey tunes. As he gained confidence in his writing, and, perhaps more important, acquired the emotional poise to express what was within him, his songs became more and more personal, he started to write autobiographical numbers like "Uncle Pen," "Memories of Mother and Dad," "I'm On My Way to the Old Home," which he refers to as "true true songs." And although the lyrics are often somewhat abstract, you can, if you care to, gain momentary insight into the emotional intensity of Bill Monroe's life.

I like to write that kind of a song, but you don't do it all the time. I have a lot of true stories, but I guess a lot of people don't care that much about you, you know, to care what kind of feelings you've got. I guess you have to be around a man to really know how he stands, or how his life goes or what he thinks about. No, I don't think I was shy [before he started to write his "true" songs] — I just didn't know how to write that kind of song more so. Of course on the Opry I always sung the numbers that made hits. Just like Acuff, Tubb, Hank Snow, people like that — people always looked forward to you being there on Saturday night so they could hear you do those songs, and records wasn't so important back in them days. But I would come with a new number every now and then, too. And that's something else that the Grand Ole Opry people don't do that they should do. They've sung the same things for forty years, some of 'em — and still doing it. That's the trouble with a many entertainers — not learning nothing new, don't write nothing.

I'm not bragging, but that's something that I've always done. You try to write something, you know, that you thought people would like. I write a lot of instrumentals; then I go to adding and putting words to it. A lot of times I write the melody before I ever start writing the words. Sometimes when I pick up my instrument, the first time I make a note I'll start in on a new melody.

Some of the songs are biographical, some are pure imagination, some are almost historical musings. An instrumental like "Land of Lincoln," for example, he conceived as an evocation of a particular time and mood.

"Land of Lincoln," I think, is a wonderful title for a fiddle tune. To picture Lincoln when he was a lawyer, you know, going to try somebody and passing an old fiddler on the street — that's what I had in mind, the way that would have happened. He'd stop a little while to listen to the fiddler, then he went on. Damn, but I think that's a really good number, it goes way on back in the way of sounds and everything, like it would have been in Lincoln's days. No, I don't think a lot of people even think about that, the way things started — a lot of people are just out for the dollar, to put on a show — but it's played a big part in my life from the time I was a kid on. The lay of the land, the people, the people I knew when I was a kid, like my father, my mother, and on back — Lincoln down to Roosevelt, I mean Wilson, and people like that, that you knew as presidents. Back in those days they respected the president of the United States; they didn't talk about the other man all the time.

Perhaps most remarkable of all is this role as conservator as well as innovator, the way in which Monroe has consciously set out to preserve the past at the same time that he has forged ahead with a music that was so fresh as to be considered revolutionary when it first appeared. In the last decade and a half, he has even resurrected many of the tunes he first learned from his Uncle Pen forty and fifty years ago.

I'd run over them, say, a few times a year, but they would never have died. I could have remembered them if I'd never played them, but it don't hurt to go over them, you know, to remember the sound of it and everything. I wanted to save those numbers and do 'em as near like Uncle Pen would have played them, so that people would know that.

Then it would be doing something good for him, too, rather than just let the number die away. It gives me a great feeling, because he would never have thought that this would have happened. He was a wonderful uncle and a good man.

It is only when the interview is over that Bill Monroe unbends a little, and his dry, laconic responses take on a certain playfulness as he accepts an invitation to lunch by asking, "You boys sure your money'll hold up now?" At the restaurant, a comfortable family-style coffee shop, he is greeted warmly by several men and women who appear to be regular customers. One couple holds up a copy of the Nashville daily paper, *The Tennessean,* with his picture on the front of the Living section. "He's a hardworking man," Bill Monroe says, with what appears to be a twinkle in his eye. "You've got the talent," says the husband, offering him the newspaper. "It's held up pretty good," Bill Monroe agrees, thanking the man for the paper and returning to his lunch. He is a brisk eater, as efficient at this activity as in every other aspect of his life, and he wipes his plate clean long before his two companions are finished.

After lunch he says that he has a surprise for us. We follow him in his pickup out onto the highway toward where we know he lives. As we pull into a shopping center at the side of the road, I wonder if he is going to stop at a Fotomat or a drive-in bank, but instead he gets out of his pickup, appears to be sighting something, then shakes his head, pulls the truck up a little further, and nods with a faint smile of satisfaction. "There," he says, "over the Dollar sign, you can see it now," and he directs our attention over the supermarket sign up into the hills. Well off in the distance, nestled on high ground, is a substantial tract of cleared land obviously put to agricultural use. "That's my farm," he says with pride. It looks beautiful, we murmur, and we stand there for a few minutes admiring it. Then we shake hands all around, he wishes us good luck, and we watch Bill Monroe drive off up the highway toward his home.

Earlier he had asked what the last lines of the story were going to be; he wanted to make sure that they said something appropriate, something fitting, and I reviewed the last exchange on the interview tape. I had asked him if he had any regrets, and after a long silence he volunteered, "Well, I guess a man could be more saving when he's young. He could put more money away to help him when he's older." But what about his family? I wondered. Did he ever regret the isolation that an entertainer's life necessarily entails? "My family knew that I was going to have to do this kind of work, because I had got into it, y'see, and I had a daughter and my son James—Melissa was my daughter. But I reckon they allowed for it, and they was always waiting for me when I'd get back Friday evening or Saturday. I guess if you love each other it'll take care of everything."

But, on second thought, I think Mr. Monroe might have preferred for me to save something a little less anodyne for the end. So, at the risk of repetition, let me give it another try.

"You see, to me bluegrass is a music that'll let you know you can do things in music. Bluegrass is a challenge. You got to get out and work hard, you got to go out and do your best, or it's gonna outdo you. Bluegrass," he declared with total conviction, "is a music that'll learn you a lot." It was the kind of school, he seemed to be saying, from which you never really wanted, or intended, to graduate.

SEVEN

Lonnie Mack: Funky Country Living

I was raised on funky country living
Eating chickens, chasing girls, and home-made wine
Yes, I was raised on funky country living
And I'll be funky country living till I die

—*"Funky Country Living"*

"I AIN'T NEVER BEEN SO UNHAPPY in my life. I ain't in it for the money. I'm in it for the fun. That's why I'm leaving, man. I ain't having any fun."

Lonnie Mack, bearded, bearish, the man who turned Chuck Berry's "Memphis" into an unforgettable instrumental hit, possessor of one of the most searing electric guitar styles and spine-chilling gospel screams this side of Bobby "Blue" Bland or Wilson Pickett (Five Blind Boys lead singer Archie Brownlee, a singer without peer in the spine-chilling department, was an early inspiration), cradles an acoustic Epiphone in his lap, smiles shyly, and shrugs when asked what he's going to do. "Whatever," he says with characteristic, if noncommittal, faith in the future. The half dozen people in the room, friends and relatives and fellow Hoosiers, nod agreement. Lonnie, who has just resumed recording after a self-imposed exile of six years and spent the winter of 1976-1977 in Nashville putting together a band and preparing to tour behind his new album, *Home at Last,* has today announced his intention to head out for Oregon, go back to the woods, leave the sterile urban surroundings and "sterile studio pickers" behind, and reclaim the kind of lifestyle, and happiness, which he has found for the past five years in the hills and hollers of Indiana where he was born.

Not surprisingly, record company and management express mild surprise, venture disappointment, but never try to remonstrate with Lonnie Mack, whose brooding demeanor, shaggy appearance, massive torso, and sometimes staggering excesses all bear out the mountain man image which he cultivates. For the five days that I am in Nashville all the talk is of leaving, a house is rented for $40 a month by phone, plans are excitedly made, recruits are sought to add to the household of nearly ten (brother Billy, eight-months-pregnant wife Gail, Billy's wife Janet, recently divorced cousin Bob Sizemore, children, and roadie Randy Bush) who are prepared to make the great migration west. Lonnie alternately broods and is seized with enthusiasm, throws himself into the process of getting rid of all the possessions, TVs, hi-fi, sound equipment, which he has accumulated in his stay in Nashville ("I ain't never had so much junk. Seems like the times I've been happiest in my life is when I've possessed the least. The best way to do it is to just never own nothing"), and schemes to make it like it was back in Friendship, Indiana, where from 1973 to 1976 he operated a combination campground and music park so far back up in the hills you had to ford a creek three times to reach the site and the law never ventured in at all.

> *1950 in a little shack*
> *The hobo jungle by the railroad track*
> *Had a lot of friends there when I was just a kid*
> *I used to go down and sit a spell*
> *I played them a song, they'd tell me a tale*
> *Tell about the places they'd already been*

The road to Friendship was neither a direct nor an easy one, although the town is no more than fifteen miles from the area around Aurora, downriver from Cincinnati, where he grew up. He was born Lonnie McIntosh on July 18, 1941. Named after harmonica player Lonnie Glosson, he comes from a large family to whom music was as natural as breathing. His grandfather played the spoons, his uncle sang Jimmie Rodgers, his father picked the banjo, and his mother taught him guitar. By the time that he was six he was chording, and his only good memories of school are of traveling around the district with the music teacher, playing "Silver Bell"

Photograph by Randy Jennings—Captured Live Photography

With band, ca. 1963. Clockwise from lower right: Lonnie, Gene Bieruns, Jimmy Thomas, Dumpy Rice, Kenny Blackburn. *Courtesy of Rien Wisse*

and Gene Autry songs for music classes. Most of his time was spent hanging around the hobo jungle, playing for tips from the railroad workers or diners at Aurora's Nieman Hotel, or picking up pointers from a blind gospel singer and guitarist named Ralph Trotto, then in his early twenties, who lived down the street.

By the time that he was thirteen he had abandoned school altogether and joined a sixty-year-old drummer named Hoot Smith, who played a cymbal "as big as a beer barrel" and whose only qualification as a bandleader was that he could get steady work in the world of honky-tonks and beer joints which would serve as Lonnie's home for the next fifteen years. Tales of those years are legion, and indeed they have taken on a mythology all their own. Lonnie's twenty-four-year-old brother, Billy, can tell you all about Shady Grove, Kentucky, the dirt floor, broken-off beer bottles, and the older woman who stole cousin Bob Sizemore's heart back in 1955. His wife, Gail, who only met Lonnie in 1967, can recount stories of some of the rougher joints of that era — the good times and bad times and all the bloody brawls — in vivid detail. It all tends to blend in after a while, but eventually Lonnie ended up at the Twilight Inn outside of Hamilton, Ohio, where the owner, Frog Childs, dubbed the group Lonnie Mack and the Twilighters, and to get the job Lonnie had to beat out a local band led by a singer and Fender bass player named Troy Seals. Seals, who would one day co-write the country standard "There's a Honky Tonk Angel (Who'll Take Me Back In)" with the piano player in his band, took a job across the road from the Twilight Inn and shortly thereafter, when Hoot Smith went back to blacksmithing and Lonnie's cousin, Harold Sizemore, quit the Twilighters in a dispute over musical direction, joined forces with Lonnie in an association that has continued off and on to this day. It was seven nights a week, three matinees plus a dinner dance, with bookings scattered throughout the tristate area. It was a rough education, but "my parents never really minded, I guess. They was just old downhome people who was into it themselves. Besides, I was making more money playing the joints than my father was working in the factory."

It was working the joints, too, that gave Lonnie the basis for his seemingly limitless repertoire not just of songs but of styles. He started out playing rockabilly and country, added blues sounds off radio station WCIN, worked with local black musicians like guitarist Maurice Gibson and drummer Greg Webster (later one of the founding members of the Ohio Players), and put it all together in a style that emphasized volume and the sheer, naked passion of voice and guitar. Many of the musicians that Lonnie started with are still playing the honky-tonk circuit, and Lonnie might never have escaped it himself if Harry Carlson, who operated a photography studio and record company in Cincinnati, had not recorded his instrumental version of "Memphis" at the tag end of a girl-group session for the Fraternity label in 1963. By then he had long since acquired his space-age 1958 "Flying V" Gibson guitar, seventh off the line of only ninety-eight originally manufactured. (When Lonnie saw a pen-and-ink illustration of "that big arrow-looking guitar, I said, 'Boy, I got to have one of them'"—it incorporated both his distinctive vision of the future and his pride in his father's Creek Indian heritage, though clearly few others at the time shared his taste for a guitar that would one day be considered a classic.) He was on the road working in Troy Seals' band when the record was released. They were in Florida backing up Jo Ann Campbell at the Peppermint Lounge when a friend reported that it was getting a lot of airplay back home. In Minnesota they played on a bill with the Fendermen, who told Lonnie that the record had gotten a four-star rating in *Billboard*. By the time they got back to Dayton, Ohio, where Seals was slated to back Chubby Checker, Lonnie Mack was top-billed.

> I ain't trying to impress nobody. I played with the best in the world, and I played with the worst in the world, and there ain't that much difference between the two. I just want to pick, man; I don't have to prove anything. You see, my idea is, I've already done it, as far as being whatever I set out to be. I've had a million seller. I've traveled all over, been known, had a fancy job with Elektra Records in Hollywood. The way I see it, I'd rather get it close a whole bunch of times and back off than go all the way and have nothing else to look forward to. Just so long as I can keep on making albums and leave something behind, I'm gonna live like I live, and I don't care if I ever write a commercial song or not. You just have to keep on creating, like a painter; you can't paint the same picture over and over. That's just the way I feel about it, and every time I get close to ever really making it, to climbing to the top of the mountain, that's when I pull out, I just pull up and run.

Lonnie never really capitalized fully on "Memphis." He toured, had some hits in the South, put out a classic album on Fraternity, did studio work for James Brown, and was working Fort Walton Beach in Florida when Elektra Records vice president Russ Miller caught up with him and signed him to the label in 1969, both as an artist and as a salaried a&r man (technically artist and repertoire, but in Lonnie's case this came down to talent scout, producer, and musician, all rolled into one). The three albums that resulted embodied all of the strengths, and some of the weaknesses, of Lonnie's music. The first in particular (*Glad I'm in the Band*) stands out, with its unique combination of country, blues, and gospel feel, all set off by Lonnie's blazing, thick-textured guitar and a vocal style which assigns less importance to articulation than to pure emotionalism — it is, really, one of the great soul albums of all time. The second, *Whatever's Right*, is just as straightforward, just as straight-out and soulful in its own way, if somewhat marred not just by its being recorded in part in what Lonnie calls "the world's worst studio" but by the attitude that he adopted that "once I've recorded it, it's out of my hands." By the time that he made *The Hills of Indiana*, his third and final album for Elektra, something in Lonnie Mack's life had radically changed. For one thing the "Wham of that 'Memphis' Man" (as his original Fraternity album was irrefutably titled) was blunted by the record's primarily acoustic focus; then, too, for the first time Lonnie wrote a number of very personal, almost private songs completely outside of the more extroverted blues and country mainstream to which he had previously confined himself. The central concern of the album in fact is spiritual, and shortly after it came out in 1971 Lonnie gave up his a&r job with Elektra and went home to Indiana.

> I seen a lot of changes
> Traveling around the land
> And I've had a lot of bosses
> Putting money in my hand
> Well, I give up a lot of luxury
> Just to gain what I got
> And I'm just glad that I'm home at last

The Friendship campground seems to have marked a watershed in Lonnie Mack's life. He bought it for five dollars down, built a log-cabin stage, and for three and a half years put on once-a-month shows which embodied all the good feeling, the "oneness" which Lonnie Mack had come to seek in music. There were good times and good fellowship, a 275-gallon oil drum for a barbecue pit, roasted hogs and roasted chickens and Van Frazier, That Hog-Eyed Man (who would be insulted if the food wasn't all eaten up), ginseng hunters and Fiddlin' Dick, a junkyard dealer who could fiddle in tongues. Most of all there was music, from sundown to sunup and then off and on all through the day. It was the kind of place, Lonnie says, where motorcycle gangs, hippies, and hill country families could all mingle peaceably, and there was never any trouble.

"I think I learned to play in all bags from that, or at least to get comfortable enough to enjoy it. That's what I really miss, man, pickers who are loose enough just to play a song through and not really give a shit if they make a mistake or not. At Friendship we'd just pull songs off the top of our head and play them right through, and most of the time they'd come out sounding all right. You see, it don't really matter if you do it right or wrong, sometimes it's better if it's wrong, but you can't find too many people in the business with that attitude. I know, 'cause I was there. But that's what I'm trying to get back to now."

Friendship came to an end in a welter of misunderstanding. Lonnie had a falling-out with his partner, and then he was shot by an off-duty policeman in Cincinnati and locked up in the Cincinnati Jail, the basis for a biting blues and a lawsuit against the city which, "if I ever win it, you ain't never gonna see me again." In the wake of these misfortunes, he set out for Nashville, leaving a lost Eden behind and resigned to trying to scale the mountain one more time.

> There was a time the woods surround me
> And the wildflowers grew to my door
> Then the world moved in around me
> Now I'm living on the outskirts of town

We are sitting in the multicolored school bus which Lonnie has been fixing up behind his rented house just down from Music Row. The transmission is out of it now, in preparation for getting back on the road, and Lonnie is whiling away another long afternoon with family and friends, drinking beer and attempting desultorily to dispel his bad feelings about Nashville with his music. All afternoon Randy, the bearded roadie, has been trying to round up some bluegrass pickers on the phone but everyone is busy or expresses regrets and Lonnie delivers himself of yet another diatribe about people who would rather make music for money than for love. The mood is somnolent, everyone is referred to as either Joey or, if female, Josephine, and the long drawn-out silences are disconcerting to anyone whose sensibility is not strictly country. The talk is of Indiana mostly—Billy and Janet are thinking of making a run up that night—and of Oregon's soon-to-be-seen Cascade Mountains. Lonnie seems sunk in his depression, but gradually the music starts to get to him, the bass player, Bucky, throws in a harmony on "I Wonder How the Old Folks Are at Home," and Lonnie's Epiphone gives off a ringing clarity that fills the bus. As Lonnie plays by himself, or with his brother seconding him, the

With one of his early guitar heroes, Robert Ward (founder of the Ohio Untouchables).
Courtesy of Nancy Wright

old songs come to life, as do his own compositions, in a way that is not even hinted at on his new album. He plays "Funky Country Living," one of his best new songs, "the way it should have been recorded (it don't mean nothing on the album)," with a presence and an immediacy and a rhythm riff that are buried in the overdubs.

Why didn't he stick to his own musical vision on the record? Lonnie shrugs. It was just another deal. He made a demo and left it with a friend. The demo was overdubbed, and someone bought it for a good price. It's hard to understand his attitude toward the music. The songs, as he plays them on the bus, are like a personal journal of his life. There is none of that on the record. The closest that you come to any sense of personal investment is the back cover painting that his wife, Gail, has done at

Lonnie's direction. In it you see a rocking chair, a Faultless wood stove, an acoustic guitar, and, propped up against the wall, the fabled 1958 Gibson Flying V — all that is missing from this catalogue of some of Lonnie's most cherished possessions is his boxy Magnatone amp, with its shimmering vibrato sound, to which he was introduced by legendary Ohio Untouchables guitarist Robert Ward. On the bus he plays the music the way it was meant to be recorded, as real, solid, and well crafted as the objects in the picture. All the joeys and josephines respond as he follows one song with another, throws in tunes that he has been working on or musical ideas that just pop into his head. It is homemade music of the sort that Lonnie has been talking about all along, and at last after five or six hours it is beginning to take effect.

As I leave, he is speaking animatedly of his uncles Woodrow and Bill Sizemore, his father and his grandfather. "Uncle Bill was Bob's father and he was the best fiddle player I ever heard. Dadgum, it'd tear you up to hear them play. You ought to get Uncle Bill and Woodrow in the story, man, 'cause they're dead, and they was the start of the whole thing." As the memories and music warm up, so do Lonnie's plans for the party that Capitol Records is planning for him this weekend. "We'll get Fiddlin' Dick down here," says Lonnie excitedly. "We'll get some of them bluegrass pickers from Friendship to come down here and play some of that old holler music." He is answered by responsive whoops. "We'll give these people something they ain't never heard before."

I got friends up the road
And food in the fields
Horses to ride
And no telephone bills
They say I'm over the hill
But I don't care
I'm just glad that I'm home at last

The only person to show up for the party outside of invited industry guests is an old marbles-playing competitor from Aurora named Thanny Schuck, whose wife, Darleen, is an aspiring country singer for whom Lonnie has produced a single. To Thanny, Lonnie is "the greatest guy in the world," a person of boundless talent and just as boundless generosity. Thanny, a born-again Christian who neither smokes nor drinks, beams at every song that Lonnie plays, but it is obvious from the first note that something is very wrong. Lonnie is playing his old Flying V, and the band — with Billy on second guitar, Bucky on bass, and drummer Beau Dollar, who goes back fifteen years with Lonnie — sounds as if it could have been any one of the numerous incarnations of the original Twilighters. They have only completed five or six songs, though — at a volume so deafening as to drive most of the small audience that is in attendance out of the room — when Lonnie stomps off the stage.

At his table he is virtually inconsolable. For a few moments he rails against the crowd, inveighs against the sparse turnout and the incompetence of the band — but most of all his disappointment and his anger are directed against himself. "I ain't never played worse in my life," he declares, his great bearded face gray with hurt and mortification. "I'm never going to play another note with this band, and that's the truth. You can put that in your story. I ain't never been so embarrassed in my life." Attempts are made to assuage him, but Lonnie is insistent on his despair. He is savage in fact in his dismissal of help, and you glimpse for a moment the raw potential for violence which has never really disappeared from his nature, the kind of destructiveness that has most often taken the form of self-destructiveness but has without question hurt others as well. The party has already begun to break up, the sound equipment is being dismantled, people have started going home, when Lonnie at last rouses himself and, yielding to the coaxing of friends, takes up his acoustic guitar to begin a second set. For the few people still present it is a rare experience, as he sings the songs that he has sung in the bus two days before with all the feeling and all the vulnerability that he seems so reluctant to show the public. It is Lonnie Mack Folksinger, Lonnie Mack Granddaddy Hippie, as he likes to conceive of himself now, and he draws everyone around him to join not only in the occasion but in the music. "We're all friends and neighbors, or whatever. I don't want to perform for you. I'm just the one who's doing the singing." And that's all he wants to be. There is talk of a new band out in California. A friend suggests, "He's just afraid that he can't cut it anymore." But really what it comes down to is that Lonnie Mack doesn't want to be who he has been for the last twenty years, he doesn't want to play that kind of music anymore, and he doesn't seem to know how to admit it to himself. By the end of the evening his music has once again salvaged his tenuous faith in himself — but just barely — and he says in a puzzled tone of voice, "Rock 'n' roll and blues used to get

At Streeterville Studios, Chicago, ca. 1986, with blues singer Lonnie Brooks; Alligator Records head Bruce Iglauer (bearded) and engineer Justin Niebank at the board; Mindy Giles standing. *Photograph by Kirk West*

it for me. Now it's just bluegrass that gives me that feeling, and I don't know why. I never even liked bluegrass when I was a kid." In a few weeks he will be heading for Oregon, figuring, like Huckleberry Finn before him, that he'd better "light out for the territory ahead of the rest." Like Huckleberry Finn, Lonnie Mack wants to be neither adopted nor civilized, for, as Huck said, "I can't stand it. I been there before."

POSTSCRIPT

Lonnie did make it to the Cascades, but from what I understand he didn't stay long.

In 1983 he moved to Austin at the invitation of Stevie Ray Vaughan, the young white blues singer from Dallas, who with his best-selling debut album, *Texas Flood,* had recently ascended to the top of the blues world. Vaughan never failed to name as his principal influences Albert and Freddie King, Albert Collins, Jimi Hendrix—and Lonnie Mack. Through Vaughan, Lonnie made a record two years later, his first in seven years, *Strike Like Lightning,* for the blues label Alligator and embarked upon his first real round of national touring, with guest appearances by Vaughan, Ry Cooder, Keith Richards, and Ronnie Wood, capped by a filmed appearance at Carnegie Hall with fellow blues and rock guitar virtuosos Albert Collins and Roy Buchanan. Over the next few years he found a whole new generation of followers, but by 1990 he had stopped recording and wound down his touring over the next decade. When he died in 2016, he had not made a scheduled public appearance in eight years, though a self-described "roadhouse musician" from whom he borrowed a guitar for a single song in 2009 at a "dive bar" near his Smithville, Tennessee, home blogged that he "officially [tore] the roof off the place. He made my rig come alive in ways I've never heard—[it] sounded like the breathing of a large wild animal. . . . People were screaming [and] everybody started dancing." And there the account breaks off, and one can only assume that, after accepting the plaudits of the crowd, Lonnie simply strode out the door.

EIGHT

Delbert McClinton: Night Life

Thanks but no thanks, baby, I've already got
more trouble than I need
Thanks but no thanks, baby, I've already got
more trouble than I need
I don't want no lonely lustful woman's irate
husband after me . . .

— *"Honky Tonkin'"*

DELBERT MCCLINTON IS EXHAUSTED. It could be any one of the approximately 300 annual dates that he plays — in Austin or Boston or New York's Bottom Line — both to keep his name in front of the public and to maintain a working band. His voice, perhaps best described as scoured to start off with ("My voice used to be smoother. I liked it smooth, but I like it rough, too"), is just about blown out; his hair is tousled, his short-sleeved polo shirt is soaked with sweat, and he is hanging on to the microphone in his customary pose almost as much for support as for effect. In an unselfconscious gesture he holds the shirt away from his body and fans himself, and it is almost as if some secret signal has been given to the well-dressed women who fill the front row. Journalist Martha Hume described one of them for *Rolling Stone* readers. "The woman wore a stylish two-piece business suit, and her hair was cut in a regulation pageboy; a briefcase wouldn't have seemed out of place. But the expression on her face was one of pure lust. . . . The woman looked as if she were going to need an oxygen tank any minute." Delbert just smiles

Delbert. *Courtesy of the Delbert McClinton Archives*

wearily. With his thickish lips, doe-like eyes, and boyish charm, he looks a little like a younger lustful Jimmy Carter. You think he is on the verge of collapse, but then he reaches back to some hidden reserve, cues the band with a gesture, and declares, "You might have noticed I'm a little bit hoarse, but if you can live with it, goddamnit I can, too. Because you know I'm gonna go for it every time." And he does, somehow summoning up the energy to turn "Please, Please, Please" or Big Joe Turner's "Rebecca" ("Rebecca, Rebecca, get your big legs off of me") into an ironic cry of love. It is what Delbert calls "dealing with the adjusted flaw," making the best, in other words—like every blues singer from time immemorial—of what you have. It is Delbert's mark.

Watching Delbert McClinton on stage is like entering somebody's living room. Not that the music is casual or overstuffed—it's hard, uncompromising music, and Delbert presents it bam bam bam without pause or punctuation, directing the band with forceful energetic gestures. But Delbert is totally at ease on stage; there is nothing artificial or calculated about his presence. He simply stands up there, clasps his hands around the microphone, blows into his harmonica, and wails. And for the audience, whether it's made up of the famous (some of Delbert's more celebrated admirers include the Blues Brothers, Emmylou Harris, and songwriter Doc Pomus) or your ordinary every-night honky-tonk fan, it's always a little bit like old home week at Delbert's shows. There's always something reassuringly familiar—rhythm and blues and honky-tonk standards mixed in with originals, which in their own amiable, sprung-rhythm, oddly off-center way present a vision just as spare, just as classic, but made fresh at the same time by the wry poetic consciousness of one Delbert McClinton.

> *Honky tonkin', I guess I done me some*
> *I've seen the bullets in the chamber from the other end of a gun*
> *Well, I've been in lots of battles that weren't even worth being won*
> *Honky tonkin', I guess I done me some . . .*

More than many of his equally talented contemporaries, Delbert McClinton has managed to escape the pitfalls of success—mostly by avoiding it. Well, that's not entirely true, and then, too, it all depends upon your definition of success. "I'm already a success," says Delbert, "in doing what I set out to do in the first place—which was just to make a mark, you know. The only thing I haven't done is make any money." But more than most of his contemporaries, Delbert has actually managed to enjoy The Life, to roll with the punches and appreciate the battles and the bullets, the buses and the marriages that break down, the economic impossibility of it all (on a showcase tour to launch a record Delbert is likely to lose several hundred dollars a night), the pronounced raunchiness of the road. There's a feistiness about Delbert, and a boyishness, too, which enables him at forty to maintain the same uncompromising vision of "doing something for real and enjoying it, whether there's two people there or 2,000." Which in turn gives him the impetus to put together yet another band made up of yet another generation of players (guitarist Billy Sanders and Robert Harwell on sax are the only holdovers from the "old" old days) who, like their various predecessors, hold forth with a rare and single-minded dedication that alone would distinguish them from all the other bar bands with similar aims and repertoires. Up on stage they respond with the assurance, precision, and tight ensemble arrangements of a crack James Brown outfit, almost as if Delbert has consciously put together a *sound* to offset the decided non-spectacularness of his act. Between choruses Delbert and Billy joke and fool around, perfectly at home, perfectly at ease, as though it were Fort Worth, Texas, 1958, and they were eighteen and seventeen years old. "I Feel So Bad," "Lovey Dovey," "Little Red Rooster," "Stormy Monday" — these are the songs Delbert still sings. The only difference is that now, twenty-two years later, with his latest single, "Giving It Up for Your Love," seemingly Top 10-bound, Delbert finally has a hit.

> *I'm a victim of life's circumstances*
> *I was raised around barrooms and*
> *Friday night dances*
> *Singing them old country songs*
> *Half the time, ending up some place I don't belong*

"He was always either playing guitar or harp or piano," says Billy Sanders, who grew up on the South Side ("Delbert was a West Side boy") and, with the exception of a few years in the '70s when he gave up the life for a used car lot in Fort Worth, has been playing guitar behind Delbert pretty much since he was sixteen. "This friend had a record collection. We used to listen to all the black players — B.B. King, Lightnin' Hopkins, T-Bone

Walker. Ray Sharpe was in Forth Worth, and of course C.L. [Cornell Dupree, the crack New York session player who has worked extensively with both King Curtis and Aretha Franklin] was playing out at the White Sands Supper Club after hours—he just bent over backwards to encourage us, get us up on the bandstand, what have you. Other guys got into Elvis, that sort of thing, but this group of people like Delbert and myself would go to see Gatemouth Brown, Bobby 'Blue' Bland—nobody'd ever know 'em, what the hell are they? It's hard to explain. It's just that Delbert was inspired, and once he was, he never let it turn around. It's probably the thing I admire about him most of all: once he got started, he's been going head-on all the way."

"There's no way I can explain it," Delbert himself says. "In fact my mama, I remember she told somebody once, she was talking to somebody about how I got into music and she said, 'One day he just became obsessed.' And she's exactly right. I was coming back from squirrel hunting down on the other side of the freight yard, kind of out on the edge of town, on Old Stove Foundry Road, and there was this old black barbecue place—where you drive up and they put the tray in your window, with these outside speaker things. And we was coming back from squirrel hunting, and I heard [Big Joe Turner's] 'Honey, Hush.' The closer we got—I mean there was no words for—like, what is that? Maybe it was just—I was tingling all over. Goddamn. Because it was definitely not Patti Page. Boy, the closer we got, the more excited I got. My heart went to pounding, and I said, 'Who is that, and what is it?' I'll never forget that. It was like hitting up with speed or something. You just went nuts, man. Boy, that stuff still does it to me—I mean, goddamn, you was hearing somebody's heart beat."

He had already started playing guitar. Born in Lubbock in 1940, Delbert moved with his family to Fort Worth when he was eleven and his father took a job as a switchman on the Rock Island railroad. His first real exposure to music came through live performance, and in fact live music has always made the biggest impression on him. "I wasn't a record buyer. Never was—and still am not. It's always been live music for me. The first time I ever sang anything in public, I called a square dance—I used to go up and square dance on Friday night at elementary school. Some of my friends would go up there and go to the movies, but I'd go square dancing with my folks, sit up there at the edge of the stage and listen to some little country band backing up the caller. The first time I ever heard anything live other than the square dance call, I came home from school one day,

With mother and brothers, Fort Worth, Texas: Jack Bridwell, Vivian Bridwell McClinton, Randall Bridwell, with Delbert in front. *Courtesy of the Delbert McClinton Archives*

and I walked in the front door and I heard somebody singing 'The Wild Side of Life.' And we lived in this little shotgun shack, every room stacked behind, so I started making my way through the house. In between the kitchen and the dining room there was this archway, and right in the archway was this long, lanky, cowboy-looking motherfucker — no doubt about it, he was real, you know — and he's setting there, and he's got his feet propped up across the archway, and he's got this little Martin with a hole in it where he stepped in it. His name was Ray Harden, and he was a friend of my older brother — I was just, I don't know, I couldn't believe it. I don't know what I did before that day. It seemed like that was the day I was born."

Within days Delbert and his brother had bought themselves a guitar, an old F-hole Kay with the strings high off the neck, for which they paid

$3.50. Within a couple of weeks they had put a band together—five guitars and a drummer who had a snare and a couple of congas. That was the start of the Mellow Fellows.

THE MELLOW FELLOWS have passed into legend now. As have the Jubals, the Fiats, the Twisters, and John Deutschendorf's high school band (Deutschendorf, a self-described "wimp" according to Delbert, later became better known as John Denver). By Delbert's account the Mellow Fellows were a little weak, although they did add a bass drum when they played the *Big D Jamboree* on the same bill with Jerry Lee Lewis. Delbert got the band gigs by just "going in and telling them that they needed us. We'd play anywhere, anytime, free and otherwise." They played all the little clubs out on the Jacksboro and Mansfield Highways, passing a kitty box to pick up change, getting home in the early morning hours and then going off to high school when they could make it. The Mellow Fellows became the Straitjackets, who in turn became the house band out at Jack's, a semi-notorious roadhouse two blocks outside the city limits where high school kids could go to drink, no questions asked, except on nights when the mule on the sign wasn't kicking (this meant there was going to be a raid). The featured entertainment at Jack's was the blues (on weekends the Straitjackets backed up established stars like Big Joe Turner, Sonny Boy Williamson, and Buster Brown), and the featured dance was "a dance known as the Push. It was not like *a* dance, it was *the* dance, done behind a real good strong shuffle beat. That was the reason I think the blues got to be so popular in Fort Worth—'cause it was the kind of music all those people liked to dance to. In fact they *still* do; they've still got Push clubs in Fort Worth." Around the same time, the Straitjackets were supplementing their musical education out at the Skyliner, where they were the only white band to play Blue Mondays and where Delbert, who had up until this time confined himself for the most part to guitar, was first exposed to blues harmonica.

"The Skyliner Club was one of them old ballrooms built in the '30s, crooked wooden dance floor that looked like it was about a half mile square. And Blue Monday—that was the black night out there. The guy that owned the place would sell them poor people—you'd pay to get in, then you'd pay for a tablecloth, then you'd pay for how many chairs you wanted around this little table about this big. Then you had to pay, buy

Delbert and the Straitjackets. *Courtesy of James Pennebaker*

all your setups and everything. Boy, he'd squeeze every penny he could get out of you. We were playing there one night — actually, we'd already finished playing, we was listening, you know, and it was one of these big old orchestra-sized bandstands, and they'd drop a sheer down to make it a smaller bandstand. All of a sudden they kicked off this song, and I heard a harmonica — it was the first time I'd ever heard anyone actually playing harmonica, and, boy, it got my attention. I was looking on the stage, I was looking all around, and I couldn't see anyone. And just that minute Jimmy Reed come walking out from behind that sheer — it just boggled my mind, you know, he's doing all that with that little bitty motherfucking harp. This was when I was about seventeen. Then when Sonny Boy'd come through, he really liked us a lot. We'd usually back him up on Friday and Saturday night, and then we'd go with him up to Lawton, Oklahoma, back him up on Sunday night at a black club they called Mother's Place. All I can remember is from the minute he'd start, I'd stop — I just couldn't play from just looking and listening, I hung on every goddamn thing he did. I really felt like I was lucky to be right in the midst of all that, you know. To sit in the dressing room with Buster Brown and Jimmy Reed—I missed that show, I was trying to drink whiskey with them—but I knew that I was in the presence of something I should make myself very aware of. Man, you *know* they were heroes to me—and they still are today. There ain't nothin' like standing there listening to Joe Turner sing—goddamn, boy. I was just awestruck."

His parents worried about him, his brothers wondered why "I didn't do some more country songs and be somebody" (according to Billy Sanders, "I like to broke my daddy's heart when I went the blues route"), at nineteen he got married in a tempestuous union that eventually blew up. So far as conventional schooling went, "I tried. I gave it a helluva try. I went summers, I went nights, I even went back when I was twenty-one. Because I had had it hammered into me, if you ain't got that, you ain't got nothing. My mother even wrote me a letter one time, eight pages, she mailed it to me at the house because she could never get me long enough to talk to me. I guess I just about worried my parents to death, but they never really gave me a hard time, at least they never discouraged me musically."

And the music just kept on expanding in the unique musical ambience that was Dallas-Fort Worth. Back in the '50s you could catch Ray Price, Ornette Coleman, King Curtis, Roger Miller, Bob Wills, T-Bone Walker, and Doc Severinsen, all comfortably coexisting within the same musical setting. C. L. Dupree was the reigning guitarist ("All the guitarists worth a shit had to go out to the White Sands to hear him play"). And the blues was king on radio station KNOK, where Delbert McClinton would soon become the first white artist to have a featured hit with his version of Sonny Boy Williamson's "Wake Up Baby." It was an extraordinarily fecund atmosphere in which, as one Ray Price bandleader told writer Dave Hickey, "You could play hillbilly one night, swing the next, jazz the next, and if you had enough coke, play the blues till dawn on every one of them. There wasn't any division, music was music, until the radio jocks and record guys got scared of rock 'n' roll."

Delbert McClinton, it is obvious, never got scared of rock 'n' roll, nor of the blues, nor of country music either. "We included about fifteen minutes of country songs for variety, I guess you might say, but we didn't do 'em in a hokey kind of a way. We always did 'em good. To tell you the truth, we just played the way we knew how to play, we never really thought

With Billy Sanders (left) and James Pennebaker (right), 1980. *Photograph by Kirk West*

about it that much. No one ever seemed to say, 'Reckon we ought to do it this way or try it that way?' We each had a certain amount of freedom, and it worked." The Straitjackets in fact became something like local celebrities, for a while they were *the* band around Fort Worth, much like Doug Sahm's group in San Antonio and a legendary unit out of Bossier City, Louisiana, known as the Boogie Kings, who, while never encountered by Delbert in the flesh, were generally conceded to be the Straitjackets' only other rivals.

There were records, too. From the late '50s on Delbert was hooked up with local legend Major Bill Smith, an entrepreneur with the style, if not the track record, of Colonel Tom Parker and Huey Meaux. ("Fast and shady," says Billy Sanders. "He was subject to making the sunshine a little brighter than it really was.") There was never any suspicion that the Major might be for real, says Delbert, "because he was so full of shit. But I don't know, I was so wrapped up and excited about just playing music that I didn't care if anybody was for real or not. I thought I could overcome anything." On various labels, under various names — he was even Mac Linton for a while — Delbert achieved a good deal more local celebrity and airplay ("We was on top and we knew it and had all kinds of special little privileges around town"), until a demo he cut with Bruce Channel called

"Hey Baby" went to number one on the national charts in 1962. Delbert was just sitting in on harp on the session, but when Channel toured England it was with "Harmonica Star Delbert McClinton," who in Liverpool gave harp instruction to an eager young opening act, the Beatles. "Hey Baby" proved to be kind of a fluke, and Delbert formed half a dozen different groups, the best known of which was the Ron-Dels, whose one chart entry, "If You Really Want Me to I'll Go," was written by Delbert and covered by Waylon Jennings. Eventually local stardom palled, his marriage, shaky to start off with, came apart, and like fellow Texans Janis Joplin and Doug Sahm, Delbert headed out for the Coast.

> *We came out west together with a common desire*
> *The fever we had might have set the West Coast on fire*
> *Two months later got trouble in mind*
> *Maggie moved out and left me behind*
> *But it's all right, 'cause it's midnight*
> *And I got two more bottles of wine. . . .*

> *I'm 1,600 miles from the people I know*
> *Been doing all I can but opportunity sure comes slow*
> *Thought I'd be a star by today*
> *But I'm sweeping out a warehouse in West L.A.*
> *But it's all right, 'cause it's midnight*
> *And I got two more bottles of wine.*

The song just about says it all. Delbert describes himself as "a total idiot, a personality wreck, I didn't know what to do next," when he hooked up with "this young lady I had just fallen in love with for a while, and she had just got a divorce and a '66 Chrysler and a pocket full of money. I said, 'Hey, baby, you want to go to L.A.?' She said, 'You bet.' I said, 'Let's go.'" Out in California the romance wore off, just like the song says, but he got together with hometown friend Glen Clark, with whom he started playing and writing seriously for the first time ("My own songs were something that was pretty alien to me, altogether different from the music I'd been playing"), and working in a veterinary supply warehouse in, of course, West L.A. Together they made a couple of albums as Delbert and Glen for Atlantic-distributed Clean Records. The records, though highly regarded and very much prophetic of the cross-pollinated country music which would become popular in the '70s (they also provide the basis for a good part of Delbert's repertoire today), didn't sell, Delbert moved back to Fort Worth, and in 1975 came out with his first ABC album.

"I took it as a good stroke. I was thirty-five years old. The '60s were pretty much a blur. And it was crazy the way it happened, too. We [he had recently remarried] had a brand-new baby, just bought a twenty-three-foot travel trailer, and were fixing to get the hell out of there and at least try to do some good in Nashville. A friend of mine, Charles Stewart, was the branch manager for ABC Records in Fort Worth. He was one of the faithful dancers back in the old days. I hadn't seen him in years, and one day he just called out of the blue and asked me what I was doing. I told him not much, and he suggested we do something, and we went over and cut some demos at a little four-track studio in Pantego. Most of them songs was the songs that ended up on the album."

It's hard to describe the full impact of *Victim of Life's Circumstances*. It sounded, and still sounds in a way, like the summation of Delbert McClinton's life in music. There are blues, kickers, r&b, and careless evocations of classic rock 'n' roll, all put across with a kind of casual panache that is dependent neither on tricky arrangements nor vocal pyrotechnics. All of the elements with which Delbert has come to be identified are present on the first album — a stabbing horn section, contemporary blues modulations, spare but eloquent lyrics, a thick musical texture, and the kind of soul-blasting r&b feel that is straight out of the honky-tonks. More than anything, though, there is the presence and energy of Delbert McClinton himself. Each of the songs was written by Delbert, there is nothing forced or out of place about any of them, and every one possesses the easy assurance, loose vocal rhythms, straight-ahead sincerity, and elliptical craft that characterize his best work.

"That's when I really started trying to do something career-wise," Delbert agrees. "'Cause I had the energy, the songs were *ready,* and I wasn't shy about presenting them either." That was when he set about putting together what was left of the old band, too. He called up Billy Sanders, then doing pretty well with his used car lot. "He came by one day and asked me if I wanted to go to Europe. And I'd always told him if he ever went to Europe without me I'd kill him. He said, 'Well, if you do, you're gonna have to get with me now.' Well, I had the business going, I was making decent money, and I was married and all this and that — and I wasn't going to do it. But then I agreed to help him a week here, a week there, and before I knew it I was right back in the mainstream again, riding around in the back of an old pickup truck with the equipment. And we *still* haven't gotten to Europe."

He called up Robert Harwell, too, who had started out as a guitar player in the days of the Twisters and then graduated to sax under the influence of Leon Childs, another after-hours player who provided inspiration around Fort Worth. Robert had been off the scene for a while himself, quitting a Vegas-type show band in disgust to study music at the University of Texas at Arlington. "He called up and said, 'Come on, we're gonna make it this time.' Well, I guess we all had the same background and roots that pulled us back to play our kind of music, but there wasn't many of us to get back together. This time we had to find a whole new generation that wanted to learn how to play simply again. Well, I went along with him then, but it's been five fucking years, and we haven't made it yet!"

> *My luck ain't been too good,*
> *The other day, you know, a mad dog bit me*
> *I stopped to help a lady on the street, and her husband hit me.*
> *Don't nothing seem to make much sense to me*
> *My whole world's gone crazy*
> *I guess it's just another lesson in the pains of love.*

Delbert's recording career since 1970 has had its ups and downs, but it's been marked by one constant: until now every recording company that he has signed with has gone under. Clean was a flash in the pan; ABC was absorbed into MCA not long after they dropped him; Capricorn, for whom he made a couple of more rock-oriented albums, went into bankruptcy before the third could be released. Nonetheless Delbert has always maintained his audience, not least because Delbert is first and foremost a live act. In some ways none of the albums, with the exception of *Victim*, has done full justice to his talent, simply because they lack the directness, the dangerous incandescence of a live set. In other, equally important ways, though, they have always remained close to Delbert's vision. Speaking of the music he grew up on, Delbert characterizes it as "raw and unpolished maybe, but that shit was not mediocre. You might talk to a technician, and he might tell you how pitiful the mix was and all that — but goddamn, but goddamn, boy, when you'd get right down to it, you'd burn all the machines and shit and hand somebody a guitar, and that's what it gets down to. You sit down in front of somebody, and you can either move them or you can't. *And it don't have nothing to do with turning knobs*. And that to me is what I want to keep alive, is the excitement of a live set."

That's what Delbert *has* kept alive, without serious concession or compromise. That's why you'll hear Delbert feature the old songs as much as his own songs, no matter what the occasion or the showcase. To Delbert clearly there are no musical divisions; he neither considers the old music old-fashioned nor the new music "progressive." It's all just good music, it's all real, "it's music that makes you want to move, it's a gut thing. I guess it's good therapy or whatever. 'Cause there ain't no way it can be anything but right."

He has reacted strongly, Billy says, to suggestions that he soften his impact. "He told me one time, they were trying to get us to change, to do something different to try to get ahead, and he said, 'We'll do it till we die. The hell with it.' He was letting me know where he stood, and I admired it, and I said, 'Doggone it, put my ass in hock, I'm going with you.'" Even on the new Capitol-distributed Muscle Shoals Sound album, clearly an attempt to snare Delbert a larger audience, and a largely successful attempt at that, it's still just Delbert, it's still for real. It may not be like seeing Delbert live — even Delbert will concede that hearing Bobby Charles' heartbreaking song, "The Jealous Kind," live is quite a different experience than listening to it on the album. ("It's a world of difference when you got somebody to sing it to. I told them while I was cutting it, man, there's nothing in the world louder than the silence of them headphones.") And the absence of any new originals (Delbert is a notoriously slow writer, who "can't just sit down and intend to write a song. When I write, I write pretty quickly, but I can be stuck for years for a line") is a distinct disadvantage. But at the same time the new album is an honest attempt to come to terms with something different in Delbert's life.

"Well, you know, this last year was a big turn in everything for me. Dope quit working like it used to. I wasn't writing. I wasn't twenty-one anymore. You know, I started feeling all those things. Like I just turned forty. In the last year it just all caught up with me. One night I had a couple of drinks of tequila, and it just put me on my ass. I went in to do this album with a sobriety I never had before. I mean, I wanted to know exactly everything that happened. I didn't want to be told afterwards, You must have been drunk, you must have been high — I even took notes, you know, of little spots in songs where I thought . . . I guess you might say this was my first involvement in producing to any degree. I think vocally it's the best work I've ever done, and Barry Beckett [the producer and head of Muscle Shoals Sound Records] said something to me that really made me feel good—we were both busting our ass, we knew from the first time we started working together that we could do something, you know, and we just about had the record finished, we was real proud of it, and he said, 'You know, it's very nice working with someone who knows what they're doing.' And, you know, I thought about it, and I thought, I really went about it right this time. I want to make records instead of drunken madness."

Drunken madness it is backstage on the Willie Nelson tour at the Austin Opry House. Delbert has finished a strong opening set and is surrounded by friends, family, and well-wishers. Everyone is happy for Delbert, it seems. "Giving It Up for Your Love" really looks like it's going to be the big hit that has been predicted for him for years. If anyone was ever ready for success, it would appear to be Delbert. ("If this had happened when I was with Clean, I'd be dead, either dead or the burned-outest sonofabitch you ever seen. Maybe I got stars over my head, 'cause it held off till I was too weak to destroy myself.") His five-year-old son, Clay, a miniature version of Delbert, even down to the reddish slicked-back hair and the cocky, almost challenging sway to his walk, is shooting darts with some of the band members. Delbert's wife, Donna Sue, is talking with Billy's wife, giving herself over for a moment to fantasies of success. "New bus, new house, new car, a roadie for me."

Delbert softly shakes his head. "It's hard to fool yourself anymore. You can't say, Boy, this is fun, when it's not. I mean, how many nights can you spend in a beer joint? Not that I don't still enjoy it. I do. But it's just not like it used to be. I'm not after the same things. It's like right now with this record—this record's doing better than anything I've ever had going, every day it's picking up forty to sixty stations, the single jumped nearly thirty spots, and if it does that next week it's going to be a big record. But I still—something won't let me believe it yet. It's been too many years and too many times of thinking, Boy, next week—but now you've got to show me. I don't want to get too up, because I don't know if I could take it, I don't know if I could smile my way through another. . . . I ain't got the years left in the first place, you know. It takes a year for each record just about. It has with me, even with the nothingness I been doing; it takes a

Doc Pomus with Delbert at the Lone Star, 1984. *Photograph by Stephanie Chernikowski*

year to go from nothingness to vanish, but at least once it's done it's there and they can't take that away. That's the way I feel about making records — if I can just get the motherfucker pressed, then I've got it beat. Because I could care less that anybody knows who I am anymore, you know? When I was in my twenties I wanted to be a big star, but I don't want that anymore, from what I've seen it's a little too awesome. People think you know something, it's really hard to keep a handle on who you are when you feel everybody's looking at you. You know, when I was a kid, I used to go out to the Boulevard Drive-In Theatre, and I used to dream that it was me up there with the bright lights on me. Nowadays, when they put them lights on, put them fuckers out, man."

Still, there's the satisfaction of having stayed true to his vision, of simply having survived. "If you had told me in the '60s that I would be as happy a person as I am today," says Delbert, "I would never have believed you. In '65 I was twenty-five, and I thought it was all over." And, too, for all of the ugliness, for all of the disappointments and all of the rage

(Delbert is not exactly the most even-tempered of men), there is what has been loosely called the fraternity of the road. For Delbert and Billy it's still the Jacksboro Highway, and as Billy says, with an explicitness that will undoubtedly embarrass Delbert, "He's probably the best friend I've ever had. I'd do anything in the world for that sonofabitch, and he's already shown me he would do the same for me. All we gotta do now is keep each other from going crazy."

Up on stage in any case it's always the present—there is no future, there is no past, and consequences don't have to be weighed in the balance. You see Delbert, a small, commanding figure brimming over with energy, truculence and vulnerability mixed in equal parts in his voice. You hear the band chugging away at this unpretentious good-time music, raising up "Chicken Shack" or "It Should've Been Me" from the dead well of history, Billy's red B.B. King guitar flashes, Robert takes another perfectly constructed solo on sax, the band is really churning now with a hot ensemble sound, and the audience responds as they always have, as they always will, caught up in the moment as much as the musicians themselves. This is what it's all about. And Delbert at the mike is sweetly, sensuously lost in the music, as he sings: "Well, the night life, it ain't no good life, but it's my life," and the sound comes crashing down all around him.

NINE

Joe Tex: Hold What You've Got

YOU CAN SEE THE HOUSE from the Navasota highway. It's a long, low, comfortable-looking ranch house with a basketball hoop in the driveway and a swimming pool out back. It's still in the process of completion, since its present occupants have lived here only five years, and plans are being made for additional landscaping and home improvements. The chickens and the horses and the occasional swirls of dust add a comfortable touch, and in fact there is only one incongruity to this familiar suburban scene: a small gray weathered shack sitting up on cinder blocks between the house and the highway. It looks like any one of the thousands of sharecropper shacks that dot the Texas landscape. That is where Joe Tex's grandmother lives.

It is the source of as much chagrin to Joe Tex himself as it would be to any other upwardly mobile professional who seeks to take care of his obligations and his family. This is the grandmother, after all, who raised him, the oft-repeated reason for his entrance into show business not "to become famous but to build my mother and my grandmother a house. But she refused to move when I built the house. Come on, I'll show you her room," he says in that familiar hoarse whisper of a voice. And he does. It's a beautiful room, sunny, open, decorated in gold and white, with paneled walls and white china figurines of geese. He shows the room off proudly, without self-consciousness. He is wearing running shoes, high athletic socks, dungarees, and a straw cowboy hat. His battered red pickup is parked in the driveway, and his round friendly face with its mischievous expression and smooth, scrunched-together features looks much the same as it did during his heyday — and the heyday of soul music — some fifteen years ago. There is gray in his beard, but his eager manner, the rushed stammer of his words, his enthusiasm not only for telling his own story but for talking about his grandmother, his forebears, his family, his *roots,* all bear out a youthfulness that belies his forty-five years. Once he gets going you can't hold him back, and his conversation is punctuated with little giggles, affectionate squeezes, and bursts of emotional generosity that seem genuinely artless.

Everything is documented. He speaks of his childhood sweetheart, as many men and women might do, then touches your knee and asks if you'd like to see a picture of her. There she is with Joe in Las Vegas a couple of years ago, flanked by Gladys Knight and Lenny Wilkens and pictures of Joe with Kareem Abdul-Jabbar, with Sammy Davis Jr., with his caftaned wife Bilaliah and their four-year-old son, Ramadan. We sit in the living room, sunk down on the cushions of the comfortable black sofa, surrounded by plants, a pool table, a Naugahyde bar, all the emblems of the good life which Joe Tex has legitimately come to enjoy. Meanwhile, his grandmother, from whom Joe Tex got his gift of humor, lives just several hundred yards away, on the very land that she and her family once sharecropped, in living rebuke to the whole concept of fortune and fame. And Joe Tex appreciates that, too.

HE WAS BORN Joseph Arrington Jr. on August 8, 1935, not in Navasota but in Rogers, 100 miles away, because his mother had words with her boss man. "She was about eight months pregnant with me, she was at home down here, and that boss man told her, if she didn't get out in the field working, he said, 'I'll come over in the yard and kill you and the goddamn baby.' So my mother told my daddy, said, 'Let's go, man. I'm not gonna stay here. Let's go.' But my daddy was scared, it was right in the middle of harvest time, and he was one of them toms — work like a dog all the time — so my mother put some clothes in a pasteboard box and tied it up with string. Back in those times you could stop the train anywhere, just wave and they see you and they stop. So she got on the train and went to Rogers to her mother, which is my grandmother. And that's where I was born."

He was raised by his grandmother with a younger sister in the little town of Rogers, "population 911 when I left in 1948, I don't know if it's decreased or increased, I know there's one gone, though, and it's me." His mother lived and worked in Baytown, outside of Houston, and summers they would all go back to Navasota to pick cotton. As anyone who has listened to his records would have to realize, Joe Tex is nothing if he

"I've enjoyed this life." *Courtesy of Joe McEwen*

is not country, and those fictional "characters" who were "eating barbecue and drinking red soda water on the nineteenth of June" were not figments of his imagination but friends, relatives, and fellow townspeople. In fact the whole town was so full of Arringtons, Warrens, and McGintys that, Joe says with a show of mock gravity, "I never could get no pussy when I was growing up. Every time I say something to one of these girls, you know, 'You're my first cousin's uncle's daughter's son by a second marriage.' I mean, relatives all up and down this whole road!"

There was a more serious side to it, too. Like James Brown, the young Joe Tex got his start in show business shining shoes and selling papers. "I used to shine shoes on Saturdays and make me a little change. And I'd dance along with the shoe shine, make me a little show. Then when I was in school I'd sell newspapers. There were three white boys that were selling them, too, at one of those intersections, so I put a little song and dance into mine, into my newspaper. When the people would pull up to the red light in the cars, I'd jump out there in the street and do a little jitterbug for them. They pay for them with fifty cents or a dollar and say, 'Keep the change.'"

He was not, he insists, in any way disadvantaged. "I guess I was spoiled in a sense. It's not an ego thing about it, but I'm spoiled to women waiting on me, you know, my shirts being ready when I come in or food being cooked. See, my daddy and mother divorced when I was two, and there was never a man image. I was raised by women all of my life, and this is why I hold women, I look at all women in the world as my mother. Even if she's my wife or my sweetheart or girlfriend. It became a part of me, you know. I just felt that a man was supposed to go out and make a living, and that's what I used to do in Rogers. I used to go out, I was about five or six years old, and I'd go hustle up a little job, I'd steal out of the stores, anything my grandmother said she wanted, she had it. See, my grandmother worked, she worked in people's houses—it weren't but for a little bit of money, but she worked and she brought home food and stuff that they give her. And we survived. If she said, 'I ain't got no money, but I sure wished I had me some liver,' I was gone. I'd go, and if the man wouldn't let me work in the store, I'd steal the liver. Or pick me up some soda pop bottles and sell them. And get enough money to get my grandmother some liver and rice. So I just grew up knowing the man go out and make the living and the woman had the dinner cooked, the shirts ironed, and the house cleaned—and those are my roots."

His roots were also in the little Baptist church in Rogers where he and his sister used to sing gospel duets, and at St. Martinsville Baptist Church in Navasota, where he and some friends formed a Five Blind Boys–styled quartet. He listened to country radio, too, to KTEM, a station in Temple that played Hank Williams, Webb Pierce, and Hank Snow, "the music that I love the most. The first blues record that I heard that I guess touched my soul was 'Drifting Blues' by Charles Brown. Somehow that song really inspired me, I really don't know exactly what it was. See, we lived next door in Rogers to a beer joint, right next door, man, and they used to play all these records—Louis Jordan, Charles Brown, Amos Milburn. . . ."

His mother came to get him and his sister when he was twelve and carried them back to Baytown, where she was living. "I was happy to be out of Rogers, 'cause Rogers is a little spot, man, no one would ever come through there and try to look for any talent or anything." And it was in high school that his talent was discovered.

It's not hard to imagine Joe "Tex" Arrington (the "Tex" was bestowed upon him by a Mr. Lang, the owner of Club Ebony in Houston, where Joe performed at the amateur show on Monday night in a cowboy outfit) at George Washington Carver High School in Baytown. He would have been the class cutup, the class clown—not the one who was always getting in trouble with his teachers necessarily but the one who always kept his classmates laughing with jokes, mimicry, and comedy routines. His enthusiasm then, as now, must have been infectious; he was obviously industrious and directed; he ran track, high and low hurdles; and his sensitivity came out in the poems he wrote for his childhood sweetheart, Jean, and the book of poems, "The Flowers of Linnell," he left as his graduation gift to the school. At one point he persuaded his mother to buy him a trombone to play in the school band, "and she went and bought me an old trombone for $35. She's paying a little bit on it every week. I got the horn, got in the band, and played it for about two weeks and put it down. I wanted to play football instead. So one night my mother is listening to the football game on the radio, and the announcer says, 'There's an extra point made good by Joe the Toe Arrington. My mother said, 'Lord, the band's playing football!'"

Judging by his energy level today, he must have been indefatigable, always hustling, always looking for the opportunity to get ahead, drifting naturally into show business because "I like people, you know, and I like making people happy." He considered college—and would no doubt have been successful at it, going on to a career in business, selling himself or insurance in much the same way that he sells a song—but ruled it out after talking it over with Jean. "Most of the ones I graduated with went on to college, but Jean and I sat down and talked about it, and I told her I wanted to help my mother and my grandmother that raised me, 'cause they lived hard all their life, and I said, 'If I take four years to go to school, there would be that much time wasted—not really wasted, but that I could be helping them.'"

His motivation, then, was clear. His vehicle for entering show business was equally decisive. He entered a citywide amateur contest his junior

Amateur show in Houston, early 1950s. *Courtesy of Bilaliah Hazziez*

year in high school and took first prize over such notable performers as Johnny Nash, Hubert Laws, and Ben E. King imitator Acquilla Cartwright. Joe did a comedy sketch, "It's in the Book," and won $300 cash and a week in New York City at Harlem's famed Hotel Theresa. While in New York, Tex appeared at the Apollo Theater and won *their* amateur show two weeks in a row. "I called up my mother and asked her if I could stay two more weeks," he told writer Joe McEwen. "Well, two weeks later I had been a four-time winner." He had also met Solomon Burke, later to be an eminent colleague and key influence upon his work, who, as he recalled, placed second doing a Roy Hamilton song.

What happened next is not so picture-book clear. He went back to Texas and finished high school, graduating in June of 1955. A collection was taken up to send Joe back to New York to pursue a show business career, and the money was being held by one of his teachers. The night before he was scheduled to leave, there was a going-away party, but when the guests arrived at the club where the party was supposed to be held it was closed. The partygoers went out to the teacher's house, only to discover that the money was gone, though the teacher was apologetic. Like so many recollected incidents in Joe Tex's life, though, this one is the occasion not for recriminations but for celebration and praise. "Another of my schoolteachers—I have to mention her because she was very inspiring, Mattie Belle Durkee, she was the director of the music department at Carver—she and the physical education teacher, Mrs. Addison, went around the city of Baytown with a Roi-Tan cigar box and solicited funds from the businesspeople, and they all contributed, and I didn't even know she was doing it. I had just sort of resolved it by saying, 'I'll get me a job, and I'll go to school, and me and Jean can get married.' But then Mrs. Durkee and Mrs. Addison come back with the money and say, 'Here, you can go to New York.' And I cried, man. It really touched me. Mrs. Durkee carried me to the train station and give me a little motherly talk—you know, Watch the big city, this kind of thing—and I got on the train, and you *know* I was determined to make it 'cause I wasn't going to let her down."

He started off staying with relatives in Hempstead, Long Island, and working as a caretaker in a Jewish cemetery. Whatever connections he may have made on the earlier trip don't seem to have done him much good, and after leaving the cemetery he worked in a clothing store, then in a furniture store for several weeks, until he heard about a place called the Celebrity Club in Freeport, a showplace for black rhythm and blues performers. When he went out there looking for an audition, the white club owner wouldn't even listen to him but told him to contact Jimmy Evans, a tough manager of the old school, who booked the club. "I don't know no Jimmy. The man give me no address, no phone number, no nothing. So I'm supposed to go up there to Broadway and holler, 'Hey, Jimmy Evans, here I am, hey hey.' So I went on back to Hempstead and continued to work at the furniture store. One day, man, I just said to myself, I just said, 'I'm going back to that club.' I said, 'They gonna hear me . . . *tonight.*'" He brazened his way into the club, told the MC he had been hired by the owner, got a tremendous reception when he sang B.B. King's "Woke Up This Morning," and had the same owner who had rejected him just weeks before come running out of his office to declare, "You're great. They love you. What's your name?"

"I said, 'Man, are you kidding?' Then I said, 'Let that go.' I said, 'Joe "Tex" Arrington.' He say, 'You want to work here? You got a job every Friday, Saturday, and Sunday.' He says, 'I don't care who is appearing, you are the main act.' But, you see, I made an enemy in that, too. 'Cause everything that happens good, there's always something left behind bad out of it. The MC I was telling you about, who let me in in the first place—I took his job, it was for him. And I could see the jealousy that night, the envy, the cold treatment. And I asked the man, 'Can't you keep your house MC?' I really tried to get the club owner to keep him, but he said no, and I took the job. I started performing at the club, and that was through August, September, the first part of October of '55, which was the night that Arthur Prysock [a popular Billy Eckstine-influenced r&b singer] was in the audience. When the show was finished, he sent for me to come to his table. He said, 'You done any recording?' I said, 'No, that's why I'm up in New York now, trying to get a recording contract.' Prysock told me, 'I have a friend of mine who is an a&r man for King Records named Henry Glover.' He said, 'I'd like for you to meet him and see if you can get something going. Do you know how to get from Hempstead to Jamaica?' And I said no, so he wrote it down."

Despite other accounts that have Glover discovering him at the Apollo, this appears to have been the way Joe Tex came to record for King. His career with King was not particularly distinguished; his first release was "Davy, You Upset My Home," a novelty song that complained about the Davy Crockett craze of the time, and while he wrote the majority of his songs they amounted more to parody, or imitation, than to a personal style of his own. One of the more blatant cases of borrowing was "Pneumonia," a takeoff on "Fever," which came about, Tex says, because he was supposed to have had the original version instead of Little Willie John and gave away his arrangement, a variant of "16 Tons," because he thought it was imitative and thus subject to litigation. The main thing about his two years at King was that they established him as a professional. They didn't make him any money to speak of, because, he says, there were no writer's or artist's royalties. The night before his first King session at the Beltone recording studio, "I didn't sleep because I was so excited. I was thinking about the Roi-Tan cigar box and about Jean and about my hometown and about all this stuff. I didn't sleep that night at all, and the next day I got up and went to the studio and on the session were some of the great names in music, man. I wasn't nervous. I just wanted to get on with it."

When he got his $200 for the session, "I said, 'I need to cash this, 'cause I ain't ever had $200 since before the World War.' I got an $80 money order and sent it back home to my mother, 'cause that was the first time since I left that I was able to send any money. So I sent her $80 in a money order—and then I'm still so excited I bought a train ticket and go home to Texas. Came back home, they was playing the record around Houston.

I was so happy, I was so excited, then a call came from Universal Attractions [booking and talent agency] — Glover had given them my number — and they said, 'You want to work? Okay, we got a gig for you.'"

So he embarked upon the life of a journeyman r&b singer. His first job was in Florida, and he was almost shot by the woman club owner with whom he had moved in. ("Peter, I'm thankful to God today that that gun was not loaded.") None of his records ever really happened, but like so many of the events in Joe Tex's life, one thing led to another, and before long he was being booked on a regular basis by Ben Bart, the head of Universal, who would soon become James Brown's longtime manager. He played on package shows all around the country and rapidly gained a reputation for being dependable. While other singers were messing up personally, he remained focused on what had been his motivation from the first. "Because I was determined to make it, man, and I didn't want to do anything that would mess up my business. [Comedian] Nipsey Russell, Arthur Prysock, Percy Mayfield, Roy Hamilton — they schooled me a lot, they really were the people that gave me the early teachings of this thing out here. They schooled me about the streets, you know, how to stay away from certain things, how not to fall into the hands of these slicksters and pimps and hustlers that was all up and down the streets." He played the Howard, he played the Apollo, he played the Regal in Chicago, and he played the little clubs, too, the gambling houses and numbers fronts and hangouts for the small-time gangsters. "Little Willie John went by me, the Midnighters went by me, '5' Royales went by me, Dinah Washington, James Brown, all them people booked by Universal. I wasn't — I'm not a jealous person and envious of their success. But I say, 'Hey, man,' I would look at other entertainers that were making it, and I felt that I was just as good as they were. I never lost faith that it would happen. There were a lot of times that I wanted to quit, but I never lost faith. I knew that if I stuck with it — now, if I stopped, that's another thing — but if I stuck with it, I knew that one day it was gonna pay off. And I was just waiting for that day."

Then two things happened to change his life. One was the song — actually it was a song stemming from personal experience — that changed his musical direction. Another was the chance meeting that changed his professional direction just as radically.

In 1960 his childhood sweetheart, Jean, whom he was still hoping to marry, got married to someone else. Joe was living in Baton Rouge and playing at a club called the Apex. He was singing a song made popular just that year by Etta James, "All I Could Do Was Cry," about a jilted lover at the wedding of his (in Etta's case, her) sweetheart. In the middle of the song, "I was just talking. Jean had just gotten married and I was despondent about it, and I just told the band to tone it down, and I started in to talking. I was in my hometown and lost the only girl I ever loved, it was real and the people just went, Ooh-wee! So the disc jockey, Samuel Douglas, they called him Rootie Tootie — he's in South Carolina now, Greenville — he said, 'Man, what was that?' He said, 'You knocked them people out. You got to record that.' I said, 'That's about my childhood sweetheart. I don't want that to get on a record, I just got carried away.' He said, 'Man, let's record that.'

"It was the first record that I had to hit the national charts. And I played the Apollo not for the first time, but the first time with a record. It was just one little freelance-type thing, but that record got me moving." And it was the genesis of a style, the basis for a succession of talking sermons that would come to characterize all of the best work of Joe Tex right up until "Hold What You've Got" some four years later.

The other event was even more of a happenstance, and that was Joe's meeting with Buddy Killen, one of country music's most successful publishers, who took charge of Joe's career and produced all of his records from the time of that first meeting in Nashville in 1961. Actually, according to Killen, a prosperous-looking, florid-faced man who looks more like an honest banker than a denizen of Music Row, it was not strictly speaking their first meeting. "The first time I saw Joe Tex, I was a musician on the Grand Ole Opry, and he came backstage at the Opry one Saturday night. I saw him, but I didn't know who he was. He was dressed in a cowboy outfit, with a purple shirt, boots, the whole works. Back in those days he wanted to sing country music."

Their first formal introduction came through Robert Riley, a former member of the Prisonaires (they were residents of the Tennessee State Penitentiary when they recorded for Sam Phillips in 1953 and helped put Sun Records on the map), who worked for Killen's Tree Publishing Company and caught Joe's act at the New Era Club in Nashville. He brought Joe to Buddy, and "Joe sang a couple of songs for me and just knocked me out. Boy, what a fabulous talent this guy was." By his own account Buddy had no idea what to do next, but he knew that "I'd never seen a greater entertainer — bar none." So he formed a production company, Dial

Records, pretty much for Joe Tex alone at the beginning, and cut a series of records with limited commercial success at first. Because of his past experiences Joe had to overcome an initial degree of suspiciousness, but he quickly learned to trust Buddy, and it was Buddy who educated him for the first time about such things as writer's and performance royalties. "When I first met Buddy, man, he was so mad with the people at King. He said, 'They did what, man?' He said, 'You don't get no BMI?' Damn, ain't nobody told me about none of that. Buddy got on it, got on the case, man, it really did make him angry. After that I started getting statements, I never did get any money from King, but at least I started getting statements. You know, with the treatment we received in the South in the early days, I never did think the day would come that I would call a white man my friend, but Buddy Killen and I, man, are like brothers. He was born in Alabama, but he's got no racial hang-ups: you're not black or white, you're just a human being to him."

He and Buddy continued to have mixed success over the next three years, gaining in mutual respect but failing to fully share a musical vision. ("I didn't quite understand what he was looking for," says Buddy, "and he didn't understand what I was looking for.") The records they put out were something of the same mixed bag of novelty songs ("Looking for My Pig," "The Peck") and moving preachments ("I Had a Good Home [But I Left]") that would eventually become their formula for success. Most were recorded in Nashville, generally with Nashville musicians, and though some came close to commercial success, none could fairly be labeled a hit. By the time they went into the studio in November of 1964 — this time in Muscle Shoals, for the first time with Joe's band — Buddy's distribution deal with London Records was up, and according to both Buddy and Joe their partnership was just about finished, too. "Joe called me and said, 'We've tried it all and, well, every time we go in the studio we sort of get crossways a little at each other' — he said, 'Why don't we terminate?' I said, 'I'll tell you. Let me record you one more time the way I want to, and if we don't happen I'll turn you loose and let you have your contract.'"

Joe pretty much concurs. "I said, 'Buddy, it's been four years, and we ain't got anything, and I don't want to waste your time, and I'm damn sure you don't want to waste mine.' I said, 'If this session doesn't come off, you give me my release. I can go somewhere else.' He said sure. So I went down, and at the time I talked with him, I was in Charlotte, North Carolina, I was gonna meet him in Alabama, and on the way down I jotted down a few lines to 'Hold On to What You Got.' I was just sitting there in the car, and I got to thinking about Jean, and at the time I was married in Baton Rouge, and my wife, Johnnie Mae, was pregnant with my son. And I was thinking about leaving Baton Rouge, the whole thing. Try to get Jean back. Jean was married, but I was gonna figure out some kind of way and get her back. So I was sitting in the car, and I was thinking about it. I said, 'Well, she's married now, and she probably won't take me back.' I said, 'Might as well hold on to what I got.' Went over and over in my head, 'Keep what you got, keep what you got. . . .' I got a bag of food in the back, and I just tore a piece of paper off the bag and got me a pencil and jotted down that much of it. I was gonna work on it later, 'cause I didn't have a melody or anything. And we got down to Muscle Shoals, and I did the four sides that I was prepared to do, and we finished those, and I'm hoarse, could hardly speak above a whisper. And Buddy says, 'We got an hour of studio time left, got to pay for it anyway. You got any more songs?'

"I said, 'No, I've got one here on the paper that I'm writing on, but I haven't finished it yet.' He said, 'What is it?' I read him the lyrics off. He said, 'Sounds pretty good to me.' He said, 'We'll take a break, and you give it to the fellows and see if you can work on it.' Well, I got to thinking and try to come up with a melody. This was November, and I said, 'If Buddy released this song and it could come out during the Christmas holidays — I wanted to give it a kind of spiritual flavor. So I thought of some Christmas songs, but the melody was too obvious. So I came up with one that was not too obvious, that I could get away with — it's "Holy, Holy, Holy, Lord God Almighty." We recorded it, and I was too hoarse, and I was trying to reach the high notes. Buddy said, 'When you get to that part, just talk.'"

The way Buddy remembers it, as soon as he heard the song, "I said, 'I think that's a smash. Let's do it.' I told the guitar player, 'I want a straight country chord in front and everybody just fill it out.' I never will forget, everybody said, 'You got to be kidding.' I said, 'No, I'm not.' So we did the song, and we didn't have multiple tracks back in those days, and we kept having breakdowns, and I finally got two or three takes on it, and I said, 'Joe, I'd like you to sing some harmony.' He said, 'I can't sing harmony.' I said, 'I'll show you exactly what I want.' So we went from mono to mono, and he sang the harmony part, but it was still ragged, and Rick Hall [the owner and engineer of FAME, the Muscle Shoals studio] apologized and said, 'Sorry you didn't get anything'; the band said, 'Sorry you didn't get anything'; and Joe said, 'Buddy, I'm really sorry. We tried.' We all left, and

Joe and Buddy Killen in the studio ca. 1970, with producer Brad Shapiro to Buddy's right.
Courtesy of Buddy Killen

I came back to Nashville the next day. I sat down in my office, and I said, 'I'm not giving up that easily.' So I called RCA and booked some studio time and took the tapes over there, and I had them run copies, and I started editing. And if I found a piece that was good, I'd use it. I used the same chorus all the way through. Every time you hear the chorus, it's the same one, because it's the only one that I could find that was good enough to use. Well, I sent the record to Jerry Wexler at Atlantic, and he said, 'It's a smash. Let's make a deal.' He put the record out immediately, we didn't wait, just put it right out."

The record took off from the moment of its release. "We put that record out," says Buddy, "and the first week it sold 50, 60,000 copies. In the first two or three days it just boomed. Jerry called me and told me what was happening, and a few days later Joe called. He said, 'Buddy, you told me you'd turn me loose if nothing happened, and we tried and we didn't get anything.' I said, 'Joe, the record's a smash.' He said, 'You put that thing, that piece of garbage out?' I said yes, and he hung up on me. About a week or ten days later he called and said, 'Look, man, you told me you were gonna let me out of the contract, and I expect you to do it.' I said, 'Joe, we sold a quarter of a million records.' He said, 'Look—' He said, 'What!!' I said, 'The record is a smash. I been hearing it on pop stations.' After that, of course, we cut a lot of big hits over the years."

The first royalty check was for $40,000. "Buddy gave me the check, I was in Nashville, and I said, 'Man, I'm gonna go to the bank and cash this and put this in a briefcase.' He said, 'You gonna go down to Baton Rouge with all this money?' I said, 'Yeah, for once in my life I'm gonna run my hands through all these dollar bills.' He said, 'Okay, but, Joe, you be careful.' I went to the bank and cashed the check and put it in an attaché case, and I was sitting in the front seat of that car going down the highway. And I employed some people to start building a house, 'cause up to that time Johnnie Mae and I were living with her mother and father. And I came back to Texas and gave my sister some money, gave my mama some money, came to Navasota and gave my grandmother some—she didn't even have an inside toilet. So I had an extra room put on the back, had a toilet put in there. She didn't have any gas at that time—I'm talking about '64, she was still burning wood, burning oil lamps. So I had the house wired, put lights in, run the gas line, the whole thing, I just splurged. Because, you see, I'd wanted to do this for them all my life. I fulfilled that dream that I had lived with for ten years. I just wanted to help my people."

"THIS IS GREAT. This is really nice. You know, coming out here, man, it's really a big, big thrill for me. I remember when I used to come up here when I was a little boy—you know when you go somewhere, when you get a special feeling about being there? Well, this is what Navasota—of all the places that I played, this is what Navasota did for me. There ain't nothing here that much, but it was just something about the place . . . I would feel at peace, contented."

We are driving through fields once planted with cotton. It is a cool December day, and John Lennon has just been murdered. All around us are landmarks of Joe Tex's childhood. St. Martinsville Church, sitting just off the highway—with its worn white boards and cupola, dirt yard and outbuildings, where Joe used to sing gospel numbers with his own homegrown quartet and the congregation would arrive in old Fords and Chevrolets and after the service buy hoop cheese and crackers at the little boarded-up store across the way. The big brick house with the white curtains drawn where the boss man used to live and from which curious white children stare as we drive along dusty dirt roads. Here are the places where Joe and his cousins, the Warrens and the Arringtons, used to work and play, in these deserted, grown-over fields and woods that used to be thriving farmland. "All along this road, man, cotton used to be. That's where my grandmother used to live, the house has been moved, and her aunt and daughter lived in the next house. We'd work over there, hunt rabbits over here, kill snakes over there. Lot of berry vines, can't see them now, but a lot of blackberries. They grow, every year they grow beside the railroad track. We used to be down there picking them berries, making them berry pies."

Looking at Joe Tex driving down these little turnrows, you get the feeling that here is a man completely at peace with himself. Cowboy hat perched securely on his head, casually taking another can from the six-pack of Bud sitting beside him on the seat and flipping the empties out the window, he surveys his life, present and past, with perfect equanimity. Here is Joe Tex, here is Joe Arrington, both flawed, both human, both content. "Salaam alaikum," he greets a cousin. "Hi, Joe," she says to her famous cousin in reply.

We drive by a little country cemetery where most of Joe's forebears are buried. It is surrounded by a log retaining wall and a low fence, and some workmen are fixing up the fence. We pass a deserted shack where a cousin used to live and another where his uncle, a Warren who married an Arrington, lives now. Joe tells me about his great-grandfather, a Baptist preacher, who according to family legend swam the Mississippi River in 1877, breaking the ice to escape the Delta and make his way to Texas. Then there is Richard A. Arrington, the current mayor of Birmingham, who Joe is convinced must be some kind of distant cousin. Was everyone in his family this interested in roots? I ask, surprised at the depth and enthusiasm of his knowledge. "I guess they know about it, but they're not interested enough to do anything about it. If you ain't got no roots, though, you can forget about it. 'Cause the roots of something, man, is all that it leads to. *Roots* I saw myself, I could have played that part, that was me. I wish I'd have met Alex Haley, and he'd have given me one of those roles. 'Cause I know about that. I ain't been on no ship, bottom of a ship, but I was out there picking that cotton."

We drive by another ramshackle little shack, and Joe suddenly brings the car to an abrupt halt. "Now, that house there—let me back up. You should have your camera, man, because you see that house there—that's the house where I was conceived. Right there. That house has some history, man, you don't often see that. I was conceived in that house. At lunchtime. My cousin Daisy lived there then, McGinty, and she set it up. My mama come in at lunchtime, she was seventeen years old, and she got her little piece. And then I was born in Rogers. . . ."

We continue to drive around Navasota, past the house of Mance Lipscomb, the late blues singer, whom Joe met when he was in his seventies. ("Used to come over to the house, my wife would cook some dinner, and he would tell stories. They loved him here, man, over at Texas A&M he was like a god.") It seems as we drive around as if everyone in Navasota either knows Joe or is related to him. Joe kids with some, defers to others, has a word of encouragement for all. He speaks with great admiration of his cousins and uncles and aunts. "These are some funny folk, man. They talk, you know, they accent with their feet when they talk. They're makeshift people, you know. If your car breaks down, they don't know nothing about no mechanics, they figure out a way, some kind of way, just to get it running. See, they know the earth, can pick up some dirt and rub it between their fingers and say, 'We need about fifty sacks of fertilizer, that's about what we need.' Then they get them those 50-, 60-pound melons. You know, when you can get close to that dirt, man, take something out there in its raw state and shape it and form it into a beautiful edifice — builders and architects, carpenters and bricklayers — that's reality, man, it's wonderful and you can't get away from it, 'cause it's part of you. Hey, there's somebody I really want you to meet. I got an uncle, my grandfather's brother, Charley Warren, he's a funny dude, man."

We pull up in front of his uncle's house, which is opposite a newly erected housing project, where woods used to be. Inside the house the heat is stifling but Charley is wearing several layers of sweaters, a loose-fitting corduroy jacket, and a red-and-black hunting cap with the earflaps tucked up, and his wife, Frances, sits bundled up in front of the gas stove making a patchwork quilt. "I don't know you," says Charley without expression at the door. "Who are you?" says Frances reproachfully. It is their way of scolding Joe for not visiting in a long time. Joe soaks it all in, jollies them along, treats them with respect and good humor. ("They're practically like Abbott and Costello, man.") At Joe's prodding Charley takes us out back to show us his treasures, a hand-painted ax handle, a plow that he acquired fifteen years ago for which he still has not found a use. He shows us his small garden of collard greens and mustard stalks, laboriously unlocks a pen fenced in with chicken wire and crammed to the gills with used automobile parts, rusted bicycles, broken saws, stamping stencils, and the detritus of a lifetime as a handyman. Then he hobbles around to the front to survey the house he built in 1944 ("I did the best I could do," he says with the dry chuckle of a Yankee farmer), and shows us where the glass marbles he set into the porch would shine at night before grandchildren and local kids took them. "Sure was pretty, the way they'd shine." "Come on," Joe mutters impatiently when Charley is out of earshot, "he could go on all day like this." Before he leaves he promises to pick up his aunt the next day and take her to the doctor. "He's a good kid," says his aunt, "I don't care who he is." "What they're doing is kind of like folk art," says Joe. "Can you imagine if they had some education?"

And you believe somehow that this is where he really chooses to be. There are not many so-called stars, after all, who would keep about them these daily reminders of their past life, live sincerely as Yusuf Hazziez but remain at peace with Joe "the Toe" "Tex" Arrington in the midst of this hard-shell Baptist community. By showbiz standards Joe Tex is not doing so well nowadays. He keeps a six-piece band, Buckboard Express, out of Atlanta, and his two go-go dancers now employ a reggae motif. He goes out on three- to four-day trips, flying out of Houston, and the phone rings fairly regularly with offers of new dates. It is a far cry from the old days, though, and in many ways Joe Tex has no one to blame — or perhaps to thank — but himself.

He quit in 1972 at the height of his popularity. "I Gotcha" was on the charts, the only platinum seller of his career, when he told Buddy Killen that he was going to devote himself full-time to his Muslim beliefs. He had been introduced to Islam in 1966 by his road manager, Norman Thrasher, an ex-Midnighter and an old friend of Muhammad Ali's, converting in 1968 "because I was searching for a little more than Christianity had to offer me. I'll say it this way: there were a lot of questions in my mind, and they weren't being answered." His conversion led to the breakup of his marriage, and he returned to Navasota and his grandmother in 1970 with his life in disarray. "I had intended to move to Atlanta. I got in the car to drive off, and something came in my mind, saying, Why don't you go back to Navasota, to your grandmother who raised you? Just like that. I came back, moved in with my grandmother in that little house, I was broke 'cause I just gave my wife everything — house, car, everything." He continued touring, but the hits dried up, and there was no real satisfaction, until he met the Honorable Elijah Muhammad in 1972.

"When I accepted Islam," he told writer Joe McEwen, "I wanted to do something to show my appreciation for what he had done for me spiritually. I tried to meet him through the '60s, and when I finally met the Messenger, I asked him what he wanted me to do. 'I Gotcha' was getting hot, and I offered to raise some funds. He said, 'No, brother, if you want to help me, will you help me the way I want you to?' I said I would. He said, 'Let the band go. Our people are so full of music, that's all we've been doing. Let that go for a minute and go and preach.'"

That is precisely what he did. Buddy Killen was surprised. "He wasn't angry," Joe says, "but he said, 'You know, you're throwing your career away. We waited to get to this point; we've been working together all these years waiting for this particular time, and now this is where you're going to drop it.' He said, 'Why don't you take a vacation and think about what you're about to do?' He says, 'Have you thought about it?' I said, 'Yes, and I'm doing what I want to do, nobody's forcing me to do this.' He said, 'Well, can you still record? Like Muhammad Ali is doing some preaching, but he's still boxing on the side. You don't have to do personal appearances, but we could still make records together.' I said, 'I really don't want to do a double deal, man. If I'm going to do this, I'm going to dedicate all my time to it, and if I decide to come back, I'll let you know.' He said, 'The door's always open, man. You can always come back. I hope you are happy. Keep in touch.'"

For the next three years he toured the country, working harder than he ever had as an entertainer, he says, preaching under his new name but sometimes preceded by the announcement: "Coming: Sunday—Yusuf Hazziez (Joe Tex, 'Hold What You've Got,' 'Skinny Legs and All')." When Elijah Muhammad died in 1975, he returned to show business with the blessing of the faith, not out of any burning desire to go back to the Life but because "there's only two jobs that I've had, you know, as a farmer and an entertainer—and they ain't picking cotton no more." In 1977 Joe Tex had a Top 10 hit with "Ain't Gonna Bump No More (With No Big Fat Woman," just as Elijah had prophesied. ("He told me, 'When you desire to go back in the business, Allah will put you back where you were.'") Since then it has not been quite so easy. There have been one-record deals, gimmick albums like *He Who Is Without Funk Cast the First Stone*, lots of failed projects, but Joe has never ceased to have faith in himself and Buddy has stuck by him despite the usual Nashville rumors and insinuations. "Oh, people would tell me things they said they'd heard him say. But I always

Jusuf Hazziez preaching. *Courtesy of Bilaliah Hazziez*

maintain, if you're somebody's friend, you're still their friend. I never question a man's religious beliefs or political beliefs, and I don't give up on people that easily."

As for Joe, "I got over my little — what would you call it? — little bright light thing very early. Because I didn't come in the business, as I told you, to become famous. I just wanted to generate some money for my people. I just go out and try to give the people the best of what little bit I have to offer. Never was on that ego trip, star thing, 'Music is my life, and I can't live without it.' 'Cause I wasn't born singing."

THE BRIGHT LIGHT THING was bright enough for a while, though, and by all appearances no one enjoyed it more than Joe Tex. By his own admission — and by any accurate reading of the fun-loving aspects of his character — he did not exactly abstain from the good side of the good life. "I used to travel in a long limousine. I had a pocketful of money, a telephone and a television in the car." And if you ever saw Joe Tex in the glory days, you would know that there was no one who exuded more good-humored charm, more pleasure at simply being there to entertain than the microphone manipulator, the dapper rapper himself. James Brown may have had more charismatic presence, Otis Redding more intensity, and Solomon Burke a more soul-stirring voice, but it was Joe Tex who sent the customers away satisfied every time, chuckling to themselves at the "Skinny Legs" dance contests, the microphone tricks (he would always catch the microphone with his foot in a move that went back to a high school talent show, when he overturned the mike stand by accident), the sly homiletics ("You're Just Buying a Book [For Some Young Man to Read]") and earnest social messages ("Don't Make Your Children Pay [For Your Mistakes]"). It was always *fun* to see Joe Tex, there was never a time when Joe Tex didn't work hard for you and your party. When others adapted his routines, when Wilson Pickett pulled women out of the audience to dance with him, when Percy Sledge did Elvis imitations and other singers did country boy routines ("Give me a piece of that barbecue, and kiss me with your greasy mouth," declared Joe Tex), it could often take on the harsh edge of humorless parody. When Joe Tex did the same things, the good humor was infectious. He paid court to his audience—and the women in his audience in particular—in much the same way as Bobby "Blue" Bland; his chuckle was his safety valve, bringing the audience back down to earth, letting them know they were seeing a show and enjoying it. He appeared often in the company of the very top soul men—Pickett, Otis, Solomon—and many was the time he could be said to have stolen the show. Whenever I saw him, he always gave the crowd its money's worth, and he always sent them off into the night feeling good.

He has warm memories of those days, too. Of James Brown in Macon in the '50s, when neither one was a star but James was already renowned for "Please, Please, Please," which Joe says he had been doing in his stage act for some time. Playing at the City Auditorium, in a James Brown-proclaimed Battle of the Blues, he got numerous requests for the song. "I said, 'No, I can't sing it, 'cause the man that made the record is on the show tonight.' They said, 'You sing it, you sing it, we want to hear you sing it.' So I went ahead and did a little bit of it, and, by the way, I was working with his band. See, he had told the cats in front of me, 'Back the man up good. Don't rush the man, play good for him.' And then he got behind the curtain somewhere and told them something different. So they tried, they didn't want to do it, they wanted to play right for me, but they were working for James Brown and they knew how he was. He brought in about ten suits that night, and every ten or fifteen minutes he'd leave the stage and change clothes. And he'd come back on, the band would still be working and the Flames would still be harmonizing, and he be back there changing."

In another well-known version of the story Joe openly mocked James at this Homecoming concert, appearing in a cape "made out of a raggedy blanket, with holes all in it," according to one musician, then falling to his knees just the way James always did but then getting tangled up in his cape and thrashing around on the floor while screaming, "Please, please, please, get me out of this cape." Which led, understandably, to James becoming a little irate and coming after him with a shotgun and shooting up the club where the after-party was. But even if that happened in the dramatic manner that some say it did, it seems all but forgotten now, and in Joe's telling he and James crossed paths without incident many times over the years, just as he and Otis shared equal booking on many celebrated tours. There was always rivalry, but it was always friendly, Joe says, except for one well-remembered time "when 'Hold What You've Got' was real, real hot, and I was playing the Apollo and the Isleys were on the bill. They had me headlining, and the Isleys didn't want to go on. So I told my manager, 'Man, if they want to close the show, let them close it. 'Cause I don't have no hang-ups about all that star business.' He said, 'No, man, this is my damn show, you my artist, you got a hot record, and you gonna headline.' So I said, 'Listen, man, do me a favor. Let them headline, but I want to come on right in front of them. I don't want any intermission or nothing.' Man, for seven days they just could not get on. And I know that they was sorry that they did that, man. 'Cause we smoked out a good group. They'd be standing in the wings looking down, and them little gals would be screaming and applauding and standing. I did everything that they might have done by the time they got out there. That was a hot week there. I said, 'Let them close it. Just put me in front of them.'"

Then there was Solomon Burke, pharmacist, licensed mortician, a bishop in his own church, and the one singer Joe admired most and was personally closest to. Of all the soul singers, Joe firmly believed, there was no one with greater talent, originality, or imagination than Solomon. "He's got that big sound, that preaching sound, Solomon Burke could do anything that he want to do. He's got a lot of gimmicks, a lot of old funny ideas I myself wouldn't dare try, but he just jump off on it and bam, he be successful at it. He brought food on the bus, man, he went out and got bread and mayonnaise and cheese and bologna and fix up a big old box of groceries, and when we get down the road a bit, he'd sell those sandwiches for a dollar apiece and throw in a free beer!

"One time we were playing in Atlanta, and the next day we were going to Birmingham, this was in '65. So all of us had our cars. They had a bus, the tour, but all of us had our cars on the road—Solomon had one of them big long old-time limousines, give him a nice ride. He said, 'Come ride with me, send your car on to Birmingham, come ride with me.' So I said okay. Here I am sitting in the back, and the man driving, and we go out of Atlanta to Decatur, and Solomon wanted to buy some whistles, some police whistles. Everybody was giving away gimmicks and stuff like that. On the show some nights Solomon would give away roses, on the next night whistles. So Solomon bought a whole box of green plastic whistles, and the man gave him a deal on it. Then Solomon went to look at some guns. The man say, 'You want one?' 'Yes,' he said, 'let me see that one over there. And that one over there. And that one.' He wound up buying a rifle, a shotgun, a .45, and a .38. And the man say, 'You gonna buy all these, I'm gonna throw in the cartridges for free.' Put the guns in the trunk, they wasn't loaded, and here we go out of Decatur on our way to Birmingham, just out of the city here come six police cars, the whole thing. Pulled us over. Solomon was about to get out, he say, 'Let me handle it.' And he got his Bible, took his cross out of his briefcase, big old cross—'Yes, officer,' he said. 'I'm Reverend Doctor Solomon Burke, a man of the cloth, can I help you?' So the man says, 'Where are you all going?' He said, 'We're on our way to Birmingham for a church meeting.' He says, 'Y'all carrying any weapons?' 'No, no, I'm a man of the cloth.' The man says, 'You mind opening the trunk, driver?' The driver got out and opened the trunk, and goddamn, there were the guns. He says, 'Follow me back to the police station.' And they charged Solomon a $100 fine and confiscated the guns and the bullets, took them all away. I said, 'Man, do you know what happened? That man wanted his guns back!' He said, 'I believe you're right.'

"But that Solomon, he's got a lot of heart, man, a lot of guts, he don't back up off of nothing. I admire people like that, never say die, you know. And he's the kind of cat that if Solomon ain't singing today, well, you just give him a lawn mower and he'll go cut him some yards and don't give a damn—and that's the same way that I am."

With Solomon, and with Don Covay (and, for a time, Wilson Pickett and Otis Redding, too), Joe formed a group called the Soul Clan that was meant to solidify, and in a way came to symbolize, the close feeling of an era. Although they only put out one single, and the whole thing eventually dissolved in a wash of recriminations, the idea was to have "something like a Rat Pack kind of thing — we were going to tour together, set up funds, and take some of the money and put it away until we got some capital. There would be a trust fund for our children, in case something would happen like with Otis, and we were planning to build some motels and things. But we just never did get beyond the talking stage, the baby never was born."

To Joe and Solomon Burke in particular there is some question about whether their record company even wanted the baby to be born. ("The Soul Clan was deliberately destroyed," Solomon says, with a broader sense of metaphor perhaps than Joe would subscribe to, "because we were becoming a power structure.") In any case the Soul Clan is widely scattered today, the soul revues have come to an end, and Joe hasn't seen Solomon in a while. And while there is a growing craze for soul music in Japan, and the improbable success of John Belushi and Dan Aykroyd's Blues Brothers act over the last couple of years (first the act, then the movie) has sparked a mini-revival of its own, so far none of it has really touched Joe. As Jerry Wexler, the man who helped create Southern soul as a commercial phenomenon at Atlantic Records, says, "You can't replicate the sounds of something when it's past. I don't know what it is, something in the ambience, something in the atmosphere, you can play the same notes, but it doesn't sound the same. You can't go back."

Joe Tex would probably agree. I don't think he would want to go back anyway. Sitting in his comfortable den with the omnipresent TV interspersing banal bulletins on the death of John Lennon ("He came along just at the right time," says Joe Tex of his near contemporary) amid the equally banal regular game-show programming, it all seems equally irrelevant. Four-year-old Ramadan is bouncing on the cushions on the floor. The phone rings from time to time with promises of deals in the offing, bookings made, bookings broken. Cousins, nephews, a friend named Rufus Foreman all pass through the room, confer with Joe, eye the TV. And Joe Tex seems genuinely content, that rare individual who can savor the past, who gets a big kick out of recalling it, but who at the same time is not afraid to let go. As he speaks on the phone in a soft husky voice, much like Muhammad Ali's, I take another tour of the room, looking over the various pictures, the plaques that commemorate places and dates and offer gratitude for shows given, services rendered. Here is one for "Meritorious

Service to Humanity," presented by Northwestern High School in Zachary, Louisiana, Elmer T. Glover Sr., Principal. Here is another, presented by the Human Rights and Black Economic Development commission. Here is one "For the Notorious Song of the Year—'Men Are Getting Scarce.'" Like Solomon Burke he, too, obviously has had to come to terms with racial indignities, and his songs—like Solomon's, like Sam Cooke's and Aretha Franklin's radical reinterpretation of Otis Redding's "Respect"—served as a rallying cry for solidarity, came to stand for some element of black pride. Did he see music as a unifying force, then? It is the only time I hear bitterness creep into his voice.

"Music don't draw nobody together except the public, and they be too busy dancing to even get the message. There's been some great things said in lyrics and songs, but if they listen, then they go on to the next message — going so fast and doing so many things and nobody even remembers. I wasn't into marching too much either. That marching—besides your feet getting tired, bunions and corns—marching ain't gonna do nothing but exercise. I was asked many times by some of the Civil Righters to come and join them on the march. I didn't see no sense in it. You got your brain, you got your five senses that was given to you by God, so instead of walking and singing your ass off, sit down and do something constructive, get some land, generate some jobs, pool your resources, put up a motel—but to hell with that walking shit!"

Like his uncle and his cousins, the family that he has cherished, he is a man of the earth. Whether he is engaged in a deep philosophical discussion or graphically demonstrating a dance craze like the Dog to his wife, Bilaliah, in the living room, he is always irrefutably himself, without pretense or embarrassment. "Joe is a very deep person," says Buddy Killen admiringly. "He's got a lot of depth and a lot of understanding. That street understanding, you know. When he writes a song, he knows who he's talking to out there. To me he's one of the greatest talents that ever came down the road and I guess I get—I've had more thrills working with him in the studio than anybody I've ever worked with."

"I don't worry about making it," says Joe Tex. "Peter, material things have never been what I was looking for. It was family, and learning more about God and creation. It was this family, you know. We were poor, we never had anything, and I never worried about it, you know. When I got to

Joe "Tex" Arrington. *Courtesy of Bilaliah Hazziez*

where my records started selling, and I was able to afford a car and put some gas in it, and have what I wanted to eat, it didn't change me —'cause I still had the basic things that I grew up with, wanting my family to be close together. A newsman asked me in Europe this last trip we made about the same things we're talking about now, and I told him, it's been nice out here, man. A lot of ups and downs, the way life is, but I've enjoyed this life. I was glad that I was able to come up out of creation and look all around and see a little bit, grass and trees and cars, fish and steaks, potatoes. Everywhere I've gone, I can always go back, and I can always find a friend. I don't go trying to make nobody like me, I just be me, you know, and it has worked out. And I thank God for that. I'm thankful that He let me get up and walk around and take a look around here. 'Cause this is nice."

While we are talking, Buddy Killen's office calls. It sounds as if a new record deal is going to come through. "He wants me to come in with some strong r&b material," announces Joe good-humoredly. "R&b, huh?" says Bilaliah equally good-humoredly. "What is that?" "It'll always come back," says Joe with perfect assurance and returns to discussing the details of a new water tank with his friend Rufus, an older white-haired man, who dreams of someday joining Joe on the road. Ramadan plays on the floor, a handsome well-turned-out replica of his father. I wonder if there will be a place on the new album for Joe's latest opus: "Is There Room for One More Colored Singer in Country Music?"

EPILOGUE

M Y VISIT with Joe Tex in Navasota took place in December of 1980. No one could have been more alive — or, I thought, taken more joy from the life he was living.

Less than two years later he was dead, just days past his forty-seventh birthday. There were rumors that it was cancer, a heart attack. Well before that, though, it had become evident that something was seriously wrong. I saw him perform in May of 1981, just five months after our initial meeting, and he was a mess, unable to put together a coherent performance and cursing out the owner of the club backstage. A disastrous Soul Clan reunion in New York two months later ended up with Wilson Pickett quarreling vociferously with Joe backstage, his dancers doing a striptease to "Ain't Gonna Bump No More," and Don Covay with a tambourine around his neck. When he died in August of 1982, there was a Muslim service, with Don Covay, Wilson Pickett, Percy Mayfield, and Buddy Killen among the honorary pallbearers, and Solomon conducted a family prayer service back at the house in his black bishop's robes and big silver cross. There was much talk of drug use even from those closest to him (after a lifetime of preaching abstinence from drink and drugs, Buddy Killen wrote in his memoir, "it was as if he were trying to make up for lost time"), and both Buddy and Bilaliah suggested a loss of hope. "In the end," Bilaliah told me with muted disappointment, "people that he did things for turned against him." There really wasn't anything more to say.

His joyous, sharply observant spirit in any case lives on in his songs. And he continues to be warmly celebrated in Navasota. He has been nominated five times for the Rock and Roll Hall of Fame. The last time, in 2016, I wrote a piece of advocacy called "Reunite the Soul Clan in the Rock and Roll Hall of Fame," but each year that he fails to be elected renders the future prospect of his induction more unlikely. It is, I think, a grave injustice—but as I'm sure Joe would point out, nothing in the end can erase the warmth of his presence on earth, the sheer exuberance of his personality, the life force that propelled him in both his travels and his art, the memories that we continue to hold and pass on.

TEN

Dick Curless: The Return of the Tumbleweed Kid

At eighteen I went out in the world. I thought I knew it all. On that tour, I was back in my home state of Maine and making $12, sometimes $15 a night. I thought, man, this is the life. This is it. But if I could go back and find that boy, knowing all the things that would happen to him, I'd tell him, "Boy, stay and sing with your family. They're not going to be there very long. Yeah, you stay home and sing. Be happy in your little town."

THAT IS THE VOICE of Dick Curless toward the end of his life: warm, intimate, direct, with a sentimentality so open and unabashed that it doesn't even begin to hide the hurt. It is not unlike his singing voice, which is as pure an instrument of emotional conveyance as you are ever likely to hear. What is surprising about that voice is its unflinching insistence on the truth, whether it makes for a pretty picture or not. Ordinarily, one might expect a singer of such consummate skills to leave off with a silky-smooth caress, and there was a time in his earlier life when Dick might have been satisfied simply to deliver the practiced vocal intimacies of a master craftsman. Now there is another level of communication: Dick Curless, the Baron of Country Music (for no very good reason, this became his moniker not long after his first national hit in 1965), is delivering home truths which shrink neither from a jubilant cry of triumph nor an outright yowl of pain. "I sing the learning and growing songs that are painful, that are real, that are life itself. I mean, life is so very real. It's not happily ever after, the white picket fence—you know what I'm trying to say. There are ups and downs and peaks and valleys, and I sing that to people—and I relate to them—because I've been through them."

The Tumbleweed Kid. *Courtesy of Terry Curless Chinnock / Richard Weize —...and more bears*

FULL CIRCLE

I DON'T THINK I've ever been more taken with anyone on first acquaintance than I was by Dick Curless. Not because I was unfamiliar with him when we first met at a recording session that my son, Jake, was producing. I had seen him perform a number of times, and he was never anything less than thoroughly ingratiating, with his black eye patch, rumbling baritone, and warm, self-effacing manner. We had even met in passing once or twice. But I can honestly say that nothing prepared me for the profundity of either the man or the music that I would encounter at the Long View Farm recording studio, just before Christmas 1994. It was so startling, so unexpected, so *transformative* an event, I don't think anyone in the room, with the possible exception of Dick (and for all of the faith that he was prepared to invest in the project, I'm not so sure about him), could have imagined just how uplifting an experience this was going to turn out to be for us all.

This is how it came about.

Earlier that year Jake and I had produced an album by Sleepy LaBeef (it's a long story, but Jake produced: I was along for the ride), with our friend Bob Kempf engineering. It turned out to be a wonderfully shared musical moment bursting with energy and creativity, and in its aftermath, Michael "Mudcat" Ward, the bass player in the band that Jake had put together for the session, suggested to Jake: Why not reassemble the group and cut an album on Dick Curless, whom Mudcat, a native of Lewiston, Maine, knew through the New England country music circuit? Totally by happenstance, or then again maybe not, Dick got in touch with Rounder Records, where Jake worked, at just about this time. Jake heard an announcement over the intercom that Dick Curless was on the line for Ken Irwin, one of Rounder's owners, and took it as a sign.

"Dick was pretending to be looking for a Merle Travis video that we distributed," Jake later wrote, "and I was pretending to be taking a message for Ken—but our mutual deception was quickly revealed. Dick wanted to make a record, and I asked him to send a demo of the type of stuff he wanted to do. A few days later I received a DAT tape of five songs of Dick playing and singing by himself, including Merle Travis' 'I Am a Pilgrim,' 'I Get the Blues When It Rains' [a '20s pop blues standard], and a variation on Ivory Joe Hunter's 'Since I Met You Baby,' with 'Jesus' substituting for 'Baby.'" Jake was totally enthralled by the music's intimacy and warmth.

When he played it for me, I was, too. Jake reassembled the rhythm section from the previous session, with the notable addition of guitarist Duke Levine (the most unassuming guitar virtuoso you'd ever want to meet), and through Bob Kempf, the engineer, set up a session at Long View Farm in North Brookfield, Massachusetts, a live-in recording facility, where everyone from the Rolling Stones to Arlo Guthrie and Uncle Tupelo had worked over the years. I volunteered — well, I *applied* — to do the liner notes.

From the beginning, it was clear that this was going to be a different kind of session — though exactly how different took a while to figure out. Just for a start, Dick showed a rare ability to draw everyone in, not just the musicians, whom he immediately dubbed the Kids in the Barn (he was sixty-two, the musicians and producer by and large half his age), but everyone else in the room as well. This would be one of the few times since the start of his career some forty years ago that he would get a chance to play his own rhythm guitar in the studio. ("I call it my mumbling guitar," he told Jake. "It's kind of tunking with a backstroke, and I got it out of ignorance, really, trying to copy Josh White's finger style with a straight pick.") Right away it was obvious that that guitar style would set the tone for the session, even though he used it not so much to lead as to encourage the other musicians to set off in idiosyncratic directions of their own which they might not otherwise have felt emboldened to explore. He began every song with his own strum, and he didn't back off of it, even if at first it didn't sound quite right. "I know it might sound a little funny," he said, "I know it's in the cracks. But that's why I did it, and I need to keep it like that."

But it was his own quiet certitude most of all that established the mood, a mood that quickly took hold and convinced us unquestionably (though I must admit, the question still lingers in my mind; did Dick himself need any convincing?) that we had all set off on a spiritual journey, a journey that was likely to lead to exaltation and grace if we were simply willing to commit ourselves to it in our own way, with or without explicit belief. The musicians themselves, all seasoned studio players, were clearly won over. In fact, there were times when they became so mesmerized by the sound of Dick's voice, never anything less than a gorgeous instrument but now invested with such an overwhelming sense of purpose and resolve, that they sometimes lost their place in the song. I know that sounds like an exaggeration, but listen to what Bob Kempf, normally the most objective and dispassionate of observers, wrote to me in the immediate aftermath of the session, as if to question whether or not what we had all experienced had actually taken place.

> *I've been sitting here wrapping Christmas presents this morning and thinking of little else but being on the Farm with Dick, Jake, you and the band. I don't know why exactly, but I feel some need to write some stuff down and send it to you. The session was without a doubt the best I've ever been involved in from all points of view, and I still can't get over that, because as you know, it never (or now I would have to say "rarely") gets this good. How this happened is hard to explain, but there were some scenes that are worth relating. . . . You saw him set up some of the songs with stories that felt almost like a prayer or a remembrance of a friend or relative. I think it was his humble, gentle way of being that drew us in so completely, and then when he sang, Oh, my god! As you know, the band members said on more than one occasion how they had trouble focusing on their parts as they were playing them because they were so caught up in Dick's singing.*

Another contributing factor — and it's hard to say whether this actually complicated or furthered the sense of mission and mood — was that it was clear to everyone that Dick was very ill. I suppose we were all content to accept his explanation that this was just the latest flare-up of the stomach problems that had plagued him for years, but it certainly did not escape anyone's attention when he would announce at the conclusion of a particularly satisfying take that he was worn out and needed to retire to his room to rest. He always returned refreshed and full of positive thoughts and ideas. "Oh, you guys are something else," he said, as if the band were setting a standard that he was struggling to maintain. "I mean, you guys make it happen [the way] you complement each other. Nice, nice, nice." "This may be my swan song," he declared more than once, even as the band was making plans to get together for the tour that would surely accompany the album's release the following summer. For the first time, Dick said, he could hear the sound of his father's voice in the studio. "There are certain things that he left me, but I never heard this closeness till I did this album."

I picture Dick now, gaunt and handsome, a backwards baseball cap planted firmly atop his head and wearing his trademark black eye patch (he was born with a weak eye, and over the years it just got worse) and a favorite old leather vest. He looks like an old trucker, an image that would surely please him, and never speaks much above a melodious whisper, with a quiet chuckle that sets everyone at ease. "You know," he said at several points, as though the thought had just occurred to him, "this is where I started out. Right here in North Brookfield, I think it was at the town hall." He paused, as if to muse upon the coincidence that the studio should be situated in the very town where he began. "It was my first show all by myself, out there with the posters and everything. I never will forget it. I sang 'Lovesick Blues,' and I was scared to death, I'll tell you. I was seventeen years old, and I was shaking—but I did it." It was as if, he said with quiet conviction, this recording was meant to be. It was like coming home.

BOYHOOD

H E WAS BORN on March 17, 1932, in Fort Fairfield, Maine, up by the border, to a couple of eighteen-year-olds, both of whom came from families with twelve children. His mother, Ella, grew up outside Fredericton, New Brunswick. ("We're going over to the province," his mother would tell him and his brother, Phil, not quite a year younger, every time they would go to visit.) She played piano and organ and was a great whistler, while his dad, Big Phil, a truck driver and steam shovel operator, a big bruising man (six feet two and a half inches, 215 pounds) but light on his feet, played guitar and a little banjo. There was always music. One uncle was a yodeler, another a noted step dancer who offered lessons—in fact, all of his mother's family were great dancers, and if they couldn't play an instrument, they played the bones. Whether at home or across the border, "the fiddles would come out, and the guitars and harmonicas and the spoons, and they'd roll back the rug, and everybody would dance on the floor, my grandfather, everybody." His father and his father's friend Emery Fields, a heavy equipment operator, too, would bring home Jimmie Rodgers records at the end of the week (though Rodgers had died of tuberculosis in 1933, his enduring popularity and influence, as the "Father of Country Music," would continue well into the '50s) and would sit around singing and playing some of the sad old story songs themselves—*tragic* songs like "Little Blossom," in which the child or the mother or the sweetheart would always die. "My dad was a marvelous singer, but sometimes he'd get to a point in the song where he'd just tear them up, I mean, my goodness, everyone in the room would be crying." Including his dad — the tears would just be coursing down his cheeks, and he wouldn't be able to finish the song.

Times were tough in Fort Fairfield, and in Caribou, ten miles further north, where the family moved when Dick and his brother were five or six. He could remember going to bed sometimes with nothing but crackers and canned milk for supper. "We burnt pieces of rubber tire in the stove and willow trees, whatever you could get — these were Depression times, I mean, we weren't alone. And the music was [always] there, everybody smoking and drinking and singing and picking and working, just like everybody does — but *as a family,* that was the best part." He could remember sitting in his father's lap as his father operated the first steam shovel in Fort Fairfield, "it had these great big levers, and this great big bucket would come back, and he'd drop it right in front of me. He had the knack of treating a steam shovel or a bulldozer like it was just part of him." The first song he ever played in public, his father took him down to the fire department, and "they turned over a ten-quart pail, sat me down, and had me pick a little tune that my father taught me on the banjo."

In Caribou he'd go down to the railroad tracks, "they were right down over the bank, where we lived, and I'd talk to the hoboes heading south. They'd say, 'Hey, kid, you got anything to eat up at the house?' I said, 'Sure, I'll be right back,' and I'd run up and get some bologna and bread. Then they'd get talking to me. I can remember this one guy in particular, standing by a trestle. He had an old tin mirror with a little ring on it, he hung it up on a sliver of wood on the trestle beam and started shaving with cold water, and while he's shaving he's telling me where he's going." It brought so vividly to mind the song his father always sang, Jimmie Rodgers' "Waiting for a Train." It brought the whole *experience,* and Jimmie Rodgers' deeply affecting lyrics about being "1,000 miles away from home, sleeping in the rain" so sharply into focus that it made him realize for the first time the poetic and literal power of music.

In the winter of 1940, when he was eight, his father moved the family down to Barre, Massachusetts, outside of Worcester, where the Great New England Hurricane of 1938 had caused terrible floods, and so many of the bridges and roads were still out or needed repair. Emery Fields had already moved down there, and so had two uncles, also heavy equipment operators, who reported back that there was plenty of work to be had. "Dad and Mom sold all the furniture for $50 to get us down there, and we took the train

The Curless family, ca. 1937:
Big Phil and Ella, Dick and
Phil Jr. *Courtesy of Terry
Curless Chinnock*

from Fort Fairfield. I remember my brother, Phil, and I had on our macki-
naws and gum rubber boots, and Dad bought us some ice cream, and we
had it up against the window and it melted in the heat of the train. You'd
lean forward and bang on those velour-type seats, and you'd see the dust
rise up in the sunrays coming through the windows. You're going clickety-
clack [he makes the sound] down the tracks, and it was just a wonderful . . .
adventure." It was like he was "one of those hoboes," he told *Yankee* magazine editor Mel Allen in 1992. "I felt like I knew where they were going
now, I knew why they hopped that train." It wasn't a long ride, but it
remained fixed indelibly in his memory. And every step of the way the
sound of the train told him, "We're going to a new place to get some work."

They moved around the Worcester area, living in a succession of tiny
towns and hamlets before finally settling in Gilbertville, an unincorpo-
rated village in the town of Hardwick, with a population of less than
1,000. In Dick's view it was a marvelous place for a boy to grow up, a real
melting-pot experience, with Lithuanians, Germans, French, Italians,
Irish, and Poles all freely mixing and intermingling. "We lived in a

tenement house," he told *Yankee*, "and everybody knew everybody. It was a mill town, a drinking town. If you fell down in one barroom, you'd get up in another." He played basketball and went out for track at Hardwick High School. ("I looked like Ichabod Crane, thin as a rail, but I was trying to do all I could while I was there.") He joined the Boy Scouts and bought his first rifle for $35, part of a matching Winchester rifle-and-pistol set, paying out five dollars a week until he finally owned it, and using it to shoot his first deer in Maine. But music remained his great love. He wrote his first song, "That Poor Little Girl of Mine," during school recess in the eighth grade and listened to Jimmie Rodgers and Gene Autry on the compact little 78 record player his dad brought home after work one day. Before long, Ernest Tubb and Eddy Arnold and Cowboy Copas singing "Filipino Baby" were added to the mix. His father and Emery Fields, who lived in Ware, about seven miles away, would come home with new records all the time, announcing, "Oh, you ought to hear this one, Dickie, got a new one here." They were "heart songs" like Eddy Arnold's "Many Tears Ago," and "I'm Throwin' Rice" — but then somehow or other "I got hooked on a blues 78 by a black man called Josh White, and then Hank Williams come along with a different kind of blues that really got my attention.

"Emery gave me my first guitar — I've still got it — and after my father didn't have any more to teach me, Emery taught me how to play. He had these huge, meat-hook hands, and he would play the E chord, and I would say, 'Emery, how many strings you covering up there?' 'Tragic Romance' [a hit for Cowboy Copas in 1946] was always his song. It was a great story song, and I loved the way he sang it. He didn't sing like anybody else, good and country, boy, down-homish. That's how I got started. Emery taught me, and then as he and my dad got working more, their hands got bigger, and they didn't play the guitar that much, but I was around to play [for them], they would just say, 'Dickie, go get the guitar and come over here. I got another song for you.'"

His father and Emery came to all his shows, the school plays and old-time "minstrel shows" that were still popular in the area. He took every opportunity that was offered, and Emery and his dad were always there to support him — the only way they would miss a show was if their work took them out of town, and they just couldn't get back in time.

He celebrated his fifteenth birthday with fifteen draft beers at Ballard's, where his grandmother cooked and he shucked clams for her occasionally, wandering out in his apron to sing a few songs for the customers.

"It was my favorite place, where old cronies came in after work, had drinks, played a little shuffleboard, and played the jukebox. It was Saint Patrick's Day, my birthday, and they had a venison supper. All the guys in town were there — they probably didn't see how many beers I had, and I thought, If my father knew, he would kick my butt. Fifteen glasses, one for every year of my life, and I walked home and, you know, I had to laugh. I said, 'I guess I've arrived.' Because back then, in the hard days of factories and working and war years, that's the way you were brought up. You were taught to — if you smoked and drank and swore, then you were a man."

He worked hard at everything he did. Summers he worked on a farm. ("It was like the old cowboy movies, get up at four o'clock in the morning, [splash] water on your face, go out and get the cows. Twenty-five dollars a week, $10 room and board, so you'd come home with $15.") Three or four weeks a year he picked tobacco in the Connecticut tobacco fields — a bus would carry him and some of his schoolmates and the other day workers down and back each day. He worked at the movie theater above Ballard's, too, cleaning up and splicing the film when it broke and soaking up the music from the crazy Spike Jones novelty features and cowboy movies that they showed. His dad told him, when you worked for somebody, be sure to always give them more than what they asked for, which became a lifelong rule. But there was something else on his mind, something that kept eating at him, no matter how lucky he felt, and knew, himself to be. "I wanted to play basketball a whole lot harder. I wanted to pick a whole lot harder. And I wanted to get out of there a whole lot harder. Because the world was *moving*."

That was when he met Yodeling Slim.

YODELING SLIM CLARK

IT DIDN'T HAPPEN BY ACCIDENT. Emery and his dad were drinking buddies of Slim's, and they all hung out together in the taverns and bars around Gilbertville. Everybody in the area knew Yodeling Slim Clark. He was a local star and it seemed like he had been a star forever, even though he was just thirty years old. He had his own show every Saturday morning on the radio station in Ware, and he even had a regional hit, a cover of Tex Ritter's 1948 smash, "Rye Whiskey," that he had cut in New York. He was born in Massachusetts, grew up on a farm, and modeled himself first on Jimmie Rodgers, then on the great Canadian yodeler Wilf Carter (Montana Slim), coming up on what was then called the "kerosene circuit" (no lights, no mikes), from the age of twelve on. "He bummed and he hoboed, traveled the rods, he went out west and sang and picked everywhere. He's one of the last of the real cowboy singers," Dick declared, speaking of a man who in his late seventies continued to exert an influence on his life. "You know, he'd make you a good story."

"Dick's dad used to drink a little bit, and so did I," Slim told country music historian Kevin Coffey. "Sometimes we'd have a beer and get to talking. He'd say, 'You ought to come and hear my son.' Of course, I heard a lot of that stuff, being back from New York and the big time. Everybody thought I could make a star out of them. So I said, 'Oh yeah, I'll bet he's good. I'll listen to him someday.'" Then one night, having had a few more beers than usual, he decided to "get the painful task over with. At the Curless home, proud father handed his teenaged son a guitar and told him, 'Sing to this fellow.'" The way Slim tells it, Dick was scared to death, but Slim just said, "Sing to me like you're singing to anybody," and he did, and the next thing he knew, Slim said, "How'd you like to go on the radio with me someday?"

Which was exactly what happened. It was 1949, and he was beginning his senior year in high school. "He took me under his wing," Dick told *Yankee* magazine. "I just watched him, the way he handled a crowd, the way he performed. I just did what he did. I used to carry Slim's guitar around to different places. I was hooked on Slim Clark and cowboy songs and radio. I was hooked on show business."

Soon Dick was performing regularly with him on the air. Sometimes, when Slim came through on his way to prerecord his radio show for a station in Keene, New Hampshire, Dick would show up, thumbing his way over to the station. Slim would always say to him, "Ain't you supposed to be in school," but Dick would just shrug it off, knowing his parents wouldn't really mind, because they knew Slim and knew that he was looking out for their boy. Through Slim he acquired his first radio moniker. "Slim said, 'You got to have a handle in this business.' I said, 'What do you mean?' and he said, 'You see them on the movie screen: Tex Ritter and Whip Wilson and Lash LaRue. I'm Yodeling Slim Clark. You got to have some sort of [identifier].' Then I sang 'Tumblin' Tumbleweeds,' and he said, 'That's it. You're the Tumbleweed Kid. That's what you're going to be known as.'

Yodeling Slim performing with the Trail Riders: Jim Finn, Dick, and Don Calvi on lap steel.
Courtesy of Terry Curless Chinnock/Richard Weize — ...and more bears

"He taught me everything. He taught me the basics of radio and the entertainment business, and he taught my brother, Phil, the basics of art. Slim's a realist painter, he's very good, does outdoor scenes. And my brother's a marvelous artist, too. But Slim showed me how to [use] a mike to put your songs out in front of you, how to do a little gab to show your personality and try to identify yourself with the music you're doing. And talk like you and I are talking, only to the radio audience. He taught me to be comfortable around that."

Before long Slim started taking him out to do live shows. "He had me on a couple of dates, where we were just singing with our guitars and the power of our voices for the audience. Slim was used to it. He'd been part of that whole circuit. I hadn't. But I got a little taste of it." Slim preferred to perform solo, or with just Dick's rhythm guitar seconding him ("That's the way I started," he said, "and that's the way I figured cowboy singers

Dick, Jim Finn, and Don Calvi (the Trail Riders) at the Opry House, Millinocket, Maine, August 9, 1950. *Courtesy of Terry Curless Chinnock/Richard Weize — ...and more bears*

should do"), but he put together a little trio, the Trail Riders, to fill out the bill. Mostly they performed as a separate unit — three guitars, with Don Calvi on lead and lap steel, Jimmy Finn occasionally picking up the bass, Dick on rhythm, and all three sharing the vocals — but sometimes they backed Slim, when Slim felt like doffing his hat a little to modernity. He helped Dick get his own radio show, too, as the Tumbleweed Kid, in a fifteen-minute slot right behind his. Dick had to come up with his own sponsors — Mickey's Furniture Company in Gilbertville and Klem's Tractor Sales in Spencer proved willing to foot the bill — and every week his mother recorded the show on a wire recorder so he could pick up on his mistakes. At school he became a kind of celebrity, and for a school project he brought in a mike and speaker and guitar to show them what a radio broadcast was all about. There was no question in his mind that things were really starting to happen for him, with posters up all over town advertising his first solo appearance, in North Brookfield, and when Slim told him he was planning a five- or six-week tour of Maine and the Maritimes starting in May, he didn't hesitate for a moment in giving his answer. It was just a month till high school graduation, he had tried on his cap and gown, and his parents had already given him a Benrus watch as a graduation gift, plus $100 for the class trip to New York City—but all of that would have to wait. He knew what he wanted to do.

"I'll see New York someday," he told his parents, who completely understood. He told his high school principal that for him there was simply no turning back. "I loved him, he was a great man. He was also our scoutmaster, and he called me on the carpet and said, 'I wish you'd reconsider.' I said, 'Well, I got to go on this tour, 'cause I'll never have another crack at it if I don't go now.'" And with the money for the class trip in his pocket, he got Slim to take him to Greenfield, just north of Amherst, where Slim had connections, and he bought his first Stetson, a pair of cowboy boots, a jeweled Western shirt, and a pair of officer-pink gabardine pants— "my first outfit, it was great." He couldn't wait to wear it onstage.

ACADIAN DREAMS

THE TOUR was everything he could ever have imagined. They played all over, in town halls, Grange halls, dance halls, town and county fairs, drive-ins, and amusement parks. "We were out for weeks, I was making $12, sometimes $15 a night. We went up through Plaster Rock into New Brunswick, Canada, back to my roots. We ended up in Sebago Lake, fishing. It was a wonderful tour, a very successful tour, and when we got back home, Slim promised we'd do another one soon." But for some reason nothing happened. Dick was never able to figure out why, but there was some holdup on Slim's part. "We're just sitting around in Gilbertville, waiting and waiting, and nothing's happening. So we got together, the Trail Riders, Don Calvi, Jimmy Finn, and myself. And I said, I mean, I'm just a kid, I'm eighteen years old, I said, 'Look, let's go back to Maine. I've got relatives there. I mean, we had a successful time up there. Let's go back ourselves.' So we ended up on my uncle Charlie's farm in Levant [just outside of Bangor], he had a chicken farm, some whiteface cattle, too, and we stayed out there, practiced in the barn, and started playing places on our own."

Before long the Trail Riders had their own noontime radio show, the *RFD Dinner Bell,* on Bangor's WABI, and were beginning to be booked on shows at places like Auto Rest Park, a sprawling amusement park in Carmel with a motel, restaurant, rides, animals, and arcade, as well as the somewhat unchallengeable claim of being "New England's Largest Jamboree!" But for Dick his most memorable moment at Auto Rest Park was not a Trail Riders booking but a fall appearance by Hawkshaw Hawkins, star of the *WWVA* [Wheeling, West Virginia] *Jamboree.* Hawkins, known as "Eleven Yards of Personality" for his six-foot-five-inch height and expansive nature, was one of Dick's biggest idols, with both "Sunny Side of the Mountain" and "Rattlesnakin' Daddy" staples in his repertoire. "Oh, I admired him so much, I copied a lot of things from him. He came up with the Kentucky Twins and Sammy Barnhart on bass, and Billy Grammer was playing guitar, and he called me up on stage, and I got pictures!" He was offering some of his stage outfits for sale, too, "and I wanted them so bad—I could fit into them, you know, because we were both over six-footers." But he knew he couldn't afford them at that stage of his career and happily contented himself with the memory and the pictures.

With the radio show going, things really started picking up for the group, and more and more gigs started coming in, everything from honky-tonks and barrooms to movie theaters, social clubs, and the roofs of drive-in refreshment stands, where the honking of car horns and the blinking of lights served as encouragement to the band. Through Yodeling Slim's connections, the Trail Riders even got a chance to record, driving down to Boston and laying down four sides at the Ace Recording Studio, including "Coast of Maine," which sounds like a Dick Curless original, even if its authorship was attributed to the label owner. Things couldn't have been going better. And then he met a girl.

It was early in the winter of 1950–51 that he first saw Pauline Green. She was one of thirteen kids and had recently started working at the Emple Knitting Mills. She was not a fan of country music in the least. In fact, her favorite singer was popular opera singer and movie star Mario Lanza, and she took the radio to work with her every day in hopes of hearing him on the air. But a friend of hers was going with Don Calvi, and she begged Pauline to accompany her to a show.

Onstage with Hawkshaw Hawkins at Auto Rest Park, October 1950: Dick is playing guitar, with Hawk beside him and (left to right) Billy Grammer, Don Calvi, and Betty Jo Wilson (with the Kentucky Twins and Sammy Barnhart hidden). *Courtesy of Terry Curless Chinnock*

The Trail Riders were playing on Main Street, upstairs at the American Legion Hall, and Dick spied her through the curtain and asked Don's girlfriend to intercede for him and ask her for a date. From the beginning it was serious—well, it was lots of fun, too, but Dick made his long-term intentions clear. Right at the start, she met his whole family, including his parents, who had recently moved to Levant and were staying with his Uncle Charlie and Aunt Hattie on the chicken farm. "They were a family where there was [always] music. On weekends, they'd be drinking and singing—fun time, party time. He had one uncle that tap-danced, Fred, and we loved to hear his dad sing and pick—there were certain harmonies where you couldn't tell the difference between him and Dick. They all just sat around, picking and singing, [while] the rest of us would be up dancing." Pauline had always considered herself something of a homebody, but she was drawn to this big, open, emotionally demonstrative family. "His dad was a wonderful man, he was the type who didn't say a lot, he just had to say a few words, and you couldn't help but [pay attention]. He gave Dick good advice when he was wrong. Of course, Dick didn't always listen. But he tried."

She came to embrace the music, too, because she knew how much it meant to Dick. "He told me music was his life. From the moment I first heard him, I was hooked." It was, she said, not just the sound of his voice but what lay behind the words, the depth and sincerity of his delivery. Certain songs he sang could make her cry, just the way he sang them. And she knew, no matter what visions she'd had of the kind of life every girl she knew dreamed of, with church on Sunday with the kids, and roses on a white picket fence, that her future was now going to have to include something she'd never envisioned: life out in a raw and raucous world with which she'd never felt entirely comfortable. She accompanied him only occasionally to the clubs or the drive-ins or the other shows on the circuit. When she first started going with Dick, he took her to a bar to meet some friends, and all she could think was, "I don't belong here." So she never ran around after him—once in a while she might go with his folks, but "I never chased him into them places," and she never thought to try to change him either.

The second winter in Bangor there was a record cold. "We couldn't get out to the shows," Dick recalled, "it was so bad. The snow was so deep, and there was so much of it, we just couldn't get out. I ended up shooting a deer, because we had to eat. But the people over in Brewer [across the river from Bangor] where we had room and board supported us for a few months till we got on our feet." And he wrote a song for Pauline, too, called "Cottage in the Pines." He surprised her with it. "I was up at my dad's, and he said, 'I've written a song for you. Do you want me to sing it?' Well, I mean, it was freezing cold, so I said, 'Hurry up.'" But she was enthralled not so much by the story it told as by the sentiment it proclaimed, as he sang of a day (and not, she was almost certain, too far off either) when "With my sweetheart by my side / Down these trails we will ride / In the land that's the answer to my prayer."

Dick and Pauline,
with Vi Kimbell,
wedding day 1952.
*Courtesy of Terry
Curless Chinnock/
Richard Weize—...
and more bears*

In the spring of 1952, Dick and Don Calvi finally persuaded Slim to make his long-delayed return to Maine. "I guess Slim was in a slump and probably drinking," said Pauline, who had been hearing so much about him but had never actually met him. "His wife, Celia, came up before him—she was a singer and she was pregnant at the time—and also a girl named Billy Jo, who was part of the show." Dick couldn't have been more excited, but then when it came time to sign their new contract with WABI, Slim and the boys "kind of eased me out." It was a bitter disappointment, but he had worked too hard to get to where he was to give up now—he was just twenty years old, and he was known throughout the region. So he signed on almost immediately with Hal Lone Pine, playing rhythm guitar and doghouse bass and occasionally featured (as the Tumbleweed Kid) on vocals.

Hal Lone Pine (Harold Breau) was probably the best-known country performer in the area, an RCA Victor recording artist, who with his wife, Betty Cody (born Rita Coté in Sherbrooke, Quebec), had the radio show right behind the Trail Riders on WABI. Their show, too, was called *RFD Dinner Bell*, but it had an ABC network coast-to-coast pickup and featured their ten-year-old son, "Lone Pine Jr."—"Sonny" to his family—on guitar. For Dick it was like having a whole new extended family, and the Breaus tried to take in Pauline, too, but she lost a lot of respect for Pine when he told Dick, right after they got married at the beginning of July, "You know, you'll sell a lot more pictures if you take your ring off, Dick." And she knew he wasn't just talking about pictures either.

Not long after their marriage, Dick got a job in the production plant at the *Bangor Daily News*. ("I wanted to settle down, get myself a job, and try to act like a family man.") They moved into a little apartment on Main Street, which they started to fix up and had nearly completed when, in November, Dick was drafted. It was almost unbelievable to them both. Pauline had just gotten pregnant, and Dick was legally blind in one eye, but there was nothing to be done about it with the Korean War still going on, and everyone knew that the state had a quota to fill. Dick was so sick with apprehension he had to be hospitalized at the Dow Air Force Base in Bangor before shipping out, first to Fort Devens, then to Camp Gordon in Augusta, Georgia. Although as a "C-profile" soldier he was assigned to the Signal Corps, he went through the same basic training as everyone else. In Georgia they were all thrown into what was called the "struggle pit," where you went in and had to "fight one another bare-fisted, down to the last man. You were taught to kill and [told], 'It's just part of your training of being a soldier, that's all.'" But for Dick, no matter how hard he tried to rationalize the experience, it was something altogether different.

He was alone in the barracks on the evening of New Year's Day when he heard on the radio that Hank Williams had died. "I wept like a baby, and I had nobody to tell, 'cause they had all gone to town. And I thought, you know, it struck me, 'Gee, he was only twenty-nine years old' — I mean, to me, I'm twenty, his age wasn't that old. But I didn't know if I was going to make twenty-nine."

THE SUNNY SIDE OF THE MOUNTAIN

THE WAR ENDED, and an armistice was signed on July 27, just three months after he arrived in Korea and two weeks after the birth of his son, Ricky (Richard William Jr.). He was slated for duty at the infamous POW camp on Koje-Do Island, but then he heard there was an opening with the Armed Forces Korea Network. "I went in and took a five-minute tape — you know, read the news. And at the end, one of the [questions] was, 'What makes you think you'd make a good disc jockey or staff announcer here?' And I said, 'Well, I used to do my own MC work in Bangor, Maine, and I'm a country and western performer, play guitar'— [and] they needed a guitar player in their band!"

He was stationed in Pusan to begin with, broadcasting over a satellite AFKN station, but before long he got transferred to the flagship station in Taegu. He started with a five-minute show, right after the Grand Ole Opry broadcast, which arrived weekly on sixteen-inch transcription discs shipped to Armed Forces Network stations all over the world. After the Opry, there was always five minutes left over for the news. But Dick talked the station manager into letting him have the five minutes, just him and his guitar. From the beginning he called himself the Rice Paddy Ranger, and he adopted as his theme Hawkshaw Hawkins' jaunty "The Sunny Side of the Mountain," a song his father had always told him would make a great signature number for his show. "Then I'd do another song, maybe two, do my theme again, and I'm out. And I'd say in all my write-ups, 'Someday I hope I can be right there where the Opry is.'" Before long the show was extended to fifteen minutes, and he was getting dozens of letters from homesick GIs with requests for songs they'd like to hear him do. "I'd start with the theme, and I'd go into a little gab and do one with just me and the guitar. Then for a third I'd do a multiple-track recording, [the way] Les Paul and Mary Ford were putting out their records at the time." Les Paul, Dick knew, was a genius, but he and his engineer, Bill Burig, figured out a crude way to reproduce his overdubbing technique, with Dick playing all the instruments and adding his own vocal harmonies to create a fuller, more "sophisticated" sound. His most popular number was a sentimental Japanese song, "China Nights (Shina No Yoru)," well known in one version or another to American troops throughout the Far East, which in Dick's multitrack rendition—with alternating English and Japanese lyrics set off by familiar "Oriental" effects—seemed to suggest equal elements of nostalgia, displacement, and romantic yearning, and perhaps for that reason got requests throughout the far-flung AFKN network.

Maybe it reflected his own loneliness, too. He couldn't really articulate all the things he felt, but when he wrote home to Pauline he couldn't hide from her how lonely he was. Nor was it lost on her that he seemed to have found ways to take care of the physical part of it anyway. One time he asked her to send him a bolt of cloth, which she didn't think twice about at the time, but later he explained—a little cruelly, she thought—that it had been for the mother of a girl that he and some of the guys had been with. It worried her when he wrote about being in and out of the hospital with debilitating attacks of psoriasis, a skin condition he had never suffered from before, which, he said, the docs put down to a kind of "nervous condition." She could tell that he was drinking, too—at least she thought she could—not the normal, social kind of drinking that he and his family had always engaged in, but something else, something that she couldn't put her finger on, without being able to see how he really was, without being able to talk to him about it.

More and more stations added his show. Soon he had all nine stations in the Korean network, and by 1954 nine more in the Far East Network in Japan. GIs throughout the Far East, and in Hawaii and the Philippines, too, knew his name, and he remained busy with his club work in Taegu. By now he was getting "bushels of letters" every week, but perhaps his most devoted fan was a young California GI named Alan Franklin, who Dick sometimes thought believed in his music more than he did himself. Alan had grown up in Hollywood, his mother, Mary C. McCall Jr., was one of the founders of the Screen Writers Guild and had served three terms as its president. She had dozens of screenwriting credits, including both the wildly popular *Maisie* series and some of the most prestigious literary adaptations of the '30s and '40s, but her son, a twin who had been born just twenty-four hours after she completed the script of *A Midsummer Night's Dream* for her longtime friend Jimmy Cagney, had little interest in the movie business. He had fallen in love with country and western music as a kid, his first idol was Bob Wills, and when he heard Dick, he had no doubt that he was hearing the real thing. For Dick it was a welcome form of affirmation. "The other guys at the station were all professional people, Casey Kasem [future originator of the internationally syndicated *American Top 40* radio show] was one of them and there were writers and actors who came from Hollywood. I was the only one doing country, and Alan loved it. He come to see me one day, and he just started pulling records. The others didn't seem to believe [he was] who he said he was—the son of Mary McCall and so on. I mean, he didn't make [anything] of it, he just said it and that was it. I believed him, and I didn't care. But to tell you about Alan, he believed so much in me and my talent, [after] he got home, he just went knocking on doors. I come back to Maine, and he lived in Beverly Hills, but he never gave up."

When he mustered out in October of 1954, it seemed like he was at the start of a whole new chapter in his life. "When I got off the boat in Seattle, I had my guitar and my duffel bag, but I put them down and I kissed the ground — I know it sounds corny, but I really did, right there in Seattle, Washington." It took five days to travel across the country by troop train, and he saw television for the first time in a little bar in New Jersey outside of Fort Dix, where everyone was scheduled to be discharged. "It was Liberace, with the candelabras sitting on top of the piano!" Then it was off to Maine — he was practically counting the minutes. He knew that everything was not quite right — things just somehow felt . . . different. But he figured that time would fix that. And he set about to pick up his life where he had left off.

SOLDIER'S HOME

I couldn't understand what was wrong with me. I came home a different person. I wanted to settle down with my family. I was just so tickled to be home. But I got here and I couldn't fit in. I couldn't relate to the people that were here.

HE WENT BACK to his old job at the newspaper, under the GI bill the position had been held for him with seniority and benefits guaranteed. "I just [figured], 'I'll settle into this, I'll get back and have something stable.'" For the time being, he thought, he'd put his musical career on hold and build something that would last for his wife and fourteen-month-old son. But he just couldn't do it. "I couldn't take it. I could not take being in there with those folks [at the plant]. All nice guys and everything, but I just could not stand to be cooped in."

Pauline could see right away that something was wrong. But she didn't know what it was. "He was trying to find his place, he was trying to find where he belonged. 'Cause, you know, in Korea it was drinking and playing, playing the clubs and setting around, and he had taken his radio show over there very seriously." It bewildered her almost, when he confided to her some of the things he had done, some of the thoughts he had had, things she didn't want to hear — she didn't know why he felt like he had to tell her. And he was different now when he drank, she saw a side of him she had never seen before, there were times when it seemed like he was taking it out on her. He became loud and abusive, sometimes even physically abusive. "Maybe it was his conscience. I believe that played a big part. It was [as if] the only way he could justify the way he was living was to get angry at everybody else in the household. It was like that was the only way he could divert attention away from what he was doing or cope with it himself." She tried to put it down to his age — they were both so young, just twenty-two. She told herself that everyone went through stages, he was just trying to find himself, but for someone who had always thought life would simply continue to go on as it was, to someone as strong in her belief that her husband was a good man in every way, it never ceased to come as a shock that this was actually happening.

He was forced to check into the Togus VA Hospital, outside of Augusta, with a severe attack of psoriasis — it had gotten all into his scalp, and the doctors at the VA, like the doctors in Korea, were convinced that it related to the "nerve problems" he was having. When things got really bad, he went "into the woods" — to a remote hunting and fishing camp on Mattaseunk Lake that his family maintained — just to be by himself. But nothing seemed to help, and to his own and Pauline's consternation things seemed to go from bad to worse, until finally he told her he just couldn't go on this way, there were things that he needed to do, he was an entertainer and, for better or worse, he was going to be one all his life. And in a way she was relieved. Because if that was the problem, it seemed like a solvable one. She had faith in him. She wanted him to be happy. She would never have wanted to be the one who forced him to abandon his dreams. She could never be that.

He couldn't remember a time when he had been so out of practice, there hadn't been a time when he had gone so long without playing or entertaining in public since he first left home with Yodeling Slim. Recording tape was expensive, but he had a bunch of tapes of his old "Rice Paddy Ranger" shows. They took up only one channel of his two-track tape recorder, so he recorded on the other channel — him and his dad and whoever else was around for the parties they would have on weekends — just to hear what he sounded like. He started seeking out old contacts, too, and before long he got back together with Hal Lone Pine and Betty Cody, who had been all over the country recently with the RCA Country & Western Caravan tour, an all-star revue that was headlined by Hank Snow and supervised by Snow's new manager, Colonel Tom Parker, in the spring of '54. Parker had in fact tried to lure Betty, who had had a number-ten country hit in 1953, to Nashville in order to make her a star, but he made it plain that he was not interested in her husband, and that was the end of that. Pine had his own TV show on WABI now and, with the addition of Dick, "he did it like the old days, him and his guitar and myself, just a few people." Dick got a big kick out of Pine and Betty's son, Lenny ("Lone Pine Jr."), who was thirteen now and just beginning to get into jazz. In fact the story would often be told of how, two or three years later, Pine slapped Sonny onstage for interjecting some jazz licks into one of Pine's rigidly traditional numbers. (Pine wanted every song played note for note, another musician said, no matter how many times you played it.) This would precipitate the son's inevitable departure from Lone Pine's Mountaineers and, eventually, the beginning of a career, as Lenny Breau, that would see him hailed as one of the most daring improvisational players of the day, before his tragic early death. Sonny's early musical experimentation didn't faze Dick in the least, in truth he tended to appreciate Sonny's adventurous spirit more than his father's plodding commitment to the music. But more than anything else, he was just happy to be back in the life that he loved.

He worked as many one-nighters as he could, gradually reestablishing an identity of his own. Finally, in the summer of 1955, he got a sit-down gig, opening up Bangor's "first nightclub," the Silver Dollar Ranch House, and he was still working there a year later, when his daughter, Terry Leigh, was born. Not long afterward he was forced to check into Togus again with what was diagnosed as a severe case of ulcers, but by the end of the year he was back on his feet with a featured spot on the *Rhythm Ranch* television show in Poland Spring, outside of Casco, and he was touring throughout New England and Canada with Roy Aldrich's Wagonmasters, the show's resident band. And most important of all, he had a record out of his own.

ONCE AGAIN IT WAS PINE who led the way. A twenty-five-year-old bluegrass musician and dedicated record collector from Westbrook, Maine, named Al Hawkes had started his own label, Event Records, in the spring of '56. Hawkes, the proprietor of a flourishing radio and TV repair business, had maintained a fanatical love for country music since he was a kid, growing up on a small farm on the outskirts of Portland. Without realizing it was illegal, he had started his own radio station in his father's barn while still in high school (he put up the antenna on a windmill tower), running it for almost a year before the FCC started snooping around to find the source of the signal. The TV repair business, which he had started in 1952 after his Army discharge, was growing all the time, and he was busy with various bluegrass and hillbilly groups of his own, but then he ran into an old friend from high school, Dick Greeley, who, courtesy of his own Army experience, had an extensive background in electronics, and told him he was thinking of starting a record company. Together the two built a studio in his father's old blacksmith shop, equipping it with two Ampex 350 tape recorders and Altec mikes and bringing to their shared enterprise all the technical expertise (if not the financial acumen) that you needed to get a small record company up and running. There wasn't a musician who passed through the area who didn't recognize his commitment to the music. In fact, the first Event session, by Charlie Bailey of the Bailey Brothers, early bluegrass performers on both the Opry and the *WWVA Jamboree*, with whom Hawkes had become friendly on his frequent visits to the area as a solo act, was recorded, purely on the basis of mutual faith, five months before the label was actually launched. (It was Bailey who in effect gave Hawkes both the impetus and the name, when, upon seeing his vast record collection for the first time, he suggested that Al really ought to start a label of his own, and if he were to record Charlie Bailey, it would be a real *event*.) The second Event release, some months later, "Prince Edward Island Is Heaven to Me," was by Hal Lone Pine and His Kountry Karavan.

Dick came in to audition at Pine's suggestion in July of '56. He did a bunch of Johnny Cash songs at first, but Al Hawkes was not impressed — the world didn't need another Johnny Cash, he told Dick, and urged him to dig a little deeper. Dick came up with "Streets of Laredo," a mournful western ballad that went back long before the days of recorded sound (it derived from the eighteenth-century British folk song "The Unfortunate Rake"). Dick had loved the song ever since he was a kid, he knew Burl Ives' 1941 version (as "The Cowboy's Lament"), and he had heard his dad and Emery sing it often, but he had developed his own slow and stately approach to the subject matter, one well served by his increasing inclination to utilize his deep lower register. Hawkes was immediately sold. "We're gonna record him," he told his partner. And so they did, just one month later.

The song came in at four minutes and ten seconds, and the flip side, "Foggy, Foggy Dew," another old English folk song which Dick had adorned with a bluesy filigree he had adapted from the Josh White version, was

Dick and Al Hawkes at the Event Records studio, 1956. *Courtesy of Darleen Hawkes Doughty and Terry Curless Chinnock*

just ten seconds shorter. Both were propelled by Dick's rhythm guitar, which, along with the steel on "Laredo," supplied a moody feeling to set off the clip-clop rhythm of the first, the sensual crooning of the second. When they took the record around to DJs five months later (this amounted to the whole of Event's marketing plan), there was as much talk about its length as about its quality, with jokes that it could provide the DJ with a welcome bathroom break. Al Hawkes was as aware as anyone else that they didn't have any way to sell a whole lot of copies, but he was equally aware that in a catalogue that never failed to strive for quality, their third single release was in its own way a quiet classic.

Then, in the spring of 1957 with his second Event single, a full-throated reprise of "China Nights," about to come out, the station manager at

"Lone Pine Jr." (Lenny Breau), 1956. *Courtesy of Terry Curless Chinnock / Richard Weize —*
... and more bears

WABI, Lee Nelson, a fellow Korean War vet, suggested to Dick that he
might think about expanding his horizons by trying out for *Arthur Godfrey's Talent Scouts.* Godfrey at the time had two top prime-time television
shows running on CBS, *Talent Scouts* on Monday night and *Arthur Godfrey
and His Friends* on Wednesday, and he had already broken such top talent
as Pat Boone, the McGuire Sisters, Johnny Nash, and, recently, Patsy
Cline, who had debuted her single, "Walkin' After Midnight," on the show

in January. (A twenty-year-old Elvis Presley was one of his more prominent turndowns.) He was known for his faux-folksy manner, but Dick
knew little about the show, in fact he didn't think he had ever even seen
it, but with his station manager's endorsement, he signed up for the tryout, which required him to finally make that long-delayed New York trip.

There was a series of preliminary auditions at the beginning of June.
The way it worked, you started out with something like twenty songs, then
winnowed them down to five and, finally, to a single featured number.
"Hi, honey," he wrote to Pauline from the Hotel Forrest just west of Times
Square. "Miss you. Passed one audition for Godfrey. Got the big one
tomorrow afternoon. I need your prayers and faith now. I'll bring you here
if I ever make it. You'll be amazed, I know!" And then, contrary to both
his fears and his expectations, he won. Which meant that he would be
appearing on the show itself, set up as a talent contest whose outcome
was determined by audience applause, in September. At Pine's insistence
he had brought Lenny Breau to the tryouts—Pine paid Sonny's expenses—
but even though he had cautioned Sonny to give his age as sixteen (sixteen
was, evidently, the cutoff age for *Talent Scouts* "professionals"), after shaving his sideburns and ditching his lavender pants at the show producers'
insistence, and then dazzling one and all with his classical, semi-classical,
and hot Merle Travis- and Chet Atkins-influenced licks, Sonny couldn't
help but blurt out his real age when he was asked. "We had a great time
anyway," Dick said ruefully. And the funny thing was, if he had won, he
would have been sixteen by the time they came back. "But he was raised
a Catholic and he wasn't going to lie."

He took Pauline with him, as promised, when they returned for his
network debut at the end of September. Everyone had to have a "talent
scout" to introduce them on the show, and she was his. It was her first
time in New York—they flew down and stayed once again at the Hotel
Forrest. She was scared to death, going on national TV, "but I thought, 'I'll
do it if it kills me'—and it almost did." You can hear the tremor in her
voice as Arthur Godfrey does his best to set her at ease, asking the ages of
her children ("four and fourteen months"), and what her hubby did for a
living. But gradually she gathered confidence, telling the audience that
her husband was a professional entertainer who had his own radio show
five days a week and appeared on television, too. At present, she said, he
was appearing at the Silver Dollar Ranch House in Bangor, and he recorded
for Event Records. And then Dick stepped into the Toni (Home Permanent

and Hair Care Products) Spotlight, with the song he and the show's musical producer had eventually settled on, Merle Travis' "Nine Pound Hammer," a tale of the Kentucky coal mines. Dick did all he could to approximate
Merle's bright, shimmering licks with his own "mumbling guitar," and he
tossed off the dancing succession of two-line verses with aplomb, while
at the same time bearing down on the sober recitation about working
conditions in the mines that was an integral part of Travis' 1947 original.
And while his nervousness may have shown a little in the somewhat
rushed tempo of the song, there are moments when the artificial trappings
of the show seem to disappear, and you see, simply, twenty-five-year-old
Dick Curless in all his unabashed charm, you see nothing but the natural
ease and grace of his demeanor shining through.

Arthur Godfrey, as choleric in private as he was easygoing in public,
was obviously taken with both the performer and his performance. When
it came time for audience applause to measure the winner (there was no
scientific applause meter, just the highly open-to-interpretation evidence
of the ears), the first contestant, a Dixieland band called Chain Gang, got
a good response. So did the classical soprano, Mary Gay Nelson. But when
it came Dick's turn, even though his applause appeared to be roughly the
same as that of the others, Godfrey unhesitatingly declared him the winner, while quickly adding (as perhaps he did many weeks) that they were
all so good, he thought he could use all three on his regular show.

Dick was featured for the rest of the week (as were the others) on
Godfrey's afternoon radio show, with multiple opportunities to interact
with his host, who introduced him each day, with slight variations, as "a
great big handsome guy [who] sings folk songs accompanying himself on
the git-fiddle, and he does a beautiful job." He couldn't seem to get over
the anomaly of a country singer named Curless ("That's C-u-r-l-e double
s," he informed the audience again and again) coming from Maine of all
places, and he kept prodding Dick as to how in the world he could have
acquired such an authentic approach to the music. Dick never lost his
equanimity, in fact he seemed altogether at ease with the situation, taking
the opportunity to give his host a quick primer on the music and, when
he sang another beautiful Merle Travis number, "I Am a Pilgrim," suggesting that Godfrey might be more familiar with yet another of Travis'
compositions, "16 Tons," which had been a number-one pop hit for Tennessee Ernie Ford the previous year.

It was, all in all, a marvelous opportunity. Pauline had gotten paid for her role as talent scout ("By the time they took out the [deductions], she made more money than I did!"), and with her earnings was able to go on a real shopping spree. Dick bought himself a new topcoat that got swiped from the lobby of the Hotel Forrest. But it didn't really matter, in every other respect the week was almost like a dream, and best of all he was approached by a real professional manager. Dick already had a manager of sorts, a DJ from Hudson, New York, named Jim Small who was connected with Event Records, but this was different. Sol Tepper was a veteran of the business, a club booker who had extensive connections with entertainers like Dean Martin and Jerry Lewis and handled a lot of other big names, including Marion Marlowe, for several years a featured singer on *Arthur Godfrey and His Friends*. Tepper saw something in Dick, he shared with him that he saw big things in his future. Dick told him that he already had an agent. "He said, 'Well, you don't need him for sure. I'll be your agent, your manager.' So I signed a contract. He says, 'You go home and get some rest, 'cause I'm going to be calling you shortly. You're going to be a very busy fellow.'" His idea was to put Dick on the new ABC-Paramount label, whose most recent signing, sixteen-year-old Paul Anka, had just seen his first release go to number one. Just go home, Tepper told him, and wait for my call. So Dick went home — he was practically walking on air — and waited.

H E WASN'T WORRIED when nothing much happened at first. These things took time, he knew. And after all the national exposure, he found that things had really changed for him back home in Maine. He was greeted at the radio station with a newfound respect, his one-nighters picked up, and the crowds at the clubs turned out like never before. He and Pauline and the kids were living in East Auburn now, not far from Casco, in the heart of Maine's tourist-rich Lakes Region. They had moved there in the spring after he started getting more and more work in the area, but they kept their place in Bangor, where most of the work was in the wintertime. He carefully studied the 16mm film of his *Talent Scouts* performance, looking for ways to improve. He saw a number of things, including the way his bad eye was hanging after all the beers he had gulped down to give himself "Dutch courage" for the show. But most of all, for the first time in his life, he saw that he had a style of his own. "I could never see what [other people] were seeing in me. I thought I was just another singer. I never realized that I had anything different than anybody else." But now he did—and he resolved to build on that.

He still hadn't heard anything definitive from Sol Tepper—evidently it was taking longer than Tepper had expected to make the deal with ABC-Paramount and set up business. But that was all right. There wasn't any hurry. He had several recording sessions for Event at the beginning of November, then on November 10 recorded "Nine Pound Hammer" in two versions, one with the recitation that he had included in his *Talent Scouts* appearance, one—thirty seconds shorter—without. The musicianship was impeccable, the sound a little fuller, and, with Sonny's guitar setting the pace, the rockabilly touch a little more confident—it was the kind of session that was relaxed enough that everyone could break up when Sonny passed wind just at the point in the recitation where Dick intoned, "Sometimes the air gets so foul back there [in the coal mines] that you can't get a good, deep breath." "No laughing, goddamnit," Dick declares, but he couldn't keep from laughing himself.

Within days of the session, he was off to Nashville for the very first time for the sixth annual Country Music DeeJay convention. Driving in from the airport with half a dozen other hillbilly singers, some of them evidently just as new to the business as he was, one of them asked the cab driver, "Gee, what kind of a place is Nashville?" And the cabbie said, "Aw, it's just like a rotten egg. You can't beat it." Which really tickled him. The convention was held at the twelve-story Andrew Jackson Hotel on Memorial Square, just down from the capitol, and everybody got a chance to hobnob with everyone else, Jim Reeves and Hawkshaw Hawkins and Ernest Tubb, who was very kind to him—he had the room above Johnny Cash, and he met the Everly Brothers, too. He wanted to compliment Jim Reeves on his huge number-one hit "Four Walls," it was the kind of song that Dick could imagine himself doing someday. But then, it was just his luck, he got sick with the flu and was pretty much confined to his room for the rest of the convention. So he never did get to tell Jim Reeves, or anyone else at this point, how much their music had meant to him.

By the time that he got home "Nine Pound Hammer" was about to be released as a single in both versions, but Al Hawkes had lost control of the company. He had come to realize he simply didn't have the means to distribute his own records, so he entered into an ill-fated partnership with a Boston distributor and label owner, which in effect sealed the doom of the Event label. In the meantime, Dick was still waiting to hear from Sol

Tepper, but he was beginning to wonder more and more if it had all just been a misunderstanding, if Tepper had simply been talking through his hat and didn't really care about Dick or his music at all. He wrote to the address Tepper had given him without hearing back, until, finally, one day, he got a letter from someone he had never heard of, saying that Tepper had died of a heart attack not long after their initial meeting. He took it as a kind of judgment. He knew it didn't really mean anything, things like this *happened,* but still — it felt as if it had somehow never been meant to be. Here he was waiting and waiting, telling everyone about his big-time New York manager, not boasting about it, just telling people and seeing how his estimation rose in their eyes — and now it was as if fate had simply chosen to mock him and mock his dreams. "He just didn't seem to [want to] pursue it or to push from that point on," said Pauline, who watched helplessly, as she so often had since his return from Korea. She knew Dick couldn't express all the things he was feeling, or the guilt with which he was consumed for things he couldn't seem to help, for actions she knew he didn't mean to hurt her or the children. He just seemed resigned to the fact that everything he had been given had for some reason been taken away. "I wondered so many times over the years [about] the pain and the fears that were consuming him. At times it became unbearable. Of course, the alcohol didn't help — but I think it eased the pain."

THE COAST OF MAINE

HE WAS, HE DECIDED ONCE AGAIN, done with this ill-omened business. He was sick of the drinking, sick of spending night after night in smoky bars, sick of all the people you had to please, sick most of all of all the temptations of the spirit and the flesh that you had to contend with. So he bought an old truck and started logging in the woods around Casco. He would get up at four o'clock in the morning and not come home till eight o'clock at night, then fall asleep in his chair before going up to bed. It was the best he'd felt since his service days. He would go out in the woods every day and spot the trees, cut them down and limb them out, then, after he had built a "brow" for lifting and loading the logs, load them onto the truck himself. "I felt like I could whip nine men every morning when I got up," he said. "That's how rugged I was. That's how good I felt." It was real, satisfying outdoor work, the kind of work he thought you could do for years and feel good about yourself. But then he got sick, and he loaned the truck to a friend, and the friend came back and told him shamefacedly that he had blown the engine. It was an old truck, an old engine, but for Dick it brought to an end what he would always look back on as an idyllic dream. "I think it lasted a few weeks," said Pauline a little caustically, though she did not fail to register the depth of her husband's disappointment. He was trying to rehabilitate himself, she knew, he just didn't want to go back to the VA hospital in Togus. For Dick the choice was now clear-cut. "I got away from music because I wanted to. I wanted to break from it because of what it was doing to me. But after the truck, I said, 'This is it. I can't make a living at this no more. I'm going back to picking and singing.' So I got the guitar out, and I got a tape recorder, and I went upstairs and stayed in that room." Once again Pauline became his refuge and his nurse. She brought him his food, she brought him whatever he needed, and he stayed with it, "trying to get my fingers back in shape, getting my voice going again, every day," until he was satisfied that he could emerge from his room and be himself once again.

THEY WENT BACK AND FORTH between Casco and Bangor, where he had started playing a new room at the Hotel Belmont. Then his old Army buddy, Alan Franklin, got in touch with him about a Las Vegas booking. Alan was working as an EMT, driving an ambulance for the Schaefer Ambulance Service in Los Angeles, but he had never lost his passion for country music, and he had never lost his faith in Dick, or his belief that Dick would one day be a big country music star. And with his family connections (his mother was still active in the film industry, his twin brother was a successful attorney, and his sister wrote for the *Los Angeles Times*), he was always on the lookout for opportunities to get Dick seen and heard. He had gone to Capitol Records about Dick as soon as he got out of the service, and when they turned him down (they said they didn't need another Tex Ritter on the label, Alan told him exasperatedly), he went to the Liberty label with no greater success. "He never gave up on me," Dick said. "He just kept knocking on doors." So when he called and said he had an offer for three weeks at the Saddle Club in Las Vegas in February of 1959, Dick jumped at the opportunity. As it turned out, the contract called for four shows a night, seven nights a week and, given the environment, it was no surprise that his ulcers kicked up and he was

Father and son, Levant, Maine, 1950s. *Courtesy of Terry Curless Chinnock*

forced to go back to Maine before the booking was over. It was a disappointment, certainly, but he was grateful for the opportunity. And he jumped right back into his regular bookings, picking up a tony gig at the Thorndike Hotel in Rockland, eighty miles up the coast from Portland, which billed itself as "a summer mecca for theatrical and art world luminaries," movie stars like Robert Montgomery and James Cagney and Claude Rains and well-known artists like Andrew Wyeth, who seemed to genuinely appreciate both him and his music.

In the meantime, through some of his new friends in the area, he had acquired a small farm in Casco—"a gentleman farm," with a big barn, a brick house, and a little cottage that went with it—somehow or other he and Pauline were able to scrape together $4,000 for the down payment, and then he persuaded his mother and father, who were still living on the chicken farm in Levant, to move into the little cottage that went with it.

It was like old times, there was always music and, always, singing with his father and brother. "When the three of us would sing, you couldn't tell us apart. Certain songs like a Hank Thompson song or a Hank Snow song, I'd play dobro, my brother would play rhythm, and my father would play harmonica, and we'd all sing—just a little trio in the house." One time, when they'd moved back to Bangor for the winter, his dad was working with his mother's brother Ronnie over at Dow, the recently designated SAC base, the two of them were running a big machine, cutting the seams in the cement for the new runways for the giant bombers. It was hard work, but his father would come home from work every night, it seemed, with a new song. "Listen to this, Dickie," he would say, just like when he was a kid. "One night he said, 'Boy, I heard a guy on the radio, got a good song. Good singer. He's going to be happening.' I said, 'What's his name?' He said, 'Buck Owens.' And he sang it to me: 'Since you went away, I've had the blues.' 'I said, 'Yeah, that's good, Dad. That's a corker. Where did you get that?' He had learned that thing and sang it to me before I got a hold of it. And I'm an entertainer!"

In the summer of 1960, Alan Franklin set up a series of gigs for him in Southern California, where he first met Wynn Stewart and Ralph Mooney, two mainstays of the booming Bakersfield scene, from which Buck Owens was just beginning to emerge. He played places like George's Round-up in Long Beach and the Foothill Club in Signal Hill just down the road. Alan got him a television spot on *Town Hall Party,* the biggest country music show on the West Coast, which was hosted by Tex Ritter and featured such headliners as Lefty Frizzell, Skeets McDonald, Joe Maphis, and one of Dick's biggest heroes, Merle Travis. Alan never stopped trying, he continued to contact label heads, and he even took Dick out to the Warner Bros. lot for a tryout for a Western television series. "I walked in for my audition, I weighed about 225 pounds, mostly liver bloat, and I was told, 'If they ask you, Can you ride?, say yes.' I said, 'Well, I can ride a little bit.' They said, 'Just tell them yes. And if they ask, Can you shoot a six-gun—' I said, 'Well, I'm good at rifles.' 'Just tell them you can.'"

He didn't get the part, but as it turned out, it wouldn't have mattered, because on September 12, 1960, he was sitting in a little bar on Pacific Avenue when he saw a headline in the paper that Hurricane Donna was making its way up the East Coast, heading straight for Portland. He got on the phone right away and called Pauline, but he hadn't gotten any further than hello when there was a snap and she screamed and he was cut off. "Man, I canceled everything and got on the next plane home. When I got there, the storm had knocked down some tree branches and a little bit of the roof of the barn — no big damage — but I didn't know. And when it happened, I could care less about movies or picking or anything else, and I never went back." And the opportunity never came around again.

For the next five years very little changed, and it seemed unlikely it ever would. His father died in 1962, just forty-eight years old, which sent Dick into a real tailspin ("We were more like brothers than father and son"), though his mother continued to live in the little cottage next door. Pauline tried to talk him through it, but she had troubles of her own. She felt like Dick had drifted away from her, and it was only natural that she should drift away from him. He became more violent when he was drinking now, and she wasn't really sure how much more she could take. But she still felt like she needed to try. "I told him, 'If you're serious about your career, and you want to do something meaningful with it — I mean, you can stay here and play the honky-tonks all your life if that's where you're comfortable, you can be the big frog in the little puddle if that's all you want out of life.'" But she knew it wasn't, and yet he didn't seem able to rouse himself from a lethargy that was interrupted only by bursts of anger and frustration and acts of self-destruction. "I probably sound a little angry when I say it, but I had such faith in that man, I had such belief. I knew he was good, and he had everything to go with it. But he didn't have direction, he just seemed to lack self-esteem." And she was never able to figure out exactly why.

A TOMBSTONE EVERY MILE

IN THE FALL of 1964 Dick got a call from Dan Fulkerson, who had worked as a salesman and copywriter at a number of Bangor radio stations before ending up at WABI. Fulkerson had never met Dick, but he had heard him many times on the air and in fact had been stationed in

Korea at the same time Dick was making a name for himself as the Rice Paddy Ranger. "He used to perform at the Pier Seven enlisted man's club right below my office [as] harbormaster, and I could hear him play down there." But Fulkerson, a native of Stillwater, Oklahoma, had never been drawn to country music until his subsequent transfer to Germany, where the director of the Armed Forces Network in Bremerhaven gave him his own hillbilly show simply because of where he had been born. The music grew on him then, and after moving to Bangor with his wife, a Maine native, and their young son, he started jotting down lyrics for songs that had yet to be written. After they separated, his wife moved to Mars Hill up on the border. She took the car, so he was reduced to hitchhiking whenever he wanted to see his son. He got picked up mostly by truckers, and, as he told writer Kevin Coffey, he was intrigued by the stories they recounted about a desolate stretch of road in Aroostook County, Maine, and the treacherous road conditions that prevailed on the journey through the Haynesville Woods. In Coffey's account:

> "I just made some notes and finally wrote some lyrics," Fulkerson said. A WABI staff musician tried his hand at some music, but Fulkerson wasn't satisfied. "So I just started writing my own music. And I hate to say it was easy, but it was really easy. . . . I'll tell you the truth, I was writing for Johnny Cash. I picked up his structure. If you ever listened to 'Please Don't Make Me Go' [another of the songs that Fulkerson wrote at this time], you can almost hear [Cash guitarist] Luther Perkins in the background."

Fulkerson completed eight songs in this manner, then demoed them himself at the WABI studios. ("Poorly, I might add.") Hal Lone Pine offered him $200 for the lot, but then a friend brought him a copy of Dick's first Event single, "Foggy, Foggy Dew," and he was knocked out by the timbre and expressiveness of Dick's voice. At his initiative, they got together and hit it off, particularly after Dick heard the doom-filled trucker song Fulkerson had written, "A Tombstone Every Mile," which recalled some of the stories his father had told him about logging up in the remote reaches of Aroostook County in the early days. That was all it took. He and Fulkerson decided to record a single—Dick had a song for the other side, "Heart Talk," which he had written for Pauline, and they pooled their money and went into the WABI studios with Dick's band, which Fulkerson firmly believed was the best stage band he had ever heard. They added a whistling-wind effect ("That's what made it a hit," said Dick), and put out the single on their own newly formed Allagash label in the late fall of 1964. Then they set about selling it, driving all over the state and, between the two of them, managing to stop at just about every radio station and record store along the way.

The record was an instant smash, not just locally but up and down the East Coast. It was the truckers, in Dick's opinion, who turned out to be their best sales force, "they hand-carried [it] down Route 1, all the way to Florida." Dick and Fulkerson had ordered 5,000 copies initially from the custom pressing division of Capitol Records in Scranton, Pennsylvania, but by the time they were ready to reorder, Capitol Records itself, which represented the "western" half of country and western, with Bakersfield fully as much of a commercial hub at this point as Nashville, had gotten in touch and wanted to re-release the single on their own Tower subsidiary. It was like a dream come true, as the skeptical dismissal that Dick had encountered all his life (*"a country singer from Maine"*) became the very vehicle for his success. The record went to number five on the national country charts, and Dick was signed as a Tower recording artist. The next release, Fulkerson's "Six Times a Day," backed with Dick's cheerfully generic "Down by the Old River," went to number twelve, and by the time he flew down to the annual Country Music DeeJay convention in Nashville in October of 1965, his new single, "'Tater Raisin' Man" (even Dick could see the limitations of this new identification), was just beginning to make some waves. The convention was celebrating the Grand Ole Opry's fortieth anniversary and Dick received three industry awards, including "most promising new artist" of 1965 (the same award that Bakersfield newcomer Merle Haggard got from the West Coast-based Academy of Country Music that year), on the Opry's fabled stage.

The song on which his newfound reputation was based was well suited to his talents, the kind of brisk, up-tempo Western storytelling that he had learned at his father's, and Yodeling Slim Clark's, knee — but it didn't begin to express the range of his talent. For that he and Dan had gone back into the studio — a professional recording studio this time (in spite of the whistling wind, Dick was never satisfied with the sound they had gotten on "Tombstone," he wanted to work on it some more, but there was a dance class coming in) — and quickly laid down ten more tracks. These included such familiar titles as "China Nights" (on which Alan Franklin, in town for the occasion, played the Chinese gong), an updated "Streets of Laredo," and the two follow-up singles, which gave Tower all the cuts it needed to schedule a full-scale album.

With plans for their own booking agency already in the works, Fulkerson and Dick booked a northeastern tour for the band, ignoring any flak they got about their bass player, Buddy Johnson, who was black. Dick went out as a single, too, playing shows all around the country, the *Midwestern Hayride* in Cincinnati and the *WWVA Jamboree* in West Virginia, even shooting a pilot for what was intended to be a syndicated television series in Cleveland.

But then Buck Owens called. The same Buck Owens whose song his father had sung to him with such enthusiasm just five or six years earlier, when no one really knew who Buck Owens was. Buck Owens was now on top of the country music world, with four number-one hits in 1965 and the Beatles recently on the pop charts with his 1963 number one, "Act Naturally." Owens initially contacted him about performing at the Heart Fund benefit he was doing in Wheeling in January of 1966. They met briefly before the show, and Buck seemed to size him up, then invited him to come back to his hotel room afterwards. "And, you know, he's combing his hair in the mirror, we're just visiting, but he's interviewing me. He says, 'We've got some plans for putting a show together, and you might be interested in being a part of it.' He said, 'I'm going to call it the All-American Road Show, Buck Owens' All-American Road Show, and I'd like to have you as part of the show.' He's combing his hair, and he's got his back to me, and he says, 'Do you drink?' and I said, 'No.' I paused. 'I inhale it." He kinda grinned, and I said, 'But I do my job, Buck. That's my time. Wherever we go, you give me an hour to be there and be ready, and I'll be there. Just give me an hour's notice—two hours if you can.' But I said, 'What I do when I'm not with you, that's my business.' And he bought 100 days off me that year, 1966."

From Dick's point of view, that pretty well established the terms of their relationship. He joined the show within a matter of weeks, signing an exclusive booking, management, and publishing contract with Buck, which brought his partnership with Dan Fulkerson to an abrupt end. Fulkerson didn't fail to register deep disappointment that Dick should make such a decision "without talking to me at all," but although he was fond of Fulkerson (he was like an intrepid adventurer, Dick told an interviewer some years later, "every time he learned something, he'd leave it right away and try something else"), Dick never hesitated in making the move, and he never looked back.

Over the course of the next year there were more peaks than he could count, as the All-American Road Show played every state but Hawaii and sold out two shows at Carnegie Hall just a month after he joined. He only wished his dad could have been around to see it. And he wished his dad and Buck could have met. He felt like he'd found in Buck a true soul mate, with the same wry sense of humor that he had grown up with. They played chess together, and Buck was never reluctant to remind him, *as a friend,* of the current score. Which was, he wrote on August 29, as of the last two tours, "25 wins — ME — 2 wins — YOU! Pardon me while I laugh!" Dick appreciated the kidding, and he could give it back. "I warmed 'em up for you, Chief," he told Buck, after getting three encores at Carnegie Hall, though he wasn't sure that in this instance Buck was all that amused. And in the end there was never any question of who was boss. Buck and his manager, Jack McFadden, kept their business strictly to themselves, and there was never any doubt in Dick's mind that every penny was going to be accounted for — and not necessarily to the advantage of the artist. But he appreciated that, too. Business was business, after all, and it was a wonderful opportunity in ways that could never be quantified or qualified. Because if playing Carnegie Hall, and a sold-out Hollywood Bowl the following year, were the professional highlights, unquestionably the musical highlight was a tour with Merle Haggard, another rising artist in Buck's stable and well on his way to becoming one of the most significant musical voices of the twentieth century, in the spring of 1966. Merle, who had been released from prison and relocated to Bakersfield at around the same time as Dick's 1960 Southern California tour, was just beginning to really make a name for himself, with "Swinging Doors," his first self-written hit, on its way to number five on the country charts. They were in the middle of an Alaskan tour when he and Merle and Merle's new wife, Bonnie Owens (previously married to Buck), shared a fifth of bourbon while sitting cross-legged on a chilly motel-room floor in Kenai and sang Jimmie Rodgers songs all night long. Merle loved Jimmie Rodgers as much as Dick, and vice versa — he felt the same way about trains, too — and they struck a bond that night that prompted Merle to spontaneously give Dick two of his best recent compositions, "All of Me Belongs to You" and "House of Memories," both of which he had yet to record.

That was a moment Dick would return to again and again, as he would to the time he was out on tour with Buck in Canada—"I was sitting on the bus, and snowflakes as big as silver dollars are hitting the windshield. I was in the front reading [Oscar Wilde's] *The Picture of Dorian Gray* and Red Simpson and Tommy Collins and some of the boys were in the back playing cards." He was in the middle of the novel, which he found fascinating, when "I just put the book down—I never finished it!—and grabbed a legal pad and pencil and wrote [the song] 'When Dad Was Around.' It's almost like it flowed out of me, and I had the tune in my mind, like someone was guiding my hand."

The next stop on the tour was a hockey arena in Moose Jaw, and everyone was sitting around in the locker room that served as their dressing room, when Dick said to Buck he had just written a song that he'd like to play for him if he had a minute. Buck said that he didn't really have a lot of time, but he'd like to hear it, so Dick sang it to him, tenderly teasing out the lyrics with which he had tried to invoke his feelings for his father ("Those man-to-man talks / From twenty to thirty / Taught me not to balk / If I got my hands dirty") as the room quieted down and Buck fixed him with an unwavering stare. When he finished, there was silence at first, "and then Buck just said, 'You sonofabitch,' and walked away." Which left Dick completely baffled at first, he couldn't understand how Buck could react that way—but later when they talked, he came to see that was just Buck's way of telling him how deeply the song had touched him, and Buck told him about some of his own recent losses, and at that moment, Dick thought, they were as close as two men could possibly be.

He moved Pauline and the kids out to Bakersfield, the hub of all of Buck's business and music activities, the following year. It was a move that had come about only after what amounted to an ultimatum from Pauline. They couldn't keep going the way that things were. From the moment that "Tombstone" hit nearly two years ago, success had brought nothing good to either one of them. Sometimes, she thought, she no longer recognized the man she had married. It was no longer just the drinking, it was the pills they all took, too. It was as if they had unleashed in him a different person—not so much a different *person* as a person who was no longer immune to temptation of any sort and yet could no more enjoy it than the sweet boy she had first met. She always knew when he was in trouble, because he always came to her and confessed. She watched as his behavior became more and more erratic, more and more reckless, and, although God knows she was not blameless herself, she found it almost unendurable as the rage and resentment, the burden of guilt that he carried around with him always, increasingly seemed to focus on her. Finally she told him she was going to leave, and his first reaction was to accuse her of being with someone else. She thought at first he was going to kill her, then himself. But then he begged and pleaded and he promised he would turn his life around, until finally she agreed: they would try to make a new start in California. But she would not go back to Casco, she said, she would never go back to Casco—there were too many bad memories there. And so they picked up, lock, stock, and barrel, at the age of thirty-five, the first time in either of their lives (with the exception of Dick's two years in the service) that they would be living anywhere but where they had grown up.

It was a fresh start in some ways, but not in others. Dick *tried,* she knew that, he really tried. And it was better. But she could see when she got out there how Dick was around Buck and the others. He acted like someone who, for whatever reason, despite the wealth of talent and personality that had been bestowed upon him, could never really believe in himself. She tried to tell him—she knew it was just his shyness, or that strangely misplaced conviction that everyone else somehow or another was more deserving than him, but it came off as standoffish. She knew he didn't mean it that way, but "he kind of hung back, and then he would think, 'Well, they didn't come up [to me],' or 'They weren't real friendly'—but, you know, [I told him] it works both ways." But he really couldn't help himself, she realized, he took everything so *hard*—it was almost like, despite everything he had been through, he counted on his innocence to protect him. It didn't make any sense, she knew, but that was the way it had been ever since he came back from Korea, and she knew it wasn't likely to change now.

He might have been better off taking Merle Haggard for his model. He admired Merle for his sensitivity and creativity, in many ways they were two like-minded artists of similar temperaments and talents. But, for all of his sensitivity, for all of the tenderness of his sensibilities, Merle didn't seem as fazed as Dick by the demands of celebrity, or the demands of the Buck Owens machine. He was able to express himself in his own stubborn way without ever giving in to the locomotive of success that swirled around Buck. He remained prickly and pissed off, where Dick allowed himself to be so easily intimidated.

The records were an indicator as much as anything else. Through

Buck's connections Dick got to work with nothing but the most accomplished studio musicians — James Burton and Ralph Mooney and Tommy Collins and Gene Moles, the very musicians who were the foundation for the "Bakersfield Sound" — but in a way that was the problem. "It was Buck's sound, or Wynn Stewart's sound," Dick said. "The moan on steel, the Don Rich [chicken] picking, it's the definite West Coast sound. I mean, I'm in the flow of what's going on there — but I'm not getting *me*." The same with the material. There was no question that it was good material, but it was good *generic* material. It seemed like everything Dick wanted to do on his own was just slightly out of step. The new Tom T. Hall story songs that were just starting to crop up on the radio, the Josh White blues and Dixieland treatment of old pop tunes like "I Get the Blues When It Rains," the acoustic-oriented "folk" that he had always been drawn to, the subtleties of Merle Travis' or Lenny Breau's up-tempo picking were all "backlogged," set aside for another day. He didn't get to play his own guitar in the studio anymore — he was told it would disturb the recording balance. When you got right down to it, he was beginning to feel a little bit like a lost sheep in the fold — and, to top it all off, the records weren't selling. With the exception of Merle Haggard's "All of Me Belongs to You," which Buck produced on him in the spring of 1967, he hadn't been able to crack the Top 30 since "Tombstone" came out more than two years earlier.

But then something happened that he could never have imagined. The deal with Buck blew up. It was, like so many other things, a simple matter of finances — in other words, who owed who money. Dick said Buck owed him for his television appearances on Buck's show. Buck said Dick was way overdrawn on his commissions and appearance money. Dick got a lawyer. Buck attached his car. Except for the personal element — the strong bond that he felt he had had with Buck from the beginning — it shouldn't really have come as any surprise. As Buck's biographer, Eileen Sisk, wrote, Buck had recently attached Joe and Rose Lee Maphis' house over a similar matter of equity, and Kay Adams, a fellow member of the troupe with whom Dick had recently recorded an album of duets, would have to leave nearly $2,000 on the table when she left the show. Pauline tried to tell him it was only business. He had to be prepared for things like this. She didn't know anything about business herself — she wasn't sure Dick knew all that much more — but she knew you had to have someone around you who did. Above all, she told him, you can't take it person-

Dick and Buck. *Courtesy of Terry Curless Chinnock/Richard Weize — ...and more bears*

ally. But that only enraged him all the more. His emotions crested and crested, until they crashed—just like they always did. And he felt, she could see it in his eyes, she could hear it in his voice, he felt utterly diminished, he felt like he was a laughingstock in the eyes of the world.

They remained in the house on Montgomery Avenue in Bakersfield until their lease ran out early in the new year. Dick still owed a few dates to Buck, and he fulfilled them. But he got new management, and he and Pauline made plans to move back to Bangor, to the house on Silver Road where they had been living since 1964, and even though he was still technically under contract to Buck for a few more weeks, he scheduled a session at RCA's Studio A in Nashville in December, which he hoped would mark the start of his new life.

Nashville was like a breath of fresh air. Jack Clement, just coming off three Top 10 hits with Charley Pride, country music's first—and so far, only—black superstar (he would go on to have thirteen number ones in the next half dozen years alone), was slated to produce. Clement, an early protégé of Sam Phillips at Sun Records, was one of the great eccentrics, not just in country music but in—well, suffice it to say, he was one of the great eccentrics. (His masterful biographical documentary was entitled *Shakespeare Was a Big George Jones Fan,* after one of his many enigmatically epigrammatic sayings.) Not surprisingly, Jack recognized Dick's potential from the beginning, in his view Dick just needed a little more latitude to express himself. The highlight of the session, the song that Dick had been saving for over a year now, was "When Dad Was Around." He wasn't going to be able to do it more than once, he told Jack, and Jack cut out all the lights and had the band gather together in the center of the studio, with just a single pink bulb illuminating them. He was still barely able to get through it ("You can hear me almost break up on the very last word"), but to his mind that recording would forever stand as testimony both to his music and to his dad. It didn't so much set the mood as establish a tone for the session, a tone in which all the Buck-era holdbacks were thrown out. "Jack was a clever producer," Dick said, and he encouraged every kind of experimentation in the studio. He gave Dick a novelty number called "Wrinkled, Crinkled, Wadded Dollar Bill" that he would later give to his friend Johnny Cash for his best-selling *Hello, I'm Johnny Cash* LP, and Dick even got to sneak in his own guitar on lead rhythm for a playful treatment of Jerry Lee Lewis' "End of the Road." For the first time in years, he was given free rein to follow his own creative impulses (one of the highlights of the session was his version of the old pop blues standard most recently popularized by Louis Prima, "I Ain't Got Nobody"), and even if the arrangements were occasionally more tricked up than he would have liked, the musicianship and songwriting, the overall *camaraderie,* were as close to his original vision of the music, the kind of music that was free of categories and divisions, as anything he had experienced since his earliest days at Event Records.

After a couple of days, he felt so good about the way things were going that he called up Pauline in California and invited her to come to Nashville and celebrate. He assured her that everyone wanted to meet her, and he wanted her to meet all of his new friends, too, not just his producer but some of the pickers, like guitarist Jerry Reed, who was a real cutup, and songwriter Hank Cochran, who had written great country standards like "Make the World Go Away" and "I Fall to Pieces" and had contributed some wonderful songs to the session. She was reluctant at first, but since her mother happened to be visiting and could take care of the kids, and Dick had been on the wagon for six months now, and besides Jack had made all the arrangements, gotten her on a "champagne" flight, with everything taken care of, she eventually agreed. A group of them came out to the airport to meet her, but from the moment she stepped off the plane, she knew it was all wrong. She could see that Dick had been drinking, and the others had, too, and when they went out to dinner later, at the Captain's Table, she just wanted to weep. "Of course, I didn't know any of them, Buck and Pat Trent, and Hank Cochran, and the rest, but they were all great people, and being country folk they made me very comfortable and just made a good evening of it. And Dick was so excited, well, he was so happy about it—but he was half bombed. And they all drank, they all drank."

"I was so happy when Pauline came in," said Dick, "it was a happy time, a wonderful time. [But] I had started drinking again. And I never did quit."

PROMISES TO KEEP

H E HAD NEW FRIENDS. He had a new sound. He even had a new look. He had noticed how badly his right eye had started to droop, it would even spontaneously "weep" sometimes, and he started wearing an eye patch most of the time. With the cover of his new album, *The Long Lonesome Road,* he unveiled his new image, sitting hatless on his guitar case on an oddly antiseptic but undeniably lonesome stretch of road. The stern expression on his face was only reinforced by the black eye patch, with "Recorded in Nashville" stamped in the lower left-hand corner. In many ways it could be argued he didn't look all that different—he was still a big, handsome guy, albeit a more somber-looking one, he was still the Tumbleweed Kid, one of the good guys, but a Tumbleweed Kid who had clearly seen some hard times. But whatever the look (and maybe it was simply a look that was more in keeping with the times, which were about to give birth to an Outlaw country movement spearheaded by Waylon Jennings and Willie Nelson), he couldn't have been more pleased with the new album, and he couldn't have been more pleased with the bookings he was getting through his new Nashville agent.

He and Pauline and the kids moved back to Maine—to Bangor, as they had agreed, although Pauline thought it was a mistake to return to Maine at all, for both personal and professional reasons. Once he had played all the bookings he owed to Buck, he started picking up new ones. In August there was another album session with Jack Clement in Nashville, which in many ways was nearly as satisfying, if not as hard-hitting, as the first. He contributed the title track, "The Wild Side of Town," and there were a couple of strong Hank Cochran originals thrown in for good measure. Two of his favorite tracks were a 1949 Elton Britt number he had learned from Yodeling Slim Clark, "Maybe I'll Cry Over You," and a tenderly highlighted version of the old Bessie Smith standard "Nobody Knows You When You're Down and Out," even if the accompaniment was a little schmaltzier, a little less "authentic" than he would have liked.

He returned to the road right after the session, playing Atlanta on Labor Day just one week later, but he barely made it through the show before collapsing backstage with what he would later term "a complete nervous breakdown." Once again he retreated to the woods, to the camp on Mattaseunk Lake, with just his dog, Honcho, for company. There was something elemental about the experience, living like he imagined his father must once have lived, living like the Native Americans, whom he had increasingly come to admire for their independence and ability to cope with whatever came their way, far from the worries and disquieting uncertainty of civilization—no electricity, no plumbing, no resources to depend upon but your own. Finally, in December, he was forced to return home, after a big snowstorm hit and threatened to shut off all avenues of escape. Several months later he started playing again, first in the little clubs where he would always remain a favorite, then back out on the road, where the drinking and the pills, the fears and the insecurities and his own inexplicable, and inexcusable, actions made him afraid and ashamed, most of all of himself.

His career didn't pick up again for another full year, and then only with the aid of an unlikely mentor. There were virtually no recording sessions, and just one single, the title track from his last album, *The Wild Side of Town*. In January of 1970, with his label ready to give up on him, he returned to Nashville for an abbreviated three-song session—but he went into the studio with new hope, a new plan, and a new direction, all from the same surprising source. Dick had just recently met Vaughn Horton, a rumpled fifty-eight-year-old songwriter and music-business insider whose songwriting credits included top pop, country, and r&b hits (he would be elected to the Nashville Songwriters Hall of Fame later that year)—but he was well aware of his reputation, and the older man wasted no time in telling Dick that he had been a fan of his, too, ever since Dick recorded Horton's Sons of the Pioneers classic, "Teardrops in My Heart," on his first Tower album.

Despite their apparent differences, the two men immediately clicked. Horton was a canny, self-assured industry veteran whose brother Roy, with whom he had started off as a New York–based hillbilly duo, oversaw the country catalogue of Peer-Southern, one of the largest song publishers in the country. (The company's founder, Ralph Peer, had discovered and recorded both Jimmie Rodgers and the Carter Family and had all their songs in his catalogue.) For all of his experience, or perhaps because of it, Horton, one of eleven children of a Pennsylvania coal miner, possessed a healthy skepticism of the usual music-business bromides, and he seemed taken not just with Dick's talent but with his roving intelligence and intellectual curiosity.

What he had never understood, he told Dick, was Capitol's failure to follow up on Dick's initial success, but in his view it was not too late, and he had a surefire way to do it. In fact, he said, he was surprised that it had never occurred to Dick or the record company before. Truck-driving songs had been around for a good while now, but with all the new CB lingo and the increasing identification of the trucker as the "last American cowboy," Vaughn Horton was betting that the trucker mystique could only pick up. And he was just as certain that Dick, with his deep voice and rugged good looks, not to mention the enduring popularity of his one and only hit, "Tombstone Every Mile," couldn't miss in this rapidly expanding field. With that in mind he brought in one song, "Big Wheel Cannonball," a 1967 trucker rewrite of Roy Acuff's "Wabash Cannonball," to Dick's truncated January session, then another, "Drag 'Em Off the Interstate, Sock It to 'Em, J.P. Blues," to a follow-up session in April. And true to his promise, over the next ten months both became Top 30 hits, and both would be prominently featured on his next LP, *Hard, Hard Traveling Man*, which included a remake of "Tombstone," a cover of Dave Dudley's signature truck-driving song, "Six Days on the Road," and another honky-tonkish Vaughn Horton original, simply entitled "Truck Stop."

It never occurred to me to ask Dick whether he had any misgivings about taking on such a self-limiting role—well, I suppose it occurred to me, but it wasn't a question I felt comfortable asking. In speaking of his trucking hits, he seemed genuinely proud of their success, and if he had any doubts about abandoning some of the scope of his musical ambitions, he never expressed them. It may simply have been that he was grateful just to be given another chance in a world that he thought had been permanently closed to him. And the songs were certainly clever enough—good-humored, professional, as it turned out both well sung and well received. But perhaps more to the point, he was taken with Vaughn Horton, the impressiveness of the man, the breadth of his knowledge, his sure sense of himself both within and outside of the country music community. And Vaughn was the first person in the business in such a long time to give him unqualified approval, to take him under his wing and be willing to do everything in his power to make him a success. It wasn't just a matter of recording Vaughn's material—they talked about life, and the music business, and everything under the sun; he just loved listening to the older man talk. And when Vaughn spoke of the inequities of the Nashville pecking order, the unfairness of the way outsiders were treated, it all rang true, because Vaughn, too, was an outsider, he, too, had come here from somewhere else, and yet somehow he had managed to beat the system.

Pauline took a somewhat more dubious view. It wasn't that she didn't like Vaughn, or even that she doubted that Vaughn had her husband's best interests at heart. He was, she knew, a true friend. But he didn't recognize her husband's fundamental core of vulnerability, his intractable naïveté. "Dick was too [impressionable]. He didn't use his own common sense. If someone talked negative, Dick would take it literally. And, you know, Vaughn told Dick a lot of things, he was very critical of different people and players and the politics of it all, [how] it's not really done on your merits. Well, Vaughn could [handle that], but Dick took stuff like that very serious, and he would get down on Nashville because Vaughn was so negative on Nashville—because Vaughn said it, it was so. And then he would lose his trust."

As if to bear out her worst forebodings, Dick came home from Nashville in a terrible state in August of 1971. He had recorded just two songs, but one of them, "Darby's Castle," was by Kris Kristofferson, a virtual unknown to the world at large until Johnny Cash recorded his "Sunday Morning Coming Down" the previous summer and Janis Joplin had a number-one pop hit with "Me and Bobby McGee" several months later. Dick was so excited about the new song, it hadn't hit for anyone yet, he told her over the phone, and he had had a struggle persuading his new producer, George Richey, to let him record it. Pauline couldn't wait to hear it—and the first thing he did when he got home was to put it on the turntable. But somehow his mood had shifted since their telephone conversation, and when she told him how much she liked the song, he just got angry—he had obviously been drinking, and the more she told him how much she liked it, the angrier he got, until finally she got out of him what Vaughn had said. Evidently, when the two of them sat down and listened to the dub just before Dick left for home, Vaughn started talking about Nashville producers who didn't know what they were doing, and all these musicians who could play anything in the world but weren't really playing anything at all, they were just putting in their time. And Dick was just crushed. And after a while she stopped trying to mollify him. Because everything she said just made things worse. Until finally he struck out at her, in a way he never had before, and she became fearful of him in a way she never had before. And she ran out of the house, scared for her life, she ran out into the driving rain, her feet sliding all over the place in the mud, and all she could think was, "I'm done, Lord. If he lives, or if he dies, he's all yours." She was certain she would never go back, this just was no way to live—but in the end she gave in when he promised, once again, he would stop drinking, he would get help, he knew he needed help, and he called the doctor at Togus, but then he only went once because he said the guy's office was so claustrophobic, you felt like you were locked up in a closet. So he came home, and his uncle helped him dry out, and he stopped drinking just like he promised he would, and life went on much as before.

O N LABOR DAY WEEKEND the following year, he and Vaughn Horton put on the first annual Truck Drivers Jamboree in Wheeling through a production company they had formed together. They presented an all-star lineup, including such trucker favorites as Red Sovine, Red Simpson, and Dave Dudley, along with a crack Nashville session band to play behind all the acts and back Dick on a live album to be produced by Big Wheel Productions for release on Capitol. It featured all of Dick's recent truck-driving hits, including his not-yet-released "Chick Inspector," which Vaughn had written for him, but it also included an assortment of such personal favorites as Josh White's jaunty "Evil Hearted Me" and a beautiful, soulful version of the country, blues, and pop standard "(Look Down)

That Lonesome Road." The album would go on to sell well, and Dick continued to have midlevel Top 40 country hits, while remaining true to his vow of staying sober for the rest of 1972. But then it all came to a crashing halt in Malta, Montana, on New Year's Eve.

Malta was a place where he would always go when he wanted to escape from humdrum reality, "go out there with them cowboys and Indians and just roar. I mean, just flat get out of it. You could belly up to the bar with those guys, and they could care less [who] you were, they took you for what you were as a person, and we'd do it up right. You know, we had some awful times!" He should have known better, obviously, but it was a booking, and he had remained sober for well over a year, but then when he got out there and he saw old friends, he smelled it, like it used to smell, the liquor, and someone offered him a drink, and he said, "No, thank you, I better not," and then he took a sip, "one little sip, in a champagne glass," and it was as if the whole last year had never happened, "I took that one little drink, and it kicked me right in again. I was sneaking it at first, but finally I'm right back where I was, I had to have two fifths of vodka every day, half a fifth when I got up, half a fifth during the day, the other one was at night. And that was just to live."

In many ways he could rationalize that it was no more than a continuation of the life he had been living for so many years, the product of an ungovernable, unruly nature that he no longer could see the point in trying to control. ("We had a nice home in town, all the neighbors around me were professional people, but I was [still] sowing my wild oats.") But then one night he was awakened by the sound of Pauline's screams, and he found his hand wrapped around her throat. He had been experiencing what he described to himself as "little blackouts," finding himself in his office down the street and not knowing how he got there, little things you could ignore or pass off as forgetfulness—but this time there were no excuses to be made, people could see in him what they wanted to see, but he alone knew the monster he had become. "I begged the Lord, I didn't know Jesus then, but I begged God, 'Please let me die.'" And then Pauline was gone. It was summertime, and he was all alone, except for Pauline's brother Charlie, who he was later told stayed with him through it all.

"I could feel the air in the room around my body, I could feel the air going down. I said, 'Oh, this ain't too bad, it's like going to sleep, it's all right.' And He put me right down, I went right down into the blackest black, and now I'm there and I'm bound, I've got no body, but I'm bound, and I can't move. I'm all alone, and there's nothing. Complete silence and complete black, black, black. I can't emphasize that any more. I'm all alone. So, boy, I started begging. 'If this is it, God, I don't want no part of this. If you spare my life, I'll go back, I'll go back and change my life, I'll make it up to the ones that I've hurt. I do love them, I do. Give me a chance,' I pleaded — it seems like it was for years, [it seemed] like an eternity. But He kept me. I kept begging and praying, and pleading, and finally I came out of it, they said it was like three to five days. And when I woke up, I said, 'Whoa, man, He listened!'"

That, for Dick, was where everything started, and when Pauline was finally persuaded to return, he started trying to make amends. But it wasn't over — he knew it could never be over, for him, or anyone whose life he had touched. For Pauline, it was almost beyond endurance. However much she loved him, however far they had come, and however far they would travel together over the next twenty years, she could never — *they* could never — altogether escape the consequences of the path he had gone down. "My heart ached for him. Because I knew he threw away a beautiful career. He let the garbage consume him." But for Dick — for them both — in the end there could be no other way of thinking about it, really, other than as the start of a new life.

PROMISED LAND

DICK HAD BOUGHT an eighty-acre property two years earlier not far from the house on Silver Road, but until now he hadn't given much thought to moving in. He had acquired a couple of railroad cars from the Bangor & Aroostook line in 1972 — a snowplow that went back to 1905 and a passenger car that was exactly like the train they had ridden down on from Fort Fairfield in 1940 — and since then he had acquired a boxcar, another passenger car, and a caboose, all sitting on a set of tracks that he had extended off a nearby trunk line. He thought he would like to farm the property — raise chickens and beef cattle, it would make a marvelous place to stable his daughter Terry's twenty-eight-year-old palomino, Sugarfoot. And it would certainly fit with his idea of living off the land, going back to a time that was more like it was when he was growing up in Fort Fairfield and his dad and Emery were operating steam shovels and going into the woods not just to commune with nature but to hunt for food to put on the table. But then it suddenly struck him with the force of a revelation: this could be his opportunity to start to make amends. He didn't need to go back in time — that was a pipe dream. What he was going to do was to build a theme park, a family entertainment center, a little along the lines of the Carmel Auto Rest Park, where he and the Trail Riders used to play, but different in that this would bring together some of the most important elements of his life: trains, music, nature, and social justice. And it would be there for the whole community to enjoy.

He had it all mapped out by the time they moved out to the farm in 1974. The train cars were already in place, but he still needed to get Pauline's permission. He needed to be sure that she was okay not just with the whole concept but with the fact that some of the plans they had made for remodeling the house and creating the kind of comfort that he had always wanted to give her would have to be deferred. That was fine, she told him, as he knew she would. What she didn't tell him was how worried she was about the finances — she didn't think he had any idea how much it was going to cost to get this project off the ground. They were already in debt for the railroad track and cars — by now he had plans for a whole Western town, and he had located a station house that he was hoping to buy in order to re-create an old train depot. He got a good price on an old 1949 American LaFrance fire truck in working condition, and he was working on a model logging operation with a steam sawmill. In addition to which, he had plans for an Indian village, which the local Penobscot tribe ("We're working hard to get some of their land back, to preserve their rights," he declared in his official publicity biography, "you wouldn't believe the injustices that have been done them") had agreed to help out on. To Dick this would be the centerpiece of the park, with a pond he had dug next to the village for them to display the ways in which they used their canoes. Pauline was racked with worry — she just felt like once again Dick was getting into something he didn't fully understand. But it was all so *real* to him, and by now he had been dropped by his record company — she just didn't have the heart to voice her objections.

In 1975 he almost died. The stomach problems with which he had been afflicted for almost twenty-five years now had gotten so bad that he was eating baking soda right out of the box, but when he went in for the operation, he was certain that he was going to be all right. Otherwise, why would he have been spared? "I was full of ulcers that were ready to perforate," he said. "That's why my headaches were so bad. Then my left lung collapsed, and I almost died on the table—they took out the gallbladder and the appendix at the same time" and in effect made him a new stomach. When he finally got out of the hospital, the leaves were coming off the trees, and he had lost fifty-five pounds, but he never wavered in his belief. "And when I came home, a little voice says to me, 'Now I want you to sit down and learn and know my word.' Just like that. A little, small voice. A truck driver's wife gave me a Living Bible, and that opened up the whole world to me." For the next nine months he and Pauline studied that Bible every day, stripped of the "begots" and "begats," just focusing on the underlying message of salvation.

Then in the bicentennial summer of 1976 he had a painter come out to work on the train—he had decided to paint the railroad cars red white and blue, even though Pauline kept reminding him that they could barely pay their bills. The painter was an old friend ("I used to drink and roar with him years ago"), but there was something different about him now. Dick could tell from his countenance that he didn't drink anymore, in fact, he told Dick, he had cured himself, didn't go through the DTs, or anything—"and that got my attention. I [had to] tell him, 'I don't know how I'm going to pay you. I'm not working. But I know I'm going to.' So we contracted it. And all the while he's down there doing the train, him and Ray, his helper—Ray was seventy-something at the time, and on his little paint cover it said, 'I love Jesus, Jesus loves me'—all the while they were [working], I was down there bugging them about the word, I'm *hungry* for the word, and they're explaining Scriptures to me. Then one day I'm down there, and my friend said, 'It's right under your nose, Curless. All you have to do is—Do you believe in Jesus?' And I said, 'Yes.' 'Do you believe He died for you and rose again?' 'Yes.' 'Do you believe in eternal life?' 'Yes.' 'Well, what's so difficult, then?' he said. 'What's so difficult about you accepting him into your life, and getting on with your life? If you can do that with your alcoholism—you licked that—why can't you—' I said, 'Because it's a very serious thing. I got to make sure if I make the decision that I'm going to live up to it.' He said, 'It's right under your nose, Curless. All you got to do is confess and let Him come into your heart.'"

And that was just the way it happened. He was lying in bed with Pauline—the date, August 3, would be forever etched in his memory—and all of a sudden he *knew*. It was like when a drink of wine goes down you, that first taste, "you've been in the desert for five days, and that drink of wine goes down, and you can feel it going all the way down, all warm, and

I'm going, 'Oh my God, dear God, Jesus, thank you.' I didn't think I could take it anymore. It kept coming — and it was the sweetest, most gorgeous feeling. I didn't want to tell Pauline. I didn't want to move a muscle. I became selfish. I said, 'Gee, I'm going to lose it if I turn to tell her. I don't believe I'm going to be able to handle all this.' It probably lasted a minute or so, but I was like a wet rag when that came through me, and then I looked over, and Pauline said, 'What ails you?' And I told her, and she grinned, because she *knew*." She knew, because she had been trying to tell him this very thing since early summer. She had had the same feeling, the same revelation — but every time she tried to tell him, he would get angry, as if, as if — she just didn't know — as if he just wasn't ready yet. So she kept it to herself and secretly took out their marriage certificate and renewed her wedding vows, by herself. And then when he told her, she was as happy for him as she had ever been in her life, she was just happy for the new person he had become.

For Dick, it not only marked the turning point of his life, it gave him the signs and the signals that he had been craving, without knowing it, since the first song he ever sang on stage, "Lovesick Blues," at the North Brookfield town hall. There would never be a time when he felt he reached the end of his journey — it was, he knew, a path you were on for as long as you were on this earth, filling your lungs with air, delivering the gift that had been given to you with your music. "That's where it started," Dick said. That was when he first recognized his music for what it was, for what it had always been: learning and growing songs that were real, learning and growing songs that as often as not reflected suffering and pain, learning and growing songs that represented life itself.

COUNTRY CARAVAN

HIS CAREER AT THIS POINT was almost entirely confined to the still-bustling (but increasingly cash-starved) New England country circuit. He continued to do both radio and television, even hosting a short-lived *Dick Curless Summer Show* on Bangor television in 1978. He was getting a lot of local commercial work, too, both radio and television, including ads for Howard Johnson's, General Tire, and Nissan/Datsun, for whom he cut a series of jingles in Nashville with an all-star session band. He was particularly proud of his work for Alcoa aluminum, briefly becoming a kind of "national spokesman" in an award-winning series of television and radio spots. One of the most important lessons he had learned long ago from Arthur Godfrey was, "Know your product," and he did — many of the products he sold, he used himself, and he could reel off with conviction the pluses of every brand he was selling. The one thing he would not do were ads for smoking or drinking.

He formed an alliance with Dave Dudley and Red Sovine, originators of two of the most popular trucker hits, in a doomed campaign to clean up trucker music and go back to the "knights of the road" image he had always admired. And he was enjoying life vicariously through his kids. Ricky, who had played drums with him off and on from the age of eleven or twelve, and had come off the road to help out while he was recuperating from his operation, had moved to Nashville in 1982 with his wife, Tina Welch, a teenage sensation on the New England country scene, and Dick kept urging his daughter, Terry, and her husband, Bill Chinnock, to follow suit. Bill was a talented singer-songwriter from New Jersey (he had moved to Maine in the mid- '70s because of his newfound love for country music) with vast rock, country, and blues ambitions. His early bands on the Jersey shore had included what would become the nucleus for Bruce Springsteen's E Street Band, and his first two albums had been produced under the aegis first of Springsteen's discoverer, John Hammond, and then of consummate Atlantic Records engineer and producer (Ray Charles, Aretha Franklin, John Coltrane, Eric Clapton) Tom Dowd. Although in many ways Dick and his new son-in-law could not have been more different, to Terry's delight they became fast friends (the only way she could explain it was that Bill seemed drawn to Dick's sensitivity, Dick to Bill's assured sense of purpose), and in fact Dick became so convinced that there was a future for his son-in-law in Nashville that he got in touch with Harold Bradley, the legendary Nashville session player (with his even more legendary brother, Owen, he had helped build Nashville's first studio on Music Row), who had been the leader on Dick's last series of Nashville sessions as well as the recent Datsun commercials. Terry and Bill moved to Nashville in 1984, and Bill made his first "country-rock" album, *Rock & Roll Cowboys*, which, as the Nashville *Tennessean* described it, "fuse[d] his East Coast 'street' songwriting attitude with the crisp production of Nashville veteran Harold Bradley."

I think this must have been around the time I first met Dick in passing at Alan's Truckstop in Amesbury, Massachusetts, where Arkansas rockabilly stalwart Sleepy LaBeef had been playing regularly ever since his bus burned up on the Maine Turnpike. Prior to that, I had seen Dick a number of times over the years, at the Hillbilly Ranch next to the Trailways bus station in Boston and the Indian Ranch in Webster, Massachusetts, close to where Dick had grown up, very likely at one of the Country Music Showers of Stars that WCOP, Boston's country station, put on in the '60s, or any one of the dimly lit clubs and bars that dotted the local country landscape. Dick was a given on that landscape, an accomplished performer who always went over well with his fans — but I can't say that I ever picked up on the depth of his music, or the feeling that informed it. I can still remember the extravagant terms of admiration and respect, though, with which Sleepy, a mountain of a man with a reverence for history as well as a genuine appreciation for human difference, introduced Dick to me — it might even have caused a blush to come to the cheek of this strangely shy, almost reticent man, who with his cowboy hat stood nearly as tall as Sleepy's six foot six — but I'm sorry to say it went right by me. Dick was as charming as ever that night, the audience loved him as he served up all his truck-driving hits and showed his fans the kind of respect that Yodeling Slim Clark had taught him what must have seemed a lifetime ago. With his deferential manner and the kind of shy stammer that kept his deep voice from ever becoming overbearing — his spoken introductions alone created a bond of intimacy between performer and audience — for all of that, the show for me was just that, a *show,* and I'd like to be able to say I'm not sure whether it was him or me.

To give myself the benefit of the doubt, part of it, I suppose, may have had to do with his own uncertainty about his place in the world at this point. He was, certainly, secure in his faith — or as secure as anyone who is a constant seeker of truth can ever be. And yet he was still floundering, stuck in Maine, with no real sense of direction or safe harbor in sight. He was waiting for God to use him, it seemed — but, as Pauline couldn't help but remind him, if God had a plan for him, it had yet to be revealed. "I'd say, 'How can you be up here in Maine and make a [living]?'" They treated him like a hometown boy, she told him with more than a degree of asperity. The local clubs — not just in Maine, all over New England — couldn't afford to pay him what he was worth, and even if they could, Dick was always giving breaks to old friends, making sure they came out okay even if he had to walk away without any real money for himself. "How can you be up here and know what's going on?" she said to him almost angrily at times. "These people don't have a clue." But it was who he was comfortable with. He was back with the people he knew.

He had given up on the idea of the family entertainment center by now. The model logging operation, the Indian village, the train depot were all finished. He had run into zoning problems, and though his lawyer advised him that there were legitimate grounds for appeal, all the wind seemed to have gone out of his sails. From Pauline's point of view it was a relief—with all of his health problems, how could he ever have sustained the work that would be necessary to build an enterprise of this sort, let alone the money and the worries? Because he continued to be afflicted with debilitating attacks of illness. He drove down to Wheeling at the beginning of 1983 as one of the first fifty country music luminaries to be honored by the brand-new WWVA Walkway of the Stars. He hadn't been feeling well for some time, but it was important to him to be there. But then when they arrived, he couldn't even get out of the black Suburban he and Pauline had driven down in. The doctors in Wheeling couldn't figure out what was wrong with him, so they transferred him to Pittsburgh, and it looked like he was going to be stuck there for a long time until Jim Sutton at WABI, who had gotten him the Alcoa ads, organized a rescue operation and got him back to the VA hospital in Togus. There, after an extensive series of tests, it was determined that the muscle relaxant the doctors had had him on for the last five years to help him digest his food was supposed to have been taken only on a short-term basis. It was only when he got off it that he finally started to feel better for the first time in years.

But he still had no clear sense of where he was heading. For all of his certainty that he had found a true spiritual home, he felt no closer to understanding how best to employ his earthly gifts. Sometimes it seemed as if his faith could almost get in his way. "I was so overzealous I drove people from me. I was so happy, I just wanted to share it [with everyone], and friends of mine, even my son couldn't figure it out—I just drove them right from me." Other people, Pauline felt, just tried to take advantage of him in his newfound Christianity. "He's a very emotional person, and they *used* his emotions, they'd have him almost crying," she said—to get things out of him that he couldn't afford, financially or emotionally, until finally she had to be the bad guy and step in. And all the while she was trying to get him motivated to go down and visit the kids in Nashville, to see what it was like down there, "to bounce him back and get him going again." To get him back to what he loved most. The music.

Dick and Pauline. *Courtesy of Terry Curless Chinnock/Richard Weize — . . . and more bears*

Then one night he was lying in bed listening to the Opry, "and I'm eating my heart out, thinking, 'Gee, I really miss that, you know?'" And all of a sudden he heard the announcer, Charlie Douglas, interviewing some other old-timers that he knew, and they were talking about this organization, R.O.P.E., Reunion of Professional Entertainers, that had just been formed, and you had to have twenty-five years in the business to be a member. And somehow, for some reason, that was what finally struck the spark. Terry and Bill had been calling him from Nashville ever since they arrived, telling him that everyone still remembered him. "Come on, Dad," Terry said. "They all ask about you." And Pauline had been after him for as long as he could remember. But it was his own recognition of how much he missed it that finally did the trick.

They went down to visit in February of 1984, and he looked up the R.O.P.E. people and saw that they were putting on a show, and who should he run into but Smokey Rogers, who was MCing the evening? He had originally met Smokey, always the kindest of friends, and the author of "Gone," among a number of enduring country standards, when he first went out to California and played Smokey's club in El Cajon. Smokey immediately called out his name and invited him to sing a song, and afterwards they all sat around and reminisced. "I mean, they hadn't seen me in a long time. They all think I'm still drinking—they haven't heard anything from me, and they think I'm still the same old Curless, but I haven't [had a] drink for ten years. So I got up and bared my soul. These are all my peers that I'm talking to—Mac Wiseman and Jack Greene and Hillous Butrum and George Morgan's brother Bill, all great people. And gee, I'm glad to be back. And I'm hugging people that I never could hug before. It's a marvelous, marvelous turnaround in my life."

Later that night Smokey sought him out and told him how good it was to see him again, that he had thought of him often, and Dick asked if there might be a place for him on the show, which had recently begun traveling under the banner of promoter Bill Boynton as the Country Gold Caravan. Smokey told him they didn't have anything right now, but there was a showcase coming up in New Orleans in the fall, if he could wait that long. "Man, I hung on to that string from February to that fall, and I went down to New Orleans [just] to get some work. There was a bunch of us on the show—Smokey was the MC—and they said, 'We like what you do.' And I've been with them ever since [ten years, as of 1994], tour[ing] every spring and fall."

That was the change he had been waiting for. He and Pauline moved to Nashville and moved in with Terry and Bill, who were renting the downstairs apartment of a large white-stucco mansion on a wooded estate overlooking the city. It was owned by a retired military man who just took to Dick from the start, and before long he and Pauline began visiting Lieutenant Colonel Beasley and his wife at their other home on Ten Mile Lake in Minnesota. There was plenty of room in the apartment for Dick and Pauline—it was a welcome return to family living—but living with the Beasleys was like acquiring a whole new family, too, with the new tenants invited to enjoy the full run of the house. Nashville was a wonderful home base for travel, and their life quickly settled into Nashville in the winter, Maine in the summertime, with the road a constant that never got old. This was the life he had originally signed up for. There was nothing on earth he would rather do.

He and Pauline drove from gig to gig in the Suburban. They took turns driving, and many nights they slept in the car. Ricky had outfitted it for them with a makeshift bed, and they had a little TV. Dick's bags were piled up in the back, his boots and hatboxes and guitars and all his costumes — but even with all that clutter, Pauline said, "I had things organized so we always had room to get in the bed! We laughed [about it], we never complained, we made do, [because] what we were doing was worthy of it." There were some lean times, to be sure, but they were *good* times, and it was, said Pauline with a laugh, a kind of adventure. "We enjoyed all our trips. We knew each other's needs. We could drive along and talk for hours, or we could say nothing at all." It was hard on Dick, no question about it. His health, never better than precarious, required constant vigilance. Pauline was the only one who knew what he was feeling, what he was going through. "I was always protecting him. We couldn't stay with people. He had to have his privacy. But he knew that I would be there for him. And he was at peace, doing what he wanted to do. These were the best years of our lives."

He took over as MC when Smokey Rogers got sick and couldn't do it anymore. Not long afterward, a war broke out within the company, and Dick was devastated to hear words spoken and roiling emotions expressed that he could never have imagined lay beneath the placid surface. For a time it looked like his own position with the troupe might be threatened, but he kept his feelings as much as possible to himself, and in 1992 went to Branson, Missouri, with a revamped version of the show, now known as the Shower of Stars. (Branson was the place where big country music stars of the recent past, from Roy Clark to Ray Stevens, Glen Campbell, and pop singers like Wayne Newton and Andy Williams, purchased their own theaters and created a profitable year-round sit-down gig for themselves.) Branson proved a little disappointing, with morning performances and limited pay, and Dick wasn't feeling that well anyway, but they took the show out on the road, too, and met receptive audiences everywhere.

He never lost his ambition, but it was a different kind of ambition now. It no longer centered around dreams of stardom, there was no longer any thought of molding himself to public demand — he was focused now on saying what he had to say, communicating his own message, not a Christian message exclusively, though that certainly entered into it, but the broad, humanistic message that the songs he had been singing and writing from early childhood on conveyed. Music was the most effective way he had found to deliver that message. Music remained the single most reliable source of uplift in his life. There was always music, with his son, his son-in-law, his brother — his mother always had a tape recorder running whenever he visited, and some of the most wonderful moments came from just sitting around the kitchen table, picking and singing, just as they always had.

The two albums that he made during this time reflect that rediscovered sense of ease. The first, *Welcome to My World,* cut in Norway for the Rocade label, is almost entirely "unplugged" and, in the absence of drums, presents a program of deeply felt traditional songs driven by Dick's own distinctive rhythm guitar. The other, *It's Just a Matter of Time,* was self-produced a couple of years later in Nashville and stands as Dick's loving tribute to Smokey Rogers, with half the album devoted to Rogers' songs. And while it is certainly more commercial-minded (Dick used his friend Mel Tillis' band, plus guitarist Jerry Reed), it conveys no less a sense of intimacy, as Dick returns again and again to the stylistic mark that had always set him apart — his unique ability (paralleled only to my mind by Bobby "Blue" Bland) to "croon" the blues. Both albums offer eloquent testimony to Dick's renewed embrace of the music that he had always loved. Both convey the sense of a man who is doing his best to find his way home. On *Welcome to My World,* he recorded his version of "Tragic Romance," the song Emery Fields had taught him when he was growing up — "I finally got it right!" And when he played it for Emery at an outdoor show, "I made him stand up, and I said, 'This is for the man who taught me how to play the E chord,' and gee, he just come apart."

He was confident of himself now in a new way, he was confident of the truth that his music expressed — but he still couldn't always embrace himself in the way that he had learned to embrace others. He couldn't help but be haunted by things he had done, people he had hurt, actions for which he had not taken responsibility at the time. They haunted Pauline, too. She knew that he was trying, he was doing all that he could, but that didn't always ease the hurt. And yet it was as if, Pauline said almost wonderingly, when you were in Dick's warm, enveloping presence, you couldn't help but be persuaded of his innocence. It served, unwittingly, to protect him, it covered up so much of what he was feeling, from everyone but himself. "I mean, he could be up there giving testimony, saying, 'I've done this, but I've changed my life around, and you look at me now in a different light' — but all the time he's trying to ease his own pain. I mean, his life had changed, and beautifully, but — I know him — there was still a lot that he was trying to justify. I think it balanced out pretty good," she says with a sorrowful shrug, "but there was still a lot within him that he was trying to make right and do right. I think it would have come to completion if there had been more time."

TRAVELING THROUGH

IT WAS AROUND THIS TIME, in the summer of 1994, that Dick got in touch with Rounder Records, with the ostensible purpose of ordering a videotape, and my son, Jake, intercepted the call. A flurry of letters and phone calls ensued. Dick sent the five-song demo tape that provided the template for the album, and there was an exchange of ideas for other songs to fill out the album. In several instances, Jake's suggestions were not only well within the range of what Dick would feel comfortable singing (that was the whole idea) but turned out to be songs that were already in his repertoire. Classic "heart" songs like Eddy Arnold's "I'll Hold You in My Heart (Till I Can Hold You in My Arms)" and "Many Tears Ago" should perhaps have come as no surprise, but Lefty Frizzell's bleak, late-period "I Never Go Around Mirrors" definitely did. Dick brought in a couple of originals, one of his own, a long-promised tribute to his mother, still very much alive (it was intended as a belated bookend to "When Dad Was Around"), and one by his son-in-law, Bill Chinnock, written a few years earlier especially for him. Perhaps the biggest eye-opener, though, was his instantaneous response to Chris Gaffney's "King of the Blues." I don't think Dick had ever heard it before, but as he listened to its painful lyrics ("I see a man whose face / Shows the trace / Of where his life has been / I see the telltale signs of bitterness setting in"), he seemed already to have committed them to memory, and after just one listen told Jake he was the guy in the song.

Dick immediately hit it off with thirty-one-year-old guitarist Duke Levine, a match for any of the most accomplished Nashville guitar pickers in both talent and taste, who quickly assumed the role of band leader. Duke in turn had brought in a steel player friend of his from the Worcester area named Tim Bowles, whose father, Francis, it turned out, much to Dick's delight, had started out as "Chuck Owens" on the New England country music circuit not long after Dick, and would in fact eventually become a regular on radio station WARE, where Dick had made his debut on Yodeling Slim Clark's show in 1949. As if to complete the circle of coincidence, the lineup was filled out by a guitarist Dick had told Jake he was bringing down from Lewiston, Maine, named Denny Breau. This was Lenny Breau's nine-years-younger brother, but apart from his family lineage (everyone in the room knew who his brother was, but I'm not sure anyone else was familiar with his parents, Hal Lone Pine and Betty Cody) no one but Dick had any idea what to expect.

In the event, it instantly became apparent that Denny was a brilliant musician who could have played anything asked of him. But Dick made it plain to everyone from the start, including Denny, that Denny was here strictly to second Duke and to flavor the music, at Duke's suggestion, on acoustic guitar. And even when Duke offered him a lead on electric, it was almost as if he had to get a sign-off from Dick to accept the invitation.

At first it was unclear just why Dick had brought him, and I'm not sure it was even clear to Denny himself. Even though he had known him since childhood, Dick was a distant figure to Denny, and they had barely played together except at events like the Maine Country Music Pioneer Show, where Denny often supplied the band. Under other circumstances, one might have thought it was simply to make Dick more comfortable in an unfamiliar situation, and, of course, Denny was thoroughly conversant with the light, syncopated, Merle-Travis-via-Lenny-Breau style to which Dick had always been drawn. But in the end I think comfort had nothing to do with it. Dick wanted to provide Denny with an opportunity — there were lessons, he said, that Denny had to learn. Because Denny — and I'm going to paraphrase here to try to convey what Dick seemed to have unexpected difficulty articulating — Denny was the boy who, unlike Dick and his brother Lenny, had stayed home to play and sing with his family, he had never really ventured out into the world and been bruised by it, and there was a big part of Dick that admired him for that. But Denny had recently shown an interest in expanding his musical horizons, and he had expressed his disappointment to Dick when Chet Atkins, his brother Lenny's mentor and one of the chief architects of the Nashville sound, informed Denny that there was nothing he could do for him unless Denny came to Nashville and took his chances like everyone else. With this session Dick wanted to give him a glimpse of another kind of opportunity. He wanted to provide him with a different test of his resolve ("I haven't told this to Denny, and we've had some good talks") by putting him in with a musician like Duke and giving him a chance not just to shine but to share. "I wanted to plant in his mind to do what he loved best," Dick said. Whether that was to stay home and be with his family or take Chet Atkins up on his challenge, he needed to have a plan. Don't let life just toss you around like flotsam and jetsam upon a raging sea. He had a wonderful, original style of his own, Dick told him, but whatever you do, you want to have a plan, you need to have a kind of storyboard for your life.

THERE WAS NO QUESTION that everyone was excited from the start. But there was equally little question that, with the exception of Dick, everyone was a little nervous, too. It's hard to describe in a credible manner how swiftly, or how smoothly, he was able to defuse the situation, but he seemed to possess the ability to set even the most self-conscious of skeptics at ease with a manner made up in equal parts of self-confidence and self-effacement. All I can say is that I've never witnessed anything like it before or since, as he won over the musicians with a pep talk in his room (Long View Farm was a residential recording facility) before even entering the studio. He spoke to them quietly as he ran through the changes of "I Am a Pilgrim," the beautiful Merle Travis folk hymn that he had sung on the Arthur Godfrey show almost forty years ago. He had a pretty good idea of how he wanted to do it, certainly, and he established the lead right away with his own bluesy guitar, but then he discreetly solicited suggestions from each individual present, and gradually the song acquired a different kind of flow. A rehearsal scene like any other? Well, sure, I suppose. But what made it different — and this is where I get stuck, because it remains in memory so utterly unique — was the quiet *intensity* of the experience, the sense of immanence and intimacy that attached to it. I know, I know, it sounds corny, and I've got to admit I'm a little embarrassed to convey my own instantaneous emotional buy-in, but I'm going to take my cue from Dick and dispense with all the normal self-protective filters. It was as if, all of the musicians later agreed, Dick was singing privately to each and every one of them, whispering in their ear with such hypnotic familiarity that none of them could resist the lure of his song. "Oh, this is gonna be fun," said Dick at one point. And he was right.

The next day in the studio only confirmed his confidence. What was perhaps most surprising was not just how seamless the whole experience was, but how fearless it was, too. It was obvious how important this was to Dick—he made it clear that he saw it as some kind of summing-up—but on the other hand, there was no pressure either, no sense of having to deliver a particular kind of musical statement in a particular amount of time. Dick might take off on a verse or two of "Up a Lazy River," throw himself into an up-tempo version of the old Dixieland standard "Darktown Strutters Ball," which Dick rebranded as "Downtown Strutters Ball" ("We're gonna do a twist!" he announced exuberantly), introduce obscure titles by everyone from Grandpa Jones to Little Jimmy Dickens, turn to a thoughtful Tom T. Hall composition or an uninhibited Elton Britt yodel. The aim was never perfection, it was always *surprise*.

Soon everyone had nicknames. Duke was Dukey-Do to Dick's own occasional Dickie-Do. The bass player, Mudcat, was already Mudcat, of course, and Denny, like his brother before him, became Sonny. "Oh, you guys got me sittin' in a great big rocking chair," he would say appreciatively from time to time to one and all. "I'm just so proud of you guys."

Dick never tried to hide the fact that he was ill—though just how ill he was I'm not sure he knew himself. His bedroom was right off the studio, and it became apparent right away that he would need frequent rests. But this only served to heighten the sense of emotional commitment. From Jake's point of view the trick (and "trick" is a misnomer, really, for a process that was so purely translucent) was to capture "that magical moment where the band had just gotten the song down, and Dick, who knew every song inside out, was not losing momentum." And that's what happened again and again—over the course of nearly thirty songs. There was no barrier to direct emotional expression. "At the end of some of the cuts," Denny said, "we'd all just sit there, with Dick's last chord ringing in the air and everyone practically in tears, and Dick would just say, 'Okay, time to go to bed now.'"

D URING BREAKS IN THE STUDIO, or in the evening in his room, Dick would tell stories not just about the songs he was singing but about the forgotten world from which the songs came. There were tales of Lefty Frizzell and Hawkshaw Hawkins and Wynn Stewart, he loved to tell the story of how Lenny Breau had used a coat hanger to get the sound that legendary steel player Bud Isaacs had achieved on his pioneering pedal steel recordings. "Remember," he would say, as if everyone in the room shared the same memory pool, which by now to all intents and purposes they did, "we just gotta get the feeling right."

In all of those quietly beguiling conversations, Dick's voice rarely rises above a whisper, but when he opens his mouth to sing, the room is filled with a flood of sound. Even the musicians are transfixed. Studio veterans all, they simply forget what they are doing sometimes, and then with a mixture of admiration and embarrassment are forced to apologize. It doesn't faze Dick a bit. He gets lost in the music, too, he admits. "You guys are so good," he says, "you got *me* drifting off." And you get the feeling as Dick plays to them, as he croons to them, eyes closed, head thrown back, his expression beatific, that he feels somehow in the innermost part of his being he is telling them something that for some reason they were simply unaware they already knew.

On "Since I Met You Jesus" he asks for it explicitly. The song is the old Ivory Joe Hunter blues, "Since I Met You Baby," but, merely by the insertion of a single word, with an unequivocal spiritual twist. It is always a high point of his live show, he explains, with room for everyone in the band to solo; it is, in a sense, a kind of spiritual offering, and it works every time. So why don't they just listen to it on the run-through, see if they don't get inspired, and then just play whatever they feel.

There is a certain amount of consternation among the musicians at first. The drummer and bass player, Billy Conway and Mudcat Ward, do not see themselves as soloists, and even the guitarists and steel player seem a little taken aback. But Dick is not about to give up. "Just give me what's in there," Dick coaxes them. "Oh, that's good," he says encouragingly to each of the players in turn, and while the song is actually being recorded, there is a point of such stillness, a moment of such utter lostness and tranquility, that it makes you want to cry. Even when they are done and everyone is listening back to his part, Dick still is not through. "Oh, gosh," he says sincerely, and not for the first time either, *"you guys are something else."*

I don't have any doubt that this quality comes through on record. If you listen to the songs carefully, you will discover that each one is constructed in layers, every one yields hidden meanings. Like any great singer, Dick Curless can't help but give a virtuoso performance, but here the focus is not on the notes, and Dick knows it. "We're here to confuse everybody," Dick says contentedly at one point. "You never know what's coming out." At the end of the session, though clearly exhausted, he still has nothing but encouragement to offer, even as the room fills up with ghosts. There is the Tumbleweed Kid and Yodeling Slim Clark, Big Phil

At Longview Farm, with Peter, Jake, and Nina Guralnick. *Courtesy of Nina Guralnick*

Curless and Emery Fields, a whole vanished tradition, an America that is something more than nostalgia and warmed-over apple pie. It may seem incongruous to some that country music, which has been built into a national industry with Nashville as its manufacturing base, should originate in Maine, too, should connect with an Acadian tradition that never made the journey south. But music has no geographical locus, perhaps country music and the blues least of all, and all you have to do to understand that fact is to listen to the music with your eyes closed and your judgment unimpeded. As Dick said to Denny Breau toward the end of the session, "You know, Denny, it's not really where you go, it's who opens the door."

When the album was finished, there was a sense of almost palpable relief, as if, without ever acknowledging it to ourselves or each other, we had all been holding our breath, not really sure if the results could bear the burden of the emotional expectation. And when they did, there was a sense of unequivocal elation. There was much talk of getting together again soon, as everyone gathered for picture taking in front of the barn, and Dick tried to teach Riley, the Long View Farm dog, to harmonize on "Old MacDonald," as Honcho had for years over the Bangor and Bakersfield airwaves. The one thing that everyone was certain of was that they would all be getting together again for the tour at the end of the summer when the album was scheduled to be released.

Dick listened to the tapes of the album over and over again at home — there were about two dozen roughs, and Pauline couldn't keep from crying when she listened to some of them. "He was so excited about it. He couldn't stop talking about it. He was like a young kid — he was singing it, he was living it, he was feeling every word."

He was operated on again just after Christmas, but by the time I went to see him at the end of February he seemed pretty much recovered. He was full of plans for the future. A new home entertainment center. Another European tour once the album came out. "This is going to be our quality time now, Ducky," he told Pauline. "I've done what I had to do." Visiting him in the rambling old farmhouse, on Ohio Street at the railroad tracks, was like encountering yet another manifestation of the adventurous spirit that had revealed itself in the studio. This was Dick as passionate historian and ethnomusicologist, with a yard full of old railroad cars crammed with business files, personal archives, antique furniture, and memorabilia that went back to the beginning of his career. Dick gave me a fat file bursting with stories and clippings, documenting nearly every phase of his life, with a number of the articles displaying small handwritten notations that sought not to soften the story but merely to correct some names and dates for the record.

There are two clippings that he pointed to with particular pride, each describing the ceremony that took place in the building that housed his old high school in Gilbertville, where, on his last birthday, he had finally received his high school diploma. He had earned his GED in Nashville and gotten all his records together, but it took his old principal, Ed O'Connor, who had gone on to become superintendent of schools before retiring, to get an official seal of approval. "In the late spring of 1950, Richard came to my office and informed me that he was leaving school to play in a band," O'Connor reminisced for an audience that included a dozen classmates and one or two old teachers. "I said, 'Richard, hang on for a few weeks, then go with this band.' He said, 'Sorry, Mr. O'Connor, this is the chance of a lifetime.'"

"This is a wonderful, wonderful birthday present," Dick said, announcing that he was going to make a copy of the diploma right away and present it to his eighty-year-old mother. "I can hear Mama now," he said. "'Sixty-two years old, and he's just coming in with his diploma. Where did I go wrong?'" Then he reminisced with his classmates and led the group in singing "America" and the old Hardwick High School anthem, before seating himself on a stool and singing and recalling the wonderful life they had all had growing up, and the difficulties he had contended with for so long after coming back from Korea. "I just couldn't figure things out," he told them, until, finally, he was saved. Everyone feasted on jelly beans and coffee, as he sang "Sentimental Journey" for his old homeroom teacher, Miss Kelleher, and "When Dad Was Around," which he dedicated to Mr. O'Connor.

In March he went out on an eight-day tour of the Midwest with Melba Montgomery and Country Music Hall of Fame member Bill Anderson. Pauline didn't want him to go, he just wasn't well enough, but he was determined to do it and in the end he went out on his own. He was drained when he got home and about a week later went back into the hospital, missing the annual Maine Country Music Pioneer Show, a remarkable panorama of seventy years of Maine country music history, which had already in essence been dedicated to him. It was a remarkable show, with Denny Breau's mother, seventy-three-year-old Yodeling Betty Cody, one of the highlights, and the tributes to Dick from the stage growing ever more emotional.

In the hospital, Dick continued to make plans for the future, if on a somewhat reduced scale. He had Pauline go out and get him a table, so that he would be able to sit on the porch and read his newspaper while he was recuperating. There were so many things he still had left to do, he said, there were so many mistakes from his past that he still wanted to amend. Eventually it became clear to everyone but Dick that he wasn't going to get better. Pauline almost couldn't believe it, after all he had been through. It had been so many years, and, with the exception of one doctor in Nashville who suspected that it might be a rare form of abdominal cancer most likely stemming from his service in Korea, no one had ever been able to give them a plausible diagnosis. Pauline would never forget

Dick's stricken look when they tried to tell him. "Bill started to say, 'They can't operate'—and I seen that look on Dick's face. And he said, 'Aren't they going to operate?' and I looked up at Bill and kind of made a thing like, 'Please don't tell him now,' and Bill said, 'Yes, they're gonna try.'"

Jake was finishing up the mixes for the album, and the artwork and the notes were just about completed, but it still didn't have a name. I think we may all have gotten a little carried away, brainstorming for something that could summon up the scope, the grandeur, the spirit of the music. Just a week or two before he died, Dick named it with a phrase from "I Am a Pilgrim" that could be taken for both the music's message and his sense of his own life's journey. He wanted it to be called *Traveling Through*.

CODA

PEOPLE TURNED UP at the funeral at Bangor Baptist Church that I thought I would never meet. His father's friend, the bulldozer operator Emery Fields, who had given him his first guitar, was there. So were Yodeling Slim Clark, and Alan Franklin, who had recently moved to Maine from California and remained Dick's staunchest fan, and, of course, his mother and brother and all the rest of Dick's family. Al Hawkes, whose Event record label had first launched Dick, drove to the funeral with Betty Cody, and they reminisced about the time Merle Travis had called her older son, Lenny, out of the audience, because he had heard there was a fifteen-year-old kid from Lewiston, Maine, who could play just like him. Many of the musicians Dick had met when he first started playing the New England country circuit were present, along with a big contingent of Korean War veterans. So was Don McLaughlin, the painter who had led him to embrace his faith not just in Jesus but in himself. Dick was vividly alive in all their memories, but the minister who gave the eulogy didn't seem to know Dick at all—or if he did, had failed to register any of the lessons that Dick taught. He took as his text Dick's best-known song, "A Tombstone Every Mile," and wove from it a dark tale of danger and temptation, with monsters lurking around every curve and death in the end the only relief from this life of suffering and pain. There was no place for music in this vision, no credit was given to Dick's music at all, other than as a temptation that he had finally, by the grace of God, been able to overcome.

I don't know how it struck anyone else — maybe they didn't hear it that way, and maybe I'm being unfair. But it struck me as a strangely graceless send-off for someone whose music was so full of grace, it seemed so sadly wrongheaded and contradictory to the spirit of a man who had contended so desperately with the very real demons in his life and had in the end reconciled faith and mission with secular songs of living and learning that, in their own way, conveyed the redemption he had found through the gift he had been given. If you had asked Dick how *he* felt about the sermon, I think he would have just chuckled and fallen back on the broad philosophy of compassion and empathy he had always striven to live up to. "Hey, don't take it so seriously," he might have said. "He's entitled to his beliefs. You know, he might just be having a bad day."

As for himself, how could he have considered himself anything but blessed? He had known what he wanted to be from the time he was twelve years old, and he had achieved it. "Tall, blond, and handsome," read the tribute in his high school yearbook, "'Tumbleweed' has kept the gals running by his prowess on the basketball team and over [radio] station WARE. His deep bass voice . . . has won many a girl's heart, no doubt, but he casts them all away for a night with 'Tex' or 'Slim.' Dick's ambition is to be a great Western singer.

"Here's luck, Dick, we're all for you," concluded the entry for RICHARD WILLIAM CURLESS, Hardwick High School Class of 1950, set off by the inscription

YOU OUGHT TO SEE HIM WHEN HE'S ALL DRESSED UP —
HE'S THE BEST DRESSED COWBOY IN TOWN.

ELEVEN

John R. Cash: I Will Rock and Roll with You (If I Have To)

I T ALL CHANGES the moment he hits the lobby at the Dallas/Fort Worth International Airport. That's when Johnny Cash becomes public property again. Fresh from a six-day break in Tampa, where he says he mostly slept and went fishing with his wife, June, and their ten-year-old son, John Carter, he is surrounded first by a small cluster, then by a swarm of fans, who shyly seek to make his acquaintance almost from the moment he strides off the plane in Wranglers and black Civil War–styled cross-buttoned shirt. He handles the requests gracefully, nods at shared experiences and memories ("Really? You were born in Lepanto, Arkansas? That's just a few miles from where I grew up"), poses for pictures, and is only mildly distracted when John Carter starts careening his mother about in the wheelchair in which she has disembarked from the plane. "No, no, she's all right," he reassures anxious well-wishers, to whom June explains that she simply threw her back out the night before. Even after all the luggage has been claimed, he stands beside the limousine for "just one more picture," smiling and exchanging small talk until the last fan is satisfied, the last snapshot snapped, and, amidst eager waves, the limousine pulls away from the curb.

On the way in to Dallas, preparations for the evening's performance, a convention-hall appearance for Home Interiors and Gifts, Inc., are discussed; John Carter expresses curiosity about where the other J.R. might live (the television series *Dallas'* J. R. Ewing seems to have supplanted J. R. Cash for a moment even in the imagination of his son); a family in a pickup truck pulls alongside before realizing excitedly who is in the limo; and Johnny Cash points out a little town just outside the city limits where

At Nashville recording session, June 1965. *Photograph by Don Hunstein.*
Courtesy of Sony Music Archives

fifteen years ago he and Waylon Jennings, then at the height of their pill-taking days, visited Waylon's first wife and three sons. At the hotel the airport scene is reenacted, with hotel management offering official greetings, a lobby full of people gesturing excitedly, and fans and employees crowding around for pictures and autographs, so that it is at least fifteen minutes before the elevator is gained and the crowd at last shut out. I am a little surprised. There have been many wilder scenes, I'm sure, in the career of Johnny Cash, and Cash's fans are sedate by comparison with rock fans. All the same, many stars would arrive by a less conspicuous entrance; most are surrounded at least by a small retinue and express a conventional distaste for the public mobbing that goes with stardom. Johnny Cash, true to his image, seems almost to thrive on this contact with people. And, one imagines, whether he is alone or fitted out with the full trappings of stardom, there is never any question of just who is in charge or of the fact that John R. Cash is doing just what he thinks is right, just what he knows he ought to be doing.

"Well, I have my refuges. I *have* to have my time alone, to restore whatever might have gone out of me on a tour, to regroup my forces. There's no way that I won't do that, because I've always done that. But when I'm around people, no matter how tired I am or how far we've gone, when I know that I'm going to be around people, I don't ever remember getting upset or getting mad or refusing to sign autographs or take pictures or whatever. When I know I'm going to be around people, I know I'm public property, and I let 'em have me. You can't say no when somebody says, Can I take your picture, or Can I have your autograph? That's really a compliment. It really is. I can't get over it. I still think like I did, always did, about something like that. I know of entertainers who refuse, and I can't understand that at all. I can't in my wildest dreams fathom an entertainer who would refuse someone their autograph."

From the very beginning of his career twenty-five years ago Johnny Cash seems to have had a perspective, both on himself and on his goals, that eludes many people, whether in the entertainment field or not. Perhaps it was his upbringing in Dyess, Arkansas, a federal "colony," where not only physical strength but strength of purpose was prized. The fourth of seven children, born in 1932 to a mother and father who never hesitated to uproot their family to make a new start in the depths of the Depression, J. R. Cash (the name was a compromise because his parents couldn't come to a better agreement, with the "J" coming to stand for John, his mother's preference, the "R," he says, for nothing, though his father's name was Ray) grew up in a community that was started "as a social experiment, really. It was a rehabilitation project that was done by President Roosevelt for farmers in Arkansas that had lost out during the Depression. My dad was informed one day in Cleveland County, where I was born, that he had been chosen (if he *cared* to) to have a house and a barn and twenty acres of cotton land in Dyess Colony. Nobody in our family had ever been up there—it was 250 miles then, it's not that far now, but to us it seemed like the other side of the world. We loaded up in an old truck everything that we had, all the kids, and moved to Dyess. Everybody was in the same boat there. Everybody knew that the man down the road next to them didn't have any more or less money than he had. It was a socialist setup, really, where if there was a profit made from the cotton gin, or the grocery store, or the bank, or the cannery, the people of the community shared the profit. We had the biggest co-op school in the state of Arkansas. Nobody had a lot of money, but everybody had a little—and we got by."

Cash has spoken (and sung) often of the values he derived from this upbringing, of the strict sense of honesty he got from his parents and the sense of openness and hopeful prospects that he gained from this newborn community. "I think communication had a lot to do with the way I feel about everything now. There was no lack of communication in any area of my life that I can recall when I was growing up. Everybody knew everybody else; I don't ever remember seeing any real trouble in the community; nobody held anything against anybody else for long. You know, I can remember instances where my dad would hear that somebody had said something about him, and he'd go to that person, he'd walk a mile maybe down a gravel road and he'd have an understanding about it. Then he'd come back and tell my mother—that was just the way it was."

Music was another strong bond of communication, something that was always an integral part of his life. "My parents woke me up every morning with the radio on playing country music." When he was sixteen and still a high tenor, John's mother, Carrie, paid for voice lessons for her son, because she sensed a potential in this boy, who was always singing "Irish ballads, Bill Monroe bluegrass songs, I knew 'Don't Sit Under the Apple Tree With Anyone Else but Me' as well as 'Rainbow at Midnight,' I wasn't locked into any one kind of music. In my mind I didn't separate the songs, I loved all kinds of music when I was a kid, and I wasn't conscious of any separation until I grew older."

Neither was there any of the sense of guilt that a fellow Arkansan like Charlie Rich (like Cash, a member of the Missionary Baptist Church and descended from a long line of preachers) felt when he was growing up and playing secular music instead of confining himself to the gospel tradition that his parents would have preferred. "No, to me it wasn't like that at all. Maybe Charlie's folks were right, but I don't know, I was taught that music was a joyful thing. I just never have closed my eyes to anybody's music, no matter what kind. I think music is a beautiful gift that's been given to man, and any area that you can explore and find something in it I think you gain."

Radio was a way to widen that area of exploration, and Cash recalls vividly listening to radio broadcasts by the Louvin Brothers and Bill Monroe, Sister Rosetta Tharpe and the Stamps Quartet, Lulu Belle and Scotty and someone he remembers only as Blind Bob Steele, a cowboy singer on a local station. "Well, he was very popular. He didn't have any records out, as far as I know, but, you know, radio was much more important then, records were secondary. That's really what I wanted to do was to be a radio singer. That's one of the first things I remember in my life was a radio. When we got that radio when I was a little boy, I felt like I could tune in the whole world practically."

Movies, too, provided an alluring glimpse of far-off horizons. "Movies always did inspire me," he says. Seeing the movie *Inside the Walls of Folsom Prison* was in fact one of the principal sources of inspiration for one of his best-known songs, "Folsom Prison Blues," and early on he was drawn to the movies of whip-snapping cowboy star Lash LaRue, the original man in black—but it was books that really fired his imagination. "Well, you know, I always have been a bookworm. We had a very big library in Dyess—our library was maybe the biggest library in the state. Mrs. Roosevelt even came down to officially open it. I read all the time when I was a kid, I got into just about everything. I can remember reading *Drums Along the Mohawk* and *The Last of the Mohicans;* I read all the Indian books I could get." Was this common? I ask. Did many kids his age go in for this kind of thing? "No, I don't know anyone else in town who did read those books—on their own, you know, unless they were assigned as textbooks. But I read them because I loved them, and I still do."

At eighteen he left Dyess, first for two weeks at the Fisher Body plant in Detroit; then he enlisted in the Air Force, where he served in Germany for three years, wrote poems for the Landsberg base newspaper, bought

On Sun Records, ca. 1955.
Courtesy of the Sam Phillips Family

his first guitar, formed a country music group, the Landsberg Barbarians, to sing his own songs and those of his idol, Hank Snow, and completed his education. By the time he arrived on the doorstep of Sun Records in Memphis in 1955, he knew exactly what he wanted to do.

Johnny Cash entered the Sun studio as fully formed, it would seem, as any of his equally distinguished contemporaries (Elvis Presley, Jerry Lee Lewis, Carl Perkins, and Charlie Rich, among others). He had his own sound even then, and his voice already possessed that patented note of tremulous sincerity and vulnerability that has always given his music its special mark. "Of all the people I ever recorded," Sam Phillips said, "Johnny Cash is probably the only singer who had a great voice as such, whether you like it or not."

"I always remember Sam Phillips with very kind thoughts and with great respect," says the subject of his praise, "but one thing about it, Sam didn't come and tap me on the head and say, 'C'mon, son, let's go make a record.' I had to fight and call and keep at it and just push push push to ever get into Sun Records in the first place and make him listen. I don't feel like anyone discovered me, you know, because I had to fight so hard just to get heard. You see, I had started to radio announcing school while

I was still trying to work as a [home appliance] salesman, determined to get into radio any way that would get me to where I could start singing. It was during this time that Elvis was very popular, and Sun Records was between my house and where I went to radio announcing school. So I just started going by there, and every day I'd ask could I see Mr. Phillips. And they'd say, 'I'm sorry, he's not in yet,' or, 'He's at a meeting.' So, really, it became a challenge to me just to get inside that studio. It became a fight. Finally one day I was sitting on the stoop just as he came to work, and I stood up and said, 'I'm John Cash, and I've got my guitar, and I want you to hear me play.' And he said, 'Well, come on in.'

"I sang two or three hours for him, everything I knew—Hank Snow, Ernest Tubb, Flatt and Scruggs (I remember singing 'I'm Gonna Sleep with One Eye Open from Now On'), I even sang 'I'll Take You Home Again, Kathleen'—just to give him an idea of what I liked. He said, 'You really got a range of material that you understand and got a feel for. You say you got a group? Well, bring them on into the studio.' And we went back in a few days, just Marshall Grant on bass, and Luther Perkins on guitar, and myself [there was a steel player, too, who dropped out in the middle of the session], and that was when we cut 'Hey, Porter,' the second or third time I was in the studio.

"You see, I knew what I wanted to do, and I did it just exactly the way I planned to do it when I went in there, but Sam Phillips saw something new in what I was doing. In his mind he saw this as a way to break tradition maybe and reach more people in country music. I heard him say so many times that Nashville is locked into that fiddle and steel guitar, and country music is going to die if there's not some fresh sound, some fresh feeling put into it. He told me, when 'I Walk the Line' hit—he didn't say much until then—he said, 'Now you see what I'm talking about. The record has crossed over out of the country into the pop. Now your country music can no longer be locked into any one category.' He said, 'That's what music is all about. It should be universal.' And I said, 'Well, Sam, that's what I've always believed, too.'"

And yet for all of his self-assurance, a background more stable than many of his label mates, and the fact that he approached Phillips on a more nearly equal basis than any of the others, Cash remains both admiring and ambivalent in his feelings toward this strangely messianic man. It was Sam Phillips, after all, who got him to speed up "I Walk the Line" (it was originally conceived as a somber ballad) to the point that when

With Sam Phillips, Nashville, ca. 1962. *Courtesy of the Sam Phillips Family*

Cash first heard it on the radio he was so discomfited he called up Phillips and begged him to halt its distribution. It was Phillips who persuaded him that *Johnny* Cash was better than plain John Cash when it came to selling records in the teenage market. "You know, one thing about it, though, I never heard Sam say a lot of the things that I've read that he said. Sam, matter of fact, was a very quiet-spoken man — unless he was drinking. Which he started doing a lot [in later years]. Still, even when he was drinking, Sam always had his wits about him, he still was a genius, in that he knew what the music business was all about. He could see me as I was, and I couldn't. He could see Elvis as he was, and Elvis couldn't. Elvis wanted to sing a slow love song to his mother, and Sam Phillips saw him as what he was: a national hero with a new style of music just turning the whole world around."

Nonetheless Cash left Sun Records with few regrets and seemingly none of the trauma that accompanied the departure of some of his label mates. To Carl Perkins, Sam Phillips *inspired* the early records, and Phillips himself characterizes his relationship with his artists as "almost like a father-son or big brother–little brother relationship." When they inevitably left — as Elvis did first, for the greater vistas of RCA and Hollywood — it was described by both sides in terms generally reserved for the breakup of a family. For Johnny Cash leaving Sun for Columbia Records after only three years on the smaller, independent label was simply the logical next step. "There were so many things I wanted to do, I had all these ideas about special projects, different album ventures like *Ride This Train, From Sea to Shining Sea,* the Indian album, but I felt like at Sun I would be limited in what I could do, where with a major company I could do all that and reach more people with my music. I think I was right, too. Sam couldn't understand it back then, we had a little misunderstanding at the time, he couldn't see me wanting to go to another record company — *but I could.*"

It worked out, in the end, pretty much the way Cash foresaw it. His style continued to evolve. The records that he produced over the years — many of them "concept" albums before the term was widespread — were a continuing chronicle of engagement and exploration, even as they remained anchored in the bedrock simplicity of his musical origins. When he made *Ride This Train,* he created a genuinely "Stirring Travelogue of America in Song and Story" by scrupulous research and painstaking attention to detail; when he recorded his gunfighter *Ballads of the True West,* he went straight to the authentic sources, read all the books, played pool with Texas historian J. Frank Dobie. For his blues songs he pored over old Library of Congress recordings and carefully studied the research material of John and Alan Lomax. He takes pride today, whether in concert or in private, in tracing in painstaking detail the genesis of his version of "Streets of Laredo" or "The Legend of John Henry's Hammer." Even at his lowest ebb, in the years during which by virtue of his admittedly self-destructive, drug-dependent behavior John Cash should have been lost to the world, some of his most worthwhile projects still emerged (*Bitter Tears: Johnny Cash Sings Ballads of the American Indian,* for example, came out in 1964, *Orange Blossom Special* in 1965), outgrowths of the same restless intelligence which more recently has prompted Cash to write, to actually *write* an incisive, well-paced autobiography (*Man in Black*) and take a year to produce a movie on the life of Christ (*Gospel Road*). "You see, I always have considered myself a student, still do." With his voracious reading and his interest in such a wide variety of subjects, did he ever consider college? I ask. "Never thought of it," comes the reply, almost too quickly, softened only by the familiar hedge of the self-made man, "I guess I just had to get my education in my own way."

Probably he did. Like many another self-made man he has led a life riddled with contradictions, of which his reliance on pills and not infrequent lapses from the righteous path since his well-publicized spiritual rebirth are only the most prominent examples. Like the best of self-made men, though, Johnny Cash has never swept the errors or contradictions under the rug, has faced up to them instead in interviews, autobiography, and casual conversation. What I wonder is whether this penchant for self-examination and voracious desire to explore new worlds may not outrun his own faith or his audience's limits. "You know, I've thought about that. I've been careful about that. I don't think I'd ever get ahead of my audience. If I ever feel like I might have, with my fancy suit and my eight-piece band, I'll just tell five of them to be quiet, take the other three, and do 'Give My Love to Rose.'" What about politics, though? Cash's populist leanings have been well publicized and have on occasion perhaps created false expectations. What if Indian rights or prison reform or something else in which he deeply believed turned out to be something with which his fans simply could not go along? "Well, I don't know. I've pretty well stayed out of the whole issue of prison reform, actually; I've just sung my songs. I've gone to the prisons, because, you know, I was concerned, but I've stayed out of the political battles because I'm not a politician. I guess a lot of people thought I wanted to be, because I spoke out on these issues, but I'm not. So I kind of quietened down on those things."

Even with his TV series and specials, which have consistently broken fresh ground in their treatment of country music and its heritage, he has steered clear of controversy for the most part. One story, though, is illustrative of the kind of problems to which this instinctively cautious approach can lead. For the first show in his groundbreaking 1969 weekly series he got the idea of presenting Ervin Rouse, the little-known author of "Orange Blossom Special," an old man at the time living in the Florida Everglades with the Seminole Indians. Cash went to the trouble of tracking him down and bringing him to Nashville for the television taping. "I talked with my producers about really doing it right, about really giving the people an original country show, something nobody had ever seen on network television." Rouse's first version of the song ran to over seven minutes; the producer talked to the star, and the song was cut to five and one-half minutes. "Well, they kept that, and said 'Thank you very much,' and paid him, and

Johnny and June, 1970. *Photograph by Raeanne Rubenstein. Courtesy of the Country Music Foundation*

he went back to the swamps and kept writing and writing, wanting to know when was he going to be on. And when they edited the show this was when I got an education about what TV's really all about. Ervin Rouse was not on the show. And I was the one who had to call and tell him."

Surprisingly this experience only reinforced Cash's inborn conservatism. "That was about my first fight with network TV. It was about my last one, too. I was determined from then on that I wouldn't stick my neck out, that if I was going to do TV—I didn't own the networks, so I'd [just] have to do it their way." But isn't there a place for outspokenness? I wonder. He seems to ponder the question for a moment, but there is no hesitation in his response. There are songs he might like to sing, but only if they are appropriate to the occasion. Many people will be there just for the songs "that brought Johnny Cash to their attention in the first place." And he feels honor-bound to deliver them. "Well, I really don't want to get politically involved," says John Cash, then adds, seemingly without irony, "Now, as far as patriotism is concerned, I'm *never* afraid to speak out on patriotism. . . ."

The audience at the Dallas Convention Center obviously is not afraid of patriotism either. It is, as one of the ushers from Criswell Bible Institute says, a "godly" crowd, made up almost entirely of women who are sales representatives for Home Interiors and Gifts. Some of them wear gold crowns to symbolize sales success, and the motif of the convention hall is Camelot, complete with lavender castle and battlements as a backdrop. Two years ago they brought in Bob Hope, and not surprisingly they love Johnny Cash, as their flashbulbs create a strobe effect for an already thoroughly modernized show. Dressed up in familiar black frock coat and pipe-stem black pants, Cash himself is a masterful entertainer, singer, and storyteller. The cordless mike and pickup system, a recent experiment about which he is very excited, gives some trouble, but the Great '80s Eight (this is 1980, after all), the solid new group which includes two horns, all-purpose instrumental virtuoso Marty Stuart on fiddle, and Joe Allen replacing original band member Marshall Grant on bass after twenty-five years of continuous service is flawless after no more than a half dozen appearances together. (A pending lawsuit by Marshall Grant will soon call attention for the first time to Cash's ongoing drug use and its painful costs, both personal and financial.) It is in any case a joyous musical occasion. A couple of times the band even threatens to get out of hand as they rock out on one of John's wittiest new songs, "I Will Rock and Roll with You (If I Have To)," or heat up dangerously on a blues solo from another new member, guitarist Jerry Hensley—but each time the audience is gently brought back with a gospel song or June's acoustic tribute to her legendary Carter Family country roots or, the greatest crowd-pleaser of all, ten-year-old John Carter doing a takeoff on "I Walk the Line" followed by a gospel testimonial to his own Carter Family heritage. The film sequences that play behind "One Piece at a Time," "Casey Jones," and a lyrical "John Henry" are well chosen; the well-oiled Johnny Cash machine is on the move, with Johnny Cash himself always at its center—a touchstone, a verity, someone the audience wants to reach out and touch, like the old cowboy heroes he admired, someone they can believe in. Seemingly without a second thought, he satisfies that belief. Johnny Cash presents himself as a pillar for everyone to lean upon—friends, family, band members, strangers. It is a surprising position for someone who not much more than a decade ago had just about given up on himself, and even now by his own admission is still teetering, but then that appears to be part of his strength.

And yet heroes fade, and that is one of the things that haunts him, as he has supper up in his hotel room after the show and talks about his own

heroes, Ernest Tubb and Hank Snow in particular, and the lack of respect they get in today's instant-trend world. "Well, that really bugs me. This has been a bone of contention with me for years, for ten years at least. There is a group of about four or five singers that have been grossly neglected at all the awards shows and all the big specials — that's Webb Pierce, Faron Young, Ferlin Husky, Carl Smith, Ray Price, and Little Jimmy Dickens, that's six. And these guys at one time in the '40s and '50s were the top male singers, the top entertainers. All these guys — you talk about heroes, all these people ought to have the chance to show people what they've got. Not what they *had,* but what they've still got. Because these people are still very effective, they still work, they still tour, they still have huge followings and fan clubs. It's just like these producers will ask Ernest Tubb or Roy Acuff or Hank Snow to come on just for kind of a token performance. 'Let's have one of the oldies on the show.' Well, that's really *terrible.* I say, 'If we can get Hank Snow to do a show, then let him be a regular guest and do his songs and let me talk to him and do a song — because *that man means a lot to me.*' Maybe that's why it bugs me. I'm not concerned that this is going to happen to me because I can handle it, but it does bug me that the people forget — hey, it's not the people, these old heroes of mine are getting pushed aside because they don't mean ratings to the television producers."

What about his own career? I ask. It seems as if in the last few years he has announced several new directions, and now with the Great '80s Eight and the "contemporary rockabilly sound" that he is tentatively reaching for, I wonder if he is looking to get back to basics, to cast off excess baggage like so much excess weight. Is it a struggle to simplify? There is, he suggests — and it's hard to tell whether he's thinking here of his faded heroes — no easy answer. "It's impossible to free myself of a lot of the baggage of success," he says, "but I've fairly well learned how to handle it. As far as making a fresh start — no, I'm not doing that anymore. I'm doing what I do now. I'm continuing stronger than ever, I believe."

John and Merle Haggard on the steps of the Cash Cabin Studio, Hendersonville, Tennessee, 2000. *Photograph by Marty Stuart*

TWELVE

Tammy Wynette: 'Til I Can Make It on My Own

ONCE WHEN SHE WAS WAITING for her mother to get off work in the summer of 1954, they came clattering by with their instruments, the young singer a startling study in pink and black, his long sideburns yet to fill in completely. "My my my," said Auzella Moore, whose husband, Carney, owned the dry cleaner's and whose brother-in-law, Scotty, worked as a hatter there and played guitar in the band. "Look at the stars," she said, as the young girl stared after them.

"They all just laughed and chuckled," she recalled wistfully years later, "and walked off. They rehearsed every day in the hat department upstairs, they had just started, actually, and were very nice—but I never saw him after that, well, I never got to talk to him, and I really wanted to." The group was made up of just the three of them: Scotty Moore on electric guitar, his friend Bill Black on bass, and, of course, nineteen-year-old vocalist and rhythm guitar player Elvis Presley, the one she would have liked to talk to, whose first record had come out just a month earlier and set Memphis ablaze. That was when Tammy Wynette (then Virginia Wynette Pugh) was twelve years old, living for a brief time with her mother in Memphis, until her grandfather wrote to her "and told me Shirley Anderson was fixing to get my basketball uniform. I went back home in a hurry."

Home was the 600-acre farm (cotton, corn, and Black Angus cattle) in rural Itawamba County, Mississippi, where she grew up with her mother's parents after her father died. "I had a *great* childhood. It was a hard life but very fulfilling," says Tammy today unselfconsciously, thinking not of picking cotton ("I did everything that could be done on a farm; if they really wanted to punish me they'd set me to churning—that was one thing I really hated") but of the warmth and security she got from a family that, while it may have had its share of division, would always remain close-knit. Her music, she says, she got from her father, Hollice Pugh, though he died of a brain tumor when she was nine months old. "He left me his guitar, his mandolin and accordion and big bass fiddle — he could play them all. He went blind before he died, but he'd hold me at the piano and put my fingers on the keys and say to my mother, 'If you do one thing, give her piano lessons if she shows any talent at all.' My father and his people were all very musically inclined — my uncles played with my father, but they never picked up a guitar after he died other than just to teach me a few chords. He died at twenty-six, and I just put up a new headstone a couple of months ago after my aunt died that says: 'An Inspiration Even After Death.'"

She did get piano lessons, though it was not always her mother who drove her to Iuka, thirty miles away, because "when my father died she moved to Birmingham for a while and went to work in an airplane factory where they made B-29 bombers, and that's the reason for me living with my grandparents. Well, there was no future for her on the farm, there was nothing for her to do there, except just live with Mama and Daddy, so I understand, you know, why she had to leave me. But I grew up feeling towards my mother like a sister, because my grandparents, I called them Mama and Daddy, and I called her Mother, but still she's like my sister — we argue, if it's over the color of a dress. She remarried when I was four, and I would live with her for two or three weeks, and then back to my grandparents. I'd get mad at her for something she did and go back to Mama; then Mama would do something I didn't like, and I'd roll my Army cot across the road to my mother's house — she was right across the road from us — until my granddaddy told me one day to park it one place or the other. So I parked it at his house until I was thirteen. And I slept with Daddy every night until I was thirteen. Then he moved me out of the bed and put me in the bed with my Aunt Carolyn, and that lasted for about a year, and then I moved home with Mother and stayed with her for about two and one-half years — until I got married at seventeen."

Though life in the Russell household may not have been luxurious (her grandfather, Chester, a forty-year board member of both the local college and the bank, was known and respected in the community as a man who didn't advertise his wealth), Wynette Pugh certainly grew up under comfortable circumstances. Still, she worked in the fields like everyone else. "It's very strange. We didn't get paid very much, maybe two dollars per hundred pounds of cotton we would pick. But we did get paid, and the only thing we would save it for was the county fair in Tupelo every September. That was our big thing, it was the only place we had to go to spend our money. Oh, Mother would give me a quarter on Saturdays, and I'd go to Red Bay, Alabama, which is actually what I call my hometown—you see, our [farm] joined the Alabama line—and I'd go to the movies in Red Bay. We'd pick cotton until noon, and then we would have a half day off, and we'd go every Saturday without fail, we couldn't wait to get there. A dime would get me into the movie, a nickel would buy popcorn, a nickel would buy a Coke, and a nickel would buy a bar of candy—so I could buy three different things and watch the movie. It was continuously all day, you know, and we'd watch them over and over—the cowboy pictures and all those old outer space things that had just started up—we'd stay as long as we could stay in there, until they ran us out."

The only live entertainment that she saw was Lash LaRue ("I'll never forget it, we thought he was the most fabulous thing in the world, popping that whip"), Flatt and Scruggs once in Tupelo, and the Chuck Wagon Gang and other leading gospel quartets that the whole family would drive to see once a week in Memphis or Birmingham, 120 miles away. She listened to records, of course, country records to begin with that her mother would bring home, by Kitty Wells and Hank Williams. "I can remember one record by Hank Williams so well—'No One Will Ever Know' was on the album, which is my favorite Hank Williams song—and I had a little tiny record player, just a little bitty thing, the record itself actually stuck way out over the little player, and I'd put it on a chair by the side of my bed at night, and I can just see my room. I'd go to bed at night, and I'd put that record on, and I'd sleep on my stomach with my hand out, and when it started to go off of 'No One Will Ever Know' and the next song that followed it, I think it was 'Cold Cold Heart,' I'd take my finger and slide it back over, scratch that record to pieces, but I'd play it every night when I'd go to bed."

She can't ever remember buying a record herself, but "I loved the Coasters, the Platters, Buddy Holly, Patsy Cline (I just idolized her), and Ray Charles." As she got older, she started driving over to Hamilton, Alabama, with a girlfriend named Linda Loden. ("She was [country singer] Sonny James' third cousin.") They would sing sometimes on the radio show of their pastor, Brother Verde Collier ("It was a thrill for us—we didn't

Tammy, May 1970. *Courtesy of Sony Music Archives*

know you could get paid for anything like that"), and then go over to the Skatetorium, where "we'd go skating on Saturday afternoons when we didn't go to the movies. That's where I first met Carmol Taylor, when I was about sixteen, and he's written so much for me since I've been in the business. He used to play there, and Rick Hall, who's over in Muscle Shoals, he used to play the fiddle for Carmol, Carmol Taylor and His Country Pals. We'd sing with whoever'd let us sing. We had one guy, oh, we thought he was Elvis, he had the long hair and all the movements — oh, what was his name, I saw him in Chicago about two years ago, he wasn't playing anymore, in fact he was teaching school — but we thought he hung the moon. Everything was played there, from country to Elvis to r&b." And Billy Sherrill was there, too, playing saxophone in an r&b band in the Hamilton, Alabama, Skatetorium.

Neither Billy nor Wynette Byrd (Tammy's first married name) remembered that first contact right away when they met again in 1966. She had married Euple Byrd, the brother of a friend of hers and five years her senior, just a few months short of high school graduation in 1960 because "I was really, I'll have to say, running away from the farm. I was just so tired of farm life, I thought anything was better than this. My stepfather signed the marriage license; my mother refused to sign. I was seventeen years old, and I just had to get away."

She didn't get very far. She enrolled in Mrs. McGuire's School of Beauty in Tupelo, had a couple of kids, moved to Memphis briefly, and then "moved into an old house of Daddy's. Daddy paid our light bill, we had no water bill, we had no inside plumbing. I didn't even have a stove, I cooked in a fireplace in the kitchen. And that's only been sixteen years ago! It's been a drastic change for me." She still harbored dreams of singing stardom, but her husband only said, "Dream on, dream on!" When they separated in 1964, she moved to Birmingham to live with her Grandmother and Grandfather Pugh, who were already sharing a tiny two-bedroom house with her aunt, her aunt's husband, and their child. She was three months pregnant and discovered that her beauty operator's license wasn't valid for the state of Alabama. "So here I was with two kids, no job, no money, no nothing, moved in with my grandmother, and I had to start all over again at the American Beauty College in Birmingham. I went for three months, worked fourteen or sixteen hours a day, and Tina was born at a little less than six months, weighing a pound and a half." It was at this point that for the first time she started to move toward what she had wanted all along: a musical career. "My mother thought I was crazy, she was totally against what I was doing. Not that she didn't believe in me, but she said, 'You're twenty-three years old, have three kids, you're divorced—' Well, I can understand it now. If one of my girls just up and said, 'Mama, I'm going to Hollywood to be a star,' I'd say, 'You've got to be kidding.' Because I know what it's like now, how difficult it really is."

She started going up to Nashville on weekends, leaving the children with her grandmother, who was the only one who seemed to truly believe in her. ("She is the most fascinating woman, one of my biggest inspirations, really. She's eighty-eight now, and she goes on the road with us every year for a certain length of time. She loves to play rook with the boys.") She was writing songs with a Birmingham DJ named Fred Lehner, appearing on the *Country Boy Eddie Show* on TV station WBRC at 6:00 A.M., and then working a full day (eight in the morning till six at night) at the beauty parlor. For one very brief period she went on the road, singing back-up on the Porter Wagoner Show, but though she was hoping for big things, nothing came of it. "I did ten shows with him in Alabama and Georgia. That really, I think, set me on fire to traveling. I drove my little Volkswagen behind that big bus, I followed that big bus and my aunt went with me every night." Shortly afterward came the move to Nashville — no connections, no prospects, three kids in tow. It was 1966, and Loretta Lynn's "You Ain't Woman Enough (To Take My Man)" was at the top of the charts.

Billy Sherrill had arrived in town himself just a few years earlier, getting his first job and education at Sam Phillips' new Nashville studio. Sherrill, one of the protean talents in country music, has attracted a number of very different reputations in Nashville over the years. He has been described as a genius, a racist, a deliberate provocateur, and a man with the surest commercial instincts in town. To Tammy he may be any or all of these things, but more than anything else, she insists, "Billy's a very old-fashioned person, basically shy and hard to get to know unless you really get to know him very, very well. Our backgrounds are just exactly the same, and I feel like I know him like the palm of my hand." It was Sherrill into whose office at Epic Records Tammy walked with her guitar one day in the summer of 1966. "His secretary had just moved to the Coast, which was a good thing for me. I knocked on the door, and he was in there completely alone, and he said, 'Yeah? Come on in. Who is it?' And I went in and told him my name and that I wanted to sing for him. He listened to me do a couple of songs, and he had his legs crossed on his desk

With Billy Sherrill. *Photograph by Raeanne Rubenstein. Courtesy of the Country Music Foundation*

and he was leaning back in his chair and never said a word till I finished, and he said, 'You know something else?'" Almost the very next day he heard a song on the radio, "Apartment #9," which he tried to lease in its original version from the small label that had put it out, and then, when he couldn't, called Tammy back in and offered it to her to record. By this time he had obviously made the connection in their backgrounds. "He was standing just inside the door, I almost hit him when I opened the door to go in his office, and he was standing throwing darts at a huge map almost the size of that wall, and he said, 'What're you doing?' And I said, 'Nothing. What're *you* doing?' And he took a dart and said, 'We're gonna put Red Bay, Alabama,' and threw a dart at Red Bay and then he threw one at Haleyville [the small Alabama town where he had grown up] and said, 'We're gonna put Red Bay and Haleyville on the map.'"

That is exactly what they did. "Apartment #9," "Your Good Girl's Gonna Go Bad," "I Don't Wanna Play House," "D-I-V-O-R-C-E" were all carefully chosen, constructed, orchestrated, and tailored to an image that both Billy and Tammy (Billy had selected the name because "you look like a Tammy to me") agreed was suited to her, all designed to bring out what Sherrill calls that "little tear in every word," which is the special quality of her voice. Then came "Stand By Your Man."

"It was the first thing Billy and I had written together, just a fast thing, twenty-five minutes during a session. We had two songs for the session, and Billy wasn't satisfied with either one of them for a single, so he told the musicians to take a break and we had about thirty or forty minutes to play with. So we went upstairs and he said, 'Do you like the idea of 'stand by your man'? And I said, 'Yeah, I do. With the old-fashioned Southern Baptist upbringing that I've got, I like that idea.' So he said, 'Well, let's write it.' So we just sat down and he asked me how I felt about what I would do, and I said, 'Well, if I was back home in Mississippi, being a Mississippi farmer's wife, you'd stand by a man regardless of what happened because you wouldn't have any reason or hope to do anything better. Because you have no education, you work in a shirt factory or something, and there's just no way that you could better yourself if you wanted to.' So we just put our ideas down and wrote 'Stand By Your Man.' Well, I hated that high note in it worse than anything in the world, I just felt like I was screaming, and I had been so used to doing the kids' things, too [songs, like "D-I-V-O-R-C-E," that focused on the effect that a bad relationship might have on the children], that I just really didn't like the whole song. And, two, Jones [country music superstar George Jones] and I had just been living together two weeks, and I took the song home to George and I played it for him and he said, 'That one's different from what you've been doing. I don't like that one.' And I said, 'What don't you like about it?' I didn't tell him Billy and I had written it. I said, 'My singing?' He said, 'No. You're singing okay.' I said, 'The arrangement?' He said, 'No. Billy did a good job on the arrangement.' I said, 'Well, what don't you like about it then?' He said, 'Well, I just don't particularly like the story.' And I started crying. I said, 'Well, I *wrote* that.' He said, 'Well, let me play it again. I might like it better after a while.' So I just got started off wrong with 'Stand By Your Man.' From the very beginning it was just wrong for me. We wrote it so fast, and I didn't have any faith in our writing, and I didn't like the high notes in it, I just thought I sounded like a rhythm and blues singer in the country field. But I have really learned to like it since then."

As well she might, with a song that, whatever its explicit message (and, for all the mockery that it has endured, that message is definitely undercut by the ever-present tear in her voice), went on to become not just the biggest seller in her career but one of the biggest-selling country singles of all time. And she and Billy have stayed together, in a musical marriage more stable than any of her well-publicized domestic alliances (including an on-again, off-again affair, and then friendship, with movie star Burt Reynolds). Just how close they are can be illustrated by the way in which she broke the news to Sherrill of her recent marriage to George Richey, a longtime associate of Billy's ("They're like brothers"), as well as writer and arranger for some of Tammy and George Jones' biggest hits. "When we first decided we were going to get married, I said to Richey, 'We better go tell Billy first of all.' So we walked in, and it was the funniest thing in the world, I'll have to tell you this regardless of what it sounds like in print. We walked into Billy's office, and I had been sick and lost a lot of weight, which I keep losing—but Sherrill has always been like a brother to me, and we walked in and he said, 'What have you two been doing? Writing?' And we said, 'No.' He said, 'What have you been doing?' And I said, 'Nothing. Just walking around—you know—just riding around.' And he said, 'Well, sit down.' He said, 'Your boobs are bigger.' I said, 'They are not. I've lost a lot of weight.' He said, 'Well, they *look* bigger.' I said, 'Well, they are not bigger.' And he said, 'Well, I guess they're not, it's just probably what you've got on.' Well, we sat there for a few minutes, and Richey and I started laughing, and I said, 'Billy, I've got to tell you something.' I said, 'Richey and I are going to get married.' And he said, 'Oh my God, I just told you your boobs was bigger.' We laughed till we just about cracked up. We started out the door that day, and he says, 'Go home. Just go on. I guess now there'll never be any more sad ballads written. Everything'll be happy, up-tempo, and gay—and fun.' He said, 'Who's gonna write the slow sad tearjerkers anymore?'"

There was no problem with material, as it turned out. Sherrill's familiar stable—"our little group," Tammy says, made up of writers like Carmol Taylor, Glenn Sutton, Bobby Braddock, and Curly Putman from the start—continued to supply Tammy with suitable (and suitably sad) material. In addition, as she has herself grown more confident, she has contributed as many as two or three songs of her own to each album. Most of her writing centers around longing and loss, the sad aftermath to fairy-tale romance, the very discrepancy she seemed to note in her description of how "Stand By Your Man" was composed. "I write exactly what I feel," she says, and indeed compositions like "Singing My Song," "Another Lonely Song," "The Woman I Am"—even though they may have been co-written with Sherrill or Sutton or George Richey—express very precisely the sense of deep personal hurt, give life to the proud but bedraggled persona which the world knows as Tammy Wynette.

"I write very fast, and strictly on inspiration. I'm not a pressure-type writer, unless I'm with Sherrill or Richey—they can pressure me into writing something, but they push me into it. I think I have more confidence in something I've done with somebody else, I don't know why. I really enjoy writing, and I do an awful lot of writing by myself, but I like somebody else's view." She feels no embarrassment at writing about "anything that's happened to me, anything I've gone through or experienced or just been mad about. I'll write about it and pretend it happened to someone else. I won't talk about it, but I'll write about it—and I guess that's just my little fairy-tale world. But I always figured the public knew everything about me anyway." She gets her inspiration not just from real-life situations but from the passing remarks of strangers, too. One recent song ("Love Doesn't Always Come on the Night It's Needed") came from a book of thoughts that her biographer, Joan Dew, gave her; several songs, "That's the Way It Could Have Been" among them, stemmed from a brief affair she had with a married man. "It's not a very easy thing to talk about; it was something I had sworn would never happen to me, we knew it was ridiculous from the first. But a lot of times I'm around the person I was involved with when I [perform] the song. And it's a very strange feeling to know that somebody's in the room that inspired to me a very pretty song." A song like " 'Til I Can Make It on My Own"—whose refrain, " 'Til I get used to losing you / Let me keep on using you," she frequently quotes as an example of lines she is proudest of—comes like so much of her recent work from the public debacle of her marriage to George Jones.

"Jones and I had just separated and were in the process of getting a divorce, and Richey had brought up the idea of the song—till I can make it on my own, till I can do something by myself, I mean, what would you do? And we tried to write it that day before a session, but Billy said, 'My mind is just too befuddled. I'm thinking about the session. Let's wait and write it tomorrow.' So I went home that night, and Richey called and said,

'Can you drive over? We're fixing some popcorn [Richey was still married to his second wife, Sheila, one of her closest friends], and let's finish writing that song.' So I said okay, and it was snowing, and he said, 'You know that idea we've been talking about today? Now, how would you feel if you'd been married to a guy and everything and dependent on him for so many years and all of a sudden he just up and left?' And I said, 'You fool, that just *happened to* me! How do you *think* I'd feel?' And he laughed, and he absolutely idolized Jones—he wrote 'The Grand Tour,' 'The Battle,' 'Picture Me Without You,' and so many things that Jones did—and he said, 'Well, write it down.' So I did, and it was very easy to write once we got those two lines, and we wrote every bit of the song until we got to four lines from the end, and it was 2:30 in the morning, and we were just beat—we had eaten popcorn and Cokes, and Richey hadn't left the piano stool all night, it was just one of the easiest songs to flow together. But we didn't know how to end it.

"We talked about it and talked about it, and then he said, 'I'm calling Sherrill. This is ridiculous. He started this song with us, and I'm calling him.' So he got up at 2:30 in the morning from the piano stool and called Sherrill, and Sherrill said, 'I'm too sleepy, and it's snowing outside. I'll come over tomorrow.' So I went home, Richey called me the next day and said, 'Sherrill's over here. Can you come over and we'll finish the song?' So I went over, and Richey and I played for Billy what we had, and Billy said, 'Oh, I like it. I really like it. You've really used the idea well.' But he said, 'I'm interested in the football games right now. When that goes off we'll finish it.' So Richey and I just looked at each other and laughed, and Sherrill was running from room to room with two different television sets, and he'd say, 'Oh, lost that game. Well, I won that one. Oh, they gotta make a touchdown. I'm gonna lose my money on this one.' Well, finally I got up and said, 'I'm going for a ride. You two can finish the song. I've had it.' And I got back about thirty minutes later, and they'd finished it!"

Tammy Wynette as just one of the boys? It's an unlikely image, and yet in the rough-and-tumble fraternity of Nashville songwriters she can more than hold her own. Even the songs she does not write, an otherwise generic song like Kenny Rogers' "Sweet Music Man," for example, can extend that sense of personal intimacy, bear out the unique persona she has created for herself, almost as if each new release will bring with it the latest installment in the running diary of her life. And yet for all the care she invests in her writing, her singing, her art, the self-belief that she has

With George Jones and Tamala Georgette, 1975. *Photograph by Raeanne Rubenstein. Courtesy of the Country Music Foundation*

invested in her career, she still does not get to go over any of the material that she hasn't written herself until two or three hours before a session. "Well, I'm very fortunate in that I learn a melody very quickly. I meet Billy in his office usually between ten and eleven, when we have a two o'clock session, and we gather together all the material in that time, and I learn all the melodies to everything before the session, between eleven and two." The song will almost always improve in live performance, she concedes, as she gets to know it better, as she gets to feel what it is really trying to say, but at the same time, she says, for Billy it's a matter of that first spontaneous reaction, and obviously he knows what he's doing, because the records have touched her listeners deeply over the years. And just as the method has become ritualized by virtue of its success, she is reluctant to alter the image she has established, too. "Well, Billy won't let me cut very many cheating-type songs or the running-around-type songs, because he says that isn't what the public expects of me. And it really isn't. Sometimes I hear songs that are different, that are totally away from what I'm used to doing, that I would very much like to do. And then again I think of the different reviews and all the things people write about the top songs I do, and I'm almost forced to stay where I am."

Don't feel sorry for Tammy Wynette, though. As she herself says, "If I never had another hit record in my career, for the past twelve years I've been so lucky, the average wouldn't be so bad." Plucky, determined, hardworking, ambitious, above all emotionally, vulnerably open, she has carved out a place for herself that no one else can usurp. Being a woman, she says, has never worked against her except at the very beginning of her career, when it seemed like every booking agent that she approached said that they didn't have very good luck with female artists, "that female artists didn't like to play the clubs, they didn't like the drinking or the dirty jokes and things like that. Well, that aggravated me, because I knew I was willing to work anyplace, within reason, where I could earn a living. I didn't care [about] working the clubs, it didn't bother me at all—they weren't my favorite place to work, but I didn't complain about it, because I earned money there." And while she can certainly betray a kind of fragility (and not just in her romantic affairs), she is more than capable of summoning up the grit that permits her to make hard businesslike decisions, too.

Just recently, she broke off with Shorty Lavender, the booking agent she was finally able to find and with whom she and George Jones had even gone into partnership with a booking agency of their own, to go with the much bigger Tulsa-based Jim Halsey organization. "I struggled with myself for weeks wondering if I was doing the right thing, but I just felt like I had to do something. We'd been playing the same places over and over, it was getting really stale, and I felt like it was time to do something different." Halsey meant Las Vegas, Johnny Carson, movie tie-ins ("I still love Shorty," she says. "Shorty and I will always be the best of friends"), and she is well aware of the need to "compete with all the other shows that are on the road, to do a show that's equal to theirs." For that reason, she is determined this year to add another bus, which will allow her both to carry more sound and put together the kind of visual backdrop to illustrate her songs that she first saw Ann-Margret use in Las Vegas. Her own brand-new Vegas act is so carefully crafted it would be slick if it were not for the undeniable feeling in her voice; even the jokes, which focus innocuously on some of the comic inconveniences of traveling on the bus with a bunch of guys, are retailed with the timing of a professional comedian. "You know, you can't just get out and tell jokes like a guy can and hold 'em in the palm of your hand. You've got to do something cute or make fun of yourself. You've got to just kind of put your own self down in some way. It's about the only thing a woman can get by with."

She seems comfortable with her newfound celebrity, with hobnobbing with the superstars, with accepting the gift of Wild Turkey and a bale of hay that arrives backstage at the Frontier courtesy of Evel Knievel. And yet there are the disquieting shadows, the bad luck that continues to dog her—the unexplained house fires, the marriages, the deaths of those close to her, the hospitalizations, the rumored affairs and the real ones, culminating in the widely publicized, frequently debunked "kidnapping" that took place in Nashville just one month ago, in the early fall of 1978. Not to mention the all-too-apparent physical fragility. ("Don't tell George," she says, as she pours a glass of milk down the sink. "You know, I haven't eaten anything in two days.") What she really likes to talk about most are her children—Gwen ("a very independent child"), Jackie ("she's my fashion girl"), eight-year-old Georgette (so anxious to record that last summer she tried to "solicit a record contract" from a disbelieving Billy Sherrill), and Tina ("she's always being grounded").

"I'm so mad at Tina," she says, "because she's got the same break in her voice that I have, but she can put it where she wants it. She'll sing a line, and she'll sing it straight, and then she'll turn around and she'll break her voice at least three or four times. She doesn't realize what she's doing—she's only thirteen—but I told Richey, 'That makes me so mad, I could just wring her neck, because she can control it and I can't.'" Of her own voice she says, "I was never aware of having any particular style." She says nothing of the subtle dynamics that allow her to capture a full range of emotion, from the delicate breathiness of a little girl to the full-throated wail of a Billy Sherrill–orchestrated crescendo, while all the time holding on to that deep well of sadness which Sherrill first spied in the "beat-looking chick" who wandered into his office twelve years ago. "When she says I love you," Billy has said, "you believe it."

So Tammy is riding the crest. With her current appearance in Vegas (she opened, with special billing, for country music megastar Roy Clark, Halsey's top client and a frequent guest host on Johnny Carson's *Tonight Show*), her autobiography coming out, increasing movie and TV work, she would appear to be scaling new career plateaus. About the kidnapping, from which she still carries a pronounced facial bruise that makeup can't hide (she was, she told *People* magazine, abducted from a Nashville mall parking lot by a masked gunman who beat and choked her, then abandoned her on a country road eighty miles from town), she is almost resigned to the widespread doubts and skepticism, which range from baffled speculation that it was no more than a publicity stunt gone awry to the unspoken accusation that would surface explicitly many years later in her daughter Jackie's memoir that the story was invented to cover up clear evidence of spousal abuse. With me there is no acknowledgment of either embarrassment or remorse. In fact, she brings up the subject herself, even offers to pull up her blouse and show me the bruises on her stomach. "I'll have to say that I've lost a lot of respect for the police department," she says. "Maybe I shouldn't say it, but I have. Because it just seems they've dragged their feet and haven't really done the things they promised they would do. I told Richey last night that I think they must have needed a body, and he said, 'Well, they had one, yours.' I still have problems sleeping because I wake up at night sometimes thinking, Where is he? Will they ever find him? Will he do it again? To anybody else?"

It is her forthcoming autobiography about which she is most excited. "I turned it down the first time when Simon & Schuster called, because I laughed and told them I didn't think my life was over yet. But then they called back and said, 'Have you ever really stopped to think that fifteen years from now nobody might care?' And, gosh, that like to drove me crazy. And so I did it, and I don't regret it, it was just a lot harder work than I ever thought it would be. But I have a great memory. When I'm asked a question, I can really, I can just see it as if it were yesterday. So we really did have fun doing the book. And if it comes out and is ever made into a movie — which hopefully someday it will be — I'd love for Faye Dunaway to play my part, and I'd like Jack Nicholson to play Jones' part." It would be inspired casting.

POSTSCRIPT

TAMMY DIDN'T GET THE CASTING she wanted, but she did get the movie. Three years after our conversation, in 1981, CBS aired a television movie based on her book, *Stand By Your Man*, with Annette O'Toole in the starring role and Tim McIntire as George Jones. It got good ratings and was even nominated for an Emmy, but I think everyone can agree: Tammy had the right idea. And we can only dream of the picture that might have been made with the actors she envisioned, fresh from *Chinatown*, and John Huston taking over the directorial reins.

Sadly her own life ended in 1998, at fifty-five, in a tailspin of sorrow and darkness. Although she continued to tour, she suffered from what seemed like a never-ending cycle of illness and hospitalization, accompanied by a growing addiction to pain medication. Even in death she was not permitted to rest, with her body exhumed a year after burial in response to wrongful death claims against both her doctor and her husband. "We once made a record called 'One of a Kind,' said Billy Sherrill, who hadn't worked with her in years but who would always cherish her not just for her talent and the tear in her voice but as that strangely familiar figure he had first met, full of innocence and driving ambition, the girl from Red Bay, Alabama. "There are no more words," he said with characteristic emotional restraint. "The words have all been said."

THIRTEEN

Lee Smith: Telling Tales

ON WRITING

*I didn't have an image of a writer [as a child]. I didn't know any writers.
I grew up in the midst of people just talking and talking and talking and
telling these stories. My Uncle Vern, who was in the legislature, was a famous
storyteller, as were others, including my dad. It was very local. I mean, my
mother could make a story out of anything; she'd go to the grocery store and
come home with a story. And I was a reader. I read everything I could get my
hands on. I didn't know anybody [else] that was reading; I didn't have
anybody that I shared this with. I was just always reading. I mean, nothing
else affords me the kind of intense pleasure that reading does. So it just
seemed like writing was the next step.*

*It was never a question whether I would do it or not. I don't think it
mattered whether I got published. It [was] just really necessary to me.
I mean, it's my work, but it's also my deepest joy, just to do it every day a
little bit — and do it a lot other days. I think it's my religion. It's my
religion — it's what I do.*

*I guess my favorite thing is before you even start writing, when you're
sitting down every day just thinking about [it], and it's all completely fluid
in your head and there're all these people running around, and there's
infinite possibilities of what they might or might not do in the course of
the novel. And I'm always thinking about this for several months before
I actually start. And I love it. Everything is all intensely alive, and it's just
total possibility, [but] as you write it, in a certain way you're nailing them
down. I mean, it's very exciting, but it's also — you're nailing them down.
And when you finish, when you put the book in a little box to send to
New York — and a writer I admire, John Ehle, used this image — it's like
putting it in a little coffin. That's how I feel — you know, it's just the
process of it.*

First book signing, Atlanta, 1968. *Courtesy of Lee Smith*

Y OU WOULD HAVE TO HEAR Lee Smith's voice to fully absorb its
range of expression and moods. Of course, anyone who has read
one or more of Lee Smith's seven previously published novels and
two collections of short stories (her new novel, *Saving Grace,* was just
about to come out at the time of our conversation in the spring of 1995)
will have gotten a good sense of the accent, the passionate and puzzled
humanity, and fine appreciation of the absurd, but for further insight into
its variousness, its unpredictable, almost desperate humor ("I mean, it's
a wild world out there"), the true beauty of its Appalachian song, you
would almost have to attend a reading, as I did that spring at the Cameron

Village Regional Library in the Raleigh-Durham-Chapel Hill area of North Carolina, where Lee Smith has lived and taught for the last twenty years. There, a roomful of listeners with no apparent common denominator (some were students, some were housewives, some might have been both or neither) was transported, without hesitation or exception, to the world of Lee Smith's latest novel, transfixed by the voice and tale of Florida Grace Shepherd, the daughter of a serpent-handling preacher, and her struggle for salvation. I had read the book carefully, I thought, and appreciated it thoroughly, but Smith's reading added new dimensions of humor, and of gravity, to it as well. There was a lilt to the language, and an *attitude* to the words, that almost invited the author's voice (imagine Mark Twain reading *Huckleberry Finn* to us, without the intervention of an impersonator or the passage of the years). There was, as always, a fine, and unbuttoned, declaration of individuality (think of Zora Neale Hurston transported to the mountains of Appalachia), a celebration of the striking uniqueness of her characters and their world.

"Lee Smith taught us to be proud of who we are," is the way one admirer put it ("If she can get that stuff published, we know we must be OK," was the way the quote went on), but the author could just as easily turn the expression around. It was her embrace of her own past and the particularity of her own experience that made her proud of who *she* was, and she could well be seen at the center of a movement, loosely defined as New Southern regionalism and incorporating everyone from Bobbie Ann Mason, Jayne Anne Phillips, and Cormac McCarthy to Jill McCorkle, Kaye Gibbons, James Wilcox, and Larry Brown, which has found fresh inspiration in this simultaneous acknowledgment of past and present, this insistent chronicling of the small, heroic battles of the human spirit, a recognition of the dignity, and absurdity, of the commonplace.

Regionalism alone, of course, could not account for the diverse appeal of all this work, and in many ways the label has served as something of a barrier to its broader acceptance, as critic Louis Rubin, Lee's teacher at Hollins College and, later, founder of Algonquin Books, the publishing house that has served as a cornerstone for Southern regional expression since 1983, points out. "If Lee's a regional writer, so is Thomas Hardy. I think the relationship of the literature to the society is very intense, no question about it, but to see that as a limiting factor . . . I mean, Eudora Welty is an American writer *because* she's a Southern writer, not in spite of the fact." Or, as Lee's friend, humorist Roy Blount, said a little less reverentially (but no less appreciatively) of one of her books, "The closest thing to reading this would be reading *Madame Bovary* while listening to Loretta Lynn and watching *Guiding Light*."

GRUNDY GIRL

L EE SMITH WAS BORN in Grundy, Virginia, in the coal-mining country in the far western corner of the state, in 1944. She was a "town girl"; her father, Ernest, operated the local five-and-dime, her grandfather was county treasurer for fifty years, various uncles owned and operated the local movie house, the Piggly Wiggly, and the Ford dealership in town. Her mother, Gig, was a "foreigner" from Chincoteague Island on Virginia's eastern shore, who'd "come to do good, she'd come to teach." Still, it would be wrong to get too much of a sense of privilege in a town like Grundy. There was, says Lee, no real class system. Everyone in town went to the same school; if you look at a picture of the neat little house on Main Street that she grew up in, you will see the Dismal River right behind it and, rising in the background, just across the river, Hoot Owl Mountain. "Grundy, Virginia," wrote Dennis Covington in his National Book Award–nominated *Salvation on Sand Mountain: Snake Handling and Redemption in Southern Appalachia*, "[is] a mining town on the lip of a widening river between mountains so steep and irrational, they must have blocked most of the sun most of the day. It is difficult to imagine how children can grow up in such a place without carrying narrowed horizons into the rest of their lives." "Which I just loved," cackles Lee. "When I finally met Dennis, he said, 'I'm sorry what I said about Grundy.'" But you *know* she takes it as a compliment.

What set Lee apart was neither geography nor class but her own situation and imagination. She grew up as what she might herself describe as a "deeply weird" kind of girl, consumed with reading on the one hand ("Oh, I was always having nightmares and little nervous breakdowns and every kind of thing—*Raintree County* put me to bed") and social success on the other ("I was Miss Grundy High; I *was*. I got a set of Samsonite luggage and a steam iron"). She was an only child, born to parents in their late thirties who were themselves not like everyone else, even if her father was "the most loved man in the community" and her mother was elected queen of the junior prom every year by the girls in her home ec classes.

Grundy. *Courtesy of Lee Smith*

For both parents were what would now be called manic depressive, her father alternating driven, workaholic activity with periods of complete shutdown, her mother suffering similar bouts of crippling depression. "They were the sweetest people—I mean, they were just wonderful, but it was almost like they were too sweet to live. I mean, they were not tough. And it was interesting because when one of them was having a hard time, the other would be the strong one, except one time when I was thirteen and they were both in the hospital at the same time."

It did not, Lee insists, stigmatize her in any way. To the town the Smiths were just "kindly nervous"; if they had to go away from time to time, "things would go on running, my dad's dime store would go on, I might live with my cousins for a while, but, you know, in a town like Grundy there was a high tolerance of any kind of abnormality or unusual behavior, in fact eccentricity was not only tolerated but prized. It was just, I did have a sense that the world was kind of precarious, and there was stuff you couldn't understand, and there were sad things, and there were complications."

Perhaps the reading was a kind of retreat, then ("I think in every

Miss Grundy High. *Courtesy of Lee Smith*

writer's childhood there's something that's not okay, or they wouldn't want to be a writer"), and one that threatened on occasion to get out of hand. The librarian, Mrs. Lillian Elgin, a friend of her mother's, probably said nothing when Lee read *Jane Eyre, Little Women, Johnny Tremain,* and all of Mark Twain over and over again, "but every now and then they would try to exercise some control, because I was reading things like *The View from Pompey's Head* and *Forever Amber* by Kathleen Winsor. But nobody else had read the books, so they didn't know what to tell me to read or not, so I just read everything." With other neighborhood kids she put out a magazine called *The Small Review* ("One time when I was about nine I wrote an editorial about: George McGuire is too grumpy—he was a grumpy adult that lived across the street—and then we had to apologize to George McGuire") and wrote plays that they would put on in the breezeway of her friend Martha Sue Owens' house. Her first story, written at the age of eight and printed out on her mother's stationery, was about Adlai Stevenson and Jane Russell, who went West and became Mormons, the very themes, she says, she is still writing about today. "You know, religion and flight, staying in one place or not staying, containment or flight — and religion." She went to the movies every Saturday night, worshipped Grace Kelly and tried to look like Sandra Dee, and wept for days at the tragic, *unfair* denouement of *Imitation of Life*. She frequently visited A. P. Carter's store in Maces Spring and heard various members of the legendary Carter Family sing and play when she went to buy her school clothes in nearby Bristol, Tennessee, and she saw the Stanley Brothers when they performed at her uncle's drive-in on Saturday night before the movie went on. She lived a worldly life, and yet was saved again and again in spectacularly demonstrative fashion — to her mother's acute Methodist embarrassment. One time at summer camp she heard God speak to her, and "I told everybody about it, and they put me in the infirmary and called my parents — this is really true." At sixteen she went off to boarding school in Richmond ("My father was worried that I would marry my high school boyfriend. Which I probably would have"), where she worked her way through a considerably more extensive library. Then in the fall of 1963 she arrived at Hollins College outside Roanoke, Virginia.

FINDING A VOICE

It's hard to tell why a kid's a writer. Sometimes it takes a writer a long time to get going, and then there are the ones who are extremely good as undergraduates but for some reason or other never go beyond that. But then you get the occasional writer like Lee, who you just knew from the very beginning she was going to write. I mean, Lee's a real writer. She writes all the time. She writes when she's down. She writes when she's up — that's just her way of dealing with the world. And you could tell that from the very beginning.

— Louis Rubin

S HE FELT A SENSE OF RELEASE when she got to college. It was the old Jane Russell–Adlai Stevenson story: containment or flight. "I think I had just felt so circumscribed and pigeonholed. By the geography *and* by the sense that your life is totally determined by who your family is. It's like, You have to go home with the one that brung you. Don't get above your raisin'. All this sense of determinism. So I had this kind of breakout period, I just went kind of wild."

At the same time Hollins, Class of 1967, was exuberant enough en masse to promote a sense of wildness in almost anyone creative enough to dream. "This group came in in the fall of '63, and they cut a wide swath," says Louis Rubin, who had begun his teaching career six years earlier at the age of thirty-three and would remain at Hollins through the group's graduation. "There were seven or eight of them who kind of grouped together. I think three have PhDs, one of them became a good newspaper-woman, Lee, of course, writes fiction, and Annie Dillard writes various things. Remarkable group of kids — they were there for four years, and they just took the place apart."

For Lee the experience offered not just liberation but reinforcement. "What I fell into at Hollins was like a womb. It was like the warmest, most nourishing possible surroundings for a writer, for a would-be writer. I was with other girls who wanted to be writers, we had a creative writing pro-gram that was totally nourishing — I mean, they read a work like it *deserved* to be read. Which it did. And it was just wonderful. And I can't help but think if I had gone to, you know, East Tennessee State, or anywhere else where I might just as likely have gone, that I would have become a much more sort of social person. I mean, a women's college was really important for me. Because I was raised as a Southern girl, where you're not supposed to put yourself forward, you're not supposed to be too smart, if you're weird, you try to hide it. And I can just see myself never having written — or written with the enthusiasm, or come out into the open as somebody who was passionately interested in this, if I had gone to a coed school. I really think that's true."

She read passionately, and all over the place, both for her classes and for herself, working her way alphabetically through the school library: Mark Twain and Virginia Woolf (she and Annie Dillard were go-go dancers for an all-girl rock band made up of English majors called the Virginia Woolfs), Harriette Arnow and Marcel Proust. When Richard Adams, author of *Watership Down,* appeared on campus, a group of students dressed up in rabbit costumes to get in the spirit of his animal allegory. There was a strong commitment to work but an equal commitment to exploring the broad "terrain of the imagination," wherever that voyage might go. "Women's colleges are not fashionable now," says Louis Rubin, "but at Hollins, at that stage of the game, they got to do all kinds of things that they never could have done if they'd gone to Washington and Lee or UVA: edit the newspaper, run the government, be in charge of this, be in charge of that. Freshman year they weren't satisfied with the college liter-ary magazine, so they published a little one of their own that they called *Beanstalks,* and by the next year they could just take over: it was extremely good training."

The summer after junior year Lee and a half dozen other girls decided to emulate *Huckleberry Finn* and take a raft down the Mississippi. They succeeded in constructing it in Paducah, Kentucky, but then ran into bureaucratic red tape which required them to have a licensed captain. "So we were all on TV crying, right? And Captain Gordon Cooper—he was a riverboat pilot who had retired into the Irvin S. Cobb Retirement Home and never expected to go on the river again—he saw us on TV and emerged from the door of the Irvin S. Cobb in his white outfit and said, 'I will take these girls down the river.' And he loved it—I mean, he just had the best time. He was a real storyteller, and he never shut up." The story of that journey, how a free-spirited voyage of exploration was transformed into a media field day ("Well, you know, we had imagined just floating along the river, and then we were on *Huntley-Brinkley,* and we got famous and people bugged us, and we were met by a jazz band from Preservation Hall when we got to New Orleans, and it was all different than what we thought"), makes for a wonderful tale, but in the end it only goes to show how inextricably art and life are linked both in their clarity and in their confusion.

Because at the heart of Lee's Hollins experience, of course, was her writing. The stories that she composed to start off with, and for which she received encouraging Cs, dealt with "stewardesses living in Hawaii [and] evil twins," nothing to do with Grundy or the mountains or the world she came from, until she was assigned a story by Eudora Welty and then, in her sophomore year, heard Welty read. She has described the impact of the experience in a number of different ways, including the manner in which Welty disarmed a passel of academics seeking to know how she had come up with the powerful symbol of a marble cake. "Well," declared the author, "it's a recipe that's been in my family for some time." A response which would have had to delight Lee Smith, who revels in "the things of this world" while raging against abstraction to this day. Probably, though, her first response was her truest. "It was like a *revelation,* really, kind of like, oh, well, okay, well, I can write about just *anything.* I can write about the people that I knew growing up and everybody I heard my daddy talking about—I mean, I can write stories about this!"

She devoured Welty's work, and the work of James Still, a transplanted Alabamian who had come to Knott County, Kentucky, in 1932 to "keep school," and whose 1940 *River of Earth,* a kind of Appalachian *Grapes of Wrath,* she discovered all by herself under the S's in the Hollins library. "At the end of the novel," Lee has written, "I was astonished to read that the family was heading for—of all places!—Grundy! . . . I read [the] passage over and over. I simply could not believe that Grundy was in a novel! . . . Then I finished reading *River of Earth* and burst into tears. Never had I been so moved by a book. In fact it didn't seem like a book at all. *River of Earth* was as real to me as the chair I sat on, as the hollers I'd grown up among."

What she had found in these writers was not just an echoing voice but an echoing *sensibility.* The first story that she wrote after her revelation reflected this newfound sense of kinship—"it wasn't even a story, it was just a sketch. It's funny, my last image of leaving Grundy to go to Hollins was, I kept waiting for my dad to come home from the dime store so we could drive over. And some of my aunts were over there, too, and they were having what I felt was this totally interminable conversation about whether my mother had colitis or not. And it just went on and on, and I thought my father would never come, and I would be stuck on this porch forever. So I just wrote a little sketch about some women sitting on a porch and talking about whether one of them had colitis. And then later, in the next course, I wrote something about this club we'd had in my neighborhood when I was a kid, and it later turned into my first novel."

Life at Hollins sounds like a great adventure, just the right mix of seriousness and silliness, free-spirited explorations and the usual high drama. There was the sophomore year abroad program, from which Lee got kicked out, and then when she came home, through the intervention of Louis Rubin, she went to work at the *Richmond News Leader.* There was the conquest of the Mississippi River, books, and romance. And when she graduated she got married, moved to Tuscaloosa, and published her first novel.

THE WRITING LIFE

"I WAS STRANGELY FORTUNATE [in that] I was published when I was real young, but I didn't pay any attention to it. I was married and having babies in Alabama [Lee's two sons were born in 1969 and 1971],

Lee with her son Josh, summer 1970. *Photograph by Susan W. Raines*

and I didn't know anybody in New York, I didn't even know my agent. I mean, I was an idiot. I was just totally immersed in my writing and my babies, and it didn't occur to me that it should be any different."

She published three novels with Harper & Row in rapid succession; her third, *Fancy Strut,* a direct foreshadowing of the movie "mockumentary" *Waiting for Guffman,* is a charming and frequently hilarious account of the small-town misadventures engendered by the theme-park staging of a sesquicentennial celebration, the direct result of two years of reporting for the *Tuscaloosa News.* But then, under the influence of events in her own life and a sense of wanting to return to her "mountain material," she wrote a disturbing fourth novel, *Black Mountain Breakdown,* about flight and freedom and the impossibility of ever really getting out ("It was real dark")—and no one wanted to publish it. "Harper & Row wouldn't touch it, and then my agent didn't want to handle me either. So I sent the book around to about twenty publishers, and it was turned down, and everybody said, 'This is so dark, this is so depressing—bleuu!'

"This was a very difficult period of my life; I was having a hard time even sustaining the idea that I might be a writer, and I decided I needed to find an agent that I could talk to, a woman agent, so I went to New York, and I thought I had found one, but she went to Greece to find herself, and

I never heard from her again. Finally, my great good friend Roy Blount hooked me up with Liz Darhanshoff [who would become her agent for life], a woman I could really relate to, that I loved—she was real funny, but she taught me something about taking myself seriously. I mean, I had always taken my *work* real seriously, but she read *Black Mountain Breakdown* and she liked it, and she called up on the phone, and she has this real northern voice, real businesslike, and she said, 'Well, send me some clips.' And I said, 'What do you mean, clips?' She said, 'Reviews, I mean reviews of your earlier books.' And I said, 'Well, I don't think I have any.' And she said—I'll never forget this, this was kind of a turning point for me, *'Well, how can you expect me to take you seriously if you don't take yourself seriously?'* And I said, 'Good point.'"

Black Mountain Breakdown was finally published in 1980, seven years after she first started sending it out and not long before her divorce from her first husband, poet James Seay, with whom she had moved to North Carolina in 1974. In the meantime she had begun her exuberantly informal, deeply impassioned documentation of the mountain material, the life, the people, the family bonds, the alternating push-and-pull of the past, the landscape amid which she had grown up and to which, it seemed, like Crystal, the broken heroine of *Black Mountain Breakdown,* she was inexorably drawn. *Black Mountain Breakdown* was not the direction in which she wanted to go, though; for all of its impact, for all of the disturbing power of its portrait of a woman's defeat at the hands of society and self-doubt, it failed, she felt, to capture the vitality of the mountains, the *life* that Lee was driven to celebrate in all of its splashy colors, in all of its messy, beautiful, ugly, anarchic reality. To find that, she had to go home.

Almost without being aware of where it was taking her, she began taping relatives, neighbors, friends, "anybody that would talk." Weren't they, wasn't *she* self-conscious? I ask, from the perspective of my own self-consciousness. "Are you kidding?" she says. "They loved to talk." As for herself, it became "my hobby, my avocation, I began to get addicted to 'going around.' And it made me realize—well, it made me doubt the possibility of ever getting it *right* from an omniscient point of view. I mean, in any given novel. And, finally, I began to get a sense that it's the storyteller's tale, that the storyteller tells the story the best he or she can, but that it's always according to the needs, or the vision—and the particular *angle* of vision—of the storyteller. And so the events themselves don't mean as much to the story as that it's coming out of somebody. And when

I did decide I wanted to deal with some of [this] Appalachian material and history, it seemed to me: Who knows what happened in the past? Who can ever say?"

That was the genesis of *Oral History*, a 1983 novel which incorporated a chorus of diverse voices and remains in many ways one of her most ambitious undertakings. It offers the complex interweaving of myth and experience, a fragile web combining lyrical realism with gritty lyricism in a form that is very much, and very originally, its own. And yet it is framed by what Lee describes as the most "ramshackle" of devices, as a city girl named Jennifer goes back to her people, and her unexplored roots, for a college paper for her professor, Dr. Bernie Ripman. At the beginning of the book she leaves her tape recorder up on top of Hoot Owl Mountain, deserted now because it is thought to be haunted, and the 250-page body of the novel is made up of the ghostly voices which the tape recorder captures.

"Well, you see, Jennifer was my excuse, it's like Jennifer goes into the house at the beginning, and there's Jennifer at the end. And in between are all these voices. And the reader has to participate, you know, to get a sense of the truth, or what *might* be the truth. Well, you know, you said to me, and I thought it was a very interesting thing—this is a little like psychoanalysis!—that after my third novel the sense of the well-made novel falls apart. And it really does. But that was also—you see, I was trying to be a certain way, and finally my marriage wasn't going to work out, and I wasn't going to be able to be that way, you know, and my sense of reality and the world and politics and everything was just—I just had to drop, I guess, the well-made novel as a means of expression."

She started out writing the book in the third person, "I started writing just straight, standard English, but one of my main intentions was to document and transcribe the mountain speech that I had grown up hearing. But when I wrote it down accurately, it sounded so stupid, juxtaposed alongside the proper English; it made them all sound like they were on *Hee Haw*. And it made it sound like I was condescending to my characters. So, finally, I just realized that this wasn't going to work at all, and I decided to let each person speak for herself or himself, and that was the only way I could do it. And just pray that the language that they were using was close to the way it had been. 'Cause you never really know—but it *had* to be their own voices, the characters' own voices, and not me talking about them."

LISTENING TO VOICES

THE NOVELS AND STORIES poured out of her. *Family Linen* (1985) was a multigenerational "comic mystery"; *Fair and Tender Ladies,* an epistolary novel (1988), is her most beloved novel, touching in a way that narrowly avoids sentiment by means of the same comic ferocity that has increasingly come to dominate her work. Its genesis was a packet of letters she bought at a yard sale for six dollars, and to date there have been at least four babies that she knows of who have been named for its heroine, Ivy Rowe. What seems to have captured the imagination of her readers is the indomitable tenacity of its heroine, her dedication to forward motion in the face of life's many obstacles, a quality that echoes Lee's own philosophy. ("After a while," she told one interviewer, "you just can't go on being bitchy. . . . You've been through all this stuff and you have to take a lighter view, don't you think?") Women come up to her all the time to tell her how they have been inspired by Ivy, to let her know how Ivy's example gave them the strength to go on, something I witnessed one evening at dinner when a woman who recognized Lee from her book jacket photograph tentatively approached. She had read the book when her mother was dying, she said, and it had meant so much to her. In a way this doesn't seem to surprise Lee all that much, because Ivy gave *her* the strength to go on, too; the novel was written at a time when her own mother was dying, she tells the woman, and she faced other domestic crises as well. Writing the book helped her to keep *her* life together.

In 1990 she won a Lyndhurst Foundation grant to study the history of country music as background research for the novel that would become *The Devil's Dream* (1992). It is the story of a family very much like the Carter Family in many respects, told through several generations up to the present day. Once again it is a conflicted tale, in which success carries within it the seeds of failure, the very independence of Katie Cocker, its present-day heroine, who directs her own life, who produces her own records, doesn't come without a price. Empowerment is always at the expense of connection. It's the eternal conundrum of country music, it's the eternal conundrum of life: as you sing a song that arises from a particular place, "what you want, of course, is to be successful, and as soon as you're successful . . . that's never your place again. You're always singing of home, but you're never home. And there's something about that—I think I feel like that about a lot of things, this intense ambivalence. To me that is the perfect ground for fiction."

That ambivalence was extended into the real world with the publication of *The Devil's Dream*. For Lee it represented something of a crisis of self-definition, as up until that time she had steadfastly resisted the idea of pushing herself in the marketplace, both for practical reasons (she had two boys at home) and because she still clung to the idea that it was her job to write, not to promote. "But with *The Devil's Dream* I felt like if it was marketed in the right places, in the right way, that it might really sell. I mean, I know my other work is weird, it's very regional, I'm obsessed with things that nobody else cares about, but [here] I felt like, This music is universal, there are a lot of people interested in it — people in all walks of life. But I think the publisher's perception was that people who are interested in country music can't read. And the people that can read would never presume to be interested in country music. They were just really uninterested, *really* uninterested in this particular book. And I really got my feelings hurt, because they didn't care at all.

"So *The Devil's Dream* kind of broke my heart, and it made me just about decide, well, I'll just forget about, you know, selling. But then two of my best friends, Susan Ketchin and her husband, [the novelist] Clyde Edgerton, were upset that nothing more was being done for the book, so for a reading I was going to do in Raleigh, they said, 'Well, we're going to sing some songs.' And it was just so much fun, we had so much fun, and other people started asking us to do it, and we got up this *Devil's Dream* show, and it was hysterical. We did it on campuses, we did it in Nashville at the Southern Festival of Books, and, of course, I got to dress up in a glitter outfit, even though I can't carry a tune. So we just had the best time in the whole world, and it ended up — I was kind of pissed off, but finally the publishing of it was so much fun, because we did this show."

PILGRIM'S REGRESS

THE NEW BOOK IS, as Lee likes to say, "profoundly weird." The primitive Pentecostal world that it portrays, whose practices and premises *Saving Grace* simply presents as a given (the story is told by the daughter of a serpent-handling preacher, who doubts her faith but never her father's power), represents both "what terrifies me and fascinates me the most about the South in a certain way. I see it both ways. I see it as real attractive and also very, very dark. It's all about giving over yourself, giving up yourself, issues that to me somehow also have a lot to do with being a woman, and particularly a Southern woman. It's that desire to affiliate, you know, that terror of being on your own and thinking that you shouldn't be on your own, I mean it's always easier to do what you're expected to do and get with the group that will tell you what to do — I'm not articulating this at all, but there's something about that kind of religion, that kind of fundamental religion, and that kind of father, that is both totally compelling and desirable, and terrifying, to me: *then you don't have to make any decisions — ever."*

From the opening passage of the novel to its bleak conclusion, you never doubt the voice or the winning, disturbing humanity of the main character. "Oh, I just loved Gracie so much. In a certain way it was like giving birth to a terrible child." Much of the narrative consists of Grace's stubborn struggle to deny her heritage ("I am and always have been contentious and ornery, full of fear and doubt in a family of believers"), and her embrace of it in the end can be taken as either triumph or failure, or both. In the end, like all of Lee Smith's books, it is nonjudgmental and pretty much non-categorizable; there are "no big sociological explanations," there are no more explanations in fact than there were for Eudora Welty's cake. It is all, as Lee sees it, just another manifestation of experience, "these people are doing this because they want to feel that passion, they want to feel God move on them directly — which I think is [the same reason] why I write. It's like this woman told me one time, she said, 'Honey, I don't know, all I can tell you is, when you have the serpent in your hand, the whole world has got an edge to it.' Isn't that great? I mean, you know what she means — that's really true."

She wrote the book in a fever, breaking off from the story cycle which was going to be her next book when Gracie's voice started calling to her (she was born under a different name as one of the voices in Lee's introduction to a wonderful book of photographs, *Appalachian Portraits*, by Shelby Lee Adams) and then refused to be still. "I didn't mean to write this novel, I knew it wouldn't be something that my publisher would want, or anything, really, that I wanted to write, but sometimes a voice will just come to you so insistently — you know, it was almost like automatic writing once it started." She has always looked for inspiration in her reading, sought out a familiar, appropriate touchstone for each book, and for this book, of course, it had to be Flannery O'Connor. She went to Milledgeville, Georgia, last spring for the annual Flannery O'Connor Festival, reveled in the landscape and in re-reading all of O'Connor's work, returned home and wrote nonstop until she finished, delivering the manuscript to her publisher a year early. "So I never felt like I wrote it, actually — it just came like ee-uuh, and all I could do was just kind of keep up."

LEE'S VOICE

A ND SO HERE SHE STANDS, once again on the brink of publication, on the brink perhaps of wider fame, about to start a publicity tour of the South by automobile with her husband of ten years, Hal Crowther (his collection of syndicated columns, *Unarmed but Dangerous,* is being published at about the same time as *Saving Grace,* and Lee has been sending out press releases for it under the name of "Scooter" Marshall). She has just been awarded a three-year Lila Wallace-Reader's Digest Writers' Award, and she will use it both to support her writing and to maintain her commitment to the Hindman Settlement School in Knott County, Kentucky, where she will teach writing workshops in the adult learning program for those who can read and story workshops for those who can't. There is a musical adaptation of *The Devil's Dream* which has just opened in Raleigh (an earlier one-woman presentation of *Fair and Tender Ladies* had its world premiere in Grundy several years ago and has an independent life of its own), there are Grundy connections to maintain, maybe even brandy to be sipped with James Still, and while she will undoubtedly miss her students at North Carolina State (from which she has taken a three-year leave of absence after fourteen years of full-time teaching), you have the feeling that everywhere she goes she will be teaching — and learning. "Very few of your students will actually become writers, but the ones that don't, you know, have had a chance to really express things, to hear things that they wouldn't have heard otherwise, to have been in this very special relationship with a group of people. To have read together and to have talked about things that mean so much to them. I mean, it's a wonderful thing, it's a wonderful sort of *process* to be engaged in together. And I just think you have to understand, if you're a young writer, that it's a life, you're embarking upon a life, and everything else is going to have to [fit in] around finding you the time to do it. It's a life, and it won't ever be

With father at Going-Out-of-Business sale, 1992. *Courtesy of Lee Smith*

a living probably, it's just a process, and the product is really not all that important for a long, long time.

"I have always felt, you are simply moved by what moves you. That's all I can say. You're interested by what interests you. My husband is always accusing me, you know, he got mad at me one day, and he said, 'You know, you'd rather hang around at the back of a drugstore in North Wilkesboro listening to people than go to Europe.' Which is true. It's always been true. I mean, I'd like to go to Europe, but I don't know, you're just drawn to what you're drawn to.

"I don't write anything unless I am totally moved by it. I mean, it's a totally emotional experience for me. It's never a rational experience. And it's always something I feel deeply ambivalent about. I don't know. I just think when you're young you're more arrogant, and you think that you can fathom out the truth, and then the older you get, it's like the more paths go off into the forest, and you can't, you just can't find your straight way.

"A lot of times for me it has really just been like salvation to write. Because, you know, real life is real chaotic, and you can't control what happens to anybody — even the people you love the most. Terrible things are going to happen to them. Terrible things are going to happen to you. And you can't control any of it. But to write is to order experience, to make a kind of ordering on the page, no matter how fragile it is. And it is, of course, profoundly, deeply satisfying — even though it's not real. It's like prayer, I think."

FOURTEEN

Call the Doctor: The Further Adventures of Doc Pomus, Part I

OUR OR FIVE times a week you can probably find him at one little club or another, but mostly at the Lone Star Cafe, where he sits at his own table, against the wall and stage right, laughing, discoursing, gesticulating with arms that seem like flippers in comparison to his giant torso, his leonine head thrown back, hand cupped to his ear to catch the dialogue that is being flung in the teeth of the room's clattering din. There is a constant stream of visitors, old acquaintances and new, faces that possess the blurred familiarity of fame mixed in with beat, sorrowful countenances that light up with the greeting that this jovial gray-bearded eminence in cape and cowboy hat bestows upon them, punks and critics, stars and sidemen alike — everyone is welcome at Doc Pomus' table.

If you didn't know Doc, you might put it all down to sentimentality: this steady flow of music industry figures and hangers-on come to pay their respects to the Legendary Songwriter whose reputation was made by such '50s and '60s classics as "A Teenager in Love," "Save the Last Dance for Me," or, for those prone to Elvis kitsch, "Viva Las Vegas." If you're not close enough to overhear the conversation, you will probably imagine that most of the talk rests firmly in the past, and that this lovable old gent in the wheelchair is merely soaking up some well-earned praise. "Bullshit!" Doc Pomus might say — if he is in a good mood. For though there is no one with a greater appreciation for people and talent of all varieties, though I can't think of anyone with a greater generosity of spirit than Doc possesses, there is no one with a greater disdain for phoniness of any sort either. Ask him anything; he'll tell you exactly what he thinks. But don't try to con Doc with kindness, because he's got a built-in bullshit detector. "I am blessed with knowing every asshole in the world of music," he will

Photograph by Sharyn Felder

confide if it's not such a good day—or maybe if it is one, too. "This guy's the worst," he will say of some fawning sycophant. Or: "It reminds me of the old days—it's just as fucked up," of a particularly untogether act, on which he will expend a good deal of energy, and much of his considerable knowledge and charm, if they should merely ask him for advice.

I first met Doc Pomus under just such circumstances as these, at the Bottom Line, where we had both gone to catch Delbert McClinton, one of Doc's favorite people, in 1980, some eight years ago. We started talking, and we've been talking ever since. "Peter, you got a minute, you ready for this?" Doc's familiar voice will come over the telephone line. And then we're off. History, philosophy, good-natured gossip, complaints, crises, and political outrage, life, loves, a good joke, you name it—but all of it informed with the most compassionate insight, the most unabashed appreciation for the absurd, an absolute openness with regard to his own feelings, emotions, and opinions. It is all, of course, an education in perspective. "So that's it," Doc will wind up in the flat tones of the native New Yorker, which are never able to fully disguise the natural enthusiasm that propels him. "What can I tell you? Just the same old nonsense." From the beginning I felt that I was included. Like Delbert and Billy Swan and Sleepy LaBeef and 996 others, I sensed that I was immediately one of Doc's 1,000 favorite friends, a fact which remains as much of a cockeyed honor today as it was on the day we first met. I don't think there's any question, it was the blues that brought us together, just as it has been the blues that has put Doc together with some of the most important people, and some of the most important events, in his life.

For a fact, it all changed for me when I was about fifteen or sixteen and I heard a Joe Turner record, "Piney Brown Blues." From that moment on I knew what I wanted to do. That to me was everything music was supposed to be. It was the way the male voice was supposed to sound. I can't explain. I never even knew there was music like that. It was the transformation of my life. Up until then—well, you know, my family was so dead set on my becoming a lawyer or an accountant, something safe, that they, in a certain way they terrorized me. I became, underneath, so frightened by my inability to cope with the world that there was a part of me that was convinced that I was never going to be anything or do anything, except maybe end up on the streets. The other side of it was that for some insane reason, don't even ask me why, part of me was convinced I could do anything: I was going to be the first professional baseball player on braces and crutches, the first boxer, I really believed that. Which really wasn't too realistic. From the moment that I heard Joe Turner sing, though, I knew what I wanted to do: I was going to be a blues singer.

Doc Pomus was born Jerome Solon Felder (his father was a lawyer, hence the "Solon") in Brooklyn on June 27, 1925. He grew up in a respectable section of Williamsburg, where his father was a precinct politician and, Doc says, middle-class appearances were far more important than emotional self-expression. At six he went off to summer camp in Connecticut to escape a citywide polio epidemic. At camp, in a cruel development whose accidental nature might stand for Doc's whole take on a universe that is neither just nor unjust, simply indifferent, he contracted polio. "I woke up one morning, and I couldn't move. My family rushed me to Long Island College Hospital, which I believe was in Brooklyn, and I was placed in plaster casts from the neck down."

This was the formative experience of his life.

As he describes himself, struggling to learn not only how to walk but how to accept himself in this new, diminished state, "I was lonely and lost, I lived in a dream world. I invented all kinds of imaginary characters, just to escape dealing with the reality of being Jerome Felder. You know, truthfully, I have few happy memories of my father. The vast majority of the time, I just knew him to be bitter and sullen and what I felt was completely unsympathetic to my needs. Much later I figured out that I was supposed to be his living flower — you know, a great athlete, a man among men — and when I turned out to be a cripple, he was just devastated. But at the time I didn't understand any of that. I was just totally ill equipped for the world. I was a very strange, reclusive kid, reading all the time, living in my own little world. In retrospect I think my father was just so frightened for me he didn't know what to do."

That was when Doc met the blues.

When I was eighteen years old, I started going down to Greenwich Village to hear Frankie Newton's band playing at George's Tavern. It was a hot summer night when I first wandered in and I was with Sy Ovryn, a neighborhood sax player whose left-wing leanings made him familiar with the Village avant-garde style. George's was small, crowded,

With Otis Blackwell, fellow songwriter and lifelong friend from Verona Café days, at the Maine [Arts] Festival, summer 1990, Brunswick, Maine. *Photograph by Sharyn Felder*

and smoky—and very democratic.... The talk was all of music, art, politics, and sometimes even sex. Everybody was real and dug *le jazz hot*.

Frankie Newton was one of the greatest trumpet players I have ever seen. He played sitting down, with his knees casually crossed, a great big black guy with huge, sad eyes who didn't dress like a musician but wore corduroy patches on the elbows, conservatively cut slacks in solid colors, and loafers....

That first night I discovered that if you stationed yourself to the left of the bandstand with a glass of beer in your hand, there was enough of a crowd to hide you from Dominick and Jerry, the owners of the joint.... Unfortunately my luck didn't hold. By the second set Dominick spotted me and had me pegged as a deadbeat trying to look cool with no coins. He walked over to me and, in his most eloquent and heartwarming broken English, said, "Why doncha spend some money or getta the fuck outta here?"

My eighteen-year-old heart was pounding like crazy, but I couldn't, or wouldn't, leave. It was like I had finally found myself, I was finally home, and in a gush of enthusiasm, a spasm of inventiveness, I presented my new self. "I'm a blues singer," I said, "and I'm here to do a song."

It didn't faze Dom. "If you're really a singer," he said, "let me hear you sing." He then signaled to Frankie Newton and told him to play a blues for me. . . . "What key?" Frankie asked. "Blues in any key, any tempo." When Frankie started to play, it was a beautiful slow blues in B-flat. I did the only blues I knew, "Piney Brown" by Joe Turner. From that moment on I was a blues singer, in B-flat. . . . The next night I was back at George's with a new name. I called myself Doc because it sounded like a hip midnight character; Pomus sounded foreign and mysterious. Then I started Brooklyn College in the fall. College student by day, professional blues singer by night. By now I was making $40 a week playing at George's. I was an eighteen-year-old cool wonder trying to convince the world and myself I had been doing this forever. . . . I now wore a dark stubble to make myself look older, and I had discovered that women like singers, even singers on braces and crutches. I was a white boy hooked on the blues, but it was a habit that I would never try to shake, because it wasn't a monkey on my back—it was a midnight lady with a lovelock on my soul.

—from *Call the Doctor: The (Unpublished — and Unfinished) Autobiography of Doc Pomus*

Obviously, in an account of this sort you are bound to leave out some of the notable influences. Rector Bailey, for example, a sometime fellow student at Brooklyn College and a mainstay of the music department who would soon include future r&b session stalwart Mickey Baker among his many pupils, introduced Doc to the world of black nightclubs, where, far from being taken as a freak, this heavyset white boy on crutches was embraced as a singular star. "Rector asked me to come with him one night to Brooklyn, and we went to this club called the Verona Café. I sat in with the band, and I'll never forget it, I had never experienced anything like it before in my life. Those people went crazy. For a fact, I said to myself, *This* is the way people are supposed to react to music. I never wanted to go back—and I didn't, not really, not for ten years. But to tell you the truth, it was probably at the expense of a career."

He started making records at nineteen. The first was for Leonard Feather. He cut sides for the Danish jazz critic Timme Rosenkrantz, for Chess, for Savoy, he even had a turntable hit with a clothing commercial for a Brooklyn outfit called Alley's Clothing Store. "The commercial was so popular that Apollo Records asked me to do a full-length version. Everywhere I went they knew me by 'Alley, Alley,' the record never did too much, but the commercial was played on all the hip radio stations, and my act even began with it. Once they heard the first couple of notes from the orchestra, everybody'd just go crazy. Which is what it was, looking back on it. I was a regular half-ass celebrity—and all because of Alley's pants!" Over the years Doc sang and recorded with such well-known jazz and r&b musicians as Rex Stewart, Tab Smith, Taft Jordan, King Curtis, Van Walls, Buddy Tate, and Mickey Baker, standing at the mike and all the while imagining that there must be dozens of others just like himself. "I just figured there must be somebody like me doing this in every big city, in every state. I had no idea. My reality was so strange. . . ."

One night—it must have been around 1951—I went to this club, and I heard Joe Turner sing for the first time in person. It was guest night, a Monday night, at the Baby Grand on 125th Street, and Dan Burley, a great boogie-woogie piano player who was also a columnist for the old *Amsterdam News,* did a thing called the Skiffle Session, where he got guests coming up out of the audience and doing numbers in between the scheduled sets. Well, this particular night Dan called me up, and I did my number, and I didn't even know that Joe had heard me—this was my idol, you understand, I don't know if you can even imagine, this was the *boss* of the blues. Well, the next day I go to peddle songs at Atlantic; I might have had a few numbers recorded at this point, for a fact the first song that I ever wrote that I didn't record was done by Gatemouth Moore for National Records in 1946—Tommy Dowd [who would soon become Atlantic's first, and for many years only, recording engineer] engineered the session, and Herb Abramson [the founding partner, with Ahmet Ertegun, of Atlantic Records in 1947] was the producer. So I know Atlantic Records from the beginning, from *before* the beginning. Anyway, I go in there on this particular day, and Herb comes out of his office and says, "You won't believe this, but Joe's inside, and he was just talking about you." Naturally, he didn't know my name, he was just telling them about this singer he'd seen the night before at the Baby Grand. But when I went inside and they told Joe I was a songwriter, he said, "Why don't you write a song for me?" And Joe always asked for my songs after that, and for a fact years later, in the last years of his life, he became one of my closest friends. It was the weirdest experience.

In this, as in all else, chance unquestionably played a part. First he had become a blues singer by being thrust, almost literally, upon the stage. Now he was a professional songwriter, too, writing songs for singers who had been his heroes while continuing to put out a steady stream of unsuccessful releases ("I just wrote songs to support my singing habit") and working a weekend circuit that encompassed New York, New Jersey, and sometimes Connecticut. This went on until 1956, when Alan Freed jumped on a song of his that had been released on a little label called Dawn, and RCA picked it up and killed it. "To this day I don't know why. I suppose they had their reasons. Maybe they just wanted to cover the song themselves with one of their own artists, some such silliness — but it depressed me. I just figured that was it, the handwriting was on the wall, and I quit singing. My last job was at the Musicale on West 70th, with Mickey Baker and King Curtis in my group."

In 1956, while he was still singing, he started writing with a high school student named Mort Shuman who was dating his cousin Neysha. "The idea was that he was in touch with young people, since he was just a kid himself. At first I gave him 10 percent just to sit in the room while I wrote. Gradually he began contributing more and more until, after a couple of years, we were full partners. At the beginning I even had him following me around on gigs, but eventually we mastered the technique of writing together." Doc also got married to the actress Willi Burke and, while he was on his honeymoon in upstate New York, he and his wife went into a little luncheonette, checked out the jukebox, and found a song that he had turned over to writer-producers Jerry Leiber and Mike Stoller in unfinished form just a few weeks before. The song was "Young Blood" by the Coasters.

"You see what had happened was, I had written this song, demoed it with my band — Mickey and Curtis were really wonderful on the demo — and played the demo for Mike [Stoller], who was looking for material

"He's Got a Right to Sing the Blues!" *Courtesy of Sharyn Felder*

because Jerry had just been in an automobile accident. Mike said he loved the title, but he asked, 'Do you mind if we make some serious changes in the song?' I said, 'Great.' They made the changes and gave me a third, which I thought was very fair. Well, I went way back with them, they'd always be kidding me by calling me 'Alley' (from the commercial, you know), and they'd always been very supportive, I mean in every way — technically, professionally, they'd always be trying to pull my coat about what I should be doing. Just the nicest guys. But I never even knew that the record had been released until I was on my honeymoon. So then I think, 'Well, maybe I'm into something,' and I called Atlantic Records from that little diner, and they wired me a huge advance — I think it was $1,500 — and that was what we lived on for a while."

It wasn't too long afterward that he and Mort Shuman hooked up with Hill and Range, the burgeoning young publishing house founded in 1945 by two Austrian-born brothers, Jean and Julian Aberbach, who had only recently made a lifelong connection with Elvis Presley (Hill and Range had helped facilitate RCA's purchase of Presley's Sun contract in 1955) which would soon enable them to move into the penthouse suite of the legendary Brill Building. Doc's introduction to Hill and Range came about through the good offices of Otis Blackwell, a blues-singing pal from Café Verona days (he and Doc had been scuffling on the same Brooklyn-New Jersey mainline for years) and the recent composer of "Don't Be Cruel," "All Shook Up," "Great Balls of Fire," "Fever," and a host of others.

It was as if a whole new world opened up, a world in which it was possible "to try to transpose the kind of feeling you got in the honky-tonks to where everybody would understand—that to me was rock 'n' roll." It was a world with steady money coming in ($200 a week to Doc as a draw against royalties, $100 to Mort, still a bachelor and a junior partner), in which Jerome Felder for the first time had a regular gig, a home of his own ("I swear, it wasn't until I was thirty-two that I lived in a hotel where I had my own bathroom. I don't think I'd ever made more than two grand a year in my life"), an office to go to, and something like professional status. "The manager at Hill and Range was a guy by the name of Paul Case, absolutely brilliant music man, he could spot a weakness in a song, just pinpoint the place where it didn't work, or he'd hear a song and know that the song was great for one particular artist and not good for another. He was like a father to me, I mean I can't tell you, I felt like he was always looking out for me, he'd hear an act and say, 'This act is great, you've got to get involved with it.'"

Between 1958 and 1965 Doc and Mort Shuman wrote "You Be My Baby" for Ray Charles, "This Magic Moment" and "I Count the Tears" for the Drifters, Dion's "A Teenager in Love," plus, of course, Doc's signature song, "Save the Last Dance for Me," as well as a couple of dozen movie-track songs and Top 10 hits ("His Latest Flame," "A Mess of Blues," "Little Sister," "Surrender") for Elvis Presley. The money was flowing, there was an eleven-room house on Long Island, it was a new kind of music, a far cry from the blues. That's the picture postcard view, but, Doc insists, the picture postcard view can never reflect reality—reality by definition is neither better nor worse, just funnier, sadder, and, in general, more interesting in all of its random complexity.

I would go in to work every day at twelve or one, we'd work in this little cubicle. At the beginning, when we first started having hit records, they gave us this plush office in the Brill Building with paintings by Bernard Buffet on the wall—because the Aberbachs sponsored Buffet's career

"A Teenager in Love"

(POMUS-SHUMAN) BY DION AND THE BELMONTS, 1959

Frankie Lymon's "Why Do Fools Fall in Love?" was the first song of this particular genre that I ever heard. At the time I was still a singer, and I went in to do a radio show, this all-night show, and while I was in there this old promotion man brought in a Frankie Lymon record. Well, he fell asleep while they were playing the record, but I had never heard anything like it — and it just kind of stayed in my subconscious, I guess. And later on I wrote this song called "(It's Great to Be) Young and in Love" — that was what we originally called it. Mort and I had carefully studied Dion's style, and this guy, Gene Schwartz, who owned the record company, specifically wanted a certain kind of medium-tempo song for him. So we showed him what we had, and he liked it, but he wasn't too happy about the message. Then I said to myself, "Kids when they're in love usually have a lot of problems, it's not always smooth sailing." So that was how it evolved into "Why Must I Be a Teenager in Love?" But for me in a certain kind of way the Frankie Lymon song really epitomized the whole thing that was going on: the transition between music written for adults and music written for young people.

"Lonely Avenue"

(POMUS) BY RAY CHARLES, 1956

I definitely remember writing the song in a car. I was still living on and off with my family, and I was riding somewhere. It has a kind of quasi-heartbeat, it's almost like subliminal writing. The really interesting thing to me was that I've always heard from a lot of people heavily involved with drugs that this was their song. Because there's a certain kind of monotony in it, a kind of strange, in-depth monotony that I guess has something to do with the half-living reality of drug people. Something like that. I never was able to figure it out. But the thing that happened that was interesting, almost all the drug people thought I was a junkie because I wrote that song.

for a long time, you know. But after Morty and I sat there for about three days in this great office, looking at the paintings, looking at each other, and not doing a thing, I just told them, "Look, you better get us a funky little office, the kind of place where we can't do anything but work—'cause we want to get out of here in a hurry." So they did. They gave us this little room, battered piano, two broken-down chairs, that was it—it opened right up onto the roof. In other words, you could step out a window and walk around, the type of thing where we could have killed ourselves. You *had* to get out of there in a hurry, it was so confining. But that was how we wrote.

I had the house on Long Island, but during the week I used to live at the Hotel Forrest, which was right across the street from the side entrance of the Brill Building, on 49th between Broadway and Eighth. In the morning I would just walk across the street to go to work. Everyone I knew, I used to meet at the Hotel Forrest. There were fighters and fight managers, professional gamblers and thieves, con men and songwriters, these great Runyoneseque figures and Damon Runyon Jr., too. Who occupied the penthouse suite, very sweet guy but the most depressed man I ever met in my life, eventually they found him floating in the Potomac River with his press card in his hand. We were lobbyites. We'd sit around telling stories all night long, Phil Spector and I would write songs in the lobby, and every song we wrote, for some reason we'd get a record on. Phillip had just come back to New York, and before he hooked up with Atlantic, he was actually living in Leiber and Stoller's offices—a very nervous character, very intelligent, funny, eccentric. I was always very fond of Phillip, we're good friends to this day. And, you know, what was interesting, he was a fine guitar player, not many people know that, and we'd sit around the lobby playing old songs, I would teach him a song like "Cottage for Sale," he'd play and I'd just sing along—it was great fun. Well, another thing a lot of people don't know about Phil, he's a great practical joker. Of course he had a cruel streak, too, he'd play some really rotten tricks, I think it stemmed from this desperation that he had, this terrible need to prove himself, but my best memories of Phil are of these long political discussions—I mean, really vituperative discussions, he was very left-wing, and I used to like to bait him about Franco or J. Edgar Hoover, I could always get him going—and of some of the practical jokes that we pulled. You wouldn't believe the lengths we'd go to sometimes! I think we took it as a real challenge.

The songs were at least an equal challenge. Sometimes it was a matter of tailoring a song to an individual talent, sometimes it was a matter of convincing an individual that the song was written specifically for him. When Atlantic, after months of delay, finally put out a single on "Save the Last Dance for Me" by the Drifters, Doc had to convince Jimmy Clanton, who was just about to record the song himself, that really, "Go, Jimmy, Go" was much better suited to him, even though, unbeknownst to Clanton, it had originally been written for Bobby Rydell as "Go, Bobby, Go." When Bobby Darin couldn't get a good cut on "Little Sister" and "His Latest Flame," the songs went immediately to Elvis Presley, who had a double-sided Top 10 hit with them.

One of the reasons that his and Mort Shuman's songs have had such a continuous life, Doc theorizes today, is that they were never written just to fill a slot. "Well, it's always easy to come up with explanations after the fact, but I feel like we weren't writing songs that could be pigeonholed, we weren't writing songs that were intended as follow-ups, and we weren't writing songs in a single voice. You see, one of the problems with the singer-songwriter is that he writes songs according to the way he sings. So, often those songs are not going to be recorded by anyone else, they just don't have a life. Now, you take a song like 'Save the Last Dance for Me,' or any of the Latin songs that Mort and I wrote together, I was trying to get the lyrics to sound like a translation. Now this is something very few people would realize, but Mort used to go to Mexico all the time, and—he was always very, very good rhythmically, he just had an uncanny ear—when he'd come back he would always have these interesting rhythms. My job was to bring the thing back to some elemental point, something palatable to the recording industry, and I wanted the lyric to sound like a Spanish translation so, subconsciously, you would have the image in your mind. With 'Young Boy Blues,' which I wrote at the Hotel Forrest with Phil Spector, I had this concept of writing an entire song in one sentence. I thought if I did it the right way, no one would ever know—I don't know why, but it was just a fascinating concept to me. And that's what I did, with all these dependent clauses, conjunctions, dangling participles, and everything. Interesting!"

Mostly, though, Doc's idea was to put technique at the service of feeling; his entire aesthetic was centered on writing from within, like the great blues singers that he admired, even if the form he adhered to was not necessarily the blues. The song that he continues to hold up as one of

"I'm a Man," "Turn Me Loose"

(POMUS-SHUMAN) BY FABIAN, 1959

There was this kid, this marvelous-looking kid, who had made some records, but they didn't sell at all. But he was doing these record hops with Dick Clark, and the young girls would go crazy. So they knew that he had something, but they had to get him a song. The only problem was, he didn't have much chops. Well, we had written a couple of songs for Presley, but Paul Case, this great professional manager at Hill and Range, told us, "Hey, listen, with Presley it's hit or miss, there'll be hundreds of guys shooting for every cut, but if you get a song with this kid now, you're gonna really be in, because they're gonna really appreciate it. Nice guys got him, you know, Marcucci and DeAngelis, and you'll be in there all the time." So we had these two songs written specifically for Presley, and we took the lyrics and we watered them down, and we took the melody and made it where he could almost talk it. We were writing a song for a particular situation, and sometimes when you do that you take the path of least resistance. But by the same token it's a tremendous challenge: trying to write a hit song for someone who can't really sing.

"A Mess of Blues"

(POMUS-SHUMAN) BY ELVIS PRESLEY, 1960

"A Mess of Blues" was the first song that Presley ever recorded of ours. We wrote the song in Brooklyn, thinking about Presley, but he was in the Army. Then a year or so later — the history is kind of interesting — Mort and I were in England to do a television show, because we had three records of the same song in the Top 10. It was "Teenager in Love," and I don't think that ever happened before or since. Anyway, Granada Television had a big show devoted to us, with all the British artists doing our songs. And Lamar Fike happened to be there, because he was over in Germany with Presley. Well, Lamar told us that he could get a song to Presley, and we thought it was just some more jazz. But Mort went in the studio and made a piano-voice demo, I think it was the sparsest demo of all time, and Presley liked it — I think maybe he really related to it because of the blues content, and he cut it on his first session after he got out of the Army.

his two or three all-time favorites is "Still in Love," a typically straight-forward, almost limpid blues ballad and the first song that he specifically wrote for Big Joe Turner, because "it was exactly what I wanted it to be." Apart from the great bluesmen, his one consistent model as a songwriter has been Irving Berlin, "because he always tried to write so simply. He never lost sight of the fact that a straight line is the shortest distance between two points." His other models have all come from real life, which provided both the inspiration and, for a period of ten years, the interruption to Doc's long sojourn in music.

In 1965 Doc took a bad fall, tearing all the ligaments in his legs. He ended up in the hospital for almost two months, and while he was in the hospital, not only did his marriage come to an end but Mort Shuman, his principal songwriting partner for the last eight years, left for France. There was no question in his mind that it was all over. He had had his run as a songwriter, just as he had had his run as a singer. When he got out of the hospital, he was despondent for a time. He saw the market changing along with his life. "I just figured it had to be all downhill from there. You've got to remember, we had no idea this was going to last. Rock 'n' roll was just a way I happened to make a living. In America it was never treated with any dignity." He changed his life, and he changed his lifestyle. When he got out of the hospital, he never got back on crutches again. And he became a professional gambler.

I'll tell you, you make exchanges. I had gotten along very well for many, many years on braces and crutches. As a matter of fact, I very rarely sat down, partially because it was difficult and also because I felt better about myself just standing up. But I was always under pressure from the weather, anytime it was rainy out I was practically risking my life. Also, because there was no more infantile paralysis, the art of making braces was gone. When I was a kid, there was this whole heritage of brace making up in Yorkville, German immigrants, descended from generations of craftsmen, who had come to this country; as a matter of fact, when I went up to Yorkville to have my braces fitted, the guy had a little bust of Hitler right there in the shop. So you had a Nazi making braces for you, but he was a master craftsman. Anyway, all these things came together, and truthfully it wasn't that hard to make the decision. I resented it in certain ways, but in other ways I was much better off. My nerves were better. I used to get fits of nerves you wouldn't believe. Since then, of course, I gained a lot of weight, and people say when you're heavy it's not good for your life span, but I'm sixty-three years old and I'm telling you, I would have died from a heart attack from the strain by now. So I made a choice, and in a lot of ways I wasn't sorry at all.

The gambling was the same kind of thing. I knew I had to find another way of making a living, and to tell you the truth, I always felt that writing songs was like gambling, a profession where the odds were definitely loaded against you. I think to me the idea of being able to overcome those odds and come out ahead — well, I always liked sporting events, but I never liked to bet on them. But the idea of being able to bet on yourself. . . . Maybe it comes down to the feeling somewhere deep in my soul that I wasn't destined to be a winner. Playing cards in a way was just an extension of the rest of my life.

Gambling, like music, offered its own form of fellowship, and its own intangible rewards. The man who introduced Doc to the ways, and the world, of professional card playing was one of his closest friends from the Hotel Forrest. "Johnny Mel was a professional gambler who knew all the tricks but prided himself on being completely legitimate. Johnny was one of the most honorable, honest people I ever met in my life. He was a high school All-American football player and a war hero who dismantled a whole field of land mines with one other guy. He came from a very nice family, and when he got back from the war — as a matter of fact he won $50,000 shooting craps on the boat, he used that as a stake — he opened up a cigar store in Pawtucket, Rhode Island, where he was from. Johnny loved cigars, he used to smoke ten five-dollar cigars a day — but he found he couldn't get the product. There were other, bigger cigar stores in town with more money and more access. So he went to the Veterans Administration, and he said, 'Look, I don't want your money. If you could just help me get a contact so I could be competitive.' Well, they turned him down. And he swore he'd never do anything legal for the rest of his life. And he never did.

"He was the sweetest human being. He showed me all these great tricks, but he prided himself on being completely legitimate. If he had to stoop to cheat — well, it would just be beyond him. So he taught me, and I had pretty good instincts and got to where I was able to survive at it. Well, he used to go out to Jersey, and one night he asked me, 'You wanna be my partner?' I said, 'Yeah.' He'd put up $100; I'd put up $100. And, you know something? I never questioned him. At the end of the night he'd either say we had no money left, or we had $500 to split, something like that. And it went on like that for months and months — I made plenty of money with him, and I was getting an education, too."

For nearly ten years this was how Doc made his living. After a while he graduated to running a game of his own, in his or other people's apartments. He got held up. A friend of his was kidnapped right out of a game. A well-known tough guy offered to sponsor him, "supposedly the toughest shylock in New York, and he wanted to be partners with me in a game. I told him, 'Ruby, I don't want to be involved.' He said, 'What are you worrying about? Nobody fucks with me.' Two weeks later they found him floating in the river, with his arms and legs cut off." Although this is one of the few sides of his life about which Doc is the least bit reticent, you get the feeling that he appreciated the people as much as he did the life, and he profited from his own appreciation for it. In the end, though, it simply proved too risky, the players too filled with a sense of their own doom. The blues clubs in which Doc had originally found himself were full of life and a violent sense of possibility; the games were simply violent.

It really had me upset at the end. That's why I stopped. It's a very, very strange, rough kind of life. You meet some strange people. A lot of it is very sad. You know, when I was a kid I had a way of blanking myself out from my surroundings. Sometimes I'd leave George's Tavern, and it'd be snowing, but the only way I'd know it was snowing was when I got home I'd be all wet and I'd realize that I must have slipped and fallen a few times. I had worked out this way of shutting off all the ugly reality.

Later on, you know, it worked against me, because a lot of times if something should happen that I didn't want to deal with, I would just shut it off. There are whole parts of my marriage that I don't recall at all. There'd be times I'd lock myself in a hotel room for two days at a time, I'd be so paranoid and petrified and scared. Because I was convinced I was doomed — well, 70 percent of me was convinced. The other part of me shut it all out, the other part of me really believed that I was gonna beat the world, I was going to be larger than life, a man among men. And I gotta tell you, you must realize, I only gambled because I thought I wasn't a songwriter any more.

With Big Joe Turner, late '70s. *Photograph by Sharyn Felder*

He gave it up around 1975 out of the same combination of instinct and inevitability that had guided him through every other major shift in his life. Gradually he began to reemerge on the scene and discovered to his amazement that the world which had grown up around him was a world in which he still had a place, a more congenial place as it turned out than he had ever occupied within the strict confines of Brill Building politesse. His advice was wanted. His songs had lasted. Old friends like Ben E. King, whom he had originally recorded with the Crowns (before the Crowns became the Drifters) on a little label that Doc ran "for a minute" in 1958, were still around. New friends came along. Through one of those new friends, Joel Dorn, he got involved in a couple of records with the singularly funky New Orleans artist Dr. John (Mac Rebennack), who remains his most frequent songwriting collaborator to this day, and with Dorn he co-produced the first album by a promising new r&b revivalist group, Roomful of Blues, in 1977. When his old partner Big Joe Turner returned to New York after many years in a triumphant 1976 comeback at the Cookery, they picked up their friendship where it had left off, and Doc found over $25,000 in back royalties for Turner as well as producing a Grammy Award–nominated album for him on the Muse label in 1983.

Most important, perhaps, he started writing again, as prolifically and as well as ever. Soon he became involved with a whole new generation of riffraff and unregenerate ne'er-do-wells like himself. The only flaw in this perfect picture of Doc in his Dotage, the happily honored Elder Statesman, is that, unlike other latter-day prophets, he has never taken any steps to protect himself or his reputation. Despite his well-earned, and well-thought-out, aesthetic of cool, Doc has always remained the very antithesis of cool (except in the coolest sense)—loyal, peevish, tolerant to a fault, willing to deliver himself of an opinion on any and all topics with a seeming guilelessness that betrays anger, sentimentality, testiness, wisdom, and a desperate need for love in turn, and that leads one above all to the irrefutable conclusion that he is deeply, passionately, irrevocably *involved*. If he is, as he says, a target for every asshole on the street, the mark for every alternative record company that comes along to rip off the artist in the same old fashion, without even the saving grace of honest venality—he wouldn't have it any other way. The one thing in which Doc has always believed, Doc's entire faith is centered on the notion that you *must* put yourself on the line. This is the way in which Jerome Felder was able to become "a man among men."

Doc Pomus today is engaged in a myriad of different projects. At any given moment at least three or four things are happening, or not happening, as the case may be. At various points in the last few years there have been: a Jimmy Witherspoon album which Doc and his songwriting partner Mac Rebennack wrote and produced; a 1981 Grammy Award-winning album by B.B. King; any number of fervent attempts to get somebody to make a new record by Little Jimmy Scott, a heartbreakingly fragile-voiced jazz and r&b pal from the '40s (whose beautiful niece, Aida, Doc used to date), which for all of Doc's indignation and passion have yet to show any sign of bearing fruit. There was a wrestling LP that Cyndi Lauper was involved in and for which Doc wrote the opening cut; an Easter Seals musical revue; a recent blues benefit for HAI (Hospital Audiences, Inc.) at the Lone Star. There are always movie projects in the offing; a new cut on an old song; or a songwriting session scheduled with one of his two or three songwriting partners of the moment. Once in a while Doc will offer a six-week songwriting seminar for the dozen or so students who can fit in his book-crammed, memento-strewn West Side apartment. More commonly he will fire off letters, out of love, rage, or, in the case of his not-

Doc and Mac, writing in Doc's apartment on West 72nd Street. *Photograph by Sharyn Felder*

infrequent missives to the trade publication *Billboard,* just to correct the historical record.

Money is no longer a problem. When Dolly Parton cut "Save the Last Dance for Me" a few years ago, for example, both Doc and Mort Shuman saw more money as an advance against royalties than they once would have gotten from a year's worth of work.

That, Doc will tell you, is about all that's changed — and it really doesn't mean that much. The problems that remain are no different from the ones with which he has had to contend since childhood: "mechanical" problems, the inevitable preoccupation of the handicapped — and not, Doc hastens to add, simply the predictable concerns of finding a dependable driver, getting a wheelchair or lift repaired, ascertaining that a club or public event to which he has been invited affords wheelchair access. It is just as much a matter of being prepared, psychologically, to venture out into the world, "of being able to go to a club in a certain way, being able

"There Must Be a Better World Somewhere"

(POMUS-REBENNACK) BY B.B. KING, 1981

Here again, this has a lot to do with my philosophy about the way things are, or at least the way things are for me personally. Well, you know, let me tell you, I guess if you're leading a certain kind of life, these are the kind of songs you're gonna write. It's like you're fighting heavyweight champions with one arm tied behind your back. I think everyone involved with writing blues, or singing the blues, feels like that. There was a situation in the studio, and I think I'm going to relate it to you accurately, as far as I can remember. The evening of the recording session, the weather was very bad and my van was in bad shape, so I never got to the session, and I was really torn up. Because B. was recording in New York, and it was a great opportunity, so it just killed me to miss it. But the story that Stewart Levine, the producer, told me — he called me up about three o'clock in the morning — was that they were sitting in the studio and B.B. King was studying the lyric, and suddenly he broke down and started crying. And he was like that for a long time, and nobody knew what to do. And what happened, finally, after a while he told Stewart he had had that lyric for so long and he finally understood what the lyrics meant. So after that he went in and did it in one take.

"A World I Never Made"

(POMUS-REBENNACK) BY B.B. KING (1982) AND JOHNNY ADAMS (1987)

This was a favorite phrase of mine from the poet A. E. Housman, and I was always determined to write a lyric around it, without paying that much attention to what his message was, really. What can I tell you? It's like with Edward Hopper, when they asked him, "Who are those paintings about, all those late-night diners?," and he said, "They're all me." That's what it's all about. It's all me. It's not me all the time, but it's me a lot of the time. But, you know, let me tell you something, to Dr. John I think it meant something different. You see, there's two ways of approaching that thing. One way it just means you had nothing to do with the making of the world, right? And the other approach is, "It's a world I never understood." Which is a subtle difference.

to create a kind of free flow so you can stand up in front of the world and be the person you want to be — or the person you *think* you want to be. It's so ridiculous, really, and it takes such an extreme amount of preparation. I don't know why this stuff even bothers me at my age — but there it is, there's nothing you can do about it."

It's hard to believe, when you see Doc in action, that he is not by nature a gregarious person, but he insists that his social skills, his extraordinary ability to *make contact,* are nothing more than an acquired response, an instinctive way of dealing with his disability. Maybe so — but I've never known anyone with more friends, and self-appointed aides-de-camp, than Doc, and I don't mean that in a sentimental way either, since Doc can be just as much of a pain in the ass (as he himself will be the first to tell you) as any of the rest of us. He seems to thrive on habits, and relationships, of long standing. On any given day he will get several dozen phone calls, from friends, acquaintances, and would-be biographers, from his daughter, Sharyn, his brother, Raoul, or his longtime friend Shirlee, whose infant son, Joshua Jeromy, takes his middle name from Doc. No matter what the circumstances of his life, no matter what his state of mind, Doc continues to work. "What is so remarkable about his writing today," says Rounder Records producer Scott Billington, to whom Doc has given some of his best recent work for projects by Johnny Adams and Irma Thomas, "is that it's so much like his songs of twenty-five years ago — only it's deeper. It's almost as if he's past the point of mere craftsmanship — even though all of Doc's songs are craftsmanlike by nature — he's writing songs that call for great singers. He's writing songs that *demand* a commitment on the artist's part; he brings out the best in a great singer."

"Hi, Doc. Brother Ray speaking." That is the way Ray Charles will announce himself, as he did just the other day, even if the phone call should follow a silence of several years. They first met when Charles signed with Atlantic at the age of twenty-one, and Ray always insisted that the song-writer demo his own songs because he liked the sound of Doc's voice. The reason for the recent call was to let Doc know that he had recorded one of Doc's new compositions on his upcoming CBS album, his first pop effort in some time. "I was walking on air for two weeks; there wasn't a thing that could get to me," Doc will confide with the same gleeful enthusiasm that he must have showed over thirty years ago when he got his first Ray Charles cut with "Lonely Avenue." A number of other old friends were in town recently for Atlantic Records' fortieth anniversary (though Doc would

At the Lone Star Cafe: Doc in front, unknown, Ben E. King, me, Solomon, and Don Covay.
Courtesy of Peter Guralnick Archives

argue, not enough), and Doc spent time with many of them, some of whom wanted to get together, some of whom merely wanted to telephone reminisce, some of whom were still desperately trying to score good weed. Maybe, Doc muses, thinking out loud, the Lone Star would like to do a Mickey Baker show. Maybe Ahmet could be persuaded to set up a retirement fund for some of the old-timers. Maybe a new generation could be led to recognize the contributions of the old through some kind of star tribute or special project—but then again, maybe not.

"I'm doing the same shit I always did. I'm acting the same way I always acted. The only difference is that now I talk about it. At one time I wouldn't express my opinions except to maybe my closest friends, because it wasn't cool to be that animated. Now I don't hold anything back. I do it because I have the confidence, I guess, and because I'd rather be vocal about it than not say anything. I don't know, maybe it's just so I'll get noticed, but I really don't want to live to see a day where the space that I take up in this world is like some musty closet, some little broom closet somewhere — I want to be able to talk out, even if I'm wrong.

"I'll tell you, Peter, there has been such an element of luck, surviving. Half the time I didn't have a clue to what I was doing. I don't even know if you *can* know what you're doing. Right now I'm backing off a little, because it's started getting on my nerves again. You know, when you first get back in, you always forget the reasons that got you disgusted in the first place. Now I'm back in it, and I'm dealing with these record producers, record companies, publishers — it's a nonsensical thing because you're dealing with people who do what they do out of choice. In other words, it's not accidental, the way they deal with people. You take a pure singer like Jimmy Scott, he's sixty-two, sixty-three years old. He'll die, and maybe there'll be some kind of hot funeral. They'll all show up in hip mourning clothes and talk about how great he was. Well, I'm tired of going around hustling money to pay for funerals and hospital bills, explaining to the world all the reasons that this shouldn't have happened. I'm getting good and pissed off at the affluent members of the music community who sit around and pontificate but let those tragedies happen again and again. I read an interview with this rock star who said if Jonas Salk was in a bar with him, people would just ignore Jonas Salk and pay attention to him, and that was terrible! Well, my thought is this: if they all paid attention to Jonas Salk, that rock star would be hiding in the bathroom. He wouldn't appreciate it too much, you see. I think it was just something that sounded good at the time."

EPILOGUE

D OC DIED OF LUNG CANCER three years later, on March 14, 1991, just nine months after a blowout sixty-fifth birthday celebration (it was actually a combined 121st, for him and his fifty-six-year-old brother, Raoul) at Katz's Delicatessen in lower Manhattan.

He kept writing almost up to his last breath, scribbling lyrics, as he always did, in his notebook or on scraps of paper. One time Dr. John came into the hospital with a portable keyboard to finish up a song they were working on for B.B. King.

The funeral was an all-star event, with various industry luminaries in attendance, and Dr. John and Little Jimmy Scott, two of Doc's favorites, contributing the musical accompaniment. Mac sang "My Buddy," accompanying himself on organ, and then accompanied Jimmy Scott on one of his signature tunes, "Someone to Watch over Me," which drew emotional gasps at first, then sustained applause. And, miracle of miracles (I can see Doc shaking his head—but in a way it *was* a fucking miracle), Jimmy was signed off this performance by Seymour Stein, founder of Madonna's label, Sire Records, who had been impervious to all of Doc's previous appeals, both public and private, all these years. (*"What is everybody waiting for?"* Doc had written as recently as 1987 in an impassioned plea in *Billboard.*)

Ahmet spoke. So did Doc's newfound buddy Lou Reed, and Charles Jones ("Jonesy"), who had operated a restaurant in Bedford-Stuyvesant when Doc was still singing the blues in the black neighborhoods of Brooklyn. "He had a healthy appetite, good eater, good sense of humor," Jonesy said—just one of the many encomiums this lifelong friend delivered ("He treated everybody the same, whether you were on the lowest rung of the ladder or the highest"), his face agleam not so much with regret as with undimmed appreciation. Phil Spector and record producer Joel Dorn spoke of their friendship and love for Doc, and so did I, while Mac declared himself to be "a degenerate scumbag dope fiend—excuse me, Rabbi, but it's the truth," before singing one of his and Doc's most uplifting compositions, "There Must Be a Better World Somewhere." And Allen Klein, always an admirer of Doc's, started a standing ovation as the casket was rolled out to the strains of "Save the Last Dance for Me." At least Allen took credit for it.

My last memory of that day is of going back to the new apartment that Doc's daughter, Sharyn, had found for him while he was in the hospital, more spacious, more gracious than the one we had all visited so often over the years (it even had a terrace in the back)—but one which Doc never got to see. There must have been seventy-five people there at one time or another—but no more than fifteen or twenty at the end of the evening. Phil Spector was in a fearsome mood (he was angry at the universe, it seemed) and was passionately haranguing Doc's son, Geoffrey, and Sharyn, in what I recall as a walk-in closet (it must have been a pretty big closet, because Geoffrey was an ex-football player of no small size). The subject of his harangue was that Doc had been cheated of his songwriting royalties all these years and that Geoffrey and Sharyn needed to get Allen Klein, who had recently enrolled Phil as a client, to recover them. Ahmet Ertegun was shaky on his feet (he had recently had hip replacement surgery) but was also clearly, and happily, under the influence — and he had by now abandoned the two canes on which he had made his entrance for the support of two beautiful young women, on whom he leaned with the satisfied grin of a Cheshire cat.

In the end everyone who was left gravitated to the Wurlitzer piano in the living room, where Phil took the treble keys and *Late Night with David Letterman* bandleader Paul Shaffer the bass, and everyone sang "Save the Last Dance for Me." At the end Ahmet held up his hand. "That's enough," he said. "You've got me in tears. Don't spoil it, don't do any more." Everyone else was in tears, too. But for whatever reason, the music went on, and we all kept singing, until finally it stopped. And Ahmet was right — but it didn't really matter. Nothing could take away from the magic of the moment, not even Doc's spirit gently remonstrating, "Ah, what can I tell you, it's all a lot of nonsense." But I don't have any doubt he would have been pleased.

Twenty-one years later, after overcoming enough obstacles to qualify as the twelve labors of Heracles, Doc's daughter, Sharyn, was finally able to bring to the screen a documentary that had originally started out under her aegis (the final product would be produced and directed by others but always retained her touch) as *Magic and Flying*. I want to go on record here as stating unequivocally that *AKA Doc Pomus* is one of the most soulful documentaries I've ever seen — and not, as Doc would have been the first to point out, because of technique but because of *feeling*. As Doc said, "I don't want to live to see a day where the space that I take up in this world is like some musty closet," and the documentary shows over and over again that it was not. But more than that, *AKA Doc Pomus* enlists all of Doc's friends to prove the point. I've got to admit that even though I participated enthusiastically I was prepared to be suspicious of what could have turned into a sentimentalization of a man who despised phony sentiment. But thanks to Doc's personality every sentiment that could have been phony is imbued with deeply felt, realistic love — and while not all of Doc's friends may have liked each other, I think we could all see in the film the qualities that Doc saw in each of us. He could in no small measure be said to have elevated us all.

FIFTEEN

Me and the Colonel

I FIRST MET THE MAN known as Colonel Thomas A. Parker at the Elvis Birthday Celebration in Memphis in January of 1988. I had just begun work on my Elvis biography, and I was there (this was actually my first Elvis Birthday Celebration and the only one I would attend for another twenty years) solely because Colonel Parker was advertised as one of the featured guests and, knowing the rarity of his public appearances, let alone any appearance blessed by the Elvis world, I figured this might be my one and only chance to absorb a little bit of his aura.

I was sitting with Sam and Knox Phillips and the rest of the Phillips family when Sam announced that he thought he would like to go over to say hello to his old adversary, Tom Parker (never "Colonel"—"he ain't no damned colonel," Sam declared on this and many other subsequent occasions), probably for the first time in close to thirty years. Being the opportunistic soul that all writers are meant to be, I tagged along, and in the aftermath, I wrote to the Colonel, saying how much I had enjoyed our meeting and telling him about the book I was embarking upon, about my serious intentions and how I meant this book to be different from other Elvis books. Most of all, I said, I hoped he might rethink his policy of not doing interviews ("I know you have never done this before, so let me at least make my pitch!") and, possibly, see this "as an opportunity to set the record straight" by involving himself in what I hastened to assure him would be a long-term and what I hoped he would find to be a fair-minded process.

Not surprisingly, he didn't take me up on my offer—but he did write back almost immediately on stationery that looked like it might have been resurrected from another age, with its Conestoga-wagon illustration

Colonel's office at 20th Century Fox Studios. *Courtesy of Elvis Presley Enterprises*

Colonel's calling card. *Courtesy of Peter Guralnick Archives*

advertising "All Star Shows" on the wagon cover, the promise of "Exclusive Management" just below, and, in a single concession to the altered circumstances of the present day, "CONSULTATION" typed in faintly on the wagon underneath. He greeted me not with his customary salutation of "Friend Peter" (that would have to wait until the second letter) but a gracious acknowledgment of "the honesty of your request" and an offer to put my name "in a file of literary friends that I know I can trust," when the time came for him to publish his own book. He also enclosed a poem he had written called "My Memories of Elvis," which paid tribute to the parental love with which Elvis had been blessed and his discovery by a "man name[d] Sam," but most of all, by a recitation of their titles, to the songs that Elvis had sung and the emotional impact that they had had, and would continue to have, upon the world.

Thus began a correspondence that more closely resembled a chess game in which, with all the goodwill in the world, I attempted to gain an advantage on the Colonel, and he, with all the goodwill in the world, blocked me every time.

One time out of the blue he wrote a "Sad Old Colonel" letter, in which he declared that he had had no idea that I was writing a book on Elvis Presley. I wrote back, perhaps more than a little disingenuously myself, "Dear Colonel, I feel terrible," but not to be outdone, he replied by return mail, "Friend Peter, Don't feel terrible, as it has nothing to do with our friendship. . . . I want to remain completely neutral in this situation, but I am your friend."

Another time, after we had had time to get our epistolary styles in order, he wrote back in response to a rough chronological outline of the beginning of his association with Elvis that I had sent him: "Friend Peter, I do not wish to waste my time to make corrections regarding the most misinformed information I have ever read in all my career in show business." And then proceeded to waste some of his time feeding me information that might be of help and signing off, of course, "Good luck from your friend, Colonel."

The upshot — well, the upshot of our first year of correspondence — was that he invited me to his eightieth birthday party in Las Vegas in June of 1989, a wonderful occasion in and of itself at which I met many luminaries in the Elvis world as well as the moving men who had recently moved Colonel and his wife, Loanne, from his Hilton headquarters into their new apartment.

At the end of the evening I went up to thank him. He was sitting on a throne-like chair surrounded by various images of elephants, including a giant ice sculpture behind him, tusked and trumpeting, with Sam Phillips standing just to his left. The two of them were engaged in a spirited discussion that had to do with the events that had occurred between October 29 and midnight on the night of November 15, 1955, essentially the sale of Elvis' contract by Sam's Sun record label to RCA.

They were going at it hammer and tongs, each armed with what appeared to be an unbreachable memory accompanied by a steel-trapped intellect unprepared to concede the possibility of error. The discussion proceeded not week by week, not day by day, but hour by hour, with neither giving any quarter and each telling the same story — but from an entirely different point of view.

This might have gone on all night, but I had to catch a plane, so I inserted myself into a rare pause in the conversation, stated my name, and congratulated and thanked the Colonel. He looked at me a little balefully, I thought, and then said in that surprisingly thick, guttural accent: "I put you on the list." Well, I know, I acknowledged with some puzzlement—of course he had put me on the list, how else would I have been invited? This went on in an Alphonse-and-Gaston sort of way for quite a while until the obvious finally dawned on me. What he was saying was: HE HAD PUT ME ON THE LIST.

Which meant, quite simply, he had given me the chance to meet maybe two dozen of the most elusive and central figures in Elvis' life, and while I was certainly not so ill-bred as to bring up the subject of my book at Colonel's birthday party, I recognized the opportunity I had been provided—and, finally, the manner in which it had been offered. And so I followed up with letters to Tom Hulett, Freddy Bienstock, Julian Aberbach, and many others, whom I might never otherwise have gotten the opportunity to talk to if, quite simply, Colonel had not—PUT ME ON THE LIST.

As for Sam and the Colonel, I left them arguing, in the most ferocious but friendly sort of way. "You ought to join us for breakfast tomorrow morning," Sam said, "for a continuation of this discussion." And I could only curse the fate that dictated that I had to catch a plane in an hour.

Now, let me back up a little. Actually, quite a lot. One of the most commonly misunderstood myths about Elvis is that he was always a pawn in somebody else's game. In other words, that he was little more than a raw, instinctive talent, a "natural," to use the term that people so often assign to great athletes, too, when they want to dismiss the intelligence and sense of direction that allowed the artist or athlete to find their way on their own. That was the Svengali role sometimes assigned to Sam, Elvis' original discoverer, as the Colonel's poem attests, who played an indisputable part in developing Elvis' artistic talent but who would be the first to admit that he neither created nor dictated that talent: he merely did all that he could, with the genius that *he* possessed, to bring it out.

As for the Colonel, he has always been assigned another, more sinister role. He is said to have been the person who swooped in and devoured that talent. He is not infrequently painted as the man who stole Elvis Presley's soul.

Nothing could be further from the truth. The first thing that has to be understood about Elvis and the Colonel at the outset of their relationship is that it was Colonel Tom Parker who was the superstar in his field when he first came into contact with Elvis Presley. It was January of 1955, and Elvis was a rising twenty-year-old regional star with unlimited talent, unbounded ambition, and untapped potential, but with just two singles on a tiny Memphis label to his name. The Colonel meanwhile had managed Eddy Arnold to heights of stardom never before imagined in the world of country music and unmatched in popular success until Garth Brooks came along.

With the Colonel's close guidance (Eddy Arnold was Colonel's only client for nearly ten years), Arnold left the Grand Ole Opry, the safe harbor for nearly every other country music star, and hosted his own network television show, played Las Vegas, and even, somewhat reluctantly, starred in two singing-cowboy movies, while at the same time achieving more than fifteen number-one country hits in six years, remaining at the top of the charts for forty weeks in 1948 alone. At the time that Elvis and the Colonel first met, Parker was managing Hank Snow, another of Elvis' idols, and Elvis' first real opportunity to break out of the narrow regional success to which he had so far been confined came when Colonel put him on a Hank Snow tour in February of 1955. If there are any doubts about Elvis' feelings at the time, they should be dispelled by the telegram he sent to his new mentor some eight months later, the day after the RCA deal was signed.

"Words can never tell you how my folks and I appreciate what you did for me," he declared. "I've always known and now my folks are assured that you are the best, most wonderful person I could ever hope to work with. Believe me when I say I will stick with you through thick and thin and do everything I can to uphold your faith in me. Again, I say thanks, and I love you like a father. Elvis Presley."

It was during his time with Eddy Arnold that the Colonel first got his sobriquet. It was, of course, an honorary title, awarded as something of a carny's quid pro quo by Louisiana's singing Governor Jimmie Davis (Davis is credited as the composer of one of the great pop-country classics of all time, "You Are My Sunshine"), and Colonel, whom Elvis in later years would not infrequently address as Admiral, took it, I'm sure, in the spirit in which it was offered. But, as someone who never failed to recognize with a certain degree of amusement that the height of your chair can determine your status in the world, he also took it one step further.

"In the future," he told Eddy Arnold's bass player, Gabe Tucker, "you will make sure that everyone addresses me as the Colonel." And by and large everyone did, with the exception of a few old friends and associates like Eddy Arnold, Sam Phillips, song publishers Jean and Julian Aberbach, and William Morris executives Abe Lastfogel and Harry Kalcheim. It was in a sense just an extension of real-life role playing, the Colonel's straight-faced approach to a genre Richard Pryor would later take in a somewhat different direction (but one no less subject to misinterpretation): comedic reality.

It wasn't all just smoke and mirrors, though. It wasn't even mostly smoke and mirrors. Colonel took his role as manager, promoter, and one-man band altogether seriously. For example, when Elvis appeared at the 12th Annual White River Water Carnival in Batesville, Arkansas, on August 6, 1955, just as Colonel was about to take over from Elvis' first manager, Bob Neal, a number of patrons strongly objected not to the music but to the off-color jokes that the singer and his bass player, Bill Black, bandied back and forth — and to the brevity of the show. Colonel refunded $50 to the promoter and, he wrote to Bob Neal:

> You must definitely set up a new deal with Elvis where he gets on the
> stage as a singer, stays on the stage as a singer, and comes off like a
> singer. . . . To be exact, I just can't have any more comedy on Elvis
> Presley's part of the program. . . . Elvis has great talents, and he does not
> have to resort to smutty comedy to sell his attractions. When we ask for
> more money for Elvis, we definitely must give better production or we
> should sell him as a comic and you know how much we can get for his
> doing that. I think the most important thing is that he needs guidance.
> He is young, inexperienced, and it takes a lot more than a couple of hot
> records in a certain territory to become a big-name artist, [you must be]
> level-headed, courteous, and carry the responsibility that goes with being
> a star as Elvis wants to be. There is no way we can play this down — even
> if we tried — as we would only be fooling ourselves and would be out of
> business in no time. My reputation is more important than my
> friendship and belief in the talents that Elvis has. He can cash in on this
> to the fullest, but he must contribute all the qualities that I know he has
> or can have if he makes up his mind to do so.

Not long afterward he got permission from Elvis' parents, Vernon and Gladys, to assume much of the burden of responsibility himself, and just three months later he managed to convince RCA to pay the unheard-of sum of $35,000 to purchase Elvis' contract from Sun, putting up $5,000

of his own money at the start of that two-week sequence that he and Sam
Phillips would still be debating thirty-three years later.

One of the other things in which he resolutely believed, and which he
had gained for Elvis as a contractual guarantee from RCA, was the power
of national television exposure, something which much of the industry
saw as being of highly dubious value because of the way it was feared it
would undercut the value of personal appearances. In the aftermath of
the signing, RCA, despite their commitment to obtain a minimum of
three national television engagements, did nothing. Nor did the William
Morris Agency, to whom Colonel next assigned the task. So he took matters into his own hands, and within three weeks of the signing had gotten
Elvis a four-appearance booking on Jimmy and Tommy Dorsey's *Stage
Show,* with an option for two more. Not, however, without a scathing
rebuke for his old friend Harry Kalcheim, the head of William Morris'
New York office, with whom he had done Eddy Arnold business for years.
"Knowing you as I do," he wrote:

> *I will be very frank. . . . Steve Yates called me with an offer for the
> Gleason show [this was the* Stage Show, *which Jackie Gleason produced],
> one shot, and the price he gave me was way out of line so I told him what
> I wanted for Presley and he got it. I called you up right after this and
> asked you why your man had not worked on this set-up. . . .*
>
> *Harry, you know as well as I do offering a new artist is one thing but
> selling one is another. I can't go for a pitch that my artist has been
> submitted and then wait till you hear from someone that wants him.
> That way you can write 100 letters and just sit and wait till someone
> comes up with a deal. . . . I don't think that this artist was pitched full
> force, for the reaction that I got on my own deals have been very good and
> so far we got nothing from William Morris . . .*
>
> *If I waited for someone to call me with deals all the time, I would
> have to start selling candy apples again. Nuff said. . . . You know my
> feelings towards you and William Morris but I can't let my friendship
> keep my artist from working, so let's all dig in and keep things rolling. I
> think this will work out for the best [for] all of us. But I do hope that
> your man will at least dig in a little more often and tell everyone so they
> will know who they should call. My best to you and the family, Your Pal,
> The Colonel [with a handwritten "Tom" appended]*

With Ed Sullivan, *Ed Sullivan Show*, October 28, 1956. *Courtesy of Elvis Presley Enterprises*

He worked on Elvis' movie deal some four months later in much the same way — pretty much on a wing and a prayer. Once again he saw the movies as integral to broadening his act's appeal, bringing in more people in just a few weeks than any performer could hope to reach in years of personal appearances. But Hollywood almost universally — I think you could amend that to *universally* — saw Elvis as a novelty act, and had it been up to them, the Hollywood moguls would have cast him in one of the numerous one-shot, low-budget exploitation pictures, like *Rock Around the Clock,* that were springing up. This was not for Colonel — nor, he felt, for Elvis Presley. Instead, he approached Hal Wallis, one of the most successful independent movie producers of the day, and after what Wallis somewhat patronizingly described as "one of the toughest bargaining sessions of my career," signed a one-picture deal with options at the

On the set of *Love Me Tender,* August/September 1956. *Courtesy of Elvis Presley Enterprises*

producer's election for six more, paying just $15,000 for the first, $20,000 for the second, up to $100,000 for the last. It was a *terrible* deal, in other words, but one which Colonel made, as so often in his career, with the idea that, once he got his foot in the door he could improve it almost immeasurably by relying on his own wits and Elvis Presley's boundless talent.

He did. Over the years, whatever you may think of Elvis' cinematic oeuvre, he turned Elvis into the number-one box office attraction in the country — or at least the number-one moneymaker — and he bedeviled poor Hal Wallis in a way that this wily veteran of over thirty years in show business could never have imagined. To the grand high poobahs of Hollywood, as Colonel never ceased to delight in telling Elvis, and Elvis never ceased to delight in hearing, they were nothing but rubes — but when the

At Nashville recording session, June 10, 1958. *Courtesy of Elvis Presley Enterprises*

negotiations were over, as Colonel meticulously pointed out to his client, who was the rube then?

One time, when they were shooting *Blue Hawaii*, Colonel halted filming by walking in front of the cameras and demanding a conference with Wallis. Wallis, who thought something must be seriously wrong, inquired anxiously as to what the problem might be. "Read the contract, read the contract," the Colonel replied, although by now Wallis was beginning to catch on. "You know, if Elvis provides his own clothes, he gets $10,000 more." Wallis surveyed the scene, in which Elvis was wearing nothing but a bathing suit and riding a surfboard, and arched his eyebrows. "He's wearing his own watch," declared the Colonel without batting an eye. And the scene did not proceed until he took off the watch.

The upshot of it all—well, what can I say? Poor Hal Wallis. For the final picture they made for Wallis, *Easy Come, Easy Go* in 1966, Elvis got $500,000, plus 20 percent of the profits, which, as Colonel gratuitously pointed out to Wallis, was a bargain price he would offer no other studio. After nearly six months of negotiations, and excruciating renegotiations over what appeared to Wallis to be little more than exquisitely fabricated talking points, Wallis finally begged his partner, Joe Hazen, to please remind him in future, no matter what the inducements, never to do business with the Colonel again.

It was all in a good day's work. The irony was not far removed from the business of doing business — in fact, often it was inextricably linked. Colonel had long since established his own club, the Snowmen's League, a W. C. Fieldsian celebrity roll without meetings or reality outside of the Colonel's sardonic imagination, which cost nothing to join but $10,000 to get out of ("We've never lost a member yet," Colonel boasted) and into which he had by now managed to enlist virtually everyone with whom he had come in contact since his arrival in Hollywood. It was nothing less, in short, than a celebration of the age-old concept of "snowing," somewhere between selling and conning, to which the Colonel had dedicated his life, its name a takeoff on the Showmen's League of circus owners and carnival operators from whom the Colonel had drawn his inspiration, its membership booklet a map of the League's method of doing business.

The table of contents gave a hint of methodology, with references to the "melt and disappear technique" and the concept of "directional" snowing (which required the ability to make one's approach simultaneous with one's departure) as well as consequences of the snowing life ("with sufficient training one can develop the ability to go nowhere with devastating results") — but the real core of the book was the thirty-two blank pages and Complete Listing of Paid-Up Members in Alphabetical Order (also blank) at its center. Over the years induction into the Snowmen's League came to be taken as a high honor in Hollywood, and its bemused membership included everyone from Hal Wallis and Joe Hazen to RCA executives, William Morris agents, newspaper columnists, and such prominent show business personalities as Frank Sinatra, Milton Berle, Bing Crosby, Gene Autry, and Bob Hope. It was the Colonel's sole concession to Hollywood social climbing, and, inevitably, one in which he dictated all the rules.

Unquestionably Colonel's biggest snow job of all was the very matter of his improbable origins. As the world well knows by now, he was born Andreas [Dries] Cornelis van Kuijk in Breda, Holland, on June 26, 1909, to a father who was a liveryman and a mother whose parents were floating peddlers, setting up a booth to sell their wares at local fairs and markets throughout the country. After his father's death he entered this country

Andreas Cornelis van Kuijk, ca. 1926–27.
Courtesy of Elvis Presley Enterprises

illegally on a freighter from Rotterdam, joined the Army, probably as André van Kuijk, and served with the 64th Regiment, an antiaircraft unit of the Coast Artillery, at Fort Shafter, just outside of Honolulu.

At some point, around the time of his honorable discharge while stationed at Fort Barrancas in Pensacola in 1932, he took the name of his former commanding officer, Captain Thomas R. Parker (note the difference in the middle initial if you have any concerns about identity theft), while claiming to come from a circus family (the Great Parker Pony Circus) in West Virginia. At this point he moved to Tampa, joined the Johnny J. Jones carnival and then the Royal American, married his first wife, Marie, whom he met working the Hav-a-Tampa cigar stand on the grounds of the South Florida Fair, and settled down with her and her son in Tampa, where he became Chief Dog Officer, selling an imaginative range of pet services, including a pet cemetery that included provisions for perpetual care. From there it was just a short leap into show business, where the Colonel's natural talent for promotion in the Florida area was enlisted by, among others, 1920s and '30s pop superstar Gene Austin (Austin's 1927 version of "My Blue Heaven" sold over five million copies and was the biggest-selling single of all time up until Bing Crosby's "White Christmas"), with whom he continued to be associated (and whom, in old age, he would continue to support) until Austin's death in 1972. He started booking Roy Acuff, perhaps the Opry's biggest star, on his frequent tours

Coast Guard Artillery, Fort Shafter, Honolulu, ca. 1929. *Courtesy of Elvis Presley Enterprises*

of Florida, and Acuff, who never had anything but the highest praise for Tom Parker, tried to persuade him to move to Nashville and become his manager. It wasn't until he met Eddy Arnold, though, on an Opry tent show tour with Jamup and Honey in 1944, that he saw the opportunity he had been waiting for.

In all this time no one ever seems to have questioned his origins, despite an accent that clearly was not Appalachian and the fact that at moments of high excitation he occasionally burst into Germanic apostrophes, which, if asked how he knew German, he was perfectly willing to explain away as Dutch. Then in 1961 his brother Ad saw him pictured in a magazine write-up about Elvis and got the Dutch magazine *Rosita* to sponsor him on a trip to Hollywood to reunite with this long-lost relative that no one in the family had heard from since 1932.

The Colonel didn't do much to avoid the reunion, simply postponed it until the filming of *Blue Hawaii* was complete. When Ad arrived, his brother's only instructions were that he must be addressed as Colonel at all times. When asked why he hadn't written in all these years, Colonel simply fell back on the same fabulism to which he treated the rest of the world. It was because, the Colonel said without blinking an eye, he and his wife had been destitute for much of that time.

"Sometimes," he said, "we had to live on a dollar a week. We slept in horse stables behind the horses. I did all kinds of things then. I went to the Indian territory, where I pretended to be a big wise white man. It so happened that sometimes I really predicted the future. I also had a canary and a few sparrows that I sprayed yellow and then sold. After a couple of weeks the people came back to me and said, 'This bird only says, "Peep!"' 'That's right,' I told them. 'It takes six weeks. It's got to feel at home.' I've been a dogcatcher, and I sold hot dogs. But I didn't want you to know all the things that I did. Besides, most of the time I didn't even have the money for stationery and a stamp. After that, the war came. I organized parties for the Army, and that's how I got into the world of show business."

His brother accepted it all in the spirit in which it was offered, staying in the storeroom of the Colonel's modest apartment, where he slept surrounded by stuffed animals, promotional items, and Elvis Presley merchandise. Something of an entrepreneur himself, he was bemused by his brother's sheer audacity. In the course of his seventeen-day visit he met a number of Colonel's friends and associates, including his brother-in-law Bitsy Mott, and, of course, Elvis Presley. He and Dries went out to Elvis' home in Bel Air, he liked to boast, and the Colonel introduced him simply as "my brother."

When he returned home, *Rosita*, something like the *Life* magazine of the Netherlands, ran a three-part series chronicling his visit. During this period *Time* magazine called the Colonel to find out what the story was with this guy from Holland who claimed to be his brother, but Colonel characteristically brazened it out. And in fact it wasn't until after Elvis' death that the world came to learn of the Colonel's true origins — and then only because Colonel declared in a lawsuit brought against him by the probate court on behalf of Elvis' only heir, his eleven-year-old daughter, Lisa Marie, that he couldn't be sued because he was a man without a country. (He won the lawsuit, incidentally — or at least was paid a good deal of the money he said he was owed, rather than having to pay anything back — but I'm not sure to what extent his claim of statelessness weighed on the decision.)

"How Much Does It Cost If It's Free?" was the title that Colonel always assigned to his unwritten autobiography. As sardonic and impenetrable as nearly all of the Colonel's public pronouncements, it masked a serious point: nothing was worth anything, you could not properly respect the effort or achievement that had gone into it, if some value were not placed on it. The Colonel's measure of value appeared to be primarily pecuniary.

But not always. Chris Hutchins, the British music reporter, in Hollywood for a *New Musical Express* profile of the Colonel, sat in on a merchandising conference in 1965. There were, Hutchins wrote, a couple of big-shot businessmen from New York who were there to make an $80,000 merchandising deal.

> Just before the businessmen arrived, an old friend of the Colonel's from his carnival days showed up. The friend had fallen on hard times and had with him a box containing several hundred balloons, which he offered to sell the Colonel for forty dollars. To help the man keep his pride, the Colonel bargained with him for half an hour, and finally bought the balloons for thirty-eight dollars.
>
> As he closed the deal, the Colonel invited in the tycoons who had been waiting in an outer office. When the man had gone, one of them stormed at the Colonel: "You kept us waiting twenty minutes to buy thirty-eight dollars' worth of balloons when we have a deal worth eighty thousand to discuss?" Replied the Colonel: "It so happens that his deal was more vital to him than yours would be to you. I say 'would,' gentlemen, because I've just decided not to do business with you. Good afternoon."

Colonel valued loyalty above all else. Toward the end of his life he liked to boast that everyone with whom he did business he had worked with for at least forty years. That included not just RCA and William Morris and Hill and Range but the printing firm he used in Florida, reporters whom he knew from the early days, and friends and associates like Grelun Landon, Al Dvorin, and his faithful lieutenant and confidant since Eddy Arnold days, Tom Diskin.

That was the underlying basis for his relationship with Elvis. It was a very dark time for Elvis when he was inducted into the Army in March of 1958. And when his mother died in August, just a month before he shipped out for Germany, he went into a tailspin of doubt and depression, desperately trying to deal with the fear he had felt since the day he had first gotten his draft notice: the irrational sense that his luck had run out, his fans would desert him, all of the things for which he had worked so hard, all of the hopes in which he had invested so much belief, would simply shrivel and die. The Colonel, who, of course, could not travel to Europe, even in the days before there was a Homeland Security Department, wrote him letter after letter, trying to buck up his spirits, devoting himself exclusively to his single client, at considerable financial risk to himself. Then in November he wrote Elvis and his father, Vernon, this letter.

Dear Vernon and Elvis,

Well here is the other news you have been waiting for. Have just received the report that 20th Century Fox also is picking up the new deal I worked on the past 8 months, so this brings the outlook for Elvis in a pretty solid picture for his future, better than it was before he went into the service.

I am sure you both will be pleased with this information, this also will prove to Elvis that he is not backsliding in any way. . . . Now at least I feel that we have what I always wanted to get on the Wallis contract ever since we first started out with them. Elvis knows how I felt about this set-up, but there was not much I could [do] at that time except get a little more each time we made a picture for Wallis and Hazen. The facts are now we do not have to call on Wallis everytime with our hat in our hands to ask for a little extra each time. The improvements I have been able to make will run into at least a couple of hundred thousand dollars more for the first Wallis and Fox pictures when Elvis comes out plus a percentage which we did not have on either before he went into the service. . . .

I know this should make Elvis very happy. With the extra gimmicks on photos and the special RCA Victor gimmicks we were able to include this year, Elvis will do even better this year than he did last year even while he is in the service. . . . Write a line with all the news so we at least know what is going on there. Give our best to Grandma and the boys, also from Mrs. Parker. Take care of yourselves.

The Colonel [hand-signed "Col"]

ELVIS' POST-ARMY CAREER is something that has been both much maligned and much misunderstood. John Lennon was famously quoted as saying, "Elvis died when he went into the Army." But in fact Elvis returned home from Germany with a renewed sense of ambition and an expanded sense of purpose, which included the determination to broaden his artistic horizons. That ambition was indisputably borne out not only by the brilliant *Elvis Is Back!* album sessions and the fulfillment of his lifelong dream to record the gospel album that became *His Hand in Mine,* but by his notable success as a song interpreter, a song *stylist,* particularly with the beautifully crafted ballads of Don Robertson and Doc Pomus and Mort Shuman over the next few years.

So what went wrong? With both Elvis — *and* Elvis and the Colonel? This clearly is not the place to recount the whole story — but suffice it to say, I don't think Elvis ever got over the death of his mother, or the sense of confusion that this introduced into the sure purposefulness with which he had conducted his march to success. Another way of saying it perhaps is that, apart from the music, he lacked the confidence to seek out a new path. Contrary to the widely held myths, he *did* make serious pictures after he got out of the Army — *Wild in the Country* and *Flaming Star* in particular — he just wasn't very good in them. For two and one-half years, from 1964 to mid-1966, he got lost in his spiritual studies (he at one point declared to the head of the Self-Realization Fellowship, founded by *Autobiography of a Yogi* author Paramahansa Yogananda, that he wanted to become a monk in the religious order), and neither the Colonel nor RCA nor anyone else was able to lure him into the studio for a non-soundtrack session, not even to fulfill his contractual obligations. Finally, in desperation, and because it was, really, the only thing he knew to do, the Colonel hit on the strategy of negotiating an almost unimaginable upgrading of his RCA contract (unimaginable, because Elvis' records were at this point in a steady spiral of decline) and then, using the contract as a wedge, inducing Elvis to go back into the studio to record the one thing that, in the absence of external pressure or persuasion, he might have chosen to record at this point: another gospel album. Which became *How Great Thou Art* — and which led in turn to the last great renaissance (stretching through the 1968 television "Comeback Special," the magnificent 1969 sessions at the American studio in Memphis, and the only slightly less successful 1970 and 1971 Nashville sessions) of Elvis' music.

If he had differences with his manager over this or any other matters, Elvis never raised them. Eddy Arnold, for example, wrote Colonel a letter in August of 1953 essentially stating that he had reached a point where he was no longer happy, did not agree with Colonel's brusque manner of doing business, and was convinced that further association would be in neither of their interests, concluding with the age-old bromide: "We started as friends, Colonel, let's end the same way."

Which, after a time, they did. But Elvis could never bring himself to that kind of confrontation. Instead, he seemingly became more and more uncertain about the direction he wanted his life to take until, in the spring of 1967, depressed about starting yet another movie and under the influence of a variety of medications, he fell in the middle of the night, postponing the start of a picture that had already been needlessly postponed, and causing Colonel to banish Elvis' spiritual adviser, Larry Geller, from the entourage, along with the books that Colonel felt had fueled his confusion. It was around this same time, too, that he redefined their business relationship as a kind of modified shared enterprise, in which for the first time Colonel would receive 50 percent of some of the non-guaranteed moneys (profit participation, for example, in the movies), based, I'm sure in his own mind, on the extra duties and extra-motivational requirements that had been forced on him.

Still they went on to new heights and new triumphs, with Elvis' Las Vegas opening on July 31, 1969, marking a culmination of Elvis' broad-scale ambition to incorporate all of the strands of American music that had influenced him into a single show. That very night the Colonel achieved a culmination of a different sort, as he outlined his terms for a contract extension on a hotel coffee shop tablecloth, raising Elvis' salary from $100,000 to $125,000 a week, effective immediately, and guaranteeing him one million dollars a year for just eight weeks' work annually — at least through 1974.

None of this was enough to stave off the inevitable effects of drift and depression from which Elvis was suffering more and more from at least 1972 on, but Colonel did his best to lift Elvis' spirits (and, not coincidentally, line both their pockets) with a live satellite telecast from Hawaii in January of 1973. This was advertised as the first entertainment event to approach anything like instant global dissemination and had come to the Colonel in a flash from watching President Nixon's live broadcast from China the previous February. It did indeed inspire Elvis for a brief time — he lost a lot of weight and dedicated himself momentarily to the challenge — and when it was over Colonel wrote to him at three in the morning, in as emotional a communication as survives from their years together. *They had no need to hug each other to show their feelings*, Colonel wrote, because they could tell just by looking at one another from the stage and from the floor how each one felt. "I always know that when I do my part," Colonel wrote, "you always do yours in your own way and in your feeling in how to do it best. That is why you and I are never at each other when we are doing our work in our own best way possible at all times."

Life was short, he went on, and many were quick to take credit after the fact, but Elvis knew who was really responsible for this idea, "this brainchild . . . came from you and me." The others — except for Mr. Parkhill from RCA Record Tours and Mr. Diskin and his troupe "and all your own selected talent" — were just Johnny-come-latelies. But Elvis didn't need to be reminded of that. Because "you above all make all of it work by being the leader and the talent. Without your dedication to your following it couldn't have been done."

Six months later Elvis fired Colonel, in an incident that might have been a replay of the 12th Annual White River Water Carnival in Batesville, Arkansas, eighteen years earlier. Onstage at the Hilton in Las Vegas, Elvis delivered an out-of-control, stream-of-consciousness diatribe against the Hilton hotel management for firing his favorite waiter. The Colonel was understandably upset, but when he remonstrated that this was no way to behave, that Elvis should always remember that he was a *professional,* Elvis fired him in front of everybody, and Colonel, sixty-four years old now and tired of it all, responded with the classic comeback, "You can't fire me, I quit." In the end he didn't stay fired, Elvis owed him too much money in deferred commissions, and, perhaps more to the point, lost his nerve. So they continued in an uneasy alliance that did credit, really, to neither one. It was like a marriage gone bad, a folie à deux, in which neither could be the first to say goodbye.

But I'm not going to dwell on that now. (You can read *Careless Love* for all the sad details.) The way I like to think of the Colonel is as a man caught up in what he always called, what always *was* for him "the wonderful world of show business," a world in which he remained surrounded by images of elephants and windmills to the end. The way that Elvis and he chose to think of each other in better times was as an unlikely and unmatched team — not Don Quixote and Sancho Panza exactly but possessed of no less impossible a dream, sallying forth into a world that refused to take them seriously at first but that was eventually won over by the illimitable talent of the one, the indomitable resourcefulness of the other. I'm not sure that either could have succeeded to the degree that they did without that initial appreciation for each other — and the scorn that each felt for the limits that the world wanted to set on them. Each in his own way approached life con brio, and their marriage was based for many years on

Sam Phillips, Colonel Parker, and an Innocent Bystander, June 24, 1989.
Photograph by Sally Wilbourn

a combination of mutual respect, mutual trust, and a finely honed sense
of boundaries that were never to be crossed.

In fact, in all their years together, Colonel never encroached on Elvis'
musical territory, except on one occasion when he recommended a song
that had long been his wife Marie's favorite in his first client Gene Austin's
rendition. He knew it was old-fashioned, he wrote to Elvis almost delicately in March of 1960, it was a ballad with a dramatic recitation that
had first been a hit in 1927, but he thought the song, "Are You Lonesome
Tonight?," could be right for Elvis' "new" post-Army style, and he had a
hunch that it could be a hit all over again. Elvis listened to it carefully, and
when he recorded it, he turned out all the lights in the studio, delivering
the recitation in the dark. He apologized to a&r man Steve Sholes after
flubbing the first take and said, "Mr. Sholes, throw that tune out, I can't
do it justice." But Sholes refused to listen to him, engineer Bill Porter

recalled, and they finished the song successfully with Elvis' customary vocal quartet, the Jordanaires, providing the perfect, hushed backdrop.

In his last few years Colonel would call me from time to time, volunteering information even as he insisted that while he wished he could help me, his hands were, somehow, inexplicably tied. I attended his eighty-fifth birthday celebration in June of 1994, and he was thrilled with the success of the first volume of my Elvis biography, *Last Train to Memphis,* when it came out a few months later — he referred to the review in the *Los Angeles Times* as an advertisement and wondered how I had arranged with the paper to get so much space. In fact, he seemed altogether pleased with the overall picture that the book painted, although he scolded me mercilessly for its title. "Well, you know," he said, and I could never be sure if his adamant linearity was serious or a joke, "Elvis took a train from New Jersey to Memphis when he got out of the Army — and it was snowing, too. Then we took a train to Miami to do the Frank Sinatra television special. But we took a bus back. You know, money doesn't grow on trees." (Sam Phillips didn't take any more benign a view. "Last train?" he said. "What do you mean, *last train*? That wasn't no last train. There were plenty more trains. And there are going to be a helluva lot more to come!") Which only goes to show, Never reveal your title too soon.

Colonel called me on my fiftieth birthday and sang "Happy birthday" on the message tape. He volunteered to help coordinate my book tour and advised me to confine it as much as possible to Waldenbooks, which, he said, did very good business at its Las Vegas location and was very well run. I've often wished I could have taken him up on his offer. My last real attempt to draw him out in his own behalf came in March of 1995 and was no more successful than any of my previous efforts. "The last time we spoke," I wrote to him, "you said that you felt your point of view was not as well represented as some others' in my book. I agreed, and agree. As I said to you at the time, the problem is that you choose not to speak or explain yourself — a policy to which you have consistently adhered and which I can fully understand and respect."

But, I suggested, there were questions that were bound to come up, questions that he alone could answer, and I then proceeded to ask some of them.

His immediate reaction was — well, I don't want to say that Colonel was nonplussed, because he remained to the end a man of stern self-governance. But there is no question that he was thrown a little (and this is something I regret) by having to confront once again questions that he must have thought had long since — with me at least — been laid to rest. He never responded directly to me. Instead he called up Jerry Schilling the moment he received the letter. Jerry had met Elvis when he was twelve years old, gone to work for him at twenty-two in 1964, and had come to appreciate Colonel more than any of the other guys both in his years with Elvis and in the nearly twenty years since Elvis' death, when he had become a manager himself. Colonel knew Jerry and I were friends, and he put it to Jerry that I was trying to "pin him against the wall." Jerry reminded him that many of the points I raised were true (Jerry had been there, for example, when Elvis fired Colonel in Vegas in 1973 and carried notes back and forth between the two of them), and eventually he managed to calm the Colonel down. After that we resumed our correspondence (well, *I* resumed our correspondence, which, aside from the phone calls, had become a little one-sided in the last year or two), and a couple of months later Jerry and I had a wonderful visit with Colonel and his wife, Loanne, which was accompanied by a good deal of helpful advice about things I needed to look out for in the making of the motion-picture adaptation of my book. (He never mentioned the greatest danger of all: that, after the expenditure of what would seem to anyone but a Hollywood habitué like vast sums of money for film scripts and rights, the movie might never get made.)

That was the last time I saw Colonel, who died eighteen months later.

Eddy Arnold, his first superstar, once said of Colonel, "He lives and breathes his artist. I said to him . . . 'Tom, why don't you get yourself a hobby — play golf, go boating, or something?' He looked me straight in the eye and said, 'You're my hobby.'"

Which was certainly true as far as it went, but I think he might have appended to that the delight he took in putting on, and matching wits with, the world at large, ready to take on anyone who might emerge from the crowd, fully confident of his ability to turn whatever might be directed at him to his and his client's advantage.

SIXTEEN

Henry Green: A Personal Memoir and Appreciation

"I WAS BORN a mouthbreather with a silver spoon in 1905," wrote Henry Green in his interim autobiography, *Pack My Bag,* published at the outset of the German Blitz, "to put down what comes to mind before one is killed, and surely it would be asking much to pretend one had a chance to live." "Children in my circumstances," he noted in a 1950 sketch for the *New York Herald Tribune,* "are sent away to boarding school. I went at six and three-quarters and did not stop till I was twenty-two, by which time I was at Oxford, but the holidays were all fishing. And then there was billiards."

Those are the kind of juxtapositions — heralding passion and absurdity in the same breath — in which one finds the essence of Henry Green. A member of the Eton-Oxford generation that included Evelyn Waugh, George Orwell, and Anthony Powell, Green has sometimes been hailed as the most talented of them all, most notably by John Updike. "Green, to me, is so good a writer," wrote Updike in his introduction to a 1978 collection of three of his novels designed to stimulate a posthumous revival, "[he is] such a revealer of what English prose fiction can do in this century, that I can launch myself upon this piece of homage ... only by falling into some sort of imitation of that liberatingly ingenuous voice." "As a novelist of the imagination he stands almost alone," wrote Eudora Welty. And W. H. Auden called him "the best English novelist alive" in a 1952 *Life* profile. And yet he was largely unknown in his lifetime, an acquired taste at best, too often dismissed as mannered, eccentric, provocative, or perverse, labeled almost reflexively as "a writer's writer."

Which always seemed a little inexplicable to me. What seemed more inexplicable is what drew me to Henry Green in the first place, just coming up for air at seventeen from my first immersion in Hemingway, Salinger, and Camus. Mad I was about him, though (sorry — there's that inescapably

inverted echo, though I'm afraid not a very good one), from my very first taste of *Loving,* and then I read in fairly short order all nine of his novels as well as the autobiography and two critical studies (including John Russell's model of appreciative textual analysis, *Henry Green: Nine Novels and an Unpacked Bag*). In fact so taken was I with Henry Green that when I went to England in 1963 I wrote to him in care of his publisher, overcoming every scruple of self-consciousness, every crippling inhibition, which, Green says, is the burden of adolescence. I don't have my letter, which I slaved over to achieve just the proper Greenish tone, but I do have his altogether astonishing reply. "By all means come to see me," he wrote to his nineteen-year-old admirer. "Any day, any time after noon. You will be very disappointed. But come now ... I'm ill, that's why I can't write (though I do still but don't print it). So come along in April and please. Your servant Henry Green."

I can scarcely express the thrill of both anticipation and sheer, stark terror that I felt as I was ushered into a high-ceilinged living room in London's posh Belgravia section. ("My house is a fourth-rate historical monument," muttered Green. "It's down at the very bottom of the list, but it's there all the same. It shall be something to pass on to my son — or a place for my widow to live.") I sat on tenterhooks while he sank back onto a comfortable sofa, close enough to touch my arm, his celebrated deafness (it could "roar or falter according to his spirit," wrote his friend Terry Southern) requiring the proximity. My own attention shifted from the well-known Matthew Smith portrait of a sleekly mustached businessman, faintly dashing and aristocratic ("It's a great nuisance, we're always having to lend it out, but when the Home Secretary asks, you can't very well refuse, after all") back to its model, gone unexpectedly seedy in late middle age. The bristle on his neck and chin was white, his neutral smile gap-toothed, and while he maintained a proudly aquiline profile, he had about him the ruined air of an old man who shuffles when he walks and always has to pee, as he frequently complained. "Once, during the Blitz, no it was before, a fireman came up to me, that was very unusual in those days. [Green volunteered for the Auxiliary Fire Service during the War, a branch of service very much resented by the London Fire Brigade regulars.] He said, 'You're fucking bloody well out of your mind.' 'Why?' I said.

Henry Green, 1949. *Photograph by Cecil Beaton © The Cecil Beaton Studio Archive at Sotheby's*

'Because you'll have fucking arthritis.' Naturally I didn't believe him, but it is true, it's an occupational hazard. You know, I wore scarfs, I even wore a waterproof thing under my tunic, but it did no good. Here I am—I'd be wearing a scarf now, only I put a tie on specially for your visit, but you have to rub with your fingers all the time. But, of course, I'm nearly sixty. You get everything at that age. . . ."

I listened transfixed as he reeled off stories, literary gossip ("You know how cutty writers are"), and bons mots, taking me into his confidence ("Strictly between ourselves," "Now, don't repeat this to a soul. . . .") and favoring me with a whole passel of well-intentioned advice. "A piece of advice from a man who's old enough to be your father," he said at one point. "Don't try to do too much. God knows, I did, and look how I am now." I was not to: study English, associate with other writers, or try to write abroad. "Don't kill off your characters, because people go on living after all. . . . It's dreadful to write autobiographical novels. They can only cause a family quarrel—which is not a thing to be sneezed at. . . . Go into the Army. You'll meet some wonderful people there. You'll have some wonderful laughs. But don't, above all, let them know that you write. They'll show you all their stuff. Some of it is just bloody awful. . . . Don't ever volunteer for anything. That's my one piece of advice!"

Throughout my visit he was courteous, animated, deferential, the very model of civility and genuine consideration. ("Would you like a drink? Would you like a smoke? Would you like a pee?") Many of the characteristics so delightful in his novels—of eccentricity, wit, and the comic contretemps, the almost willful misunderstandings which plague human intercourse ("I don't follow," he once said to Terry Southern, interviewing him for the *Paris Review,* in response to a question on subtlety. "*Suttee,* as I understand it, is the suicide—now forbidden—of a Hindu wife on her husband's flaming bier. I don't want my wife to do that when my time comes—and with great respect, as I know her, she won't")—all these qualities were present in abundance in his conversation, and just before my departure he thrilled me by asking, "Have you written a novel? Is it published?" He then offered to read the novel, promising to send it on to Chatto & Windus, his publisher, if he liked it. If he didn't, "I'll promise to have it back to you within five days—no, better make that seven days." He then signed a copy of the *Texas Quarterly*—in which an excerpt from his most recent never-to-be-finished work, *London and Fire 1939-1945,* had been published two years earlier—with the inscription, as inexplicable to me then as it is now, "With the admiration and respect of Henry Green Ap 20/63." When I left, I need hardly say, I was walking on London air.

I write books but I am not proud of this any more than anyone is of their nails growing.

HENRY GREEN'S literary career began with almost unsettling precocity. His first novel, *Blindness,* was published in 1926, when he was twenty-one and up at Oxford, but it was begun while he was still a schoolboy at Eton, "its nature unrevealed," notes Anthony Powell in his own memoir *Infants of the Spring,* "though the fact admitted; an undertaking not regarded overseriously by relations and friends." Green, or Yorke — for that was his given name; Green was merely a pseudonym of convenience — left Oxford after two years, determined, he wrote in *Pack My Bag,* "to drive out what they taught me there. . . . I had a sense of guilt whenever I spoke to someone who did manual work. As it was said in those days I had a complex and in the end it drove me to go to work in a factory with my wet podgy hands."

The factory was his father's, H. Pontifex and Sons, in Birmingham. "Yorke usually defined his family's engineering firm as making lavatories," sniffs Powell, "though sanitary fittings were subsidiary in the production to such equipment as beer-bottling machines." Subsidiary to that was the effect upon young Henry Yorke himself. "I like the proletariat," he said to me, with an ingenuousness of which he was well aware. "I suppose that sounds snobbish, but that's the only way one can express oneself here." Elsewhere he told Nigel Dennis that "proletarian inspiration" was essential to his development as a writer and that the writer's duty is "to meet as many pedestrian people as possible and to listen to the most pedestrian conversation." The direct result of going to work was that in 1929 he published the first of his great novels, *Living,* a kaleidoscopic picture of factory life, a unique triumph of experimentally humanistic prose. From that point on — for the next quarter of a century anyway — he combined but never mixed his business and writing lives, and perhaps this is what gives his almost whimsical literary excursions so unlikely a solidity of structure, of theme and character. He continued to maintain his anonymity because, he said, it protected him in business dealings and in his relations with the factory workers. "Some years ago," he told Terry Southern ruefully in the

Paris Review interview, "a group at our Birmingham works put in a penny each and bought a copy of a book of mine — *Living*. And as I was going round the iron-foundry one day, a loam-moulder said to me: 'I read your book, Henry.' 'And did you like it?' I asked, rightly apprehensive. He replied: 'I didn't think much of it, Henry.' Too awful."

With the War came his second great immersion in the cauldron of everyday experience, as he joined the Auxiliary Fire Service. Out of this came a second circumstantially autobiographical novel, *Caught,* and an intense creative flurry which, he would have us believe, stemmed initially from fear of dying ("That is my excuse, that we who may not have time to write anything else must do what we now can") and concluded, appropriately enough, with *Concluding,* the visionary novel which served in many ways as a model for John Updike's *The Poorhouse Fair.* His last two novels, *Nothing* and *Doting,* represented something of a parlor trick, either bearing out his recently formulated dictum that the novel of the future must be conveyed in dialogue alone or serving as the inspiration for that theory.

Throughout the novels run a number of common threads. The most startling, of course, is style, though Green insists in his *Paris Review* interview that a writer "can't do anything else. His style is himself, and we are all of us changing every day." Nonetheless, even granted that this is true and each writer's style is unique, Green's style is decidedly more so, bearing comparison with no other writer that comes to mind, except perhaps the obscure C. M. Doughty, whose *Travels in Arabia Deserta* was much admired by the young Henry Yorke. Elsewhere it would be difficult to find even a remote parallel to Green's hammered syntax, his inversions and improbably isolated relative clauses, the displaced modifiers and strained locutions which make for an almost skittishly self-assured tone. Just listen to the concluding sentence of *Pack My Bag,* which refers to the simple pleasures of his functioning life and marriage. "It was not hunting when it was no fun, not having to go shooting, it was not having to be polite to masters who were fools, it was to lose convictions, at a blow it was life itself at last in loneliness certainly at first, but, in that long exchange of letters then beginning and for the ten years now we have not had to write because we are man and wife, there was love." Here we find not only style but as bald a statement of theme as we are likely to get from a man who believed that "Explanation kills life" and — perhaps as explanation for his own crabwise progress of style — "We seldom learn directly; except in disaster, life is oblique in its impact upon people." Thus ellipses abound, and aside from the impossibly crammed beginnings ("[I rewrite] the first twenty pages over and over again," he told Terry Southern. "Because in my idea you have to get everything into them") the method is cinematic, a matter of montage and juxtaposition rather than painstaking (or even consistent) development of plot. Equally cinematic are the vivid descriptions of flora and fauna, which establish motifs of color and symbolism and, were it not for their enlivening eccentricity, might well represent Green's most daunting single characteristic. But then all of Green's work is saved from the sterility of theory by his commitment to the everyday world itself, to the reality of his characters, to the inexplicable variousness of humankind (and human motivation), which is rendered with a brilliance of observation, a warmth of appreciation that cuts across any consideration of style, consistency, or class.

Loving (1945) is probably the most accessible of his novels. Certainly it was his most popular, both in the United States and England, and in fact it led to the one significant revival of interest in his work in his lifetime. A tale of English servants at an Irish country house during the Second World War, it is typically oblique both in its view of the war as seen from a neutral country, and in its point of view, which is that of the servants rather than the masters. ("In the war," Green wrote not cynically of the earlier Great War, "people in our walk of life entertained all sorts and conditions of men with a view to self-preservation. . . . That is not to say the privileged did not fight, we did, but there were too few of us to win.") Just as typically the plot hinges on a number of small actions which are echoed, mostly in dialogue, throughout the text — echoed, amplified, exaggerated, and laid to rest so that gradually, almost unknowingly the reader is drawn into the seemingly trivial web of events and obliged to worry with the characters over their outcome.

The novel starts with the old butler, Eldon, dying, and in fact Green told Terry Southern, "I got the idea of *Loving* from a manservant in the Fire Service during the war . . . he told me he had once asked the elderly butler who was over him what the old boy most liked in the world. The reply was: 'Lying in bed on a summer morning, with the window open, listening to the church bells, eating buttered toast with cunty fingers.' I saw the book in a flash." Indeed the book begins with the dying butler's cry of "Ellen" over and over and his successor Charley Raunce's unexplained admonition to the pantry boy to "clean your teeth before you have to do with a woman." Raunce, the nominal hero, is in love with Edith, the maid, who discovers their mistress' daughter-in-law, Mrs. Jack, in bed with a Captain Davenport in a scene that reverberates throughout the novel. The book quivers in fact with a wealth of erotic suggestion and imagery, from the lovemaking of the doves while the children's nanny tells a fairy tale of "six little doves lived in a nest" to the crying of the peacocks which accompanies the lovemaking of just about everyone else.

The book is filled, too, with the kind of comic misunderstandings which attend all of Green's work, conversations at cross-purposes, motivations darkly hinted at, confusions of identity, and rude intrusions, like the appearance of the cook's nephew, Albert, perhaps her illegitimate son, evacuated from war-torn England into the tranquil nursery of Mrs. Tennant's castle. When an insurance investigator comes about Mrs. Tennant's missing ring, with both the mistress and her daughter-in-law abroad, the servants are thrown into confusion enough to elicit a false confession from Raunce's lad, also Albert. When the investigator leaves his card, all the dark fears of Irish perfidy are brought out. "Holy Moses," exclaims Raunce. "I knew it all along. See 'ere. 'Irish Regina Assurance.' Don't you read that the way I do. . . . I.R.A. boy. So 'e was one of their scouts, must a'been." This in turn causes an atmosphere of total panic, which upon the return of Mrs. Tennant and her daughter-in-law, through an intricate and misunderstood process of association, very nearly leads to a muddled confession of adultery. "I shall get to the bottom of it," announces Mrs. Tennant, of whom we know no more than her words and actions — we are treated to the private moments of none of the characters, and yet, Green would argue, we know them as well through inference as we are likely to know anyone in this world, because "we are all of us changing every day."

Living (1929), too, is about love, as equal parts liberation and imprisonment. Taking as one of its recurrent symbols the homing pigeons which "never fly far from house which provides for them (except when they are taken off then they fly back there), as they might be tied by a piece of string to that house," this is the closest to autobiography that any of Henry Green's novels will come until he flirts with the form once again in his fourth novel, *Caught,* as he tells the parallel stories of the workers in a Birmingham factory and the effect upon them of young Mr. Dupret's elevation to the directorship upon the death of his father. Henry Yorke's own father did not retire until his eighties. "Such a burden," Green complained to me. "Good Lord, he lived to be eighty-two, no eighty-three, I think, and he was such a bother. He used to come around, and he took up so much of one's time, poor man." Was he alive at the time that Green wrote *Living*? I asked. "But that was fiction!" In any case here, as in *Loving*, Green adopts an omniscient, somewhat superior tone that allows for both commentary ("So he thought and he was wrong," writes Green affectionately of one of his characters) and previews, or flash-forwards, which set up expectations. ("Craigan seemed to shrink and now for ever, except for one time later, his old authority was gone.") What is most immediately striking about the book, and has occasioned its greatest criticism, too, is the bold, virtually article-free prose which Green used to try to capture the industrial rhythms of Birmingham. "Bridesley, Birmingham," he starts out. "Two o'clock. Thousands came back from dinner along streets." And again: "Noise of lathes working began again in this factory. Hundreds went along road outside, men and girls. Some turned in to Dupret factory." This, it must be admitted, takes a certain amount of getting used to, but once you get caught up in its narrative cadences (which match the sharply colloquial speech of the characters), it stands as one of Green's boldest stylistic breakthroughs.

More to the point, the characters themselves provide a unique glimpse of Green as a full-blown Dickensian (or perhaps Joyce Cary–like) portraitist. It is a family portrait that takes up much of the canvas, for some reason, as in most of Green's work, a fragmented non-nuclear family which revolves here around the old man, Craigan, who appropriately enough passes much of his spare time reading and rereading Dickens. ("Don't you ever read any but the works of Dickens?" another character asks him. "No why should I?" Craigan replies, for Dickens contains multitudes.) Craigan is one of Green's most vivid creations, non-romanticized, philosophical about his limitations ("I wouldn't educate my son above the station 'e was born in . . . what is there in it, old Dupret 'ad to work 12 hours a day to keep 'is money I'll be bound 'e did"), and yet . . . heroic. But heroism, like love, is scarcely an unmixed blessing, and Craigan's effect on those around him is not altogether benevolent. Lily, who keeps house for the man she calls "grandad," feels crushed by his attempts to control her life; Jim Dale, the young man Craigan has picked out for her and has taken to live in his home, throws away opportunities for advancement; and Lily's father, Joe Gates, reacts to the old man's despotic hold and in the end comes across, like so many of Green's characters, as ambiguously sinister. Meanwhile, the proto-Henry figure, the young Dupret, is shown in relatively unsympathetic parallel to the busily engaged lives of his employees, making a shallow round of social visits, casting about for some function in life. Typically his only contact with the other principals comes in oblique and wrongheaded fashion. "What a beautiful face," he says of Joe Gates, and the works manager worries over that. Later, after his bull-in-a-china-shop approach has thrown Craigan and all the other old-timers out of work (and has upended the safe predictability of their lives in other ways as well), he passes Lily on the street "and did not notice her, she was so like the others." At the end of the book the ambiguity of living, of loving, of *involvement* is once again expressed, as Lily instinctively reaches out for new life, watching the neighbor's baby in its pram. "Suddenly with loud raucous cry she rushed at the baby, and with clatter of wings all the pigeon lifted and flew away, she rushed at baby to kiss it. Mrs. Eames hid her son's face in her hand, laughing: 'You're too young, that's too old for you' she said."

Caught (1943) and *Back* (1946), written amidst the fury of war, with *Loving* in between, represent, if anything, a heightening of this consciousness of the division between the apparent mundaneness of everyday experience and the limitlessness of the imagination, as well as the words that can be used to express it. Each book offers up soaring flights of unexpected metaphor bolstered by equally soaring flights of uninterpretable fancy. *Caught,* which would not be published in unexpurgated form until 2017 (its fevered sexuality is captured in descriptions like "his hands went like two owls in daylight over . . . the fat white winter of her body"), is a vivid, highly particularized evocation of his Auxiliary Fire Service experience, though in a setting (and with plot devices) rendered in so surrealistic a manner that, as the novelist Alan Hollinghurst has written, it creates the "somehow incandescent impression of being miraculously both humdrum and visionary."

Once again the various plot strands hinge on multiple misunderstandings, in this instance more often dark than comic, and the inherent difficulty for both characters and author to comprehend the heart of their experience. Just as in *Living,* only more so, Green corrects his protagonist Richard Roe's attempts to convey some of the fearfulness and beauty of encountering fire for the first time, after "we'd waited a whole year . . . then suddenly to be pitchforked into chaos." In the end, and in very short order, nearly all the principal characters we have met in the pages of the book are dead—killed off in Roe's lengthy, and strangely impersonal, account of the experience to his wife. But, the author insists with almost ill-tempered lyricism, in only one of several long parenthetical corrections to his character's narrative, "it had not been like that at all. What he had seen was a broken, torn-up dark mosaic aglow with rose where square after square of timber had been burned down to embers, while beyond the distant yellow flames toyed joyfully with the next black stacks which softly merged into the pink of that night."

Back is no less lyrical, no less hallucinatory, and perhaps even more marked by moments of serial confusion and mistaken identity, though in this case it all adds up more to a comedy of manners with a conventionally (if no less strangely Greenish) happy ending. The principal source of confusion lies in the mind of Charley Summers, who after four years in a German prisoner-of-war camp has returned home missing a leg and lacking the ability to grasp anything whole. ("His day to day sense of being injured by everyone, by life itself, rose up and gagged him.")

The measure of his confusion can be gauged by his refusal to believe that the love of his life, Rose, who died the week he was taken prisoner, is actually dead. Throughout the book he, and the reader, are assaulted with images of roses, verbal cues, even songs like "Honeysuckle Rose," that evoke his lost love's name, and when he first meets a hitherto unknown, out-of-wedlock half sister, Nancy, she is so close to a "living image, herself, Rose in person," that Charley simply faints dead away. It is their father, a somewhat rapscalliony character with multiple mysteries of his own, who urges Charley to look up this young war widow, without providing any information as to who she actually is, and for much of the book Charley cannot be persuaded that this is not Rose herself, embarked for one inscrutable reason or another on a delusional journey of her own.

In the end the resolution comes not so much from Charley finally coming to grips with reality as with the alteration of reality itself through multiple novelistic devices, so that when Charley accepts Nancy's proposal of marriage, which comes only after he is able to accept the reality of Nancy herself, the world explodes in a welter of roseate imagery not dissimilar to Richard Roe's ecstatic experience of fire. Nancy has one condition for their marriage, "that they should have a trial trip," and so, as she lies naked on the bed and beckons to her intended, "a lamp with a pink shade at her side . . . he knelt [and] the pink shade seemed to spill a light of roses over her in all their summer colours, her hands that lay along her legs were red, her stomach gold, her breasts the colour of cream roses, and her neck white roses for the bride." It is, simply, too much for poor Charley, and "he burst into tears [and] buried his face in her side just below her ribs, and bawled like a child. 'Rose,' he called out, not knowing he did so, 'Rose.'" But Nancy is undaunted, even as "the salt water ran down between her legs. And she knew what she had taken on," the novel concludes with inscrutable good humor. "It was no more or less, really, than she had expected."

Prose is not to be read aloud but to oneself alone at night, and it is not quick as poetry, but rather a gathering web of insinuations which go further than names however shared can ever go. Prose should be a long intimacy between strangers with no direct appeal to what both may have known. It should slowly appeal to feelings unexpressed, it should in the end draw tears out of the stone. . . .

IN REREADING Henry Green recently I was reminded once again of some of the pure pleasures, not to mention challenges, that reading can provide. It had been a while since I last read Green, and I approached the task with some trepidation, in the same way that one will so often approach any familiar landmark of childhood, fearing that it may have radically shrunk, or, worse still, that one may have radically changed. In Henry Green's case the jauntiness of tone, the jaggedness of style, the graceful lyricism which suggests an almost airy appreciation not only for his characters but for the very participial construction of life, only reinforce the nagging question of why he has not been more widely appreciated.

Evidently the same thought occurred to him, too. Henry Green never published a full-length work again after 1952. He never wrote another novel, whether because he was embittered, or found the effort too exhausting, or, as I suspect, had theorized his talents into an attenuated state. When I visited him, he had only recently given up a commissioned work on firefighting, of which two excerpts had been published. ("They will always pick what you know to be no good at all.") He was working oddly enough on a book which was to be not a sequel but a parallel to "the autobiographical one, about the Blitz, oh damnit what is it? — I'm not putting it on, as you get older you'll find you can't remember your own titles — well, no matter. What the hell is it, though? What's the one that begins 'I was born with a silver spoon in my mouth?'" "*Pack My Bag*?" I ventured.

That settled, he went on to explain that he was dictating this version, without reference to the first, which, like all of his books he had entirely forgotten, and with more emphasis on billiards. He had no intention of publishing it, though. "It's marvelous not to publish," he crowed with little conviction. "I never made any money out of it anyway, it's so funny to confound the buggers." At another point he suggested, "As you get older, you think increasingly of your readers. Pornography would be the simplest, because everyone's interested in that. But you get in trouble." According to Anthony Powell, who was obviously very much of two minds about his old schoolmate, he should have been satisfied to appear "in standard works of reference on writers of his period; perhaps a small recompense for a life's work, but one writers of respectable distinction often fail to pull off." Green himself, when I visited him, though, was speaking of receiving the Nobel Prize the following year (1964) through the intervention of "that American fellow who won it [presumably Steinbeck, since Hemingway and Faulkner, a more logical stylistic choice, were both dead], I shan't mention any names, but he was terribly nice." He was, as Powell remarks in his memoirs, "not in very good shape" in his last years, withdrawn, suspicious, "something of a hermit"—but, of course, there was no way I could know that then. To me he was simply a great man, a bit down on his creative luck—I think I must have pitied him a little and from the vantage point of my nineteen years wondered that a great writer could ever lack subject, or confidence, to write. His drinking, his chain-smoking, his aura of physical decay only heightened the romantic self-destructive image which I constructed for him.

I was soon to discover another side to his eccentricity, though. At the conclusion of our conversation he asked me again and again to come back and see him; when I demurred, thanking him for being so polite but really it wasn't necessary, he insisted once more, claiming that no one came to visit him, that he had no other relief from boredom. Somewhat dubious, I took him at his final word and, when I wrote to him suggesting one more visit, added, "I don't know what your feelings are. If you think it's pointless that's all right. This is no attempt to be disarmingly frank but direct." The response came by return post without a stamp and with Private & Confidential scrawled across the top. What could it mean? I wondered as I paid the postman and then tore open the envelope. *Dear Guralnick,* I read. *My dear chap I think we must "call it a day." I did what you wanted & that should be enough.* And that was that.

It was an incident which, fictionally, would have delighted any other Henry Green reader, a typical misunderstanding and appropriate send-up of a romantic young upstart. Unfortunately I wasn't in any position to appreciate the joke. I was shattered and, I thought, altogether in the dark. Oddly enough in reading over the account I wrote before receiving that second communication, I find myself theorizing, "He turns upon old friends, perhaps because they desert his advocacy," and Powell's neat summation ("'I'm not well,' he said. 'People say it's drink. It's not that. I'm not well. I think I'm going to die'") might have provided me with some cold comfort. But on that day, and for many days thereafter, there was no comfort for me, as I went over my behavior, analyzed my actions, and sought to discover where I had gone wrong. I only read of Green's 1973 death in Updike's appreciation in the *New York Review of Books* five years later. It rekindled memories which I had suppressed, along with an admiration which had never wavered. And while I am hopeful that Henry Green will someday receive his due in the literary pantheon, where in E. M. Forster's conceit all the great writers from every age are seated together in a vast, illimitable space, all spinning their tales simultaneously, I am reminded of what I noted with such sad and passionate naïveté in my journal when we met: "The fucking bastards," I wrote in an angry, illegible hand that I scarcely recognize anymore as my own. "He deserves something more."

SEVENTEEN

Some Cats Know: Words and Music by Leiber & Stoller

Some cats know how to take it nice an' slow . . .
But if a cat don't know, a cat don't know

"WE NEVER *considered* being celebrated or in the limelight," says Jerry Leiber, almost irritated at the naïveté of the question. "That was not what we did. Any more than a stage-rigger would figure to have his name up in lights on Broadway—that's not what you did, that wasn't your job. And that wasn't what your goal was."

"It was very important for us to do," adds Mike Stoller. "But we didn't consider in any sense that it was 'important' in relation to anything else. We did not figure, for example, that there would be any lasting thing. We used to assume that when the record was over, it was over and the songs were over, too. They had the longevity in our minds of a newspaper."

What they did, of course, was to write songs. "Hound Dog," "Kansas City," "Along Came Jones," "Charlie Brown," "Jailhouse Rock," "There Goes My Baby"—a whole generation grew up on Leiber and Stoller, who at the age of forty-five (they were born roughly within a month of each other in 1933), with twenty-eight years of collaboration behind them, may be "the longest-running partnership—since when? Gilbert and Solomon?" "None of them," murmurs Mike, "had the ability to withstand pain like we do." Even in dialogue their talents complement each other. Jerry, whom *Time* once described as "bouncy, wordy, and uncertain," sets the conversational pace, his manner sharp, his gravelly voice alternately expressing engagement and mild exasperation, his verbal agility steering a comfortable path between candor and diplomatic evasion. The interview takes place in Leiber's new apartment, austere, comfortable, book-lined, filled with paintings and objets d'art which reflect a very personal, contemporary

Jerry Leiber and Mike Stoller at the piano, with (standing left to right): Lester Sill;
Jerry Wexler; the Coasters (Carl Gardner, Will "Dub" Jones, Billy Guy, and Cornell Gunter);
Ahmet Ertegun. *Courtesy of the Leiber & Stoller Archives*

vision. Stoller, whom his partner has described as being "withdrawn, practically comatose" when they first met, speaks slowly, carefully, with a
precise memory for names and dates and an almost painfully unassuming
manner. Both Leiber and Stoller are witty, sophisticated, and casually
urbane—probably much like their original models, Cole Porter, Johnny
Mercer, and George Gershwin. They are vitally involved in the cultural
life of New York—art, theater, literature, "serious" music—and bemoan
what they consider to be the current cultural stasis. "There used to be a
kind of thing going that was more coherent," says Jerry, "that split, just
like the music business. That kind of centrifuge of activity that used to
be—there just isn't that kind of thing happening anymore. Everything's
turned into big business, and I think that's part of it."

He stares, a little challengingly, the rasp in his voice seemingly calling up a trace of aggressiveness that is buried, the stare betraying, yes, there it is, the famous "look" — one eye brown, one eye blue — that caused Lester Sill, the well-connected sales manager for the Bihari brothers' pioneering r&b label Modern Records, to listen to a song presented to him by a teenage record clerk at Norty's Music Center. Which stopped Mike Stoller in his tracks, too, when he was first confronted with a mad seventeen-year-old lyrics writer at his door. ("I just looked at him for a while," Stoller told British music journalist Charlie Gillett. "He had fiery red hair, and one blue eye and one brown eye. So after about three months of just standing there I said come on in.")

"All righty," says Jerry Leiber, direct and to the point. "Where do you want to start? In the beginning, naturally."

They met in 1950 in L.A., where Leiber had moved with his mother in 1945 and Stoller had come out with his family the year before. Leiber was writing blues lyrics, a product, he says, of growing up in a poor neighborhood in Baltimore. "I always associated with black people, always felt comfortable with black people." He had a drummer friend at Fairfax High writing the melodies, but the arrangement wasn't satisfactory, and the drummer told him of Mike Stoller. Stoller, a freshman at Los Angeles City College, had grown up on Long Island, falling in love first with boogie-woogie, then with bebop. "Where I lived was not an integrated neighborhood, but I went to summer camp at a very early age — it was a totally integrated summer camp run primarily by some trade unions and I think the Harlem Y was involved in it. My interest in black music came from listening to the older black kids playing piano, an old upright piano they used to have in the barn there." At ten or eleven he took lessons, remarkably enough, from the great stride pianist James P. Johnson — "I had maybe four or five lessons. It was a marvelous experience, but I would say in a sense I was probably not sophisticated enough and a little too young to appreciate what he could have taught me. I used to love to listen to him play. He always had a bottle of Southern Comfort on the piano — which I think shocked me a little. I mean, whiskey — right?"

Meeting in California, they discovered in each other, in Leiber's words, "a buddy from a secret organization." "There were not," says Stoller with typical understatement, "as many young white people who were involved with that kind of music at that particular time." In fact there were hardly any, and the initial reaction Leiber and Stoller encountered from black artists to whom they tried to peddle their tunes was "very supportive," says Leiber. "If they showed anything outside of what they might have showed anyone else, it was mild amusement, and they were a little bit surprised that our work was as 'on' as it was." "We tried," says Stoller, "particularly in the early days, to be what we felt was 'authentic,' lyrically and musically." Evidently they succeeded, because within months of their first meeting Lester Sill introduced them to jazz and r&b DJ Gene Norman, who in turn introduced them to all their r&b heroes, including Jimmy Witherspoon, who sang a composition they had written specifically in his style, "Real Ugly Woman," at Norman's first Blues Jubilee. His performance was recorded, but before it could be released, once again through the advocacy of Lester Sill, they got a jaunty studio recording of another of their songs, "That's What the Good Book Says," by a local r&b group called the Robins. "That, of course, was the big thrill, the affirmation of it being real, even with our names misspelled [Lieber and Stroller], as they were most of the first early years." By the end of 1951 they had had their first national r&b hit, sophisticated blues singer Charles Brown's "Hard Times." They were all of eighteen years old.

"We found ourselves writing for black artists," Jerry Leiber told rock 'n' roll critic and cultural historian Robert Palmer, "because those were the voices and rhythms we loved. By the fall of 1950, when both Mike and I were in City College, we had black girlfriends and were into a black lifestyle." Casually, though, they now insist. Certainly without any of the romantic intensity of Norman Mailer and Jack Kerouac, whose purple passages express a kind of heedless excess that was even then altogether alien to them. Nor, for that matter, with the single-minded determination of Johnny Otis, the famous r&b bandleader who passed for black and, in Leiber's words, "never even associated with white people." To Otis, looking back from the vantage of a bitter court battle over the copyright to "Hound Dog," their first real smash (which Otis ultimately lost), Leiber and Stoller were "young kids, they would bring songs and I would help rewrite them. For instance, once they had a song that had razor-cuttin' and gin-drinkin' and dice-shootin', and they didn't understand, this was derogatory to black people. They were just young guys who meant well, they weren't racist in the true sense of the word."

To Leiber and Stoller what they were doing was the product of a legitimate passion, and when they met Big Mama Thornton, one of Otis' featured singers, they were inspired to write a song for her — and to fight Otis

Big Mama Thornton.
*Courtesy of Dave "Daddy
Cool" Booth / Showtime
Archives*

for the credit when the song ("Hound Dog") came out with his name on
it. That was their second classic hit of '52 (actually it entered the charts
in early '53 but was recorded the previous August); their first was "Kansas
City," known in its original version by Little Willie Littlefield (who has
claimed at times that *he* wrote the tune and sold it in a moment of weakness) as "K.C. Loving." Leiber and Stoller shrug off such talk as sour grapes
mostly, as well they might with the track record they possess; for the most
part, they say, the business was on the up-and-up, although few of the
label owners were willing to "pay us properly, but that was the going ticket.
If you sold 100,000 records, you might get paid on sixty — you just knew
it, that was the rule of thumb. But they were all very nice to us." In any
case by this time they were bored, prepared for one of the periodic
retrenchments that would take place throughout their professional life.
In 1953, in partnership with Lester Sill, they started their own record
company, Spark, and, with Sill's guidance, entered into the full-scale world
of production, promotion, packaging, the record business.

What they set out to do artistically represented a distinct departure
from the world of straight-ahead blues which they had already conquered.

At the West Coast offices of Atlantic Records and Quintet Music, ca. 1956: Lou Krefetz (front), Jerry Leiber, Lester Sill, Mike Stoller. *Courtesy of the Leiber & Stoller Archives*

They took the same group, the Robins, with whom they had achieved their first studio recording, and wrote songs for them, which, while modeled on the Atlantic work of the Clovers, had no real analogue except in the terms — satirical "playlets," "little burlesque inventions" — which Jerry Leiber has assigned to them. These songs (with titles like "Riot in Cell Block #9," "Framed," "Smokey Joe's Café") were marked from the start by a blend of humor and implicit social commentary virtually unique to Leiber and Stoller. They were couched in a convincing but somehow timeless street idiom so stylized that, like Hemingway's written dialogue, it sometimes seemed realer than real life. So successful was this new form that, with Spark struggling due to lack of financing, Atlantic Records not only took on the Robins, whose current release, "Smokey Joe's Café," was

Spark's biggest hit and became even bigger when it was reissued on the Atlantic subsidiary Atco, they hired Leiber and Stoller on a non-exclusive basis (in other words, they could work for anyone else they liked, and did) as the first independent producers in the modern record business.

So it was that in 1956 they moved back to the East Coast and embarked upon a string of Atlantic smashes with the Coasters (the Robins in a new configuration) that probably remains their best-known work. They were "behind the scenes" men; despite the urging of Atlantic head Ahmet Erte-gun's brother, Nesuhi, save for one brief pseudonymous excursion by Jerry they never even thought about recording themselves in their chosen field, because the whole idea of a white blues singer seemed totally inauthentic to them; and yet they were as much the auteurs of their work as if they had sung every part and played all the instruments. Those humorous vignettes ("Searchin'," "Yakety Yak," "Charlie Brown"), which sound so spontaneous with their call-and-response ("Look-a there, look-a there, look-a there"), disbelieving bass voice, and King Curtis' sputtering sax, were the product sometimes of as many as thirty to sixty takes and count-less splices to do everything from minimizing the "ess" sound to getting the timing just right. "Every sound on the record we were controlling," says Stoller. "I don't mean to say that we put a clamp on anybody's head, but we were controlling—" "There was a design for every record," Leiber puts in. "Absolutely. From the beginning to the end."

With the Drifters, and then their lead singer, Ben E. King, as a solo artist a few years later ("Up on the Roof," "On Broadway," "Spanish Har-lem," all Top 10 pop hits), they carried this style of technical overlay to an even greater degree, introducing strings to r&b in a crazy mélange of Rimsky-Korsakov, Borodin, and deep-down gospel-shouting soul that reached its apogee with the Drifters' string-laden, Brazilian *baion*-influenced "There Goes My Baby" in 1959. The production techniques that they pioneered would soon be adopted with grandiose sonic results by their young assistant and guitar player from the Coast, Phil Spector, but for Leiber and Stoller even the Drifters' music was getting beyond what they had set out to do. After the early hits (actually it was midcareer for the Drifters, who had been through several metamorphoses already)—and with the outstanding exception of Ben E. King's "Spanish Harlem," which Jerry Leiber wrote with Spector—they assigned the writing for the most part to protégés like Barry Mann and Cynthia Weil, or Gerry Goffin and Carole King. "I mean, we could write any kind of a song," says Leiber matter-of-factly. "But I think we preferred either straight blues or those burlesque inventions that we did for the Coasters. The straight romantic blues ballads were not quite . . ." "Quite as inspired," puts in Mike. "Yeah." Here, as elsewhere in talking with Leiber and Stoller, you are struck by the same combination of professionalism and passion which allowed them to write for Perry Como and Jaye P. Morgan at the same time they were creating a new teenage vocabulary in their work with the Coasters, the same capacity for compartmentalization that created a near-perfect symbiosis of voice and vision with the Coasters over nearly two decades, without ever leading to the slightest inclination on their part to see the group perform live.

And then there was Elvis. The work with Elvis doesn't fit neatly into any logical progression, because there was nothing logical about it. It was pure accident that he was doing "Hound Dog" as part of his act in 1956 and then was persuaded by RCA to record it. When he did and it went instantly to number one, where it remained for three months, Leiber and Stoller, who had an affiliation with his publisher, Hill and Range, were invited to submit more songs. They suggested several titles, and he chose "Love Me," which was "originally written as a spoof almost of country-western style," Jerry says, flying in the face of the fact that it was originally recorded for Spark as an impassioned r&b ballad by Willy and Ruth. For Mike and him, Leiber insists, "'Love Me' was really what [the comic country duo] Homer and Jethro might have done to a legitimate lyric. Or Spike Jones. But then it was taken seriously. And we never argued." And while it seems obvious from his silence that Mike may not entirely agree with this or some of his partner's other more extravagant expostulations, silence is as much of a comment as he is inclined to make.

The success of "Love Me" in late 1956 (it went to number two pop, number seven r&b, and number ten country, in the immediate wake of the release of Elvis' first film, *Love Me Tender*) led to more Elvis cuts, extensive soundtrack work, uncredited production chores, and occasionally even sly, tongue-in-cheek "playlet"-like songs, like the title track for Elvis' third movie, *Jailhouse Rock,* for which they also wrote three other numbers. It was in many ways an ideal marriage between two writers who had captured the perfect irony of the age and the artist who in their view personified it. Leiber and Stoller may have appreciated Elvis ("He knew an awful lot of songs. He knew what Ray Charles was doing at the time. . . . We just didn't think that any white boy would know about that kind of

With Elvis, 1957. *Courtesy of the Leiber & Stoller Archives*

stuff, and he surprised us") but, they both say, they found the musical constrictions stifling. "If something didn't fall within the parameters of three or four different styles, right? A country blues ballad, a shuffle rhythm tune with a certain content, a verse chorus hook with a certain sound in it, if it didn't fall within the parameters of something that was very familiar to them — *at that time* — they wouldn't consider it. And for us it got to be rather boring — fulfilling that obligation; we actually did stop writing for Elvis because of that."

They left Atlantic in early 1962 — "for a number of reasons." "It was a business deal," says Mike. "Our objectives," Leiber said in an interview some years later, "were that we wanted to make a lot of money. And I guess we were a little bit cynical and a little bit depressed with the scene." They went back to freelancing for a while, then started up their own label, Tiger Records, with the idea of "re-creat[ing] an Atlantic-Chess-Specialty type label." They cut some great r&b sides (Alvin Robinson's "Something You Got," Bessie Banks' "Go Now"), "but we couldn't get to first base [in terms of sales] with rhythm and blues records." They had what they judged to be just a few months of financial life left, when in an altogether unanticipated swerve in direction, they suddenly struck it rich with what could only be described as bubblegum music.

Bubblegum music?

"Yeah, it *is* puzzling," says Mike.

"Well, I can tell you very quickly what happened," says Jerry.

What happened was that in these desperate circumstances Jerry happened to run into George Goldner, a music business character, inveterate gambler, and "man with a golden ear," who had had a string of breakthrough Latin-music hits (he was known as "the Mambo King") as well as seminal rock 'n' roll records like Frankie Lymon and the Teenagers' multimillion-selling "Why Do Fools Fall in Love?" He had accomplished all this on a succession of different labels, all of which he had started and then lost to his gambling habit.

"He was out of a record company, out of a job, and looking for some action, and I offered him a partnership in our label." Goldner stayed up all night listening to a stack of their demos and unreleased masters, and when they came into the office the next morning, Jerry says breezily with a triumphant note of fatalism in his voice that I'm not sure Mike altogether shares, "he held up an acetate and said, 'I'd stake my life on this record.' And he played it, and it was 'Chapel of Love' by the Dixie Cups. I hated the record, it was teenybop music, but we put it out [on their brand-new Red Bird label] and it sold a million two, something like that, and that more or less determined the character of the record company."

Stoller picks up the story.

"After a couple of years involved with this, Jerry and I looked at each other one day and said, 'What are we doing? This isn't our cup of tea —'" "Meaning Red Bird." "And so we said, 'You know what? It's hanging us up.' And we sold our shares in the company to George Goldner and said, 'Enough. We got to move on.'" "Which is something we usually do every five to seven years." "Catharsis — on some level."

It's important to mention something here — and not just in parentheses. The part of the story that they explicitly left out of our interview was their shock at learning one day that they had a new "partner" — because Goldner had once again lost his share of the company at the track, only this time it was *their* company. They found this out when Jerry was summoned abruptly to a meeting with a tough-talking Broadway "wise guy," who announced, first to Jerry's bewilderment, then to his dawning realization, that he had called the meeting simply because he always liked to meet his partners face-to-face. He seemed uncertain of the company's name. Red Bird, Blue Bird, what difference did it make, it was all green, it was all money. Which led Mike and Jerry to a radical reconsideration of their options and their gift of the company to Goldner just a few weeks later for the price of one dollar. But none of this, understandably, was brought up in our conversation, which took place just ten or so years after the event.

Since that perilous moment they have been involved in various projects of one sort or another — a suite of darkly ironic cabaret songs for Peggy Lee, 1975's *Mirrors;* work with English rock artists like Stealers Wheel, Procul Harum, and Elkie Brooks; a blues album with T-Bone Walker that turned into an unintended exercise in nostalgia; plus assorted other ventures, most in the end unrealized, into musical theater, movies, and the mordant cabaret tradition for which their talents seem so well suited. What comes across most vividly in their telling of the story of their professional life together — apart from the almost staggering output and ambition involved — is how easy they choose to make it seem, what smooth sailing two seventeen-year-olds in search of adventure had in shark-infested waters. Both Leiber and Stoller explicitly deny this — the shark part; the business that they knew was made up of ex-schoolteachers like Aladdin head Leo Mesner, label salesmen turned mambo dancers like George Goldner, and small businessmen whose only fault was to believe too much in the American system of free enterprise. Race was no obstacle, at least as far as family and friends were concerned; the disagreement with Johnny Otis was essentially a business quarrel; and the breaks with Atlantic, Jerry Wexler, Phil Spector, even the Coasters are all glossed over. The one rule of thumb has been that whatever they did "we had to be excited" by it.

For Leiber and Stoller in any case you get the feeling that all of this is long ago and far away. What they are interested in right now is establishing themselves as serious artists. "We've always," says Jerry Leiber, "had a broader spectrum of interest than our early work might indicate." Which might or might not be a statement to be taken literally. Or perhaps it is just a form of the same hip self-deprecation that permeates their talk, which never admits too clear-cut a goal or too straightforward a satisfaction if that goal is actually achieved.

They continue to write in fits and starts, blocking out words and music separately, working intensely for a time and then taking off several weeks. Mostly they write at one or the other's apartment, though they still maintain an office on the Brill Building's eleventh floor. Clearly it isn't the same, though, any more for them than for anyone else. "Well, the world has changed," says Jerry Leiber. "It's not just the music industry. Right now I think we're in a very boring hiatus. Movies are worse than ever. The Broadway theater is deader than a doornail. A lot of contemporary painting today is pretty dull, certainly in comparison to the abstract expressionists and even in comparison to the pop painters of the '60s. Everything more or less right now seems a little dismal. Content is lacking, originality is lacking, individuality is lacking, and I think a tremendous amount of spirit and conviction and belief is lacking—but, boy, the packaging is dynamite!"

They see themselves, you feel, on a precipice. They might argue that this does not inhibit their art, it has *never* inhibited their art, nor is it a matter of day-to-day concern. But from talking to them one gets the feeling that in some ways they are not all that aware of, nor all that affected by, what's happening in the world they left behind.

They remain restless, wary, holding on to the cautious, not-quite-satiric pessimism that runs through all of their work. Perhaps Leiber's lyrics sum it up best in a composition that both call without undue irony "as simple and straightforward a song of joy as Jerry Leiber is capable of writing," the self-explanatory "I've Got Them Feelin' Too Good Today Blues." Could the dark side of feeling good represent a loss not just of the contradictions that have fueled all their best work but of the creative impulse itself? Where would any of us be without a healthy injection of bad news?

POSTSCRIPT

IT MAY SEEM ODD, and more than a little ironic, that their greatest success in later years, 1995's long-running Broadway smash, *Smokey Joe's Café*, the first in what has become an almost endless succession of "jukebox musicals," should in many ways echo Jerry's description of the bleak contemporary cultural scene. None of the grand schemes worked out: a musical based on the life of Oscar Wilde; an adaptation of Mordecai Richler's *The Apprenticeship of Duddy Kravitz*, the bitingly satiric tale of a young Jewish Montrealer on the make; various other films and theatrical ventures. In collaboration with David Ritz, they did deliver a colorful account of their own life and times, *Hound Dog: The Leiber and Stoller*

Autobiography, which rolls out their story in a smooth alternation of conjoined monologues, and their relationship remained very much a partnership, even if the focus was more on business than new songs, until Jerry's death in 2011. With his wife, Corky, a noted jazz pianist and harpist, Mike has continued to be extensively involved in progressive political causes and philanthropy and has had a number of recent compositions in movie scores and animated features, while co-writing the music for the 2011 Tony-nominated musical *The People in the Picture.* Inevitably, in every interview that he gives and every public appearance that he makes, the sixty-year partnership ("longer than Gilbert and Solomon") always comes up. "Jerry was sick for a long time," he said not long ago, "and his passing was expected, but it was still a shock. There are still occasions, when I have an idea or hear good news, that I find myself reaching for the phone to call him."

EIGHTEEN

Producing a Legend: Willie Dixon and the Blues

"**B**LUES IS THE FACTS OF LIFE. Blues is the true facts of life — and they're expressed with words, inspiration, feeling, understanding, wisdom, and knowledge. A poor man have no chance for justice, you know. That's why I write a lot of the kind of songs that I do: to explain the facts of life. All of my songs are actually message songs. 'I Just Want to Make Love to You'? Well, yeah, that's a message, too. That's a different kind of message, you see. Facts of life."

"Willie said one time if you've ever worked at something that's not going to happen, well, then, that's the blues, and that's true. Actually that's a pretty good description. In that sense I guess we've all experienced the blues."

The two speakers could not be more different. The first, blues composer and bassist Willie Dixon, garrulous, gargantuan, a man with a pure entrepreneurial spirit who has survived on his wits and his charm for fifty-two years now, ever since first arriving in Chicago from Vicksburg, Mississippi, in 1936 at the age of twenty-one, will offer an opinion, or even a dissertation, at the drop of a hat. The second, forty-year-old Fort Worth native T Bone Burnett, who has recently produced Elvis Costello, Los Lobos, the BoDeans, and Roy Orbison, among others, is lean, lanky, and virtually consumed with self-consciousness. It seems painful sometimes for him to come out with just what is on his mind, even though it is evident that he does not lack a sure sense of himself either. The two came together through the offices of Bug Music, a song-publishing firm that administers publishing for them both and recently set up a label deal with Capitol Records, for which the new Willie Dixon album will be the first release. They are currently in their third day of recording, and there is some concern that things are not going altogether as planned.

Originally the idea was to record the session digitally, live to two-track

T Bone and Willie. *Courtesy of T Bone Burnett*

with no overdubs, in four working days. This was the impromptu way that blues was recorded in its heyday, and this, it was reasoned, was how the blues was *meant* to be recorded, as a way of spontaneously capturing the moment. By the time that I arrive on the third day, that idea, like so many perfectly good theories throughout history (there may even be a blues about it), has been abandoned. Willie's voice is a little ragged, and he is going to have to overdub his vocals; the backing musicians, a seasoned and thoroughly empathetic group of professionals, are somewhat at musical odds, mostly because of the confusion arising from Willie's unending stream of new, and frequently contradictory, directives with regard to each song; the producer, whose manner suggests a thoroughly urban insecurity grafted onto an open-faced innocence modified by ubiquitous dark glasses, seems to be getting a little discouraged; and although the blues is often thought to be a simple music, the problems which these blues are creating have become exceedingly complex.

None of this, however, all of the participants hasten to assure each other as well as a crew from the *Today* show and assembled friends, family, and visiting firemen, is to be taken as any cause for alarm. The situation is perfectly normal, it's just a little bit fucked up.

For Willie Dixon, who wrote, conducted, arranged, orchestrated, and

A very young Willie Dixon (seated), newly arrived in Chicago. *Courtesy of Mary Katherine Aldin*

produced some of the biggest blues hits by singers like Muddy Waters, Howlin' Wolf, Little Walter, Sonny Boy Williamson, and Willie Mabon, at Chess Records' Chicago studios in the '50s and '60s, there certainly doesn't appear to be any reason to panic. Nothing seems to faze Willie, whose 300-plus pounds may have shrunk a little since a recent bout with diabetes (his right leg has been amputated just above the knee, pretty much keeping him from playing the bass, and he uses a gray metal cane or crutch to get around) but whose Barnum-like spirit is unquenchable. Never exactly a household name himself, Willie is more like a household product, with literally hundreds of his songs ("Hoochie Coochie Man," "Little Red Rooster," "Spoonful," "Seventh Son," and "I Can't Quit You, Baby," among others) familiar in one version or another by everyone from Otis Rush, Mose Allison, Muddy, and Wolf, to Cream, the Allman Brothers, and Led Zeppelin. While he could never be described as self-effacing, Willie is not an impatient man either, and it has always been his contention that if it is your time it is your time—and if it is not, no one, and nothing, is going to force it.

T Bone would probably subscribe to this philosophy. A conflicted Christian with a contemporary existential flair (he is the person frequently credited with having been a catalyst for Bob Dylan's Christian awakening on the 1975-76 Rolling Thunder Revue tour), he is a longtime admirer of Willie Dixon who once even started to write a song called "The Willie Dixon Story" intended to show how white America had ripped off the African American heritage. The song never worked out, and I'm not sure that T Bone would still subscribe to its straightforward, non-ironic premise (though he would never disavow the basic truth behind it), but the session eventually came about, not surprisingly, because Willie Dixon was as open to the idea of T Bone Burnett, or someone *like* T Bone Burnett, producing him (prior to the session, he was only passingly familiar with T Bone's name, let alone his work) as T Bone was to the idea of reclaiming a blues legend like Willie. In T Bone's mind "this was an opportunity to do something a little different. I wanted to do some songs that we could really collaborate on and make something a little bit new." In Willie's mind this is what he has been doing all along. He has always tried to make blues with a difference, introducing three-part harmony and the popular-song "bridge" to the blues, sometimes with the idea of expanding boundaries, sometimes simply to create a novelty number that might sell. "People are always trying to brand blues as a twelve-bar music. I was always against this because I felt, why should you brand something [as] one thing? In dealing with twelve-bar music you could never get a chance to express everything or tell a complete story. And so I started putting introductions to these songs and also middles and changing ideas within it."

"Changing ideas within it" turned out to be the bugaboo of this particular session. As someone once said of Willie, "He has a lot of ideas, and some of them are good." The band that has been assembled for this session is admirably equipped to adapt, but even they express perplexity, albeit in respectful and somewhat muted fashion, at the fecundity of Willie's vision.

Three of the musicians come from one edition or another of Willie's last touring unit, the Chicago Blues All Stars. Guitarist Cash McCall, a forty-seven-year-old native of New Madrid, Missouri, was a house musician at Chess in the '70s and is comfortable with everything from country and western to modern jazz. Harmonica player Sugar Blue, who was touted as the new hope of the blues not too long ago by the Rolling Stones and appeared on their 1978 album, *Some Girls,* is at thirty-eight the young Turk of the session, with his Jesse Jackson buttons, modified Afro, and black beret. Finally, Lafayette Leake, one of the last surviving masters of the blues piano, who has been with Willie off and on ever since Willie first arrived at Chess in 1951, is absolutely imperturbable at the keyboard, fingering the keys even during playbacks as if he were imagining a counterpoint to his own lyrical solos, filling the big, high-ceilinged room with music at every break in the action. The rhythm section consists of transplanted New Orleans drummer Earl Palmer, who has anchored more sessions than anyone can count, from Little Richard's first Specialty sides to Elvis Costello's 1986 *King of America,* which T Bone produced, and seventy-one-year-old bassist Red Callender, another longtime session stalwart who arrived in L.A. with Eddie Heywood Sr. on January 1, 1936, and had his first recording session with Louis Armstrong on "Sunny Side of the Street" the following year. Although they have never played together as a unit, and each comes from a background considerably different from the others' (Earl Palmer started out life as a six-year-old tap dancer on the black vaudeville circuit with his mother; Red Callender has played with the Honolulu Symphony as well as the NBC and CBS orchestras, while Sugar Blue grew up as James Whiting in Harlem and came up under the tutelage of the otherwise obscure Professor Six Million), they fall in like old friends, perfectly fulfilling T Bone's eclectic vision. They are patient with each other, and more than considerate of both artist and producer, but to a man they express their frustration in different ways. The talk is frequently of food and the environment, and the effect of each on the other; there are jokes to dispel the tension, and shared reminiscences of small-town black Southern life of another era. "People really cared back then," says Lafayette Leake in his quiet, confident voice, looking a little like a brown bespectacled Buddha in gray cap and earphones and grinning while everyone nods agreement. "Love is a caring, you know, but money eliminates caring." "That's right." "You can never go back to that time," declares Leake with finality.

"We just need to relax a little," T Bone says more than once, sometimes conducting from the control room, sometimes joining in on a borrowed National steel guitar while bent over his headset in the studio. "It sounded a little nervous from time to time."

"You're even more laid-back than the band," says the engineer, when everyone else is out of earshot.

"I don't consider that an indictment," says T Bone, to whom the producer's principal role is "to support and encourage the artist, and to stay

The Big Three Trio, ca. 1947: Ollie Crawford, Leonard "Baby Doo" Caston, and Willie.
Courtesy of Chess Records

out of the way as much as possible." In fact, says T Bone, listening intently to a playback and scratching his head, "I guess I consider it a badge of honor."

Finally, on the fourth day, it begins to come together. Some overdubs and a couple of tunes are quickly dispatched and now at last, with everyone about to scatter in different directions (Earl Palmer has a couple more sessions scheduled before taking off for Brazil with Ray Conniff; T Bone is just about to fly to Ireland to embark on Elvis Costello's new album), the feeling begins to seem right. From the first day of the session T Bone has had it in mind to cut some sides informally, with just Willie and Lafayette Leake ("like two old running partners, you know") and perhaps Red Callender's bass joining in. The idea has never quite coalesced so far, but now for the first time it seems appropriate to try something along those lines, and Willie and T Bone together come up with the idea of doing a new version of Willie's classic "Don't Mess with the Messer" with strictly acoustic instrumentation. Willie hoists himself up wearily on a stool beside the piano to rehearse, and Cash picks up the silver-bodied National guitar. Cash and Leake confer on a progression, and someone asks Willie how many verses the song has. "How many you want?" "All of 'em, Will."

Willie at home. *Photograph by Kirk West*

"Oh well, then, we could be here all week." As the song develops, it some-how transmutes into a kind of country blues of the sort that Willie Dixon might have heard from both black and white musicians in Vicksburg, Mississippi, over sixty years ago. "That's beautiful, Leake," says Willie. "You playing harmony with it. Man, that's nice." "There's a lot of ways you can do it," says Leake, grinning shyly. "Hey, Will," says Cash, "Louis [Satterfield, a session bass player and longtime musical associate of Willie's] told me to ask you to do that whistle, you know, where you got two notes going at once." Willie pushes his black horn-rimmed glasses back on his head and does it, to everyone's gratification, while Leake keeps on playing. "We need more of that bass ambience," says Cash, pretending to be the kind of producer that T Bone is not. "Red, listen to that chord," says Earl Palmer to his rhythm mate. "Don't that sound like Basie? You can tell that man's heard more than just the blues."

Finally Willie goes back into the isolation booth to try a master take. The results are charming, but they could never be quite as charming as the informal scene that has developed like a grainy, slightly out-of-focus photograph in the studio. "Man, that's really country, Will," someone says, listening to the playback. "It's all country," mutters Willie cheerfully, "one country or another." "I feel just like Minnie Pearl," says Cash. "I'm just so damn proud to be here."

Goodbyes are not much different than goodbyes ever are. Everyone exchanges phone numbers and addresses and promises to keep in touch. Red introduces his wife, Mary Lou, to Willie's wife, Marie, and everyone else that she doesn't already know. Leake concentrates on his dinner, which consists of the same medium hamburger he has consumed at every other meal (he believes, he says, in "keeping up with a regular routine of meals," a statement which draws a good deal of teasing attention). There are still overdubs to do, and while no one ever really knows how a record is going to turn out, there is at least a good feeling in the air.

"I believe in writing songs that are different from what the average person who is writing or singing out there is doing," says Willie in a predictably expansive mood. "Right now everybody has that push-push style, everybody has that thing in their mind that when you go up to sing, you've got to come up preaching, or hollering and screaming and all that kind of stuff. But a good sweet reasonable song is a different kind of thing. And I believe what the world is looking for today is a more understanding thing. I think the world would really appreciate something different."

"I had a very difficult upbringing," says T Bone, in response to a question about something else, "which I think gave me in one sense the sensitivity required to be a record producer. I think to produce records well you have to be sensitive and understanding of other people's narcissism and fear, which is something I'm rife with. The way I approach every project, every record, I don't even want to do it if I don't feel like the person really loves me and that I really love them — or at least that there's the possibility of love. There's only one time where I did a session where I felt that that didn't happen, and it was very debilitating. It was a horrible feeling."

"Hey, T Bone," says Willie, with his lazy gold-toothed grin, "maybe I ought to produce *your* next album."

T Bone, who has been bemoaning his own lack of success as a commercial artist with characteristic self-effacement, grins at the thought. "You know, Will," he says, "maybe that wouldn't be such a bad idea."

NINETEEN

Meeting Chuck Berry

THE FIRST TIME I met Chuck Berry he was playing a club called Where It's At, which, in contradiction of its name, occupied the second floor of a drab business building in Kenmore Square and was operated by longtime Boston DJ Dave Maynard and his manager, Ruth Clenott. It was 1967, and I was in my senior year of college, working at the Paperback Booksmith, as I had for the last four years, both in and out of school. I was making $65 a week. The reason I know this is because Chuck Berry signed my paycheck.

Well, it wasn't my paycheck exactly, it was my paycheck *stub,* and the reason he signed it was because I didn't have anything else to present to him for an autograph. He had just given an exhilarating performance with a pickup band of Berklee College students (unlike Bo Diddley, say, whom I had recently seen at the same club, Chuck Berry never carried his own band, and the result was inconsistent, to say the least). But tonight, for whatever reason, Chuck was thoroughly engaged, and rather than performing tired rehashes of his familiar hits with a rhythm section that didn't have a clue, he followed what I'm sure was the unintended lead of the band, jazz players all, freely improvising on the hits, while throwing in unexpected bonuses like "Rockin' at the Philharmonic" and Lionel Hampton's "Flying Home" as well as a few jazz-inflected T-Bone Walker tunes. He was clearly in good spirits, but it took a while for me to work up the nerve to approach him as he stood to one side of the foot-high stage, packing up his guitar and getting ready to leave.

He regarded me with a quizzical look, casting an even more quizzical look at the book I was attempting to give him—"book" might actually be a little bit of a stretch for the pamphlet-sized booklet I was finally able to

Chuck Berry, 1965. *Photograph by Brian Smith*

hand him, with its smudged white cover and stapled-together pages. What's this? his noncommittal expression seemed to say, in a manner that betrayed neither receptiveness nor hostility. More to the point, that blank stare seemed to suggest, without meaning to get all in your face about it, who the fuck are you? I have no idea what I said. I'm sure I wished that the book could simply declare itself. The stark black lettering on the cover announced "*Almost Grown and Other Stories,* by Peter Guralnick," and it had originally been published three years earlier, when I was twenty. I must have mumbled something about how the book had been inspired in part by his music, that the title obviously came from his song, that I hoped he would like it. (Help me, I'm trying to paint a sympathetic picture here.) He flipped through the pages and placed the book carefully in his guitar case. "Cool," he said, or the equivalent, and flashed me what I took to be an encouraging, if inescapably sardonic, smile. And then he was gone, off to the airport to fly to another gig, or maybe just home to St. Louis. I still like to think that he read the stories on the plane on his way to wherever he was going.

It would be another forty-four years before I actually *met* him.

But first, perhaps I should say — well, you tell me, do I really have to say? — that there is no end to my admiration for Chuck Berry's work, even if his commitment to performance has at times proved wanting. As much as Percy Mayfield remains the Poet Laureate of the Blues, Chuck Berry will always be the Poet Laureate of — what? Of Our Time. Has there ever been a more perfect pop song than "Nadine," a catchier encapsulation of story line and wit in four verses and a chorus, in which the protagonist (like all of Chuck's characters, a not-too-distant stand-in for its author but never precisely himself) is introduced "pushing through the crowd trying to get to where she's at . . . I was campaign-shouting like a Southern diplomat." I mean, come on — and the song only gets better from there. When he was recognized in 2012 by PEN New England (a division of the international writers' organization) for its first "Song Lyrics of Literary Excellence" award, his co-honoree, Leonard Cohen, graciously declared that "all of us are just footnotes to the work of Chuck Berry," which was itself a footnote to Bob Dylan's salute to him several years earlier as "the Shakespeare of rock 'n' roll."

Which is all very generically well. But perhaps the most persuasive tribute I ever encountered was delivered by the highly cerebral New Orleans singer, songwriter, arranger, and pianist extraordinaire, Allen

Toussaint. I was trying to get at some of the reasons for the dramatic expansion of Toussaint's own songwriting aspirations (musically, poetically, politically) in the '70s, when he graduated from brilliant pop cameos like "Ride Your Pony" and "Mother-in-Law" to more ambitious, post-Beatles, post-Miles, post–Civil Rights Era work. Was it the influence of Bob Dylan, say, that allowed him to contemplate a wider range of subjects, a greater breadth and length to the songs? Oh, no, not at all, Allen replied in his cool, elegant manner, he wished he could agree with me, but his single greatest influence in terms of lyrics and storytelling from first to last was Chuck Berry. And with that he started quoting Chuck Berry lyrics, just as you or I might, just as Elvis Presley, Carl Perkins, and Jerry Lee Lewis do on the fabled "Million Dollar Quartet" session. "What a wonderful little story that is," he said, speaking of "You Never Can Tell," Chuck's fairy-tale picture of young love in Creole-speaking Louisiana, "how he lived that life with that couple, you know. Oh, the man's a mountain," said Allen unhesitatingly, and then went on to quote some more.

I saw Chuck in performance many times over the years, everywhere from Carnegie Hall to a decommissioned state armory. I wrote to him at one point at the invitation of Bob Baldori, who started playing with Chuck in 1966 and had remained close to him ever since. Chuck had just begun work on his autobiography, and Bob thought, a little fancifully perhaps, he might welcome some help. ("Dear Mr. Berry," I wrote in effect, "You won't remember me, but . . ."—then cited Bob as a reference and suggested that while I didn't know that I had anything to offer as a writer, maybe he could use me as someone to bounce ideas off, if he were so inclined.) I never heard back, which was probably just as well, because when the book came out two years later, in 1987, it was a masterpiece. "It is at once witty, elegant, and revealing," I wrote of it for *Vibe*, "and (or perhaps *but*) ultimately elusive. Every word was written by its author in a web of elegant, intricate connections that are both coded and transparent. Very much like the songs." And it was all Chuck—with a little help from his editor (and later mine), Michael Pietsch, who traveled to Chuck's amusement park/residence, Berry Park, outside of St. Louis, to retrieve it.

It was not until New Orleans, in 2011, though, that I got beyond that first monosyllabic exchange. We were both there to fulfill a date that was initially labeled, without the requisite irony, as "The Summit Meeting of Rock," because it was to include filmed interviews with Chuck, Jerry Lee Lewis, Little Richard, and Fats Domino, both as a group and, in the case

In New Orleans, with Chuck and Jerry Lee, September 2011. *Photograph by Ultan Guilfoyle*

of the first three, individually as well. It was part of a *Rolling Stone*-sponsored oral history project for the Rock and Roll Hall of Fame that had only recently begun, and I was the designated interviewer. Do I have to stipulate that it was one of the most challenging things I've ever done, and also, unquestionably, one of the funnest? *You* try facing down Jerry Lee Lewis, Richard, or Chuck, each with his own keenly intelligent, widely divergent, and informed point of view, and attempt to get a go-ahead smile out of them on their own uncompromising terrain. I think I'd be safe in saying that, overall, unaffected warmth and affection prevailed, stimulated as much as anything by everyone's genuine love for Fats, but at the same time it was not an entirely smooth and mellow meeting. Religion, politics, personality — all of the usual sources of conflict were present in good measure. Little Richard at one point wanted to thank God for bringing them all to New Orleans, but Jerry Lee, an intensely religious man himself, demurred at what I think he took to be a too-casual appropriation of faith. "I don't know about you," he muttered, "but I came here on a plane. And I think you came by bus!" Someone suggested that Louis Jordan was one of the key figures in the development of rock 'n' roll, and someone else objected that "Ain't Nobody Here but Us Chickens" was not in *their* view anything *like* rock 'n' roll. It was incredible! The interview with Jerry Lee was probably the most wide-ranging; Little Richard, for all of his avid study of history and precise recollection of it, was not about to abandon his theological texts; but it was Chuck who proved the most surprising, as, robbed of the constraints of filter and short-term memory, he abandoned, if only for a moment, his lifelong habit of emotional indirection and spoke unguardedly of his family, his mother and his father, the expectations they had of him and the inspiration with which they provided him growing up.

He was as slim and stylish as ever, wearing the jaunty captain's hat that has become almost ubiquitous since the departure of most of his beautifully coiffed hair some years ago. Communication was sometimes a challenge, because not surprisingly he had left his hearing aids at home, despite repeated admonitions from his family and his friend Joe Edwards, proprietor of Blueberry Hill, the St. Louis club where he played off and on for almost twenty years before "taking a break" from performing in 2014, at the age of eighty-eight. He spoke of poetry and politics (just to clarify, nearly everything is "politics" to Chuck, from the endemic chicanery of the music business to the endemic racism he has encountered over the years), and he insisted for the most part, just as he always has in his art, on speaking metaphorically, if unmistakably.

He spoke, too, of the sources of inspiration that he always points to for much of the flair, if not the full scope, of his creativity. (There is, Chuck will never fail to tell you, nothing new under the sun.) He cited Charlie Christian and T-Bone Walker and Louis Jordan, not to mention Louis Jordan's great guitarist Carl Hogan (just listen to "Ain't That Just Like a Woman" if you want to hear one of the fundamental sources for the Chuck Berry guitar style)—and Nat "King" Cole, too, for his diction. But as to his idea of reaching *everyone*, not just the "neighborhood" (the Ur-definition, of course, of rock 'n' roll), well, that was something he derived from the concept of get-ahead capitalism that he got from helping out his father in the grocery business as a young boy. "By then," he said, describing himself at ages ten and eleven, "I had a bit of politics in my head. My dad had a business of his own, selling groceries, and he worked for himself, so I came to handling money at that age. He carried vegetables in a basket and would go by someone's door and knock on it. 'Would you like—' You know, *the material looked so good.* [But] I sold a lot [of it] because of the *ingenuity* that I [showed] trying to sell."

That was the very idea that he applied to the music, when, after driving up to Chicago to introduce himself to Leonard Chess on Muddy Waters' recommendation, he presented himself to the world at the age of twenty-eight by employing that same sense of ingenuity, that same sense of "politics." Meaning, he said, "M-O-N-E-Y. What sells. What's on the market. Now, I knew the market. There had to be a market in order for you to be successful in a business. The market had to need your business, or the product of it. So I tried to sing as though they would be interested, and that would *become* a market." And then, he said, you multiplied that market, and you added another market to it, and it was as if you were still traveling from neighborhood to neighborhood, and pretty soon you had a constituency that included nearly everybody. *That* was the constituency that Chuck Berry was aiming for as an artist. And that was the constituency that he ultimately reached.

We started out our interview talking about poetry, and we came back to poetry in the end. Remember, this is a man whose older brother was named for Paul Laurence Dunbar, the great African American poet, whose "We Wear the Mask" should be required reading in all the schools. It had always tickled me the way that Chuck would end so many of his concerts with a poem. It was a poem I had never heard in any other context, though it reminded me of "Ozymandias" by Percy Bysshe Shelley, in which a traveler from some "antique land" stumbles upon the tomb of one of its ancient kings. "Look on my works, ye Mighty, and despair," proclaim the words engraved on the faded stone at the base of the ruined monument, while "boundless and bare / The lone and level sands stretch far away."

The poem that Chuck recited, while nowhere near as bleak (it takes a more positive, transcendental spin), was certainly in the same philosophical ballpark. It was called "Even This Shall Pass Away," and, as I discovered from asking him about it, it was not an original poem by Chuck Berry at all; it was in fact a poem that he had first heard his father recite ("That's my dad," Chuck said. "I get a little choked up when I think of him") when he was no more than six or seven years old, some eighty years ago. The author, I would later learn after a little research (very little—it's all over the internet), was Theodore Tilton, an American poet, newspaper editor, and abolitionist, and the poem was first published in his collection *The Sexton's Tale* in 1867. With very little prompting, Chuck recited the poem, and as he did, he got more and more choked up. "My dad," he said, "was the cause of me being in show business. He was not only in poetry but in acting a bit. He was Mordecai in the play *A Dream of Queen Esther*. [This was a church production by a prolific white playwright and meteorologist,

Henry Berry's van. *Photograph by Harry Davis © Bill Greensmith Collection*

Walter Ben Hare.] He was very low in speech and music, and he came out onstage, he came out to tell the king, 'Sire, sire, someone is approaching our castle.' And I knew his voice—I'm five years old right now—I knew his voice and I hollered out in the theater, 'Daddy!' I don't remember it, but they tell me I did. His position in the choir was bass. Mother's was soprano and lead. That's all there was in our house, poetry and choir rehearsal and duets and so forth; I listened to Dad and Mother discuss things about poetry and delivery and voice and diction—I don't think anyone could know how much it really means." Who were some of his favorite poets as a kid? I ask. Edgar Allan Poe, he said after some consideration ("I can't think of them [all], my memory's really bad"), and Paul Laurence Dunbar was his mother's. On second thought, he offered, Dunbar was his favorite, too.

But getting back to that recitation—he couldn't do it as well as his father, Chuck said, after completing several verses of "Even This Shall Pass Away," "my dad's voice *rang*. But here's something for you." And with that he launched into the fifth verse (out of seven), searching for the

The Camera Club, late 1930s (Chuck is fifth from left, with camera; his uncle Harry Davis is third from left, with hand on tripod). *Photograph by Harry Davis © Bill Greensmith Collection*

words, searching for the memories, concluding triumphantly, "'Pain is hard to bear,' he cried / 'But with patience day by day / Even this shall pass away.' Oh, I'm breaking up again." And with that he concluded, to the applause of everyone in the room, the film director, the sound and camera operators, his son, Charles Jr., a woman who carried a card that said "Sherry with Berry," and assorted other bystanders — no more than twenty-five or thirty in all. He was in tears. He was in triumph.

The problem for Chuck Berry is the same one we all face: the painful depredations of mortality. His work, of course, is his immortality, though as Woody Allen has often said, "I don't want to achieve immortality through my work; I want to achieve immortality through not dying"—and

Chuck might very well agree. He is, like many of us, his own best advocate and his own worst enemy, but the particular problem for Chuck is that, for all of the accolades that have come his way (listen to Elvis, Carl Perkins, and Jerry Lee Lewis celebrate his genius on that Million Dollar Quartet session, just for a start), to this day he has not been unambiguously embraced in the full artistic terms he deserves. There are undoubtedly a multiplicity of reasons for this (race would certainly have to be factored in), but the principal reason that Chuck has not been lifted up on a wave of critical and biographical hosannas is Chuck himself. His unwillingness to ingratiate himself. His unreadable distance. The deep-seated sense of anger and suspicion that can unexpectedly flare up and turn into overt hostility, with or without provocation (check out the star-studded sixtieth-birthday performance documentary, *Hail! Hail! Rock 'n' Roll*, which is both brilliant for its uplifting artistry and maddening for its self-inflicted failures). Most of all, I would guess, it comes down to his determined, uncompromisingly defiant refusal to conform to anyone else's expectations but his own.

He is not like any other popular performer that I can think of (oh, Merle Haggard might be a distant cousin, maybe a second or third cousin once removed, but no closer). For all of the canny "political" (read *artistic* here) inclusiveness that established both his career and his legacy, he has from the beginning chosen to set himself apart. Or *been* set apart. By a juvenile conviction for armed robbery before he ever thought of entering show business (remember: this was an upwardly mobile, middle-class kid, by his own description). Later by two mid-career prison terms, one coming at the height of his success in 1960 (a contested Mann Act violation, which could certainly be seen as a form of "political" [read *racial* here] reprisal). Not to mention some of his well-documented sexual proclivities and peccadilloes (and I don't mean to minimize these either), what his biographer, Bruce Pegg, writes represent the actions of "a man whose detachment from society made him feel immune to its mores and taboos." (For disturbing details see Pegg's *Brown Eyed Handsome Man: The Life and Hard Times of Chuck Berry*.) Sometimes that sense of detachment has served him well (by allowing him to speak in another person's voice, for example, in his songwriting), sometimes it has not — but it has always been a non-negotiable part of his personality. And it has at times alienated his own audience at the very moment that, were he but able to admit it, he might have needed them most.

Which has tended to make his transition to lovable icon, to venerable (and much-venerated) elder statesman, a little daunting. In the last few years he has enjoyed a round of gracious honors: a larger-than-life duck-walking statue in St. Louis (his stylized duckwalk was from the beginning the hallmark of his live act); that PEN New England "Song Lyrics of Literary Excellence" award, conferred at the John F. Kennedy Presidential Library, where Chuck took great delight in snapping pictures, and having his own picture taken with images of JFK; his celebration in a weeklong series of events as an American Music Master at the Rock and Roll Hall of Fame; the $100,000 international Polar Music Prize, which has often been referred to as "the Nobel Prize for Music." At each of the first three (he was not able to attend the Polar Prize ceremony in Sweden in 2014, three years before his death at ninety), he acquitted himself with more than a hint of sentiment and a large dose of his own brand of idiosyncratic charm. "I'm wondering about my future," he told *Rolling Stone* reporter Patrick Doyle at the Rock and Roll Hall of Fame festivities. When pressed to be a little more specific, "I'll give you a little piece of poetry," he said. "Give you a song? / I can't do that / My singing days have passed / My voice is gone, my throat is worn / And my lungs are going fast." Or as he put it ten years earlier, in 2002: "In a way, I feel it might be ill-mannered to try and top myself. The music I play is a ritual. Something that matters to people in a special way. I wouldn't want to interfere with that."

TWENTY

American Without Tears:

Elvis Costello and Allen Toussaint Go on a Journey

TWO MEN ARE CAUGHT in the spotlight, both middle-aged, both impeccably dressed. One is black, one white, each is wearing a dark suit, and, altogether inadvertently, both are wearing purple ties. It is a Monday night in February of 2006 at Joe's Pub, an intimate show-case club in New York City, and Elvis Costello and Allen Toussaint are previewing their new album in a two-man performance for their record label and its foreign distributors. Elvis, the more rumpled one, rakish in a purple shirt and Stetson-style dress-up hat, takes on his familiar front-man role, eloquent, witty, and characteristically generous with praise for his sixty-eight-year-old musical partner, who sits erect and attentive at the piano, a small smile playing about his lips. Allen Toussaint, with a perfectly sculpted gray Afro and mustache, is a New Orleans legend. He has produced hits on such other New Orleans legends as Irma Thomas, Ernie K-Doe, Lee Dorsey, and the Neville Brothers as well as providing assistance to rock stars from Paul Simon, Paul McCartney, Dr. John, and the Band to—Elvis Costello. But he is, as he will be the first to tell you, a man who has always operated behind the scenes, the "proof of [whose] labors still gets out there, it's just not brought out there by me."

Elvis has decided at their brief soundcheck-rehearsal that afternoon that he will play guitar on only one song, so he looks to Allen for his cue, and from the first notes it is clear that he is as drawn in as anyone in the room by the spare and stately power of the music. They lead off with one of their first collaborations, "The Sharpest Thorn," guided by Allen's ele-gant, almost classical accompaniment. They sing old songs and new songs alike, with Elvis almost invariably providing the lead vocal and Allen, as on so many of his hit productions, providing the indispensable second voice. There are echoes of Allen's mentor, New Orleans piano legend

Professor Longhair ("the Bach of rock," as Allen has dubbed him without a trace of irony), throughout the program, but only on Allen's "Who's Gonna Help Brother Get Further?," a song that Allen wrote in 1970 which brilliantly delineates the African American urban experience in the twentieth century without ever sacrificing its wryly idiomatic tone, does Allen take the lead. There are angry songs by Elvis focusing on the current political situation, there are tender love songs, there are songs that work as sheer entertainment, but the mood of the evening never falters, the sense that each and every person in the room, including the musicians, is lost in the music. By the very joyfulness of its expression this is, decidedly, music to make you smile.

*I think the marriage of [our styles] is very interesting inasmuch as how
bold Elvis is, how attuned and aware of what's going on. He's not a
coward, and that's good: for someone to have such a talent and be able
to bring it forward. He says things that many people would like to
but don't know how to say. Elvis has taken me by the hand and said,
Let's take a trip.*

— Allen Toussaint

*Allen is a tempering influence on my tendency to really — I mean, if I'm
let off the leash, I will go into it quite a bit [but], you know, he will say just
the right thing. It's not to say that either of us expresses our ideas better
than the other, but he's got such an instinctive and natural ability to lend
each of his talents in a different way and in different proportion — and,
most important, [with] generosity.*

— Elvis Costello

IT IS THE MOST IMPROBABLE of collaborations. For the last twenty years at least, Elvis Costello, the former Declan MacManus of London and Liverpool, at one time a certified pop star, has been a whirling dervish of creativity. In the last two years alone, since reaching the age of fifty, he has been working on an opera about Hans Christian Andersen for the Royal Danish Opera, put out a raw roots album, *The Delivery Man,* with his band, the Imposters, sung and recorded with a fifty-two-piece jazz

Photograph by Jimmy Katz

orchestra from the Netherlands, Metropole Orkest, for whom he has written a number of ambitious orchestrations of some of his old songs as well as lyrics for Charles Mingus and Billy Strayhorn compositions, and showcased a fifteen-minute suite from the ballet he was commissioned to write for Italy's Aterballetto dance company's adaptation of *A Midsummer Night's Dream* (it was released as the Deutsche Grammophon recording, *Il Sogno,* on the same day as *The Delivery Man* in the fall of 2004) with symphony orchestras around the world. In the last few months he has performed at the Apollo, sung on a duets album with Tony Bennett, performed with Emmylou Harris and Gillian Welch at the Grand Ole Opry, shot a VH1 tribute to his music with Billie Joe Armstrong, Death Cab for Cutie, and Fiona Apple, and embarked upon numerous other plans for a far-flung series of events in virtually every one of the seven lively arts. As Allen Toussaint says admiringly of him, "Elvis operates at one speed: top speed. If you wound him up any tighter, I think he'd explode!"

Allen, meanwhile, has led what can only be described as a quiet, somewhat reclusive life in New Orleans—if quiet reclusivity can be said to include a gold Rolls-Royce and a Mercedes convertible to tool around town in, a home, a production company and a well-appointed recording studio, Sea-Saint, all in the same comfortable Gentilly neighborhood, and a position of sufficient prominence in the world of music that for close to three decades everyone came to him. He saw no reason, and no likelihood, of ever leaving his hometown ("Everything that was dear to me was near to me")—until Katrina. With Katrina he made the same preparations he always had: he boarded up his home and studio with the same numbered boards he had used before, and he prepared to wait out the storm at the Astor Crowne Plaza on Bourbon Street. When it became obvious that Katrina wasn't just another storm, he hired a school bus to take him to Baton Rouge, flew to New York, and there embarked upon a life he had never envisioned. With the help of his friend and business partner, Josh Feigenbaum, he found a comfortable midtown apartment, started playing a solo Sunday-brunch gig at Joe's Pub ("This was something that was totally foreign to me"), and joined in the fund-raisers for Katrina victims that were sprouting up all over, but particularly in New York City.

That was how he met Elvis Costello. They had worked together previously when Elvis joined the legion of musical pilgrims coming to New Orleans for an infusion of impeccable funk (it is Allen's piano you hear on *Spike*'s "Deep Dark Truthful Mirror" from 1989). Elvis had begun singing Allen's "Freedom for the Stallion" as a kind of salute to New Orleans in the immediate aftermath of Katrina, and then they performed it together at Lincoln Center in September, reprising it the next day at Joe's Pub. That, according to Elvis, was where the idea for the album was born. At first it was going to be a salute to Allen's work in the form of an Allen Toussaint Songbook, but within days the concept had expanded to include Elvis' fiery new composition, "The River in Reverse," written the afternoon of the "Parting the Waters" benefit at Town Hall, and then very quickly, as Elvis continued to connect with Allen on an almost daily basis, it grew to incorporate a more ambitious collaboration. Allen had by now learned that his house and studio were lost. He and Elvis were backstage at the Madison Square Garden "From the Big Apple to the Big Easy" benefit, and Elvis came up to him, "and I just said quietly, 'So sorry to hear it,' the way you would, and he just said, 'The things I had served me well when I had them.' Which I thought was a remarkable reaction. And then he said, 'I'll have to write some more.'"

"I loved New Orleans so much," says Allen, "it took a lot for me to leave." He was still not certain, even after coming to New York, that he was ready to step into the spotlight, but on the other hand there was no denying that the ground had shifted. In the last decade the stars had stopped coming to New Orleans, and Allen for his part resolutely — some might say obstinately — refused to leave home for any of the opportunities the world might have to offer. Looking back on it, Allen says, "I was busy every day, I was making music and making tracks. I stayed with the music as if I was on a mission — *but without a mission.* Because I didn't have something that I had to have ready the next day or the next week. When Katrina came, it's almost as if Katrina said, 'Okay, you've been here doing this, let's go put it to use.'"

The music itself — not only the words — has a subtext. I don't know that Allen's ever thought about it or analyzed it — I don't think that's in his nature. There are certain writers who are analytical, and there are others that just accept the thoughts that come to them. Whether they are about matters of the heart or matters of the world, they treat them equally. I might be opposite to him in that. You know, I consider everything that comes to me. But sometimes you can be in the middle of a song and recognize what it's actually saying, and that's the power of [the music].

— *Elvis Costello*

ONE OF the THINGS that drove the album from the start was the growing realization not just on Elvis' part, but on Allen's as well, of the richness, depth, and complexity of Allen's old songs. Elvis had known most of the compositions they were considering for the album for at least twenty years, but the full range of their social, political, and emotional implications had never occurred to him, probably as much as anything else because of the good-time New Orleans feel of their original presenta-tion. Allen, too, was surprised at some of their nuances. He had never seen himself as political. He was not one to "shake a fist at the politician or the political scene — or beat someone over the head about something, even if it's artistic. But Elvis found some of these songs of mine that were written thirty or thirty-five years ago totally applicable to the [present-day] situation, and when I hear them I see now that, yes, I guess that was their destiny."

Perhaps it was the fluidity of their composition that allowed them to

The Flamingos, July 15, 1953: with (from left to right) Walter Lang (trumpet), Allen at piano, Ferdinand Bigeou (trombone), Benjamin Gregory (tenor sax), Snooks Eaglin (guitar), James Jackson (drums), Frank Morton (clarinet). *From the collection of Frank Morton*

find so unexpected a new life. Perhaps it was simply Allen's evolution as a songwriter. He looks back on some of his classic early compositions as embodying the "soft-shoe approach—you know, lighthearted, debonair, not thick in any fashion. But then I guess I got to a point in my life where it became, 'Okay, I got this, but now it's got to have *"and then some."'* Not to be different but because it deserved to go somewhere else. Because I found pleasure in that. Sometimes," Allen says with a shrug, "my son says 'Daddy, why don't you write like you used to, before you started wearing those suits and ties?'" He laughs, and his voice trails off. "I don't know...."

There was never any question about what he was going to do with his life. Allen knew, he says, from the time he was six and one-half years old, and his parents simply accepted it because they had no other choice. At thirteen he started his own group, the Flamingos, with blind rhythm and blues singer-guitarist Snooks Eaglin. He made sure that Snooks got all the words right, and he painstakingly wrote out note-for-note arrangements for the band for much the same reason that Elvis would learn to read and write music in his forties: to be able to present the music properly, even if it was, in Allen's case, just the jukebox hits of the day. Once he entered the recording end of the business in the late '50s, he began writing songs himself for the most natural reason: the artist that he was recording needed a song. "They need a song? Of course, write a song. Sometimes at a recording session they would need another, so we'd go on break and I'd write another right then and there. Ever so humble, I must say, but song it was."

He rehearsed the singers at home. "Guys and girls [Irma Thomas, Art and Aaron Neville, Betty Harris, Benny Spellman at one time or another] would get together in the front room of my parents' house, and we would have a jam session all day long." He would work out background vocals for each song, with every singer not featured on that particular number making up the chorus. He passed out the arrangements to the musicians in the studio, and they would do four songs in three hours. They were, he says, simple songs and fun times, at a time when the world seemed like a kinder place. On his own Allen listened to everything: gospel and hillbilly, the Metropolitan Opera and Professor Longhair, Grieg and Chopin. The first classical piece he learned was Grieg's Piano Concerto in A Minor, he taught it to himself from a record when he was barely in his teens, "and the piano I was playing it on was flat, so for two years I was playing it in the wrong key!"

With the same mix of determination, originality, and self-invention, he sought his true voice. In Lee Dorsey, an auto repairman, or body-and-fender *artiste*, as Allen dubbed him, he found it: an instrument as curiously original and idiosyncratic as his own. "I can always see Lee moving through the world," he told New Orleans music historian Jeff Hannusch, "and me back there watching and writing about it." For Dorsey he wrote and produced "Ride Your Pony," "Working in the Coal Mine," and "Holy Cow," all pop and r&b hits, in the mid-'60s, writing and arranging (percussion, bass, and horn parts were all fully written out) for a voice that he heard in his head, creating "pockets" for Lee to fit right into. With Dorsey's 1970 album, *Yes We Can*, and a singles session from the same period, for the first time he seemed to find a way to explore some of the more ambitious concepts that he had unconsciously been yearning to express. "Those songs," he told Hannusch, "would probably never have been written if it hadn't been for the kind of guy that Lee [was]." "Who's Gonna Help Brother Get Further?," "On Your Way Down," "Tears, Tears, and

Lee Dorsey, Body-and-Fender Artiste. *Photograph by Michael Smith © The Historic New Orleans Collection*

More Tears," and "Freedom for the Stallion," which provide much of the template for the new collaboration with Costello, all stem from those Dorsey sessions, while the Pointer Sisters' version of the album's title song, a big pop hit, was one of the first productions out of Allen's new studio, Sea-Saint, in 1973. From this point on his horizons just kept on expanding, both as producer (he was responsible for Labelle's 1975 number-one pop hit, "Lady Marmalade"), songwriter (Glen Campbell's 1977 "Southern Nights," a simultaneous number-one hit on the pop, country, and adult-contemporary charts), and artist, a career on which he embarked with more than a little ambivalence in the immediate aftermath of all the attention that *Yes We Can* had brought him. From Allen's point of view it was almost as if he was pushed into it. He still saw himself as "the one who made a demo for someone with the zeal for being front-stage center. My life [had always] been, Okay, here comes John — I'm ready for John. Here comes Sally — I'm ready for Sally. Then here comes me. . . . No, I'm the one waiting for John and Sally."

This collaboration with Elvis is a luxury. Most of my life I've been used to having everything to do, from evaluating what kind of song the artist should sing to writing the song and teaching it to the artist to setting up the proper environment for the artist and musicians so that we get the best out of every one. Not that I consider those things tedious, it's what I do — but I didn't miss [them either]. Collaborating with Elvis was like collaborating with a whole collection of knowledge and information. I had already thought in my mind that he would be the general, because after all he invited me in. But when we did start, we were [both] very reluctant about the take-charge. Which was odd.

— Allen Toussaint

THE PROBLEM WAS, simply, finding an approach that worked. This wasn't a question of Elvis fitting himself into someone else's established style, as he did with Burt Bacharach, nor was it a matter of submitting finished songs for Allen to arrange. The intent was a true creative partnership, but at first, Elvis says, there was just too much politeness. In the end it was Allen's piano playing that furnished the inspiration. He had recorded "Tipitina and Me," an elegiac, minor-key variation on Professor Longhair's exuberant signature piece, for *Our New Orleans 2005,* one of the first of the benefit albums. Now, as he fooled around with the figure at the end of a somewhat dispiriting first day, Elvis asked if it would be all right to write some lyrics to it. He came back the next morning with "Ascension Day," a moody gospel piece for voice and piano ("Not a soul was stirring / Not a bird was singing, at least not within my hearing") — the music, Elvis says, had "opened up a series of images. When I heard that piece for the first time I felt like a curtain came back and I was looking into a world not of people standing around with stained T-shirts and no shoes, trying to drag their few possessions out of the way of a body of water, but more of a roomful of people of great nobility and gentility. There's no irony, there's no self-regard, I'm sure Allen's doing it just because he loves the way it sounds and feels."

From that point they were on their way. The first collaboration after "Ascension Day" was on a song idea of Elvis', "The Sharpest Thorn." It was, Elvis says, about "somebody who goes out full of pride to a celebration, a parade, and comes home at the end of the day with confetti in his hair, his pockets picked, a little poorer, a little wiser. It wasn't a serious song [at the start], but it was lifted up by these images that Allen suggested almost out of thin air. He just suddenly said to me, 'Could it be about good and evil?' And I said, yes, it could absolutely be about a moral dilemma. Then at another point he said, 'Is there any place for the Archangel Gabriel in this song?' It was the most extraordinary thing. Allen literally put us in a reverie with those few remarks and his response to the music, the way he asked questions about certain cadences and articulated the changes [with] a gospel accompaniment."

Oh, no, Allen demurs in a separate conversation, "Elvis already had the plot going." And as far as the music was concerned, he simply felt "very reverent about it. When I first heard it going in a certain direction, I thought — I actually wrote down in my notes — I will funkify this. I will make it funky. But I noticed when I was playing it, I didn't dare touch it. It felt like it would have been sacrilegious to do anything but the purest form of what it was."

Along with writing and song selection, they quickly settled on a format for recording. They would, if at all possible, work in New Orleans, and they would employ both Allen's customary four-man horn section and guitarist, along with Elvis' band, the Imposters, to achieve the abrasive edge that Elvis felt the album needed. Had they simply worked with New Orleans musicians, Elvis says, it would have been like remaking the old records, only with a new vocalist. This way you "get to play with your own interpretation, but when it comes to the articulations that lie above the beat, it wouldn't have been the same if we'd got a New York horn section." The idea was to create an authentic original voice.

Within a month they were in the studio. They started off in Los Angeles, because New Orleans was still closed down, and they got the first three songs in twenty-five minutes, before the horns arrived. "I thought, Wow, we're not even going to get to New Orleans," says Elvis. "We're going to finish this record in three days!" "We were," Allen agrees, "really spoiled." When the horns finally got there on the second day, things slowed down considerably because Elvis was committed to the idea of cutting everything live. It was definitely harder, says Allen, who had been cutting separate tracks for convenience sake for over thirty years, but it was a revitalizing experience, "because the horns were playing the song, they were not just playing parts — they were hearing the song coming at them, [just like] Elvis was hearing the horns coming right back at him. I must say, it was wonderful to see that happen. I don't recall fixing anything."

Writing and rehearsing for the album. *Photograph by Joshua Feigenbaum*

Everyone left for New Orleans the first week of December, as soon as New Orleans began to reopen and they were able to get into a hotel and recording studio. For Allen there was nowhere else on earth to be, and for Elvis the same allure that had originally drawn him to the city's music remained, in a heartbreakingly different way, as he drove through desolate, deserted streets seeking out a vanished world. New Orleans was where they recorded Elvis' angry "River in Reverse," the song with which the *idea* for the album had started, but it was also where Elvis was determined to get Allen to step out front and center on his own wide-ranging portrait of a world, "Who's Gonna Help Brother Get Further?" "I was *tricked* into singing it," Allen says laughingly, as he recalls the way Elvis had him teach everyone the precise syntax of the chorus ("Pray tell what's gonna happen to brother / Who's gonna help him get further? / 'One another'") and then demo the song, which paints a vividly detailed picture of life in a world of inescapable dualities, where social progress can only come from embracing the pain (and the richness) of this world, then forging a new path together.

"I WILL TEND TO HEAT UP QUICKLY," says Elvis to guest host Bill Flanagan on the *Charlie Rose* show, "[whereas] with Allen you'll be laughing at the wit of the line before you've realized the seriousness of what he said." What gives Allen's songs their sense of mystery and power, he says, what permits them to open up, much like Sam Cooke's songs, from their commonplace expressions and everyday settings, are the layers of nuance and suggestion that lie just beneath the surface. On the other hand: "John actually has a face," Allen says with some amusement, referring to a character in the song with "two dollars in his pocket, talking loud [but] thinks he's rich." "He used to wear gray pants and a red shirt!" In response to my assumption that he was the one who came up with the idea for the angry — or let's just say humorously indignant — trombone solo by Big Sam Williams in the middle of the song, "No way," says Allen. "No way — and let me say it again. It was the expertise and awareness of Elvis that caused that to happen. Someone told Elvis, 'You know, that trombone player can really play,' and he came over and said, 'Why don't we consider having a trombone solo?' Now, when was the last time you heard a trombone solo on a record? I would have missed that. But Elvis don't miss. He sees the moment." He pauses. *"I think that's why his life must be joyful to him."*

The recording of the album, Elvis says, was in fact "the most joyful experience I've ever had in the studio. You go in a room, you do it right, and then it's done." Because it was conceived as a three-act "entertainment," in the end beautiful versions of Allen's "What Do You Want the Girl to Do?" and "The Greatest Love," both of which are highlights of the live show, were left off the final mix — because, Elvis felt, they would have thrown off the balance of the presentation. The album, as it is now constituted, begins with three of Allen's most accessible songs, each transformed by Elvis' passionate performance, followed by "The Sharpest Thorn," before embarking upon the album's second, and more overtly political, movement, introduced by "Brother." The last act kicks in with "International Echo," with words by Elvis and music by Allen, once again in an unmistakable Professor Longhair vein. Speaking of joyfulness, this is surely as rollicking a number as Elvis has ever written, a tribute not just to the impact of music in general but to the impact of Allen Toussaint's music on Elvis, and Elvis' perhaps on you and me. It's about how music can work on the imagination, how it "comes from one city, travels around the world, and then rebounds back," Elvis says. It's a song about how Elvis first heard Allen Toussaint's songs in various versions by English beat groups, how he heard "Wonder Woman," one of the most obscure numbers on the album, in a wonderfully unself-conscious version by his friend (and longtime collaborator) Nick Lowe's pub-rock band, Brinsley Schwarz, in the early '70s, "and then I sought out the Lee Dorsey version and found they'd copied it note for note!"

Send out a message and it's sure to rebound. . . .
What is that sound? Seems to be coming from under the ground
International echo

FOR ELVIS there is no greater expression of truth than art. Not politics, not posterity ("I have no concern for posterity," he has said. "I believe when you're gone, you're gone"), just a dedication to process and aspiration. He loves "the way painters used to paint the roofs of churches [as if there were] always a world beyond." That had to do with belief, of course, but it is all to do with conveying a vision that has its own imperative, he has come to feel, it's all about communicating something that demands expression.

This has been a hard-won realization for a man who was originally assumed to possess a post-punk sensibility whose only lyrical reference points were "guilt and revenge." He did a great deal, he recognizes now, to play up that image, and he didn't really question the confinement that it imposed upon him ("There was always the unwillingness to be vulnerable") until he began work on 1986's *King of America* with producer T Bone Burnett. That was when he relearned the lesson he had taken from all the records that had inspired him since he was a kid, from Mingus to Hank Williams, that it should not be about keeping the meaning secret but about being "generous with what you've got," as he described it to Bill Flanagan, "giving the song enough space to be what you actually intended instead of trying to turn it into something else."

Since then the expression of his ideas has come in many different forms. *North* (2003), for example, is a nakedly unadorned confession — "there's no flashy language to speak of, it's not dressed in any poetic clothes or conceits or any of the devices that I've employed that [can] develop like barnacles, you know, on a ship." Some of the other projects have been more rococo, striking different audiences in different ways, but

Elvis and T Bone, 1984. *Photograph by Sherry Rayn Barnett*

they all represent an attempt to emphasize what Elvis calls "creativity, not positivity or negativity," to access in one way or another some form of direct emotional communication. He would like to think he is not so quick to judge others by their image nowadays, particularly young singers looking to make their mark. Image is one thing, he says, music another. And while he may regret some of the choices he made starting out, he has always, he says, cared deeply about the music. "I always took it seriously."

I ask Allen what kind of song he would create for Elvis if he were writing for him today, as he once wrote for Lee Dorsey. "I would probably write a very, very simple song," he says, after giving the matter some thought, "one that is easy to be hummed. With a comical chorus, whether it had lyrics or not. Elvis is very bold in his speech, and he admits himself that many times he writes to the dark side. I would find no validity in going in the direction [in which] he goes so strongly and drives his own bus. So I would take all of that power of a giant and submit it as tenderly as a lamb. The way he delivered his spirit of it would make it as emotional, or as spiritual, as it needed to be."

And if he were to write and produce for himself, if he were given the impossible assignment of trying to spotlight the real Allen Toussaint in the same way that he has shone the light on so many others? Here the

Jazz & Heritage Festival, 1994. *Photograph by David Gahr*

answer is not so easy. He *might,* he says, just before the start of the *River in Reverse* album tour, bring Allen Toussaint more to the forefront today, "just because of the endorsement of other folk." But left to his own devices, he suspects he would probably still do much the same thing he has done in the past: surround himself with as many beautiful ambient sounds as he found pleasing, put in the trees and the wind, write bass lines and counter lines—"and to me any of those things is just as important, and most of them are more important, than me. When I am recording other artists, I don't feel that way. I feel that they are most important. With me [it's] everything else."

But maybe that is changing. After showcasing the album with Elvis in England, Europe, and Japan, after playing San Francisco, Chicago, New York, Atlanta, and a host of other cities on a full-scale band tour this past summer, it seems as if Allen, almost against his will, is coming closer to center stage. The show is accompanied by all the accoutrements and triumphalism of a standard rock presentation, but at its heart are those same moments of private reverie, shared by artist and audience alike, that made the two-man Joe's Pub preview six months earlier so remarkable. Elvis performs many of his most familiar songs (though, he is quick to point out to the audience, with new arrangements by Allen), the wit and patter are all Elvis', and Allen for the most part remains a bemused, if dignified, spectator, his quizzically raised eyebrows his most explicit commentary on the proceedings. But over the course of the tour he has begun to do more and more vocals, always with Elvis' enthusiastic onstage endorsement ("I get the best seat in the house," he frequently says as he stands there for Allen's beautifully realized tribute to Professor Longhair), and if Elvis' "The Poisoned Rose" is invariably one of the soulful highlights of a soulful evening, so too is "Who's Gonna Help Brother," no less than Allen's recent addition of Paul Simon's "American Tune." There is something for everyone here, brought to you unquestionably by way of Elvis' extraordinary graciousness, energy, and generosity of spirit, but Allen Toussaint simply playing the piano conveys no less extraordinary a presence. "Allen Toussaint for President," someone calls out one night, and Elvis, who has just introduced the show's single stage prop, a tiny action figure of President Bush, can only assent with the broadest of grins.

To Allen there would have been little point in making a sad and doleful album: the significance of the music, the significance of music in general is simply too great. "This is not a sympathy record," he has said. "The songs here can live in war and peace, anytime, anywhere." He and Elvis, he hastens to point out, did not set out to make speeches. "We were making the music we love." The view is no different even from Elvis' more political perspective. When all is said and done, it is the music that will survive. "God gave me something to hold on to," Allen says, "so that the things that happen around me are only as dramatic as I perceive them." He is meditating on matters of race, on the divided world he was born into, the way that things have and have not changed, but he could just as easily be speaking of Katrina. "Everything costs something," he says gravely. "The world is better now. . . . It's better."

TWENTY-ONE

The Song of Solomon: A Triptych

THE VOICES OF SOLOMON BURKE

S OMEDAY I'm going to write an epic narrative (maybe it should be an epic narrative *poem*) about My Travels with Solomon Burke. The thing about it is, with Solomon there was no need to travel very far. In fact, there was no need to travel at all. You would only have to spend a day or two with Solomon — maybe just a few hours — to have enough material for a film, a book, or a life-changing experience.

If I were to say that life with Solomon was a three-ring circus, it would be selling his circus short. There's no telling the number of rings that he could keep going at the same time — *or* the number of voices. You could be sitting with Solomon, and he might call someone up, someone with whom, let's say, he might be having certain problems of a fiduciary nature, and he would take on the mien — the mien, the manner, and the voice — of a Dr. Stein, Dr. Burke's comptroller, explaining that there had been an unanticipated problem with the transfer of funds, or the conversion of foreign currencies, but he could provide full assurance that it would be taken care of forthwith. Or under certain exigent circumstances he might become Dr. Burke the brain surgeon, as he did when longtime club owner/ manager/booking agent Jimmy Evans had in fact *had* brain surgery and was incommunicado to everyone except his family and medical team. Occasionally he was Solomon Berkowitz (this was more of a joke between friends), confidently throwing in a wide range of Yiddish expressions that he said he had learned from the kosher market where his stepfather worked as a chicken plucker (sometimes he said his stepfather was a black Jew). Or, on the other hand, he might be a Muslim brother (I can't remember what name he went by in that guise), if the occasion so demanded — you just never could tell.

Gettting back the crown: New Orleans, 1985. *Photograph by Alan Edelstein*

I first met Solomon in 1980, just as I was beginning work on my book *Sweet Soul Music*. I had written a lead review about him in an early issue of *Rolling Stone*, in 1969. It was one of the first pieces I wrote for them, and it was all about — well, what it really boiled down to was a line from one of Solomon's early hits, "Everybody Needs Somebody to Love":

"There's a song I sing," Solomon proclaimed, "and I believe if everybody was to sing this song, it would save the whole world."

Well, the way he sang it, I believed that, too, and my review was the template for the book proposal for *Sweet Soul Music* which I sent around for the next eleven years.

When I finally got a book contract in 1980, the first person I went looking for was Solomon. I had pursued a bunch of false leads, run down a lot of out-of-service telephone numbers, and spoken to any number of people who professed to have no knowledge of Solomon whatsoever. Then J. W. Alexander gave me the name of a man who he thought might still be Solomon's lawyer. (J. W., Sam Cooke's friend and business partner, had managed Solomon for a minute in the late '60s, and still chuckled fondly over their misadventures, all precipitated by Solomon's penchant for real-life "spontaneity" over any kind of long-range planning.) Anyway, I called the lawyer's office and didn't get any further, it seemed, than I had with anyone else, and was going out to play tennis one day when my wife, Alexandra, came rushing out after me, saying, "Peter, there's someone on the phone who I think has something to do with Solomon Burke. I think he may have said he *was* Solomon Burke," she added, as we walked back into the house, "but I think I must have misunderstood."

Once I got on the phone, it wasn't hard to grasp the reason for her confusion. I had listened to all his records, seen Solomon perform in little clubs and headline all-star Supersonic Attractions soul revues — but the voice I heard on the phone didn't bear any resemblance to the commanding voice I thought I knew so well. *This* voice was the voice of a mild-mannered (for that you can read "white," if you like) insurance salesman. Maybe an accountant — or a very cautious lawyer. Maybe, it occurred to me, this was a different Solomon Burke altogether.

This Solomon Burke carefully went over the pronunciation of my name, which he had already established with Alexandra. Then he inquired in an exceedingly circumspect and mild-mannered way about the purpose of my call. Still thinking that this must be some kind of a joke, I started to explain that I was writing a book, it was a book about soul music, it was about *Southern* soul music.

"Of course, of course," interrupted the voice at the other end of the line, suddenly warming to the conversation and abandoning all pretense of polite neutrality. "And how," said the man who bore the title of "King of Rock 'n' Soul" in a newly commanding tone, "could you write a book on soul music without speaking to the King?"

Well, that was it. That was the beginning of my adventure. I went down to New York a few weeks later when he was playing at Tramps. I met him in the dressing room upstairs, surrounded by a small coterie of friends, family, and longtime acquaintances, and he welcomed me into his world.

After the show, which was as inspired as virtually every show I would see over the next thirty years (including the one whose second set consisted entirely of a spur-of-the-moment wedding ceremony—remember, Solomon was a bishop in his grandmother Eleanor A. Moore's Daddy Grace–inspired church, whose name, he always insisted, should really be changed from the House of God for All People to the House of God for All People, Let It All Hang Out), Solomon wanted to cap the evening with a visit to the famous Stage Delicatessen, so we drove uptown—but it was closed. As was every other familiar landmark that he wanted to introduce me to. So, undaunted, we ended up at an all-night diner in Times Square, where Solomon interviewed the hookers who had ducked in out of the cold, asking them with great good humor about their life and work as he used a salt shaker for a microphone and told them they were being filmed by hidden cameras.

It was a great beginning, and it never stopped, taking place over a period of three decades, two continents, any number of Northern, Southern, and Western states, and a smattering of churches, both Solomon's own and others that he had his eye on as potential acquisitions.

It was the most fun I've ever had in my life, with every real-life adventure a lesson in improvisation, intellect, wit, and spontaneity. Sitting in a somewhat seedy, down-at-the-heels New Jersey Holiday Inn, eating cold french fries and listening to him describe the Chateaubriand steak he was being served in the Presidential Suite at the Plaza to someone on the other end of the line who he felt, for whatever reason, needed to be impressed—the thing was, as he described it, against all evidence of the senses, you could almost, no, Solomon might insist, you could *actually* taste it. Watching him empty all the money in his pockets for the audience at a gospel program at a sad old broken-down church in Brooklyn, moments after the promoter told him to his grievous disappointment that she was not going to be able to pay him for his performance that evening. Attending a gathering of all his affiliated churches in Los Angeles, where he made me sit onstage and, handing me a souvenir from his recent trip to the Holy Land, said, "Bless the yarmulke, Pete." Atlantic Records vice president Jerry Wexler once described him as "the best soul singer of all time, hands down—with a borrowed band." But I wouldn't even put that qualification on it. He was without question the greatest singer of *any* kind that I've ever seen (remember, there's a lot of singers that I haven't seen, including, for example, Sam Cooke), one of the most inventive showmen, also one

Backstage after the wedding, May 1, 1993: Solomon, Red and Georgette Kelly, and me.
Photograph by Sharyn Felder

of the most brilliant, profound, and certainly the funniest person I've ever met, onstage or off—which tended to cost him in the pulpit. ("I couldn't resist the joke, Pete," he said to me one time after bringing his congregation to a point of mass hysteria, then throwing it all away with a punch line of dubious taste.)

This was the Experience of Solomon. Sometimes, as you might imagine, it could be a struggle to keep up, not just because of his ingenious inventions and capacious imagination but also because, as I realized early on, Solomon's zest for multi-dimensionality simply did not permit him to believe that he should be governed by the same rules as everyone else. Not to put too fine a point on it, he was addicted to the con. (I was going to say the game—I've tried to soften it in all kinds of ways—but it really *was* the con, and it was his own con he was addicted to most of all.) Early on he tried to enlist me in one of his more intricately imagined schemes, which involved the acquisition of a million-dollar house for no money down—and no money risked on my part, he hastened to add, just the quick cancellation of a newly established bank account in my name. I told him with no small amount of misgiving (this wasn't the first time a subject of this sort had come up, though it was the first time that he had suggested there was a role for me to play) that much as I loved him, we couldn't continue like this—that I didn't play. To my relief a big smile wreathed his face. "That's what I love about you, Pete," he said. "You always take the long view." Which never stopped him from delivering home truths from time to time that could impact on either one of us, or both. One time he was miffed with me for inadvertently getting in the way of a social situation that he was trying to promote for himself, and he raised a question that he might just as easily have asked himself: "Tell me," he said, "when you're alone in your room at night, who is it that's Pete the Writer?" A question that I've never ceased to ponder, with no more of a clue to the proper response today than I had at the time.

From that point on in any case he never failed to respect the "boundaries" that we had established, while I for my part always tried to provide what seemed to me the most helpful advice you could offer to anyone thinking of going into business, in whatever way, with Solomon: don't let yourself get overextended. Don't put up more money than you can afford to lose. My rationalization, obviously—if I were being totally honest, I would have to admit that it remains my guilty rationalization to this day—was that this was a man capable of so many extraordinary acts of kindness that surely this side of his nature had to outweigh the financial legerdemain in which he so frequently chose to indulge. And besides, I reasoned (*rationalized*—I know there was no reason involved), wasn't it true that Solomon was drawn at least as much to the game as to the reward? One time, toward the end of his life, he was both tickled and taken aback when an old friend who knew his proclivities insisted not just on paying him in advance but on *over*paying him, in 250 crisp hundred-dollar bills, without even a chance for negotiations. "Can't we just go in the back and do this like gangsters?" Solomon protested. As Queen Mother Taylor, the doyenne of one of Los Angeles' first "Cadillac" churches, which Solomon was doing everything in his power to take over from her son, once said to me, "I know he's a con—but I love him."

But at the same time I was well aware that not everyone was as charmed—nor should they have been. And almost inevitably I got caught up in one of Solomon's schemes, as someone I had introduced him to took exception to what could only be described as Solomon's deceptive business practices. Unbeknownst to me, he filed suit against Solomon, seeking to garnish his wages and evidently naming me in the suit as someone who would substantiate his claims. I didn't know anything about any of this, but I did know that something had changed in our relationship when I stopped hearing from Solomon two or three times a week. And when he did call, I couldn't miss the chill in his voice. It wasn't until we arrived in Italy for the 1998 Sweet Soul Music Festival in Porretta that I finally understood. There was a fierce scowl on Solomon's face that I had never seen before, as we stood in the parking lot across from the hotel and, flanked by two of his daughters, whom I had known since they were little girls, he delivered his message. "You know what you've done," Solomon declared in thunderous tones, and when I protested that I didn't, I had no idea what he was talking about, his expression only grew darker, his voice more cold, as he provided just enough details for me to guess at what must have happened. "You've made your money," he said, and now I got mad, as his daughters grew more uncomfortable. I would NEVER, I protested—and it was true. But there was no assuaging the anger or the hurt that he felt; nothing could persuade him that he had not been betrayed by someone he trusted.

It took two or three years to patch things up, and then only through the intervention of a mutual friend, Dan Rabinovitz, a thirty-six-year-old Boston lawyer who played trumpet in the band whenever he could. Dan had brought to Solomon's attention the plight of a white Newton, Massachusetts, firefighter named Ray McNamara, who, after suffering burns over 90 percent of his body, in addition to losing his ears, nose, hair, and eyesight, confided to a newspaper columnist in 2001 that his ambition had always been to sing onstage with the great soul singer Solomon Burke. Dan thought it would be nice if Solomon could send him some kind of memento, but Solomon said, "You know a CD would be nice, and a call would be beautiful, but we can do better. Put a band together, and I'll come to town. It'll be a monster. And I don't want no money either." So Danny arranged it, and at the benefit, which took place in the ballroom of the Bradford Hotel and drew an audience of close to 1,000, made up largely of firefighters and their friends, Solomon called out my name and without further preamble simply declared, "I made a mistake," as the band continued to vamp. "Once I didn't believe you were my friend," he said, "but I found out you were the best friend I ever had. Will you ever forgive me"—pregnant pause—"for being such a hamburger?" And then he improvised lyrics about friendship to the strains of "Spanish Harlem."

After that we were pretty much back on track. And Solomon found himself caught up in a run of unprecedented success which, despite his

At the Ray Mac benefit, November 19, 2001. *Courtesy of Kurt Andrews, Dan Rabinovitz*

gift of second sight, I'm not sure even he could have anticipated. He won a Grammy. He was elected to the Rock and Roll Hall of Fame. He was honored by the Blues Foundation and the Rhythm and Blues Foundation. And he found a whole new audience that took him all around the world, where he played for kings and queens (well, popes, cardinals, and billionaires anyway — in Italy he had his own personal cardinal, to whom he dedicated songs like "My Way" and "O Sole Mio" at every show) — and whenever funds were available put together ever-expanding Orchestras of Soul. (He even had his own "Soul Harpist," Julia Cunningham, a strikingly beautiful, classically trained musician who toured with him for several years.) All the while he continued to reach the audience that had recognized him from the first, the fans who turned out for him wherever he played, the stadiums, the churches, even the little clubs you might have thought he would have long since abandoned, and they never failed to respond to the warmth of his embrace.

And yet, it seemed, somehow something had changed. You could put it down in part to his weight, I suppose. He was always heavyset—even as a teenager he weighed over 200 pounds—but when I first met him, he was still mobile enough to play touch football with his kids when they came to visit me at my hotel. Toward the end of his life, even after a monthlong stay at the Duke [University] Diet and Fitness Center, where he briefly took off more than 100 pounds, his weight ballooned to close to 500 pounds, and he was for the most part confined to a wheelchair, specifying in his personal appearance contracts an oversized throne built to his specifications, from which he was able to preach with no less power or gestural effectiveness. But for all of the joy he took in performing, and the emotional energy he derived from it, he was clearly frustrated by the increasing difficulty he had, and the increasing health problems he faced, simply attempting to navigate the everyday aspects of his life. And I would say, despite the love with which he surrounded himself (he claimed twenty-one children, ninety grandchildren, and nineteen great-grandchildren plus or minus at the time of his death, all of whom he sent forth into the world with his full faith and support), there was, it seemed, a loneliness at his core that was almost unquenchable. Solomon was a man of such wide-ranging intellect, exquisite sensitivity, and unfailing good humor, it was easy to forget sometimes how deeply he felt things. He was, said one longtime music industry observer, who only met him late in life, "one of the most self-aware men I've ever known," an acute student of human nature who, as he himself was the first to admit, had been through his own Dark Nights of the Soul.

The last three times I saw him, he burst into tears at different points in the conversation each time.

The first time we were in Memphis for a Stax reunion concert to celebrate the opening of the Stax Museum of American Soul Music and the Stax Music Academy. As usual, a documentarian was trailing him—I think there may even have been *two*—and Solomon was in an expansive, if inconclusive, mood. (None of the multiple documentaries, begun with Solomon's equivocal commitment, and so much hope and promise, was ever completed, with the sole exception of *Everybody Needs Somebody*, a wonderful shoestring operation on which its British director, Paul Spencer, simply would never give up.) We were sitting around in Solomon's suite at the recently opened Hotel Madison, the self-styled "Blues Hotel," when all of a sudden the fire alarm went off, there were repeated announcements over the hotel's PA system that everyone must immediately vacate their rooms, we could hear doors slamming, and Solomon's close friend and aide-de-camp Jane Vickers gathered up all the valuables in anticipation of our departure. When Solomon announced in response to increasingly urgent messages from the front desk that he was not going to leave the room, the hotel sent up two burly security officers to carry him out in his chair—but still Solomon refused to leave. A few years ago, I knew, he had prayed away a hurricane in New Orleans in the midst of a recording session, and this he was certain was a false alarm. I'm not sure how convinced any of the rest of us were, but we stayed—and it turned out he was right. Maybe that was what put him in the mood that seemed to come over him—for all I know, maybe he had recently gotten bad news about a loved one, maybe he just wasn't feeling well—but all of a sudden, it was as if everyone and everything else in the room faded away, and he was talking about the transience of everything, the impermanence of life, the fragility of relationships. I thought at first maybe he was testing me, I couldn't figure out where he was going, and I tried to jolly him along. But Solomon would have none of it. When I realized how upset he was, I tried another tack. Think of all the joy he had brought into the world, I said, how all that joy and love would never go away—but Solomon just shook his head, as great tears coursed down his cheeks. "It's not the same," he said inconsolably. "Things change."

The next time, a year or two later, in Cleveland, the tears were tears of joy—but he was no less emotionally unglued. The occasion was a salute to Sam Cooke in the American Music Masters series at the Rock and Roll Hall of Fame. Aretha Franklin was headlining, but Solomon was coming back to close the show with Sam's soaring civil rights anthem, "A Change Is Gonna Come," which would lead into an all-star (Elvis Costello, Otis Clay, William Bell, original Soul Stirrers guitarist Leroy Crume, and the Manhattans, among others) reprise of the song.

Solomon had offered to do the show for free if he could sing with

Aretha and Solomon. *Courtesy of the Rock and Roll Hall of Fame and Museum*

Aretha (I'm not really sure how serious he was about waiving the fee), but she had evidently turned that down as well as the opportunity to do the closing herself. (She had first choice of songs and had selected three relatively obscure songs, while passing on "A Change Is Gonna Come.") So Solomon began in fervent and stately fashion — he not only had the crowd riveted, he was riveted himself. He had just gotten to the verse that centers around betrayal ("I go to my brother, and I say, 'Brother, help me, please . . .'") when all of a sudden an echoing voice was heard from the wings. The look on Solomon's face as Aretha came strolling out onstage two and a half minutes into the song cannot be described. "Ladies and gentlemen, the Queen of Soul," he announced, and then it was not so much that he gave the song over to her as that he gave *himself* over to one of the most joyously uplifting and (coming from this most spontaneous of singers) genuinely spontaneous moments that I ever saw him achieve, onstage or off. It's the only time I ever saw Solomon Burke upstaged — and he wasn't even upstaged, he was simply carried away by a tide of emotion that he could not control.

Afterwards, he sat there onstage on his throne, stunned, it seemed, by what had just happened, bathed in a glow of expectation and regret. I went out to him from the wings as tears rolled down his face. "Did you see that, Pete?" he said over and over, as if he needed somehow to convince himself. "Did you see that?" he repeated, as if a prophecy had been fulfilled.

He seemed certain at that moment that everything had changed, he spoke as if this was to be the dawn of a whole new era, which had only been suggested by the Grammy he had won in 2003. And though the moment was never to be repeated, he kept that hope alive for the rest of his life. When in 2009 Bill Clinton went over to North Korea to bring back two American hostages in a plane he had borrowed from his friend Steve Bing, Solomon was on the phone to Steve, whom he had met some three years earlier on a Jerry Lee Lewis project that Steve had initiated, almost before the plane landed. He had an idea for how they could use the plane, Solomon told Steve. Everyone knew about Aretha's fear of flying, he said, but with Steve's plane he was certain she could overcome it. He would book a tour of Europe for the two of them which would climax with a command performance for the Pope. And all Steve had to do was supply the plane. To which Steve, a great admirer and supporter of Solomon from the moment they first met, but no less a realistic student of human nature, agreed that it was indeed a great opportunity and that he was sure that Aretha would think so, too — all Solomon had to do was pay for the fuel.

And if you'll permit a brief digression, through Steve, Solomon and Jerry Lee went on to become fast friends, forming one of the most improbable mutual admiration societies I've ever seen. If you want to see the dramatic moment of their meeting, just take a look at their duet on "Who Will the Next Fool Be?" in the performance documentary for Jerry Lee's album *Last Man Standing*. Jerry Lee had no idea what to expect (and seemingly not a lot of interest) until Solomon opened his mouth to sing, and the expression on his face as Solomon leaned into the lyric, matched only by his own redoubled commitment to the song (never let it be said that Jerry Lee Lewis turned away from a challenge) says it all. They had a ball that day, and they continued to have a ball right up until Solomon's death four years later, sharing a sly wit, a clear-eyed recognition of human foibles, and a deep-seated spirituality, not to mention an abiding reverence for the music, and person, of Gene Autry.

The last time I saw Solomon, we were talking about the same thing we had been talking about ever since my biography of Sam Cooke had come out a few years earlier. "You know, it's a great book," he told me backstage in Cleveland, just after the book was published. "But when are we going to do *The* Book?" And in all our conversations since then, whatever the subject, however much time might have passed, he would always bring up *the* Book, *our* book — he had had other people approach him, he said (I don't know if he did), but we had to do the book together.

There was no holdback on my part. It was something I absolutely wanted to do. The only thing was, while with Solomon you could always count on the moment — there was never any question of the immediacy of the moment you were in — for all his vatic powers, the future was never anything less than murky. Dates, flights, firmly fixed plans — they might all work out, but on the other hand they might not, and then for all the good intentions you might very well find yourself stranded in a city or on a continent that Solomon had long since left for greener pastures. Perhaps you notice a reliance on my part — maybe even an overreliance — on the advice I had so often offered others. Don't allow yourself to get overextended, unless you have a Boeing 737 to lend. You just never knew with Solomon. But at the same time I was well aware that it was almost as bad an idea to let Solomon overextend *himself* — in other words, to get his entrepreneurial hopes up, which in this case would have meant conflating what even to me was a million-dollar idea with a commercial enterprise that was worth a million dollars. Which in a certain sense it may well have been, just not in convertible currency.

That was why, at our last meeting, backstage at a show in New York, I returned to the idea I had been suggesting all along, why didn't he just start by talking into a tape recorder? Or better yet, he could respond to questions from his daughter Victoria (she was the closest to him of all his kids, she was the most like him — in fact, she followed him into the funeral business, and when he died, it was Victoria who prepared the body). He could just talk to her, I explained, she might prompt him, but she probably wouldn't even have to do that — don't think of it as a book, I told him. Just focus on one or two periods in your life to start off with, things you've already told me, or maybe things I had never heard, and then he should just tell everything he could remember about them. Like the time he and his friend John Brooks were working at a mental hospital in Philadelphia and set off for California in a horse and wagon. (Years after Solomon first told me the story, I met John Brooks, and he confirmed it without any prompting, though without most of the most colorful details.) Or how about the time he found himself inadvertently booked to play for the Ku Klux Klan? ("Man, they was 30,000 Ku Klux Klanners in their sheets — the whole time we played that show those people kept coming. With their sheets on. Little kids with little sheets, ladies, man, everybody just coming up, just moving under the lights, everyone dancing and having a good time.")

Or — and this was the place I thought we should really begin the story, when he was broadcasting on the radio as a little boy, traveling from church to church as the Wonder Boy Preacher. He could just start when he was seven, eight, nine.

"How about when I was ten?"

"Well, sure," I said, a little taken aback. "Sure, when you were ten. Why? Did something happen when you were ten?"

"That's when they put me out on the street," Solomon said, as his face — that beautiful, unwrinkled baby face — scrunched up and he started to cry.

Once again I was bewildered. I had no idea where this was coming from, or what I had started.

"Well, why?" I said, at a complete loss. "Why did they put you out on the street?"

"That's what I could never figure out." Solomon was really bawling now.

"Well, who—" I couldn't stop myself now. Whatever was prompting this memory was clearly heartbreaking, but I just didn't understand. "I mean, who put you out on the street?"

Solomon looked at me with one of the bleakest expressions I have ever seen. "That's what I could never understand."

And that was the end of it. What could possibly have happened in the life of this blessed boy who was so cherished by his family, his community, most of all his grandmother, who saw his arrival on earth as the result of a divine prophecy? "It was such a big deal when he was born," his mother, Josephine, once said to me. What could have happened?

I'll always wonder.

Bile will consume you, Solomon said to me one time, in summing up his own struggles with envy and regret. This was something with which, like so many of Solomon's keen-eyed observations and sayings, I could whole-heartedly identify. Who doesn't struggle with envy? Who doesn't struggle with regret? And sometimes, when I call to mind all the moments and all the people (family, friends, Doc Pomus, Solomon Burke) who have meant so much to me, I think, Well, I really don't regret very much, except maybe not getting a chance to write about Satchel Paige, or not playing baseball anymore. But if I'm really being honest, I don't think I'll ever get over the regret I feel that Solomon and I never got around to writing *The* Book.

The following piece ("Christmas Presents from Heaven") isn't it, but it's the closest I came. . . .

"CHRISTMAS PRESENTS FROM HEAVEN"
OR HOW SOLOMON BURKE GOT HIS START IN THE
RECORDING BUSINESS: A MONOLOGUE

M Y RECORDING CAREER came about, in a way, as part of a prediction. In 1954, when I was fourteen years old, I wrote a song for my grandmother as a Christmas present. God gave me the song on December 10, I finished the song on December 17, and on the eighteenth my grandmother said that she wanted to speak to me. I came into her room and she said, "I want you to see your Christmas present." I said, "Now?" She said, "Yes, look under the bed." I looked under her bed, and there was a guitar wrapped up in a pillowcase. And I was so excited 'cause this was my Christmas gift, this little guitar. And I said, "But Santa Claus won't bring me nothing," all that kind of stuff. And she said, "I want to tell you something. I want you to have this now, because it's important that you have it. Seriously." And then I sang for her the little song that I had written called "Christmas Presents from Heaven," not knowing it was a prophecy for me, to alert me to the future.

On the morning of the nineteenth my grandmother passed in her sleep, so she had only heard the song on that day, and the whole day she was briefing me, telling me the different things that were going to happen, the homes, the women, the children, the cars—and I'll never forget the most exciting thing she ever said to me, and the most depressing thing, too. The most exciting thing was that I would be able to reach out and touch people and help them spiritually, thousands of people, millions of people. But then she said to me that I would go to the pits of hell and submerge at will, and I've been there, I've been there, too.

It was just within a very short while, no more than a few weeks, I think, that God opened up a way for me to fulfill my grandmother's prophecy. There was a talent contest for gospel singers down at the Liberty Baptist Church, and all the big record companies were going to be there. I had a little group called the Gospel Cavaliers, and Viola Williams, [Philadelphia DJ] Kae Williams' wife, suggested we come down. Well, one of the guy's mothers had just bought a TV, and this was back in the days when having a TV was really something. And another guy says, "No, my father's taking me to a football game. We ain't gonna make no money anyway." Well, I couldn't get any of my little group to go with me, and my only suit was at the cleaner's, but I wasn't going to disappoint Mrs. Williams. So I borrowed a pair of pants from my uncle and a pepperpot jacket from my father that he didn't know I had taken (it was sharp!), and I went to this concert. I didn't even have my guitar with me, I had to borrow one from one of the groups on the program. I wasn't even on the program, but Mrs. Williams said, "Let him sing," because she had heard me at the church a couple of weeks before, and I always give her credit for the start of my career.

Well, I'm standing there onstage trying to get the guitar tuned up so I can play in Vestapol (which is the only way I know how to play), and I could feel the tension of the crowd rising, so I said to myself, "My God! I'd better do something. I'm a preacher, so I better start preaching." Which is how I started talking about "That Old Ship of Zion."

Well, how was I to know that was Bess Berman's favorite song? She was there for Apollo Records, Jimmy Bracken was there for Vee-Jay, Dave Clark from Duke, somebody else from Savoy — all the big gospel labels were there. But when I started singing, Miss Berman kind of moved up to the front right past Jimmy Bracken till she was right in front of me just kind of encouraging me with those eyes, saying, "Sing that song. Come on, sing it, sing it. You'll be all right." I mean, I didn't know who she was at that point, but she was the most attractive, well-dressed, well-groomed lady I had ever seen. She reminded me of royalty the way her personality shone through. She had hypnotizing eyes. And as I sang, I wondered who was this lady giving me confidence; I thought, "She's probably looking at my pants" — which were pinned up!

Well, I got through it okay, and I finally got everyone in the congregation to sing along, and when I got done Mrs. Williams came up to me and said, "Oh, I really liked what you were singing." And just as she was talking to me, Bess Berman came up and said, "You are mine, you are mine." I didn't know who she was or who she represented, but I was hers.

Mrs. Williams said, "That's Mrs. Berman."

I said, "Great!" I still didn't know.

She said, "You are going to make records for me."

I said, "Where do I sign? Let me sign the contract."

It was no time before they brought me to New York to record. The first time I came in on the train with my mother. We stayed at my aunt's house in Brooklyn. I had never seen a project before, and my twin cousins, Mary and Martha, who are both blind, were taking me around, introducing me to everyone as the recording star. I was going from floor to floor with them, and I'm thinking, "Holy God, the blind is leading the blind!"

We were recording at the Apollo studio on 45th and Tenth Avenue, and I was Bess Berman's personal project. She said I was going to be the next Harry Belafonte. She didn't want to record me strictly as a gospel singer, but the first things we recorded were spiritual, because I was still in a mourning period for my grandmother, you understand, and each of those songs—"Christmas Presents from Heaven," "I'm All Alone," and "To Thee"—referred in some way to her. Except for "Christmas Presents," there were no lyrics written down on paper, the songs just came to me as I was standing at the mike. Well, sometimes they came hard. I'd be standing there in the studio, and everybody would be saying to me, "Where are your words?" And I'd say, "Oh, I know them all by heart." "But we don't know 'em!" "Well, gee whiz, do you all know how to follow?"

I think I was more fascinated than I was nervous. I had recorded before on a home recorder, because I always wanted to hear the sound of my own voice and there was a little man on my street named the Reverend Mongo who had one of those machines that make records that come out on a little paper plastic kind of disc. So I had had a little bit of experience, but never on such a large scale—with a real orchestra with three great big mikes with big heads and a guy in a booth with red and green lights and flashing yellow for caution and someone to run and get pastrami sandwiches. There was a big fat guy ten times bigger than I am right now who ate corned beef and pastrami on white bread with mayonnaise and a kosher pickle on the side, and when he walked around you could see the mayonnaise dripping from his mouth—this was the guy who put the needle down on the lacquer to make the record. He was the engineer. It was all just so fascinating to me, it really was walking in a dream, all these musicians coming and going and shaking hands and talking about the Harlem clubs and "I just blew in from Chicago," or "I'm on my way to Detroit." It was really just so exciting.

Early Apollo Records publicity shot. *Courtesy of Jimmy Evans*

The original records were God-given, really—God-given lyrics, God-given arrangements—there was no producer needed, nothing directing the proceedings but God, the spirit of God. It was after that that the hard work started. You see, once I got past the spiritual element, I was actually fantasizing. "I'm in love." "Why do me this way?" I didn't know anything about these kinds of things. I mean, I'd never had any real problems, not really; I was probably thinking in my mind of what I'd heard on the radio, of Amos Milburn or Ivory Joe Hunter or Chuck Willis, that kind of stuff. You take "Why Do Me That Way?" [the title of his second record]—now, that's like the first rap record, but I was talking because I didn't know what to do next, and the musicians didn't know whether to keep playing or stop. Those guys were more glad to get through that song than I was— "Is this the end or what?" There was one session, I think it took us almost two weeks to do three songs. That was when they brought in Howard Biggs. Howard Biggs was brought in because of Roy Hamilton, I think. If Mrs. Berman hadn't hired him, Bill Cook [Roy Hamilton's manager] would have. Now, Howard Biggs was *it,* he was a story in himself. He was a very successful black bandleader and arranger whose story would take a month to tell. Let me just try to sum it up by saying that Mr. Biggs was a complete genius who utilized Scotch like soda pop. He was also a deputy sheriff of New York. One time he was driving me down the Long Island freeway in his Mercedes, and we were going 100 miles per hour—on the wrong side. I thought God wasn't hearing my prayers, and I never could understand how Mr. Biggs could take an exit where the sign said "Do not enter," but he said, "It's okay, they know me." It was such a great thrill to get to his house that you would never want to leave. His wife would say, "Aren't you ready to go back to the city yet, Solomon?" "No, ma'am!" When I made "No Man Walks Alone," I really wanted to say, "No man drives alone either," because God certainly rode with Howard Biggs.

Howard tried to work with me on my songs, and I think that just made him drink all the more. He'd say, "Okay, Solomon, sing into the Wilcox. That's fine. Now let me write this down. Fine. Now do that part again." Well, I'd go back and do it completely different, and Howard would say, "No, no, no, no, no. I need a drink. This man keeps changing the songs." And his wife would say, "Solomon, can you remember what you sang the last time?" I'd say, "No, ma'am." "Well, do you have a problem with your memory?" "No, ma'am." "Well, why can't you remember what you sang the last time?" "Well, God don't give it to me that way." "There we go. Why can't this boy be a Catholic?!?"

Howard was the one that brought in the musicians. Most of the time we had Al Lucas playing bass, Coatesville Harris on drums, Mickey Baker on guitar, a young kid named King Curtis showed up for one or two of the sessions, and we even had Lester Young on tenor one time and Lionel Hampton on vibes. We had the Ray Charles Singers behind us, the number-one choral group in the country (this is the *white* Ray Charles Singers), with all these hits of their own—this was big-time, I'm telling you, with people writing up charts and saying, "Do you want us to dot that note, how about putting that in C-sharp natural?" And then they would look at me and say, "All this orchestration for this little kid? What's he going to do?" And I would respond in my big bass voice, and they would just go, "Ohhhh."

I would go out on tour behind the records, what I thought was a tour. Philadelphia; Reading, Pennsylvania; Coatesville; Harrisburg; Morristown; Camden; Newark, New Jersey—like I say, this was the big time. Sometimes we'd get as far as Baltimore, Washington, Florida—places I had never been before in my life. I had a Buick Roadmaster of my own. I think at this point it was a little difficult to tell me I wasn't a star. So the hat size changed that I was wearing. As a matter of fact, I wouldn't wear a hat at all—because it messed up my bangs. Thank God that's over. Now I wear bangs and mess up my hat.

Everything was going great. Joe Louis, the heavyweight champ, brought me a song called "You Can Run, But You Can't Hide"—well, actually that was his slogan in the ring, and we just kind of borrowed it from him and gave him writer's credit on the song. Joe traveled around with me for several months introducing me on stage, and we got quite a bit of national acclaim until one time we got on *The Steve Allen Show,* and Steve said, "Joe, I want you to introduce the young man you've brought with you tonight," and Joe couldn't remember my name. He's going, "Well, uh uh—" And Steve says, "The young man, you know, Solomon—" And poor Joe goes, "Oh, yeah, and Dick Haymes has the same record out on Decca Records." I think my poor little record company just about had a heart attack.

You know, I think Bess Berman would have done just about anything for me. She even wanted to legally adopt me—I'm serious—just to develop my career. My mother got a $10,000 couch out of it—camel's hair couch, beautiful couch—but she didn't go through with the adoption. That's why I'm still Solomon Burke; just think, I could have been Solomon Berman. They thought I was going to become Jewish, the way I loved those kosher pickles!

But those days came to an end, and in a funny way, too. You see, I was playing a club in Newark, New Jersey. I think the record we had out then was "Don't Cry," and the manager was so overwhelmed with the crowd that we had drawn that he came up to me and said, "Mr. Burke, listen, I've got to get back to the box office. I just wanted to give you your money. Here's the $2,500 balance, because I already paid your manager $2,500 in front." And, you know, it was crazy, I thought he was crazy, because *I* thought I was making $750 total, that was what my manager had told me. So I said, "This isn't my money." And he said, "Yes, it is. It's your money. Here's your contract." And I said, "I didn't sign any contract. We just go on faith." And he said, "Well, you signed this one." Well, I looked down, and I saw my name, and I said, "Man, okay. This money's mine?" "Yeah, this is yours." By this time my manager had come up, and he said, "Did you pick up that money? Did you give him the money?" And I said, "The gentleman came and paid me." "You give me that money, or I ain't gonna book you no more. You know, you're getting the big head."

Well, I didn't know about that, but I knew I didn't want to work with my manager anymore. Then he told me if I didn't work with him I wasn't going to work with anyone. He told me that I couldn't record for anyone, that I no longer had a contract with my record company, that I would be blackballed all over the world. So I became a bum, because I was just really terrified, I thought my whole little world had crumbled. Well, it had. And I'll never forget, I asked a guy standing on the corner of 16th and Ridge in Philadelphia in the summertime to loan me fifty cents, and he took fifty cents out of his pocket and kind of tossed it to me. Well, in Philadelphia we have grates on the sewers, and the fifty cents landed right on one of those grates and you had to be very careful how you picked it up, because otherwise it would fall down the sewer. So I got down on my knees and very gently tried to get that fifty cents from the sewer grate, and all of a sudden something came over me spiritually that said, "If you pick up that fifty cents now, you'll be picking up change for the rest of your life." I made the decision, and I kicked the fifty cents in the sewer. And the guy said, "You gotta be crazy. You crazy nut." Well, he went to run after me, and I ran out in the street, and a lady hit me with her car, and when she hit me she got out and offered to take me to the hospital, and come to find out she knew me (her name was Othella Thompson) because I had been dating her niece. Well, she took me home with her, and that whole cycle of my life was over. That's when I went back to school and became a mortician.

I graduated from Eckels Mortuary College and served an apprenticeship with my Aunt Anna, at the A. V. Barkley Funeral Home in Philadelphia. I could have been very content simply to become a successful mortician and build an empire of funeral homes, but then a gentleman by the name of Babe Chivian came along, a heavyset Jewish guy with a receding hairline and a beautiful smile and the biggest diamond ring I ever saw in my life—he walked with a little tilt and dressed very nicely and had a chain of body shops, but he *loved* show business. And he had a way of convincing you to do things that you didn't even think you wanted to do, and he said to me, "You got to be out there singing. Baby, can I manage you?"

Well, I wasn't into singing at all at this point—I had the church, I had the funeral home—but Babe convinced me by giving me this red Lincoln limousine, he kept it sitting in front of the funeral home for almost a week, and there was no way we could let this red Lincoln convertible sit in front of the funeral home, it was just the wrong place for it. So the family talked to him, and he said, "Man, you need to make a record." And I told him about being blackballed. And he said, "Man, it's all okay. We're all friends. Everybody knows everybody. All you have to do is sing."

What happened next I don't really understand to this day. This is a story I can't even make up, but let me try to tell you how I *think* it happened. Babe Chivian put me on a little label called Singular Records in Philadelphia—it was just Babe and Artie Singer and a disc jockey out of Philadelphia, a Mr. Brown. Now, we cut these two sides, and nothing much happened with them because we didn't have any national distribution, and then we went back to cut a couple more sides, only this time we went into New York to a guy named Herb Abramson, who I thought was the president of Atlantic Records. Well he *had* been the president of Atlantic Records; as a matter of fact, his ex-wife, Miriam Bienstock, still *was* with Atlantic Records. But I didn't know anything about that; when I walked into his little studio—and this happened by sheer luck, really; somebody just told Babe he should go see Herb because he was connected with Atlantic—well, when we walked in that studio, I thought, "Great, I'm on Atlantic!" Well, nothing happened this time either, and I wasn't on Atlantic. As a matter of fact, neither was Herb. But this is the funny part—Paul Ackerman, who was at *Billboard,* turned out to be a fan of mine, and when he heard the little record we had put out, he contacted Babe and said, "Listen, this is a nice record you sent me, but I don't think you guys can handle it. I think that Solomon deserves a shot with a major label. Why don't you bring Solomon into New York and let Jerry Wexler at Atlantic hear it?"

So Babe got me all dressed up, and we rode into New York—again!—in our red convertible Lincoln, yes, it was *the* red convertible that got me out of the funeral business. So we drove up and parked this red, big, giant box of a car in front of Atlantic Records—the real Atlantic Records this time—and everybody looked at the car. We got out, and there was a little sign on the window that said Solomon Burke that rolled up when the window rolled up. And Babe said, "Listen, if it don't work here, we'll go to RCA Victor, Columbia, or even Capitol." So we walked in, all nervous, just about ready to turn around, and Jerry Wexler says, "Hey, great, where have you been, sign here, come back a month from now and we'll make a record." Well, he showed us the pictures of Chuck Willis and Ray Charles and Ivory Joe Hunter, and he says, "You're going to be right up there with them." And I say, "Oh, my God. This is *it*." So Babe says, "You've got to have a corned beef and pastrami on white with mayonnaise — today." So he bought me five of them at the Stage Deli, and we sat there and different musicians were coming up to us and saying "Hey, I hear you're on Atlantic." And I was so impressed that word had gotten out within an hour that I was on the Atlantic label.

And that was the beginning of the new Solomon Burke.

PRINT THE LEGEND:
AN APPENDIX IN SEARCH OF A DIGRESSION

I'M KIDDING, kind of.

But I just got curious.

Like all of Solomon's stories, the narrative of his discovery is such a wonderful tale, and Solomon was so precise in dating the events leading up to it, all tied to his grandmother's death on December 19, 1954, that I started trying to square the story with the facts.

The way that Solomon told it, it all happened within a matter of weeks — and it all fit together so perfectly. And it still does. I have no doubt of that. But not quite — or not *precisely* — in the same way. Because if in fact his grandmother died in December of 1954, it took nearly a year for her prophecy to come to pass.

Eleanor A. (for Alma) Moore was unquestionably the most significant influence in Solomon's life. According to family legend, she arrived in Philadelphia sometime following the St. Valentine's Day Massacre in Chicago in 1929, in which Solomon's grandfather, a numbers runner for Detroit's Purple Gang, was among the dead. The loss of her husband caused a change in Eleanor Moore's life, and not long after her arrival in Philadelphia in the Packard limousine in which Solomon many years later would learn to drive she experienced a conversion to Sweet Daddy Grace's United House of Prayer for All People, which she served for the rest of her life.

Sweet Daddy Grace, born Marcelino Manuel da Graça in the Cape Verde Islands in 1881, was probably the second most important influence in Solomon's life, for his eloquence, his style ("Sweet Daddy was very attractive to the ladies," said Solomon's sister, Laurena, "whatever Sweet Daddy wants Sweet Daddy can have, Brother drew his glamour, I think,

from Sweet Daddy"), his charismatic message, and his profoundly entrepreneurial spirit. Along with Father Divine he was unquestionably the
most successful African American evangelist of the first half of the twentieth century, drawing hundreds of thousands of adherents with his gift
of prophecy, his healing powers, his flowing hair, and his long curling
fingernails, painted red, white, and blue. He preached a gospel of salvation
through upward mobility (he was one of the first, and most convincing,
of the prosperity preachers), sold practical Sweet Daddy Grace household
products like soap and toothpaste, and openly defied the laws of segrega-
tion in the South with his mass baptisms and revivals. "He was my godfather, the man I idolized," Solomon said, "a fabulous man with a great
message of deliverance. He was dynamic, colorful, charismatic, just magical. His guards marched like real soldiers, and they had silver and gold
swords, and the bands played, and he'd wave from the top of his big Cadillac limousine. It's the one true church in America that I can truly say does
everything it says it's gonna do. There's no hanky-panky, no wishy-washy.
It's a *church*."

And it was a church that was founded on the premise that God was to
be celebrated through the power of music ("Praise Him with the sound
of the trumpet; praise Him with the harp and lyre," in the words of the
psalm), and in particular through the shout band music that the House
of Prayer for All People pioneered, which included special steps and
rhythms and the thundering power of a chorus of trombones, tubas, sou-
saphones, cymbals, and drums. But most of all trombones. This was the
very tradition, Solomon would always declare, from which he drew one
of his biggest and most memorable hits, "Everybody Needs Somebody to
Love"; in fact, he said, it was a march taken directly from his church.
Which led him to question, sometimes humorously, sometimes bitingly,
the co-writing credits that went to Jerry Wexler and his producer Bert
Berns on the song.

With the encouragement of Daddy Grace, Eleanor Moore started her
own church, most commonly known as the House of God for All People,
sometimes as Solomon's Temple (if you can believe Solomon — and I don't
mean you shouldn't *always* believe him — he came to his grandmother in
a dream some years before his birth, and it was on the basis of that dream
that his grandmother founded her church), but fundamentally it was a
branch of the United House of Prayer for All People, with its own United
Praying Band. She had prayer services every night of the week in the living

Eleanor A. Moore. *Courtesy of Selassie Burke*

room of her home at 3836 Mount Vernon Street in Philadelphia's "Black Bottom," the very home in which Solomon was born on the second floor as his grandmother was having church below.

His grandmother was known for her kindness, her healing powers, and her ability to "read" people—"the gift she had was almost unthinkable," said her grandson, who was clearly blessed with the same gift. And what she prophesied for her grandson certainly came true in every respect. It's just that it doesn't seem to have come true in quite the condensed version that her grandson recalled.

Solomon appears to have been discovered in the late fall of 1955, about a year after Mother Moore's death, when it was announced in the November 26 issue of *Cash Box* that "Kae Williams, Philly deejay, took over personal management of Solomon Burke, spiritual singer, who will turn to r&b [and has been] signed on Apollo label." Then in January of 1956, three weeks after the Christmas 1955 release of Solomon's debut on Apollo with "Christmas Presents from Heaven," Kae Williams told the *Philadelphia Tribune*, the oldest continuously published African American

newspaper in the country, all about his fifteen-year-old discovery, a ninth grader at Shoemaker Junior High School, who, as Solomon always said, had actually been spotted first by Williams' wife, Viola, at a gospel program. Williams pointed out that his new discovery had been "a gospel singer in this city for about eight years, and has learned to sing with as much soul as a 40-year-old." All of which was indubitably true of a young man who had been preaching and singing, "standing on a fish box," since he was seven.

And the subsequent chronology? *Billboard* reported that Solomon appeared with Joe Louis on *The Steve Allen Show* at the beginning of January, 1957. He was booked at the Apollo with Mickey and Sylvia, Big Maybelle, and the Drifters the following month and then with Ray Charles a year later. As for his time in exile, this, too, bears out, with his total absence from the scene from December 1958 until his first Singular release on December 21, 1959. (For the real trivia nuts, his signing by Herb Abramson to his brand-new [and very short-lived] Triumph label was announced in December 1958 but evidently fell through because he was still signed to Apollo, which may provide some insight into Solomon's confusion about the role that Herb Abramson played in pointing him to Atlantic some two years later.) He recorded "Just Out of Reach," the country song that was his first real hit, at his initial Atlantic session on December 13, 1960, which came about (both the song and the signing) through the advocacy of *Billboard* editor Paul Ackerman, who, as Solomon always said, believed not just in his talent but in the unique *potential* of his talent. And the song only hit, according to Solomon, when, eight months later, he met one of his idols, Gene Autry ("I was so excited about meeting him I never asked for his autograph"), who had recently acquired the publishing on the song, and "was so kind as to say, 'I love what you did with [our] song, but you're not getting any airplay, and we're going to do something about that — *as of next week.*'" Ten days later, Solomon said, "nine major stations were playing it." And while I can offer nothing in the way of documentation here, the song did take off in September of 1961, not long after it was finally released by Atlantic, eventually going all the way to number seven on the r&b charts and into the pop Top 30.

Whew! Too much information? Maybe so — but I hope not. (As I told every Creative Writing class I ever taught, Prize the digression.) And I can

With Jerry Wexler: "Just Out of Reach." *Courtesy of Jerry Wexler* only think about the book that might have been, giving free range to Solomon's seemingly boundless capacity for intertwining memory and invention. As Jerry Wexler said of Solomon, with a mix of irritation and affection, "He is a card-carrying fabulist." Which could just as easily be taken as an unadulterated compliment. Like every great creative artist, Solomon felt no compunction about throwing off the yoke of the quotidian, even if it was staring him in the face, and despite the fact that he possessed a photographic memory, I don't think I ever heard Solomon recite the same story twice in the same way. And yet every story had a solid basis in fact (remember the would-be horse-and-wagon trip to California, remember the famous popcorn story in which Solomon secured the concession rights — generously understood to mean pictures and souvenirs — from the notoriously tight-fisted Apollo Theater and showed up with a truckload of soul popcorn) and with every repetition each story seemed to be seeking a newer, deeper, and almost always funnier truth.

So — Print the Legend? I don't know. Print both versions, because in my experience life and legend can sometimes merge in ways that are virtually indistinguishable. But prize the truth. And prize the truth that Solomon Burke delivered to us in his music, in his songs, in the endless inventiveness that he brought to bear in his passage through this world.

As for "Christmas Presents from Heaven," Solomon sang the song, and prized its memory, till the day he died. As well he should have. And when we listen to the song, I don't think there's any question that we can still hear his grandmother encouraging him, as she continued to do in his mind's eye throughout his life, encouraging him, telling him that he has a gift that he must never turn his back on, reminding him to speak with clarity and purpose, telling him, always, to keep the faith.

"I was born with trombones and tubas playing," Solomon said, recalling his birth in his grandmother's home. "They were having church downstairs, and they never heard me cry, because there was no need to cry — it was joy. That [was] all I knew.

"My grandmother was a great spiritual medium and seer, her friends were powerful people like Father Divine, my cousin the great Prophet Jones from Detroit, and my godfather Daddy Grace, who would come and visit and talk with her spiritually. And she asked a favor of him to help organize her church for me, twelve years before I was born.

"My grandmother believed I would be the first child bishop. She was my mentor, my guiding angel — I'm like her spiritually, physically, all my

In Addis Ababa, ca. 1971, with two of Haile Selassie's royal guards. *Courtesy of (and identification by) Selassie Burke*

children resemble her. And she believed in music as an instrument that God provided for man to be helped and healed by. If you could play an instrument or sing, you became a messenger for the heavens — the answer at Grandma's house was our big Philco radio.

"Every Saturday night we listened to the Top 40, and that [included] Bing Crosby, Frank Sinatra, Nat 'King' Cole, Louis Armstrong, Dinah Washington, and Count Basie, [but] the other fascinating thing was to listen to Gene Autry and right after Gene Autry, Roy Rogers. My grandmother would say, 'Listen to them, listen to what they're singing and how they're singing it, the diction, the phrasing: "I'm back in the saddle again" [pronounced crisply], not "Bac'nthesall again." Pronunciation is *important,* to try to make people feel you're in that position, right in the words of the song.' She said, '*Put yourself in that saddle.*'

"We listened to country music and classical, and that was our Saturdays. We listened to Mahalia Jackson, Sister Rosetta Tharpe, Marian Anderson, who was supposed to be our cousin, Paul Robeson, and of course [Philadelphia's] Ward Singers, but there was nobody like Brother

Joe May. Ivory Joe Hunter was one of my favorites, and I knew my grand-mother, as religious as she was, loved his song '(When I Lost My Baby) I Almost Lost My Mind,' which I later recorded as 'Since I Met You Baby.' When folks back in those days, precious folks, I don't want to call them old folks, when they loved somebody, you know what they'd say? 'They must be some kind of kin to us somewhere down the line. I betcha they're some kind of kin.'"

And so they were, and are, as we all are in one way or another, Solomon would insist (and I would agree — think E. M. Forster), to this day.

"You know," says Solomon reflectively, "the race is not given to the swift but to those who endure to the end — but I think I am the fastest-moving entertainer in the world, in a wheelchair. My grandmother taught me that God would never fail me. Every day there [would be] a service. The church was the foundation of all the music, and the music never stopped. There was always a band with two or three trombones, tubas, tambourines, cymbals. It was a message to God, something you feel down to your bones, your soul, your heart."

TWENTY-TWO

Perfect Imperfection: The Life and Art of Jerry Lee Lewis

E VEN THE MANNER of his arrival was out of the ordinary, according to Jerry Lee Lewis.

"I came into this world naked, feet first, and jumpin'. And I been
jumpin' ever since," he has said on a number of occasions.

Which is one way of putting it—certainly one that bears out something
of both the larger-than-life legend and its self-propelled reality. But it
doesn't even begin to suggest all of the complexities, the subtleties, the
daring, the imagination, and the sweep of either Jerry Lee Lewis or his
music, which has been, in its own way, as revolutionary as Walt Whitman's
"barbaric yawp," Marlon Brando's single-minded dedication to the articulation of raw emotion, or Jack Kerouac's call for "spontaneous bop pros-
ody," an exhortation that Jerry Lee's music could be said to match, raise,
and maybe even double.

If there was one person who instinctively embodied the aesthetic of
Sam Phillips—discoverer of B.B. King, Ike Turner, Howlin' Wolf, not to
mention Johnny Cash, Elvis Presley, and Carl Perkins—it was Jerry Lee
Lewis. What Phillips was looking for was what he called "perfect imper-
fection"—he was looking for freedom and spontaneity and feel. What he
prized most was not just individualism but individualism *in the extreme*,
where "mistakes" could give rise to inspiration, where fearless experimentation could take the artist out on a limb from which only the greatest
feats of artistic derring-do could get him back. He was looking in short
for Jerry Lee Lewis.

"He was the most talented man I ever worked with, black or white,"
Phillips once said. "One of the most talented human beings to walk on
God's earth. There's not one-millionth of an inch difference [between]
the way Jerry Lee Lewis thinks about his music and the way Bach or
Beethoven felt about [theirs]." Or as guitarist Roland Janes, whom you

hear on so many of those classic Sun sides, has observed: "I can't find anyone to compare with him. What you hear him doing on records is only a small percentage of what he's capable of doing. I don't think even he knows how great he is. He can take a solo with either hand and sing a song five different ways — every one of them great! A lot of people think he was jealous of Elvis. He wasn't jealous of Elvis. He had a great amount of respect for Elvis, they were both great in their own field — but in his mind he thought he was a much better performer than Elvis, and who's to say he wasn't?"

The first published piece I ever wrote for the fledgling *Boston Phoenix*, in January of 1967, was about James Brown. The second was on Jerry Lee Lewis. This was no serendipitous connection. I would say that the two of them — along with Howlin' Wolf and Solomon Burke — would indisputably qualify as not just the greatest theatrical events but the greatest theatrical *happenings* I have ever seen. With which (at least the part that concerns him — but maybe, in a private moment, the recognition of the other three) Jerry Lee would heartily agree. About himself he has often said, "I'm the Greatest Live Show on Earth. I've seen them all, and I've never seen no cat, nowhere, no way, that could follow me."

Now, there *are* three entertainers, he will concede, even in his more braggadocious moments, that he himself would not have wanted to follow, but they are all tucked comfortably away in the past. These are, as anyone familiar with the Jerry Lee Lewis pantheon will immediately be aware, Hank Williams, Jimmie Rodgers, and Al Jolson, whom he classifies along with himself as the four greatest song stylists in history. It's a great quote, confidently articulated from the start and just as fiercely believed, but I think it should be understood in context.

First of all, when Jerry Lee speaks of stylists, he is speaking of someone with the unique ability to transform a song, to take material almost irrespective of genre and brand it unmistakably as his or her own. In this sense Aretha Franklin or James Brown could be considered the same kind of stylist as Jerry Lee Lewis. So could B.B. King. It's the ability not simply to put your own stamp on the music but, when it works, to create something uplifting and new — even from the most seemingly shopworn material.

The other thing that should be understood is the elasticity of Jerry Lee's definition. Jerry Lee Lewis lives in a world without musical borders. Like Elvis, like Ray Charles — maybe even like *Beethoven!* — his vision encompasses the most democratic of vistas, and he is as likely to single

Jerry Lee leaps, guitarist Roland Janes looks on. *Courtesy of the Sam Phillips Family*

out Gene Autry, Sister Rosetta Tharpe ("I tell you, man, that woman could sing some *rock 'n' roll*"), Bing Crosby, Frank Sinatra, Tommy Dorsey, or B.B. King on any given day. As a youngster, he is prone to confide, he followed B.B. King's music "quite desperately . . . Man, if I could play guitar like B.B. King," he says, "I'd be President."

As a youngster there's no question that he followed music of every sort quite desperately. In fact, for all of his brashness — and I would be the last person to deny his brashness; no, Jerry Lee Lewis would be the *last* — it's

With his parents, Elmo and Mamie. *Courtesy of Jerry Lee Lewis*

With parents and sisters Linda Gail (front) and Frankie Jean. *Courtesy of Linda Gail Lewis*

clear he has been following music in the same way all of his life. Like Elvis, like Robert Johnson, like Hank Williams and other self-tutored geniuses, his eyes and ears were open to everything around him in a way that is not necessarily vouchsafed to ordinary mortals, even those growing up in exactly the same surroundings.

JERRY LEE GREW UP in and around the small town of Ferriday, Louisiana, just across the river from Natchez. His first exposure to music, not surprisingly, came in church, the same Assemblies of God denomination in which Elvis Presley was raised. The message and mood that he got from it was undeniably uplifting, but it was neither the beginning nor the end of his love of music. "I think," he says without any hint of exaggeration, "I was caught up in music when I was born. I heard music on street corners, colored people just setting around Ferriday picking the blues — I didn't know what it was, but I knew it was good. And I had to get involved with it."

His first all-out involvement came through the piano that he encountered at the age of eight in the home of his uncle and aunt Lee and Stella Calhoun (his uncle, a wealthy oilman and land speculator from whom both he and his cousin, the future televangelist Jimmy Swaggart, got their middle name, was the only person in town rich enough to have his own piano, according to Jerry Lee). He marched straight up to the instrument and picked out a tune — "Silent Night" — strictly on the black keys. "Why, I believe he's a natural-born pianist," said his mother, Mamie, Stella's younger sister, who would always believe in his talent. "Well, he might be a piano *player*," said his father, Elmo, a talented musician in his own right, who had enough faith in his son's potential to mortgage their home for $300 to purchase a rebuilt Starck player piano for him.

Jerry Lee practiced on that piano five, six, seven hours a day, every day. His mother brought him meals at the piano sometimes, and when his younger sisters complained, or failed to grasp why he should get such special treatment when they were forced to work in the fields or do ordinary household chores, he simply announced to them, "I am the great I AM" — which may not have done much to clear up the resentment or the misunderstanding.

There wasn't anybody, though, who could have missed his dedication. He played so much he wore the ivory off the keys. "It was the greatest-sounding piano I ever heard in my life," he says today. "I loved it. I worshipped it."

He had just one lesson at school, and it ended up pretty much the same way that all of his formal schooling did. "The teacher gave me [this little song] to do. When I played the song a few days later, I said, 'Don't it sound better like this?' and I did it Jerry Lee-style. He kinda slapped me and said, 'Don't you ever do that again.' That was the end of my piano lessons."

He got his musical education at home instead. In the evening the family would all sing together. "Boy, my daddy was a devoted fan of Jimmie Rodgers — he thought Jimmie Rodgers hung the moon. I can see him now, him and my mother, he would sit on a chair and she would stand by him, and he would pick that guitar and they would start singing — and it was beautiful. I didn't realize what I was hearing at the time, but it's stamped on my mind, I can hear it just like [they was] sitting here now. It was great."

As he got older, he started venturing a little further afield with Jimmy Swaggart (and sometimes with another cousin of theirs, future country star Mickey Gilley). There was a black club in town, Haney's Big House — it was owned by his uncle Lee Calhoun in association with a black man named Will Haney, "a great big man, big as a door," says Jerry Lee, "he could just pick you up and sail you like a football if he wanted to." Jerry Lee never actually tested the proposition, but Haney did throw the boys out every time he saw them because, he said, their uncle would kill him if he ever found out they frequented his club. Still, they always snuck back, because, as Jerry Lee says, "the music was speaking [to me] — and even the people." He saw a young B.B. King there, he saw the great blues pianists Sunnyland Slim and Memphis Slim, he saw Muddy Waters, Ray Charles, Bobby "Blue" Bland, and Champion Jack Dupree. "It was," he says, "like strolling through heaven. It was like it was giving birth to a new music that people needed to hear. *Rock 'n' roll* — that's what it was. That's what I was listening to. Even in church."

He made his public debut at the age of thirteen at the Ford dealership in Ferriday, which was introducing its new line of cars with a show by a hillbilly band. The piano player in the band recognized Jerry Lee and called him up out of the crowd to do a number while the band took a break — and Jerry Lee Lewis heard his voice coming out over a PA system for the first time. He got such a response to his storming version of "Hada-col Boogie," he says, that he encored with "Drinkin' Wine Spo-Dee-O-Dee," a big r&b hit by Stick McGhee earlier that year. When the owner of the

With the Statesmen Quartet. *Courtesy of the Sam Phillips Family*

dealership passed the hat and collected nearly $14, that was the start of his professional career.

He began playing piano and drums with a group at the Wagon Wheel in Natchez, making a brief excursion to the Southwestern Bible Institute in Waxahachie, Texas, where his studies were brought to an abrupt end when he introduced a boogie-woogie treatment of "My God Is Real" in chapel. He auditioned for the Louisiana Hayride and even cut an acetate while he was there. But it was when he heard Elvis' first Sun record, "Blue Moon of Kentucky," coming out over the radio that he knew his music had arrived. "I turned the speaker up in the car. 'Daddy,' I said, 'now, *there* is music.' It was new, it was fresh, and it had to happen. Daddy said, 'Yeah, I see it.'"

It took him two years to get to Memphis, after an unproductive side trip to Nashville, where he was turned down by just about every record label in town. They were, he says, simply unprepared to hear anything as original and different as what he had to offer. Back home in Louisiana he was reading a magazine story about Elvis that cited Sam Phillips as the guiding light behind all these rising stars — Elvis, Johnny Cash, Carl Perkins, even B.B. King — and he said to his father, "This is the man we need to go see." His father agreed, and they sold all the eggs from their little farm to finance the trip to Memphis. Sam Phillips didn't happen to be in when they arrived, but Jack Clement, only recently hired as Sun's first outside producer and third employee, was. This could be a long, entertaining, and almost endlessly digressive story if told in all of its iterations, but here are one or two versions in a nutshell.

Sally Wilbourn, Sun's *second* outside employee, who had been hired the previous year to help out Sam's office manager and associate Marion Keisker when Sam opened WHER, the first "all-girl" radio station in the nation, came back to the control room and told Jack there was someone in the tiny reception area who said he played piano like Chet Atkins. According to Jack: "I said, 'I want to listen to *that*,' and she brought him back, and he really did sound like Chet Atkins playing the piano. Well, that intrigued me. So I went back in the control room and put on a tape."

This is only the first place that the various accounts diverge — and it must be remembered, this is history told by two participants of the greatest creative integrity who never had anything less than the highest regard for each other. But according to Jerry Lee: "Jack said rock 'n' roll was out for me, because Elvis had it tied up, and I could forget about that. I said, '*Well, I don't think so.* I'm a HIT.' He said, 'They all say that, son. They all say that.' I said, 'Yeah, but I'm not "all." I'm *different*. And you're going to have to cut a little demo here for Mr. Phillips to listen to, because [if you don't] I'm going to set out on the doorstep until he gets back.'"

Whichever way it happened — and more than likely it was somewhere in between — when Sam returned and heard the tape, it was as if, he said, Jerry Lee Lewis had stepped out of a dream he was fixing to have. "They put that tape on, and I said, 'Where in *hell* did this man come from?' I mean, he played that piano with *abandon*." But that wasn't all; others might do that just as well. "Between the stuff he played and didn't play," Sam said, "I could hear that spiritual thing, too. I told Jack, 'Just get him in here as fast as you can.'" And when they finally met, and a goateed twenty-one-year-old Jerry Lee Lewis sat down at the piano, Sam only had to listen to a few bars to know that this was exactly what — and who — he had been looking for. "You are a rich man," he said, extending his hand. To which Jerry Lee might have responded, I could have told you that all along — but I would guess that this was one of those times when modesty, and a genuine feeling of accomplishment, entered into his calculation. Because both men knew exactly what Sam Phillips meant.

"Jerry is an informal person," Sam recognized from the start, "and the conditions had to be right. You had to have a good song, of course, but atmosphere was nearly everything else." That was what Sun Records provided first and foremost, that was what Sam Phillips and Sun Records stood for: the capacity to bring the most out of the untried, untutored raw talent that walked through the door. It was Sam Phillips' mission to find in each of his artists, from Howlin' Wolf to Elvis Presley, something they did not necessarily know they had in themselves. But Phillips quickly discovered that Jerry Lee Lewis was different from most of his other artists simply by virtue of the degree of self-confidence he innately possessed.

The other way in which he stood out was that, much like Elvis, and to a degree unlike many of the others, Jerry Lee was a true scholar of the music — of *every sort* of music — endowed, like Elvis, not just with an encyclopedic recall but with the ability to transform virtually every song that he recalled into a vehicle for his own personal style.

That was how he came to record his signature song, "Whole Lotta Shakin' Going On," at his second or third formal session. He was there mainly to cut a new Jack Clement composition, "It'll Be Me," as the A-side of his second single. (The first, labeled "Jerry Lee Lewis With His Pumping Piano" by Phillips, nomenclature that stuck throughout the Sun years, spotlighted a brilliantly off-kilter version of the year's number-one country hit, "Crazy Arms," while the original — by Ray Price — was still on the charts.) They had reached a point in the session where Jerry Lee was rapidly running out of enthusiasm for the Clement number (with as spontaneous an artist as Jerry Lee, this can easily happen after only two or three unsatisfactory takes), when his bass player, cousin, and soon-to-be-father-in-law J. W. Brown said, "How about that song that goes over so good in your show?" The song was one he had learned from Natchez disc jockey and singer Johnny Littlejohn at the Wagon Wheel, and Jerry Lee did it pretty much the way Johnny Littlejohn did — but, of course, with typical Jerry Lee *flair.* Jack, in his own vivid, perhaps slightly condensed account (there were at least three additional takes, and they may have taken place on successive days), barely had time to get back to the control room. "I turned on the machine [just as] they're playing the chord, and they did it. No dry run, no nothing. Just BLAM! Now, that was fun."

Jerry Lee was working with the musicians who would help define his

At Sam Phillips' home, with Sam's sons, Knox and Jerry, their cousin Thomas Jefferson Phillips Jr. (at left), and stuffed animals. *Courtesy of the Sam Phillips Family*

sound, guitarist Roland Janes and drummer J. M. Van Eaton, who had started out their musical life at Sun just a few months earlier as the nucleus of Billy Riley's Little Green Men. In this case, as on so many of the early sides, it was virtually a duet between piano and drums with guitar interpolations — the whole sound expanded and enhanced, as Sun chronicler Hank Davis has pointed out, by Sam Phillips' patented "slap-back" effect, a kind of tape-delayed echo that served only to intensify the throbbing, pounding beat. As Roland describes it, "The first time you heard him, it was like hearing a whole different music that you never heard before. He could do full-ons with his left hand as good as most people do with their right. And he had this rhythm, this fantastic bass rhythm — I mean, the music never stopped. He and J.M. [the drummer] could cut records by themselves, and it would sound like a whole orchestra. We were all on the same wavelength, really. We never talked about it. We just did it."

The only thing left to do was to inform the world. The record was released without a lot of fanfare on March 15, 1957. Two weeks later Jerry Lee started out on a Sam Phillips–sponsored Stars, Inc. tour headlined by

Johnny Cash and Carl Perkins, with one of the few female rockabillies, Wanda Jackson, on a number of the dates. Two things happened on that tour. Carl Perkins described the first to writer Michael Lydon, though in strict chronological terms it seems to have occurred considerably later than the second and describes a Jerry Lee Lewis that few, including Jerry Lee himself, would necessarily admit to having known. According to Carl: "Jerry, when he started, he was people-shy. He'd sit at the piano with just one corner of his face showing and play Hank Williams tunes. He came off [stage] one night in Calgary moaning, 'This business ain't for me, people don't like me,' and John and I told him, 'Turn around so they can see you, make a fuss.' So the next night he carried on, stood up, kicked the stool back, and a new Jerry Lee Lewis was born. And we regretted it, because he damn near stole the show. Four nights later he was top of the bill."

Evidently Sam Phillips' brother Jud must have foreseen the *new* Jerry Lee Lewis some three weeks earlier when the tour stopped off at the Community Center in Sheffield, Alabama, across the river from the Phillipses' hometown of Florence, where Jud, a sometime figure at Sun, just as charismatic as his younger brother but more flamboyant in his interpersonal skills and free-spending ways, was still living. Jerry Lee had never met Jud before, but as he walked offstage, "I looked and I saw this man standing there — and it was just like looking at Sam Phillips. And he [introduced himself] and walked me down to the dressing room and told me just exactly what he could do for me. Just where we could go, just *how* we could go, and just what we could do. And he didn't miss [by] an inch."

Having sold Sam on his new act's unlimited commercial potential, Jud took Jerry Lee to New York and got him booked on *The Steve Allen Show* — without an appointment, without a press kit, without even a hit record. As Jerry tells the story, "We just walked in, and the man said, 'What have you got?' Jud said, 'I got my boy here.' The guy turned around to somebody else and said, 'How do you like that? Here's a salesman without a damn thing to sell.' Then he said, 'You got your boy, huh? What does he do?' 'He plays piano and sings.' The man looked at Jud like he was crazy. I just sat there blowing bubble gum and reading a funny book. I said, 'Jud, what do you want me to do?' Jud said, 'Just cut loose on "Whole Lotta Shakin'."'"

That was all it took. Jud had persuaded his brother in effect to gamble the future of Sun Records on this one television appearance. When Jerry Lee appeared on *The Steve Allen Show* on July 28, every distributor in the country was fully stocked with copies of his three-month-old single, each one a potential return. If you watch it today, it seems impossible to believe that the result could ever have been in doubt. Jerry Lee's energy and impact are nothing short of cataclysmic. In fact, his sense of cosmic exhilaration was so infectious that when he kicked away the piano stool, Steve Allen sent it flying back, and in little more than a month the record was at the top of the pop, country, and r&b charts. It might well be called one of the defining moments in the history of rock 'n' roll—I don't think anyone attuned to the American vernacular tradition would dispute that claim—except that, as Sam and Jerry Lee might remonstrate, it was a defining moment only by happenstance, a *captured* moment that, were it to have taken place a moment sooner or a moment later, might have been just as good but would have been undeniably different. That in essence is the aesthetic not just of Sun but of rock 'n' roll.

From that moment on, Jerry Lee Lewis was an incontestable star. When he went out on tour the following year with Chuck Berry and Buddy Holly in a huge Alan Freed package, with two more groundbreaking hits, "Great Balls of Fire" and "Breathless," under his belt, he was the headliner, though every night he had to battle it out with Chuck Berry over who was going to close the show. The ferocity of the competition was such that when Chuck (whom Jerry Lee calls "the King of Rock 'n' Roll," because, among other things, he was Jerry's mother's favorite singer) was scheduled to close, Jerry did everything in his power to *make it impossible* for anyone to follow him. One night, according to an oft-repeated legend, he took out a Coke bottle full of gasoline and burned the piano to the ground, declaring, "I'd like to see any sonofabitch follow that." Did he actually do it? Suffice it to say that none of the musicians on the tour witnessed the conflagration. But did they believe he *could* have done it? Well, that's another story.

Perhaps more pertinent is guitarist Roland Janes' memory of the tour. Almost every night at the end of the show, as Roland recalls, "after they closed the curtains and all the people were gone, Jerry Lee would go back and sit down at the piano and start playing. Then people would start drifting out [from backstage], and the next thing you know you got a jam session going on with all these big stars and Jerry Lee at the piano, leading the chorus. He just had this charisma in his music and his personality that he'd draw them all around. There've been many nights when I would think, 'Man, I wish they'd hurry up and get through, we need to get on to the next town.' But [I don't think] I've ever known anyone who loved music more than Jerry Lee."

Of course everyone knows what happened next. Bob Dylan might have been thinking of Jerry Lee Lewis when he wrote the song "I Threw It All Away." Not that there was anything intentional about it. With his career at its zenith—and Elvis tucked safely away in the Army, Little Richard retired to the ministry, and Chuck Berry embroiled in legal difficulties—Jerry Lee embarked on a British tour which should have established him once and for all as the reigning king of rock 'n' roll. Instead, going against all advice, not to mention common sense, he took along his new thirteen-year-old bride, Myra Gale, the daughter of his first cousin and bass player, J. W. Brown, and, when asked about their relationship, not only acknowledged but proclaimed it. At which point the tour was canceled, Jerry Lee Lewis was unceremoniously told to leave the country, and his career ground to an ignominious halt. One hundred thousand record sleeves had been ordered for his first long-playing album—it scarcely sold at all. And with that began his long period in the wilderness.

"I don't think he ever realized," said Roland Janes, "I mean, number one, he didn't feel he did anything wrong. He dearly loved Myra. He was very sincere. But it just stopped him in his tracks. And I think it hurt him deeply. He tried not to show it. He didn't talk about it. And [whether or not] what he did was a wise thing, he had his pride."

He stayed out on the road. He went, as he has famously said, from $10,000 a night on occasion to as low as $250, playing as many as 300 nights a year, never giving less than his all. I can well remember the first time I saw him in the midst of that period when he was booked into an amusement park in New Hampshire. All of a sudden there he was, sitting in the back seat of a white Cadillac convertible, his chin tilted upward in that familiar Churchillian pose, puffing on a big cigar and towing his piano in a little trailer behind. The show itself was perfection incarnate, just like virtually every show I saw him do for the next fifteen or twenty years, every performance different, every song—even the most familiar—attacked in a brand-new way, with even the repertoire varying widely to include blues, country, ragtime, and requests for everything from "Bonnie B" ("It was a big hit in Sweden," he might announce proudly) to "Milkshake Mademoiselle," "Lovin' Up a Storm," and his definitive version of Roy Orbison's "Down the Line." He was ready to do anything that his wildly enthusiastic fans called for, anything that took his fancy—with flair, with attitude, with brio, and, almost always, with the frequent interpolation of his own name.

I don't think I can even begin to convey how great it really was—maybe greater than it would have been if his career had been one uninterrupted ascent (though I doubt it). But what was most astonishing about his performance, for all of its wildness, for all of what seemed like its anarchic impulse, was the discipline that went into it, the determination to create a moment that could somehow stave off whatever was bound to happen next. Jerry Lee was dedicated not just to the concept of art as an act of endless exploration but to an artistic life of civic obligation. As he told British journalist Cliff White, "Sometimes I catch myself cutting up when I should be working harder. I carry on the foolishness for a while, [but] then I'll get with it, because I know I'm lagging, because people pay to see a show." And in my experience (at least until health and lifestyle issues inevitably began to take their toll), that's pretty much what you always got.

If Jerry Lee discovered a slice of heaven at Haney's Big House (the real thing was always reserved for the Assemblies of God church), he found it again in country music in 1968. That was the year he and producer Jerry Kennedy decided on a different approach. "I knew we had to make a move," he said, "and it was right there under my nose the whole time. I'd been singing this kind of music ever since I was a kid—you know, it's like the farmer sitting out on a 300-acre farm, and all the time oil's flowing under him, but he ain't got enough sense to get at it. Then one day he finally hits and he's a smart man!"

For the next ten years, starting with "Another Place, Another Time," he had one Top 10 country hit after another. Which not only reestablished his popularity but confirmed something that, like the oil lying fallow under the farmer's field, had been present all along: his remarkable ability not just to deliver but to *interpret* a song. You could hear it, of course, as far back as "You Win Again," the B-side of "Great Balls of Fire," and certainly Jerry Lee has always maintained his allegiance to the Hank Williams and Jimmie Rodgers canon. But more than that, he has added to it over the years with sensitive treatments of original material by everyone from Mickey Newbury and Kris Kristofferson to Van Morrison and Charlie Rich. Although in many cases during his country years he might not have encountered the song before he entered the studio, in almost every instance, like the great actor he is, he could always find something to connect to, and with any song that really mattered to him, you could hear it expand and evolve as he continued to explore it in live performance. Many songs have been written to capitalize on his legend (he has even written

Courtesy of the Sam Phillips Family

some himself), and some of his bolder self-dramatizations—everything from "Lewis Boogie" to "I Am What I Am," "My Life Would Make a Damn Good Country Song," and his friend Mack Vickery's "Rockin' My Life Away"—are not to be discounted, certainly.

But that is not what I am talking about. What I am talking about is his ability to enter so fully into the landscape of a song like Mickey Newbury's "She Even Woke Me Up to Say Goodbye" that it truly tells his story. Or, just as effectively, to reinvigorate an old chestnut like "Somewhere Over the Rainbow" or Charlie Rich's "Who Will the Next Fool Be," which is broadened, deepened, then transformed with a whistled outro and Jerry Lee declaring wistfully at the fade: "Can't you imagine a cat with khaki pants on walking down the street whistling?"

The key to this is the same as the key to his extravagant persona: an openness to the moment, a devil-take-the-hindmost kind of emotional honesty, a willingness to tap into the subconscious and go where*ever* it might take him. "She Even Woke Me Up to Say Goodbye"? "Lord, you can't beat that song," says Jerry Lee. "That man had figured me out before I had figured myself out. Wow, it hit me between the eyes with a baseball bat." Robbie Robertson's "Twilight," from Jerry Lee's 2006 all-star duets album, *Last Man Standing,* grabbed him in much the same way. "I didn't change the words of it, the words are just terrific." It was the words that inspired him to rearrange the music and put it in what he calls his own "bluesy-type way." I asked him, too, about another song that he had left off the album—just Jerry Lee alone at the piano—which had struck me and a number of other observers as a genuine masterpiece. Well, no, he could have done much better, he said, as he might, of course, at any juncture. The thing about it was, "I was *trying* to sing—and when you try to sing a song, you can forget it."

So just remember that, all you aspiring musicians out there, don't try too hard. But, not uncharacteristically, Jerry Lee's formulation masks a serious point—and a serious tension. The point is the same as Jack Kerouac's passionate espousal of spontaneity or Chet Baker's exhortation, "Let's get lost." You have to give yourself up to the music if it's ever going to be worth a shit. At the same time dedication to a life of the imagination requires an act of bravery, demands a show of self-confidence—in Jerry Lee's case an *extreme* show of self-confidence—that in many instances may contradict the logic of both observation and experience. Which is why it's not altogether surprising that Jerry Lee Lewis' art should ultimately rest on the same high-wire act that he has carried on all his life, the same one on which so many other great artists from John Donne to Little Richard have been suspended: a teetering balance between the sacred and the profane.

Clearly the music of the church was a source of inspiration to him: it is at the heart of rock 'n' roll. And, just as clearly, it is not simply belief but a reaching out for belief—maybe even at times a reaction *against* belief—that comes through over and over again in his songs. Jerry Lee has articulated this self-debate more than some. Most notably perhaps in his passionate dispute with Sam Phillips over the recording of "Great Balls of Fire." "How can the Devil save souls?" he cries out desperately at one point, seemingly on the verge of walking out of the studio forever. "Man, I got the DEVIL in me. If I didn't, I'd be a Christian." The issue at the heart of their long-ago disagreement, he says today, was salvation. "And come to find out, he was wrong, and I was, too." But it obviously weighs on him no less heavily. At the so-called Million Dollar Quartet session—that wonderful, informal 1956 collaboration between a world-famous Elvis, Sun's then-current star Carl Perkins, and a twenty-one-year-old Jerry Lee, still waiting for his first record to come out (the fourth member of the "quartet," Johnny Cash, only showed up for the picture-taking)—there are all these moments of casual transcendence, prompted for the most part by the gospel songs on which all three have grown up. At the conclusion

The Million Dollar Quartet: Jerry Lee Lewis, Carl Perkins, Elvis Presley, and Johnny Cash, December 4, 1956. *Courtesy of Colin Escott*

of the session, Jerry says, "after we had been playing and jamming for three or four hours, I said, 'Elvis, I want to ask you one thing before we leave. This is on my mind, and I'd just like to know. If you died, do you think you'd go to heaven or hell?' And his eyes got real big, and he looked at me, and he said, 'Jerry Lee, don't you *ever* ask me that again.' And I didn't. But I know it had me scared—and it still does."

And yet, for all of the doubts, for all of the fears, for all of the setbacks, stumbling blocks, and crises of conscience that have cropped up over the years, to Jerry Lee Lewis, there is little question. "Rock 'n' roll," he says, "is the greatest music that's ever been. Or ever will be. Whether it was taken from gospel roots or rhythm and blues or black roots [or] red roots or blue roots, rock 'n' roll was rock 'n' roll. You're not gonna beat it. And if you do, then I really want to hear it!"

The only question that might be raised is, What, exactly, is rock 'n' roll music? And here, I guess, I would side with both Sam Phillips and Jerry Lee in suggesting that you can't brand it, it's a synthesis that could only have come about in the Southern part of this country — Sam might have insisted only in Memphis — it's an expression of some of the most idealistic democratic dreams, perhaps as fully expressed, irreversible, and undeniable an example of integration of both class and race as we have yet been able to manage. Who else but Jerry Lee could turn Teresa Brewer's "Music Music Music" into a freewheeling symphony celebrating American music from ragtime to rock? Or translate Stephen Foster's "Beautiful Dreamer" into a deeply felt, highly personal meditation on mortality? As Jerry Lee says, "I'm a rock 'n' roll/country/honkytonk/motherhumpin'/piano-playing man. I got rhythm in my soul, music in my veins, and thunder in my left hand." And it's true. So give yourself a treat — listen to the music. But watch out for flying glissandos. And if only to echo a self-appraisal with an appraisal of my own, see if you don't agree that Jerry Lee Lewis can cut just about anyone — but NO ONE CUTS THE KILLER.

Entertainer of the Year? That would not even begin to cover it. Jerry Lee Lewis rightly considers himself "the greatest damn entertainer in the world." Maybe even in the universe. Of course you might take into account the faintly perceptible nod and wink that will occasionally accompany his more flamboyant pronouncements. But you don't have to. Because, like so many other self-created myths — like Howlin' Wolf, like Thelonious Monk, like James Brown or Bob Dylan — the man has inevitably merged with the music; he is, in his own terms, a walking contradiction, partly truth and partly fiction. And he wouldn't have it any other way.

"I am what I am," he says. "If people don't like it, that's their problem." He may be a sinner, he says, but at least he's man enough to admit it. He is in the end an originalist. You're not going to get him to admit that anyone like him has ever walked the earth before. As to the question of whether there might ever be anyone like him again, though, you might well be surprised at his answer. "I certainly hope so," he told a reporter some time ago. "Why?" was the reporter's stunned response. "Well, Killer," came the reply, expressed no doubt with a combination of measured tolerance and rueful regret, "just think what a dull world this would be without a Jerry Lee Lewis in it." As to what he would most like to be remembered for, there has never been any hesitation whatsoever. His music, he says. "I want them to remember me simply for my music."

TWENTY-THREE

Howlin' Wolf: What Is the Soul of Man?

THERE ARE PROBABLY just so many performers in any one lifetime who can be considered truly electrifying. Jerry Lee Lewis has always cited Al Jolson, Jimmie Rodgers, Hank Williams — and himself. He might very well have added Elvis, who inspired him originally to come to Sun Records — but then again he might not.

All of us have had someone who inspired us in that unique way — some might name Aretha Franklin, others Bruce Springsteen or Louis Armstrong or Michael Jackson or, from other eras, other genres, Maria Callas or Enrico Caruso.

For me, as any reader of the previous chapter will be well aware, it's always been James Brown, Solomon Burke, Jerry Lee Lewis, and Howlin' Wolf — they represent the pantheon of performers who in my experience just tore the house down every time. I'm sure if I'd seen Sam Cooke at the Harlem Square Club or Elvis Presley at the Eagle's Nest in Memphis in 1954, I'd enlarge my list. But of all the performers I've seen in person, these are the ones who always had the ability to take their audiences to places they never expected to go, who shared a charismatic experience that I've never felt to such an extent before or since.

Howlin' Wolf, in his own way, may well have been the most commanding, not just because of his physical presence — he was six foot three and well over 300 pounds when I first encountered him — but by the fact that as a blues singer, accompanied as often as not by little more than a barebones rhythm section, he was able, through sheer force of personality, to suggest a breadth of vision, a scope of enterprise that cut across all barriers of time and place.

One of the first times I met him, in 1967, he was playing the Club 47 in Cambridge, a tiny basement room with a seating capacity of no more than 150. I had written a story about him for the *Boston Phoenix*, a descriptive preview intended to draw in the uninitiated as well as die-hard fans. It was written with the utmost respect — well, let's be honest, it was written with the same veneration that you might deduce from my present tone — about a man whose talent I considered to be virtually indescribable. Here is the best I could do at the time.

"Howlin' Wolf is bigger than life," I wrote. "He eclipses other performers with [the] size and gusto of his performance. Some bluesmen will try on different styles, will jive their audience in a shuffling attempt to ingratiate themselves. Wolf rolls on the floor, he passes a broom obscenely between his legs, he appears in farmer's overalls — yet somehow nothing Wolf does is jive, no matter how often you may have seen it before or how familiar the gesture. The Wolf is always himself."

Okay, okay, I know — I should probably apologize for some of the language. Just remember: this was 1967, and I was in love with the blues. Anyway, when I went to see him the next night, the night after the piece came out, somehow or other I got introduced to Wolf as the guy who had done the newspaper write-up about him. "Oh yeah?" said Wolf, interrupting a story he was telling to a dozen wide-eyed listeners. "Well, sit down," he said, putting an empyrean hand on my shoulder. "Sit down, boy." He wanted to see the article, he said, and after I mumblingly demurred, someone else quickly produced a copy. Glancing over it, he apologized for not having his reading glasses with him. Could someone read it to him?

Not me. That was for sure.

So the kid who had given him the story started reading it, glancing at me, I thought, with something between pity and withering scorn. This might have had something to do with the headline, I suppose, which read, "Rasping, Vulgar, Giant Wolf Howls Fierce Blues of Bitterness, Rage."

"He imitates no one," the kid read, "and as he prowls the stage, suddenly lurching heavily forward, leaning on a post waiting out the instrumental break, impatiently biding his time, the self-created public personality becomes the man. 'The mighty Wolf,' he shouts, 'Making his midnight creep / Hunters they can't find him / Stealing chicks wherever he goes / Then dragging his tail behind him.' He turns his back on the audience, and his massive hips begin to shake. His dance is awkward and ungainly, his voice overpowers with a fierce rasping force, as he proclaims, 'I'm a tail dragger. . . .'"

Awkward? Ungainly? The kid is *really* disapproving now. But it doesn't seem to faze Wolf one bit — Wolf in fact repeats the lyric, delicately savoring each phrase. "Where'd you get that from, boy?" he says to me. "You make it all up out of your own head?"

By the time the kid finished reading, sweat was pouring down my face, but Wolf seemed genuinely pleased. At the end he pumped my hand several times and once again expressed his wonderment at my sources. But it was his behavior on stage afterwards that was truly revealing.

Up until then it had been a somewhat perfunctory evening—if anything attached to Wolf could ever be described as perfunctory. But now when he went up for the second set, he seemed determined to reenact every descriptive phrase I had employed. He leapt in the air, he rolled on the floor, he cradled the microphone between his legs, he pounded at the posts that supported the ceiling with frightening ferocity. (For me this couldn't help but bring to mind the overpowering Blind Willie Johnson/Reverend Gary Davis song about Samson at the Temple, "If I Had My Way I'd Tear This Building Down"—that was pretty much what I thought was going to happen.) At the end of the evening he lay on his back roaring into the mike and struggling to get to his feet again and again. Each time he would raise himself up to a sitting position and then fall back and the whole stage would shudder, until at last he leapt up and, towering over us in the front row, announced:

"The Wolf don't *jive*. His FRIENDS know that."

They did indeed. They all did—I'm sure they still do.

The first time Sun Records founder Sam Phillips met him, the first time he *heard* Howlin' Wolf, in the spring of 1951, Sam would always recall, he had a single unwavering response. "I said, 'This is for me. This is where the soul of man never dies.'"

Phillips never altered that view. If he could have recorded just one person to the end of his days, he said, repeatedly and with great conviction, it would have been the Howlin' Wolf, the most profound talent he ever encountered. Of all the artists he ever recorded, not excluding Elvis Presley, Johnny Cash, Jerry Lee Lewis, or B.B. King, he would always point to Wolf not necessarily as the most gifted (for he had extravagant words of praise for every one of his discoveries) but as the most *inspired*. "God, what I would give to see him [again] as he was in my studio," Phillips would declare, "to see the fervor in his face, to hear the pure instinctive quality in that man's voice. You could almost be hypnotized by him just sitting in a damn chair."

Phillips had opened his studio in Memphis some sixteen months earlier

Wolf at radio station KWEM, 1951. *Courtesy of Bill Greensmith / Blues Unlimited*

with the explicit aim of "mak[ing] records with some of the great Negro artists in the South who just had no place to go." He didn't have a label of his own, he didn't *want* to have a label of his own—his idea was just to make the music and license it to record labels that had the resources, both financial and temperamental, to sell it. What he had set out to do, he knew, was neither popular nor safe within the context of place and time. "Everybody laughed at me," he said, speaking specifically of the radio station where he still worked. "Of course, they'd try to make it tongue-in-cheek, they'd say, 'Well, you smell okay. I guess you haven't been hanging around those niggers today, Sam.'" His fellow workers would chuckle then, Sam said, as if to make it clear that they weren't altogether serious, but it would have been hard to misread the malevolent underlying intent.

But he persisted because he believed so passionately not only in the justice of the cause but in the grandeur of the music, in the innate *spirituality* that was at its core. He had just had his first number-one hit on Chess Records with Ike Turner and Jackie Brenston's "Rocket 88," subsequently hailed in many quarters as the first rock 'n' roll record, when a DJ at KWEM across the river in West Memphis, knowing his predilection for *that kind of music,* called and told him they had this new guy on the air with the most unusual-sounding voice. He was doing an early-morning broadcast every Saturday, selling farm implements and dry goods and advertising his appearances in the area with on-air performances of his songs. The DJ thought Sam might be interested.

Sam listened in the following Saturday, and when he did, it seemed his life was forever changed. "I mean, I tuned him in, and it was the worst pickup you ever heard, and as I recall I heard one number, and I instantly, I *INSTANTLY* said, 'THIS IS WHAT I'M LOOKING FOR.'"

He called the station and invited Wolf to come by the studio sometime and see him, they could get together at any hour of the day or night, whatever suited him best.

The man he met was certainly imposing—he was forty-one years old, thirteen years older than Sam, with a broad handsome face, smooth, dark skin, and a manner that indicated wariness, suspicion, and a residue of deep hurt. He was someone, Sam knew, who would have been very easy to dismiss. He volunteered scarcely anything personal in that gruff, scoured voice, unlike any Sam had ever heard. And yet, Sam felt, he possessed "a certain element of confidence, he knew he had something to say," and as they talked, Sam could sense that as much as he might be reading the Wolf, Wolf was reading him, too. "He was highly, highly intelligent," Sam said, "in many ways the sweetest man you'll ever know, and the strangest man in many ways, too."

Sam was so struck by the differentness of the man, he was so drawn to the particularity of his demeanor—but he didn't want to, in his words, "overpromise" anything. He simply suggested that maybe Wolf could come by with his band sometime—they could try a few things just to see what they could get.

Wolf showed up several days later with a guitarist and drummer in tow and an assortment of harmonicas, and before long the trio was just blowing as if Sam wasn't even in the room, encouraging one another with unrestrained shouts while he switched the mikes around and adjusted the levels to get the maximum out of each individual piece. But, really, he knew he was just giving himself an excuse to listen in. Because for one of the few times in his life, *Sam couldn't think of a single thing to do.*

Oddly enough, one of the things I am convinced that drew him most to Wolf was something that neither man knew — or, for that matter, would ever know — about the other.

Sam Phillips had just had a nervous breakdown, his second, with eight electroshock treatments and no guarantee that he would ever again lead a normal life. And Wolf, who had been abandoned by his mother at an early age and had never really been off the farm until he was drafted during World War II, had had a full-blown nervous breakdown himself while he was in the Army, to the point that he was discharged with a Certificate of Disability based on a file that labeled him a "mental defective. . . . Hard to handle — must be careful not to make him angry."

This was something of which he was deeply ashamed and almost never spoke — but it almost certainly added to the affect that Sam Phillips immediately sensed: this was a man, Sam recognized instinctively, of a fiercely private, highly sensitive, and intensely mistrustful nature, someone it would not have been easy to get to know under any circumstances, let alone the sharply divided circumstances of the time. No matter what he came to achieve in later life, Wolf always sensed that others might be mocking him ("Don't Laugh at Me" was the title of one of his later compositions), but he came to feel this was just the penalty for refusing to be anything other than himself. "Anytime you stand up for what you believe is right," he said to me mournfully one time, "people are gonna laugh and say things about you. But if I wasn't doin' nothing, wouldn't nobody be sayin' nothin' about me either."

He was different in other ways, too. Here was a man who, until he entered the Army in his early thirties, had never really left home. After his discharge nothing much seemed to have changed. He returned to his father's farm, then took up farming briefly on his own — but it wasn't until shortly before he met Sam Phillips in 1951 that he finally committed himself to a career in music. Not that he wasn't well known in the area around Penton, Mississippi, and all through the Delta, where, as he said, you played all night "for a fish sandwich, and glad to get it, too."

He had taken up guitar originally, at the age of seventeen, on January 15, 1928, to be precise — and Wolf was *always* precise, consistently and somewhat mystifyingly so in this instance. He was, he said, inspired by the great Delta bluesman Charley Patton, who lived on a nearby plantation, and he adopted his performing name early on, probably taking it from J. T. "Funny Papa" Smith's 1931 recording "Howling Wolf Blues," which became his signature tune. Though, he was also quick to point out, he had come by the nickname legitimately at an early age: his grandfather used to tease him with it as a little boy because of his fear of the wolves that had once roamed the countryside.

In any case it wasn't the *name* that drew the attention of his peers. And it wasn't his size either. It was that same mystifying manner that he would retain all his life, that indecipherable suggestion of sorrow and profundity, inextricably linked, that would first draw Sam Phillips to him.

A younger Delta blues singer, Johnny Shines, met Wolf in Hughes, Arkansas, in the early 1930s when Johnny was still in his teens. "I was kind of afraid of him," Johnny said. "I mean, just to walk up and put your hand on him. Well, it wasn't his *size* — I mean, what he was doing, the WAY he was doing, the sound that he was giving off. I didn't know it at the time, but Wolf did farmwork during the week. I usually saw him only on Saturday and Sunday nights. As far as I knew he could have crawled out of a cave, a place of solitude, after a full week's rest, to serenade us. I thought he was a magic man. *That's how great I thought Wolf was.*"

That's how great Sam Phillips thought he was, too. Which was why Sam, ordinarily the most confident of men, even at this troubled juncture in his life, found himself momentarily at a loss, "blinded," as he said, "by the sound of Wolf's voice," which, with its scoured rasp and overwhelming ferocity, was at one and the same time, Sam said, both the worst voice he had ever heard in his life and, in its own inimitable way, the most beautiful.

"I didn't want anything much but Wolf," he said. "I mean, the minute I opened the microphones and that look came over his face, like, 'I'm getting ready, everybody else better be ready, too,' I was entranced." But how in the world, he asked himself, were you ever going to capture someone who sang "with his damn soul"? There was no formula for it, certainly — as far as Sam was concerned, there was no formula for any-thing even *remotely* touching on creativity — but he was determined to do all that he could to bring out of the Wolf everything that was in him, and over the next month they worked at it night and day.

Eventually they concentrated on two songs that seemed to change with every take, a pulsating midtempo blues called "How Many More Years" that was Wolf's calling card and a menacing, modal, Mississippi hill-country blues, transformed by Wolf's almost unearthly howl, more like a moan in this instance, which Sam called "Moanin' at Midnight." As far as Sam was concerned just Wolf and his guitarist, Willie Johnson, would have been enough (Willie sounded almost like he was playing two guitars at once, with his combination of crashing chords and thickly distorted single-string leads) — but Sam brought in a piano player not so much to fill out the sound as to provide a little additional form and structure. For "Moanin' at Midnight" the piano eventually sat out, and the master con-sisted of nothing but drums, Wolf's haunting vocal and harmonica, and the relentlessly rhythmic pattern of Willie Johnson's guitar.

The record was a hit from the time it came out on Chess in the fall of 1951 — it turned out in fact to be the highest-charting hit Wolf would ever have, with both sides scoring in the Top 10 r&b charts, and "How Many More Years" reaching number four.

Sam recorded Wolf over the next year and a half, until he had the last in a series of business fallings-out with Leonard Chess in the fall of 1952. Chess at this point seems to have put an embargo on Wolf doing any more recordings at Sam's studio and set about persuading him to move to Chicago — which, given Wolf's natural sense of caution, took more than a year to effect.

Although it was strictly a business matter, Sam uncharacteristically took Wolf's departure as an almost personal affront. Losing Wolf, he fre-quently said, was the greatest disappointment he would ever experience in the record business. It was the single factor that most convinced him that he finally needed to start a record company of his own. But more than anything else he regretted missing out on the opportunity to explore new creative paths with the Wolf. If they had continued to work together, he was firmly convinced, Wolf would have provided what Sam called an "entirely different approach to rock 'n' roll." He could have been "the counterpart of Elvis," Sam said — "this guy would have been huge with white youngsters, along with black.

Howlin' Wolf at Free Trade Hall, Manchester, 1964. *Photograph by Brian Smith*

"You will always take something to your grave that you regret. I'm not going to take many things because I've been too blessed. But I guess I'll take to my grave not having the Wolf around. This seems crazy, but it's a fact. I don't know that anybody else ever got the joy out of Wolf I got.

"I could not have done anything for the Wolf no matter how hard I tried, except capture what he gave to me in front of my eyes."

As for Wolf, he took a slightly different view. "I'm the onliest one that drove out of the South like a gentleman," he told music historian Dave Booth. "I had a four-thousand-dollar car and $3,900 in my pocket." And in another detail radically different from the portrait in the Chess Records feature film *Cadillac Records*, which has Wolf arriving in Chicago in a broken-down pickup truck wearing overalls, he was probably wearing a three-piece suit at the time.

He made the most of his new life. With help from Muddy Waters, he quickly established himself on the South Side as Muddy's chief rival for Chicago's blues throne, and his career on Chess, while it never took off commercially in quite the way that his initial success might have foretold, was marked by unforgettable recordings like "Smokestack Lightnin'," "I Asked for Water (She Gave Me Gasoline)," "Evil," "Who's Been Talkin'," "Spoonful," "Natchez Burning," "Little Red Rooster," and "Killing Floor."

His peers could recall, anyone who listened could clearly discern the roots that he so proudly proclaimed in his music, with the influence of Charley Patton and Tommy Johnson (not to mention the "Father of Country Music," Jimmie Rodgers, whom Wolf always cited) predominating. Some of the songs might have had Willie Dixon's name as songwriter (Wolf more often than not would have disputed that), but they were all unquestionably, inarguably *Wolf*. And even as the blues declined in popularity and many of his generation chased commercial trends, Wolf's music never deviated from its original intent. What is perhaps most extraordinary about it is that it retained its full strength, its uncompromising integrity and power, from first to last.

If you don't believe me, listen to his final album, *The Back Door Wolf*, which includes everything from a tribute to the first black astronaut (I'm not going to name it — you're going to have to look up the title for yourself) to Wolf's powerful evocation of his original inspiration, Charley Patton, with "Can't Stay Here." Or if you still need to be convinced of the force of Wolf's musical conviction, pick up a not-very-good but lots-of-fun album, *The Super Super Blues Band*, a kind of summit meeting of Wolf, Bo Diddley, and Muddy (the only time Wolf and Muddy would ever meet on record), which is dominated by Wolf's triumphant — some might say *triumphalist* — spirit, expressed in the form of his relentlessly cheerful taunts. "I'm the king, I'm the king," he shouts out again and again to Muddy, "I done tole y'all, I'm the king." Which is intended, one suspects, to motivate himself as much as it is to disparage his rival.

Just one note of qualification. In the spirit of full disclosure I should tell you: avoid at all costs 1969's *The Howlin' Wolf Album* and *Message to the Young*, two ill-advised psychedelic experiments recorded over his protests in the wake of the commercial success of Muddy's equally ill-conceived *Electric Mud*. "Man, that stuff's dogshit," Wolf told *Rolling Stone*. And it is.

A NUMBER OF YEARS AGO, when the *New York Times* asked me to write a story for a special section they were running (they just called it Favorites, but in my mind it was really about "defining cultural moments of the twentieth century"), I didn't hesitate for an instant. It was Howlin' Wolf on *Shindig!*, with the Rolling Stones at his feet.

It's difficult for me even now to adequately suggest the tectonic cultural shift that occurred when Howlin' Wolf first (and I believe last) appeared on national TV. But, in the spirit of Sam Phillips, let me at least try.

My wife, Alexandra, and I were living in what could best be described as a limited-hot-water garret apartment in North Cambridge—it may not have been Paris in the '20s, but for me it represented the writer's life. There wasn't a lot on TV in those days, but we read the newspaper listings religiously for anything that might be of unusual interest. (Remember, this was long before the age of TiVo and YouTube—in those days, if you missed it, it was gone.) One of the programs we checked out as a matter of course was *Shindig!*, by far the best music show on television and the only one ever to have earned an exclamation point in its title. The Rolling Stones were the headliners on this particular night—it was Thursday, May 20, 1965—and that alone would have compelled us to watch. But there in small type, along with a number of other pop acts, was a listing for—"Chester Burnett."

Now—one thing that I may have neglected to mention up till now, not entirely without ulterior motive, was that Howlin' Wolf's given name was Chester Arthur Burnett, named, as surely everyone will immediately recall, for our twenty-first president. And while it's all very well to possess this kind of arcane knowledge, the kind of knowledge with which blues lovers and trainspotters seem to be congenitally cursed, in this instance, like most knowledge, it only gave rise to waves of doubt. Because this was not a name under which Wolf had ever appeared professionally. And I could only wonder if this might not be some terrible misunderstanding. Or worse yet, some cruel cosmic joke.

All doubt was erased when Wolf came striding out on stage, all six foot three and 300 pounds of him, and without preamble launched magisterially into "How Many More Years," his first hit.

There was not the slightest hint of self-consciousness or hesitation as he ripped into the song, his great, expressive face providing dramatic commentary to the buzz-saw rasp of his voice, the unabashed gusto and drive of his performance. Every moment was larger than life. He looked as if he were about to swallow the tiny harmonica in his mouth, waggled his hips in a wildly elephantine dance, then leapt up and down, with the Stones sitting at his feet, as if not just the stage but the entire world would shake.

For years I would ask friends—I would catechize my kids: What were the ten greatest moments in television history? They might at one time

have gone for the Huxtable family lip-synching to Ray Charles' "Night Time Is the Right Time" on *The Cosby Show* — which was, of course, undeniably great, though it is now, sadly, almost impossible to watch — and then, as they got older and the simultaneous rise of MTV and VCRs encouraged personalized video mixes, we added any number of other similarly iconic musical moments.

But for me no one ever challenged Wolf on *Shindig!* In fact he occupied — and occupies to this day — the first three places on my television top ten, with, maybe, no, *definitely, The Wire* coming in fourth. But then, of course, there's Elvis' 1968 "Comeback Special." Not to mention any number of episodes of *The Colbert Report.* And what about James Brown on the theatrically released *T.A.M.I. Show* — well, that's kind of cheating, it's not exactly television. Okay. Well, then, maybe Jerry Lee Lewis and Jackie Wilson duetting on *Shindig!,* or Sleepy LaBeef singing "Strange Things Happening Every Day" on *Late Night with Conan O'Brien.* Or how about the irretrievably lost episode of *The Tonight Show,* on which Sam Cooke sang "A Change Is Gonna Come" in public for the first, and maybe last, time?

But Howlin' Wolf on *Shindig!* remains for me number one.

I'VE OFTEN THOUGHT there may be one common denominator for all great music, and that is its capacity to bring a smile to your lips. It's not the subject matter. And it doesn't really have much to do with mood. It's the commitment to the moment. It's what Sam Phillips called throwing yourself into the music with ABANDON. It's the one quality that unites Thelonious Monk and Jerry Lee Lewis, the Master Musicians of Joujouka and Howlin' Wolf. The sheer delight that they take in making music. The gratification that they suggest awaits us all, if we will only give ourselves over to what is going on around us, *right now.*

I never saw anyone who could outdo Wolf — for seriousness of purpose or pleasure of performance. Every night was necessarily going to be different. It was a world in which all the signposts were familiar, but nothing was ever quite the same.

Even at the end of his life, when he was so sick he was forced to accommodate his bookings to the proximity of a VA hospital where he could get

With Son House, backstage at *Shindig!,* May 20, 1965. *Photograph by Dick Waterman*

35¢

THE MAGAZINE OF ROCK 'N' ROLL

CRAWDADDY!

REVOLVER REVIEWED BYRDS / TEMPTATIONS ANIMALS / REMAINS

On the cover of
Crawdaddy!,
September 1966.
*Courtesy of Peter
Guralnick Archives*

dialysis treatment three times a week, it was almost as if—no, it really just *was* that he had made a conscious choice that this was what he was going to do and nothing short of dying was going to stop him from doing it. His bandleader, Eddie Shaw, took care of him as well as anyone could, but some nights it almost looked as if Wolf was about to pass out onstage, as all the color would drain from his face and he would just shake his head sadly, waiting for his strength to come back.

One night some of the nurses from the VA hospital showed up and requested "I Can't Stop Loving You." Wolf didn't really know the song, but Eddie Shaw did and played the melody as Wolf just sat there with his legs spread wide, his size-seventeen feet tapping out the rhythm, and a beatific smile wreathing his face. "I can't stop loving you, I just can't," he extemporized to the nurses in that gravelly voice, not singing, just reciting. "You *know* I can't get enough of you, baby," he repeated over and over, as Eddie Shaw played the familiar changes and the nurses cheered, and once again it was crystal clear that for Wolf there was no division between the music and the moment.

I remember the very first time I met him, the very first time I interviewed him, sort of, a year before the *Boston Phoenix* episode. It was the summer of 1966 — I was just there for the show, but I was pressed into service at the last minute by Paul Williams, the eighteen-year-old editor of *Crawdaddy!* (the only rock magazine to earn *its* exclamation mark), because, he freely admitted in a state of near panic, he didn't really know anything about the blues.

Well, needless to say, I was just as panicked — maybe paralyzed is the better word — and we spent most of our time naively asking Wolf some of those Eternal Questions of the Blues. What, for example, we wondered, did he think of all these white kids, like the Rolling Stones, who had so recently adopted the music? Well, he said, he liked Paul Butterfield (this was not long after the Butterfield Blues Band's first album had come out, but Wolf knew Paul and guitarist Mike Bloomfield from the clubs), "he grown up in it just like that other boy out in California, [who did] that 'Hound Dog' number."

You mean Elvis Presley? I finally managed to get out, *extremely* tentatively (I mean, what if I was totally wrong!), after trying a number of unsuccessful prompts to get him to commit himself a little more explicitly.

"Yeah," said Wolf impatiently, as if the reference should be obvious to anyone.

"Elvis Presley," he said, "he made it *his* way."

There was not an ounce of irony in the statement. This, I came to realize, represented Wolf's deepest convictions — not just about Elvis but about himself. As strange as it might seem coming from someone who was the purest of all blues singers, for Wolf there was no such thing as category, his way of thinking didn't allow for limits or labels. It wasn't, as Wolf vehemently affirmed to Paul Williams and me, a question of color, it was a matter of *belief*.

"You can't take a man's freedom away from him," Wolf said, in defense of Elvis Presley and anyone else who might have chosen the less traveled path. "I like any music that sounds good to me. It's what taste you got. It's just what [you] want to do."

TWENTY-FOUR

Living with the Blues: An Interview with Eric Clapton

AN INTRODUCTORY NOTE

I THINK THIS is the only Q&A I have ever done.

The reason, I think, will almost immediately become obvious.

This is a conversation about the blues, to be sure, but it's also a tale of mutual discovery.

"I thought it was magic," said Eric Clapton of his own introduction to the music at fifteen or sixteen. "The whole thing was such a fantastic romance. The embodiment of all my dreams, really, just the wildness of it all."

I could have said almost exactly the same thing—in fact, I'm sure I did in the course of our nearly three-hour-long conversation in 1990, which began with a question from me about Robert Johnson that was volleyed back at me disconcertingly. "Well, as you put it so well in your book *Searching for Robert Johnson* . . ." Eric began—and I may be naive, but I didn't detect a twinkle in his eye.

Let me just inject a brief historical note. The first Robert Johnson album, *King of the Delta Blues Singers,* came out, without alarums or trumpets, in the fall of 1961. I was seventeen, Mick Jagger and Keith Richards were the same age, Eric Clapton was a year younger. Without making too much of it, it seems almost as if we all discovered a brand-new cosmos on the same day. Over the course of the next ten years the album would sell approximately 15,000 copies, and I feel as if over the course of the following half century I must have met nearly every one of its purchasers. When I asked Eric in the course of our interview if he felt sometimes as if he had fallen into some kind of secret society with his discovery not just of

Eric and Buddy Guy, London, 1969. *Photograph by Dick Waterman*

Robert Johnson but, almost inevitably, of the ever-widening world of the blues, it was the same question that I have asked myself, and the same grateful realization that I have come to, again and again over the years.

Under ordinary circumstances, I would have prepared for this interview, as I did for every other profile in this book, immersing myself in the subject with as much listening, background research, and random exploration as I could possibly muster. I'm not saying I didn't do that here — but the point of the piece was never going to be a full-blown profile, it was a conversation about a shared obsession.

This was in other ways, too, a new experience for me, if only because, after so many years of writing about heroes from an older generation like Muddy Waters and Howlin' Wolf, I found myself now talking with someone who shared the same heroes and much the same original impulse. Which was, quite simply, to get lost in the blues. And so we talked about the sense of romance and estrangement that had come over us both, at roughly the same age, when we were first plunged into a world in which, in different ways, we each sought to find a home. When we spoke of Muddy Waters, a regal, almost unapproachable figure to the young Eric Clapton who would one day become very much of a mentor to him, it was with an awareness of the painful process that we all undergo (if you don't believe me, read the previous chapter, on Howlin' Wolf) when forced to confront the ambiguities of real life as opposed to the myths that we inevitably create. Nor is it something, all those painful contradictions, that we can ever leave completely behind.

These are some of the subjects that Eric addressed, both directly and indirectly, and while I'm sure I imposed some of my own preoccupations, I think, clearly, they are his as well. What it all means (the cause, the reason for this unswerving dedication to the blues) may well remain a mystery, but the description, I hope, will ring true, not just for Eric Clapton but as a reflection of the pervasive influence that the blues has had on the world at large over the last century. Its near-universal appeal can no longer be put down to cultural tourism or generational self-approbation. It has long since proved both its durability and its depth, exerting an impact that reaches far beyond the confines of form or language. As Sam Phillips said, "I mean, the blues, the blues, the blues — and sometimes the blues are so good, it's hard to pick out what you like best, in the same song. You hear something different in the blues every time you play it." A viewpoint that Eric Clapton could only echo, as he describes his struggle to find a voice of his own to match the voices that he heard calling to him.

He appears to see himself as a combination of warring impulses, who can speak frankly, but wryly, of his own hard-won growth—he portrays himself as an artisan at times, a man simply doing his job, but also, unquestionably, an artist seeking self-expression. One comes away from speaking with him with a sense of a man self-confident to the point of impatience with critics who don't understand the exigencies of real life, and self-doubting enough to be acutely aware of every whisper of criticism. He is fully aware of his status as a "star," and both discounts its importance and falls back on it at times, almost as if it constituted membership in an exclusive club. Will there be members of future generations, I ask him, who may look upon him as he once looked upon Muddy Waters? "Ohhhh . . . that would be nice if they did," he says with genuine doubt, but, at the same time, pleasure at the prospect.

AN EDUCATION IN THE BLUES

Do you remember the first time you heard Robert Johnson?

I don't think I'd even heard of Robert Johnson when I found the record, it was probably just fresh out. I was around fifteen or sixteen, and it was like a real shock that there was something that powerful. A friend of mine gave it to me, a very dear friend who was at school with me and we were both avid blues collectors. This guy always seemed to be, I don't know why, one step ahead. You know, it was almost like something he did to spite me, as if whatever I was into he would come up with something sharper. And he came up to me and gave me this record and said, "See if you can learn some of *this*." You know? I played it, and it really shook me up, because it had, it didn't seem to be concerned with appeal at all. It was like all the music I'd heard up until that time seemed to be structured in a way for recording. What struck me about Robert Johnson's record was it seemed as if he wasn't playing for an audience. It didn't obey the rules of time or harmony or anything. It all led me to believe that here was a guy who really didn't want to play for people at all, that his thing was so unbearable for him to have to live with that he was almost like ashamed of it. This was an image, really, that I was very, very keen to hang on to.

What was it about Robert Johnson that initially drew you in? Was it the lyrics, the music . . . ?

You know, it seemed to me it was almost as if he had a collection of English poetry at home or something. Like, "She's got an Elgin movement from her head down to her toes." Unbelievable! Almost Byronesque in a way. Just his turn of phrase was so classical. It was almost like I'd been prepared each step of the way to receive him. Like a religious experience that started out by hearing Chuck Berry, and then at each stage I was going further and further back, and deeper and deeper into the source of the music, until I was ready for Robert Johnson. And even then I wasn't quite ready. It was still very, very powerful for me. I don't know what it was. I really don't like to analyze it too much. I was very much of a working-class kid when that record was around. But it was as if there was some kind of radar that . . . It's far too magical to be put down as pure chance somehow. Why would it mean so much to me, or for someone like Keith Richards, to hear that in England, of all places? Why didn't we grow up listening to European music or English music? Why did black American blues get through to me? I don't know. . . .

What about when you started playing? How did you approach the problem of interpretation?

It was always the question of finding something that would have a riff or a form that could be interpreted fairly easily into a band format. In "Crossroads" you had a very definite riff. In actual fact, the riff for that came more or less from "Terraplane" in a way. It's quite similar. There are certain songs, actually, on the album *King of the Delta Blues* that I wouldn't touch. So I'd have to look for ones I didn't have so much respect for. This has changed for me over the years. Now, probably, I wouldn't touch *any* of them! But because I had less inhibition then, I would single out the ones that seemed to me accessible. Through being more sort of standard. A lot of them I would be too much in awe of, or scared of, to attempt to interpret. It was just too deep for me to be able to deal with. I recognized that. It would have been an insult to the song, to the memory of Robert, to attack it in any lesser way. But things like "Crossroads," "From Four Till Late," well, they were easier, they seemed to me fairly off-the-cuff.

How about when you were by yourself? Would you sit and play along with the record?

No, no. I don't . . . it would take too much of a sacrifice on every level to really come up with that. For me Robert was more than that. There are a lot of people who could study . . . or scholarly-approach the style of playing and get it down note for note—but then what are they going to do about the singing? What made more sense to me was to approach his more accessible songs and make them accessible to today's market in a way. So that they would like it, in a sense on a very shallow level, and then ask questions afterwards. Because to mimic Robert, even vocally and musically with the guitar, wouldn't make it accessible to people that were listening now. It would just leave it where it was and not even as good as what it was.

What about the technical aspect? Did things like tunings interest you?

I couldn't . . . I tried to work out, I think I still do now and then try to work out, how he did play in tunings—but it still doesn't make sense to me. And I don't think anyone will have the answer. Because you can take an open tuning and just move one string, and you've got a whole other story. Take a straight Spanish tuning and move like the fifth string up to normal. There's a lot of difference. . . . I mean, I don't think anyone can ever really claim to be totally right about the way Robert would have played.

Doesn't Ry Cooder come close?

He's just as much a mystery. He won't tell you what he's doing. You'd have to sneak up—I know one guy who did it, snuck up on one of his guitars while Ry wasn't around and just couldn't make head nor tail of it. It didn't fit any textbook tuning. That's . . . he's allowed that, surely, I mean that's his secret.

How do you see the spirit of Robert Johnson surviving today? Or do you?

One of the few people that inherited that kind of wildness and passion was Buddy Guy. He has a lot of whatever that spirit was. Do you know what I mean? It's like this tormented . . . when he opens his mouth and sings, it's just cold chills every time. That's what I imagine Robert to have been like. If he had kind of come through. That's probably why my adoration transferred to Buddy and still is there. He is still the man that can turn it on every, every time, without an ounce of polish. It's just brutal playing, brutal singing, and right to the point, passionate. And that's what I think came through. Maybe he's reincarnated.

Tell me about the first time you met the blues.

I guess it would have been, I think it was Sonny Boy Williamson at this blues festival they had once a year in England, around '63. Or Memphis Slim. The first guy I saw play that way live was Matt "Guitar" Murphy when he was with Memphis Slim. I ventured to talk to him after the show. This was at the Marquee Club. And he disappointed me, because he said that he didn't care about the blues, he was just doing this for the bread. He wanted to . . . he really considered himself a jazz musician. What a kind of wake-up that was! But, you see, I'd already selected my heroes at that point, and the guys that were coming over weren't necessarily my heroes. My heroes were Muddy and Little Walter. The first person I saw that was my hero was Little Walter. Somehow or another he'd got himself into a tour of England on his own. I don't know how the hell that happened because he was pretty hard to deal with, but I loved him. I mean, I saw him play with a pickup band at the Marquee Club, and he stopped—every number he would start and stop and tell them it was all wrong, and he'd start it again. It was sheer chaos. And the promoter of the club was saying, Ahhhh, what did I get involved in here? This guy is drunk. He's drinking two bottles of rum a day. . . . To me it was pure magic, just the sound that came out—I mean, he could not *not* play. You know what I mean? He was very reticent to get into anything for very long, but whenever it happened, even if it was just like for thirty seconds that he'd blow, it was heaven for me. And I just thought, Well, these guys can't, they don't understand. This is what it is, you take the rough with the smooth. You're lucky to have this guy here. You're lucky he's alive and that he condescends to play for you. No way I could complain about that. No way. I thought it was magic.

The next one of my heroes to come over was Buddy Guy, and he did the same thing. I mean, he was pretty straight, but he toured on his own. And he was doing all the tricks that Jimi later did. He bounced it on the

Little Walter. *Courtesy of Bill Greensmith/Blues Unlimited*

floor and he was playing it with his teeth, between his legs, behind his head, everything. I saw *him* at the Marquee. I called up my friend Ben Palmer, who was very instrumental in getting me into the blues, he was the pianist in the Roosters, the first band that I played in, and he was in Wales, but he came down both times, to see Walter and Buddy Guy. And Buddy was on *Ready Steady Go!* because he had a single they were trying to push, it was called "Let Me Love You, Baby." And Cathy McGowan, the presenter of the show, said, "And here from the States we have Chubby Checker." And he came on. . . . And I was just watching coincidentally, and there's Buddy Guy in this shiny sharkskin suit, with a strap, playing "Let Me Love You, Baby" live. It was phenomenal. And after he finished, Cathy McGowan came on and said, "Sorry, I was wrong. It wasn't Chubby Checker, it was Chuck Berry." So for the mass of people that were watching, they never knew who it was. Unbelievable. The whole thing was such . . . a fantastic romance. The embodiment of all my dreams, really, just the wildness of it all.

Tell me about the blues scene in London.

I was a student in Kingston, which is just on the outskirts of London, so I would go into London and bum around a lot when I was in my late teens. There was Alexis Korner and Cyril Davies and, of course, later the Stones. I found it very, very exciting. Except that Alexis was a little jazz-orientated, he was into a Cannonball Adderley kind of thing now and then instrumentally, and he wasn't a great singer, but he would do great material. You see, the thing to me, it was like the simplicity of the blues was almost impossible for anyone to master. So they would — even if they were playing a blues, they would lean towards the jazz side of things to give it some respectability. The only person on the scene then who was playing blues fairly straight, and even then with a little jazz, was John Mayall. Which is what attracted me to John, you know. He was strictly a bluesman.

What about yourself? As you started playing professionally, did you have any doubts about the authenticity of your own playing, about your own ability to play the music?

Not at all. In fact, because of the isolationist point of view of it being in England, I was actually very dogmatic, and I considered myself a kind of bearer of the flame, you know. I was very proud of what I was doing. I didn't have any self-doubts at all.

What about the racial issue?

I . . . I think my ego made me regard it as being all right in my case, but not all right in anybody else's. Do you know what I mean? So that I didn't really like any other white guy's playing. Except for mine. For some reason I believed that I had the kind of hidden key.

And you had no hesitation about playing a song by Otis Rush, say, one of your idols?

No, I would just play it. We [John Mayall's Bluesbreakers] were playing "All Your Love" then. What I was doing, even at that stage, was taking the bare bones of what Otis Rush was doing, or Buddy Guy was doing, or B.B.

Sonny Boy Williamson
in Liverpool, 1962.
*Courtesy of Dave
"Daddy Cool" Booth/
Showtime Archives*

King or Freddie King was doing, and then playing my way. For instance, [my] "Hideaway" isn't anything like Freddie King's version, really. I had the confidence to play my version even then, and when I did, and when I got a reaction, I knew I was doing the right thing.

Was this challenged at all when you were playing with guys like Sonny Boy?

Yeah, of course. I mean, then you had to kind of own up. *Especially* with Sonny Boy. I was with the Yardbirds, and we were becoming more of a pop band at the time that he came along. And you could see that he didn't think much of us at all. He made us very aware of the fact of our shortcomings.

How did you respond to that?

I did my best and tried to play the way that I thought he would like. And he did . . . on certain occasions he did seem to sort of approve. You know, begrudgingly. I found out later that he wasn't really one to give encouragement. He got the best out of you by being pretty aggressive.

Did this at all challenge your romance with the blues?

Not at all. No. Because I considered him to be right. And us wrong. You see, I knew his songs, I had *heard* them, but at that point in time it hadn't occurred to me that to know a song was different to being familiar with it. I thought it would be in a key, and it would have a tempo, I didn't realize that the detail was important. It didn't occur to me that there would be strict adherence to a guitar line, to an intro, to a solo. And that's what I learnt very quickly with him. Because he didn't just want to count it off. That's what really shook me up—because I thought we could get away with just busking it, and he wasn't at all happy with that. I mean, we would rehearse, but still, even then, we were nowhere near getting it right to his satisfaction. And it was a little bit panic-making, but at the end of the day, when we got onstage, it was, like, different. . . . In rehearsals he'd be really mean, and no matter what you did, you could never please him. But onstage, then he would forget, because he was dealing with the audience and he wouldn't be so concerned with what you were playing. . . . Given the situation that I was in—a band of musicians who were less well equipped to deal with it—I felt that it was my responsibility to bridge the gap between him and the band. Because we did tour quite extensively in England. And it had to be dealt with. I was the liaison. And what it did in a way was to strengthen my belief that that's where my root was. Which happened later with Muddy and all the other great bluesmen I played along with. They rekindled the fire.

It was an education in the blues.

Very rapid. The one other time that really shook me up was playing with Howlin' Wolf [on *The London Howlin' Wolf Sessions*, recorded in

Recording with Wolf. *Courtesy of Chess Records*

1970]. But I could see that I was better equipped than anyone else, in that sense again. And it gave me a sense of pride in myself, and in my knowledge of the genre, that I could deal with it better than, say, Ringo, who decided on the first night he was never going back in the studio with anybody *like* Howlin' Wolf. Because Howlin' Wolf, on the first night, he was just so miserable and so scathing to everyone—because we were going to approach it from a fairly ad-lib point of view. His attitude was the same as Sonny Boy's. You know, like: we're going to do "Little Red Rooster," and it goes like THIS. And it doesn't go like anything *you* think it goes like. And he was tough, and very aggressive, and a certain amount of the guys in the studio were just too shook up to come back the next day. And I was pretty shook up, too. It scared me. You see, I was already going along a different path. I was a rock musician. And it's not that I'd left my blues roots behind, it's just that I'd forgotten a lot of the ways things went. And to get it all back in the space of an evening is no easy job. But I spoke to, I can't remember his name now, the producer from Chicago [Norman Dayron], and he said, Well, come back again tomorrow, it'll be all right. And I did and it was better. But Ringo didn't come back. He didn't see the point. It wasn't that much of an issue for him. But I wanted to get it right. I really did. You see, it introduced me to the reality of playing. Because up until then it had always been a bit of a fantasy, you know, listening to the records and harboring a sense of belonging to it. Which no one else could really shake until I met the real guys, and then I felt a bit of a stranger. But it fortified my . . . my urge to get it right. Because I . . . once you got the reward it made you realize that there was something there. That I did have something there. That I could make these guys smile.

Did you have a sense of anything else going on? That there were others like you out there?

I had the first Butterfield album right after it came out. It was just by word of mouth, I can't remember how I found out about it. But I thought it was great. Especially Butterfield's playing. I thought Bloomfield played too much. It wasn't until I met him that I realized that was his character to be that way. He couldn't keep—couldn't hold himself in rein. He was just one of those ebullient characters. But I loved it all the same.

Did you see that as offering you . . .

A chance? Yeah. 'Cause they came to England, and they came looking for John Mayall, and we hung out and played together, and I realized then that if I wanted to go to America and play that it was going to be acceptable.

Did this help resolve the whole issue of actually singing the blues? Because you really hadn't sung much up till then?

Yeah, I thought Butterfield was the first one that I heard who could come anywhere near it. John Hammond I thought too much "characterized" it. It didn't seem like it was coming from him. More that he was . . . imitating. I mean, I wasn't convinced as much as I was with Butterfield. My singing even today doesn't stand up to the test, 'cause I don't — I'm not a singer. I don't consider myself a singer. I still consider myself a guitar player, and I always did.

Was it a huge leap for you to do your first vocal [on the Robert Johnson song "Ramblin' on My Mind"] on that John Mayall album?

Well, I'd been singing and playing that — in that style — for so long it was really just a question of turning the tape machines on. The leap came in accepting that this thing was going to go on to plastic and would be recorded. Accepting that took a lot of convincing from John, who really kept having to tell me that it was worth it.

You've said that Muddy Waters acted as a kind of mentor to you, that he served almost as a kind of salvation, personally?

When we worked together [on an extensive 1979 tour], yeah, he was doing a lot of character building for me. 'Cause I was losing my identity at the time. I didn't know where I was going. I'd been lured . . . I lured myself off the path of being a blues player and was trying to . . . I even got into country music. I was very heavily influenced by J. J. Cale in those days and wanted to find a different way to play. We talked about that a lot, and Muddy would say, in a very simple way he'd say, "Well, I love listening to your band, but my favorite song you do is 'Worried Life Blues.' That's really where you're at, and you should realize that. You should realize it and be proud of it." And he helped to instill that feeling in me again. Because at the end of the day I got something out of his company, and his music, that

Eric, with Muddy
Waters at home,
ca. 1980. *Photograph
by Kirk West*

I could get from no one else. And it was only by getting back with Muddy, and then occasionally seeing Buddy Guy and people like that, that knocked on the door again. The knock that reminded me where I was really from.

Did you ever talk with Muddy about Robert Johnson?

A couple of times. When we were touring together. But I didn't . . . it was not something I cared to go into too much. Because I always felt with Muddy that to talk about other musicians that had influenced him was stepping outside of what I was, I felt like I was becoming someone else . . . becoming a scholar or a journalist even, to take on that role. And so, I would almost talk about Robert Johnson as if . . . I'd known him, so it was a shared experience. You know what I mean? And he would say, you know, he would say whatever he was going to say. I mean, I think he was under pressure a lot. I think when he was touring in the later years of his life, it took a great deal of generosity of spirit for him to accept the way things were. I mean, he still excelled, and he was very generous about everyone but, you know, without wanting to give too much away.

But you obviously felt as if you got past the barriers? He accepted you.

Yeah, I think he let me in. I think the only thing that would ever keep me from feeling like I was a member of his family was just being . . . that original thing of him being a fantasy at first. And it was very hard for me to get over that, there was a lot of reticence to get over. Because it's almost more comfortable to keep your heroes at a distance in a way and preserve your fantasy about them than to get to know the real person. I was almost forced into getting to know him. You know, we went to parties at his house and barbecues, and he'd be riding around on his tricycle, and it was like this blues singer is behaving like a clown. Really a jolly guy. And it kind of clashed and jarred with all the kind of moody, soulful person. He was just a regular guy at home. With an eye for the women and everything else.

What about Buddy Guy? He was another one of your heroes. Do you ever feel any self-consciousness playing with him today?

No, I feel I've established enough of a repertoire, or a playing style of my own, that I don't need to mimic him. I mean, there's no way you can go along with what he's doing, 'cause you don't know what he's going to come up with. You just let it be and play the way you play. And he wouldn't have it any other way himself.

You've said you were drawn to his playing because he plays so close to the edge. It's always struck me that your playing seems more deliberate, more controlled . . .

Much more civilized.

Does he ever pull you over the edge?

He can do, yeah. He will . . . yeah, he *can* do. He'll put you on the spot, too. There was one night I was playing at [Buddy Guy's club in Chicago] the Checkerboard, and we'd done a gig out of town. We flew in and drove down there, and it was about twelve o'clock at night and Buddy was playing, and we told him we were coming. And we got up and started to play. It was just me, I think. I had my band in the audience, and I'm playing away, and at some point someone walked up to the front of the stage and got Buddy's attention and whispered in his ear, and he just said, "Carry on," and left the stage. And I had to kind of lead the band for another ten or fifteen minutes, just playing instrumentally. I didn't know what the hell was going on, and the next thing I knew, the police broke in. That was what the guy had whispered to Buddy, that it was going to be raided. And Buddy just shot off out of the place. And the lights went up, and the cops came in, and we were all lined up, and they wanted to see everyone's ID. And that was it. We were left holding the baby. *That's* over the edge.

One thing I wondered about. If Muddy says "Worried Life Blues" is really you, the soul of Eric Clapton, and in a way you agree, why not just do a blues tour? I don't mean for the rest of your life necessarily . . .

I'm still working my way around to it. I've made this concession. I'm doing some shows at the Albert Hall in January, and I've broken it up into four parts. I'm going to do two sets of what I would regard as my standard material. Which is rock 'n' roll verging on blues with a bit of pop. And that will be one set with a ten-piece band, one set with a quartet. And then there'll be three nights with an orchestra, where I've commissioned Mike Kamen to write a concerto for the guitar, and three nights with a blues band—and that will be [Chuck Berry pianist] Johnnie Johnson on piano, myself, Buddy Guy, Robert Cray, and Buddy Guy's bass player and Jamie Oldaker, who used to be with me years ago, as the drummer, and maybe a harp player. I'm just taking it bit by bit. And the next album will be a blues album, which we've already kind of started making plans for.

And so a lot of that is political. I still have to make records, I feel, for a record-buying public who have got used to the kind of things that I've done in the past, like "Layla," or "Cocaine," or "I Shot the Sheriff," and that they need to hear . . . And I understand that, and I *like* playing that kind of stuff. And I don't think . . . I don't know if I can be honest and play straight blues all the time. I'm too fragmented now. I've had too many other likes in other areas, you know what I mean, that I'm not ashamed of, that I really do like. I like playing rock 'n' roll. Sometimes I like playing country. Sometimes I like playing reggae. But when it comes down to fundamental lead playing, I still play the way I always did. In that scale, with that emotional content.

Is there any conflict between the satisfaction you can get from playing in private, for yourself, and actually playing out in public?

I never play alone. I very rarely play alone at home, or in a hotel room, or anywhere. I very rarely travel with a guitar. I tend to keep all of that bottled up, until there's an audience to play to. I think music is a shared experience. . . . It's like it gains value according to the certain circumstances.

With a mass audience, though, can you really expose your innermost musical feelings?

Yeah, I think you get a true . . . you do get a true picture. It's not necessarily what the whole audience is feeling, but for a fact there's a core of them out there that will recognize true emotion, will recognize the reality of honesty, of honest music when it's being played. You will always get reaction from that. If it touches them deep down, they can't help but react. On top of what I was saying about the music having a value when it's shared, I mean also with the musicians in the band, because before you're playing to the audience, you're playing for them. Which is something I should have pointed out, I guess. If you do your best to play with musicians of the highest caliber, spiritually and musically, then you're really putting yourself up against it every night. You know, you're taking a framework and trying to reinvent it every time. You've got to come up with the goods, 'cause otherwise they're let down. And then the audience comes after.

How much freedom is there in that? Can you surprise the band the way Buddy Guy surprised you?

Yeah, yeah. I wouldn't necessarily do it quite so much. I wouldn't be very popular — because in this day and age, technologically the way it is, a lot of the stuff is preprogrammed. For instance, the keyboard player has got a — you know, in between each number he's got to punch a lot of buttons to get the sound that he wants for the song that is coming next. And if I turn around and say, We're not going to do that one, we're going to do this, he is fucked. And that's not a pleasant prospect for a synthesizer player. It's not. And I understand that, so it's not really . . . it doesn't really benefit anyone to play the fool, which is what I consider that. It's all well and good to have freedom up to a point, but then to abuse that, which is what it would be, is going to make things difficult for everyone else. I mean, it would be great in a way for me to be that free, but also, you know,

I'm stepping on other people's toes. If I'm hiring a band, I want to make them happy. I want them to be happy doing what they're doing. I don't want it to be difficult for them.

You sound, from the way you talk about this band, as if there's a real feeling of closeness, almost kinship, there. But you've said in the past that, after Cream, you had a fear of opening yourself up, of exposing your own vulnerability in this way. . . .

I can retract that now. I've found a few friends that I play with that have transcended that, and I can allow myself to put myself in a trusting position again with the musicians I have now. Those guys up there are my best friends, really. I spend more time with them than anyone else. When I'm at home, I very rarely communicate with other people. I'm a bit of a loner. So my social life really is the road.

But wouldn't that connection primarily be onstage?

No, it's an offstage thing, too. I started using again in about '84, and drinking a lot, and the first people to be upset and notice it were my band. They were actually highly instrumental in getting me back to sobriety. If you spoke to the drummer, Steve Ferrone, and Nathan East, they could tell you stories about walking me around Tokyo, trying to get me away from my hotel room to keep me sober for the gig that night. They realized and I realized, it was because they loved me, too. It wasn't just the gig they were worried about, it was me as a human being. And that's when I started to put my trust and faith back into the people I was playing with. And when they found that, too, it all came around. That I got sober again because I loved them and respected them. That's where all the transactions begin. And that shines through on stage, the trust. It's very deep now.

One of the things that's struck me as unusual about your career is the extent to which you've continued to set up others as role models, as heroes, really, even after achieving great success. And then inevitably have been disillusioned at some point down the line perhaps only by your own expectations. It's almost as if you mistrusted yourself, or your own success. . . .

I've suffered a lot from that. Because of the identity crisis of having to like what you do as much as what you've liked in other people, your role models or your heroes, having to put it, you know, in the marketplace alongside what they've done. One of the things I remember Tom Dowd or Ahmet Ertegun, I think, saying to me: don't forget, when you sell a record, you're selling alongside Frank Sinatra and B.B. King and Quincy Jones, people of that stature. And you've got to think of yourself as one of them. And when you do, when you can make that comparison and be comfortable with it, you'll have got somewhere. That's the way I'm starting to think. It's taken me a long time. I'm a slow learner, and a very slow developer. And no doubt drink and drugs were instrumental in keeping me from that growth. But it's taking place now. Maybe too late — not *too* late, I don't think. But late for sure. But I've come to terms with my identity a lot better.

Along those lines, not too long ago you were talking about the songwriter Jerry Williams, whose songs you've recorded extensively in recent years, and you said here was someone whose demos were better than the finished product. Other times you've spoken about your own desire to drop the whole facade not just of stardom but of "produced" music, go back to the basics. Well, why not just drop the facade? Why not put out demos, or a less finished product, if that's what you're drawn to?

Well, in respect to what I do, because I don't make demos ... And I still think it's important for the records to be as good as you can make them. You know? When I've written songs and made them into demos — for instance, on the *August* album I had one demo which we did clean up and polish a lot. Which I could never play in concert because it never reached the level of the demo. And another one that's called "Tearing Us Apart," which I do do in concert and which is exactly the same as the demo. It varies according to how much of myself has come through. "Tearing Us Apart" — that is purely me. There's no facade in that. But I don't write that much to really qualify me being that upfront about it. So when, for instance, in Jerry Williams' case, what I tend to think is that his material is so malleable, it's so easily adjusted, that I can put myself into that and be really me, singing his words with his chord changes. You know, I don't feel that I'm hiding behind him in any way. It's just that certain songs that he writes are the kind of things that I would like to write but I don't get around to.

I guess what I meant was you've always surrounded yourself with all these uncompromising people, from Ben Palmer to Delaney Bramlett or Jerry Williams. . . . It almost seems as if they were idealized images of a submerged self or fears of . . .

That's a very accurate way of putting it. And in a sense, I tend to think — not in a malicious way — that I used those people, you know, to convey what I was feeling without me having to do the legwork. Because of my lack of belief in myself. I think I was aware of it, but my excuse was that I was taking something from them, yes, but what I was giving them was the ability to be known, the possibility for the audience to know them. Because the reason, for instance, why I joined Delaney's band was because I was in total awe of him, and I thought everyone else should see this. I knew that I had the drawing power, even from then. I could make the public aware of them just by putting my name on the bill. And I still use that a lot.

So it's a kind of insecurity on top of . . .

I think it's a combination of things that have gone back to when I was first adulated, where I was put in a position of pressure that whatever I would write or play wouldn't be as good as I would like it to be. That has been something I've had to bear with over all these years. Something that has taken a long time to come to terms with. To the point now, to give you an example, I walked onstage with Elton John on Saturday night without one reservation. Now, two years ago, or even a year ago, it would have been a lot harder to deal with. And I would have said yes at the outset, and then sat in the audience and just thought about that moment when I was going to have to walk onstage. Now I sat and enjoyed the show, and at the time when I was supposed to get up, someone came and told me, and I walked up and played, and it was just like water off of a duck's back. I really enjoyed it, and I had no idea what I was going to play, I just knew I was going to be me. And whatever came out would be me. Didn't know the song. Didn't know the changes. But felt no fear whatsoever. And that to me is a miracle. I've got to that point now, and it can only get better — I hope. I read in Laurence Olivier's autobiography where he got stage fright at the age of fifty-seven. And for a year suffered from the fact that he couldn't remember lines. Every night. So that can always happen. But at this moment in time I'm pretty comfortable with what I can do. I know my limitations, really. And try to push them—but I stay within them, too.

Do you have any sense of where the blues is going from here?

Outside of Robert Cray [with whom he had recently, and very happily, worked], no, I don't. I'm not really aware of what is happening. Stevie Ray [Vaughan] is doing as much, if not more, than Robert to play on that threshold . . . the passion threshold . . . of the blues. I tend to think that it's a dying art, that there are just a handful of people left who are interested or are playing it. And I don't know what will happen to it after we're gone. I have no idea. But I think we're all doing our bit. We're all pulling it as much as we can. I mean, you can't force it down people's throats, you've just kind of got to keep slipping it in there. That's what I try to do, is to lean that way every now and then. A lot of people have said to me that their favorite track on this new album of mine is [Ray Charles'] "Hard Times." That really shook me, because I didn't think they would like that. I thought that was almost too, kind of, ancient in a way, in its approach, for anyone to like it. But there are people out there that want that. And that's very encouraging for me to know that I can make an album in six months' time, or maybe more, that will be composed of entirely that kind of thing.

Well, that brings us back, in a way, to your interpretation, the way you've always approached what could be regarded as classic blues.

The way that I've always looked upon any interpretation of a great blues musician's material was to take the most obvious things and simplify them. Like my way of doing "Crossroads" was to take that one musical figure and make that the point, the focal point. Just really trying to focus in on what the essence of the song was. I mean, keeping it simple.

You mean you simplify to reach a broader audience?

No, no, just to make it . . . playable for me. I am very limited in my technique, really, so what matters in my playing is the simplicity of it and that it gets to the point. Rather than playing around everything.

But very few of the bluesmen are virtuosos, really, in their playing.

No, nor am I. That's how I identified with them. It's not what is said but how it's said. Not how much is said, but the way it's said. And that's what I would try to draw out of anything that was a great influence on me, trying to draw out of Robert Johnson what was the spirit of what was being said as much as the way, or the form, or the technique.

Where would you draw that spirit from?

From what I heard.

Somewhere I read that when you started out you tried to envision the car the person was driving, the smell of the car, the specific locale or milieu . . .

Yeah, the outward sensations that would echo what was going on inside.

Was it almost like method acting in a way? Was it a specific discipline you put yourself through to try to get to the core of the thing?

Yeah, it would be. It would be a discipline that you would introduce . . . to make that possible. On the surface of things, it was . . . the *sound* of the music kind of overwhelms you, you know. And then all these pictures come into your head. And then when you want to — I mean, if I want to put myself into this frame of mind now . . . say if I've got a gig tonight with Buddy, I've really got to kind of call up all of this stuff that's inside that goes right back to when, like you said, you first heard Robert Johnson, or when I first heard Little Walter live. They're all in there. All of this stuff is inside me, it's just a matter of tapping it.

Do you tap on your own reserve of emotional experience, memories of your grandparents, your mother . . .

That's all I've got to refer to. That's all I've got to refer to. It isn't labeled. It's a bag of emotions that have been untapped by — I mean, even when I was in psychotherapy for a while, I would reserve . . . Even in deep psychotherapy there was a certain place that no one . . . that I wouldn't let him go. Because that is meant to be used for my music.

That's what maintains its spontaneity? You mean, otherwise it would become formulaic for you?

Yeah, I think so. It's always fresh. And that kind of like leads me to a troubled life, in a way. My personal life really suffers from that. Suffers from a lot of . . . kind of inability to deal with relationships, things like that. Because, you know, I keep a lot of this stuff inside.

It disallows total unburdening?

Total intimacy with other people. Yeah.

Do you think this is true for all artists?

I think so. To a greater or lesser degree. There's a place that — no, you won't let anyone else go. . . . Because [you] are dreadfully ashamed, or dreadfully scared. I don't think it's a question of being frightened of losing your creativity or anything like that. It's deeper than that.

You've often said that the best of Buddy Guy has never gotten onto record, that the spirit of the music, the almost total abandon of his blues, isn't really transferable to record. Do you feel that's true of your own music as well?

To a certain extent, yes. I think . . . I still think my best playing exists separately from the songs. It's just something that is of its own. To get that onto a record is difficult because you kind of become much more studied.

Have you ever thought of taking a mobile recording unit and attempting to capture moments like those?

No, because I kind of like it the way it is. You know, there's something very true, in a way, that some music belongs to the concert hall and the audience and should remain that way. And for the gods.

In making the blues album, do you think you'll try to maintain a greater degree of spontaneity, go for more of a live feel, I mean?

No, because it would be a deliberate project. The spontaneity would come in the singing and the guitar passages. They would be allowed to be free. But then I'd still get into the thing of which take is better. So there you've got deliberation straightaway. It [can't be] carefree. Otherwise you take the first take, and what if it's not as good as you want it to be? Then you've got to do it again. So that's the studio for you. You have the time and the wherewithal to be deliberate.

Recently there's been talk of all kinds of musical reunions. With all the other reunions that have taken place this year, would you ever think of doing something like that?

No, I don't think so. My time schedule won't allow it. Because I've strictly allowed myself — I do that kind of thing by the bucketload, usually. But I'm promoting my new album as much as I can, and I'm very loath to cut into that. I've got to look after this project of mine first and foremost. From now until December I'll be promoting the album. Then I go into rehearsals for the Albert Hall, then I go to Europe and America. The blues album will be either the end of next year, or the beginning of the year after.

That's pretty long-range planning.

We have to, yeah.

Did you ever think about just running away? Leaving it all behind?

No, no. . . . where would I go? I mean, this is my life. I like it.

TWENTY-FIVE

Malaco Records: Life on the Edge of Town

KODACHROME

THE PICTURE is faintly nostalgic by now, grown familiar from semi-parodic repetition. It shows some white boys in formal dress with their dates. From their haircuts you can tell it is the late '50s or early '60s, before the Beatles discovered America. It is no earlier, though, because at the center of the picture is a group of black men, only slightly older than the couples, equally formally dressed but clearly entertainers. Everyone is looking pleased with themselves, the entertainers' grins no more fixed or formal than their hosts'. Fictionally the photograph might just as well be a still from the movie *Animal House,* with Otis Day and the Knights the featured attraction. In reality the year is 1963, the place is the Pi Kappa Alpha fraternity house at Ole Miss just after the riots that attended the admission of James Meredith, the university's first Negro student; the fraternity brothers include Tommy Couch, slight and bespectacled, from Tuscumbia, Alabama (Tuscumbia is one of the communities that make up the quad-city area of Muscle Shoals), and a muscular-looking blond young man from Columbia, Mississippi, named Gerald "Wolf" Stephenson. Both are wearing white tuxedos and squiring pretty, elaborately begowned girls they have already pinned and will soon marry; they are both pharmacology majors and evidently the best of friends. The group is Professor James Richards and the Esquire Combo, from Tommy Couch's hometown. They are getting $175 for the evening, and one of their interchangeable lead singers is Percy Sledge....

*   *   *

THE RHYTHM & THE BLUES, 1983

IN THE LAST COUPLE OF YEARS, a strange phenomenon has been taking place in the pop marketplace, or rather taking place all over again: rhythm and blues — what has been proclaimed as "bump and grind and get on down" kind of music in one recent song; "roots" music; soul music that focuses on feeling and not necessarily production values — has been gaining in popularity by leaps and bounds almost twenty years after its first incarnation. There are many explanations for this phenomenon (disco is too mechanical, rap too aggressive, there has always been a black adult audience out there who never deserted the music but were themselves abandoned by the tastemakers), and the aesthetic basis for the revival could be debated, but there is no argument over the album or the record company that spearheaded the revolution. *Down Home* was the second album by Z. Z. Hill, a journeyman r&b singer who had been making records for a succession of labels since 1963, to be released on Malaco, a tiny independent out of Jackson, Mississippi, which could best be compared to Z.Z. himself for its solid record of out-of-the-way commercial success without any special distinction. Hill's first album on Malaco, titled simply *Z. Z. Hill* and focusing primarily on Bobby "Blue" Bland–style blues, had sold about 25,000 copies, decent sales in a market that has traditionally scorned long-playing records and snapped up 45s for quick turnover in mood and trend. *Down Home* entered the black LP charts fairly inauspiciously in January 1982. Ninety-three weeks later it was still on the charts, having reached as high as number nineteen, hovered in the midrange, and in November 1983 settled comfortably at number sixty-six. It has become in the process probably the best-selling (approximately 450,000 units to date) blues album of all time, and although the two singles released off the album sold only moderately well (it was a deliberate decision *not* to release "Down Home Blues" as a single), it very likely represents the most profitable blues session ever for the simple reason that albums afford a margin of profit inconceivable in the marketing of 45s. In the nearly two years that the album has been on the charts similar hits have been scored by such soul artists as Bobby Womack, Tyrone Davis, Johnnie Taylor, and Clarence Carter, names and styles out of the '60s, on labels like Beverly Glen, High Rise, Venture, independents similar to Malaco though without Malaco's staying power. In the wake of the success of *Down Home,* Malaco has itself carefully scouted and signed

Z. Z. Hill. *Courtesy of Malaco Records*

Latimore, Denise LaSalle, and most recently Little Milton, while issuing a third album by Hill in the fall of '82, *The Rhythm & the Blues,* which has joined its predecessor for close to a year on the charts. For the first time in his life Z. Z. Hill is a star, and Malaco is being scrutinized for its secrets. Articles have appeared in the trades hailing the label's "commitment to deep-fried Southern soul and blues," its "refusal to make concessions to current musical trends." But there is no mystery, really. Malaco is just one more, perhaps the last, in a long line of Southern studios which included Stax, Muscle Shoals, and TK in Miami, an old-fashioned "hit factory" built around a solid rhythm section and a stable of songwriters in the Southern pop tradition. What makes Malaco unique is that it is like a dinosaur in the modern age, an artifact in the flesh, the last manifestation of a species that was thought long ago to have become extinct.

CHIMNEYVILLE

To GET TO THE STUDIO which Malaco has occupied for the last seventeen years, you simply turn off I-55 at Jackson, head out Northside Drive, go past the Mississippi Power and Light Company (Rex Brown station), cross the railroad tracks, and find it sitting inconspicuously in the midst of all the other light industry (Faulkner Concrete, tool and die manufacturers) that has sprung up in the Jackson countryside within recent memory. There is no point in asking directions of civic-minded citizens; no one recognizes the name, despite Malaco's newfound popularity and the fact that it has never occupied any other site. Nor has success changed Malaco to any appreciable degree; its exterior is indistinguishable from those of its neighbors, about what you would expect a warehouse for an old bottling plant with a corrugated green metal front to look like. To call the interior pretentious would be flattering. Where Muscle Shoals Sound Studio features a kind of space-age austerity, and Stax at its height had the look of a turn-of-the-century New York bordello, Malaco just looks lived-in, a warren of offices with two twenty-four-track studios (one is primarily for voice-overs), a gold record or two in evidence, and album covers haphazardly hung in plain brown wooden frames in the reception area and down the hall.

President Tommy Couch's desk is piled high with a litter of correspondence and cassettes, all of it relating to the record business with the exception of auction lists for Civil War memorabilia. (Tommy collects letters and envelopes primarily.) The wall behind his desk shows a hunting scene; to the right is a green sofa with ripped upholstery, just in case there is an overflow of visitors. Tommy, who resembles the older brother perhaps or the well-fed uncle of the young man in the 1963 picture, still boyish looking but a little overstuffed since he quit smoking and now scarcely able to turn his head because of a degenerative arthritic condition, is the most easygoing of men, seemingly without secrets or affectations and as pleased as anyone could be that he should be able to make his living from something he still loves. Like everyone else at Malaco, Tommy Couch plays several roles: secretaries sing background; promotion people write songs; gospel singers double as chauffeurs; and Tommy screens material, fields questions, and produces a session, all at the same time. Only Director of Business Affairs Stewart Madison intentionally limits his activities, sitting in a back office figuring the accounts — but even Stewart, who went to school briefly with Tommy and Wolf (Wolf is the muscular young man who looks like a football player in the photograph and is Malaco's chief engineer today), dates his love of music to hanging around Stan's Record Shop and listening to Professor Bop spin the rhythm and blues hits on the radio in Shreveport, where he grew up. All three seem more than a little bemused that they are doing something, that they are actually leading a life they could once have scarcely dreamt of for themselves.

Malaco began in real life in 1962 on the campus of the University of Mississippi when Tommy Couch, the self-deprecatingly ambitious social chairman of Pi Kappa Alpha, started booking bands from his hometown for fraternity dances. Most of the bands were well known in the Muscle Shoals area, at a time when Muscle Shoals was just beginning to get its start as a recording center, with Rick Hall's FAME Studio leading the way. The groups included the Mark V's, Fame's original rhythm section, augmented by legendary singer-songwriter Dan Penn; the Del Rays, who made up most of Rick Hall's second rhythm section and included Tommy's boyhood friend, guitarist Jimmy Johnson; the Mystics, who came up behind the other two bands and included future Muscle Shoals Sound Studio bassist David Hood and Wishbone Studio founder Terry Woodford; and Hollis Dixon, Muscle Shoals' rock 'n' roll patriarch, who included elements from each of the above as well as songwriter Donnie Fritts on drums. All of these bands were white, and they all played rhythm and blues ("When I wasn't Ray Charles or James Brown, I was Bobby 'Blue' Penn," says Dan Penn, the chief evangelist for the style, with wry amusement today), so it was perhaps not such a leap when Couch began booking some black bands on campus.

These were the days of the Red Tops, the Counts, the Dynamics out of Charlotte, North Carolina, Doug Clark and the Hot Nuts (who were said to get naked on stage), and a slew of classic New Orleans acts, and though one could scarcely point to rhythm and blues as a trendsetter in integration, many of the r&b singers remember the college fraternities, and Ole Miss in particular, with special affection. "Those college audiences were the greatest audiences in the world," recalls Rufus Thomas, whose "Walkin' the Dog" would become a Top 10 r&b and pop hit in 1963 and a featured track on the Rolling Stones' first album the following year. "At Old Miss they'd send the girls home at twelve o'clock, and we'd tell nasty jokes and all that stuff. Used to have some good times down there in Oxford." Tommy and his roommate-partner Bob Hamill brought blues singer Fred McDowell in from Como, Mississippi, where he was working at the Stuckey's gas station, to play tea dances after the football game. They brought in the Esquires just three years before Percy Sledge hit with his epochal soul smash, "When a Man Loves a Woman," and might not

Tommy, Jimmy Johnson, Herman's Hermits lead singer Peter Noone, Mitch Malouf, and Wolf Stephenson, 1966. *Courtesy of Malaco Records*

have remembered Percy at all if he had not hovered on the edge of the stage all night, even when he was not singing, because he was so fascinated with the fraternity boys' carrying on. "They getting ready to do that mop dance again," Percy explained when asked why he didn't take a break. The "mop dance" turned out to be the dance everyone else called "the alligator," when every couple got down on the floor and flailed around. "They ain't doing no alligator," Percy insisted with some bemusement. "Those people are doing the mop dance. They busy just mopping up the floor."

Sophomore year Tommy started booking bands off campus as well as on, getting groups for neighboring colleges and pretty much covering the area. He did this with his roommate under the banner of Campus Attractions, and with Jimmy Johnson co-promoted a Del Rays' dance at the King

Edward Hotel in Jackson on a Saturday night after the state high school all-star football game. "We made $2,000 apiece, I think; I didn't know there was more money than that in the world." Senior year he got married but kept booking the Pike fraternity through its new social chairman, Wolf Stephenson, while all business for Campus Attractions was conducted out of his tiny married apartment, "with calls coming in at all hours day and night." When Tommy graduated in '65 he moved to Jackson, where his wife Mayme's mother lived, and went to work in a pharmacy. This might have been the end of his life in music, except that he formed a partnership with his brother-in-law, Mitchell Malouf, who was an accountant, to carry on the booking business under the name of Malaco Attractions, a combination of both their names that his mother-in-law suggested. In 1965, 1966, and 1967 he and Malouf brought Herman's Hermits, the Who, the Dave Clark Five, and the Blues Magoos to Jackson's 10,000-seat coliseum, and Tommy quit the pharmaceutical business and even purchased a franchise from the *Hullabaloo* TV show for a teenage nightclub, which prospered for two years. "All right. Now we had a club and a booking agency going. The next thing, I thought we ought to have a studio. So we opened a four-track right here where we are now, used to be a warehouse for Pepsi-Cola. We didn't know *what* we were doing."

Malaco in fact had only two entrées into the larger world of show business. One was the burgeoning Muscle Shoals musical scene, which in the years 1965 to 1968 was becoming the hottest spot in the country to record soul music. The other source for his education was local entrepreneur Johnny Vincent, a legendary figure in the record business, then in his early forties but already finished as a commercial producer. Malaco rented its first office space from Johnny, who had put most of his music business earnings into real estate, and it was through him that they located their studio. Like many another provincial prophet, Vincent is the kind of person you can like or loathe, but dismiss him, Tommy says laughingly, at your peril. He recorded Guitar Slim for Specialty in 1953 with Ray Charles on piano, produced Huey "Piano" Smith, Frankie Ford, Earl King, and Jimmy Clanton for his own company, Ace, in the mid- to late '50s, and he can spin tales of the old days or plans for the future with equal conviction and logorrhea. When Tommy met him in 1965, many saw him as a washed-up failure, but Tommy saw a charismatic figure from whom he could learn not just business but character. More than his brother-in-law, more than the booking agency or even the artists, Vincent, I think, symbolized to Tommy Couch the limitless vistas of the imagination, the lonely strength that could grow out of a vision, the opportunity for heroics—all this to a man who had never previously imagined such possibilities for himself. "Johnny is the greatest salesman I ever met," Tommy says of his mentor. And I would suspect what he sold Tommy on most of all was himself.

In any case I don't think it would be any exaggeration to say that Tommy and his brother-in-law would have been at a complete loss if it hadn't been for the help of their friends. "They didn't have the slightest idea what to do," says someone who arrived when the four-track Scully board and twin Ampex mixers were still in their crates. "They didn't even know how to plug in the equipment." It's all true, Tommy genially concedes. They didn't even trust the first session they did for their newfound production company to their own studio but instead took the three groups they had been rehearsing to Muscle Shoals, where Jimmy Johnson engineered. Thrilled just to have made a record, they had the tape mastered in Memphis and took the master direct to Buster Williams' Plastic Products in Coldwater, Mississippi, so they could get it pressed and on the street by the next day. "There was always a certain amount of urgency anytime you came out with a record," says Tommy wryly. "I never knew why, but it had to be quick—you know, drive all night to do something and then the record sells three."

The early ventures were similar to vanity publications. Tommy hooked up with Meridian songwriters Paul Davis and George Soulé, white r&b enthusiasts with backgrounds similar to his own, and together they cut a record on a black singer named Eddie Houston from Meridian (he worked in the foundry that Soulé's family owned), which they leased to Capitol. The Capitol contact led to a 1969 album with Fred McDowell ("Some guy recorded a blues album here, and we said we can do better"), who brought harmonica player Johnny Woods with him for one of the sessions. "It must have been the first time Johnny had been out of that section of the country in years, because I never will forget, when they got here, Fred told him, 'Okay, Johnny, I told you. See, boy, you in Jackson now.' Like it was some big deal or something." McDowell's first, and only, major-label album, *I Do Not Play No Rock 'n' Roll*, won a good deal of attention while at the same time earning the fledgling producers their share of criticism (with Jerry Puckett playing electric bass and James Stroud on drums it came a little too close to rock 'n' roll, a number of purists objected)—but evi-

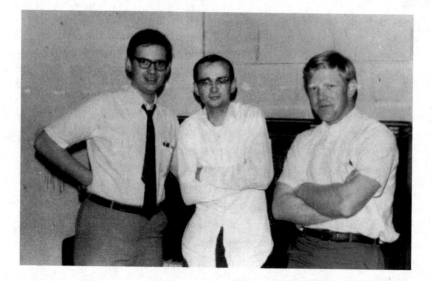

Tommy, songwriter George Soulé, Wolf Stephenson, ca. 1967. *Courtesy of Malaco Records*

dently they didn't cut themselves much of a deal with Capitol, as they barely earned back the $325 they had paid McDowell.

Most of their studio income at this point derived in fact from jingles and custom work, and even that barely supported the rhythm section they had put together in emulation of Stax and Muscle Shoals, "because we thought that was what you were supposed to do. They wound up doing more playing and socializing than they did recording, but that was all right, too." Tim Whitsett, formerly of the Imperials (one of Malaco Attractions' steadiest draws), contributed to the Malaco coffers by renting office space for his own little production and publishing company. Wolf Stephenson had by this time graduated and had been working as a pharmacist in Jackson for the past three years ("I didn't know what I wanted to do when I got out of school. I had a bunch of friends studying pharmacy, and it was good pay on graduation for back then—$650 a month"), but he came out to the studio whenever he could with nothing but his enthusiasm, his proven friendship, and mechanical aptitude to recommend him. Although he was as lacking in practical experience as Tommy and Mitchell, Wolf had always been handy, so gradually he took over many of the engineering chores, leaving record promotion to Tommy and Mitchell (by this time they had virtually given up their concert promotion, taking one last ill-advised fling in 1969 with an Ike and Tina Turner Revue show that lost $5,000), with record production covered by Tommy and lead guitarist Jerry Puckett. The Malaco name was getting around, the sound was becoming more professional, but it wasn't until 1970, after being in business for five years, that they saw any real success.

It came in unlikely fashion. A proteanly gifted New Orleans producer named Wardell Quezergue, who had written, arranged, and produced some of New Orleans' greatest hits and played trumpet in the original Fats Domino band (he would become known for good reason as "the Creole Beethoven"), found his way to the studio with an act called the Unemployed, whom he recorded doing a song called "Funky Thing (Parts I and II)." And then, right out of the box, he licensed it to Jerry Wexler, who had made so many of the Atlantic records on which Tommy and Wolf had grown up. "Now, this was amazing," says Tommy about the much-coveted Atlantic connection. "We made a record, and they just picked it up. We were extremely impressed."

So was Wardell, evidently, who, having suffered business losses in New Orleans that he couldn't immediately repay, saw in the Malaco setup something that could be beneficial for both parties. "It worked to both our advantages," he told Stax historian Rob Bowman. "We had the songs and the artists and they had the studio." So, six months later, he was back with musical arrangements for a number of acts that he and his partner, a tough New Orleans longshoreman named Elijah Walker, had signed. He came in with the arrangements, says Tommy, "and we spent about a week [with just the rhythm section] cutting tracks."

A week or two later, he returned with all of his artists, fully rehearsed. That was just the way Wardell produced, one of those artists told Rob Bowman. Long before he allowed you to enter the studio, he made sure not only that you knew the lyrics, but that "your timing [was down], you were pronouncing your words correctly, and your expression and acting of the song was done properly."

"They came up from New Orleans on a Saturday in an old school bus," Tommy recalls, "and we cut all the vocals in one day. Elijah Walker got credit as executive producer, but he wasn't even there. Wardell did the whole production, did the arrangements, played keyboards, everything, and the next week we mixed the session. I did the mix because Wolf was still working in the drugstore. The artists were Bonnie and Sheila, the Barons, Jean Knight, and King Floyd."

The only problem was, this time there was no interest from Jerry Wex-

Elijah Walker and King Floyd with Jerry Wexler and Wardell Quezergue (King Floyd's fiancée, Patricia Hubbard, is in background). *Courtesy of Malaco Records*

ler, and Tommy had taken on the risk (and the potential reward) of finding a label to license the records before they ran out of money. The first company Tommy approached, really the only one he could think of, was Stax, who, by virtue of their status as the leading independent r&b label in the country, really knew how to get records out to distributors and DJs. Tim Whitsett, until recently a Malaco tenant, had just been named the head of Stax publishing and set up an appointment for Tommy, Mitchell Malouf, and Jerry Puckett to play their new masters for a&r director Don Davis, who, in Tommy's recollection, was "very nice" — but turned them down flat. "We were crushed. The only other guy I really knew in the business," says Tommy, able to make light of it now, but at the time as close to a sense of utter defeat as I think Tommy Couch could ever be, "was Shelby Singleton, in Nashville, and I called him from the gas station across the street, but he was out of town."

It wasn't until they got back to Jackson, and a local DJ named Joe Lewis, who would later go to work for Malaco as a promo man, suggested they put out a King Floyd single themselves, that the idea of an independent label was born. For this they came up with the name Chimneyville (Chimneyville was what Jackson had been dubbed after General Sherman had reduced most of its homes to chimneys in his famous 1863 campaign to take Vicksburg), and Joe Lewis started playing the record on local station WOKJ, then took it to a DJ convention in Houston, where he plugged it to his fellow soul jocks. No one at Malaco had the slightest doubt what the hit side was. "It was a song called 'What Our Love Needs,'" says Tommy. "No question about it. That shows, really, how sharp we were. One day George Vinnett on WYLD down in New Orleans turned the record over and played the other side. The other side was 'Groove Me.' As soon as he turned it over, we were getting orders for 1,000, 5,000, 10,000 the next day. Pretty soon we couldn't handle it. Just to show you how sharp Atlantic was, they knew almost before we did what was going on. I got a call at my house early one morning, and it was Henry Allen. I knew he worked for Atlantic, but I wanted to talk to Jerry Wexler himself. So when I got to work, Jerry called, and we kind of made a deal. Atlantic moved so fast that by that afternoon they had a guy down to pick up the master. The next week Mitchell and I went to Jerry's home in Miami. He was the kind of guy we were just in awe of. This was in the fall of 1970. By December the record went gold, and they had a little kind of event to celebrate. I think Jerry Puckett and I picked up Jerry Wexler at the airport. On the way in he said he wanted to give us a little advice on how to keep having hits. He said, 'Just whatever you do, stay funky.' I thought, 'That'll be the easiest thing in the world, to stay funky.' In six months we had fifteen strings on every record, Wardell had oboes and flutes — I guess we didn't really follow his advice!"

Nonetheless, for a time Malaco continued to have hits. After the success of King Floyd, Stax picked up Jean Knight's record. "Mr. Big Stuff," a sassy production number with a snappy girl chorus, became a number-one r&b hit (number two pop) in the spring of 1971, going on to sell two million copies. King Floyd continued to sell, too, although Malaco had more and more trouble getting him into the studio. Before long everything else seemed to slow down, including studio bookings, and by 1975 it seemed as if Malaco had played out its ten-year string. Soul music was dead; Stax was on the verge of economic collapse; and the deal with Atlantic — which by now had virtually abandoned most of its black acts—was up. Jerry Puckett, the session guitarist from the start and the rhythm section's musical mainstay, quit because nothing much was happening. ("That was a big blow; I really felt it would be hard to go on without him.") And then on September 1, 1975, Tommy's brother-in-law and original partner, Mitchell Malouf, withdrew from active participation in the company out of what Wolf termed a religious awakening.

"It was a real tough time," says Tommy reflectively. "Our deal with Atlantic was over. Our publishing deal with Southern Music was [just about] finished. I was never that discouraged that I wanted to get out of the music business—but I came close." It was at just about this time that Tommy decided to put out a song by one of his background singers. The song was "Misty Blue," the artist Dorothy Moore.

Dorothy Moore was a native Jacksonian. She had been singing background on Malaco sessions for three years and lately, through Tim Whitsett, had been cutting some demos for Stax's East/Memphis publishing company. Just before Stax went under, she cut a demo on an Eddie Floyd song that Floyd, a successful Stax artist as well as writer, flipped over. Tommy had already cut a session on Dorothy, but it had sat around for five or six months; Eddie Floyd's enthusiasm moved him to finish it. Jimmy Johnson, who was down from Muscle Shoals on a social visit, overdubbed guitar, and Tommy shipped the masters to Henry Stone at TK Records in Miami. Stone, originally Atlantic's Miami distributor, a tough-talking man with connections whose funky label was having phenomenal success with an updated, groove-driven version of the Atlantic and Stax sound, put out one single from the session but passed on "Misty Blue." Tommy still believed in the song, "so I thought, 'We'll just come out with a new label and start it off with "Misty Blue."'" That was how the Malaco label came about, but it was short-lived in its first incarnation. The record shipped around Thanksgiving, was big by Christmas, and TK had it in January. As Tommy explains a little sheepishly, "I didn't think we had an [exclusive] deal, but my lawyer was Henry's lawyer—that was how we met in the first place—and he said, 'Henry thinks he should have the record.' I said, 'Well, I don't know if he should or not.' But I gave it to him anyway." From then on Malaco's (and Chimneyville's) deal with TK *was* an exclusive, and "Misty Blue" sold one and a half million.

That was the way things went, from feast to famine, with every variation in between. In January of 1973 Paul Simon had come down to Jackson on the growing strength of the Malaco name to record some tracks for his album *There Goes Rhymin' Simon*. In 1979 Frederick Knight, who had emigrated from Stax to TK and would soon move from his native Birmingham to Jackson on the basis of his connection with Malaco, produced the novelty disco hit "Ring My Bell" (number one pop and r&b) at the Malaco studio. By 1980 TK was in financial hot water, like Stax before it, leaving Malaco not only on its own but virtually alone in the once-thriving world of independent soul labels, while at the same time, due to the similar collapse of the gospel independents, Malaco's gospel division, which had only been formalized four years earlier, became the third-largest gospel label in the country.

It was during this period that Stewart Madison entered the picture, moving to Jackson from Shreveport and acquiring Mitchell Malouf's share of the company, just in time for a short-lived plunge into disco, even as the label continued to release records by such old faithfuls as Dorothy Moore, Fern Kinney (another local backup singer), and McKinley Mitchell. It was at this time, too, that septuagenarian promotion man Dave Clark, a genuine legend in his and everybody else's time, joined the company upon the collapse of TK, where he had sought refuge after the fall of Stax. This was the climate into which Z. Z. Hill, an unlikely candidate for any kind of high-profile success, arrived, dropping by the studio one fall day in 1980 looking for a label deal. They cut a single on him (#2069 — everybody remembers the number), and it sold about 70,000 copies, so Z.Z. came back seven months later to cut enough sides to make up an album. No one was expecting much. "We didn't know, truthfully," says Stewart Madison, "if these guys could sell albums. They never had."

DOING BUSINESS

THE PRODUCTION BUDGET for a typical Malaco LP comes to something like $10,000 or $15,000, including all prorated in-house costs. To give an idea of just how cheap this is, it would not be uncommon to pay as much for a producer's fee for a pop single with commercial potential. Until recently there was no such thing as a signing bonus, really, or artist's advance against royalties, which meant that royalties began for the artist as soon as production costs were recovered. Production itself is, generally, fairly basic, with a rhythm section no longer resident but still stable and quick to pick up the tunes and come up with a strong, funky arrangement. (Tim Whitsett's brother, Carson, goes back the furthest; he was playing keyboards for the Imperials as a teenager and has been in the studio off and on from the start.) String and horn parts are added afterward, as necessary, but strictly for tonal coloration. The simplicity isn't just economical, it's intentional; having finally learned to keep Jerry Wexler's dictum in mind, Malaco is going after the old-time r&b fan with a vengeance. "I consider what we're doing, we're taking over Bobby 'Blue' Bland's audience," says business manager Stewart Madison. "I say, 'Thank you, Bobby,' every time he does another slick session."

Songs come from all over. Now that Malaco has at last made a name for itself, it can be difficult sometimes to wade through all the material that comes over the transom, not to mention the solicited items from the small stable of proven "down home blues" writers (George Jackson, Jimmi "Count" Hughes, and Frank Johnson among them, with Jackson, the multitalented author of rock star Bob Seger's signature hit "Old Time Rock and Roll" as well as the Osmonds' "One Bad Apple," by far the most successful) who have found in Malaco something of a haven. Tommy Couch sorts through all the demos, driving his partners crazy as he pops even the most hopeless-looking title into the car cassette player on the way to lunch or half listens to familiar-sounding songs in the midst of other conversations. He still retains the genuine astonishment and delight of someone who came into the music business, in Jerry Wexler's felicitous phrase, "on a pass"; neither musician nor studio technician, he is often able by some improbable alchemy to recognize the commercial potential of a song, but probably his greatest talent is his capacity for putting people at ease. This is what production at Malaco comes down to, this is what constitutes the "Malaco Sound," not the technical "sound," which, as Stewart unintentionally suggests, tends to resemble cut-rate Bobby Bland, but the self-belief that Tommy seems able to draw out of everyone and for which he earns co-production credit with Wolf, who engineers all Malaco releases.

Once the record is pressed, it becomes the business of the promotion staff to market it. Basically promotion is the responsibility of Dave Clark, the self-proclaimed "oldest promotion man in the business." Clark, who resembles a wizened, walnut Jiminy Cricket, presents as unlikely a figure as anyone in this unlikely cast of characters, with his penchant for stylish flared pants and three-piece suits, purple knit jackets and red

Dave Clark, ca. 1984. *Courtesy of Malaco Records*

tam-o'-shanters or battered fedoras set at a rakish angle with thin wisps of white hair straggling out. He is, he insists, seventy-five years old, more or less, but he has always looked seventy-five years old, a spry seventy-five, say acquaintances who assumed he was that age when they first met him fifteen or twenty years ago.

He dates his start in the business to 1938, when there was no business and he was hired by Harold Oxley to do advance work for the Jimmie Lunceford Band out of Memphis. Before that he attended Lane College in Jackson, Tennessee, fronted his own band there, and then discovered a very stout, very young local singer named Mabel Smith, who went on the road with Clark's Hoodoo Men before acquiring wider fame some fifteen years later as Big Maybelle. Clark himself personified a unique blend of hard-nosed sophistication and pliant charm ("Stay away from drugs, stay away from whiskey, and surround yourself with plenty of young girls," is his motto) that obviously eased his job as what he calls the first independent black record promotion man. In the '30s he wrote a column for *DownBeat* called "Swing Row Is My Beat," became acquainted with Zora Neale Hurston ("Zora?" He hails the name across the chasm of the years. "Zora was all right. You know, in order to understand black history you've got to be able to understand black fiction"), got to know just about everyone who was anyone in the last hundred years of black entertainment, and somehow developed a manner of speaking in which he almost literally gums the words in a fashion that is certainly inimitable if not incomprehensible. ("Sing?" he responds to a question about his band-leading days. "I can hardly talk.") He prides himself on his steady record of employment. He worked for Duke Records for seventeen years, Stax for four or five, TK for the same, and looked Malaco over carefully, he says, before deciding to cast his lot with them. He has co-writing credits on something like sixty or seventy songs, including B.B King's "Why I Sing the Blues"; he was a strong behind-the-scenes presence in Bobby "Blue" Bland's career; and, while he worked for Duke and Stax, he was in the habit of traveling 100,000 miles a year by car without even carrying an address book, because the names and numbers were all in his head. There are two things on which everyone who knows Dave Clark will agree: whatever his true age, he is unquestionably the oldest record promotion man in the business; and he loves the blues. That is why he knew, when he got to Malaco, he had definitely come home.

"Dave is the kind of guy who'll always have a job," says Tommy Couch admiringly, as taken with Clark, it is obvious, as he is with Johnny Vincent. "If a record's got anything, Dave will get us airplay on it. What he did, really, was to give us credibility." There are roughly nine promotion people working for Malaco today (three or four full-time) with Clark nominally in charge, but as Tommy says straightforwardly, "Dave's a horrible administrator; his strength is on the street." And that is where he has stayed, still covering the territory, driving his latest-model Cadillac with the customized DC decal from Jackson to Memphis, from Memphis to Washington, from Washington to New York, with all the backwater stops in between. It was Dave Clark, everyone concedes, who broke Z. Z. Hill, both by collecting on old—in some cases age-old—favors and because at last he had a good *blues* record to sink his teeth into. "Dave," says Tommy, "just loves to work a blues record. With a funk act like Sho-Nuff or Freedom he doesn't get all that excited, but give him a Z. Z Hill and he'll work that record to death." That is just what he did, and just what he is still doing. I've been out with Dave Clark, and I can attest to his enthusiasm and his persistence. If he is not as young as he once was — and he probably wasn't ever that — he is just as worrisome. So that if some of the younger one-stop operators in Harlem or Fort Apache in the Bronx don't know exactly who he is, they definitely know he is somebody. How could they not when he is introduced by an old colleague at each stop with the ringing declaration: "Gentlemen, let me introduce you to the premier record promotion man in the country, Mr. Dave Clark."

The final problem any small company has to contend with, after first making a record and then selling it, is collecting the money that it is owed. This, you would think, would almost go without saying, and yet more than one small company of Malaco's size and aspirations has been put out of business by a hit. It's an old story: the orders pour in; the pressing plant requires cash; the distributors are customarily extended credit; and the record company is caught in the crunch. Johnny Vincent's active career was ended by a disastrous distribution deal he made with Vee-Jay; even Sam Phillips, whose Sun Records may well have given birth to rock 'n' roll, is said to have gotten out of the business in large part because of the frustrations of trying to collect. For Malaco this is where Stewart Madison comes in. Neither Tommy nor Wolf would be comfortable in this role, but Stewart doesn't mind the hard-guy image at all. For Stewart it is not a matter of hard or soft; it is just a matter of figuring out how to get the money that is due him.

Stewart, whose father and two brothers were lawyers, seems to have taken a while to find himself. He attended several colleges without finishing and only found a place at Ole Miss, briefly, because of the white flight that greeted the arrival of integration. (Tommy says that Wolf remembers the one time he saw Stewart at school, "passed out on the floor of our fraternity — but I don't remember him at all.") After dropping out of Ole Miss, too, he became a municipal bonds salesman in Houston until, in 1970, a studio in which he had an investment in his hometown of Shreveport was about to go under and there was no one else with any interest in trying to salvage it. Sound City Recording, which recorded blues and soul singers like Little Johnny Taylor, Ted Taylor, Eddie Giles, and Tommie Young for the Jewel label throughout the '70s, was his ten-year introduction to the music business, and a return to the kind of music he loved growing up. "I liked Lazy Lester and Little Junior Parker, Solomon Burke and Al 'TNT' Braggs, you know, the *real* r&b. *James Brown Live at the Apollo* was a real fashionable album when we were in college," he says, but his favorite album, like Tommy's and Dan Penn's in Muscle Shoals (this may well have been the most influential record of all time in advancing the crossover appeal of the newly emerging genre of Southern soul), was Bobby "Blue" Bland's *Two Steps from the Blues*. That is the record to which he likes to compare Z. Z. Hill's *Down Home*. "It's kind of a classic, isn't it?" he says with pride. "I think it will really stand the test of time."

At Malaco, Stewart says, "our areas are very separate. I make about 80 percent of the financial decisions. Tommy makes most of the artistic ones. Wolf has complete authority in the studio." The most difficult part of Stewart's job is keeping tabs on the accounts receivable, making sure that distributors get the credit that politeness and custom dictate but not so much that creditor and debtor become in effect partners. Probably as many good record companies have gone under from misgauging that balance as from their susceptibility to profligate spending and profligate ways, but Stewart has a very clear philosophy on both of these fronts, and in other areas as well.

"The greatest comfort a large company has is the ability to make mistakes and absorb them. A small company simply does not have that option. One $100,000 mistake in our lives is pretty serious — especially when we know we could make six or seven albums for that amount of money and probably get a couple of hits out of them, too. That's why sometimes you tend to become a little more conservative when you start to make a little money rather than more aggressive, but you've got to watch out for that, too.

"We don't have any artists that are problems. If you're smart enough, you can choose the type of artist and people that surround you so they're not going to give you any real headaches. It's the same with our session band. These guys have been with us for the last four years, and they're journeymen for our type of music. You can give them the songs, and in ten seconds they've got it. We trust them, they work hard, and we don't have any worries about them. I'd rather have less quality and have a good guy in there, because it's the people problems that are really gonna kill you. If I've convinced my partners of anything, it's that we don't have to put up with that. If an artist ever got to be a real headache, then I would sell him off.

"Money is important up to a point, but I wouldn't get all in a rage about it. With my distributors I have a certain credibility. I don't threaten, but they know I'm gonna follow through. If a guy's not regular with us, I won't allow discounts. Other times I'll try to do something for our regular accounts at the end of the year, give them an additional discount and all they have to do is pay their bills on time. At this point I feel like there's no kind of record we couldn't take on. After all, there's only twenty or twenty-five people you're dealing with in this business. If you have a good product and they keep buying, there's no problem; it's just that at a certain time the guy at my end has to ask the question and say, 'Now it's time for me. You got 2,000 records, and I want to be paid for a certain amount.' And if you're not, what you do is pretty simple. Nothing. You've just got to be sure you cut them off in time. And you've got to be sure they know you mean what you say.

"I wouldn't want to be a big company. We can do five to eight million and still not be a big company. If you get two or three hits all together, the cost factor doesn't go up, but we're not going to release twenty-five albums all at once. We're going to do seven or eight r&b albums in a year, seven or eight gospel, there's a spot for a couple of other records if something comes in that's good. But nothing's going to come in that's so good that it could stop us from doing what we're doing. If it's good, it's gonna be good in six months. Female artists generally don't sell as many as male. Anything under 10,000 sales is disappointing. Anything over 200,000 is pretty surprising. We're not trying to create a new type of music. We're not kids around here anymore. We've all had problems — personally, businesswise, in the record business — but I know one thing: I'm never gonna be poor again."

THE SESSION

THE SESSION THAT I ATTENDED when I was at Malaco in the spring of 1983 was a Latimore session primarily, onto which a G. C. Cameron date was piggybacked, so that two albums could be recorded at the same time. The band, mixed and of varying lengths of stay, had reassembled from scattered bases of operation, including Nashville; McComb, Mississippi; and points south. Keyboard player and arranger Carson Whitsett, of course, went back to the beginning; guitarist Dino Zimmerman, also white, came out of Stewart's old Shreveport studio; while the African American rhythm section, bass player Ray Griffin and drummer James Robertson, have provided the strong Malaco bottom for a number of

Frederick Knight, Bobby "Blue" Bland, and George Jackson, mid '90s. *Courtesy of Malaco Records*

years, and ponytailed black guitarist Vasti Jackson injects a note of contemporary funk.

Songs for the Latimore album have been collected from all over. George Jackson, who recently transferred his publishing from Muscle Shoals Sound to Malaco and gets some of the best cuts on every Malaco album, has sent in several new songs from Memphis. (He is the r&b singer-songwriter who, in addition to his smash pop hits with Bob Seger and the Osmonds, wrote the song that started it all, "Down Home Blues.") Latimore has, disappointingly, failed to come in with any new material but is planning to redo his biggest hit, "Let's Straighten It Out," and Tommy has come up with the idea of his covering the Hall and Oates number "Sara Smile" at the session. In addition, Frederick Knight, impeccably turned out in a purple pin-striped suit and polka-dot tie, and Joe Shamwell, who teaches communications at once-segregated Jackson State (Shamwell, a Washington, D.C., native, co-wrote such Stax standards as "Lovin' on Borrowed Time" and "Got to Make a Comeback"), both show up with material for which they have high hopes. Only Frank Johnson, a thirtyish black songwriter who has been brought in from Muscle Shoals and put up at a local motel, seems out of place in the relaxed, easygoing setting. A shy, high-strung man with jittery eyes and a disconsolate look, Johnson holes up in his motel room with a guitar and a cheap little tape recorder, then comes in to the studio each day with two or three new songs he is ready to try out for Tommy. Sometimes they click and sometimes they don't, but Frank has a good track record as a writer (over the years he has had cuts by Aretha Franklin, Ray Charles, Johnnie Taylor, and the Temptations), and so long as his personal problems don't intrude he would appear to be good insurance for any session.

The Latimore session itself proceeds slowly. There's nothing very glamorous about the process, and no elaborate preparations have been made beforehand. Mostly it's just a matter of hard work and hanging around, trying out the songs to see if they're a good fit and then waiting for the band to put together an arrangement. Latimore, a big genial man of forty-four with a white-flecked beard, steady gaze, and beatific smile, maintains an easy equanimity as he talks with Tommy or Frederick Knight, or listens with amusement as his road manager, Ricco Saunders, bald, fiftyish, with an earring in his left ear and a 1976 championship Los Angeles Angels jacket and cap, reminisces about the glory days at TK, the yachts, the tickets to the Super Bowl and Ali's fights, the sporting life that in the end was TK's undoing. For Latimore the session represents a four-day break in touring; he'll pick up his band somewhere outside Atlanta and hopefully be home within a week or two, to see his daughter and take up the everyday domestic concerns of house payments and IRS worries once again. He tries not to stay out too long at a time anymore ("I feel much better mentally and physically if I don't") but remains unfailingly patient, cooperative, and cheerful throughout the session, whether it appears that anything is really happening or not.

Probably half of any session consists of team boosterism, something like an intentionally induced state of group euphoria. Like baseball players, the musicians talk it up ("All right! Sounds good. That's a killer. It's hot!"), with the playbacks coming at such a deafening volume that the song can scarcely help but sound like a hit. There is no particular aim to a Malaco session, Tommy Couch is quick to explain, except to produce eight or ten good cuts. "Personally what I like to do is an album of ten singles. I don't really go for concepts. Maybe I'm just not smart enough." They work hard and get four or five tracks on the first day of this session, but there is nothing very inspired. They are working on "Take Me Down," an out-of-left-field selection by the country group Alabama, when Dave Clark comes in on the second day from an all-night party for the Bar-Kays in Memphis. Dave sits around for a while fiddling impatiently, wanders in and out, makes a few dispirited comments, then declares to no one in particular, "This session just about to disgust me. It beginning to sound like the hero gonna come riding in here on his horse in one of them Western pictures. They forgetting that they got a black blues singer here!" What the session needs, Dave declares, is a *blues,* and the blues he's got in mind just happens to be one he co-wrote for Bobby "Blue" Bland some years ago. How's it go? someone wonders. Dave jumps up as if no one would ever ask and goes off to find a copy of the record, which will eventually be recorded though it does not find its way onto the album.

Latimore for his part retains an unforced enthusiasm, a stoical willingness to do whatever is asked of him; he is just the kind of hard worker Malaco is always looking for. His first album for Malaco, *Singing in the Key of Love,* a nice collection of mostly blues-flavored originals that seems to lack a little of the spark of his TK work, has sold about 30,000 copies, and if this one sells more he should have a good future with the company. He was born Benjamin ("Benny") Latimore in 1939 in Charleston, Tennessee, near Chattanooga, was the first in his family to go to college but dropped out of Tennessee A&I after two years, in 1962, to go on the road with Joe Henderson ("Snap Your Fingers") as a keyboard player. He ended up in Miami some three years later and started making records for TK in 1973 that showcased an unlikely combination of contemporary soulfulness, down-home blues feel, and lead melodica playing. He had a number-one r&b hit with his own self-written "Let's Straighten It Out" in 1974, but since TK's demise has fallen upon hard times professionally and seems at a crossroads in his career. A student of Kahlil Gibran's *The Prophet,* he appears to take it all in stride, confessing that he has been going through a creative dry spell lately but that "you can't force your writing. For the past year I haven't been at my most prolific, but it will come back. I tend to get a little philosophical sometimes, and people take it as if I'm trying to preach to them, so then I have to back off and take it a little lighter. In life you have to have a marriage of the commercial and the artistic." He excuses himself to go out and put down a reference vocal, hoarsely singing from a little isolation booth bathed in yellow and red lights, while the band members are separated from each other by baffles. "It could get a little nastier," Tommy Couch remarks mildly as he wanders into the control booth. Vasti Jackson throws out a lick that he says "will put a little more snatch into it." Nothing wrong with a little snatch, someone says. "Hey, y'all gonna have to cooperate with the brothers," someone else taunts the two white musicians good-naturedly. "Y'all sound like you been in Nashville."

The session goes on and on. It is a long day and a long night, and Wolf's ears are beginning to hurt. He does some isometrics and shakes his head as he plays the track back for everyone to listen to. In the last few years Wolf has discovered scuba diving, and he is looking forward to taking off for Florida as soon as the session is over. Unlike Tommy, Wolf appears to have difficulty opening up; he dates everything before and after his divorce from his high school sweetheart, and it would be impossible to say for sure whether or not he is having a good time. At one point Tommy goes out to dinner, and when he comes back G. C. Cameron, former lead singer for the Spinners, is recording a song by Marvin Gaye, his onetime brother-in-law. (They were both married to sisters of Motown founder Berry Gordy.) "You are so wonderful," emerge the familiar lyrics over nothing but a rhythm track made up of a rhythm box and synthesizers. From the control booth everyone joins in spontaneously on the chorus — Tommy, the musicians, Joe Shamwell, promotion person Thomasine Anderson, and Malaco artist Fern Kinney, who has dropped by to see if there is any paid background singing to be done. "Pride and joy," they echo G. C. Cameron over and over again. "Pride and joy," they sing out — with pride and joy — until at last everyone collapses in laughter, and the session picks up again, not to be concluded until long after midnight.

"I've gotten such an education in this business," says Benny Latimore. "It's all I've ever done. And I've had the opportunity to meet so many different people in so many different walks of life, where otherwise I might not ever have had that experience. You see, people relate to me in a different way than they do to their peers. They don't feel threatened when they're talking to me, and they know I'm not going to judge them. I guess I'm just one of those people that people like to talk to, and I love to listen. Sometimes I write about these things, and it gets a little heavy. I guess you might call that art for art's sake. But, you know, this is the world, a man's got to eat and feed his family, too. TK and Malaco? The early TK was somewhat similar to this, kind of a family-like atmosphere. As it grew, it got a little bit cold. It's a better setup here, really. I had a few nibbles after I finally got out of my TK contract, but I didn't want to be just a statistic. So this seems just about right. With Tommy, if you didn't know he was the president of the company you wouldn't even know who he was."

Frank Johnson wanders in. He is distraught and distracted, flushed with the excitement of the session, and he has decided he, too, is going to move to Jackson. There is no work in Jackson, Tommy tries to tell him; there aren't going to be any more sessions until next fall; has he forgotten he has a family back in Muscle Shoals? Frank is beyond reasoning; his life has been on a downslide for the last few years; after moving to L.A. in 1979 to hook up with Motown and produce a Johnnie Taylor session, personal and professional problems got the best of him, and now he just repeats the same thing over and over. "Why don't you just do like I say?" Tommy says patiently, without giving up or getting mad. When he finally gets rid of him, he feels guilty over his part in the little scene. "Frank's got some problems but, you know, he's trying real hard to keep them under control. Then I got on him about being so down and negative, and I think he wanted to overcome that and be a little more positive, and he just got a little carried away. I guess I shouldn't have been so hard on him." In the morning Frank will catch the Greyhound to Memphis.

After the session is over and Latimore has packed up and gone, it's back to business as usual. Dave Clark is on the phone working the stations. The musicians are doing a few overdubs, and then they're on their way home to hunt up work, hustle songs, try to find themselves a stake. Frederick Knight, an enormously talented writer and producer, has dreams of writing a hit song for country star Kenny Rogers, while Johnny Vincent is talking about reactivating his Ace label once again. Stewart is in the back keeping track of his accounts, while Tommy and Wolf give themselves a brief temporary respite, reminisce, listen to a test pressing, talk about Wolf's plans to move into a new house. This is what Tommy enjoys, sitting around with his friends, talking about old times and taking care of business. This, it turns out, is the record business. "You know," Wolf volunteers in a rare burst of emotion when Tommy goes out of the room for a moment, "I've known Tommy a long time, since 1962; it doesn't seem like it. Looking at him now, the way he is with his rheumatoid arthritis and all, you wouldn't believe it, but we used to go cave exploring in northern Alabama on vacation from college." I don't know what Tommy would have to say to that. Probably not much more than a chuckle and a mild demurral, and then the honest acknowledgment that life does take funny turns sometimes. For Tommy is proud of his contribution; he has played a real part in a genuine success story and remained the kind of fundamentally decent person he set out to be, someone who never puts on airs but is never anything less than himself. He is pleased at the idea of a story on Malaco, at the recognition that the label is finally beginning to get; he is just mildly surprised, he says, that anyone would be interested.

A VERY BRIEF EPILOGUE

Z. Z. HILL DIED of a heart attack at the age of forty-eight in April 1984, but Malaco completed its conquest of the down-home blues market over the next year or so, releasing its first album by Little Milton, acquiring the contract of Johnnie Taylor, and then, through the good offices of Dave Clark, signing the artist on whom they had set their sights from the very first, Bobby "Blue" Bland, with whom they would go on to make a dozen albums over the next eighteen years. Dave Clark retired from the road in 1989, though he remained a close member of the Malaco family until his death in 1995. Tommy Couch Jr. (born 1965) started playing a larger and larger role in the company in the 1990s, taking over as president in 2013. And Malaco even survived a tornado, which destroyed three of their four buildings on Northside Drive in 2011 but not the vault that housed their master tapes. They rebuilt. Tommy and Wolf were inducted into the Blues Hall of Fame in 2016. And Malaco celebrated its fiftieth anniversary in 2018 with a major exhibit at the Delta Blues Museum in Clarksdale. It was called *The Last Soul Company: 50 Years of Excellence,* but it might just as well have been called *The Blues Is Alright,* after Little Milton's anthemic signature tune, which set the tone not just for the Malaco label but for its entire extended family, the audience that Malaco Records had so unexpectedly found and nurtured, who would carry the down-home message of Southern soul well into the next century.

TWENTY-SIX

My Father, My Grandfather, and Ray Charles

Let me just give you a little background.

In the spring of 2004, Charles Bertolami, a former student and chief resident of my father's at the Harvard School of Dental Medicine and Massachusetts General Hospital, where my father was Chief of Oral and Maxillofacial Surgery for fifteen years, invited me to give the commencement address at the University of California, San Francisco, School of Dentistry graduation. He was a great admirer of my father, but that wasn't the reason he was inviting me. Every year, he said, he asked someone from outside the field of dentistry to give the address, with the idea of expanding horizons and placing medicine within a broader humanistic framework. A couple of years earlier the speaker had been Michael Dirda, an award-winning editor and book reviewer at the Washington Post, *and Michael had told Charles about my Elvis books. Charles immediately recognized the name, of course, and got in touch.*

My original inclination was to say no (I'm a no-boy by nature), but my father urged me to think it over, he thought I might find it interesting. The UCSF dental school had pioneered a program to encourage diversity in the field of dentistry which sought out highly motivated candidates who were not fully qualified by their undergraduate preparation. So UCSF inaugurated a postgraduate program "to boost dental admission test scores and basic science grades of students who intend to practice in underserved communities." This program, in its first few years, had achieved an astonishing degree of success, with seventy-nine of its first eighty students going on to successfully complete dental school, while a number of other dental schools across the country set up similar outreach programs. There's lots more — but suffice it to say, I gave the address and in the process first of writing it, and then addressing a gathering of the most diverse parents, families, and graduates, discovered unexpected rewards of my own.

I found in it an opportunity to consider my own origins, the extraordinary achievements of my father's father, who came to this country from Odessa in

1906 with virtually no English, just the unswerving determination to become a doctor, which he accomplished when he graduated from Tufts Medical School cum laude nine years later. It led me in short to a renewed appreciation — well, I'm not sure why I say renewed — quite simply, it reaffirmed my faith in the broad diversity of the American dream.

So here, stripped of the customary honorifics and with, as you'll see, a slightly modified form of presentation, is what I had to say. I wanted to take into consideration as much as possible the imagined reader, not the newly minted Dental School graduate who is hopefully now pursuing the kind of community-serving practice that my grandfather found so rewarding, and in some cases I've provided summary transitions that take into account the fact that the reader (you) will already be acquainted with some of the subject matter, as the UCSF students were not. But the message, as important to me now as it was then, remains the same. Beginning here.

M Y FATHER, Walter Guralnick, as some of you may already be aware, is a well-known oral surgeon, someone who achieved great success in his field not just for his extraordinary technical skills but for his compassion and his lifelong dedication to the delivery of patient-centered medical services. His father, Rubin, was a pediatrician, a Russian immigrant who came to this country in his early twenties to become a doctor, after working as a pharmacist in Odessa, where as a Jew he could not hope to go to medical school.

My father's older brother, my Uncle Gene (named for Eugene Debs by his father, a lifelong Socialist, who in the following decade would become an elector for Norman Thomas in his quest for the presidency), was a surgeon. And I had a great-uncle, my maternal grandmother's brother Rob Ulin, who was an orthopedic surgeon.

So, not at all surprisingly, everywhere I went as a child, I was asked — well, I was told, really: so you're going to be a doctor like your father, your uncle, your grandfather. Everyone gave my father a knowing wink, as if to say: What else could he be? What else could be expected of any son of yours?

My father expected something much more of me, though. Without ever saying so, he demanded of me what he had always demanded of himself in pursuit of his own goals.

That I be myself.

Father and son, 2011. *Courtesy of Peter Guralnick Archives*

That I trust my own instincts.

That if I wanted to be a writer, which I told him I did from a very early age, I had to dedicate myself to becoming the very best writer I could be. And most of all (something that is very hard to communicate to a child whose only other irrational ambition is to be a professional baseball player) that I needed to believe in myself, irrespective of what the world might think.

That is what I think made my father such an outstanding physician. He is not a boastful man. He is not flamboyant in any sense of the word. But for a kid growing up with all the doubts that most kids have — and maybe more than my share of self-doubt — he always conveyed a sense of quiet conviction, to friends, patients, colleagues.

I can remember visiting his office as a little kid. There was always a sense of reassuring orderliness. By that I don't mean that emotions were unduly repressed, though I have no doubt that its 1950s formality would be at odds with the look of the world that we see around us today. But the orderliness was at the service of the patient. It was intended to set the patient at ease, and there was an unfailing sense of courtesy, an unwavering belief that the patient, not the doctor's dignity or self-importance, was the focus. I'm sure this was something he learned from *his* father.

My grandfather making a house call. *Courtesy of Peter Guralnick Archives*

My grandfather's office was in a wooden tenement in an Italian immigrant section of East Boston, up a rickety flight of stairs, with an old potbellied stove in the waiting room and patients who often could not afford to pay with anything but vegetables or some other form of homegrown barter. They didn't sign up for it, but the treatment those patients received, the thoughtful attention that was given to every variety of ailment and ill, to people from all backgrounds and walks of life, was easily the equal of any treatment you might get today signing up for the kind of concierge service that is the product of an inequitable and elitist healthcare system.

The point is, for both my father and grandfather, and for many others, obviously, of their and other generations, medicine represented a form of community service. The consideration that you gave to your patients reflected the values in which you believed — *human* values as well as scientific ones — and what you did reflected not just technical training but what you stood for, the kind of person you were.

I think this may have been the greatest lesson I took, and continue to take, from my father: there can be no distinction between your life and your work, if your work is in fact your profession and not just a job. I saw this in everything he did, and I tried to carry the idea forward in my own work. As Sister Rosetta Tharpe said, "99 1/2 Won't Do."

I tried to carry forward, too, the idea of treating others the way in which you would want to be treated yourself. It seems like such a simple idea, but so often we assume a privilege to ourselves, we arrogate a kind of primacy to our own interests and pursuits. I've certainly seen it in the way that patients can be treated even in the most prestigious hospitals, in poorly monitored waiting rooms and examining rooms where, however sophisticated the scientific equipment, patients can — perhaps unintentionally — be made to feel ashamed of their own ignorance. By an impatient manner, a haughty self-regard, maybe just by the sense that the doctor would rather be somewhere else.

The work that I gravitated toward over the years took a surprising twist. I set out to be a novelist, but it didn't work out that way. Whether because of the alignment of the stars or simply because I had a greater talent for something else, I ended up writing primarily nonfiction, mostly about music. About American vernacular music in particular, Ray Charles and Sam Cooke, Elvis Presley and Bobby "Blue" Bland.

It came about strictly out of passion — and here I'll just give a brief personal aside. At fifteen or sixteen I just fell into the blues. I can't tell you exactly how it happened, and to this day I don't know just what it was — I had never heard anything quite like it before, and I like to think maybe it was that unadorned embrace of reality that James Baldwin described as "the ability to look at things as they are and survive your losses," the "zest, joy, and capacity for facing and surviving disaster." But to this day I don't really know what first drew me to the blues. The music just grabbed me and completely turned me around.

I started writing about the blues with one idea, and one idea only. To tell people about this music that I thought was so great. Just to have the chance to put the names of Muddy Waters or Bo Diddley or Howlin' Wolf down on paper, to try to describe the greatness, the grandeur, the scope and the pure theatricality of the James Brown Show for readers who had never experienced it for themselves — to call attention to a music and a culture that had not simply been ignored but for the most part utterly dismissed as something unworthy even of condemnation by the mainstream white culture. How could I possibly turn down an opportunity like that?

But then something more was demanded of me, something that I didn't think I was prepared to give. I had always imagined the solitary life of the writer for myself—you know, starving in a garret, communing with my tormented soul. But I realized if I was going to write about the blues—well, I suppose I could have just stuck to living my own version of the blues, but if I wanted to write about it, I was going to have to tell the story of the men and women who *sang* the blues. And to tell their stories I was going to have to get out of my garret, get out of my own head, and talk to them.

The first blues singer I ever actually interviewed was a sixty-three-year-old Mississippian named Skip James, who in 1964 had only recently been rediscovered by a white folk audience thirty-three years after making his first—and, up to that time, only—recordings. He sang his own original songs in an eerie falsetto voice that sounded like nothing you've ever heard, and he played guitar in a weird E-minor tuning that didn't seem to have traveled anywhere outside of his tiny hometown of Bentonia. He was absolutely, totally unique—I felt like no matter what personal feelings might be holding me back, from terminal shyness to, simply, inadequacy to the task, I had no choice (as Sam Phillips said in another, somewhat grander context, "Had I not tried, I would have been the biggest damn coward that God ever put on this earth") but to interview him.

I told that Commencement Day audience my tale of abject self-humiliation. (If you want to read more, check out the third chapter of this book.) But it was the lesson I derived from it that I focused on in addressing the 2004 graduates of the University of California, San Francisco, School of Dentistry, almost all of whom, I'm sure, had a much greater claim on the lessons and rewards of daring to reach beyond the self-imposed limits of your background and inclinations.

"I learned a lot that day," I told them. . . .

Well, of course, I learned a lot about Skip James and about the difference between high-flown theories of art and real life. (Why'd you quit? I asked him, expecting to hear the kind of parable that would make sense of the universe. I never got paid, he said.) And whatever Skip James may have thought of the poor imposture that I was conducting, he treated me—like nearly everyone else I have interviewed over the years, from

Muddy Waters to Waylon Jennings to Big Joe Turner to Bobby "Blue" Bland — with a graciousness and a generosity of spirit that I'm not sure I had ever done anything to earn.

But the main thing I took — not just from that interview but from all the hundreds of interviews I've done since — is that the success of an interview has little to do with matters of technique. It is, rather, like everything else in life, a human connection. And without necessarily realizing it at first, what I tried to bring to bear in the interviews I conducted over the years were some of the same principles that my father and grandfather applied to the practice of medicine, lessons that never really had to be articulated, only observed: You must never think you are better than anyone else. You must never think it is *your* needs that should be served first. You must never imagine that anyone owes you anything. You must always be ready to listen to, you must always be genuinely *interested in*, other people's stories if you want to understand anything about the truth of their lives.

I've spoken to journalism classes, I've certainly been interviewed enough times myself by now — and so often students want to know: What's the trick? How do you get people to speak honestly, to speak intimately, about themselves and their work? How do you gain people's trust? Well, leaving aside the whole issue of whether this is an accurate assessment, the answer is much simpler than the question supposes.

You have to listen before you can even begin to make a judgment, whether it has to do with writing history or making a diagnosis. You have to *show* respect, as my father so often indicated to me in the conduct of his life and profession, in order to gain respect.

My father also taught the value of preparation. I don't think he ever did anything in his practice without meticulous consideration of the choices involved, human as well as scientific, without, in other words, carefully laying the groundwork — and I have certainly tried to do the same. It doesn't make sense to ask somebody in the public eye a question that has been asked and answered a thousand times. Instead, you try to learn everything you can about your subject — above all, what engaged their interest, what motivated him or her — and then get them to expound on matters that will illuminate that engagement. For example, when I first met Johnny Cash, I knew he was a great reader, so I asked him about the books he read as a child — and *that* led to his telling me about the day Eleanor Roosevelt dedicated the public library in his hometown of Dyess,

Arkansas, and how much the Rooseveltian ideals (for Dyess was in essence a utopian socialist community created by the Federal Emergency Relief Administration) had meant to him in his life and work.

I don't mean in any sense that I activated some secret switch by asking the "magic" question. You ask a lot of questions, you sit still for a lot of answers that are not strictly speaking "relevant," but the point of the exercise, like any probe, is not to show off your own cleverness but to get to the heart of the matter — in the case of a physician to try to understand just what the problem is, and what are the parameters of its treatment, in my own case to try to tell a true story as much as possible from the inside out.

This requires, I need hardly tell you, at least as much humility as it does hubris. It requires the recognition that no inquiry ever has a full-stop ending, that all knowledge is transitional, and if you truly believe that that is the case, in the end it is, obviously, the journey, not the arrival, that matters. In other words — and this can be as comforting a thought as it is a humbling one — knowledge, comprehension, understanding are ongoing pursuits. It's the excitement of what lies ahead that keeps you going — it's the *process,* of your life, of your work, that should never lose its sense of wonder and discovery.

My father had always vowed to retire as Chief of Oral and Maxillofacial Surgery at the Massachusetts General Hospital when he reached the age of sixty-five. He believed in theory that was the right thing to do — if you are not willing to make way for the new, you are no longer serving the ideal that first motivated you, you are merely serving yourself. I think about this. . . . A lot! As you attain a position in the world, it's hard not to assume a proprietary stance about it, it's tempting to spend a good deal of time defending what you have come to see as your turf. But turf is constantly shifting, and so, too, are goals. I always told my kids — you can't make your choices on the basis of a fifty-year projection. You have to be guided by your belief that this is the best course for you NOW, and if in five or ten years your priorities change, well, if you're a resourceful person, you can figure out how to adapt.

When my grandfather graduated from medical school, he went into practice as a GP. Several years later, he decided that what he really wanted

Nina and Rubin Guralnick, with Walter (left) and Eugene, East Boston, Massachusetts, ca. 1920. Courtesy of Peter Guralnick Archives

to be was a pediatrician, and he went back to school to be certified, even though at this point he had two small children at home.

I'm sure my father had real moments of doubt when he fulfilled his pledge to himself and officially "retired" for the first time — not from his beliefs, not from his self, just from his job. But then he went on to help set up the Ambulatory Care Center at the Mass. General, and after that he became medical director of the MGH operating rooms, and then at the age of seventy-six or seventy-seven he made a limited two-year commitment to revamping the Dental School clinic. And today at eighty-seven he goes into the hospital four or five days a week, makes grand rounds, serves on committees, and chairs study groups on subjects that remain of abiding interest to him. [He would continue this practice, although at a slightly reduced schedule, for the next thirteen years, until his death.] I'm sure he would tell you he is still learning. And in my own work I would certainly hope to be able to continue to say the same.

It seems to me there's only one real definition of success: so long as you can afford to do the work that means the most to you, that's really all that matters. And if you can't, you've just got to figure out another way of going about it. There's no temporal measure of success: it took the great blues singer Robert Johnson fifty years after his death to be recognized, but that's nothing. It took the poet John Donne three hundred. You keep plugging away at what you believe in, and sometimes the effort alone will have to suffice. I don't know exactly how long it took for my father to help get dental insurance established in Massachusetts, how much steady commitment in the face of fright, fear, and cries of socialized medicine. (I can't tell you how many dentists I have met over the years who loved my father but hated his "socialistic" ideas.) But he believed in making dentistry available to everyone, just as he continues to believe in universal health care today, as he has committed himself, passionately, to universal health care and expanded public health service all his life. And he also believed that even if these things were never to happen in quite the way he envisioned, or according to the schedule he would have liked, what alternative was there but to continue to fight the good fight?

It took me eleven years to write my biography of Elvis Presley. It took me fifteen to set up the right conditions to write the biography of the great soul and spiritual singer Sam Cooke that I'm just finishing up now. But if I had never succeeded, or if readers and critics had chosen to look away from my work, would that mean that I had just wasted my time? I don't think so. The world that I see around me, the world which I seek to describe in my work cannot be measured by so limited a yardstick. It is a world in which opposite impulses can coexist, a world in which moral dichotomies yield no easier solutions than they do in today's headline stories, a world in which aspiration is as important as result, in which it is understood that while aspiration may not always lead to success, disappointing conclusions are not so much deserving of condemnation as of understanding.

My father sometimes bemoans what he sees as the shortsightedness, the lack of goals that besets not just the practice of modern medicine but the world at large. But he never bemoans for a minute the hope of improvement, the possibilities of the future, the dream of progress. Or the dedication that so many people show by their service to others, by their commitment to a larger community, whatever their profession.

Sam Cooke's father, a minister in the Church of Christ (Holiness), who came to the South Side of Chicago from the Mississippi Delta so that his children could get an education, told all eight of his sons and daughters: "If you're going to shine shoes, be the best shoeshine boy out there. If you're going to sweep a street, be the best street sweeper. Whatever you strive to be, be the best at it, whether it's a small job or working in top management." He was a man of little education but much mother wit, who wrote the same familiar poem in each of his children's course books when they graduated: "Once a task is once begun / Never stop until it's done / Be the labor great or small / Do it well or not at all."

Elvis Presley, who grew up in equally difficult circumstances on the poor-white side of town, said of his own journey: "Well, I've tried to be the same all the way through. Naturally, you learn a lot about people, and you get involved in a lot of different situations, but I've tried to be the same. I mean, the way I was brought up, I've always considered other people's feelings. That's simple. It's just the way I was brought up by my mother and father — to believe and have respect for other people."

Elvis Presley and Sam Cooke, the two figures with whom I have spent most of the last twenty years, met arguably tragic ends. Each had lofty goals which, for all their success — like all lofty goals — could never be said to have been fully achieved.

But they never abandoned their aspirations.

Not long before he died, I spoke to Ray Charles on the telephone. He was describing the spiritual he had sung, forty years earlier, at Sam Cooke's funeral.

"I gave my heart to it, man," he said. "Everything that came out of me that day was truly genuine. There was nothing fake about it."

That's all we can do, but—as Ray Charles would have been the first to suggest—it's what we *must* do.

I think we owe it to ourselves to embrace that sense of possibility. I think we owe it to ourselves to strive for that elusive human connection that is at the heart of every form of communication, medical, musical, social, professional. It's a matter, as Ray Charles said to me that day, not just of hitting the note—but of hitting the note with grace and feeling.

EPILOGUE

MY FATHER DIED at almost 101 two weeks after his last day of work, in 2017. He received a diagnosis of irreversible congestive heart failure and made up his mind to do what he had always said he would do. He simply stopped eating and had his pacemaker disconnected, electing a kind of hospice-care approach administered under the aegis of palliative care.

In his last days in the hospital he exhibited the same lucidity and compassion that had characterized him all his life. There was a steady procession of visitors, everyone from colleagues of sixty years to first- and second-year residents, family, and friends. With every one, the talk was always of the future—not his future, of course, but, at his insistence, theirs. His three great-granddaughters, fourteen, thirteen, and nine at the time, who were not able to visit, all wrote letters, unprompted, about how much their relationship with him had meant, about how much—and I'm quoting from one here—"you always genuinely wanted to know what was going on in our lives," concluding in the same loving but realistic terms that he had always sought to convey to them ("I don't want this letter to sound the same as every other letter that I've written to you in my life") how much they would all miss him.

Well, me, too. And the same holds true for so many of his friends and family. Every day we think of things we'd like to tell him, every day we think of things he would genuinely relish, and other things that would make him boiling mad. We can only imagine—no, actually we really know—the disappointment he would feel at the casual cruelties of daily (better make that hourly) political life. We have become far removed lately from the social ideals of fairness and justice and democratic equality in which he believed so passionately. But there are an equal number of small things—and not always such small things—in which clearly he would take great pride and pleasure. His last great causes at the hospital were diversity and gender equality, and the signs of progress in both areas over his last few years (not victory but progress) were unmistakable.

Most of all he was devoted to the eleemosynary principle, a word which he became convinced in his nineties he might have been misusing all his life (the dictionary definition seems to come down, more or less, to "charitable," which he did not mean at all) but which remained for him in his own definition a call to political action and humanistic hope, the idea that you can always do well—no matter *what* the definition—by doing good. In your life, in your work, in the world that for a time we all share.

TWENTY-SEVEN

Reading, Writing, and Real Life

S OMETIMES I GET ASKED who or what influenced me most in my deep-seated (and very early) desire to write.

I've named books and writers: *Tristram Shandy* (don't miss the book, but don't miss the movie either), Norse mythology, and Henry Green; Alice Munro, Grace Paley, and Hubert Selby Jr.; Ralph Ellison, Italo Svevo, Sigrid Undset, and Zora Neale Hurston. For the last few years I've been working on a series of loosely connected short stories suggested by Dawn Powell's novel *My Home Is Far Away,* a book that I can best describe as suggesting the magical realism of Ingmar Bergman's *Fanny and Alexander* transplanted to the world of Winesburg, Ohio. Which could lead me to Hemingway, or *Hemingway's Boat,* or — well, I'm sure you get the point.

There were teachers, certainly. Omar Pound (Omar Shakespear Pound, son of Ezra) is the one who stands out the most. He came to the Roxbury Latin School when I was in the ninth grade and was greeted with almost universal rejection bordering on scorn by my classmates — for his oddity, for his self-determined eccentricities, for his stubborn scruffiness, both personal and intellectual. But for me, and a few others, he provided a wonderful opportunity for self-expression in the two or three extended writing exercises he assigned each week, prompted by a phrase or saying that he supplied, of which just one immediately comes to mind: "Only a fool learns from experience." True? Untrue? I didn't know then, and I don't know now. But as I recall, I wrote a short story that I hope was as open-ended in a fourteen-year-old way and lent itself as much to individual interpretation as I have intended in my biographies of Elvis, Sam Cooke, and Sam Phillips, or any of the other books that I've written.

But there's still that lingering question: What in the world would lead a nine- or ten-year-old kid to want to be a writer? It was my grandfather, Philip Marson, who taught English for over thirty years at Boston Latin

My grandfather and me. *Courtesy of Peter Guralnick Archives*

(no, not the same Latin School—it's complicated), founded and ran Camp Alton (which I would later run) in what he conceived of as a fresh-air expansion of the educational experience, dreamed of having the time one day to finish *Finnegans Wake* (he finally did at seventy-eight, over his customary breakfast of shredded wheat), and explored the secondhand bookstores of Boston's Cornhill for twenty-five-cent masterpieces like Jean Toomer's *Cane,* without necessarily passing up a side trip to the Old Howard burlesque show in adjacent Scollay Square, where he pulled his hat down over his forehead for fear of running into one of his students. I wasn't around for the Old Howard, which closed in 1953, but by the time I was ten or eleven I started accompanying him on his foraging trips to Cornhill (now the site of Government Center), which always included a mid-morning hot fudge sundae at Bailey's, where the fudge sauce was so thick it could have been a meal in itself.

My father and me,
1946. *Courtesy of Peter
Guralnick Archives*

It was his enthusiasm, I think, that inspired me most, his enthusiasm and his unfettered appetite for life, literature, sports (he was a three-sport athlete at Tufts—Tris Speaker, the Grey Eagle himself, he said, had praised him for his play in a college game at Fenway Park), grammatical niceties, and democratic ideals. More than just appreciation, it was his undisguised avidity for experience and people of every sort. "Hey, Pete," he would shout out in his high-pitched voice, to my pre-adolescent, adolescent, and post-adolescent (does that count as adult?) embarrassment, "Will you look at that?" And I'm not going to tell you what *that* was— because it's still embarrassing. But, you know, it was always interesting.

But none of that would have counted for anywhere near as much if he were not such an unrestrained fan of me—it just seemed like whatever I did was all right with him. He came to all my baseball games, naturally, but when I took up tennis, which he had always scorned as an artificially encumbered (don't ask me why), pointless kind of sport, he embraced it wholeheartedly, coming to all my tournaments and swiftly learning the finer points of the game. If I recommended a book, he was quick to seek it out. And when at the ages of ten, eleven, twelve, and into early adolescence, I suffered from fears that so crippled me that I found it difficult even to go to school, his belief in me never wavered. Or more to the point perhaps, he never seemed to see me as any less, or any different, a person.

I grew up in my grandparents' house in suburban Boston off and on from the time I was born. My father, whom I would never fail to cite as an equally inspiring, though very different, influence in terms of both character and commitment, landed in England the day I was born and didn't return from the War until I was more than two years old, close to a year after V-E Day. So my mother and I camped out with my grandparents, very comfortably for me, though I'm not so sure about my mother. (One of the short stories I've written lately tries to imagine what it must have been like for her, twenty-three, twenty-four years old, with no certainty of the future, an only child living with her only child in her parents' house.) Then, when my father finally came home, we remained for another three years, until my sister was born and we could afford a place of our own, moving into the garden apartments that had recently opened up nearby as affordable housing for returning veterans. A year or two after that, my grandparents gave my parents the house and moved to a roomy old apartment in Coolidge Corner, not far away.

Staying with my grandparents on weekends in their new apartment, even more book-crammed than the house they had just left because it was filled with the same books in a smaller space, was always a treat. We went to theater together, my grandmother, my grandfather, and I—I can remember seeing Charles Laughton in *Don Juan in Hell,* the stand-alone third act of George Bernard Shaw's *Man and Superman,* when I was nine or ten years old. (Shaw was always a great favorite of my grandfather's, along with such native-born contrarians as H. L. Mencken.) We went to serious plays, musicals, Broadway tryouts, and revivals. Along with Shaw, Eugene O'Neill undoubtedly loomed largest in my grandfather's theatrical canon, and it was as exciting to listen to my grandparents talk about seeing Paul Robeson in his first big Broadway role in *The Emperor Jones* or attending O'Neill's marathon nine-act *Strange Interlude,* which included a break for dinner, as it was to hear my grandfather tell the story of how he lost his hat when he stood up to cheer for Franklin Roosevelt at the Boston Garden.

But it was books in the end that were the instigators of the most passionate discussions, books that inspired me to want to write books of my own, books that would always provide an impetus for dinnertime conversation and home decor. My grandfather introduced me to Romain Rolland's *Jean-Christophe,* to James Joyce and Knut Hamsun, Joseph Conrad and Ford Madox Ford (he loved to discourse on what he called the shuttle-and-weave of their narrative technique), and Sigrid Undset. I'll admit, I might have been better off if I had stuck a little longer with the Landmark series of biographies that continued to excite me or the Scribner's Illustrated Classics editions of Jules Verne and Robert Louis Stevenson and James Fenimore Cooper, with those wonderful N. C. Wyeth illustrations, or any of the other children's classics that I indiscriminately devoured. But I was so bereft of self-awareness (while at the same time so consumed by self-consciousness) that I started to record my impressions of each of the books that I read in little tablet notebooks, earnest summaries not just of the books but of my own judgments of them. I could only express my "wonderment at, and admiration for, the author's scope and ability," as I put it portentously, writing about Sigrid Undset's *Kristin Lavransdatter* when I was fifteen. And struggled for six handwritten pages to express more specifically my admiration for this 1,000-page trilogy that takes place in fourteenth-century Norway, with its rare combination of epic sweep and unexpected intimacy. My grandfather considered it the greatest novel ever written, a judgment with which, as you can see, I struggled mightily to concur — and in fact for the most part still do. But I also knew, as my grandfather's own omnivorous passion for discovery suggested, that all such judgments were nonsense. In the end, like the question of who was the greatest baseball player of all time, an early and abiding conversation of ours, it was a provisional title only, waiting for the next great thing to come along.

And yet, and yet, well, you know, when it comes right down to it, it wasn't books or writing or epistemological fervor that were my primary inspiration. They would have meant nothing if it hadn't been for everything else. What my grandfather communicated to me most of all was a hunger for life, for the raw stuff of life that served as the underpinning for every great book that either of us admired. I'm oversimplifying, I know, but it just seemed like, in the greater scheme of things, with my grandfather there was no exclusionary gene. There was no sense of high and low (no one appreciated a "dirty joke" more shamelessly than he) and, save for the inviolable principles of grammar and the strict standards of a "good education," everything was in play, everything existed on the same human plane.

In many ways, I think that was what opened me up to the blues — not just the music but the *experience* of the music, the many different implications of the music — which turned out to be the single greatest revelation of my life. So many of the places where I started out are still the places

My mother and me at camp, ca. 1947. *Courtesy of Peter Guralnick Archives*

where I am. Books, writing, playing sports (no more baseball or soccer, just tennis), the blues. As my grandfather got older, his enthusiasm never diminished. When *One Hundred Dollar Misunderstanding,* a fictional dialogue between a fourteen-year-old black prostitute and her clueless white college john, came out in 1962, my grandfather got the idea that he and I could write a novel in the same manner about the generation gap, which was very much in the news in those days. We would write alternating chapters — well, you get the picture — and he was so excited by the idea that I couldn't say no, though we never advanced to the point where we put anything down on paper. When the draft briefly threatened, he decided he would buy land in Canada and we could start a commune there, and while the threat went away before he ever needed to put his idea into practice, I had no doubt it would have been a very interesting (and well-ordered) commune.

A few years later, in 1970, he asked if I would help him run camp, a close-knit community of 250 campers and close to seventy staff which he had founded and directed since 1937, the following year. I'm not sure I need to explain, but this came like a bolt out of the blue. My wife, Alexandra, and I had been working at camp for the last few years, and I was running the tennis program and coaching baseball. "No speculation," I told my twelve-year-old charges, taking my cue, as always, from William Carlos Williams. (The idea, quite simply, was, it never does any good to overestimate or underestimate your opponent, you just play the game.) It was a wonderful way to spend the summer, and it was certainly rewarding from any number of points of view, not least of which was being close to my grandparents. But not for one moment had the thought of running camp crossed my mind. I was twenty-six years old, working on my first full-length published book, *Feel Like Going Home,* and my fifth unpublished novel, *Mister Downchild,* and I thought I knew where my future lay.

At the same time, the idea of turning my grandfather down never crossed my mind. He was seventy-eight years old and had never asked for my help before — in fact, I couldn't remember him ever asking *anybody's* help. So, sure, yes, unequivocally. And yet I found it impossible to imagine how this could ever work. How exactly was I going to help? And if his idea was to defer to me, to withdraw and leave the day-to-day running of camp to me alone, well, this would require a lot more conviction, self-belief, and, above all, *knowledge* (since no one knew anything about the running of camp except for him) than I possessed. The question was, did I have it in me to be the person that I needed, that I wanted, for my grandfather's sake, to be?

As it turned out, I never had to answer that question. My grandfather got sick — it appeared at first to be a stroke, it turned out to be a brain tumor — almost immediately after asking for my help. I kept things going over the winter in hopes that he would recover, and when he didn't, it was like being thrown into the water and discovering, much to your surprise, that you actually knew how to swim. I ended up running camp by myself that summer, and I ran it for twenty-one years after that, and whatever my grandfather intended (and I suspect it was a great deal more than just providing me with an income to support my writing), it turned out to be one of the most rewarding, existentially engaging experiences of my life. And not just in the ways you might expect — camp remained a thriving, self-sustaining community of 300 people that continued to grow and evolve, as did my own views of democratic institutions and possibilities — but because it inescapably exposed me to real life, it forced me out into a world in which my feelings were not the center of everything. A world of building things and balancing books, where you dealt of necessity (and to your own incalculable experiential benefit) with all kinds of different people, benefited from the wisdom and experience of others (could that have been what Omar Pound meant?), and learned not just to stand up for yourself but for everyone else, too, because no matter how much inner turmoil you might feel (and I think back to my ten- and eleven-year-old self, curled up in a ball reading a book, afraid to leave the comforting familiarity of my room), you don't have the luxury of dwelling on your own emotions. Because — why? *Everyone is depending on you.* It forced me, in other words, to grow up, in a way that deeply affected not only my writing but my ability to understand all the different personalities and perspectives that I wanted to portray in both my fiction and my nonfiction, in my biographies and profiles of such multifarious personalities as Muddy Waters, Howlin' Wolf, Waylon Jennings, Charlie Rich, Sam Phillips, Doc Pomus, and Solomon Burke. It forced me, when you come right down to it, to embrace the world.

My grandfather used to come see me in my dreams sometimes. He always wore his tan windbreaker and stood by the tree on the right-field line at camp, where he would watch my baseball games, both as a kid and as an adult. It was always good to see him — there was never a time I didn't wish he would stay longer. But even though I rarely see him nowadays, I carry with me always the conviction that he communicated so unhesitantly: that everything is just out there waiting to be discovered. And I try to keep that belief in the forefront — well, maybe the backfront — of my mind. I continue to be drawn on by the prospect, I continue to struggle for its discovery.

A Fan's Notes

Rather than a formal bibliography and discography — this isn't that kind of book, and the totality of everything that would need to be listed could fill another book — I thought I would provide chapter notes, acknowledging some of my most important sources and pointing toward books and music (not all of which were available when I initially addressed the subject, but every one of which has contributed to my ongoing curiosity and understanding) that continue to offer an opportunity for exploration. Not random exactly, more like a product of enthusiastically organized free association. And it's certainly not intended in any way to be definitive. It couldn't be, no matter what my intentions, because I've ignored the issue of availability — there's simply not enough available back catalogue, and what there is goes in and out of print, while it seems like *everything* is available streaming and online, with more coming and going all the time. Take a song like Little Jimmy Dickens' "Shopping for Dresses," for example, a terrific song which was featured on Merle Haggard's album *Going Where the Lonely Go.* Well, see if you can find the legendary motel-room guitar pull in which Jimmy Dickens first played the song for Merle — and if you can't find that (you probably won't) look for the TNN video, which may or may not still be available on YouTube, where the two of them duet and Merle recounts the tale of writing another verse to round out the structure of Jimmy's song. See what I mean?

Taking into account the impossibility of what is, or is not, currently in print, and how, and in what configurations you may find it, you'll see that I've listed LPs and CDs that in some cases have long since disappeared from the record stores, which also, with rare and notable exceptions, have disappeared as well. And yet, if you're persistent enough, you can find just about anything you want, create your own playlists, and if you're into the physical object, you can create your own CD-Rs, and/or find new and used vinyl and CDs, both new releases and reissues, foreign or domestic, of nearly everything that's listed here. (But probably not the Jimmy Dickens motel shot.)

So take these notes any way you like. But most of all, take them as a starting point, and — I don't think I have to say this — don't stop there. There's a world — there are *worlds* — out there waiting to be discovered, and this book, like every book I've written, is intended merely as an introduction.

ROBERT JOHNSON AND THE TRANSFORMATIVE NATURE OF ART

I met Mack McCormick in 1976 to do a short article for *Rolling Stone* about his groundbreaking research on Robert Johnson. What he told me then, and over the next few years, the astonishing wealth of biographical detail that he had accumulated about a figure who had up till then existed almost entirely in the imagination, provided much of the impetus for my book, *Searching for Robert Johnson*. In 2019, at the invitation of Preston Lauterbach, Elijah Wald and I interviewed Robert's ninety-three-year-old stepsister, Annye Anderson, and her not infrequently mind-boggling information and perspective, while not detailed in this chapter (they are fully revealed in the book she collaborated on with Preston, *Brother Robert*, which was published by Da Capo in the spring of 2020), helped me gain new insights, and a very different vantage point, even after all these years. Bruce Conforth and Gayle Dean Wardlow's recent biography *Up Jumped the Devil: The Real Life of Robert Johnson* (Chicago Review Press, 2019), written without the input of Annye Anderson, is, for all of its sometimes querulous tone, an invaluable contribution to Robert Johnson scholarship, propelled by the seminal research of Gayle Dean Wardlow, a Mississippi native who began his totally independent on-site field investigations in the early 1960s (and whom I first met at the 1969 Memphis Blues Festival). And then there's Mack McCormick's book, *Biography of a Phantom*, still unfinished and unpublished, forty-four years after our initial meeting (when Mack said it was ready to go to press), and five years after its author's death. I have been told, however, by one of Mack's closest late-in-life disciples that there's more than enough finished material for at least a solid start and plenty more for a dedicated student to finish it. So, come on, someone, let's go!

As far as the music goes, I *could* say, Go out and get the original LP, *Robert Johnson: King of the Delta Blues Singers* (Columbia 1654), but that would be silly and nostalgia-serving. To me the only way to go is the most recent iteration of the complete recordings, 2011's two-CD collection *Robert Johnson: The Centennial Collection* (Columbia Legacy 85907), where twenty-one years after its original attempt, Sony finally got the digital sound right. And it spectacularly is.

WHOSE SKIP JAMES IS THIS?

I continue to be indebted to Bruce Jackson for permitting me to quote from his November 1964 interview of Skip, which was published in part in *Sing Out!* in 1966 as "The Personal Blues of Skip James." (Incidentally, you should check out Bruce's new book *Places: Things Heard. Things Seen.* [BlazeVOX, 2019].) And Dick Waterman has never been anything less than generous in sharing his photographs, friendship, insights, and memories. Don't, on any account, miss his classic book of photographs and recollections of life in the blues world, *Between Midnight and Day* (Thunder's Mouth Press, 2003).

You can get all of Skip James' original 1931 recordings, painstakingly and beautifully remastered, on *Skip James: The Complete Early Recordings* (Yazoo 2009). And a good selection of his post-rediscovery Vanguard recordings are gathered on *Skip James: Blues from the Delta* (Vanguard 79517). But don't miss his video performance on *Devil Got My Woman* (Vestapol DVD 13049), which stars Howlin' Wolf as both performer and audience member. Also, be sure to check out Sam Pollard and Ben Hedin's documentary *Two Trains Runnin'* (2016 — available on a number of streaming services), which with interviews, animation, and documentary footage, entertainingly, and with exemplary depth and deftness, links the story of the search for Skip James and Son House with the grim events taking place simultaneously at the start of the Mississippi Freedom Summer of 1964.

Ironically, as I was finishing these notes, I received a book from Stefan Grossman, proprietor of Guitar Workshop (consisting primarily of guitar instructional videos) and

Vestapol (primarily documentary and performance footage), called *Blues and the Soul of Man: An Autobiography of Nehemiah "Skip" James* (Guitar Workshop/Mel Bay, 2019), which has been edited into a first-person narrative from Stephen Calt's extensive interviews with Skip. This was the way the book was originally intended to be, writes Grossman in his preface, "but for some reason Stephen changed his mind [and] turned the interviews [into] a vehicle to present his opinions and feelings." And Stephen, writes Grossman, who was clearly a friend but just as clearly saw the deficiencies of this approach, "was a very opinionated person."

In any case, these are Skip's own words, and while I might quarrel with some of the orthographic choices, this is a story well worth reading—and never told in quite this fashion before. It can be rough, certainly—Skip can be difficult at times, fractious, argumentative, and painfully, boastfully insecure—but as my friend Donnie Fritts always used to say about any and every experience known to man, It's *human*. Plus, there's the added treat of an introduction by Eddie Dean (originally published as "Skip James' Hard Time Killing Floor Blues" in the *Washington City Paper* 11/25–12/1/94), a scrupulous chronicler of the odd, the eccentric, and the beautiful, who is putting together a collection of some of his best writings, primarily on the insufficiently appreciated, and highly original, roots music of the greater D.C. and Virginia area, which I hope will be coming soon.

COSMIC RAY: HOW RAY CHARLES' "I GOT A WOMAN" TRANSFORMED THE MUSIC OF RAY CHARLES, ALLOWED HIM TO KEEP HIS BAND, AND CREATED A MUSICAL AND SOCIAL REVOLUTION

Michael Lydon's 1998 biography, *Ray Charles: Man and Music* (Riverhead Books), is essential, shedding light in particular on the early years. So is David Ritz's collaboration with Ray on his autobiography, *Brother Ray* (Dial Press, 1978), which wonderfully captures the saltiness, tone, and rhythms of Ray's expressive voice. In addition, Robert Palmer's liner notes to *Ray Charles: The Birth of Soul,* a three-CD collection subtitled *The Complete Atlantic Rhythm and Blues Recordings, 1952–1959* (Atlantic 82310-2), are typically expansive and insightful (they are included in his posthumously published *Blues & Chaos* [Scribner, 2009], as is his 1978 feature on Ray, "Soul Survivor: Ray Charles" [*Rolling Stone*, 2/9/78]). I have also drawn upon the extensive writings and interviews of Jeff Hannusch, John Broven, Whitney Balliett, Charlie Gillett, Colin Escott, and Joël Dufour (whose interview with Renald Richard, along with Michael Lydon's, proved invaluable), in addition to my own interviews over the years with Ray, Jerry Wexler (whose book, written with David Ritz, *Rhythm and the Blues: A Life in American Music,* [Knopf, 1993], fills in some of the gaps), Ahmet Ertegun, and Zenas Sears, among others. And I would also highly recommend *Trading Twelves: The Selected Letters of Ralph Ellison and Albert Murray* (Modern Library, 2000) for all kinds of breezy and informative exchanges, not least on Ray Charles.

For a fundamental listening experience I think I'd start with the box set (it's really more like a small cardboard suitcase) *Ray Charles: Pure Genius—The Complete Atlantic Recordings (1952–1959)* (Rhino R2 74371). And you can't afford to miss the two-CD *Ray Charles: Live* (Atlantic 81732), whose first CD, recorded at Newport in 1958, is certainly uplifting enough—but it's the second, recorded at Atlanta's Herndon Stadium in 1959 by Zenas Sears, that is truly cataclysmic. Ray's slow-to-almost-a-dead-stop version of "Drown in My Own Tears" at the Herndon Stadium show might be considered the living definition of soul.

Otherwise, there's just so much to take in, including, of course, the single-CD version of *Modern Sounds in Country and Western Music Vols. 1 and 2* (Concord Records CRE00860) from the ABC years and *Ray Charles: Genius & Soul: The 50th Anniversary Collection* (Rhino R2 72859), a five-CD set which, on top of a fine selection of Atlantic staples, has nearly three CDs' worth of some of Ray's best ABC-Paramount material (including his transcendent "America the Beautiful")—oh, and then there are some soulful Christmas songs, and, and—and, at this point I'm just going to leave it to you to find your own way.

HAG AT THE CROSSROADS: PORTRAIT OF THE ARTIST IN MIDLIFE

I owe a long-standing debt of friendship and gratitude to Merle's onetime manager Tex Whitson, an unsung hero and a great pal. If there were any justice, Tex would be writing his own history of Bakersfield music. Here's a start. "Merle came to Ridgecrest, CA, to join Lewis Talley's band, 'THE TALLEY WHACKERS,' at the Porthole Café. The band was called that for years. Newspaper would NOT take the ads if 'Talley Whacker.' And a couple women customers mentioned it to Chet Elder, the Bar owner. Merle played bass. Very reluctant to sing. He wanted to play guitar. But Lewis was always trying to trick him into singing—he just wanted a break from lead vocals. . . ." Want more? Ask Tex.

Frank Mull, too, has been a great help from the first time we met, in 1980, when we flew from Nashville to Meridian in a tiny, and what seemed to me very rickety, plane. And Peter Wolf has been a never-ending source of shared enthusiasm, insight, knowledge, and appreciation for Merle's music over the years, while his late-in-life close friendship with Merle spurred all kinds of new, and fascinating, discussions, plus one classic Merle song (see below).

Tally Records publicity shot, ca. 1962–63. *Courtesy of Richard Weize — . . . and more bears*

As far as the written record goes, there's been so much published about Merle over the years, including two memoirs of his own, *Sing Me Back Home* (Times Books, 1981) and *Merle Haggard's My House of Memories* (Cliff Street Books, 1999), both of which have their moments and reflect Merle up to a point in his own filtered voice, with the addition of pointed recollections by various members of his close and extended family in the first. I'm not going to go into all the memorable portraits of Merle I've read (there are lots!), but there's one in particular, Jason Fine's "The Fighter: The Life and Times of Merle

Haggard" *(Rolling Stone* 10/1/09), that I think captures Merle's unique, not infrequently cranky voice in a canny, affectionate, and empathetic way. *Workin' Man Blues: Country Music in California* by Gerald Haslam with Alexandra Haslam Russell and Richard Chon (University of California Press, 1999) provides a fine overview not just of the Bakersfield but of the extensive Southern California country scene. And then there are the voluminous booklets for Merle's three Bear Family box sets (see below), not to mention the ten-CD Bear Family Bakersfield box, also listed below. But, needless to say, there is still a *crying* need for a great Merle Haggard biography.

Recordings—it's not so much hard to know where to start as where to stop. (We're talking about someone whose oeuvre could qualify for a Nobel Prize.) There are so many great individual LPs (*Pride in What I Am, Someday We'll Look Back, Let Me Tell You About a Song, Merle Haggard Presents His Thirtieth Album, It's All in the Movies,* just to name a few of the Capitol ones), but I'll just single out *Serving 190 Proof* (MCA 1645), the thoroughly beat, and altogether existential, autobiographical statement that was most on his mind at the time of our 1980 meeting. But, you know, I simply can't not mention *Same Train — A Different Time* (Bear Family 15740), Merle's tribute to Jimmie Rodgers, as much of a musical masterpiece as any of Merle's original work. (I know, I know, an odd statement to make about an album that is a tribute to another artist.) This is an album that you can't stop listening to, presented here in an expanded version from its original two-LP issue, with nearly all of Merle's supremely felt Rodgers songs gathered together in one place, twenty-nine in all.

Down Every Road, 1962-1994 (Capitol 7243-8-35711-2-3 in its original 1996 issue), a four-CD set compiled by Lefty Frizzell's biographer, Daniel Cooper, is probably the best overall survey of his work over more than three decades—but it's not enough. (Incidentally, you really do need to read Cooper's book about Merle's idol, *Lefty Frizzell: The Honky-Tonk Life of Country Music's Greatest Singer* [Little, Brown, 1995].) So, all right, I might as well point you toward an oddball three-CD set of his Epic recordings from the 1980s, *The Music of Merle Haggard: The Epic Years* (Epic/Legacy 88697 76095 2), which features some of Merle's best singing ever, not only on some of his most accessible hits but on captivating versions of standards like "Pennies from Heaven," "The Old Watermill," "There! I've Said It Again," and "It's All in the Game."

And while we're at it (we are still at it, aren't we?), maybe the place to start with an artist of Merle's stature is the three Bear Family box sets of virtually every studio recording from 1962 to 1981, fifteen CDs in all, each set complete with its own extensive booklet: *Untamed Hawk: The Early Recordings of Merle Haggard* (Bear Family 15744); *Merle Haggard: The Studio Recordings 1969-1976* (Bear Family 16749); and *Merle Haggard: The Troubadour* (Bear Family 17250). I really wouldn't say this about many popular artists (honest—although the Jerry Lee Lewis chapter will totally contradict this statement), but there is so much to plumb here (there's quite a bit you can skip, too), I don't think you'll ever get your fill of Merle's inexhaustible imagination. And if you want to explore some of the roots of where all this music came from, Bear Family has recently released an extraordinary aural and textual document, *The Bakersfield Sound: Country Capital of the West 1940-1974* (BCD 16036), a ten-CD boxed set with a lavishly illustrated 224-page book by Scott B. Bomar that contains twenty-nine tracks by Merle, an almost equal number by Buck Owens, and innumerable contributions from those "assorted hillbillies" who made up the Bakersfield Sound, with nary a peep from Nashville.

Which cannot be said for Ken Burns' 2019 *Country Music* documentary series, which is Nashville-centric to the core (the rest, if not dross, is simply a sideshow), but still, even as it fails to recognize either Merle's or Bakersfield's rightful place in the country music firmament, it does at least offer Merle a significant and eloquent voice. On the other hand, if you're looking for an informal introduction to Merle in a rare relaxed and expansive mood, search out the Country Music Hall of Fame link to the panel discussion in which he participated on April 11, 2012, with longtime Strangers Norm Hamlet and Don Markham for the opening of the brilliant Bakersfield exhibit at the Hall of Fame. He was not billed, because true to form he was not about to commit to something he was unaccustomed, and not ordinarily inclined, to doing—in fact, he didn't commit at all until the moment he showed up unannounced, taking the place of Fuzzy Owen, his oldest associate, and looking like a down-and-outer who had just wandered in from "Lower Broad." But here you'll see Merle as he rarely presented himself: relaxed, engaged, emotional, and funny, with a warmth and graciousness that eschewed nostalgia but instead, for just that moment, celebrated an unconditional embrace of a shared past. At one point, talking about his ex-wife and lifetime partner Bonnie Owens, he comes close to tears, but what is most striking is the way in which, without ever surrendering that keen-eyed gaze, his face continues to be bathed in smiles. As Merle himself might have put it, quoting from the lyrics of one of his more upbeat songs, "I can't say we've had a good morning, but it's been a great afternoon."

And finally, let me just list a few of the songs that I always return to again and again, both well-known and obscure, but be forewarned: some of them are kind of on the gloomy side.

"I Can't Hold Myself in Line"; "The Day the Rains Came"; "Shelley's Winter Love"; "Mama's Hungry Eyes"; "I Take a Lot of Pride in What I Am"; "Leonard" (a rare biographical ballad about one of his principal mentors, Tommy Collins); "Sing Me Back Home"; "Things Aren't Funny Anymore"; "Mama Tried"; "Tulare Dust"; "They're Tearin' the Labor Camps Down"; "I Can't Be Myself (When I'm With You)"; "Holding Things Together"; "If We Make It Through December"; "Jesus, Take a Hold"; and maybe his best-known standard, "Today I Started Loving You Again." And—and—and, I mean, I know these last two are kind of cheats because he didn't write them, but listen to the feeling he imparts to Blaze Foley's sublime "If I Could Only Fly," and the depth of despair he brings to his duet with Peter Wolf on Peter's "It's Too Late for Me," a song that sounds as if it was written to order for Merle. (It appears on Peter's 2010 album, *Midnight Souvenirs* [Verve B0013896-02].)

And finally—I'm sorry, but what's so good about goodbye?—how could I omit what is said to be the last song he ever wrote, recorded in a ramshackle kind of arrangement at his home studio when he was too sick to go out on the road anymore but still kept writing and singing, a devastatingly bleak "Kern River Blues," which is available on YouTube with a succession of eloquent still images. Just heartbreaking. https://www.youtube.com/watch?v=L5xKRv23SVE

BILL MONROE: HARD WORKING MAN BLUES

I've got to provide a tip of the hat to my photographer on this trip, Russ Barnard, publisher and editor of *Country Music* magazine, where the original story appeared. (A year or so earlier we had gone on another road trip to Johnny Cash's baronial home on Hickory Lake, where Russ presented John with a special surprise, the twentieth-anniversary issue of *Country Music*, which was dedicated to John and contained a cover story represented by the eleventh chapter in this book.)

The book that was probably most helpful to me in preparing for my interview with Mr. Monroe was Jim Rooney's pathbreaking oral history, *Bossmen: Bill Monroe & Muddy Waters* (Dial Press, 1971), both because of its warm, generous-spirited nature — and because it was in print at the time! Since then I have read, with great interest and edification, Richard D. Smith's *Can't You Hear Me Callin': The Life of Bill Monroe, Father of Bluegrass* (Little, Brown, 2000) and, for a very different take on some of the more rollicking aspects of the bluegrass life, or maybe just life itself, Tom Piazza's *True Adventures with the King of Bluegrass: Jimmy Martin* (Country Music Foundation Press, 1999). For another kind of treat, check out Bobby Anderson's contagiously enthusiastic *That Muhlenberg Sound* (revised edition, McDowell Publishing, 2005) for an extensive picture of the origins of "thumb picking" (actually a thumb-and-finger-picking roll, which would come to be known as Merle Travis–style guitar) and all the formative influences on, and connections between, Bill Monroe, Merle Travis, Chet Atkins, and Ike Everly. In addition, it's worth seeking out Ralph Rinzler's chapter on Monroe in *Stars of Country Music,* edited by Bill Malone and Judith McCulloh (University of Illinois Press, 1975) and the must-read Charles Wolfe liner notes (actually, an eighty-eight-page booklet, with a definitive 1936-1949 discography by Monroe scholar Neil V. Rosenberg, whose *Bluegrass: A History* [University of Illinois Press, 1985] is also essential reading) to the monumental Bear Family six-CD set, *Blue Moon of Kentucky: Bill Monroe 1936-1949* (Bear Family 16399). This is about as good an introduction to the Monroe biography as you can get. And the music is unparalleled.

Obviously that's not where you should stop. There are any number of individual albums and collections, including a fine four-CD set compiled by the Country Music Hall of Fame, *The Music of Bill Monroe from 1936 to 1994* (MCA D4-11048, if you can find it), and there's another Bear Family box (*Bill Monroe: Bluegrass* 1950-1958 [Bear Family 15423]), but I would say *Blue Moon of Kentucky: Bill Monroe 1936-1949* (Bear Family 16399) is definitely the place to start, documenting as it does the birth of a new music, with all of its early stars (Bill and Charlie Monroe, Lester Flatt, Earl Scruggs, Stringbean, Chubby Wise, et al.) making their dazzling debut appearances.

LONNIE MACK: FUNKY COUNTRY LIVING

Nick Tosches and Don Light got me together with Lonnie in the first place. Nick was living in Nashville at the time and working for Don Light Talent, and his enthusiasm for Lonnie and, even more, Delbert McClinton, another client, was indefatigable. Don was just a wonderful guy with whom I became great friends in later life, whose modesty, wit, and charm are chronicled in Peter Cooper's *Johnny's Cash & Charley's Pride* (Spring House Press, 2017). Lonnie's daughter Holly Mack (McIntosh) has been a great help with her encouragement and her vivid memories of her father. So has Bruce Iglauer, who introduced me to Holly, and Ben Sandmel as well as Bill Millar (don't miss Bill's collection of seminal rock and roots writings, *Let the Good Times Rock!* [Music Mentor Books, 2004]) have been champions of Lonnie from the start.

From my point of view, Lonnie's Elektra recordings capture him at the peak of his powers. There's a two-CD set, *Lonnie Mack: The Complete Elektra Recordings* (Wounded Bird WOU 1014), that incorporates all of this material, starting with his first, and most essential, Elektra album, *Glad I'm in the Band* (original LP catalogue number Elektra EKS 74040), which you can't beat for sheer naked soulfulness and distinction. But hell, all four of the albums included here are essential (and soulful) in their own way: *Whatever's Right* (originally Elektra EKS 74050), just as intense if not quite as consistent; the more muted *Hills of Indiana* (Elektra EKS 74102), which even includes a version of Bill Monroe's "Uncle Pen"; and his very first album, *The Wham of That Memphis Man!* (Elektra EKS 74077), licensed from the Fraternity label and featuring his original hit recording of "Memphis," along with several other shimmering instrumentals and two of his greatest vocals, "Where There's a Will There's a Way" and "Why." And if that's not enough for you, *Memphis Wham!*, a twenty-four-track collection of his Fraternity recordings (Ace 713), adds another dozen or so Fraternity recordings to the original album, all with beautiful remastering and presentation. Which leaves the more personal Capitol albums and blues-rock Alligator recordings still to explore. Suffice it to say that there's no one quite like Lonnie (not Stevie Ray Vaughan, not Eric Clapton, not Keith Richards) in his combination of guitar pyrotechnics and incontestably soulful vocals. Think of him at his best as a combination of Bobby "Blue" Bland, Charlie Rich, Dan Penn, and James Brown—and then just forget about the comparisons and appreciate him on his own.

DELBERT MCCLINTON: NIGHT LIFE

Much thanks to Delbert's wife, Wendy Goldstein, whom Doc Pomus first introduced me to at the Bottom Line. Also to Delbert's biographer, Diana Finlay Hendricks, whose *Delbert McClinton: One of the Fortunate Few* (Texas A&M University Press, 2017) really fills out the picture.

For a broad introduction to Delbert's music, *Delbert McClinton: The Definitive Collection* (Hip-O B0006873-02) includes a well-selected presentation of material over a period of thirty-plus (1961–1997) years—but, you know, if you had to choose one album in particular, *Victim of Life's Circumstances* (original LP issue: ABC Records ABCD-907) would be the one you would never want to miss. Then there's the charming (and highly original) early Delbert and Glen material originally issued on Clean Records and included on *The Delbert and Glen Sessions 1972–1973* (Australian Raven label, RV-CD 184). Really, there are just so many consistently rewarding Delbert albums, including *The Jealous Kind* (original LP release: Capitol/Muscle Shoals Sound Records ST-12115). There are a couple of *Live from Austin* albums from 1989 (Alligator 4773) and 2006 (New West 6099)—they're both good, but I think I'd choose the first. And Delbert is still releasing fine albums and writing pointed, up-to-the-emotional-minute songs, right up to and including 2019's *Tall, Dark & Handsome* (Hot Shot Records HSR 002), which Delbert describes as "kind of a salute to Texas blues, the music I grew up on." But don't miss him live if you have the chance—that's where Delbert always shines.

JOE TEX: HOLD WHAT YOU'VE GOT

I've stayed in touch with Joe's widow, Bilaliah Hazziez, and their son, Ramadan, and Bilaliah has continued to be a good friend and a great help all these years. Joe McEwen and I have discussed the case of Joe Tex endlessly—what a great artist he was, what a great guy, and how cruelly he has been overlooked by subsequent generations who could still learn from, and (let's be real) continue to be entertained by, him. Joe McEwen met Joe a few years before I did, and his 1977 celebration of Joe ("Joe Tex: The Soul of an Underdog," *Boston Phoenix*, 5/31/77) is well worth seeking out.

Ace Records has done their usual exemplary job of presenting Joe's music in three CDs on the Kent and Southbound labels: *Skinny Legs and All: The Classic Early Dial Sides* (Kent 114), which takes him from his first recordings for Buddy Killen to his breakthrough hits; *You're Right, Joe Tex* (Kent 117), which picks up the story with equally strong material from 1968 to 1970 more or less; and *Ain't Gonna Bump No More* (Southbound [GY]CDSEWD 043), which consists primarily, but not exclusively, of his novelty hits from the '70s. But even if you get all of these compilations, don't under any circumstances miss out on *Buying a Book* (original 1969 LP issue: Atlantic 8231), my favorite Joe Tex album and one of the most incisive personal collections of songs in the entire oeuvre of soul, with its precise observations and sly wit. Listen to "Grandma Mary" and "Anything You Wanna Know" for sharp-edged portraits of the grandmother who raised him and the town in which he grew up.

And here, just as a point of reference, are some Joe Tex songs to look out for, both pre- and post-Dial, with just a few repetitions, that you might otherwise have missed from the first Kent CD. And while you're at it, don't forget to check out the internet for some utterly beguiling videos of the Joe Tex Show in Spain, Scandinavia, France, and who knows where else, which surface and resurface occasionally on YouTube.

"All I Could Do Was Cry"; "Ain't I a Mess"; "Baby You're Right"; "I Had a Good Home (But I Left)"; "You Keep Her"; "Meet Me in Church"; "The Only Girl I've Ever Loved"; "Sit Yourself Down"; "Don't Play"; "Don't Make Your Children Pay (For Your Mistakes)"; "One Monkey Don't Stop No Show"; "Mama Red"; "I'll Make Every Day Christmas"; "Hold What You've Got" (live from the Brooklyn Fox); "The Love You Save"; "Papa's Dream."

DICK CURLESS: THE RETURN OF THE TUMBLEWEED KID

Dick's daughter, Terry Curless Chinnock, has been tireless, kind, and enthusiastic in digging into her father's archives and calling up family memories with warmth and affection. Her mother, Pauline, has provided answers to some key questions, and her son, William Chinnock, continues to scour the internet for video clips of his father and grandfather. William's late father, Bill, made a start at a documentary, *Dick Curless: Portrait of a Country Singer*, which was unfortunately curtailed by ill health, but the eleven and a half minutes of footage he assembled as part of a grant application is available on YouTube (http://www.youtube.com/watch?v=weHwwoj47hc). There's lots more Dick Curless available on the internet, more of it showing up all the time, largely due to the efforts of William Chinnock and longtime New England country music mainstay Bucky Mitchell.

So far as written material goes, Dick gave me a ton, but the best by far is "The Aroostook County Cowboy" by Mel R. Allen in the January 1993 issue of *Yankee* magazine. This is where the eloquent quote by Dick at the front of the chapter comes from. In addition, there is a fine story, "Dick Curless: Back on the Track," by the late John Morthland, a sadly underappreciated writer about rock and country, in the December 1975 issue of *Country Music* magazine. (John's *The Best of Country Music* [Dolphin/Doubleday, 1984], a "Critical and Historical Guide to the 750 Greatest [Country] Albums," remains a lively and thought-provoking introduction to the first sixty years of recorded country music.) Also, Kevin Coffey's biographical booklet for the first Bear Family set of Dick's recordings, *Dick Curless: A Tombstone Every Mile* (see below), accompanied by a meticulous discography through 1969, is absolutely essential. And Clifford R. Murphy's *Yankee Twang: Country and Western Music in New England* (University of Illinois Press, 2014) provides an overview of the

At the wheel of his father's truck. *Courtesy of Terry Curless Chinnock*

tradition from which Dick emerged and which he so greatly influenced. Cliff also shared his interview with Dick's brother, Phil, with me, and put me in touch with Dan Fulkerson, who has been back in Oklahoma for years and offered up vivid memories of his first meeting with Dick in Bangor and their early commercial success.

Returning once again to the internet, *The Eventful Life of Al Hawkes* (https://vimeo.com/16297214) is on no account to be missed, and *The Genius of Lenny Breau,* guided by his daughter, Emily Hughes, is well worth seeking out, though it seems to be only fitfully available.

The central listening experience for this book is, of course, *Traveling Through* (Rounder CD 3137). If you've read the chapter, you'll know that in my opinion anyway it's both exalted and sublime. For almost everything else I would recommend the seven-CD Bear Family set referenced above, *Dick Curless: A Tombstone Every Mile* (Bear Family BCD 15882), which covers virtually everything from his 1950 recording debut through 1969, including all his Event sides, his Event audition, various appearances on the Arthur Godfrey shows, and even some Rice Paddy Ranger broadcasts from Korea. It carries you right up through the two albums he recorded with Jack Clement in Nashville, and I think that should probably be enough. However, there *is* a second box set, *Hard, Hard Traveling Man* (Bear Family 16171), which rounds out the Capitol years and has some real gems (including the home recordings that directly foreshadow his Rounder set). But definitely start with the first. And then look for some of the lost treasures that continue to turn up, as both audio and video, on the internet. And, just as a postscript, be sure to check out Merle Travis' *Folk Songs of the Hills* in whatever format you can find it, which, while it may have aged — not musically but in the semi-didactic manner of its presentation — was an invaluable source of material not just for Dick but for a whole generation of serious-minded folk and country singers, providing a model for the influential "theme albums" of both Johnny Cash and Merle Haggard.

JOHN R. CASH: I WILL ROCK AND ROLL WITH YOU (IF I HAVE TO)

Many thanks to Mark Stielper, John's unofficial official historian, biographer, and close friend, and one too infrequently acknowledged for his extraordinary insights, information, and depth-of-field understanding and appreciation of Johnny Cash. Thanks also to Marty Stuart for much of the same. He has been a real friend, and a great resource on all sorts of far-flung subjects, since our first meeting in Dallas in 1980, just after he joined John's band. (Listen to his ardent-but-accurate testimony in the A&E documentary *Sam Phillips: The Man Who Invented Rock 'n' Roll* as well as in Ken Burns' *Country*.) Both Patrick Carr and Steve Turner were an invaluable help to me in writing about John in my Sam Phillips biography. Patrick's *Cash: The Autobiography* (HarperSanFrancisco, 1997), based on extensive interviews over the years, is probably the best of the Cash-authored books (there are a bunch), while Steve's *The Man Called Cash* (W Publishing Group, 2004) focuses with great sensitivity on his spiritual side. Robert Hilburn's magisterial *Johnny Cash: The Life* (Little, Brown, 2013) is both meticulously researched and narratively compelling, with its never-less-than-scrupulous alertness to the telling detail.

With respect to the music, just as a start why not try *Johnny Cash: Up Through the Years, 1955–1957* (Bear Family BCD 15247), a twenty-four-track, single-CD selection of the most essential Sun material? For a more offbeat, idiosyncratically comprehensive approach, check out the Gregg Geller–produced *Johnny Cash: The Legend* (Columbia/Legacy C4K 92802), a fifty-year, four-CD package that groups the songs in rough thematic sequence in order to suggest some of the breadth, diversity, and complexity of Johnny Cash's work. For even more adventurous twists and turns, try Gregg's official *Bootleg* series, Volumes II (*From Memphis to Hollywood*) and III (*Live Around the World*) in particular. On these (Columbia/Legacy 88697 60051 and 88697 93033 respectively) you will discover,

Onstage, October 1969.
Photograph by Sandy Speiser.
Courtesy of Sony Music Archives

among other things, his first radio broadcast in the spring of 1955 and some of his early demos (Vol. II) as well as rare live performances, early and late (Vol. III). And, oh, hell, while you're at it, you might just look into *Johnny Cash: The Outtakes* (Bear Family BCD 16325), which provides a fascinating glimpse of the evolution of some of his earliest Sun sides. Meanwhile, bear in mind that there remains an entire body of work still to come, with all the Columbia hits, theme albums like *Ride This Train* (original LP number Columbia CS 8255) and *Bitter Tears: Ballads of the American Indian* (original LP number Columbia CS 9048), not to mention the live ones recorded at Folsom Prison and San Quentin. And then there are all the other creative sidetracks (or, actually, I think they're on the mainline, too), including books, documentaries, and a sparkling two-DVD set, *The Best of the Johnny Cash TV Show 1969–1971* (Sony/Legacy 88697040269), which, starting with Bob Dylan's and Joni Mitchell's appearances on the very first show, definitely lives up to its title. So, as I'm sure you've noticed by now, once again I'm just going to sidestep the adjudication process — the decision is entirely yours.

TAMMY WYNETTE: 'TIL I CAN MAKE IT ON MY OWN

Tammy was working on her autobiography when I spoke with her, and it turned out to be almost everything she could have hoped for, both as a book and as a television movie. (Well, it's true she didn't get her theatrical release, and she didn't get the stars she imagined, but still. . . .) *Stand By Your Man: An Autobiography* (Simon and Schuster, 1979) is both well researched and sensitively written in Tammy's voice by Joan Dew, whom I would later meet while working on my Sam Cooke biography. (Dew and her then-husband, Al Schmitt, Sam's engineer, spent much of Sam's last night with him at a Hollywood restaurant, talking about his plans for an upcoming blues album.) Jimmy McDonough's *Tammy Wynette: Tragic Country Queen* (Viking, 2010) is worlds away from Dew's more conventional first-person approach, beginning with a love letter from the author to his deceased subject — but it is at the same time both more personal and, not surprisingly, more intimate, another recommended stop on Jimmy McDonough's own self-determined, Hubert Selby-esque literary trail, which began with his startling profile of Little Jimmy Scott, "All the Way with Jimmy Scott: For Whatever the Reason" (*Village Voice Rock & Roll Quarterly*, Winter 1988).

For Tammy's music, I can only offer my own very square-john selection — I'm afraid I'm just not that familiar with the outer fringes of her work. *The Essential Tammy Wynette* (Sony Legacy 88883741152), a two-CD set, not only has all the hits, it covers the spectrum of her career and features some of her most beautiful singing. It includes a few of her own compositions, concluding with a 1993 version of her painfully imagined fairy-tale world, "That's the Way It Could Have Been (That's the Way It Should Have Been)," with Dolly Parton and Loretta Lynn singing backup. You really should seek out more of her solo compositions, though, which were rarely released as singles and thus are not on this collection of hits. *The Essential Tammy Wynette* also includes a handful of deeply felt duets with George Jones, but once again you should seek out more, and *George Jones & Tammy Wynette: 16 Biggest Hits* (Epic EK 69969) is probably the best, and easiest, solution. But, at the risk of repetition, I really have to encourage both you and myself to keep on digging, particularly for live versions of some of their most affecting songs.

LEE SMITH: TELLING TALES

All I can do here is thank Lee for her extraordinary friendship over the last twenty-five years, beginning with our first meeting in Chapel Hill, when I came to write the story. (In fact, we should have met twenty-eight years earlier, in 1967, when we were among the fourteen recipients of the Book-of-the-Month Club Writing Fellowship award for graduating college seniors, but Lee was busy getting married, so she skipped the New York ceremony.) And, you know, I feel like I really need to stipulate that Lee is *everyone's* best friend — and I don't say that lightly. Because I very much doubt that anyone who has ever had a chance to get to know her would deny her generosity of spirit, the extraordinary way that she will extend herself for others while never abandoning the discipline of her work, or the many special, and indefinable, qualities of kindness and empathy that, even under the most trying of circumstances, will always manifest themselves, both in her writing and in real life.

Her books reward reading and rereading, not just the novels and short stories but her memoir, too (*Dimestore: A Writer's Life*, Algonquin, 2016). Maybe my favorite (though I'm not sure Lee would thank me for this—it may well say more about me than her) is the uncharacteristically dark *Black Mountain Breakdown* (G. P. Putnam's Sons, 1980). It's not a direction she chose to pursue, though the first two-thirds of *Saving Grace* (G. P. Putnam's Sons, 1995) probably comes closest. But the place you should really start (forget about my preferences) is with the novels that first won her so extraordinarily devoted an audience, an audience that would certainly have assured her of best-seller status, had family obligations not prevented her from traveling at the time. (Read her extraordinarily moving "Goodbye to the Sunset Man," *The Independent Weekly*, 10/06/04, and online.) Those books would include *Oral History* (G. P. Putnam's Sons, 1983), *Family Linen* (G. P. Putnam's Sons, 1985), *Fair and Tender Ladies* (G. P. Putnam's Sons, 1988), and *The Devil's Dream* (G. P. Putnam's Sons, 1992), all of which draw on the Appalachian heritage that was the key to her discovery of her writing voice. Each is expressed in a different but consistently engaging way. (*Fair and Tender Ladies* is an epistolary novel, *The Devil's Dream* a mythic retelling of the evolution of country music through the story of a fictionalized Carter Family.) Several of her novels and short stories have invited stage adaptations, with *Fair and Tender Ladies* inspiring a memorable musical score from songwriters Tom House, Tommy Goldsmith, and Karren Pell that can stand on its own. And while we're on musical connections, Lee and fellow novelist (and former student) Jill McCorkle, along with singer-songwriter friends Marshall Chapman and Matraca Berg, created a Southern feminist musical entertainment, *Good Ol' Girls*, which premiered in a workshop production at Chapel Hill in 1998, briefly became an off-Broadway show, and now has morphed into "An Evening of Stories and Songs" by the four of them. (Lee plays tambourine.) Don't miss it if you have the chance, especially with the irrepressibly rowdy and enthusiastic female audience (along with a less vocal, but no less enthusiastic male constituency) that it always attracts.

CALL THE DOCTOR: THE FURTHER ADVENTURES OF DOC POMUS, PART I

Okay, I think I may have gone a little overboard in my personal panegyric to Lee, but I could say the same (if slightly different) thing about Doc. There are hundreds, maybe thousands, of musicians, gamblers, elevator operators, club owners, aspirational humanists, and restaurateurs who could attest to the privilege that friendship with Doc conferred as well. But, as good a friend as Doc was, Doc's daughter, Sharyn, whose photographs are featured throughout this book, has shown equal qualities of good-ness and no-bullshit determination, albeit without some of Doc's more challenging qualities. And his good friend Shirlee Hauser has always been a truth teller, too, dear to both Doc's heart and the truth of his story.

The documentary that Sharyn started out to make, *Magic and Flying*, eventually evolved into *AKA Doc Pomus* under the direction of Peter Miller and Will Hechter (but with the full participation of Sharyn). It's as good a way as I can imagine of getting to know Doc, as soulful a documentary as I have ever seen (you can read more about it in Doc's chapter), bringing Doc to life in the company of all his friends and family, embracing emotion wholeheartedly and without reservation but eschewing sentimentalization. *Lonely Avenue: The Unlikely Life and Times of Doc Pomus* by Alex Halberstadt (Da Capo, 2007) fills in some of the facts. And if you want to get a peek at his notebooks (as well as some additional material on Doc), look for "Doc Pomus: A Special Feature" in *Antaeus on Music*, a special edition of the periodical published by Ecco Press (No. 71/72, Autumn 1993).

Here are some other ways to get to know Doc. There are three albums featuring Doc as a singer. The title track of *It's Great to Be Young and in Love* ("Whiskey, Women, and . . ." LP 713) is in fact the original demo version of Doc and Mort Shuman's 1959 Top 10 hit for Dion DiMucci, "Why Must I Be a Teenager in Love?" With liner notes about each song by Doc, I guess for me that makes it the preferred album. An earlier compilation, *Send for the Doctor: The Early Years, 1944–55* ("Whiskey, Women, and . . ." LP 700), has similar Doc notes, while *Blues in the Red* (Rev-Ola CD 148) offers a somewhat different assortment, but without the Dion demo and without Doc's notes. Then there's *The Pomus and Shuman Story: Double Trouble 1956–1967* (Ace 1152), a single, twenty-six-track CD that features some of Doc and Mort's most famous tracks ("Lonely Avenue," "A Teenager in Love," and "Save the Last Dance for Me," for example, in their original versions by Ray Charles, Dion,

With Ahmet Ertegun
and Ben E. King,
South Street
Seaport, 1986.
*Courtesy of Sharyn
Felder*

and the Drifters respectively), along with some of their most obscure ("Wake Up Miss Rip Van Winkle" by the Tibbs Brothers). There's also a well-intended tribute album, *Till the Night Is Gone: A Tribute to Doc Pomus* (Forward 71878), with contributions by Bob Dylan, B.B. King, Aaron Neville, Brian Wilson, Dr. John, and others. And then there's the Robert Altman movie *Short Cuts,* for which Doc and Mac wrote several songs, including the great "To Hell with Love." There's a soundtrack CD (*Music From and Inspired by the Film Short Cuts* [Imago 72787-21014-2]), but be sure to check out the movie first, which, starting with the Raymond Carver stories that inspired it (which could just as easily have been inspired by Doc's songs), for my money is right up Doc's alley.

Doc couldn't have been prouder of the album that he and Mac wrote for B.B. King, *There Must Be a Better World Somewhere* (MCA Records 5162), the title track in particular. But for me the crown jewel of Doc recordings is *Johnny Adams Sings Doc Pomus: The Real Me* (Rounder 2109), a project conceived of originally by producer Scott Billington both out of his admiration for Doc's songs and his sense that they not only provided a perfect match for Johnny's virtuosic voice (he wasn't known as "The Tan Canary" for nothing), they afforded Johnny the opportunity to take on broader themes and deeper meanings as well. Doc threw himself into the project and was still actively involved in the writing and selection of songs until just days before he died. Although he never got to hear the results, there is no question in my mind that he would have seen the album as the realization of his vision—though certainly not as the conclusion of his journey. In his declaratively matter-of-fact, but strangely inspirational, way, I'm sure he would have insisted that there were plenty of songs still to write, plenty of miles still to go.

ME AND THE COLONEL

Colonel's widow, Loanne Parker, has been unflagging in her efforts to help in any way she could. So has Jack Soden, longtime head of Elvis Presley Enterprises and a not-so-secret admirer of Colonel's over the years. More recently, Paul Gongaware, one of Colonel's many loyal disciples (he started with Colonel in the '70s and today, as co-CEO of Concerts West, promotes Rolling Stones tours worldwide), has shared some of his memories and thoughts about the man he continues to admire, who he strongly feels, like so many others who knew the man behind the mask, has been much misunderstood by history.

The Colonel has not been well served by books or movies either, whether in documentary or feature films. There is a Dutch documentary, *Dries van Kuijk: Het Nederlandse Geheim Achter Elvis,* which premiered in 2009 on the hundredth anniversary of his birth and includes interviews with Loanne Parker and his brother Ad—I suspect it may have a fuller, and more sympathetic, view of the man known as Colonel Thomas A. Parker, but I haven't seen it, and I don't know that it's scheduled for English-language release. You might get a kick out of watching the interview Colonel did with Ted Koppel on *Nightline* on the tenth anniversary of Elvis' death—it offers *some* sense of his canniness, directness, self-amusement, and inscrutability. I've always felt that Colonel's letters would serve him best in terms of self-portrayal—I tried to tell him this once, but he told me he was way ahead of me and showed me letters of thanks for his many charitable contributions. For twenty-five years I've wanted to put together a collection of those letters, which show him at his wittiest, most calculating, astute, and covertly affectionate best—well, I hope you'll have a chance to judge for yourself before another decade passes.

Thomas A. Parker, Hawaii, ca. 1930. *Courtesy of Elvis Presley Enterprises*

HENRY GREEN: A PERSONAL MEMOIR AND APPRECIATION

I think from reading the chapter you can get an idea of the novels I would recommend most: *Living, Caught, Loving,* and *Back,* which are available in many different packages and editions. Of the four my favorite right now is *Back,* but *Loving* might provide the easiest entrée, and I would stress that each of Green's five additional novels, as well as his autobiography, yields pleasures of its own.

John Russell's *Henry Green: Nine Novels and an Unpacked Bag* (Rutgers University Press, 1960) provides an appreciative, affectionate, and insightful view of Green's work from someone who knew him and toward whom Green clearly felt affection himself. Green in fact showed me a baseball autographed by the Atlanta Braves that Russell had given him (Russell's father, "Honey," was a legendary scout as well as a member of the Basketball Hall of Fame), which provided him with one of those occasions he so relished, combining both puzzlement and delight.

John Updike was his greatest latter-day champion, tirelessly promoting Green's work in *The New Yorker* and the *New York Review of Books,* celebrating his style, spurring on new editions of his work, providing the introduction to a 1978 collection of three of his novels (*Loving, Living,* and *Party Going*) and a 1992 compendium of his uncollected, and in some cases unpublished, writings. I still have the postcard that Updike sent me in 1962, a year or so before my meeting with Henry Green. (Are you kidding? Did you think there might be any chance that I *wouldn't*?) I had written him a letter asking whether I was imagining what seemed to me a direct link between Updike's first novel, *The Poorhouse Fair,* and Green's third-to-last, *Concluding,* to which he thrillingly replied: "Yes, quite right," in response to my question, and then went on, "I revere the man as a stylist almost above anybody living. Why not say it; above <u>anybody</u> living. . . . But no one in this country reads Green, I guess. Except me, my wife, and now you." Do I have to spell it out for you? I was walking on air.

In addition to Green's novels and memoir, there is an illuminating biography, *Romancing: The Life and Work of Henry Green* (Random House, 2001), by Jeremy Treglown. There is also that anthology of his writings introduced by John Updike and put together by Green's son, Matthew Yorke, *Surviving: The Uncollected Writings of Henry Green* (Chatto and Windus, 1992). This includes such items as the inimitable 1958 *Paris Review* interview concocted by Green and Terry Southern and a twenty-page introduction to the wartime memoir he was working on when I met him (the only piece of it that he completed), which he proposed to call *London and Fire 1939–1945.*

SOME CATS KNOW: WORDS AND MUSIC BY LEIBER & STOLLER

Randy Poe, longtime president of Leiber and Stoller Music Publishing and, like Sam Phillips, a native Florentine, has always been my great friend and go-to source over the years, an inestimable source of both information and advice—and not just with respect to this chapter either.

Mike and Jerry did finally get their own book, *Hound Dog: The Leiber and Stoller Autobiography* (Simon and Schuster, 2009), written with David Ritz in what amounted to separate-but-equal alternating monologues. Skillfully assembled by Ritz, it does a good job of capturing much of the substance, and even more of the tone, of their long-standing partnership and separate selves and lives.

For a survey of their music from first to almost last, Ace Records in England has put together a handsome trio of albums, *The Leiber & Stoller Story,* Volumes 1-3 (Ace 1010, 1116, and 1156). Volumes 1 and 2 are the indispensable ones, with their exemplary representation of early blues, "playlets," and unexpected originals. Volume 3 offers its own unexpected share of treasures (choice Red Bird tracks, Jerry Leiber's lead vocal with the Coasters on "Shake 'Em Up and Let 'Em Roll," and Peggy Lee's "Is That All There Is," among others). For a fair share of Coasters hits you really need to pick up a Coasters album, with *50 Coastin' Classics* (Rhino R2-71090), which includes their earliest tracks (as the Robins), offering the greatest depth and breadth. There are so many other directions to pursue, but one place to start would be with their earliest hitmaker, Big Mama Thornton, and probably the place to begin with her is an album that goes back to her original hit, *Hound Dog: The Peacock Recordings* (MCA 10668). But I've got to say, for pure thrills, chills, and delight, I would jump to a couple of albums that she recorded more than a decade later for the blues label Arhoolie. *Big Mama Thornton in Europe* (Arhoolie 9056) presents her at her majestic best in a wide variety of settings, and with a wide variety of accompanists, including Buddy Guy, harmonica virtuoso Walter Horton, and, in a couple of solo outings, Mississippi blues slide guitarist Fred McDowell. The second album, *Ball N' Chain* (Arhoolie CD 305), duplicates eight of the cuts on *Big Mama in Europe,* but the eight remaining tracks include six with the Muddy Waters band and a re-recording of "Ball and Chain," a song that Janis Joplin borrowed with Thornton's explicit permission and from which Big Mama probably derived more income than all of her other work combined.

PRODUCING A LEGEND: WILLIE DIXON AND THE BLUES

Much thanks to Mary Katherine Aldin, a longtime Dixon family friend, for both her photographs and long-standing friendship. And *I Am the Blues: The Willie Dixon Story* (Da Capo, 1990), written with Don Snowden, presents a finely honed picture of the facts and the fancies, as suggested by its title.

Willie never ceased to think of himself as an artist from Big Three Trio days on, and you can certainly search out his albums if you like. But for my money it's his production work and his writing for others — Muddy Waters and Howlin' Wolf in particular, but so

Courtesy of Mary Katherine Aldin

many more—for which he will always be remembered. Just in case you don't already know, let me tip you to the revolutionary recordings he produced for Cobra Records during a two-year break from his principal employer, Chess Records. The single greatest repository is *The Cobra Records Story 1956-1958* (Capricorn 42012-2), a two-CD compilation which highlights "The Songs, Musicianship and Arranging Talents of Willie Dixon." In that brief space of time Willie recorded Otis Rush, Magic Sam, and Buddy Guy, creating a new style of Chicago blues, loosely designated as "West Side Blues," while also producing priceless sides on Sunnyland Slim, Walter Horton, Sonny Boy Williamson, and Little Willie Foster, among others. All of Otis Rush and Magic Sam's Cobra singles are included on this boxed set (a couple are represented by majestic alternate takes), along with Buddy Guy's two singles on Artistic, a Cobra subsidiary. And I should stipulate, no one should be without a complete CD dedicated to nothing but Otis Rush's epochal masterpieces, complete with alternate takes and meaningful variations, which is available as *The Essential Otis Rush: The Classic Cobra Recordings 1956-1958* (Varese Sarabande/Fuel 302 061 0772) or *Otis Rush— Good 'Un's: The Classic Cobra Recordings 1956-1958* (West Side 858). These may be the pinnacle of Willie's producing prowess (you will be astonished at the difference between his own 1952 Big Three Trio recording of "My Love Will Never Die"—it's on YouTube—and the chilling transformation it achieves in Otis Rush's version) as well as one of the unquestionable pinnacles of postwar blues. But just to round things out (you know, there's so much more) don't under any circumstances miss the masterpiece that he produced with Arhoolie Records owner Chris Strachwitz in 1968, *John Littlejohn: Chicago Blues Stars* (Arhoolie CD 1043) aka *John Littlejohn: Slidin' Home* (Arhoolie CD 9019)—it's the same album, the first by a thirty-seven-year-old bluesman who had already played with everyone from Jimmy Reed to Howlin' Wolf. It's as if he had been waiting for this moment all his life—though the moment was never to be repeated—as he combines an ascendant evocation of Elmore James' slide guitar with an assortment of songs (by both Willie and himself) that, with Willie Dixon's input, can sometimes rise almost to the level of an Otis Rush.

MEETING CHUCK BERRY

Bill Greensmith, British expat, St. Louis emigré, and co-editor of *Blues Unlimited: Essential Interviews from the Original Blues Magazine* (University of Illinois Press, 2015), which offers an essential (and fascinating) window on blues history, has helped me with research, photos, information, and advice, as he has in the past. So has Fred Rothwell, author of the seminal discography *Long Distance Information: Chuck Berry's Recorded Legacy* (Music Mentor Books, 2001), which has morphed into The Chuck Berry Database online (http://www.crlf.de/ChuckBerry/cbdb/) curated by Morton Reff, Dietmar Rudolph, and himself. That's the go-to destination for all Chuck Berry information (bibliographical, discographical, epistemological, etc.) and needs.

Chuck Berry: The Autobiography (Harmony Books, 1987) is the primary clue to the Inner Chuck if not the Facts of Chuck, an indisputable masterpiece, which, unlike any of the other autobiographies that I've alluded to here, was entirely (and brilliantly) self-written. Another indispensable clue to the Mystery of Chuck is *Chuck Berry: Hail! Hail! Rock 'n' Roll: The Ultimate Collector's Edition* (Universal/Image ID3156THDVD), a four-DVD set commemorating and including the feature film made from an all-star concert put together to celebrate Chuck's sixtieth birthday in St. Louis. I don't know if I'd go so far as to call the film itself a flawed masterpiece (the ways in which it falls short are entirely

St. Louis, 1948.
*Photograph by Harry
Davis © Bill Greensmith
Collection*

due to Chuck), but it provides undeniable examples of both his shining genius and his self-lacerating flaws. Some of the highlights: rehearsal scenes with Keith Richards, Eric Clapton, and Chuck's original pianist, Johnnie Johnson, that far exceed most of the performances in the concert itself; Chuck reciting the poem "Even This Shall Pass Away," with Robbie Robertson improvising delicately on acoustic guitar ("That's beautiful," Chuck says at several points — and it is); a guided tour of Chuck's personal scrapbook, once again initiated by Robbie, which turns into perhaps the most open and revealing interview Chuck ever did. Another totally unexpected bonus is a conversation with Little Richard and Bo Diddley in which Chuck very sweetly attempts to teach them something about the music *business*. (It's all about *ownership* is the lesson he comes back to again and again, as again and again they seem to fail to grasp the point.) Overall, all these "extras" provide a fascinating glimpse of some of the strengths and all of the weaknesses of Chuck's stubborn, go-it-alone, sometimes cruel, and not infrequently self-defeating approach. This really is must viewing, even if at times (quite a few times) it can be difficult to take.

For another, very different approach, a well-researched and altogether sobering rendition of the facts, you might check out Bruce Pegg's *Brown Eyed Handsome Man: The Life and Hard Times of Chuck Berry: An Unauthorized Biography* (Routledge, 2002). But for a totally different, if no less indecipherable side of Chuck, in which Chuck cops to reading *Crime and Punishment* as well as Madame Blavatsky, read Brian Cullman's lovely sketch, "Mr. Berry and Mrs. Blavatsky," which appeared in the *Paris Review*, March 21, 2017. Oh, and one more recent discovery (by me anyway — maybe old to everyone else), a fifty-four-minute 1980 *Omnibus* BBC documentary, *Chuck Berry: Johnny B. Goode,* which provides a compelling, well-articulated, and often surprising (though very blurred in the very blurry version I've been able to see) glimpse of the inner Chuck, along with lots of performance footage of every sort.

So far as sounds go, you could do worse than go back to the first three LPs, *After School Session* (Chess LP 1426), *One Dozen Berrys* (Chess LP 1432, with a cover shot of Chuck in a sea of berries), and *Chuck Berry Is on Top* (Chess LP 1435, illustrated by an inviting photo of a sumptuous sundae with, naturally, berries — but not Chuck this time — on top). Well, I'm kidding, kind of, though they're all great and available collectively on a two-CD British set. On a more practical note, *Chuck Berry: The Great Twenty-Eight* (MCA/Chess Records CHD-92500, available in a number of different two-LP, one-CD configurations) would be one place to start. It's pretty much unimpeachable, as far as it goes, although it *is* missing such essential tracks as "Down Bound Train," "You Never Can Tell," "Promised Land," and "Tulane," all of which are available on *Chuck Berry: His Best* Vols. I and II (MCA/Chess 9371 and 9381), which unfortunately are more impeachable in other, more undifferentiating ways. Finally, for completeness' sake, you can go to *Chuck Berry: Johnny B. Goode: His Complete '50s Chess Recordings* (Geffen/Hip-O Select B0009473), a four-CD set that includes many alternate and unissued takes, some of which are fascinating, others not. None of the essential '60s sides are here, though. They are available on a second box, *Chuck Berry: You Never Can Tell: His Complete Chess Recordings 1960-1966* (Geffen/Hip-O Select B001 2465), which has some great material, but not enough to justify its size or selection. I really don't mean to be cranky—I just wish (and you know what they say about wishes) there could be one aesthetically pleasing two- or three-volume set of all of Chuck's moments of triumph in the studio, both hits and obscurities, like Library of America editions of Mark Twain or Jack Kerouac, say. But, of course, today you can always make up your own selection and listen to it in any order you like. And with all that said, in fact without any of it being said, however you seek out his music, you can be assured that your life will be enlivened and enriched by the work of the man that Bob Dylan declared to be "the Shakespeare of Rock 'n' Roll."

And, of course, the internet never stops yielding up treasures like Chuck paying personal homage to T-Bone Walker at Montreux, Chuck in Belgium, Paris, Germany (the videos appear and disappear), Chuck backed by a not altogether appreciative all-star jazz ensemble (Kenny Burrell, Tommy Bryant, Buck Clayton, Jo Jones) at the 1958 Newport Jazz Festival, Chuck in every type of setting, not all certainly but many showing Chuck at his unfailingly triumphant, pleasingly inventive best.

AMERICAN WITHOUT TEARS: ELVIS COSTELLO AND ALLEN TOUSSAINT GO ON A JOURNEY

Elvis has been a constant source of friendship and inspiration since I first met him in a whirl of creative activity (which has never stopped) on his first American solo tour in 1984.

I could say much the same about Allen's own unceasing creativity (and have tried to), even though I only knew him for a comparative minute. Gregg Geller and Joe McEwen have kept me up to date on Elvis in particular in all sorts of ways, and Ben Sandmel has played a similar role with respect to Allen, whom he first introduced me to when I was working on my Sam Cooke biography in 2001. Josh Feigenbaum was a big help in connecting me with Allen after the flood when he helped Allen relocate to New York (I interviewed Allen for the story in Josh's apartment), and in providing photographs of some of the songwriting sessions for *The River in Reverse*, which also took place in his apartment.

John Broven's pioneering book, *Walking to New Orleans,* now in its third edition and retitled *Rhythm and Blues in New Orleans* (Pelican, 2016), is required reading for any background in New Orleans music, as is Jeff Hannusch's *I Hear You Knockin'* (Swallow Publications, 1985). They are both superb, and superbly lively, portraits of the music and the era. For a more offbeat, and highly entertaining (though no less authoritative) account, do yourself another favor and take a look at Ben Sandmel's rambunctious tale of one of the music's most redoubtable characters, *Ernie K-Doe: The R&B Emperor of New Orleans*

(Historic New Orleans Collection, 2012). All three will fill you in on the world that Allen Toussaint was born into and forever changed.

Now, when we get down to musical brass tacks with Elvis and Allen, that's a little (a lot!) more difficult. Well, first, be sure to read Elvis' own fascinating, exuberant, sometimes verging-on-stream-of-consciousness (in an unself-conscious, almost Joycean way) memoir, *Unfaithful Music & Disappearing Ink* (Blue Rider Press, 2015). It will certainly reward your efforts—but, you know, if you want to see where some of the broader vistas of his artistic vision could take him, pay particular attention to his portraits of his father and grandfather, which may well point the way to a future that includes novels, short stories, plays, and his long-awaited musical version of *A Face in the Crowd*. For critical analysis of his own work, Elvis has always been eloquent on the origins and meanings of his songs in interviews and liner notes. If only Allen had been so forthcoming, we might have had a similar, though perhaps more elegant and discreet, memoir—"hip but not rowdy. Extremely hip but not the kind of guttural hip that carries a knife. Hip that carries a comb or a handkerchief," as he said of Sam Cooke. But alas, he never put pen to paper in that way.

For listening, I'm afraid I'm somewhat at a loss. There's just too much! Start, obviously, with the CD/DVD combo of the album that cemented their collaboration, *The River in Reverse* (Verve Forecast B0006801-10). It remains as vital (and perhaps even more pertinent) today as when it was first recorded, though I'm not sure I don't still miss T Bone Burnett's leavening producer's touch just a little. I'm not going to go into the entire Library of Elvis, in which there are an untold number of constantly changing and variegated rewards from first to last, but I would point you to *River in Reverse*'s two most immediate stylistic predecessors, *King of America* (RykoDisc 20281 or Rhino R2 74642) and *Spike* (Rhino R2 74286). Both are co-produced by T Bone in a manner that seems to bring out Elvis' most humble and heartfelt qualities, and both are accompanied by numerous alternate takes and previously unissued tracks as well as freewheeling, expansive, and enlightening notes, historical and musical, by Elvis.

With Allen's work—oh, man, I just don't know. For a start, how about *Finger Poppin' and Stompin' Feet: 20 Classic Allen Toussaint Productions for Minit Records 1960-1962* (EMI 7243 5 37450 2 8), which includes many of the early New Orleans hits, though no Lee Dorsey. Obviously, then, you're just going to have to check out Lee Dorsey's albums, too. (*Yes We Can . . . And Then Some* [Polydor 314 517 865-2] is a priceless collection of some of the later, deeper—though still utterly delightful—material. And there are any number of collections of the early hits.) Then there's Allen's *What Is Success: The Scepter and Bell Recordings*, ca. 1969-1970 (Kent 286), incorporating his very first album as an artist, *Toussaint*, with his own versions of "Everything I Do Gonh Be Funky," "From a Whisper to a Scream," and "What Is Success," plus a number of Bell singles from the same era, all presented in his ever-immaculate fashion. But then there's *The Allen Toussaint Collection* (Reprise 26549-2), a good representation of some of his best 1970s work as an artist, with some duplications with the last. And how about *Rolling with the Punches: The Allen Toussaint Songbook* (Ace 1354), a fine tribute album, including Lee Dorsey and K-Doe (of course), Bonnie Raitt, Aaron Neville, Irma Thomas, Solomon Burke, and Glen Campbell, as well as Allen himself. His last two albums, *The Bright Mississippi* (Nonesuch 480380-2) and *American Tunes* (Nonesuch 755979467-7, released in June 2016, seven months after his death), both beautifully produced by Joe Henry, are more in the nature of swinging, ambitious, and utterly beguiling "art albums," mostly instrumental and, were it not for their sly wit, at times almost autumnal in mood. *The Bright Mississippi*, with no original compositions, is still teeming with originality and, driven by a brilliant all-star band, stands as a tribute to his New Orleans jazz roots while at the same time evoking both Duke Ellington and Thelonious Monk. *American Tunes* continues the mood, but in more languorous fashion, with half a dozen solo presentations and beautifully calibrated vocal performances by Rhiannon Giddens on two Duke Ellington numbers, plus an expressive vocal of his own on Paul Simon's "American Tune." And if it sounds a little diffuse, it's not. It's all undeniably, all unimpeachably Allen.

But (there's always a but, isn't there?) so far as I know, and most likely because of licensing issues, there's never been the kind of comprehensive collection that Gregg Geller put together for Verve to help publicize *The River in Reverse,* and which now exists in expanded and slightly altered form on Spotify as *All These Things: The Allen Toussaint Story,* going from the original versions of "Working in the Coal Mine" and "It's Raining" to "Who's Gonna Help Brother Get Further?" and "Freedom for the Stallion," with plenty of room for versions of Toussaint classics by the Band, the Rolling Stones, the Pointer Sisters, Dr. John, and Glen Campbell. I would check it out if I were you.

THE SONG OF SOLOMON: A TRIPTYCH

Thanks, as always, to Selassie and Victoria Burke in particular but really to the whole extended (and it *is* extended) Burke family. Steve Bing has been an ongoing source of appreciation and information—it's always fun to share Solomon stories with Steve. Ditto for Dan Rabinovitz, a trumpet-playing lawyer (cf. Charlie Rich—but here the reference is positive), who is working on his own memoir of his years playing with Solomon and Sleepy LaBeef, among others. Dan, as Selassie Burke will happily attest, deserves to be included in the Solomon storytellers and appreciators Hall of Fame. But I should also mention that another good friend, Scott Billington, is working on a book about his own adventures producing Solomon, Charlie Rich, Johnny Adams, Irma Thomas, Walter "Wolfman" Washington, et al., and there you'll get the full story of Solomon turning the hurricane back in New Orleans.

For an introduction to Solomon himself in all his larger-than-life glory, Paul Spencer's 2007 BBC documentary, *Solomon Burke: "Everybody Needs Somebody"* (available on DVD from Snapper 636551505376), is absolutely indispensable. Made on a shoestring, with all

Solomon and Selassie Burke, with Nina and Peter Guralnick, 1993. *Photograph by Sharyn Felder*

the unforeseeable starts and stops that every project with Solomon entailed (but this one didn't stop—the only documentary of the numerous ones embarked upon to actually reach the finish line), it suggests all the charisma and humor you could ever hope for, set within a fascinating tour of the Philadelphia neighborhood where he grew up, "the little city within a city [between] 38th and Mt. Vernon and 40th and Mt. Vernon, where you were safe and you knew everybody and everybody knew you." And there's additional testimony from, among others, his sister and his childhood friend John Brooks, with whom he did or did not set out for California in a horse-drawn wagon. You be the judge.

For a musical representation of Solomon's multifaceted career, you could certainly start with his "inspirational," strongly gospel-flavored Apollo sides, which have been collected in a number of places, including the Swedish LP *You Can Run But You Can't Hide* (Mr. R&B 108, which also features five Singular-label follow-ups) and *Soul Arrives! 1955-1961* (Jasmine 3019), which offers some additional Singular and pseudonymous (as "Little Vincent") Apollo sides as well as his first two Atlantic singles. *Home in Your Heart: The Best of Solomon Burke* (Rhino 70284) really is (both home in your heart—even though it's the song that's being referred to here—and the best) and includes all of Solomon's essential, you-would-never-want-to-be-without-these-songs Atlantic hits, along with many other supernal musical moments. And *Soul Alive!* (Rounder 11521), a two-CD set recorded in front of a very live audience in Washington, D.C., in 1981, is as close as you'll ever get to capturing the sheer unanticipatable magic of a Solomon Burke live performance—it's amazing!

But now let me do the same thing I did with Merle Haggard, provide a list of some of the Solomon songs you (or at least *I*) absolutely can't do without. Here's *my* Solomon songbook:

"Sidewalks, Fences, and Walls"; "The Price" (this is so emotional a song that, on the few occasions that he would perform it live, Solomon would almost invariably come to a point where he announced, "I'm going to have to leave that one alone," and cut it off); "I Stayed Away Too Long" (which Lonnie Mack does in a stunning version as "She Don't Come Here Anymore" on *Glad I'm in the Band*); the semi-acoustic, jazzy, bluesy, two-guitar, exquisitely sung version of "Drown in My Own Tears" that turns up without preamble or follow-up on his MGM album *We're Almost Home*); "Goodbye Baby"; "It's Just a Matter of Time"; his majestic "A Change Is Gonna Come" on the album of the same name that Scott Billington produced (Rounder 2053); "Time Is a Thief" (like Jerry Lee's "She Even Woke Me Up," another great Mickey Newbury song); "I Feel a Sin Coming On"; "Letter from My Darling," on *Soul of the Blues* (Black Top 1095); the entirety of *Soul Alive!*; and "Silent Night," a 33 1/3 rpm "Big Single" (Savoy SCS-0002), cut live in Macon, Georgia, in the summer of 1982 in what producer Fred Mendelsohn said was 110-degree heat. ("Look, Fred," Solomon declared, pointing out the window in the midst of an inspirational Christmas sermon, "It's snowing!")

And the internet, of course, remains an ever-replenishing source of oddball and exalted moments alike, such as Solomon being interviewed by a ten-year-old boy in Holland, some 1987 *Reelin' in the Years* documentary footage of Solomon singing and preaching in a well-maintained House of God for All People church, his duet with Aretha at the Rock and Roll Hall of Fame, and his memorable performances on Conan O'Brien and David Letterman, plus innumerable unforgettable appearances in Europe and points east, north, west, and south. And then there are Daddy Grace's mass baptisms, and—and—and—oh, I'm just going to have to do like Solomon now—I'm just going to have to leave this one alone.

And finally, just a note on the brief monologue that concludes "Print the Legend: An Appendix in Search of a Digression." Most of it is drawn, with thanks, from Paul Spencer's interviews with Solomon for the documentary and from my own conversations with him over the years—but it is a construct, put together in an attempt to reflect Solomon's increasing preoccupation with his grandmother, her church, Sweet Daddy Grace, and the deep-seated roots of his music and his belief in the last years of his life. Some of the other sources with which it has been informed and assembled (all of which are well worth seeking out in their own right) are: Robert Wilonsky, "Soul Survivor" (*Dallas Observer*, 3/20/97); Jonathan Valania, "Solomon Burke Brings It Home" (*Philadelphia Weekly*, July 17, 2002); Robert Chalmers, "Solomon Burke: Last of the Great Soul Men" (*The Independent*, 6/29/08); and Charles Young, "King Solomon's Sweet Thunder" (*Rolling Stone*, 5/27/10). For a surprising early portrait (it's really more like an artifact) of the discovery of a teenage Solomon Burke, check out "Disc Jockey Hails Solomon Burke, 15, As New Sensation," *Philadelphia Tribune*, 1/17/56, which, even if it should be taken with a large grain of salt, provides a window into one of those lost moments of history that you think are irrecoverable. And for a scholarly and informative approach to the church's history of shout bands, right up to the present day, read Nick Spitzer's illuminating liner notes to *Saints' Paradise: Trombone Shout Bands from the United House of Prayer* (Smithsonian Folkways Recordings SFW40117).

Most of all, though, I just hope I have done justice to Solomon's own extraordinary powers of self-expression, the eloquence and flow of his speech, and the depth of his feeling about all the subjects he touches upon in this valedictory monologue.

PERFECT IMPERFECTION: THE LIFE AND ART OF JERRY LEE LEWIS

I've gotten lots of help over the years on this one, from Knox Phillips, Bill Millar, Cal Morgan, J. M. Van Eaton, Colin Escott, Steve Bing, Judith Coghlan Lewis, and the Zen spirit of Roland Janes.

Needless to say, there's lots of good reading, too. *Jerry Lee Lewis: His Own Story* by Rick Bragg (Harper, 2014) has all the familiar stories with some elegant literary embellishments. And, of course, everyone knows Nick Tosches' *Hellfire* (Delacorte Press, 1982), which is told with all of Nick's nihilistic panache. But the best place to go for the spirit of Jerry Lee is the largely ignored, and I think generally underrated, *Killer!*, an oral history by Charles White (Century, 1993), which comes as close to true autobiography (and Lewis family autobiography) as Jerry Lee is ever likely to get. (Charles White, aka "Dr. Rock," is also the author of the classic *The Life and Times of Little Richard: The Quasar of Rock* [Harmony Books, 1984], which occupies a deserved place next to David Ritz's *Brother Ray* and Chuck Berry's *Chuck Berry: The Autobiography* in the small pantheon of rhythm and rock autobiographies.) John Grissim's *Country Music: White Man's Blues* (Paperback Library, 1970) has an appropriately unbuttoned chapter on Jerry Lee (this is where he says, of himself, Sam Phillips, and Jack Clement, "Birds of a feather flock together. It took all of us to get together to screw up the world. We've done it!"), along with profiles of Merle Haggard and Waylon Jennings that are nearly as good. And *Good Rockin' Tonight: Sun Records and the Birth of Rock 'n' Roll* (St. Martin's, 1991) by Colin Escott with Martin Hawkins is essential reading, too, but no more essential than any number of other writings by Colin and Martin on Sun, rockabilly, country, you name it, among which are Colin's masterful *Hank Williams: The Biography* (the revised paperback edition, published by Little, Brown in 2004) and Martin's authoritative *A Shot in the Dark: Making Records in Nashville, 1945-1955* (Vanderbilt University Press and the Country Music Foundation Press, 2006).

On the video front, *Jerry Lee Lewis: Greatest Live Performances of the '50s, '60s and '70s* (Time-Life DVD MI9406), once again courtesy of Colin Escott, is a great start, but it doesn't even begin to encompass what is available on the internet, not to mention real-life encounters. You could spend all day on YouTube checking out great Jerry Lee Lewis performances (just like Solomon's, they are almost all great — seriously), but the one video that has never surfaced is the one that evidently was never made: Jerry Lee as Iago in what by all accounts was his utterly enthralling performance in *Catch My Soul*, the rock 'n' roll version of *Othello*. But barring a video or the surfacing of a full-length audio recording, definitely be on the hunt for Jerry Lee's leering Iago-channeling "Lust of the Blood," which has appeared on various private-issue CDs and once in a while on YouTube before it disappears again in short order.

Jerry Lee Lewis has been interviewed countless times and, as with his live performances, though he frequently recounts the same stories and addresses many of the same issues, he never tells a story the same way twice. And while he is never less than truthful (once again, I'm serious), he is never less than entertaining either. Here are a few of the most colorful (and informative) sources that I've enjoyed over the years: "The Devil and Jerry Lee Lewis" by Robert Palmer (*Rolling Stone*, 12/13/79); John Pugh's "The Greatest Live Show on Earth" (*Country Music*, January 1973); Cliff White's "The Killer Speaks" (*New Kommotion* 24, 1980); "Jerry Lee Lewis: Higher Than Most" by John Grissim (*Rolling Stone*, 9/17/70); "Jerry Lee Lewis: The Killer Staggers On" by John Morthland (*Creem*, March 1974); Michael Lollar, "Jerry and God: Wild Man Lewis Eyes His Soul for Final Shakedown" (*Memphis Commercial Appeal*, ca. 1996). In addition, he gave a wonderful interview to Andrew Solt and Jerry Schilling, which has never been fully screened or published, for Time-Life's ten-part video *The History of Rock 'n' Roll*. And as for my own literary adventures with Jerry Lee, starting in 1970 when he was living on Coro Lake outside of Memphis, with an extended family that seemed to incorporate nearly everyone who was important in his life, I wouldn't trade anything for any of them. As he said to me the first time we met, "Don't you take no wooden nickels or no silver dollars either along the way." Thirty-five years later, the dollars had turned to wood, but the point seemed to be the same: in the end all that matters is the genuine article.

Now, it may not seem like it from these notes (I'm sure it doesn't, because I really am trying to call up all the wonders of the vasty deep), but I am firmly opposed to the comprehensive, no-false-take-missed approach to record (or writing) anthologies. ON THE OTHER HAND, *Classic Jerry Lee Lewis: The Definitive Edition of His Sun Recordings* (Bear Family BCD 15420), produced and annotated, like so many other great Bear Family recordings, by Colin Escott, is the one box set that no rock 'n' roll — no *music* — collection should be without, an eight-CD, 246-song set, complete with some of the most amazing music, thematic variations, and incidental dialogue ever recorded. Jerry Lee Lewis said at one time that he had recorded enough material at Sun for forty separate albums to be issued, and he may well have. But this will have to serve for now. I could offer as a compromise solution (and by now I think we all know how Sam Phillips and Jerry Lee Lewis both felt about compromise) *The Essential Jerry Lee Lewis: The Sun Sessions* (RCA/Legacy 88883706092). It's a perfectly well-chosen selection, with forty tracks on two CDs, and it could certainly serve as a form of introduction to Jerry Lee's seven earth-shattering years on Sun — but then there's still the whole rest of his career to go, the country collections, the live recordings, etc. etc. But I swear, if you're looking for transcendence, don't wait, don't hesitate, go out and buy *Classic Jerry Lee Lewis: The Definitive Edition of His Sun Recordings* right now.

On the other *other* hand, here's a completely unscientific, off-the-top-of-my-and-a-lot-of other-people's-heads selection of SOME RANDOM (could it really be forty?) JERRY LEE LEWIS CUTS YOU MIGHT NOT NECESSARILY THINK OF WHEN YOU'RE THINK-ING OF JERRY LEE (but then again you might):

"She Even Woke Me Up to Say Goodbye"; "Big Legged Woman"; "Who Will the Next Fool Be?" (two versions: the one on his 1979 Elektra album *Jerry Lee Lewis* [original LP number Elektra 6E-184; Wounded Bird CD WOU 184] with an offhand-observation-and-whistling outro by Jerry Lee, plus the inspired video-version duet with Solomon Burke on *Last Man Standing Live* [Shangri La/Artists First AFT 20009-9]); "Over the Rainbow"; "Down the Line"; "Crazy Arms"; "Big Blon' Baby"; "Lust of the Blood"; "Seasons of My Heart" (duet with his sister Linda Gail Lewis); "In the Mood" (instrumental released on Sun as by The Hawk); "I Believe in You"; "Beautiful Dreamer" and "Music! Music! Music!" (from *The Knox Phillips Sessions* [Saguaro Road Records 30558]); "Hello Hello Baby"; "Down the Sawdust Trail"; "I'll Sail My Ship Alone"; "Hi-Heel Sneakers" (from *The Greatest Live Shows on Earth* [Bear Family 15608]); "Since I Met You Baby" ("Play your fiddle, Mr. Kenneth Lovelace"); "When I Take My Vacation in Heaven"; "That Kind of Fool"; "Blues Like Midnight" (with Jerry Lee on guitar) and Bob Dylan's "Stepchild" from *Rock & Roll Time* [Vanguard 78334]); "High School Confidential"; "Life Is Like a Mountain Railroad"; "Autumn Leaves"; "Take Me Out to the Ballgame" (with Neil Sedaka on *Shindig!*); his empyrean "Rockin' Medley" with Tom Jones on the *Tom Jones Show* in 1969 and, just as expressive, his instrumental backing for Tom (with Chet Atkins playing guitar) on "Funny How Time Slips Away"; the video of Jerry Lee playing "Mexicali Rose" for a beaming Gene Autry; "Goldmine in the Sky"; "Settin' the Woods on Fire"; "Corine Corina"; "Sweet Geor-gia Brown" (with Kenny Lovelace's hot fiddle); "Trouble in Mind"; "Strange Things Hap-pening Every Day" (not Jerry Lee — Sister Rosetta Tharpe performing one of the songs that most inspired him); "Little Queenie"; "Lovin' Up a Storm"; "It All Depends (Who Will Buy the Wine)"; "Hand Me Down My Walking Cane"; "Jesus Is on the Mainline (Call Him Sometime)"; "My God Is Real"; "Goodnight Irene"; "Come What May"; "That's My Desire" plus "You're the Only Star in My Blue Heaven" from *The Complete Million Dollar Quartet* (RCA/Sony BMG 82876 88935-2) — oh, hell, you'd better just get the whole album, which might just as well be subtitled *The Elvis Presley* (twenty-one-year-old superstar, on top of the world)-*Jerry Lee Lewis* (twenty-one-year-old neophyte, with his first single just out — but just as much on top of the world) *Duets Album*.

And now I'll offer an alternate take for what I said at the end of the Solomon Burke section. In Jerry Lee's own words, with a little bit of poetic license, Too much of this (and it's already too much) is going to drive (or has already driven) me plumb crazy.

HOWLIN' WOLF: WHAT IS THE SOUL OF MAN?

James Segrest and Mark Hoffman's *Moanin' at Midnight: The Life and Times of Howlin' Wolf* (Pantheon Books, 2004) is a terrific resource, and Mark has continued to be a great help to me, with his extensive ongoing research. Sam Phillips' recollections of Wolf never dimmed, and Marion Keisker had equally vivid memories, if not as many. Josh Hecht's unpublished interview of Sam for a Wolf documentary that was never completed offers some wonderfully focused memories and observations, and I am indebted to Josh for providing me with it. Ditto Peter Riley's interview with Wolf, conducted a couple of years after first meeting him at sixteen or seventeen. And I can't imagine anyone who could fail to be charmed by the warmth and affection of the brilliant Canadian-born musician Colin Linden's recollections of meeting Wolf at the age of eleven when he prevailed upon his mother to take him to see Wolf at the Colonial Tavern in Toronto. *"For the next 3 hours, he sat with me, a cup of coffee in one hand and cigarette in the other, as I asked him questions about his past, where and how he learned and from whom. He was very happy to talk and seemed to sense how much it meant for me to know the answers."* (You can find it on my website, peterguralnick.com, and I'm sure elsewhere.) Also, don't let me forget to point you to Dick Shurman, one of the world's most prominent Wolfologists, not to mention a good friend to all Howlin' Wolf researchers and to the man himself from the time Dick first met him in 1969 as an eighteen-year-old freshman at the University of Chicago. Dick was already a blues devotee (he has since gone on to produce at least ten Grammy-nominated albums) when he looked up Wolf in the phone book and called him up out of the blue, upon which he was invited immediately to dinner and to attend Wolf's performance at the Key Largo that night on Chicago's West Side. ("Wolf was more than just polite or courteous to me," Dick wrote in his thoroughly entertaining, and equally charming, contribution to *Charley Patton: Voice of the Mississippi Delta*, edited by Robert Sacré [University Press of Mississippi, 2018]. "He seemed to think that I was a young man who could benefit from fatherly advice.")

With Mick Jagger, 1970.
Courtesy of Chess Records

Pete Welding's *DownBeat* cover story on Wolf, "'I Sing for the People': An Interview with Bluesman Howling Wolf" (*DownBeat*, 12/14/67), is well worth seeking out. So is Dave Booth's interview of him, which is quoted in part in Colin Escott's liner notes to *Howlin' Wolf: Memphis Days* Vol. 1 and elsewhere. And Johnny Shines' uncompleted memoir, *Success Was My Downfall*, published in part as "A Lifetime in the Blues: Johnny Shines" by John Earl in *Blues World* Special Edition 46/49 (1973), is a must.

For visual representation, the sine qua non, ne plus ultra, or, as I call it, the Greatest Moment of Television Ever, is Wolf's appearance on *Shindig!* on Thursday, May 20, 1965, with the Rolling Stones at his feet. (That's where the picture with Son House was taken by Son's good friend and manager, Dick Waterman, who brought Son for a first-time-in-more-than-twenty-years reunion on the set. ("Man, he sure has got his growth!" Son remarked to Dick.) *Devil Got My Woman: Blues at Newport* (Vestapol DVD 13049), shot by Alan Lomax in a faux juke joint with most of the blues performers (and a few non-blues artists, too) from the 1966 Newport Folk Festival, is priceless both for Wolf's performance and his commentary during the performances of others. And then there's *The Howlin' Wolf Story: The Secret History of Rock 'n' Roll* (Bluebird/BMG 82876-56631-9) and *The American Folk-Blues Festival: The British Tours 1963-1966* (Hip-O Records B0008353-09), which also includes Muddy Waters and Sonny Boy Williamson, among others. (There are other Hip-O American Folk Blues Festival compilations, with *The American Folk Blues Festival 1962-1966, Volume Two* [Hip-O B0000751-09] offering several additional Wolf tracks.) And, and, and . . . then there's the internet.

As for sound recordings, well, start with *Howlin' Wolf: Smokestack Lightning, The Complete Chess Masters 1951-1960* (Chess/Hip-O-Select/Geffen B0015309-02), which gives a broad, deep, and infinitely satisfying survey of his career through 1960. (Inexplicably — well, maddeningly anyway — there was never a Volume 2 to complete the story.) Then there are a trio of masterpieces stemming from the very beginning of his career. *Howlin' Wolf: Memphis Days — The Definitive Edition* Vols. 1 and 2 (Bear Family BCD 15460, 15500) represent nearly all of Sam Phillips' unsurpassable 1951 and 1952 recordings of the "most profound and different" artist he ever recorded. *Howling Wolf Sings the Blues* (Ace CDCHM 1013) is nearly (but not quite — it's an infinitesimal difference) as good, culled from the RPM recordings which the Bihari brothers made when they tried to steal Wolf from Sam and Leonard Chess in the fall of 1951. But obviously you wouldn't want to miss his post-1960 work either. So I guess you could go to the comprehensive *Howlin' Wolf: The Chess Box* (Chess/MCA CHD3-9332), a three-CD collection that runs from 1951 to 1976, with a lot of duplications, obviously, but also twenty-nine post-1960 selections and a few hidden treasures, including four interspersed interview segments and a tantalizing solo version of a Charley Patton song on acoustic guitar. (But for more, and better, of that, check out the four similar tracks on *Howlin' Wolf: Ain't Gonna Be Your Dog* [MCA/Chess 9349] — I'm sorry, but it's a pretty cool selection, too, with some good talking sections.) Whatever you do, though, I implore you — don't on any account stop there. Just as with Jerry Lee Lewis, there is no such thing as too much Howlin' Wolf.

LIVING WITH THE BLUES: AN INTERVIEW WITH ERIC CLAPTON

My interview with Eric Clapton was a one-off, suggested by *Musician* editor Bill Flanagan (soon to originate *VH1 Storytellers*), who was always looking for ways to broaden my horizons, and brought about almost entirely by the graciousness of Eric Clapton.

Solely with respect to our particular discussion, without in any way intending to slight Eric Clapton's own work, here are a few places to look for some of his most dedicated blues collaborations. *Sonny Boy Williamson and the Yardbirds* (live) (original LP issue Mercury SR 21071 or 61071) and John Mayall's *Bluesbreakers with Eric Clapton* (original U.S. LP version, London PS 492 — there are innumerable more recent versions) showcase some of the earliest blues experiences he describes, but the highlight for me is *The London Howlin' Wolf Sessions: Deluxe Edition* (Chess/MCA 088 112 985-2), not just for all the obvious reasons but because it includes a guitar lesson by Howlin' Wolf on the proper way to play "Little Red Rooster." Then there is *Delaney and Bonnie and Friends on Tour with Eric Clap-*

ton (original LP and CD issue Atco 33-326), when he briefly set aside the superstardom of Cream and Blind Faith and put his talents exclusively at the service of what he considered to be his underlying passion and commitment to the music. His participation in *Chuck Berry: Hail! Hail! Rock 'n' Roll*, the all-star concert celebrating Chuck's sixtieth birthday and commemorated in the four-DVD collection cited above as *Chuck Berry: Hail! Hail! Rock 'n' Roll: The Ultimate Collector's Edition* (Universal/Image ID3156THDVD), once again underscores his "true gen," both in rehearsal and in the concert itself, where, given the spotlight, he remains true to Muddy Waters' advice and sticks to the blues, with a beautiful version of Chuck's "Wee Wee Hours."

And, of course, there is his long-planned and well-executed Robert Johnson tribute, which was released in 2004 as *Me and Mr. Johnson* (Reprise Records/Duck Records 48423-2), featuring fourteen songs that he recorded in as many days with some of his most trusted longtime collaborators. Later that year he revisited the subject with a CD-DVD package called *Sessions for Robert J.* (Reprise Records/Duck Records 38627-2). The original idea was to film some videos to accompany the CD—but then he realized he had more to say, even with songs he had already recorded, and ultimately it grew into a whole new package. On eight of the DVD tracks he uses virtually the same band, but then there are an equal number of deeply felt acoustic duets with guitarist Doyle Bramhall II filmed in the very Dallas warehouse in which Robert Johnson recorded his 1937 sessions. For me the musical high point of the video performances are three lyrical solo tracks by Clapton—I was going to speak about the palpable feeling of his playing (not a very expressive description), but hell, the whole project reflects that same feeling, obviously, including a number of interspersed interview segments in which Eric reflects upon his discovery of Robert Johnson and offers thoughtful reflections on the man and his music. I guess of the three configurations, this (the DVD) would be my preference, with the accompanying CD including five very different versions of songs that are on the first album, plus an additional six titles, with all, I think, sourced from the DVD, showing a similar fluency and (only occasionally over-the-top) commitment. Okay, I think that's enough, probably more than you need. Suffice it to say, I think Muddy would have been proud.

MALACO RECORDS: LIFE ON THE EDGE OF TOWN

I can only offer my heartfelt thanks to Tommy Couch and Wolf Stephenson, who opened themselves up to me when we first met and have been good friends over the years. Dave Clark was the one who led me to Malaco in the first place, and my adventures with him in New York, not only on his extravagant promotional excursion to Fort Apache in the Bronx, but on our trip to Lincoln Center's New York Public Library for the Performing Arts to seek out his 1930s *DownBeat* columns and ruminate on the role of Zora Neale Hurston in the ongoing cultural revolution.

For an introduction to Malaco Records you couldn't do better than to go to the six-CD box set *The Last Soul Company* (Malaco MCD 0030), which, with 112 songs, includes all the hits by every artist of note from King Floyd to Bobby "Blue" Bland, as well as a healthy dose of obscurities well worth seeking out, along with a comprehensive booklet by r&b scholar Rob Bowman. From there you should seek out all the individual albums you like, from Z. Z. Hill's landmark *Down Home* to Bobby Bland's *Members Only* and Little Milton's *Annie Mae's Cafe*—but the box set will provide you with a great start, imbued as it is with the true all-embracing and exploratory Malaco spirit. In addition there's a book coming, an expansion of Rob Bowman's comprehensive notes, entitled *The Last Soul Company: The Malaco Records Story*, to be published by the Malaco Press, with an announced publication date of 2020.

MY FATHER, MY GRANDFATHER, AND RAY CHARLES

I'm going to place some of my grandfather Rubin Guralnick's papers in my archive (the Peter Guralnick Collection) in the Southern Folklife Collection in the Wilson Library at the University of North Carolina at Chapel Hill. These will include his unpublished script for a film based loosely on the life of Catherine the Great (it's called *The Great Impostor,* with the subtitle "A Screen Play of Russian Life"), along with his 1937-38 correspondence with Norman Corwin, a budding radio superstar with connections in Hollywood, about how to get it produced. Norman, who was twenty-seven at the time, had grown up with my father and uncle (he was a fellow East Bostonite, and my grandfather was his pediatrician), and, even though it was clear that no movie was ever going to get made, he was very kind in his advice. Years later, when both he and my father were in their nineties, I got to meet him on the phone through Steve Bing, and he declared emphatically to me and Steve, "If Dr. Guralnick told you something, it was so." The script, whatever its imperfections, is just one manifestation of my grandfather's indefatigably curious and, above all, *enthusiastic* spirit, something that communicated itself in everything he said and did, from his passionate political exhortations to his teasing promise to me as a little kid that we would one day visit the Galápagos Islands to see the tortoises (maybe the very ones!) that Charles Darwin had written about.

My father Walter Guralnick's writing and records, including an extensive oral history taken on video in his early nineties, can be found at the Massachusetts General Hospital Archives and Special Collections for the most part, though some exists at Harvard's Countway Library and, as with my grandfather, his work bears scrutiny well beyond his field.

READING, WRITING, AND REAL LIFE

I'm going to deposit some of my other grandfather Philip Marson's papers in the UNC collection, too. But he also wrote a book, *A Teacher Speaks* (David McKay, 1960), part memoir (there's quite a bit about Camp Alton, whose records will be partially archived at UNC as well), part passionate call for educational reform. Some of his educational nostrums struck me as a little rigid even at the time (and remember, I was a kid who loved the sentence diagramming and grammatical puzzles he set for me). Maybe it was just that his faith in going back to basics didn't seem to reflect the remarkable ability he possessed to rise to any pedagogical challenge—or maybe just *any* challenge—that was thrown at him in real life. But he made his case with great vigor, and the book received all sorts of enthusiastic reviews in that frenetic post-Sputnik educational era. (One of the more unlikely endorsements came from Ezra Pound, still confined to St. Elizabeths, who wrote to an admirer: "You ought to back Ph. Marson to the FULL and AT ONCE. He diagnoses the syphilis in our educ." Etc.) More to the point was Leonard Bernstein's warmly affectionate introduction to the book, in which he declared (as he would reaffirm when he introduced my grandfather in person on his CBS series, *Young People's Concerts*): "If I say that Philip Marson's name, lo, led all the rest, it is not to make value judgements or com-

Phil, Rose, and Betty
Marson, with Cubby, at
Camp Emoh, Alfred,
Maine, ca. 1935. *Courtesy
of Peter Guralnick
Archives*

parisons with my other [key] teachers. It is only to say that he taught me something unique, incomparable . . . far beyond the teaching of tetrameter or dangling participles or even the glories of English verse: he taught me how to learn." And I can only echo that sentiment, with love.

And, as one more tip of the hat to my grandfather, I will always be grateful to him for introducing me to Sigrid Undset. And I think he would have been delighted with the modernized translation of *Kristin Lavransdatter* by Tiina Nunnally that was published in a single-volume Penguin Classics Deluxe Edition in 2005, providing a graceful entrée for yet another generation of readers.

Acknowledgments

I N WRITING A BOOK over so long a period (this is, if you think about it, the product for me of over fifty years of what Sam Phillips would call Big Fun), one incurs debts that can never be repaid. Literally hundreds (thousands?) of people have helped me with my research and my interviews over the years, and I thank them all. And, of course, more than anything I am grateful to all the people I have interviewed and written about both for their work and for the graciousness with which they welcomed me into their worlds. The following are just some of the people who gave me a hand in ways that I cannot begin to calculate over the weeks, months, and years that went into the writing of this book:

J. W. Alexander, Brenda Coladay, Terry Curless Chinnock and her mother Pauline Curless, Roland Janes, Sharyn Felder, Peter Wolf, Colin Escott, Tex Whitson, Colin Linden, Ben Sandmel, Gregg Geller, Wil Haygood, Russ Barnard, Jack Clement, Martin Hawkins, Dick Waterman, Steve Frappier, Dave ("Daddy Cool") Booth, Mary Katherine Aldin, Richard Weize, Joe McEwen, Jake Guralnick, Randy Poe, Steve Bing, Andy Leach, David Less, Michael Lydon, Michael Ochs, Fred Rothwell, Rich Kienzle, Galen Gart, Bill Millar, Jim O'Neal, John Broven, Pat Rainer, Red Kelly, Jack Soden, Michael Gray, Cal Morgan, William Bell, Paul Bazylinski, Irving Roberts, Peter Stromberg, Jim Jaworowicz, Don Light, the Country Music Foundation, Phyllis Hill, Roger Armstrong (Ace Records), Trevor Cajiao, Steve Weiss, Chris Murray, Mark Stielper, Lance Hidy, John and Shelby Singleton, Howell Begle, Mark Hoffman, Joe Lauro, Bob Smith, Julian Bond, Alan Edelstein, Bill Greensmith, Paul Burch, Dick Shurman, Paul Spencer, Dan Rabinovitz, Ross Kolhonen, Rob Santos, Scott Billington, Reginald and Alison Toussaint, Robert Gordon, Jim Cole, Jeff Rosen, Matt Ross-Spang, Jerry Schilling, Knox and Jerry Phillips, the Kitchen Sisters (Davia Nelson and Nikki Silva).

Once again Alexandra Guralnick patiently read, transcribed, debated, and imagined the details of the various stories every step of the way. As always, thanks to Jake and Nina for their incalculable contributions. And thanks once again to Pamela Marshall, this time for her empathetic supervisory efficiency, and to Barbara Clark, who took her place in the copyediting chair and showed the same kind of cheerfully stringent approach and occasional willingness to forsake consistency for feel that Pamela did on the last three books.

Working with Susan Marsh, whose passionate commitment to elegance of form and unswerving dedication to the text have guided the design of every book I have written since 1979, was, as always, an unalloyed pleasure. And I could say much the same about my editor, Michael Pietsch, whose honesty, loyalty, editorial insight, and friendship have served as guideposts for the last twenty-eight years.

Thanks to all, and to all those not named, from whom I drew encouragement, sustenance, and inspiration, not to mention the courage (and enthusiasm) to go on!

Index

Note: Italic page numbers refer to photographs. The initials PG refer to Peter Guralnick.

About the Author

Peter Guralnick's books include the prizewinning two-volume biography of Elvis Presley, *Last Train to Memphis* and *Careless Love; Sweet Soul Music; Dream Boogie: The Triumph of Sam Cooke;* and *Searching for Robert Johnson.* He won a Grammy for his liner notes for *Sam Cooke Live at the Harlem Square Club,* wrote and coproduced the documentary *Sam Phillips: The Man Who Invented Rock 'n' Roll,* and wrote the scripts for the Grammy-winning documentary *Sam Cooke/Legend* and Martin Scorsese's blues documentary *Feel Like Going Home.* His most recent book is *Sam Phillips: The Man Who Invented Rock 'n' Roll.*